Research Anthology on Applying Social Networking Strategies to Classrooms and Libraries

Information Resources Management Association
USA

Volume I

IGI Global
PUBLISHER of TIMELY KNOWLEDGE

Published in the United States of America by
    IGI Global
    Information Science Reference (an imprint of IGI Global)
    701 E. Chocolate Avenue
    Hershey PA, USA 17033
    Tel: 717-533-8845
    Fax: 717-533-8661
    E-mail: cust@igi-global.com
    Web site: http://www.igi-global.com

Library of Congress Cataloging-in-Publication Data

Names: Information Resources Management Association, editor.
Title: Research anthology on applying social networking strategies to
  classrooms and libraries / Information Resources Management Association,
  editor.
Description: Hershey PA : Information Science Reference, 2022. | Includes
  bibliographical references. | Summary: "This reference book presents
  contributed chapters that describe the applications, tools, and
  opportunities provided by the intersection of education and social
  media, considering the ways in which social media encourages learner
  engagement and community participation"-- Provided by publisher.
Identifiers: LCCN 2022030171 (print) | LCCN 2022030172 (ebook) | ISBN
  9781668471234 (hardcover) | ISBN 9781668471241 (ebook)
Subjects: LCSH: Social media in education. | Libraries and social media. |
  Online social networks--Educational applications | Online social
  networks--Library applications.
Classification: LCC LB1044.87 .R46 2022 (print) | LCC LB1044.87 (ebook) |
  DDC 371.33/44678--dc23/eng/20220920
LC record available at https://lccn.loc.gov/2022030171
LC ebook record available at https://lccn.loc.gov/2022030172

British Cataloguing in Publication Data
A Cataloguing in Publication record for this book is available from the British Library.

For electronic access to this publication, please contact: eresources@igi-global.com.

List of Contributors

Table of Contents

Section 2
Development and Design Methodologies

Volume III

Section 4
Utilization and Applications

Section 5
Organizational and Social Implications

Section 6
Managerial Impact

Section 7
Critical Issues and Challenges

Preface

The introduction of social media has given many communities the opportunity to connect and communicate with each other at a higher level than ever before. Many organizations, from businesses to governments, have taken advantage of this important tool to conduct research and enhance efficiency. Libraries and educational institutions have also made use of social media to enhance educational marketing, engage with learning communities, adapt educational tools, and more.

Staying informed of the most up-to-date research trends and findings is of the utmost importance. That is why IGI Global is pleased to offer this four-volume reference collection of reprinted IGI Global book chapters and journal articles that have been handpicked by senior editorial staff. This collection will shed light on critical issues related to the trends, techniques, and uses of various applications by providing both broad and detailed perspectives on cutting-edge theories and developments. This collection is designed to act as a single reference source on conceptual, methodological, technical, and managerial issues, as well as to provide insight into emerging trends and future opportunities within the field.

The *Research Anthology on Applying Social Networking Strategies to Classrooms and Libraries* is organized into seven distinct sections that provide comprehensive coverage of important topics. The sections are:

1. Fundamental Concepts and Theories;
2. Development and Design Methodologies;
3. Tools and Technologies;
4. Utilization and Applications;
5. Organizational and Social Implications;
6. Managerial Impact; and
7. Critical Issues and Challenges.

The following paragraphs provide a summary of what to expect from this invaluable reference tool.

Section 1, "Fundamental Concepts and Theories," serves as a foundation for this extensive reference tool by addressing crucial theories essential to implementing social networking into classrooms and libraries. The first chapter, "Social Media and the Future of the Instructional Model," by Prof. Soha Abdeljaber of Rising Leaders Academy, USA and Prof. Kathryn Nieves Licwinko of New Jersey City University, USA, provides the latest information on social media and its application in the instructional model. The chapter contains information on how social media enhances learning, especially at times where remote learning is necessary, such as COVID-19. The last chapter, "Facebook in the International Classroom," by Prof. Inna P. Piven of Unitec Institute of Technology, New Zealand, explores international students' learning experiences with Facebook-based activities within the eight-week study term known as the intensive mode of course delivery. By implementing participant observation and two asynchronous Facebook focus groups, the study investigates the potential values of Facebook for learning from international students' perspective.

Section 2, "Development and Design Methodologies," presents in-depth coverage of the design and development of social networking implementation. The first chapter, "Bridging Activities: Social Media for Connecting Language Learners' in-School and Out-of-School Literacy Practices," by Prof. Ellen Yeh of Columbia College Chicago, USA and Prof. Svetlana Mitric of University of Illinois at Chicago, USA, applies pedagogically-focused project design by using Instagram as a platform to investigate how the use of social media such as Instagram in a multimodal digital storytelling model could bridge the skills English language learners (ELLs) learn in the classroom to out-of-school literacy practices. The last chapter, "Social Media, Cyberculture, Blockchains, and Education: A New Strategy for Brazilian Higher Education," by Prof. Matheus Batalha Moreira Nery of Uninassau, Brazil; Prof. Magno Oliveira Macambira of Universidade Estadual de Feira de Santana, Brazil; Prof. Marlton Fontes Mota of Universidade Tiradentes, Brazil; and Prof. Izabella Cristine Oliveira Rezende of Uninassau, Brazil, contributes to the debate of the uses of social media, cyberculture, and blockchain technology for the development of educational strategies. It reviews the existing scientific literature on social networking, social media, cyberculture, and blockchains related to Brazil.

Section 3, "Tools and Technologies," explores the various tools and technologies used in classrooms and libraries for social networking. The first chapter, "Using Social Media in Creating and Implementing Educational Practices," by Profs. Inna P. Piven and Robyn Gandell of Unitec Institute of Technology, New Zealand, examines the use of social media as a couse management tool, the use of social media to enhance student-centered learning and the need for institutional support for using social media in educational contexts. The last chapter, "Is Twitter an Unexploited Potential in Indian Academic Libraries? Case Study Based on Select Academic Library Tweets," by Prof. Swapan Kumar Patra of Tshwane University of Technology, South Africa, maps the Indian libraries' Twitter activities, taking academic libraries as case study.

Section 4, "Utilization and Applications," describes the opportunities and challenges of social networking implementation. The first chapter, "Navigating the Shortcomings of Virtual Learning Environments via Social Media," by Profs. Puvaneswary Murugaiah and Siew Hwa Yen of School of Distance Education, Universiti Sains Malaysia, Penang, Malaysia, uncovers the shortcomings of the use of virtual learning environments (VLEs) for language learning in several Malaysian institutions of higher learning. It also highlights the use of social media in addressing the barriers. The last chapter, "Nexus Between Social Network, Social Media Use, and Loneliness: A Case Study of University Students, Bangladesh," by Prof. Md. Aminul Islam of University of Liberal Arts Bangladesh, Bangladesh and Prof. Bezon Kumar of Rabindra University, Bangladesh, explores how real-life social network and social media use are related to loneliness among university students in Bangladesh.

Section 5, "Organizational and Social Implications," includes chapters discussing the impact of social networking on education and library organizations and beyond. The first chapter, "Identifiable Problems in Social Media: Concerning Legal Awareness Within Academic Libraries," by Prof. Amy D. Dye-Reeves of Murray State University, USA, serves as a primer for academic librarians on helping patrons with disabilities receive, protect, and understand disseminated content on a multitude of popular social media networking platforms. The content of the chapter provides introductory material on the Americans with Disabilities Act (ADA) and the Family Educational Rights and Privacy Act. The last chapter, "Using Twitter to Form Professional Learning Communities: An Analysis of Georgia K-12 School Personnel Discussing Educational Technology on Twitter," by Profs. Charles B. Hodges, Lucas John Jensen, and Mete Akcaoglu of Georgia Southern University, USA, diescusses teacher professional development taking place on Twitter in Georgia, USA.

Section 6, "Managerial Impact," covers the internal and external impacts of social networking within education and library administration. The first chapter, "Social Media in Tertiary Education: Considerations and Potential Issues," by Prof. Ann M. Simpson of Unitec Institute of Technology, New Zealand, addresses some of the considerations and potential issues that impact our use of social media in the higher education classroom. It examines social media as an educational tool in higher education, possible pedagogies for social media use, potential educational contexts, and privacy concerns raised by social media use in educational environments. The last chapter, "Social Media Integration in Educational Administration as Information and Smart Systems: Digital Literacy for Economic, Social, and Political Engagement in Namibia," by Profs. Sadrag Panduleni Shihomeka and Helena N. Amadhila of University of Namibia, Namibia, explains that there are various groups on Facebook where youthful education administrators can use to post educational information and discuss pertinent issues concerning their institutions.

Section 7, "Critical Issues and Challenges," presents coverage of academic and research perspectives on challenges to social networking in education and libraries. The first chapter, "Making Social Media More Social: A Literature Review of Academic Libraries' Engagement and Connections Through Social Media Platforms," by Prof. Elia Trucks of University of Denver, USA, explores how academic libraries have used social media for broadcasting information, responsive communication, and engagement. The last chapter, "Social Media Usage for Informal Learning in Malaysia: Academic Researcher Perspective," by Prof. Mohmed Y. Mohmed Al-Sabaawi of Department of Management Information Systems, College of Administration and Economics, University of Mosul, Iraq; Prof. Halina Mohamed Dahlan of Information Systems Department, Azman Hashim International Business School, Universiti Teknologi Malaysia, Malaysia; and Prof. Hafiz Muhammad Faisal Shehzad of Department of Computer Science and IT, University of Sargodha, Pakistan, explores the use of social media for informal learning, barriers, benefits, and effect of individual factors.

Although the primary organization of the contents in this multi-volume work is based on its seven sections, offering a progression of coverage of the important concepts, methodologies, technologies, applications, social issues, and emerging trends, the reader can also identify specific contents by utilizing the extensive indexing system listed at the end of each volume. As a comprehensive collection of research on the latest findings related to social networking in education and library practices, the *Research Anthology on Applying Social Networking Strategies to Classrooms and Libraries* provides pre-service teachers, teacher educators, faculty and administrators of both K-12 and higher education, librarians, archivists, government officials, researchers, and academicians with a complete understanding of the applications and impacts of social networking. Given the vast number of issues concerning usage, failure, success, strategies, and applications of social networking applied to classrooms and libraries, the *Research Anthology on Applying Social Networking Strategies to Classrooms and Libraries* encompasses the most pertinent research on the applications, impacts, uses, and strategies of social networking.

Section 1
Fundamental Concepts and Theories

Chapter 1
Social Media and the Future of the Instructional Model

Soha Abdeljaber
Rising Leaders Academy, USA

Kathryn Nieves Licwinko
https://orcid.org/0000-0003-4430-9934
New Jersey City University, USA

ABSTRACT

This chapter provides the latest information on social media and its application in the instructional model. The chapter contains information on how social media enhances learning, especially at times where remote learning is necessary, such as COVID-19. It also includes problems that have been documented in schools as a result of social media. This chapter also presents information about the use of social media for professional development and how teachers are interacting and collaborating using social media.

WHAT IS SOCIAL MEDIA?

Social media have been defined as "a group of internet-based applications that build on the ideological and technological foundations of Web 2.0, and that allow the creation and exchange of user generated content" (Kaplan & Haenlein, 2010, p. 61). Hudson (2020) stated that social media refers to websites and applications that are designed to allow people to share content quickly, efficiently, and in real-time. While many people access social media through smartphone apps, this communication tool started with computers, and social media can refer to any internet communication tool that allows users to broadly share content and engage with the public. The first recognizable social media website, known as Six Degrees, was created in 1997, and the first blogging sites followed in 1999. In the early 2000s, social media website like MySpace began to emerge. Then in 2005, YouTube came out creating an entirely new way for people to communicate and share videos from around the world. Then in 2006, Facebook and Twitter exploded throughout the world and remained two of the most popular social networks (Hen-

DOI: 10.4018/978-1-6684-7123-4.ch001

dricks, 2019). According to Engel (2020), Facebook had more than 2.3 billion monthly active users in 2019, and this number is only expected to rise.

Expands Student Engagement

People from around the world use social media to engage and share their interest and passion, as well as videos and information that others can share. Educators are always looking for ways to engage students, and social media has been one tool that proved to be effective. According to Dragseth (2019), social media can increase student engagement. Social media can expand students' creativity, work ethics, and engagement (Ashford University, 2020). Since students are using social media more frequently and are already engaged with each other using it, social media expanded student engagement in learning as well (Ashford University, 2020). Teachers are assigning activities and sharing information on social media because they had a positive outcome with student engagement. Technology and social media also allow for creativity because of the various tools that students can use, which they are already familiar with.

Social media sites are usually interactive, and this keeps the student involved and engaged (Willbold, 2019). According to the Pew Research Center, teenagers are growing more comfortable sharing more information on social media each year (Lee, 2020). This will likely result in more students' engagement. Social media allows people to communicate indirectly, which could help students in social anxiety in public (Lee, 2020).

Students' perceptions towards teachers impact their motivation and learning engagement (Mahmud et al., 2016). Studies show that teachers who provide information about themselves on social media were perceived by students as more credible and relatable (Mahmud et al., 2016). Students became more comfortable participating in class, which increased student engagement. Research shows that students are more susceptible towards teachers who are active on social media because they feel like they can easily reach out to them for classroom information and instruction (Mahmoud et al., 2016).

Supports Collaborative Environment

As teachers use social media more for personal use, they are also using it to enable learning and collaboration among students in the classroom (Fuglei, 2020). Research has shown positive effects of the use of social media in education, including new opportunities for connection and collaboration (Li & Greenhow, 2015). Social media supports an open forum and collaborative learning environment. Information can be shared at a rapid-pace which can help students accelerate the development of creative, critical thinking, and communication processes (Ashford University, 2020).

Students from around the world can connect and collaborate through social media websites. According to Ansari and Khan (2020), social media used for collaborative learning had significant impact on the interactivity between students and teachers, as well as students with each other. Social media for collaborative learning also improves students' academic performance and satisfaction (Zhu, 2012). Social media also supports student collaboration where students can share work and critique projects. An educator at Penn State University created an iTunes U class which gathered more than 58,000 students where they could share work and evaluate each other's projects (Davis, 2018).

Deepens Classroom Conversations

Social media emphasizes collaboration, engagement, critical thinking, and reflection, which are associated with deep learning (Samuels-Peretz, 2017). Students' satisfaction in learning using social media was higher than in traditional classroom because students can share knowledge and send messages to peers through social media platforms (Suebsom, 2020). Social media conversations deepened academic dialogue in their classrooms because students who do not speak much in the classroom usually participate in online conversations more than they do offline (Stevens, 2013). Research shows that integrating social media in the instructional model has positive psychological effects (Jackson, 2011). Shy students feel safer participating in discussions where they can type rather than speak. Typing responses allows students to read their input before they submit and are able to edit what they want to express before sharing it with others. This provides more confidence for students. Jackson (2011) stated that "social media allows teachers to manage social anxiety and create a safe learning environment where everyone learns". Social media can enhance student relationships and interactions, especially for socially anxious or introverted students (Fuglei, 2020). Research shows that student connections through social media created a safe place for students where they could share more and not worry as much about making mistakes (Sun et al, 2017). Social media networks promote connectedness that tie students' academic and social experiences into the same learning environment (Eamer et al., 2014).

With social media, teachers can transfer the classroom discussion to social media to keep the conversation going long after the classroom has adjourned (David, 2018). Schwarz and Caduri (2016) found that school teachers used social media to increase students' active learning in core subjects to foster inquiry-based science, historical reasoning, and literary analysis. Teachers use social media features such as posts, likes, chat, share, and comments to deepen classroom conversations. Batsila and Tsihouridis (2016) found that teachers who used social media tools for digital storytelling in English classes helped enhance their students' reading and writing skills, as well as their interest in writing and students' self-confident. Thibaut (2015) found that Edmodo, a social network site, increase students' critical evaluation of writing, as well their awareness of audience and authorship. These researchers found that social media motivated students to write for an audience beyond the classroom, engage critically in the writing process, and empower students to take ownership of their learning. According to Willbold (2019), social media helps students to learn certain concepts with great efficacy. A study by Blaschke (2014) found that students perceived specific social media in conjunction with learning activities as influencing cognitive and meta-cognitive skills.

Support Differentiation

Teachers can find hundreds of tools for differentiating instruction through social media with a simple Google search and that list is increasing. Social media has been used to enhanced differentiated instruction for all grade levels. Tomlinson & Allan (2000) defined differentiation as "a teacher reacting responsively to a learner's needs. Differentiation is simply attending to the learning needs of a particular student or small group of students rather than the more typical pattern of teaching the class as though all individuals in it were basically alike." Differentiated instruction enables educators to modify their instruction to address students' strengths and needs, interests, and learning profile (Koehler, 2010).

With social media, teachers give students a variety of learning experiences that incorporate the capability to exchange ideas, offer feedback, and provide avenues to connect content with the learners' interests

(McCarty, 2016). Social media also supports differentiation by allowing the needs of creative learners to be met through a cooperative learning environment (Wenzel & Carano, 2021). Teachers can also use technology and social media to individualize and differentiate instruction for exceptional students who need additional support (Mahoney & Hall, 2017).

Social Media in Blended Learning and Flipped Classrooms

Social media in both the blended learning environment and flipped classrooms can help students improve knowledge, thinking skills and creative thinking skills, while making them more confident to share knowledge and work collaboratively with each other (Suebsom, 2020). For this reason, the use of social learning in blended learning and flipped classrooms are becoming popular tools of education in the 21st century. Blended learning is a methodology that includes both online and traditional teaching, so it essentially is a blend of learning using face-to-face instruction and technology. Many teachers use social media for their online portion of blended learning. In a flipped classroom, online teaching is an additional support to traditional teaching. Flipped classroom is a type of blended learning where students flip what they do at home and in the classroom, so what used to be done in the classroom is now done at home online, and what used to be done at home, like practicing problems, is now done in the classroom where the teacher can guide students. Mitchell (2020) stated that "content instruction takes place outside of class time, while in-class time is devoted to conceptual interaction and practice, consistent with the concept of classroom flipping". YouTube is a video sharing platform that has been a popular option for introducing flipped classroom concepts for instruction, where students are first exposed to new material at home through social media. Teachers share educational lectures in video format as a form of presenting material online.

K-12 Social Media Communities During COVID-19

When the COVID-19 pandemic caused schools around the world to begin closing, remote learning was forced on students and teachers. Essentially, teachers needed to gain immediate expertise in online learning to keep schooling going (Porter, 2020). As a result, the just-in-time professional learning provided through social media became a necessity. Educators began turning to social media to curate online resources that they felt could support their students (Karimi et al., 2020). For example, many teachers created Facebook groups after the teacher strikes of 2018, but these groups were transitioned to remote learning resources for educators during the pandemic (Hagerty, 2020). These spaces became areas where educators could share successful ideas of how they supported their learners virtually, as well as a place to post state, local, and school-related COVID-19 updates (Hagerty, 2020). In the early days of the pandemic, the educator social media posts with the most interaction were free advice and resources and critiques about the online learning transition (Harron & Liu, 2020), demonstrating teachers' needs for both instructional materials and support.

During the Covid-19 pandemic, there has been a spike in social media usage worldwide where free digital tools were used for education (Koeze & Popper, 2020). Covid-19 hit the United States hard in the spring of 2020 causing schools in all states to shut down and go to remote learning. Many K-12 schools rapidly transitioned to remote learning and used social media to bring students and teachers together (Greenhow & Chapman, 2020). Social media supports active learning to overcome the barriers of distance learning to reduce the feeling of distance or disconnect (Greenhow & Chapman, 2020). The accessibilities via social media enable learning to be less affected by physical settings (Mahmoud et al., 2016). Given that social media usage for educators can eliminate feelings of stress or being overworked (Chatterjee & Parra, 2020), these platforms were shown to be supportive during the remote learning transition.

The COVID-19 pandemic saw a rise in teachers adopting newer social media platforms. Educators began using the quick video social media tool to create engaging videos for their students (Nierenberg & Pasick, 2020). Then, when they posted the video to the platform, they generated teacher and education hashtags, which made it easier for educators to track each other's video content (Nierenberg & Pasick, 2020). Educators also turned to other social networking sites, like Facebook groups and Twitter, to share ideas. In a study of two popular remote learning hashtags on Twitter (#remotelearning & #remoteteaching) at the start of the school closures and the COVID-19 pandemic, Trust et al. (2020) found that the hashtags were used in posts over 36,000 times a month. Held within these hashtag streams were an abundance of resources to support educators making the transition to these learning environments (Trust et al., 2020). In addition, remote learning-centered Facebook groups were formed, tailored to each content area subject and age group. These groups were developed as an "emergency" community of practice where educators had an accessible space to gain resources, express challenges and concerns, and seek advice, all surrounding a common need (Gandolfi & Kratcoski, 2020).

Potentially Problematics Issues With Using Social Media for Instruction

When students post, upload, or communicate via social media platforms, such as Facebook and Twitter, that are not licensed by the university or K-12 school district, issues related to privacy, accessibility, and equity that make required assignments potentially problematic (UC Berkley, 2017). Greenhow and Askari (2017) stated that teachers have a responsibility to protect students' privacy, and this limits the teachers' use of social media as a learning tool. In addition, students can message each other privately through social media, which makes it difficult to prevent students from working together when they are supposed to be completing activities independently. Online interactions can cause miscommunication since the individuals are not able to hear the tone spoken or see the body language, so the views and ideas written may be misunderstood. There is also the possibility of inappropriate communication and cyberbullying among students. There has also been evidence of students being bullied on social media, as well as cases where students posted threats of school violence (Joosten, 2012).

In addition, spending too much time online has been shows to have an effect on the health of individuals because spending a lot of time on social media can affect the way the genes operate within the human body and weaken the immune and hormone levels, as well as the function of arteries (Zaidieh, 2012). Further, spending too much time on social media has also been shown that it has an impact on mental health (Zaidieh, 2012). Kirschner and Karpinski (2010) also found that students' grades declined as their use of Facebook increased. Junco and Cotton (2013) also found that students' college GPA dropped when they used Facebook while doing school work. Social media presents a distraction for many students who spend time interacting with peers rather than focus on their school work (Zimmer, 2018). Another issue with social media has been the spread of misinformation. Priebe (2020) stated that the spread of misinformation on social media has been a critical issue during the COVID-19 Pandemic.

Impact on Instructional Practice

Within education, social media has the capacity to influence instructional practices for teachers. Many educators are turning toward applications such as Facebook, Twitter, and Instagram, among others, for collegial collaboration, resources, and materials. The use of social media is considered an informal professional development practice, where teachers are receiving additional tools and strategies to better support their students (Rodesiler & Pace, 2015). Since professional learning is essential, including embracing changes and discovering new tools to better support learners (Darling-Hammond et al., 2009), social media has become a more popular format for ongoing teacher learning.

These online communities also have the potential to combat feelings of isolation that educators often experience, as well as allow for the opportunity to gain support and advice from teachers from around the world (Kelly & Antonio, 2016; Trust et al., 2017). These learning experiences connect to some of the characteristics of effective professional development, including an emphasis on student learning and pedagogy, the ability to make connections and create a change, and sustained support (Darling-Hammond et al., 2009). Educators who spend time investing in their professional learning through social media have reported positive results for their pedagogy (Ranieri et al., 2012). Furthermore, through the use of social media for professional learning outside of the classroom, teachers essentially become models of lifelong learners for their students (Trust, 2012).

Social media serves as a self-selected professional development opportunity that is personalized for the teacher (Trust, 2016). These platforms act as just-in-time learning, where teachers have full control of their professional development, deciding what they want to learn based on their needs and offering timing flexibility (Greenhalgh & Koehler, 2016). The asynchronous capabilities of social media allow educators to log on and participate in sharing and conversations at times that are convenient for their schedule. Although teachers are often given opportunities to collaborate with the people in their schools, social media opens the opportunity for connections to be made with other teachers from around the world (Carpenter & Linton, 2016). Despite the fact that many districts have adopted policies discouraging social media use, schools are moving toward accepting and promoting educational uses of these platforms, including teacher professional learning (Rodesiler, 2017). In fact, the United States Department of Education (2010) openly encouraged states and school districts to begin using social networking as a way to form communities of practice among educators and increase their professional learning.

Social Learning Theory's Application to Social Media

Social media has changed the platform for social interactions, and educators found an opportunity to apply the concepts of Bandura's Social Learning Theory to enhance student engagement and learning in the social media platform (Deaton, 2015). The social learning theory, proposed by Albert Bandura, emphasizes the importance of observing, in which people learn by watching others (Bandura, 1986). Students can learn from anyone, including teachers, peers, and individuals on YouTube. Bandura (1986) proposed four mediation processes for learning, which are attention, retention, reproduction, and motivation.

The application of the social learning theory presents an opportunity to promote leaps in students' achievement, which improves attention, memory, and motivation (Deaton, 2015). Social media provides a platform for improving learning in a social context by enhancing the cognitive processes of attention, memory, and motivation (Deaton, 2015). Utilizing social media outlets, such as Facebook and Twitter, in the instructional model requires for students to stay focused and attentive where they post comments, read articles, and like posts (Casey & Wells, 2015). The visual stimuli seen in the social media platforms can be coded into the students' memory, which helps students create mental images and memories based on temporary sensory experiences (Ponton & Rhea, 2006). Social media also provides a platform for interaction with peers in a low-risk environment since digital interactions are detached from many social anxieties, and this can be motivational for students, and it may translate to higher engagement and increased student learning (Deaton, 2015).

Student Learning Outcomes

Social media allows students to communicate more efficiently, so students can collaborate more and have more effective outcomes (Stevens, 2013). Javaeed et al. (2020) conducted a study to assess the impact of integrating social media in the instructional model on student learning outcome and found the outcome which included social media was statistically significant. According to Javaeed et al. (2020), "Social media integration provided better examination outcomes for the students and gave voice or space to those who never previously asked questions or participated in the class". There are many reasons for this, which include increased student engagement and collaboration as mentioned above. Social media gave a voice for students, especially those who never participated in class, allowing students to communicate with confidence (Javaeed et al, 2020). Willbold (2019) stated that social media provides plenty of information that students are more inclined to read, especially with the animations attached. Students are putting extra effort towards learning by reading online messages, comments, and news articles that interest them (Willbold, 2019).

Professional Learning Networks

A professional learning network (PLN) is the term used to define educator relationships within an informal learning space. While PLNs may loosely be defined as interactions and experiences that support continued professional growth, the term has been extended to reflect educator connections within a digital space (Krutka et al., 2017). These PLNs tend to evolve through social media, where educators begin to follow other educators and topics of interest. These groups are global in nature, allowing educators to share and learn from others around the world, and also provide an opportunity to eliminate the isolation often experienced by teachers (Flanigan, 2011). Since PLNs are active outside of an educator's school, they may feel more comfortable expressing issues they are experiencing within their buildings without colleague judgement (Smith, 2016).

PLNs directly connect to the community of practice framework developed by Lave and Wenger (1991). In these communities, participants are joined together by a common interest and shared experiences. Initially, new participants observe the community of practice until they have gained the trust of the members and feel comfortable participating in the structure and culture of the group (Lave & Wenger, 1991). As the members increase their confidence and grow in their expertise, they begin to contribute to the community more frequently, eventually extending an outreach to find newer, less experienced members to add to the group (Lave & Wenger, 1991). Aside from collaboration and a common interest, communities of practice curate and share resources with members of the group (Wenger, 1996). This framework directly connects to the idea of a PLN. Educators join based on common interests, problems, or circumstances. Initially, newcomers observe the interactions within the community. They may begin contributing questions or seek advice before diving into the sharing of their own resources and ideas.

Through the documentation within a common hashtag or stored files within a Facebook group, the PLN, much like a community of practice, develops their collection of resources to share, which is edited as time progresses.

Initially, PLNs can be described as overwhelming due to the nonstop nature of social media activity and the quantity of users to follow. Magid and Gallagher (2015) recommend reaching out to colleagues to see who they follow on social networking sites, as well as searching for and following bloggers, authors, and researchers whose work is admired. If a teacher is able to successfully navigate the continuous sharing, posting, and learning of these networks and maneuver through the number of educational users, they will earn chances to receive support, feedback, new ideas, and opportunities to collaborate with other educators (Trust, 2012). The informality of these networks paired with the access to other educators and resources make it possible for teachers to continue their professional learning, while making transformations in their instructional practices (Beach, 2012).

Benefits for Rural Educators

Educators who work in rural areas of the world have unique challenges. With limited access to resources and professional development, attrition rates for educators working in these communities is consistently a problem (Malkus et al., 2015). Furthermore, rural educators may be the only teacher in their content area within the school or district, which can lead to feelings of isolation and limit access to a professional learning community (Waters & Hensley, 2020). Social media platforms are an opportunity for rural educators to gain the resources and professional connection they need. Through platforms such as Twitter, these teachers can have access to quality instructional materials, professional development, and connections with other educators around the globe (Zimmerle, 2020). Participation in a PLN within a virtual social media community allows for collaborative learning (Waters & Hensley, 2020), which can help rural educators gain the support and tools they need for their students.

PLNs Within Higher Education

A survey conducted by Moran et al. (2011) found that many United States professors and faculty members are already using social media for both their courses and their professional learning. While educators working within higher education have use for social media communities, their professional learning networks have differing characteristics from K-12 education. Professors tend to use social media to stay current on topics and studies within their fields (Gruzd et al., 2012). However, the largest appeal of social media comes from the ability to share work, rather than consume content. Professors most often use Twitter to share their own work and subsequent resources (Veletsianos, 2012). Self-promotion on social media allows for academic faculty can lead to larger scale recognition of their work (Chamberlin & Lehmann, 2011), as well as networking experience with their peers (Veletsianos, 2012). The research suggests that there is significant potential to building innovative communities through social media within higher education (Chugh & Ruhi, 2018).

Teacher candidates, or pre-service teachers, have often been encouraged to use their social media accounts for professional growth. While many pre-service teachers already have personal social media accounts, they may be conflicted about the difference between their professional and personal accounts. However, the research indicates that these teachers should be encouraged to participate in educator social media communities (Carpenter, 2015). Since they are preparing to enter the field of education, professional participation on social media can lead to connections and engagement with current in-service educators who are already in the classroom (Carpenter & Morrison, 2018). Not only do the new teachers gain the chance to build relationships with teachers who have been in the field longer (Carpenter & Morrison, 2018), they also gain access to resources and support, which can help them become adapted to the teaching profession (Alberth et al., 2018). Aspiring educators can also gain opportunities for informal mentorship with in-service teachers through social media (Carpenter, 2015). However, Kamalodeen and Jameson-Charles (2016) also point out that both the new teachers and veteran teachers can be mutually benefited from social media relationships, as each party can learn from the other.

The research suggests that education professors tend to push teacher candidates toward the use of social media for professional reasons because it can help prepare them for their future careers in the classroom (Shuck et al., 2013). Students are encouraged to create a professional educator account and participate in the culture of the community. A study by Asim et al. (2020) found that teacher candidates commonly build on the ideas of others, such as quoting articles, share online resources, engage with speakers of webinars, and post questions to gain advice and understanding. Undergraduates who use the platforms have described it as engaging and informative (Luo et al., 2017). However, forcing undergraduate students or pre-service teachers to engage in educator social media communities for class assignments is counterproductive and can negatively impact their future use of these platforms (Kruta & Damico, 2020). Furthermore, teacher candidates need to be aware of some of the challenges within social media communities. Prospective teachers tend to share lower quality resources and can potentially engage in irrelevant conversations that can negatively influence the social media community (Keles, 2017). Instruction on proper evaluation of online resources and a review of how to determine the culture of a social media community can help early educators from making these errors.

Characteristics of Social Media Communities

Each social media platform offers a differing approach to professional learning and educator collaboration. Educators can use social media to share successes, request feedback for improvement, find others in a similar role, and share student work on a larger scale than just the classroom (Randles, 2017). However, the manner in which each of those elements is conducted within each platform is unique. Twitter, for example, offers educators a limited character capacity to share thoughts, questions, and ideas with others. Hashtags help to curate the information and allow educators to follow specific topics of interest while also creating a more permanent community (Casal, 2017). Unlike other social media platforms, most educators tend to leave their Twitter profiles public to make it easier to build a community with others (Visser et al., 2014). Due to the ease of following hashtags and fellow educators, Twitter is often where teachers go for emerging trends in education and collaboration (Friedman, 2020).

Twitter extends beyond re-tweets, where users repost interesting links and comments from other participants on the platform. Especially in the educational sector, Twitter chats are common forms of professional learning. Users who are interested in the same topic can join together, select a specific meeting date and time, and engage in synchronous conversations through Tweets (Weslely, 2013). These Twitter chats often have a moderator who facilitates the discussion by tweeting questions to the group, paired with the group's topic-related hashtag (Wesley, 2013). Participants respond to the question prompt and also add the hashtag to their posts, which allows the posts to appear on the stream in chronological order to be followed like a conversation (Wesley, 2013). This synchronous element of Twitter is unique to the platform.

Instagram and Pinterest are all about images. Pinterest is designed for content curation, where teachers can post images that link to outside sources and discover new ideas for their classroom. The outside sources direct educators to different blogs, websites, and articles throughout the web. Through this social network, teachers become curators of content, where they select items based on quality, arrange it (in the case of Pinterest, adding it to a topic-specific board), and share it with others (Weisberger & Butler, 2012). Teachers most commonly use Pinterest to seek resources based on their students, including resources offering multiple means of access and differentiation for their students' needs (Irvine, 2015).

Facebook groups are communities of educators who come together to share interest in a common topic. Friedman (2020) considers Facebook to be a combination of popular features from other social networking sites. Unlike Twitter, Facebook tends to be more private, where the norm is to limit the individuals who can see a user's posts (Magid & Gallagher, 2015). Facebook groups can be created by any user of the platform and have varying levels of privacy from public to private but searchable by users or unsearchable, where users must be invited by a moderator to join (Moreau, 2019). Each group has administrators who are responsible for accepting and adding users to private groups, as well as moderating group interactions and posts (Moreau, 2019). Groups have the capacity to create and share events, images, videos, and files (Moreau, 2019). Some groups have mentoring experiences, where participants can become or gain a mentor to work with and learn from for approximately ten weeks (Facebook, n.d.).

Educator Interactions

Just as the characteristics of each social media platform differs, there is also variance among the method of interactions among educators. Typically, social media allows teachers to have access to like-minded individuals, as well as other educators with differing perspectives and ideas (Carpenter & Krutka, 2015). Participants are able to share successes, failures, and anecdotes, as well as pursue resources and expertise of other educators regarding materials, methods, assessments, and curriculum (Alberth et al., 2018). Teachers are free to respond to and connect with educators at their own leisure, which opens opportunities to reflect on the learning one has done through discussions (Alberth et al., 2018). However, it is not just participators who benefit from the social media experience. Teachers new to the platform can still acquire the advantages of educator interactions as a silent observer (Marcià & García, 2016). These observations can help promote educator learning while still allowing them to learn the logistics and technicalities of the social networking site.

Both Twitter chats and Facebook group forums offer opportunities for users to engage in conversation and interact. Through these platforms, teachers have the ability to discover more about curricula, instructional techniques, and technology, as well as address concerns about teaching issues (Bissessar, 2014). In a study of physical education teachers participating in professional learning on Facebook and Twitter, Goodyear et al. (2014) found that the interactions encouraged inquiry while simultaneously challenged teachers to be more innovative and collaborative. Similarly, educators were able to use Twitter to form a relationship with other classrooms around the world, as well as connect with experts who could share their expertise with their students (Visser et al., 2014). Rossell-Aguilar (2018) surveyed educators about their professional learning on Twitter and found that most users have tested out an idea or strategy they have learned from others on the platform, which led to positive classroom results.

In terms of interactions between educators, there are also differences when it comes to gender and area of educational focus. For example, middle and high school teachers are less likely to try out a new strategy discussed through a Twitter chat than their elementary educator colleagues (Nochumson, 2020).

Similarly, Kerr and Schmeichel (2018) found that men and women who participated in social media communities had different types of interactions with their educational PLN. Men were more likely to engage in self-promotion, distribution of feedback or advice, or criticism of the ideas another educator had posted (Kerr & Schmeichel, 2018). Women, by contrast, were more likely to offer positive feedback to other users, at least when engaging in Twitter chats (Kerr & Schmeichel, 2018). Minimal research has been conducted about the differences within gender and participation in other social networking sites, such as Instagram and Pinterest.

Interaction Challenges

Social media communities for educators are not without faults. The development of a resourceful and meaningful social media community takes a long period of time to form, otherwise it could result in educators feeling unfulfilled in terms of learning by these spaces (Donelan, 2016). Even within functioning communities, negative interactions can occur that hinder professional learning. For example, participation in Facebook group discussions can turn pessimistic, resulting in off-topic conversations and the sharing of low-quality educational resources (Keles, 2017). Twitter hashtags for education topics often have similar problems, where threads designated for teachers can become filled with irrelevant content and single users monopolizing the hashtag, rather than acting as an ongoing dialogue and reflection on educational practice (Casal, 2017). In some cases, such as Facebook groups, there is a moderator to keep posts relevant and on topic (Bergviken Rensfeldt et al., 2018). However, the existence of these moderators within informal educator communities also run the risk of overregulation and censoring of group members.

Identity Struggles

When teachers engage in social media communities, they are not just seeking professional learning, they are looking to gain a professional identity (Carpenter et al., 2019). However, Pittard (2017) suggests that social media can lead to identity struggles for educators. In viewing the Instagram classroom pictures and lesson plans shared by other teachers online, teachers can gain unrealistic expectations and begin questioning their performance in their role (Pittard, 2017). Furthermore, the privacy settings within social media can cause "context collapse," where posts are public and can reach an infinite audience (Carpenter et al., 2019). With social media platforms like Instagram and Twitter, teachers often remain public so they can be followed by others. However, this setting also leaves their posts open to be viewed, shared, and commented on by others, even those outside the field of education. Carpenter et al. (2019) describe this situation as challenging for educator's identities because they struggle with how to present themselves professionally when their work can be viewed by other educators, students, families, and communities.

Resources Shared

The information shared on social media has the capacity to translate into real life experiences and situations (Ranieri et al., 2012). Therefore, the sharing of resources and strategies is one of the primary advantages of social media, aside from the educator-to-educator connections. While conferences often serve as a way for teachers to gain materials and instructional methods to support their students, teachers have indicated that time and money are barriers to attendance. Participation in social media, by following conference hashtags, have become ways for educators to virtually attend and participate in these workshops and sessions (Visser et al., 2014). In developing countries where access to new resources and instructional methodologies may not be as easy to find, social media provides an access point to new techniques and strategies (Bett & Makewa, 2017). Teachers might share links directly to materials, images of student work or classroom experiences, or discussions of instructional strategies.

The Influence of Entrepreneurship and Professional Branding

In recent years, social media communities have shifted toward self-promotion and personal branding (Bergviken Rensfeldt et al., 2018). A personal brand is a way that a user can set themselves apart from the other educators on these apps, allowing their life experiences and unique perspectives to be showcased (Shulman, 2019). Through this branding, educators can display their expertise and better support others (Shulman, 2019). According to Randles (2017), social media is a way to build a digital resume: to showcase conference attendance, successful classroom lessons and experiences, and blog posts. However, aside from this personal branding work, there has been a rise in educational entrepreneurs and influencers on social media. These teacher influencers use their social media presence to advertise for their products or paid resources, rather than to seek advice or connect to other educators (Berry et al., 2013). Similarly, popular education hashtags on apps like Instagram have been inundated with promotional products and for-purchase resources by influences (Reinstein, 2018). Many of these teachers are linking to their outside websites, where other educators can purchase their self-created instructional materials (Reinstein, 2018; Schroeder et al., 2019). While these opportunities on social media allow for teachers to earn additional financial compensation for their work, it also has the potential to impact the quality and types of resources used in classrooms. Torphy et al. (2020) define this situation as the influence of "teacherpreneurial guilds," where teachers develop a community of self-promotion, gaining followers to sell their personal brand and professional materials. These educators build a level of trust with their teacher followers, causing them to purchase, promote, and follow their educational practices, strategies, and resources within their own classrooms (Torphy et al., 2020).

Social Media for Posting School Announcements

Teachers are starting to communicate with their students and post announcements about instruction on social media. Many teachers are creating Facebook groups for the classes to post announcements, communicate, and collaborate (Cunha, van Kruistum, & van Oers, 2016). Teachers may also use Facebook to remind students about the instructions of assignment, post videos, and set discussions. Research has shown that teachers who actively participate in social media with students and parents are more successful at building community (Gao et al., 2012). Facebook has also been a popular website with parents in which districts share messages, stories, and information about school events and activities. Twitter has also been used by schools to update parents on school activities, projects and events Willbold (2019).

Social Media and the Future of the Instructional Model

Lenhart (2015) reported that 92% of teenagers in the U.S go online daily. In 2015, the Pew Research Center found that 71% of teens use more than one social networking site (Lee, 2020). In 2017, one million new people joined social networks every single day (Kemp, 2018). In a global study of the internet and social media across 239 countries, researchers found that social media usage will continue to grow (Kemp, 2018). According to Willbold (2019), every individual above 13 years old will have a social media account. As more and more people began to interact on social media, it became integrated in many fields that affect humans, such as politics and education. In schools, social media is becoming more popular to keep students engaged and provide quick, short responses.

Prior to the Covid-19 pandemic, there were over 3 billion regular social media users with a significant increase in daily screen time since the pandemic began (Iwai, 2020). Not only are teachers using it to enhance instruction, they have found it to be a very helpful tool to use in extenuating circumstances, such as natural disasters and during the COVID-19 Pandemic. During COVID-19 in 2020, most schools in the United States closed, and learning shifted online for students from all levels around the world and in the United States. Instructors turned to social networks, such as Zoom, YouTube, and Facebook to hold live sessions and provide instruction. COVID-19 has shifted schools and educators to implement more technology in the instructional model that as of yet is still unknown how it will inevitably change education. Social media has been an effective tool that helped teaches, parents, and students remain connected outside schools. COVID-19 demonstrated that technology can help transform traditional instructional models where the one-size-fits-all approach to education is undergoing unprecedented change (Spencer, 2020). With this change, teachers will likely use social media more to connect with their students and educate them since it has been proven to be an effective instructional tool that expands student engagement, supports collaborative learning, improves learning outcome, and deepens classroom conversations. Greenhow and Galvin (2020) stated, "Social media, with its affordances for personal profiling, relationship-building, content creation and socializing, when thoughtfully integrated into an online education plan, can help students and teachers stay connected while apart, enhance students' engagement and make remote learning seem less remote." As the world becomes more connected via technology, students from around the world can access education through live lectures on social media remote and even while living in remote areas of the world (Willbold, 2019).

Davis (2018) shared ways to use social media in education to impact student learning. These are ways that will likely be implemented more in the future, especially after the COVID-19 pandemic when learning became mostly online for most students in the United States and around the world. One way is to use social media as an online classroom. Davis (2018) suggested that teachers can created private groups on social media tools, such as Facebook, where teachers can post assignments, give live lectures, and answer questions via comments and private messages. This works well for students who are unable to a traditional classroom (Davis, 2018). Teachers can also keep students involved during school breaks by positing assignments, projects, and discussions on social media. This can help students keep us the momentum in their school work (Davis, 2018). West (2019) suggested that teachers use a Facebook page to broadcast updated and alerts, as well as stream live lectures and host discussions. Even if students are not active on Facebook, these pages are still accessible when students are not signed on.

Trends and the Future of Social Media and Professional Learning

Current trends in social media usage among educators show that there will likely be a rise in teachers looking to adopt new platforms as they emerge. Although Twitter has been the most studied app for teacher professional learning (Bruguera et al., 2019), teachers are showing signs of testing alternate platforms. The landscape of social media is consistently changing, given the transition from Twitter and Facebook to the increasingly popular Instagram among educators over the past several years (Carpenter et al., 2019).

Consider the recent increase with video-based platforms, like TikTok, it is apparent that teachers are seeking new ways to learn from their peers. Since educator sharing of curricula, instructional materials, and teaching methodologies appears to be a consistent practice over the past few years, these experiences will likely continue. However, as more educators participate in social media communities and share links and resources, teachers need to remain mindful of their material selection to ensure rigor and validity.

Social media will continue to play a role in professional development for educators. The number of studies related to social media and informal learning for teachers has increased in recent years (Bruguera et al., 2019). Furthermore, the coronavirus pandemic caused many educators to shift toward social networking as a survival tool to gain the strategies and support they needed to maneuver through the school year. The flexibility and socialization aspects of social media platforms (Bruguera et al., 2019) will make these spaces will likely serve as informal learning environments for educators for years to come. While educators may engage in new platforms and apps as they arise, the common theme is that they will likely continue to collaborate and share their practices with others.

REFERENCES

Alberth, A., Mursalim, M., Siam, S., Suardika, I. K., & Ino, L. (2018). Social media as a conduit for teacher professional development in the digital era: Myths, promises, or realities? *TEFLIN Journal, 29*(2), 293–306. doi:10.15639/teflinjournal.v29i2/293-306

Ansari, J.A. & Khan, N.A. (2020). Exploring the role of social media in collaborative learning the new domain of learning. *Smart Learning Environments, 7*(9).

Asim, S., Poyo, S., & Fecich, S. (2020). It's about how to pivot: Teacher educators, teacher candidates, and Twitter. In R. E. Ferdig, E. Baumgartner, R. Hartshorne, R. Kaplan-Rakowski, & C. Mouza (Eds.), Teaching, Technology, and Teacher Education during the COVID-19 Pandemic: Stories from the Field (pp. 279–288). Academic Press.

Bandura, A. (1986). *Social foundations of thought and action: A social cognitive theory*. Prentice-Hall, Inc.

Batsila, M., & Tsihouridis, C. (2016). 'Once upon a time there was…' a digital world for junior high school learners. *International Journal of Emerging Technologies in Learning, 11*(3), 42–50. doi:10.3991/ijet.v11i03.5370

Beach, R. (2012). Can online learning communities foster professional development? *Language Arts, 89*(4), 252–262.

Bergviken Rensfeldt, A., Hillman, T., & Selwyn, N. (2018). Teachers 'liking their work? Exploring the realities of teacher Facebook groups. *British Educational Research Journal, 44*(2), 230–250. doi:10.1002/berj.3325

Berkley, U. C. (2017). *Teaching with Social Media*. Retrieved from https://teaching.berkeley.edu/teaching-social-media

Berry, B., Byrd, A., & Wieder, A. (2013). *Teacherpreneurs: Innovative teachers who lead but don't leave*. Jossey-Bass.

Bett, H., & Makewa, L. (2017). Can Facebook groups enhance continuing professional development of teachers? Lessons from Kenya. *Asia-Pacific Journal of Teacher Education*, *48*(2), 132–146. doi:10.10 80/1359866X.2018.1542662

Bissessar, C. S. G. (2014). Facebook as an informal teacher professional development tool. *The Australian Journal of Teacher Education*, *39*(2). Advance online publication. doi:10.14221/ajte.2014v39n2.9

Blascke, L. (2014). Using social media to engage and develop the online learner in self-determined learning. *Research in Learning Technology*, *22*. Advance online publication. doi:10.3402/rlt.v22.21635

Bruguera, C., Guitert, M., & Romeu, T. (2019). Social media and professional development: A systematic review. *Research in Learning Technology*, *27*(0), 27. doi:10.25304/rlt.v27.2286

Carpenter, J. (2015). Preservice teachers' microblogging: Professional development via Twitter. Contemporary Issues in Technology & Teacher Education, 15(2).

Carpenter, J., Morrison, S., Craft, M., & Lee, M. (2019). Exploring how and why educators use Instagram. In K. Graziano (Ed.), *Proceedings of Society for Information Technology & Teacher Education International Conference* (pp. 2686-2691). Academic Press.

Carpenter, J. P., & Krutka, D. G. (2015). Engagement through microblogging: Educator professional development via Twitter. *Professional Development in Education*, *41*(4), 707–728. doi:10.1080/19415 257.2014.939294

Carpenter, J. P., & Linton, J. N. (2016). Edcamp unconferences: Educators' perspec-tives on an untraditional professional learning experience. *Teaching and Teacher Education*, *57*, 97–108. doi:10.1016/j. tate.2016.03.004

Carpenter, J. P., & Morrison, S. A. (2018). Enhancing teacher education...with Twitter? *Phi Delta Kappan*, *100*(1), 25–28. doi:10.1177/0031721718797118

Casal, S. S. (2017). Conversations, debates, and affiliation networks on Twitter. *The Turkish Online Journal of Educational Technology*, *16*(3), 47–59.

Casey, G. G., & Wells, M. M. (2015). Remixing to design learning: Social media and peer-to-peer interaction. *Journal of Learning Design*, *8*(1), 39–54. doi:10.5204/jld.v8i1.225

Chamberlain, L., & Lehmann, K. (2011). Twitter in higher education. In C. Wankel (Ed.), *Educating Educators with Social Media* (pp. 375–391). doi:10.1108/S2044-9968(2011)0000001021

Chatterjee, S., & Parra, J. (2020). Innovative design revisions on an undergraduate technology integration course for K-12 preservice teachers. In R. E. Ferdig, E. Baumgartner, R. Hartshorne, R. Kaplan-Rakowski, & C. Mouza (Eds.), Teaching, Technology, and Teacher Education during the COVID-19 Pandemic: Stories from the Field (pp. 431–442). Academic Press.

Chugh, R., & Ruhi, U. (2018). Social media in higher education: A literature review of Facebook. *Education and Information Technologies*, *23*(2), 605–616. doi:10.100710639-017-9621-2

Cunda, F. & van Kruistum, O. (2016). *Teachers and Facebook: using online groups to improve students' communication and engagement in education.* Retrieved from https://www.researchgate.net/publication/307936668_Teachers_and_Facebook_using_online_groups_to_improve_students'_communication_and_engagement_in_education

Darling-Hammond, L., Wei, R. C., Andree, A., Richardson, N., & Orphanos, S. (2009). *Professional learning in the learning profession.* National Staff Development Council. https://learningforward.org/docs/pdf/nsdcstudy2009.pdf

Davis, L. (2018). *The impact of social media in education: Student engagement tactics.* Retrieved from https://www.schoology.com/blog/impact-social-media-education-student-engagement-tactics

Deaton, S. (2015). Social learning theory in the age of social media: Implications for educational practitioners. *Journal of Educational Technology, 12*(1), 1–6.

Donelan, H. (2016). Social media for professional development and networking opportunities in academia. *Journal of Further and Higher Education, 40*(6), 706–729. doi:10.1080/0309877X.2015.1014321

Dragseth, M. (2019). *Building student engagement through social media.* Retrieved from doi:10.1080/15512169.2018.1550421

Eamer, A., Hughes, J., & Morrison, L. J. (2014). Crossing cultural borders through Ning. *Multicultural Education Review, 6*(1), 49–78. doi:10.1080/2005615X.2014.11102907

Engel, R. (2020). *Four social media platforms school districts should be using in 2020.* Retrieved from https://www.finalsite.com/blog/p/~board/b/post/social-media-platforms-school-districts-2020

Facebook. (n.d.). *What are Facebook mentorship groups and how do they work?* https://www.facebook.com/help/380533659173752

Flanigan, R. (2011). *Professional learning networks taking off.* Education Week. http://www.edweek.org/ew/articles/2011/10/26/09edtech-network.h31.html?tkn=NXCFrTi53Q/

Friedman, J. (2020, January 16). *Using social media for teacher professional development.* Houghton Mifflin Harcourt. https://www.hmhco.com/blog/using-social-media-for-teacher-professional-development

Fuglei, M. (2020). *Social medial in education: Benefits, drawbacks, and things to avoid.* Retrieved from https://blog.sharetolearn.com/leaders-link/educational-social-media-use/

Gandolfi, E., & Kratcoski, A. (2020). Building a community of practice for technology integration and educational reform in a time of crisis. In R. E. Ferdig, E. Baumgartner, R. Hartshorne, R. Kaplan-Rakowski, & C. Mouza (Eds.), Teaching, Technology, and Teacher Education during the COVID-19 Pandemic: Stories from the Field (pp. 169–174). Academic Press.

Gao, F., Luo, T., & Zhang, K. (2012). Tweeting for learning: A critical analysis of research on microblogging in education published in 2008-2011. *British Journal of Educational Technology, 43*(5), 783–801. https://doi.org/10.1111/j.1467-8535.2012.01357.x

Goodyear, V. A., Casey, A., & Kirk, D. (2014). Tweet me, message me, like me: Using social media to facilitate pedagogical change within an emerging community of practice. *Sport Education and Society, 19*(7), 927–943.

Greenhalgh, S. P., & Koehler, M. J. (2016). 28 days later: Twitter hashtags as "just in time" teacher professional development. *TechTrends*, *61*(3), 273–281.

Greenhow, C., & Askari, E. (2017). Learning and teaching with social network sites: A decade of research in K-12 related education. *Education and Information Technologies*, *22*(2), 623–645. https://doi.org/10.1007/s10639-015-9446-9

Greenhow, C., & Chapman, A. (2020). Social distancing meets social media: Digital tools for connecting students, teachers, and citizens in an emergency. *Information and Learning Sciences, 121*(5), 341-352. doi:10.1108/ILS-04-2020-0134

Greenhow, C., & Galvin, S. (2020). Teaching with social media: Evidence-based strategies for making remote higher education less remote. *Information and Learning Sciences, 121*(7), 513-524. https://search.ebsohost.com/login.aspx?direct=true&AuthType=shib&db=edsemr&AN=edsemr

Harron, J., & Liu, S. (2020). Coronavirus and online learning: A case study of influential K-12 teacher voices on Twitter. In E. Langran (Ed.), *Proceedings of SITE Interactive 2020 Online Conference* (pp. 719-724). Academic Press.

Hendricks, D. (2019). *Complete history of social media: Then and now*. Retrieved from https://smallbiztrends.com/2013/05/the-complete-history-of-social-media-infographic.html

Hudson, M. (2020). *What is social media?* Retrieved from https://www.thebalancesmb.com/what-is-social-media-2890301

Irvine, T. M. (2015). *Pinned: A qualitative study of teacher experiences of interfacing with online resources for lesson planning* (Unpublished Doctoral Dissertation). Capella University.

Jackson, C. (2011). Your students love social media… and so can you. *Teaching Tolerance*, *39*, 38–41.

Javaeed, A., Kibria, Z., Khan, Z., & Ghauri, S. K. (2020). Impact of Social Media Integration in Teaching Methods on Exam Outcomes. *Advances in Medical Education and Practice*, *11*, 53–61. https://doi.org/10.2147/AMEP.S209123

Joosten, T. (2012). *Social media for educators: Strategies and best practices*. Jossey-Bass.

Junco, R., & Cotton, S. R. (2013). No a 4 U: The relationship between multitasking and academic performance. *Computers & Education*, *59*(2), 505–514. https://doi.org/10.1016/j.compedu.2011.12.023

Kamalodeen, V. J., & Jameson-Charles, M. (2016). A mixed methods research approach to exploring teacher participation in an online social networking website. *International Journal of Qualitative Methods*, *15*(1).

Kaplan, A. M., & Haenlein, M. (2010). Users of the world, unite! The challenges and opportunities of social media. *Business Horizons*, *53*(1), 59–68.

Karimi, H., Derr, T., Trophy, K. T., Frank, K. A., & Tang, J. (2020). Towards improving sample representativeness of teachers on online social media: A case study on Pinterest. *International Conference on Artificial Intelligence in Education*, 130-134.

Keles, E. (2017). Use of Facebook for the community services practices course: Community of inquiry as a theoretical framework. *Computers & Education*, *116*, 203–224.

Kelly, N., & Antonio, A. (2016). Teacher peer support in social network sites. *Teaching and Teacher Education*, *56*, 138–149.

Kemp, S. (2018). *The global state of digital in 2019 – from Argentina to Zambia.* Retrieved from https://hootsuite.com/pages/digital-in-2018

Kerr, S. L., & Schmeichel, M. J. (2018). Teacher Twitter chats: Gender differences in participants' contributions. *Journal of Research on Technology in Education*, *50*(3), 241–252.

Kirschner, A. P., & Karpinski, A. C. (2010). Facebook and academic performance. *Computers in Human Behavior*, *26*(6), 1237–1245. https://doi.org/10.1016/j.chb.2010.03.024

Koehler, S. (2010). *Effects of differentiating for readiness, interest and leaning profile on engagement and understanding.* Retrieved from https://fisherpub.sjfc.edu/cgi/viewcontent.cgi?article=1090&context=mathcs_etd_masters

Koeze, E., & Popper, N. (2020). *The virus changed the way we Internet.* Retrieved from www.nytimes.com/interactive/2020/04/07/technology/coronavirus-internet-use.html

Krutka, D., Carpenter, J., & Trust, T. (2017). Enriching professional learning networks: A framework for identification, reflection, and interaction. *TechTrends*, *61*(3), 246–252.

Krutka, D. G., & Damico, N. (2020). Should we ask students to Tweet? Perceptions, patterns, and problems of assigned social media participation. *Contemporary Issues in Teacher and Technology Education*, *20*(1).

Lave, J., & Wenger, E. (1991). *Situated learning: Legitimate peripheral participation.* Cambridge University Press.

Lee, S. (2020). *Social media in the classroom: Creative teaching methods for engaging students though social media.* Retrieved from https://www.accreditedschoolsonline.org/resources/classroom-social-media/

Lenhart, A. (2015). Teens, social media & technology overview 2015. *Pew Research Centre, Internet & Technology.* Retrieved from http://www.pewinternet.org/2015/04/09/teens-social-media-technology-2015/

Li, J., & Greenhow, C. (2015). Scholars and social media: Tweeting in the conference backchannel for professional learning. *Educational Media International*, *52*(1), 1–14.

Luo, T., Sickel, J., & Cheng, L. (2017). Preservice teachers' participation and perceptions of Twitter live chats as personal learning networks. *TechTrends*, *61*(3), 226–235.

Magid, L., & Gallagher, K. (2015). *The educator's guide to social media.* ConnectSafely. https://connectsafely.org/wp-content/uploads/2015/10/eduguide.pdf

Mahmoud, M., Ramachandiran, C., & Ismail, O. (2016). Social media and classroom engagement: Students' Perception. *Journal of Media Critiques*, *2*(8). https://eds.b.ebscohost.com/eds/detail/detail?vid=3&sid=537b4fa4-666a-40f0-b1bc-b0ae54696570%40sessionmgr103&bdata=JkF1dGhUeXBlPXNoaWImc2l0ZT1lZHMtbGl2ZQ%3d%3d#AN=edsdoj.234643a68dd43c-49f2941804100c288&db=edsdoj

Mahoney, J., & Hall, C. (2017). *Using technology to differentiate and accommodate students with disabilities.* Retrieved from https://journals.sagepub.com/doi/10.1177/2042753017751517

Malkus, N., Hoyer, K. M., & Sparks, D. (2015). *Teaching vacancies and difficult-to-start teaching positions in public schools.* Retrieved from https://nces.ed.gov/pubs2015/2015065.pdf

Marcià, M., & García, I. (2016). Informal online communities and networks as a source of teacher professional development: A review. *Teaching and Teacher Education, 55*, 291–307.

Mitchell, S. (2020). The Evolution of Lesson Plans in a Hybrid Course: Flipping the Classroom and Engaging Students Through iPads and YouTube Videos. *HETS Online Journal, 10*(2), 1H+. https://link.gale.com/apps/doc/A627281079/AONE?u=uphoenix&sid=AONE&xid=a01d d1e5

Moran, M., Seaman, J., & Tinti-Kane, H. (2011). *Teaching, learning, and sharing: How today's higher education faculty use social media.* Babson Survey Research Group. http://file.eric.ed.gov/fulltext/ED535130.pdf

Moreau, E. (2019, November 10). *Everything you need to know about Facebook groups.* Lifewire. https://www.lifewire.com/facebook-groups-4103720

Nierenberg, A., & Pasick, A. (2020, September 18). *Streaming kindergarten on TikTok.* New York Times. https://www.nytimes.com/2020/09/18/us/remote-learning-tiktok.html

Nochumson, T. C. (2019). Elementary schoolteachers' use of Twitter: Exploring the implications of learning through online social media. *Professional Development in Education, 46*(2), 306–323.

Ponton, M. K., & Rhea, N. E. (2006). Autonomous learning from a social cognitive perspective. *New Horizons in Adult Education and Human Resource Development, 20*(2), 38–49.

Porter, T. (2020, June 22). *Reflecting on teacher wellbeing during the COVID-19 pandemic.* https://ies.ed.gov/ncee/edlabs/regions/pacific/blogs/blog28_reflecting-on-teacher-wellbeing-during-COVID-19-pandemic.asp

Priebe, M. (2020). The COVID-19 infodemic: Combating 'dangerous' misinformation on social media. *College of Communication Arts and Sciences Department of Communication, 23.* https://comartsci.msu.edu/about/newsroom/news/covid-19-infodemic-combatting-dangerous-misinformation-social-media

Randles, J. (2017, October 6). *9 things teachers should share on social media.* ISTE. https://www.iste.org/explore/Professional-development/9-things-teachers-should-share-on-social-media

Ranieri, M., Manca, S., & Fini, A. (2012). Why (and how) do teachers engage in social networks? An exploratory study of professional use of Facebook and its implications for lifelong learning. *British Journal of Educational Technology, 43*(5), 754–769.

Reinstein, J. (2018, August 31). *Teachers are moonlighting as Instagram influencers to make ends meet.* Buzzfeed News. https://www.buzzfeednews.com/article/juliareinstein/teachers-instagram-influencers-school-tpt-pinterest

Rodesiler, L. (2017). Local social media policies governing teachers' professionally oriented participation online: A content analysis. *TechTrends: Linking Research & Practice to Improving Learning, 61*(3), 293–300.

Rodesiler, L., & Pace, B. G. (2015). English teachers' online participation in professional development: A narrative study. *English Education*, *47*(4), 347–378.

Rosell-Aguilar, F. (2018). Twitter: A professional development and community of practice tool for teachers. *Journal of Interactive Media in Education*, *2018*(1), 1–12.

Samuels-Peretz, D., Dvorkin Camiel, L., Teeley, K., & Banerjee, G. (2017). Digitally inspired thinking: Can social media lead to deep learning in higher education? *College Teaching*, *65*(1), 32. https://doi.org/10.1080/87567555.2016.1225663

Schroeder, S., Curcio, R., & Lundgren, L. (2019). Expanding the learning network: How teachers use Pinterest. *Journal of Research on Technology in Education*, *51*(2), 166–186.

Schwarz, B., & Caduri, G. (2016). Novelties in the use of social networks by leading teachers in their classes. *Computers & Education*, *102*, 35–51. https://doi.org/10.1016/j.compedu.2016.07.002

Shuck, S., Aubusson, P., Kearney, M., & Burden, K. (2013). Mobilizing teacher education: A study of a professional learning community. *Teacher Development*, *17*(1), 1–18.

Shulman, R. D. (2019, December 26). *Why teachers need a personal brand and how to create one.* Forbes. https://www.forbes.com/sites/robynshulman/2019/12/26/why-teachers-need-a-personal-brand-and-how-to-create-one/#76591054177c

Smith, S. E. (2016). *The use of micro-blogging for teacher professional development support and personalized professional development* (Order No. 10141721). Available from ProQuest Central. (1807413490)

Spencer, G. (2020). *Schools after COVID-19: From a teaching culture to a learning culture.* Retrieved from https://news.microsoft.com/apac/features/technology-in-schools-from-a-teaching-culture-to-a-learning-culture/

Stevens, K. (2013). *Dipping into social media in the classroom.* Retrieved from https://www.edsurge.com/news/2013-09-18-dipping-into-social-media-in-the-classroom

Suebsom, K. (2020). *The use of blended learning: Social media and flipped classroom to encourage thinking skills and collaborate work in higher education.* Retrieved from https://dl.acm.org/doi/pdf/10.1145/3383845.3383883

Sun, Z., Lin, C. H., You, J., Shen, H. J., Qi, S., & Luo, L. (2017). Improving the English-speaking skills of young learners through mobile social networking. *Computer Assisted Language Learning*, *30*(3), 304–324.

Thibaut, P. (2015). Social network sites with learning purposes: Exploring new spaces for literacy and learning in the primary classroom. *Australian Journal of Language and Literacy*, *38*(2), 83–94.

Tomlinson, C. A., & Allan, S. D. (2000). *Leadership for differentiating schools and classrooms.* ASCD. Retrieved from http://www.ascd.org/publications/books/100216/chapters/Understanding-Differentiated-Instruction@-Building-a-Foundation-for-Leadership.aspx

Torphy, K., Hu, S., Liu, Y., & Chen, Z. (2020). Teachers turning to teachers: Teacherpreneurial behaviors in social media. *American Journal of Education*, *127*(1), 49–76.

Trust, T. (2012). Professional learning networks designed for teacher learning. *Journal of Digital Learning in Teacher Education*, *28*(4), 133–138.

Trust, T., Carpenter, J. P., Krutka, D. G., & Kimmons, R. (2020). #RemoteTeaching & #RemoteLearning: Educator tweeting during the COVID-19 pandemic. *Journal of Technology and Teacher Education*, *28*(2), 151–159.

Veletsianos, G. (2012). Higher education scholars' participation and practices on Twitter. *Journal of Computer Assisted Learning*, *28*(4), 336–349.

Visser, R. D., Evering, L. C., & Barrett, D. E. (2014). #TwitterforTeachers: The implications of Twitter as a self-directed professional development tool for K-12 teachers. *Journal of Research on Technology in Education*, *46*(4), 396–413.

Waters, S., & Hensley, M. (2020). Measuring rural P-12 teachers' attitudes, perceptions, and utilizations of social media. *Research in Social Sciences and Technology*, *5*(3), 25–54.

Weisberger, C., & Butler, S. (2012). *Re-envisioning modern pedagogy: Educators as curators*. Presentation given at SXSWedu.

Wenger, E. (1996). Communities of practice: The social fabric of a learning organization. *The Healthcare Forum Journal*, *39*(4), 20–25.

Wesley, P. M. (2013). Investigating the community of practice of world language educators. *Journal of Teacher Education*, *64*(4), 305–318.

West, C. (2019). *12 Ways to use social media for education*. Retrieved from https://sproutsocial.com/insights/social-media-for-education/

Willbold, M. (2019). *Social media in education: Can they improve the learning?* Retrieved from https://elearningindustry.com/social-media-in-education-improve-learning

Zaidieh, A. (2012). *The use of social networking in education: Challenges and opportunities*. Retrieved from https://pdfs.semanticscholar.org/76e2/1d0c5cc14238463a09eec33d5d06573a32d2.pdf

Zhu, C. (2012). Student satisfaction, performance, and knowledge construction in online collaborative learning. *Journal of Educational Technology & Society*, *15*(1), 127–136.

Zimmer, S. (2018). Social media as a teaching and learning tool. *Social Media as a Teaching & Learning Tool – Research Starters Education*, 1. https://eds.a.ebscohost.com/eds/pdfviewer/pdfviewer?vid=3&sid=721cb31c-6fc8-4e78-a11d-2f0e8aceala5%40sdc-v-sessmgr03

Zimmerle, J. (2020). Nice to Tweet you: Supporting rural preservice teachers through Twitter chats. *SRATE Journal*, *29*(2), 1–8.

Chapter 2
An Interdisciplinary Perspective of Incorporating Social Media into Teaching Practice

Margaret C. Stewart
University of North Florida, Jacksonville, USA

Julie D. Lanzillo
Neumann University, Aston, USA

ABSTRACT

The ability to use social media as a job skill among several industries is growing increasingly prevalent. From social media managers to digital content coordinators to fan engagement specialists, graduating students have tremendous opportunity to thrive professionally due to the popularity and ubiquity of social media. In collegiate and professional settings alike, a clear emphasis on the importance of effective social media management is now critical. As a result, educators are now challenged to find creative and innovative ways to prepare students through theoretical knowledge and practical experience relating to the ever-changing landscape of both the technical and industrial demands. This article presents a critical review of existing information on the use of social technologies in the classroom, a discussion on relevant perceptions, techniques, recommendations for interdisciplinary classroom implementation and student engagement, and considerations for educators incorporating social media practice into their curricula.

INTRODUCTION

The following article provides a detailed examination of the value of incorporating personal social media strategy into the college classroom, and the ways social media can serve as a teaching, engagement, and professional development tool for undergraduate students across academic disciplines. With this is mind, this paper sets forth suggestions for trial and implementation of various social media uses and activities, and describes these exercises within the respective contexts of sport management and communication

DOI: 10.4018/978-1-6684-7123-4.ch002

studies courses. Lastly, a series of legal and practical considerations are presented to aid educators in their understanding of how to responsibly integrate social media into their teaching pedagogy.

CRITICAL LITERATURE ASSESSMENT

Relevant Perceptions of Social Media for Teaching and Learning

The ubiquity of social media continues to embed in social and cultural fabrics on a global scale. As such, industries, individuals, and educational institutions are clamouring to maximize of these platforms. While social media for personal use is in its adolescence, it is still arguably in a childlike stage among brands and businesses. Organizations are readily trying to determine and employ the most effective social media strategy, which is challenged by how quickly social media and digital technologies evolve. Even more, the effective development of courses and training within higher education to accommodate these in-demand job skills are becoming an increasing reality. While research on the subject of social media for education is still relatively limited to date, recent years have brought about a demand that requires ongoing exploration and discovery.

Lebel, Danylchuk, and Millar (2015) cite a potential disconnect among the expectations of students, the digital strategies used by faculty in their pedagogy, and the standards and demands within their industry. A sample of 132 sport management faculty at an American university indicates that only roughly 60% include social media as part of course design. Their findings reveal that while faculty recognize the potential benefits of using social media for college teaching, they are not widely utilizing the available social technologies within their classroom. This is troubling, given that the 2016 job study from the National Institute for Social Media emphasized the need for experience when it comes to social media.

In fact, respondents indicate that social media experience is valued over above all when it comes to hiring someone in a social media role. One participant reveals, "It would be very difficult to get a social media position without having any formal social media experience. You can get social media internships; and you can land those for part-time jobs and smaller roles in which you start to volunteer for social media opportunities without having experience" (NISM, 2016, p. 13) Another professional cites the dynamic nature of social media, which is a huge hurdle for educators (discussed later in this paper), in saying, "So, they have to be someone that is willing to learn new things because social media is constantly changing…But, with social media, there's not going to be textbooks and the exact formula for success, so being a self-starter, as someone who's creative and a problem solver, very analytical and detail oriented is going to be super important" (NISM, 2016, p. 14).

The speed at which social media has evolved from a purely personal mediated tool to an organizational communication powerhouse is astounding. Liu (2010) notes that the commercial world has quickly adopted social media as a tool for marketing, branding, and customer service, and suggested that due to the obvious modern need for constant connection, social media has potentially tremendous benefit to educational practices. Novakovich, Miah and Shaw (2017) discover a substantial quality gap in the use of social media as it pertains to personal versus professional use.

So how might college educators prepare their students to meet the experiential social media needs within their respective industries through classroom teaching? Manca and Ranieri (2016) discover that Facebook and Twitter are viewed by college faculty members as useful tools to increase student motivation; SlideShare, academic social networks (i.e. ResearchGate, Academia.edu), and YouTube are used to share educational content and increase engagement. In turn, motivations for using social media for college teaching include increasing student engagement and involvement, to provide collaborative learning opportunities, to capitalize on student familiarity with social media tools, to improve teaching quality, to share and distribute content easily (Manca & Ranieri, 2016).

Coa, Ajjan, & Hong (2013) find that perceived usefulness, external pressures, and technology compatibility influence the educational outcomes of social media in college teaching. These external pressures may include a demand from various industries regarding the level and calibre of social media preparedness from graduating students. Nonetheless, existing research proves that use of social media in the college classroom can simultaneously be beneficial and challenging. Among the noted barriers to faculty of using social media in teaching include concerns over privacy and student integrity, grading and assessment concerns, and the ability to accurately measure and assess performance using the platforms, weakening of the traditional student/teacher roles and dynamics, implications to student distractions, and scarcity of best practices (Manca & Ranieri, 2016). Despite the paradox of social media as a classroom tool for teaching and learning, more strategies and techniques are becoming published that are helping educators better understand their uses and benefits.

For example, more recently Grud, Haythornwaite, Paulin, Gilbert, and Esteve del Valle (2018) explore which social media platforms are used in teaching and how they are utilized. Their results found that YouTube was the most popular platform for video sharing and that Facebook was most widely used for social networking. Additionally, the use of blogging, microblogging, and document sharing sites (i.e Google Docs) were also popular. When using these platforms for teaching, their research revealed distinct purposes: (1) student engagement, (2) instructor organization, (3) engagement with outside resources, (4) improving student attention to course content, (5) building practical communities, and (6) discovery of relevant resources. Their findings of these various social media factors align with existing educational research which supports the use of social media through the concepts doing so extends the learning environment into the digital realm, exposes students to social media in practice, and fostering collaborative learning (Grud et al., 2018).

Building a Classroom Community and Engaging Students Using Social Media

Due to the very definition of social media, creating a sense of community is required (Thompson, 2011). The social nature of the communication tool mandates active participation, and two-way dialogue. Therefore, it is imperative that class exercises utilizing social media are built on the understanding that student participation is required. Liu's (2010) study examines student use of a variety of social media and their perceived attitudes towards these tools. The findings reveal that the top four reasons for using social media are for social engagement, direction communication, speed of feedback, and relationship-building. These results suggest that social networks and interactive communication may be important tools for students, thus enhancing their engagement when leveraged for learning. When these platforms are integrated and utilized effectively, they seem to improve student involvement in the learning process and their perceptions of the value and quality of their education (Lui, 2010). Chawinga (2017) finds that incorporating the use of Twitter and blogs effectively into two undergraduate courses foster learner-centred teaching, and that the technologies were primarily used by students to share and discuss course materials, post course reflections, and interact among themselves and with their instructor readily.

Kuh, Kinzle, Cruce, Shoup, and Gonyea (2007) emphasize that when students are engaged in the learning process, they increase their academic achievement and likely their own self-efficacy in the education experience (Rutherford, 2010). According to Smith and Caruso (2010), 49% of participants indicate they used social networking sites to collaborate on coursework with peers. Further, 33% of the sample reveal that they used video-sharing sites, such as YouTube, or course-work related activities (Smith & Caruso, 2010). These results align with a most recent report from the Pew Research Center regarding teens and the media which indicates that 85% of teenage social media users are on YouTube, with 32% reporting to use the platform most often among social media (Anderson & Jiang, 2018).

Evans (2014) finds that among 252 undergraduate business students that a positive correlation exists between the amount of Twitter usage and student engagement and citizenship revealing that students appear motivated to use the platforms to become more involved in their learning experiences. Dabbagh and Kitsantas (2011) suggest that college students are transitioning to a more blended experience of both formal and informal learning processes, augmented perhaps by the use of social media. Rutherford's (2010) study reveals a positive correlation between students using social media to engage with their academic peers online and how they qualify the quality of their education experience. Junco, Heibergert and Loken (2011) further support this notion, revealing that the use of Twitter in an experimental group yielded higher scores on the National Survey of Student Engagement and higher semester grade point averages. In all reality, social media and learning are not at odds; rather, they complement each other well when used in harmony as sources of information and communication exchanges (Bingham and Conner, 2010).

McLoughlin and Lee (2007) suggest that the innovative features of the social web, or Web 2.0 as it is more widely known, foster collaboration, information exchange, and user engagement, thus promoting an active experience for users of social networking platforms (Rutherford, 2010). The inherent nature of social media is engaging and dynamic, thereby affording users with the chance to be active contributors to the learning process, rather than passive observers. This is also beneficial for accommodating students of all learning types and potentially contributes to a more inclusive classroom composition. Engaging students using online social networks is innately student-centred, in that students have the choice as to which content types and vehicles they utilize to engage with the learning experience. For example, students can decide if they prefer to interact with one another via textual channels, such as instant messaging (IM), or using richer channels such as video conferencing through a tool such as Skype; the students can engage synchronously or asynchronously; they can also determine their preferred formats for exchanging content and information (i.e. text, video, audio). These varied options cater to all students because they encompass the broadest possible range of content types, instructional technology tools, and engagement strategies, while simultaneously exposing students to a variety of instructional channels and materials (Baird & Fisher, 2006; Christensen, Horn, & Johnson, 2008).

Grover and Stewart (2010) suggest that the learning environment can become more personalized using this approach, reinforcing the idea that social media offer such an array of online resources that cater to all learning styles. Subsequent studies reveal that educational social media use thereby increases the chances for learner success (Rodriguez, 2011). Perhaps all of these existing research findings when considered collectively postulate that students are more willing to utilize social media for educational purposes because they already have a personal commitment to be engaged in utilizing the platforms. As such, this existing integration makes it extremely convenient for users to migrate between personal and professional uses of these tools, shifting functions between social interactions and educational collaborations. If, in fact, this willingness exists, there may be an opportunity to enhance the quality of the learner's experience by integrating social media and new technologies into existing and evolving curricula.

Certainly, this extension can be a benefit for college students, both in terms of overall engagement, as well as professional preparedness.

Innovative Techniques for Using Social Media in the Classroom

Palloff and Pratt (2005) discuss the important concept of social presence when it comes to online platforms. Defined as the sense of community, cohesion and connection among learning, which usually yields positive learning outcomes, Palloff and Pratt (2005) recognize that social presence is vital to contemporary teaching and learning. Today, most people have a personal learning network, or a group of individuals with whom people turn for immediate information sharing and seeking. Typically, these personal learning networks thrive among the pervasive nature of the contemporary social media climate (Bozarth, 2010). Connecting students among one another's personal social networks can construct a large professional networking and learning conglomerate, if students are willing and motivated to contribute to this type of learning initiative.

Thomas and Brown (2011) share three principles to comprise what they describe as the new culture of learning: (1) traditional learning methods are incapable of keeping up with rapid technological innovation, (2) collaborative learning is easier and more prevalent because of new media; (3) peer-to-peer, or collaborative, learning is reminisced by emerging technology and its inherently collective nature. They contend that people constantly learn from engaging in interactions with one another even in casual relationships. Social media not only foster support for existing relationships, but also for generating new, more fluid relationships online based on interests and similarities (Thomas & Brown, 2011).

Liu (2010) shares the top three most popular social media platforms and provided recommendations as to how to incorporate them into educational realms. The top platform – Facebook – makes a great tool for in-depth self-introductions to class and also serves as a community building and management tool, which is useful for collaboration and professional networking. The second most popular platform is Wikis, mainly acting as open-source information repositories to share resources. Lastly, YouTube, the popular video-sharing site and second largest search engine in the world, is the third most popular channel. YouTube provides a number of education affordances, including using videos for research and class examples, having students produce and publish their own videos featuring projects they create, and adding clarity to lectures and inciting class discussion over the content of a video (Liu, 2010).

O'Boyle (2014) argues that the popularity of Twitter, and its rampant use by industry professionals already present on the site as a portal for sharing real-time information, makes that platform one of the essential ones for the sport management student to use in this manner. Kitchakarn (2016) examines the integration of Facebook into a fundamental English course among first-year students who utilized the platform for exchanging comments and ideas, participating in discussion, and to do self-study. Overall, the students find Facebook to be a useful tool for their course experience and they had a positive attitude towards the use of Facebook and doing more academic activities using Facebook. Furthermore, Kim and Freberg (2016) interview 20 industry professionals about the qualities entry-level employees should bring with them as it relates to social media use. Their findings note that the hands-on experience that students gain in a classroom will greatly benefit them in their future professional endeavors. Furthermore, He, Gu, Wu, Zhai and Song (2017) find that social media use was positively correlated with employability outcomes.

Based upon these recommendations, students could potentially be asked to create and publish user-generated content (UGC). User-generated content is revolutionized in Web 2.0, whereby online actors are no longer spectators to a web of content; rather, Internet users are active authors, publishers, creators, and participants in what Rodriquez (2011) refers to as a "collaborative social environment" (Rodriquez, 2011, p. 540). User-generated content dominates social media spaces and fuels attention and engagement. Shirky (2010) states that accessibility and permanence, meaning the volume and the longevity of content, are two cornerstones of new media content. Duffy and Bruns (2006) suggest that utilizing these types of tools in an educational setting is conducive to the social-mobile reality of the modern-day, and to the expectations of the industry that awaits them in their professional future. Rutherford (2010) shares three categories of resources available on the social web that may have benefit to education and learner engagement: (1) content sharing, (2) content creation, and (3) social networking sites. Using any of these means on their own or in combination may afford students with the opportunity to interact with their peers with greater frequency beyond the classroom. Students can use social media to facilitate discussions on course-related topics, share materials and resources for the course, collaborate for group projects, assignments, and peer reviews, as well as coordinate on assignments and face-to-face meetings (Salaway, Caruso, Nelson, & Ellison, 2008).

Henderson, Selwyn, and Aston (2015) explore the realities of digital technologies as part of the undergraduate educational experience. An extensive sample (n=1,658 undergraduate students) yield findings supporting that digital technologies are helpful for organizing and managing academic logistics, researching ad seeking out information in creative and innovative ways, and for supporting basic tasks. In addition, these technologies are flexible, cost-saving, and foster collaboration (Henderson et al., 2015). The pervasiveness and power of social media appears to be determined and ever-evolving. Lee and McLoughlin (2007) emphasizes two key traits of Internet and communication technologies (ICTs): their inescapable nature and inevitable presence. Noting that educators must be prepared to surrender a degree of control over the learning process, and empowering the learners to guide more of their educational procedure, the reality of the changing state of higher education may require such adjustments (Lee and McLoughlin, 2007). Such changes to both the industry and the educational institutions preparing students to enter it, coupled with challenges to retention across higher education, warrant innovation and ready adaptation of new technologies and best practices for social engagement as essential.

Thus, social learning in the contemporary technological landscape means that people at every institution or organization, as well as within larger society, have a greater ability to maximize their learning potential through social interaction. This process is heavily augmented by the prevalence and accessibility of social media. Social learning culture, strengthened by the trends and innovations in social media, has transformed brick-and-mortar education, corporate communication, job training and are thereby influencing traditional higher education classroom teaching (Bingham and Conner, 2010).

SUGGESTED SOCIAL MEDIA ACTIVITIES FOR IMPLEMENTATION

Communication Studies: Personal Branding Activity

Thompson (2011) claim that communication is indeed a process of active participation, fostered immensely by the present climate of social communicative spaces online. It is also recommended that the students initially be instructed on the proper use of these platforms, instead of merely assuming that, because they may already be using them, they are doing so properly (Junco, et al., 2011). With active participation and guidelines for appropriate citizenship at the forefront of the experience's design, the personal branding activity gives students the chance to view, assess, and modify their existing social presence in a low stakes situation.

This activity was originally designed for a 300-level undergraduate special topics course entitled Professional Uses of New Media, and is presently being utilized in a 4000-level undergraduate course in communication studies entitled Strategic Social Media. Upper-level undergraduate students experience participating in a personal social media audit, thereby having the opportunity to reflect on their own social media presence. This four-part activity tasks students with examining their online digital footprint, in a procedure which mirrors the way that future employers are likely to when considering someone for hire. From there, students design a self-marketing campaign based on their professional goals wherein they use the techniques and strategies learned in class to promote and showcase their marketable skills.

The first of the four steps is the personal audit of online digital footprints. At this stage students are provided with instructions to conduct a professional search for themselves by name, handle, and email through basic search engines (i.e. Google) as well as the search feature of the major social media platforms (i.e. Facebook, Twitter, and Instagram), following the steps taken by many hiring managers during a professional background check. Students are instructed to make observations and reflect on their audit of your online/social media digital footprint to answer a series of questions. The items they respond to include some of the following: (a) considering what concerned them about their discoveries, if necessary, how will they address/manage these concerns, (b) what, if any, benefits or opportunities emerged about their online presentation of self (i.e. making professional contacts), (c) how does their online presence create or contribute to their desired personal brand, and (d) how does that assist with their professional marketability and appeal as a potential job candidate in their field?

In the second phase of the assignment, the students can either work individually or in assigned pairs or small groups. If working in teams or dyads, it is recommended that the instructor organize students based on common professional and/or scholastic interests in order to maximize the quality of feedback and outcome of these conversations. If working individually, the student is assigned to research their desired career field to determine some traits, qualities, or skills that are commonly sought after in individuals working in this area. If partnered or in groups, students will discuss the outcome of these audits with your assigned partner. The desired goal in step two of this exercise is for students to prepare professional goal assessments, supported by adequate career research.

Next, the third step is for the students to individually or collectively design their personal branding social media campaign. Using a variety of readings from the course, students are exposed to several strategies and techniques regarding personal branding in social media marketing. Each student should work individually or with their partner or team to come up with a creative social media campaign idea using the personal branding strategies. The goal of this campaign is to presents its contents to your consumer, who, in the context of this activity, are the hiring managers and leaders within your desired industry. The campaign should strategically showcase your brand, skills, and traits to this audience. If working in pairs or groups, a modification to this activity would be to have students interview their peers about their career ambitions and create a campaign on behalf their classmate or teammate. This has proven to be a successful tactic for students to become exposed to traits and qualities that class peers have observed about their professional potential that the student may remain unaware of prior to this type of engagement. In the last and final step to this activity, students are asked to present the campaign to their classmates. In the presentation they describe the campaign and the strategies and content which comprise it to an audience of their instructor or peers and demonstrate how the campaign they created will interact with the consumers and be used to promote their own or their peers' personal brand online.

Sports Management: Professional Development

Social media is woven throughout the sport management industry. It is a regular practice used by sports organizations and athletes to connect and engage with fans (Newman, Peck, Harris & Wilhide, 2013). The sport management educator should incorporate these everyday tools into coursework, and introduce professional development strategies for students. For professional development, the emphasis should be on the potential for positive impact when it comes to helping make initial connections with sports industry contacts, helping establish a strong digital personal brand and in shaping perceptions (Hawes, 2014). Learner participation and creation infers that students can become actors in the social media strategy and content creation processes from the classroom, long before they enter their desired career. Online identity formation can relate to individual persons, businesses, or brands, and how they establish social presence and present their personality online. By training students in the effective social media strategies in the environment of the undergraduate college classroom, sport management students are able to foster an experiential understanding of best practices for social media strategy.

There is little research on the use of social media among sport management students, for the purposes of career and professional development. There is, however, considerable research on the uses and benefits of social media for general career development (Han, 2013; Strehlke, 2010). Additionally, it is a well-known practice among organizations to use social media platforms to screen potential job candidates (Herbold and Douma, 2013). As a result, the implications for aspiring sport management professionals to learn how to effectively use these platforms is crucial to career success and professional development. It is imperative that the sport management educator incorporate these relevant and helpful tools, but demonstrate to students that they are merely vehicles toward the development of real networks, which require old fashioned human contact and interaction.

As professional networking is a cornerstone to the success of the future sport industry professional (Rice, 2016), students in the discipline are required to complete assignments that enhance and reinforce this critical process of career development. Building on the Personal Branding Activity above, sport management students are immersed in the use of social media for professional purposes in the 100-level Introduction to Sport Management Class. Students are required to complete a minimum of three informational interviews, specific to a function of sport management, including but not limited to sales, facilities, events, sponsorships, public relations, development, athletic administration, youth sports, compliance, and tourism/sports commissions. Assignment instructions specifically state that students are not permitted to interview individuals with whom they have a prior connection, and must demonstrate how they have used social media to initiate the relationship with the interview subjects.

Most students turn to LinkedIn and Twitter, after ensuring their own profiles are up to date, and reflect an appropriately professional appearance. As the assignment is initially introduced, class time is dedicated to the demonstration of basics of business communication, such as how to send an appropriate LinkedIn connection request, rather than merely click the "connect" button. Students are then instructed on how to search for industry professionals, based on job titles, organizations worked for, and the university alumni group, among other avenues.

In the next stage of the assignment, students are required to keep a database of the connections they build, and allocate one hour per week to development of their network. Each week, class time is dedicated to informal discussions and stories shared by the instructor, guest lecturers and students about how social media has been positively used for career progression in their own experiences (Donelan, 2016). As the semester progresses, students are required to give more formal presentations about the development of their professional networks, citing specific use of how social media platforms have played a role in building those relationships.

In the final phase of the assignment, students give a presentation on the development of their networking databases, and share best practices and lessons learned with classmates about their initial use of social media in this way. While many younger students may have created a LinkedIn profile in high school, or upon arrival in college, it is rare that many have used the tool for two-way communication, or relationship building. These presentations provide valuable evidence for all students in the effectiveness this strategy can have for career development.

Finally, upperclassmen who have continued to execute this exercise, are invited to class to share personal stories about the effectiveness of this practice in their own career paths. Stories shared have centered around how an initial online connection evolved into a meaningful professional contact over time, which may have resulted in an internship, entry level job, reference, or connection to others as a way to increase one's professional network. It is an essential practice for younger students to hear the stories of older students as reinforcement to the effectiveness of the practice.

CONSIDERATIONS REGARDING IMPLEMENTATION

Legal Considerations

Rodriquez (2011) reminds teachers of the careful considerations surrounding intellectual property. Original student-generated work may be controlled by the university and guided by institutional policies, stemming from the notion that students are researching with professors and making discoveries together using university-sponsored resources. Today; however, students are using their own mobile devices and computers to create and produce massive volumes of content, and this is where intellectual property could become a concern when integrating social media into an education environment. For the most part, it appears that universities are respectful of student-created work that is not related to the institution; however, there are blurred lines when it comes to using social media tools in a learning environment. Another concern that Rodriguez raised is related to the Family Educational Rights and Privacy Act (FERPA). By potentially migrating course conversations from once semi-private spaces, such as face-to-face classrooms or discussion threads hosted on a privately-secured learning management system (LMS), there is a risk of violation of privacy. As a recommendation, Rodriguez suggests keeping feedback for assignments and discussion regarding student grades to private, individual conversations, rather than in publically open online space (Rodriguez, 2011).

Practical Considerations

In addition to FERPA and intellectual property considerations, instructors face the reality of many practical considerations when it comes to social media adoption in the academic classroom. Lebel, et al. (2015) noted the disconnect among student and faculty expectations, social media classroom implementation, and industry standards of social media. Cao, Ajjan and Hong (2013) indicate the greater the perceived risk of using social media in college teaching, the less likely faculty are to utilize social media as part of their course design. Manca and Ranieri (2016) observe ambivalence towards teaching using social media among educators in higher education, and discuss that restricted use of social media by academics as a result of cultural resistance, pedagogical issues, and institutional constraints. In many ways, the ubiquity of technology contributes to the challenges of keeping everyone in class on the same page. Despite their popularity, "social media are still far from being currently used in academic contexts for teaching" (Manca & Ranieri, 2016, p. 226).

Student preferences for devices, platforms, and features, while vast and accommodating, also challenges continuity. An instructor cannot assume that all students have access to all platforms and features, and a participant in the study by Gikas and Grant (2013) shares that despite many college students today being digital natives, moments still exist where the technology is beyond them. "A lot of people in the class are very tech savvy, I've noticed. You know, a lot of people have mobile devices, smart phones, laptops, everything. Obviously, we are all wired in because we have to post online But everyone sitting around me was having a really hard time figuring out how to do the poll online" (Gikas & Grant, 2013, p.23).

Having to consider the individual preferences, familiarity, and the learning curve for all social media across all students and courses may prove to be a daunting task for educators, and may contribute to the resistance to adopting social media within course design. Further, the realities of the digital divide must be acknowledged when given full consideration to how to create universally accessible curriculum using digital technologies. For instance, Chawinga (2017) regarded logistical challenges including Internet cost and accessibility, limited bandwidth, and insufficient hardware within their study of undergraduate courses offered at Mzuzu University, a public university in Malawi. While technology is pervasive, awareness to the global technological digital divide is a necessary reality and potential challenge for digitally competent and innovative educators.

CONCLUSION

The ongoing incorporation of social media in the college classroom is unavoidable. As students are enabled to create individual content, they should simultaneously be required to utilize a variety of promotional and personal branding techniques to enhance their online digital footprint. Among the ideas suggested herein, some of these basic strategies for classroom implementation include searching and using hashtags on Twitter as well as creating digital media content to enhance the impact of their online presence. Further, exploring the variety of options for being effective communicators through peer, faculty, and industry leader networking is a crucial and imperative aspect of this type of pedagogical advancement.

As social media, and its related impact on the sport management industry, continues to evolve and innovate, faculty must stay engaged and abreast of new platforms and features as they emerge. Further, instructors are encouraged to demonstrate best practices among their engagements with the students, and create and develop experiential applications, which allow for students to be readily involved with social media for professional uses. In doing so, there are self and institutional benefits for faculty, students, department, program, and campus communities at large. When students exhibit positive ambassadorship on social media, it draws a new level of publicity and attention to the program and institution by the industry that the students aspire to enter. Thus, the networking and job placement opportunities that may surface from the integration of responsible and tactical social media use is far-reaching.

In the long-range forecast of 21st century education, faculty and students have an incredible ability to learn from one another about the latest trends, features, applications, and opportunities of using social media, particularly as new platforms surface and take social precedence. Such an experience of collaborative learning, not only promotes student engagement and professional development, but also empowers students to feel like active contributors within their constructive learning process. Surely, the academic and educational benefits of social media use are still being realized at an infantile stage; however, as social cultural adoption has proven, these technologies show now sign of scaling back across personal, educational, economic, industry, and global boundaries. The opportunity and challenge henceforth for higher educational professionals is to train students to enter this dynamic workforce, and lies in the agility and preparedness to face a social media climate that is impossible to fully realize, as its unfolding nature leaves a great deal unknown.

REFERENCES

Anderson, A., & Jiang, J. (2018). Teens, Social Media & Technology 2018. *Pew Research Center*. Retrieved from http://www.pewinternet.org/2018/05/31/teens-social-media-technology-2018/

Baird, D. E., & Fisher, M. (2006). Neomillenial user experience designing strategies: Utilizing social networking media to support "Always On" learning. *Journal of Educational Technology Systems*, *34*(1), 5–32. doi:10.2190/6WMW-47L0-M81Q-12G1

Bingham, T., & Conner, M. (2010). *The New Social Learning*. Alexandria: ASTD Press.

Bozarth, J. (2010). *Social Media for Trainers: Techniques for Enhancing and Extending Learning*. San Francisco, CA: Pfeiffer.

Cao, Y., Ajjan, H., & Hong, P. (2013). Using social media applications for educational outcomes in college teaching: A structural equation analysis. *British Journal of Educational Technology*, *44*(4), 581–593. doi:10.1111/bjet.12066

Chawinga, W. D. (2017). Taking social media to a university classroom: Teaching and learning using Twitter and blogs. *International Journal of Educational Technology in Higher Education*, *14*(3).

Christensen, C. M., Horn, M. B., & Johnson, C. W. (2008). *Disrupting class: How disruptive innovation will change the way the world learns*. New York: McGraw Hill.

Dabbagh, N., & Kitsantas, A. (2011). Personal learning environments, social media, and self-regulated learning: A natural formula for connecting formal and informal learning. *Internet and Higher Education*, *15*(1), 3–8. doi:10.1016/j.iheduc.2011.06.002

Donelan, H. (2016). Social media for professional development and networking opportunities in academia? *Journal of Further and Higher Education*, *40*(5), 706–729. doi:10.1080/0309877X.2015.1014321

Duffy, P., & Bruns, A. (2006) The use of blogs, wikis and RSS in education: A conversation of possibilities. In *Proceedings Online Learning and Teaching Conference* (pp. 31-38).

Evans, C. (2014). Twitter for teaching: Can social media be used to enhance the process of learning? *British Journal of Educational Technology*, *45*(5), 902–915. doi:10.1111/bjet.12099

Grover, A., & Stewart, D. W. (2010). Defining interactive social media in an educational context. In C. Wankel, M. Marcovich, & J. Stanaityte (Eds.), *Cutting edge social media approaches to business education: Teaching with LinkedIn, Facebook, Twitter, Second Life, and Blogs* (pp. 7–38). Charlotte: Information Age Publishing.

Grud, A., Haythornwaite, C., Paulin, D., Gilbert, S., & Esteve del Valle, M. (2018). Uses and Gratifications factors for social media use in teaching: Instructors' perspectives. *New Media & Society, 20*(2), 475–494. doi:10.1177/1461444816662933

Han, S. (2013). Social media usage in career development. *Career Planning and Adult Development Journal, 29*(3), 80.

Hawes, K. (2014, March 6). Harnessing social media for your personal branding. *Fast Company.* Retrieved from http://www.fastcompany.com/3027020/harnessing-social-media-for-your-personal-branding

He, C., Ju, G., Wu, W., Zhai, X., & Song, J. (2017). Social media use in the career development of graduate students: The mediating role of internship effectiveness and the moderating role of Zhongyong. *Higher Education, 74*(6), 1033–1051. doi:10.100710734-016-0107-8

Henderson, M., Selwyn, N., & Aston, R. (2015). What works and why? Student perceptions of 'useful' digital technology in university teaching and learning. *Studies in Higher Education, 42(8), 1567-1579.*

Herbold, J., & Douma, B. (2013). Students' use of social media for job seeking: Recruitment guide for accounting firms. *The CPA Journal, 4*, 68–71.

Junco, R., Heiberger, G., & Loken, E. (2011). The effect of Twitter on college student engagement and grades. *Journal of Computer Assisted Learning, 27*(2), 119–132. doi:10.1111/j.1365-2729.2010.00387.x

Kim, C., & Freberg, K. (2016). The state of social media curriculum: exploring professional expectations of pedagogy and practices to equip the next generation of professionals. *Journal of for Public Relations Education, 2*(2), 68–82.

Kitchakarn, O. (2016). How students perceived social media as a learning tool on engaging their language learning performance. *The Turkish Online Journal of Educational Technology, 15*(4), 53–60.

Kuh, G. D., Kinzle, J., Cruce, T., Shoup, R., & Gonyea, R. M. (2007). *Connecting the dots: Multi-faceted analyses of the relationship between student engagement results from the NSSE, and the institutional practices and conditions that foster student success.* Bloomington: Center for PostSecondary Research.

Lebel, K., Danylchuk, K., & Millar, P. (2015). Social Media as a Learning Tool: Sport management faculty perceptions of digital pedagogies. *Sport Management Education Journal, 9*(1), 39–50. doi:10.1123mej.2014-0013

Lee, M., & McLoughlin, C. (2007). Teaching and learning in the Web 2.0 era: Empowering students through learner-generated content. *International Journal of Instructional Technology & Distance Learning, 4*(10), 21–34.

Liu, Y. (2010). Social media tools as a learning resource. *Journal of Educational Technology Development and Exchange, 3*(1), 101–114. doi:10.18785/jetde.0301.08

Manca, S., & Ranieri, M. (2016). Facebook and the others: Potentials and obstacles of social media for teaching in higher education. *Computers & Education, 95*, 216–230. doi:10.1016/j.compedu.2016.01.012

McLoughlin, C., & Lee, M. J. (2007). Social software and participatory learning: Pedagogical choices with technology affordance in the Web 2.0 era. *Paper presented at the Australian Society for Computers in Learning in Tertiary Education*, Singapore.

National Institute for Social Media. (2016). 2016 Social Media Job Study. Retrieved from https://nismonline.org/wp-content/uploads/2017/03/NISM-Social-Media-Report-3.pdf

Newman, T., Peck, J., Harris, C., & Wilhide, B. (2013). *Social Media in Sport Marketing*. Scottsdale, AZ: Holcomb Hathaway.

Novakovich, J., Miah, S., & Shaw, S. (2017). Designing curriculum to shape professional social media skills and identity in virtual communities of practice. *Computers & Education*, *104*, 65–90. doi:10.1016/j.compedu.2016.11.002

O'Boyle, I. (2014). Mobilising social media in sport management education. *Journal of Hospitality, Leisure, Sport and Tourism Education*, *15*, 58–60. doi:10.1016/j.jhlste.2014.05.002

Palloff, R. M., & Pratt, K. (2005). *Collaborating Online: Learning Together in Community*. San Francisco: Jossey-Bass.

Rice, T. (2016). Sport Professionals Stress the Importance of Networking. Retrieved on August 10, 2017: https://sportsfitnessnetwork.com/2015/05/sport-professionals-stress-the-importance-of-networking/

Rodriguez, J. E. (2011). Social media use in higher education: Key areas to consider for educators. *Journal of Online Learning and Teaching / MERLOT*, *7*(4), 539–550.

Rutherford, C. (2010). Using online social media to support preservice student engagement. *Journal of Online Learning and Teaching / MERLOT*, *6*(4), 703–711.

Salaway, G., Caruso, J. B., Nelson, M. R., & Ellison, N. B. (2008). *The ECAR Study of Undergraduate Students and Information Technology, 2008*. Boulder: EDUCAUSE Center for Applied Research.

Shirky, C. (2010). *Cognitive Surplus: Creativity and Generosity in a Connected Age*. New York: The Penguin Press.

Smith, S. D., & Caruso, J. B. (2010). *The ECAR Study of Undergraduate Students and Information Technology, 2010*. Boulder: EDUCAUSE Center for Applied Research.

Strehlke, C. (2010). Social networking sites: A starting point for career development practitioners. *Journal of Employment Counseling*, *47*(1), 38–48. doi:10.1002/j.2161-1920.2010.tb00089.x

Thomas, D. T., & Brown, J. S. (2011). *A New Culture of Learning: Cultivating the Imagination for a World of Constant Change*. Lexington: Self-Published.

Thompson, J. (2011). *The Media and Modernity: A Social Theory of the Media*. Polity Press.

Williams, J., & Chinn, S. J. (2010). Meeting relationship-marketing goals through social media: A conceptual model for sport marketers. *International Journal of Sport Communication*, *3*(4), 422–437. doi:10.1123/ijsc.3.4.422

This research was previously published in the International Journal of Digital Literacy and Digital Competence (IJDLDC), 9(2); pages 50-61, copyright year 2018 by IGI Publishing (an imprint of IGI Global).

Chapter 3
Using Social Media as a Tool for Learning in Higher Education

Kathryn Woods
Austin Peay State University, Clarksville, USA

Melissa Gomez
Austin Peay State University, Clarksville, USA

Michelle Gadson Arnold
Middle Tennessee State University, Murfreesboro, USA

ABSTRACT

The use of social media has become ubiquitous in many industries, including higher education. Emerging research shows that incorporating various social media platforms into course instruction can increase student interest, participation, and engagement as well as provide instructors and students with multiple platforms for communication and research that can be used to enhance the sense of community in an online group. This study determined whether various groups of students had differing attitudes toward using social media for class assignments. The recommendations provided are intended to help instructors interested in using social media for class assignments to learn more about how various student groups perceive this practice.

BACKGROUND

Technological advances constantly create new opportunities for instructors to distribute information and connect with students in ways that will help them succeed in the classroom and beyond. The volume of growth that has taken place within the realm of social media has made platforms such as Twitter, Facebook, Pinterest, and Instagram appealing in many industries, including higher education. In 2017, 2.01 billion people were active on Facebook (Facebook, 2017), making this site attractive to organizations that wish to reach a large number of people for a low cost. About 328 million active users are on Twitter,

DOI: 10.4018/978-1-6684-7123-4.ch003

with more than 500 million tweets sent each day. Eighty percent of Twitter users are active on mobile, implying that the vast majority of regular users receives their updates while on the go (Twitter, 2017).

While Facebook and Twitter have long held the lead in number of users, Instagram and Pinterest are not to be discounted regarding the amount of people who can be reached through these platforms. About 700 million users are on Instagram, a number that doubled between the summer of 2015 and the summer of 2017 (Heath, 2017). More than 175 million users are active on Pinterest, a virtual bulletin board site (Pinterest, 2017). In the United States, multi-platform use is on the rise. More than half of all online adults now regularly use at least two social media sites. Nearly eighty percent American online adults (79%) use Facebook. This represents 68 percent of American adults. Roughly one-third of online adults (32 percent) use Instagram, while 31 percent of the same population use Pinterest and 24 percent use Twitter. Seventy-six percent of Facebook users report that they use the site daily, while half of all Instagram users (51 percent) use the site daily. Instagram and Twitter users tend to be younger than Facebook users (Greenwood, Perrin, & Duggan, 2016).

LITERATURE REVIEW

The Impact of Social Media

Social media began as a way to keep people connected by providing a way to efficiently share photos, videos, text, and web links, often in real time, and has developed into a force that has impacted and continues to impact – or in some cases, revolutionize – organizations. Marketing processes and strategies have embraced social media channels as a way to communicate with customers through relationship building and retargeting. Personally, social media has changed the way many people keep up with family or friends, so naturally it has changed the way users "keep up" with their favorite organizations. News media has also been significantly impacted by the rise of social media. Newspaper subscriptions, etc. are on the decline, and many turn to various social media platforms to keep up with the latest information. Fifty-four percent of Millennials report that their primary source for news is social media (YPulse, 2017).

Social media has also impacted the way job seekers market themselves for employment. Increasingly, undergraduate and graduate students are expected to engage in some sort of personal branding with an online presence. In many cases, job recruiters expect students to go beyond creating a great resume, and be able to prove themselves as active members of their discipline by following and creating industry-related content online, especially via social media accounts (Harris, 2015). Social media has also created a new way of influencing the public. These platforms connect users with celebrities, political leaders, industry experts, etc. in a new, more direct way. In recent years, some users have utilized these platforms to create social media "campaigns" to raise money or make changes in the world via crowdfunding. Perhaps the most well-known is the ALS Ice Bucket Challenge of 2014, in which donors were encouraged to video themselves pouring a bucket of ice on their heads, and then post the video on social media and challenge other friends to complete the dare and make a donation to the fund. In total, more than 115 million dollars was raised, and the funds were used to help fight the disease through research, care services, and public policy programs (ALS, 2014).

Social Media in Higher Education

Similar to the business world, institutions of higher education have also been significantly impacted by the rise of social media. Most colleges and universities now have some kind of presence on Facebook, Twitter, or both. A presence on a social media platform allows colleges and universities to engage in social conversations with prospective students, current students, alumni, supporters of the school, and interested community groups in new, efficient ways. Oftentimes, individual academic departments also maintain their own social media accounts that cater to different, specific audiences.

Perhaps one of the most positive ways that social media impacts higher education is in the new channels for communication that have opened between students and their peers, between students and instructors, and between students and content. Instructors in many disciplines can now show, rather than tell students about course-related events and topics, and find new ways to keep up with the latest information to share with students. Instructors can also connect with each other in a more streamlined, global way to share information with colleagues within their discipline. Instructors can also assist in connecting students with successful professionals/role models from their disciplines.

Using Social Media for Class Assignments

Recent studies show that incorporating social media usage into online course curriculum in various ways has positive implications for increasing student engagement (Dixson, 2010; Prestridge, 2014; Veletsianos et al, 2013; Özmen and Atıcı, 2014; Kurtz, 2014; DiVall and Kirwin, 2012; Junco, Heiberger, and Loken, 2011) and increasing students' sense of collaborative learning in an online group (Meishar-Tal, Kurtz, and Pieterse, 2012; McCarthy, 2010; Fox and Varadarajan, 2011; Kassens-Noor, 2012; Minocha, 2009; Buzzetto-More, 2015; Ebner, Lienhardt, Rohs, and Meyer, 2010). Social media platforms facilitate new ways for instructors to interact with students, as well as for students to interact with the course material.

Engagement

Jones and Shao (2011) suggested that complex changes have taken place in the student body, namely with the latest waves of technology. Students today are comfortable using social networking sites, uploading and manipulating digital media, and using mobile devices to access the internet. However, teachers, older students and younger students may all have varying degrees of comfort with new technologies. The researchers suggested that the gaps are not so large that they cannot be bridged. They suggested that technology should be introduced with proper expectations and levels of understanding that will allow it to be a tool and not a hindrance in the learning process. Dixson (2010) suggested that students' levels of engagement increased when multiple channels of communication were made available in an online course, specifically when opportunities were created for students to interact with one another as well as with their instructor.

Other researchers have found social media platforms used in online course discussions increase the levels of communication from student to student, student to content, and student to instructor. Özmen and Atıcı (2014) found that social media supported deeper engagement in learning as a tool to support interaction among students in a course and student interaction with faculty. Kurtz (2014) found that social media supported deeper engagement in learning as a tool to support interaction among students in a course, student interaction with course content, and student interaction with faculty. Veletsianos et al

(2013) found that instructors considered social media tools particularly valuable for students to exchange photos that sparked topical discussions and increased interactions among students.

The body of research on the benefits of incorporating specific social media platforms into online course discussions is increasing. Prestridge (2014) found that Twitter supported deeper engagement in learning as a highly effective tool to support interaction among students in a course and student interaction with course content. Junco, Heiberger, and Loken (2011) found that students using Twitter for academic and co-curricular discussions had a significantly greater increase in engagement as well as higher semester grade point averages than the students who did not.

Other researchers have observed some advantages of using Facebook as a complementary platform in online course discussions. DiVall and Kirwin (2012) found that students perceived the addition of a Facebook page as a valuable study tool that added to their learning. These students used the class Facebook page to share study tips, links, and questions about course material. The use of social media in this study supported deeper engagement as a tool to support interactions between students and faculty.

Increased Interaction

Minocha (2009) contended that social media reduced the gap between course content and the external environment, which led to an increased sense of community. Social media affords opportunities for students to join groups that are relevant to their current or future careers, allowing them a glimpse into "real world" issues that pertain to their subject. Students can also develop communication channels with industry leaders in their desired fields to get in touch with current issues and trends affecting their relevant stakeholders and communities.

Fox and Varadarajan (2011) found that using Twitter in college class assignments encouraged higher levels of interaction among students. Kassens-Noor (2012) found that Twitter fostered the combined knowledge creation of a group better than individuals' diaries and discussion, because Twitter facilitates sharing of ideas beyond the classroom via an online platform that allows readily available access at random times to continue such discussion. In this study, Twitter had a positive impact on student learning, because instantaneous peer-to-peer communication via Twitter enhanced understanding of the course material. McCarthy (2010) found that Facebook groups used with freshman courses increased interaction between students, and that international students gained a sense of comfort in using social media in class because they were able to interact with their peers using familiar technology.

METHODS

Purpose of the Study

This study was conducted to determine how students respond to using social media platforms for class assignments. Analyzed research findings presented include how various student groups (traditional, non-traditional, undergraduate, graduate, etc.) perceived this practice.

Data Collection

Faculty from various departments in social science disciplines at two universities in the Southeast region of the United States surveyed students to determine their attitudes toward using social media in class assignments. Students were given a pre-test (Appendix A) to determine whether and/or how frequently they used social media and if they had experience using it in the classroom environment. They were asked whether they believed that social media outlets can/will be an effective learning tool to enhance learning in higher education. The pre-test also asked students to report their gender, enrollment category (undergraduate or graduate), student group (traditional or non-traditional), and whether they were currently enrolled in an online or face-to-face class. The pre-test was given as each course began.

During each course involved in this study, students completed at least one assignment using social media, and the post-test (Appendix B) was given at the close of the semester. On the post-test, the students were asked to indicate whether they believed that the use of social media enhanced learning in the course, and were again asked whether they believed that social media outlets can/will be an effective learning tool to enhance learning in higher education.

In total, 239 students enrolled in fourteen courses at two universities were surveyed. One hundred fifty-five students completed the pre-test, and 105 students completed the post-test. These researchers paired usable pre-test and post-test responses for eighty-five students, which gave a response rate of thirty five percent. Data was collected in the Fall 2015, Spring 2016, and Fall 2016 semesters.

RESULTS

Quantitative Analysis

These researchers collected several pieces of demographic information on the pre-test. Regarding the sample of eighty-five students surveyed in this study, 62 students (73%) were considered non-traditional students (age 24 or older), while only 23 (27%) were in the traditional college age group of 18 – 24. Seventy students in the sample (82%) were enrolled as undergraduates, while fifteen students (18%) were enrolled as graduate students. Sixty of them (71%) were enrolled in an online course, while 25 students (29%) were enrolled in a face-to-face course. Twenty-four students in the sample (28%) were male, and 61 students surveyed (72%) were female.

Regarding the survey question "Do you believe that social media outlets can/will be an effective learning tool to enhance learning in higher education?" listed on both the pre-test and post-test, students were provided with both a "yes" and "no" response field and an open-ended text box to record their additional comments if desired. When asked this question on the pre-test, 58 students (68.2%) replied "yes", indicating that they had a positive mindset about using social media in class assignments. When asked the same question on the post-test, 73 students (85.9%) replied "yes". In other words, 17.7% more students had a positive outlook on the potential for social media to be an effective learning tool in higher education after completing at least one assignment using social media during a course than they did before completing the assignment(s).

The researchers also observed some differences between various student groups surveyed regarding the percentage increase in the number of students who replied "yes" to the pre-test question "Do you believe that social media outlets can/will be an effective learning tool to enhance learning in higher education?"

and the number of students who replied "yes" to the same question on the post-test after completing at least one social media assignment during the course. This data represents how many students in each subset had a different opinion about the effectiveness of these assignments after they actually completed them in a class environment. This information is summarized below in Table 1.

Table 1. Differences between student groups from pre-test to post-test

N = 85	n	Pre-test: Yes	%	Post-test: Yes	%	% Increase	Chi Square p value
Never/occasionally use social media	15	5	33.3	12	80	46.7	0.186
Regularly/daily use social media	70	53	75.7	61	87.1	11.4	
Traditional students	23	16	69.6	16	69.6	0	0.453
Non-traditional students	62	42	67.7	57	91.9	24.2	
Used social media in class previously	26	23	88.5	24	92.3	3.8	0.422
Have not used social media in class previously	59	35	59.3	49	83	23.7	
Undergraduate students	70	45	60	58	82.9	22.9	0.796
Graduate students	15	13	86.7	15	100	13.3	
Online course	60	40	66.6	53	88.3	21.7	0.645
Face-to-face course	25	18	72	20	80	8	
Male students	24	16	66.7	21	87.5	20.8	0.881
Female students	61	42	68.9	52	85.2	16.3	

Although none of the groups showed statistically significant differences in Chi Square calculations comparing the percentage increases between the available subsets of students, these researchers observed notable differences in the descriptive statistics. The largest percentage increase was observed when the subset of students who reported that they never or only occasionally used social media was compared with the group who reported that they regularly or daily used social media. Only 33.3% of the group who reported that they never or occasionally used social media (n = 15) responded "yes" to the pre-test survey question "Do you believe that social media outlets can/will be an effective learning tool to enhance learning in higher education?" at the beginning of their course. This percentage increased to 80% after the group had completed at least one social media class assignment – an increase of 46.7%. The group who reported that they regularly used social media or used social daily (n = 70) increased their percentage of "yes" responses on this question from 75.7% on the pre-test to 87.1% on the post-test. Similarly, the subset of students who reported that they had not previously used social media in class assignments had a greater increase in the same percentage (23.7%) than did the group who reported they had previously used social media in class assignments (3.8%). While all four subsets increased their agreement that social media can be an effective tool to enhance learning in higher education from pre-test to post-test, the groups who were less experienced with using social media at the time the course began had the larger percentage increases.

Other observations of interest included the differences between the responses on the pre and post-tests by traditional and non-traditional students, undergraduate and graduate students, and students taking online courses or face-to-face courses. The pre-test data revealed similar percentages for traditional

(69.6%) and non-traditional students (67.7%) who indicated that they believed social media outlets can/will be an effective learning tool to enhance learning in higher education. However, traditional students maintained the same percentage on the post-test while non-traditional students increased their "yes" responses by 24.2 percent. Undergraduate students showed an increase of 22.9% while graduate students showed an increase of 13.3 percent. Students taking online courses increased their "yes" responses by 21.7% while students in face-to-face courses showed an increase of eight percent. Males and females were similar with their responses to this question on both the pre-test and post-test.

Qualitative Analysis

The comments provided in the open-ended text fields for the question "Do you believe that social media outlets can/will be an effective learning tool to enhance learning in higher education?" were also analyzed, and the following perceptions were emphasized on the pre-test: (a) Social media is already a big part of students' lives, so universities should incorporate it into the learning environment where possible. (b) Information on social media can be helpful if the user is discerning. (c) Social media can be distracting for students. The following student comments from the pre-test are examples of these themes:

- "Social media outlets… point towards the current issues, news, development of advanced technologies and provide other forms of various resources to the students besides textbooks and lectures to enhance their knowledge in the subject matters."
- "Social media can be an effective learning tool in several ways, such as staying connected to news sources and being able to follow the people that are involved in the certain matters that we may be speaking about in class. Having that social connection at any given time on your phones or tablets is just a new way of being on top of the current news and what's occurring in society."
- "It helps students become aware of what people outside of our university are doing. Learning other people's opinions and learning from resources outside of those we are handed, open our eyes and minds to information. It's good to view what society is looking at and incorporate that into our own opinions."
- "Yes, I believe social media can be an effective tool if properly utilized. Usages can range from notifications to information management"
- "Social media such as Twitter can be a huge distraction for those who can't handle staying on task for what needs to be done."
- "Honestly, I think it will just make people procrastinate more…social media is way too distracting to learn from."

Comments addressing the same question on the post-test mostly fell into the same three categories, with one addition. An emerging theme on the post-test was that students found value in connecting with relevant industry professionals and learning how to apply that example to their own social media usage. The following comments are examples from the post-test:

- "The more we used social media for this course, the more it shows what is to be expected from us when we are in the field with our profession."
- "If used appropriately, I believe so. One must be discerning as to what topics and what avenues are valid for educational purposes, however."

- "I think half of the battle in learning is keeping people interested and engaged. Social media kept it fun and interesting and I found myself working harder than I normally would."
- "It's a great way to interact with others in your field, whether I agree with their opinion or not."
- "I believe there are too many false posts generated on social media outlets. It's difficult to determine when the information is factual in a tweet or other posts."

These themes helped to support the students' responses with a more robust description of their perceptions and concerns about the practice of using social media assignments in class.

Limitations

The central limitation for this study involved sample size, especially for graduate-level students. Replication with a larger sample could support a more extensive analysis of relevant data. The students surveyed were selected via a convenience sample. Additionally, since classes were diverse in subject matter, the social media assignments varied from course to course. Further, this study is intended to measure only student perceptions, and not student performance regarding achieving the learning objectives related to the assignments. Another iteration of this study could narrow down whether a singular type of social media assignment is potentially better received than another by making the assignments uniform in nature and comparing data over time.

DISCUSSION

As previously stated, 86% of students reported that they had a positive outlook on the potential for social media to be an effective learning tool in higher education after completing at least one assignment using social media during a course. This percentage increased 17.7% from the beginning of the term. This data affirms that while most students surveyed already had a positive outlook on the practice, many students who were skeptical about using social media as part of their course assignments changed their opinions after giving it a try. These changes align with the findings of previous studies which reported students rated using social media in their courses as valuable to their learning process after they completed assignments that utilized at least one social media platform (DiVall and Kirwin, 2012; Jones and Shao, 2011; Junco, Heiberger, and Loken, 2011; Özmen and Atıcı, 2014).

These researchers also observed that four subsets of students (those who used social media regularly, those who did not use social media regularly, those who had experience using social media in class assignments, and those who did not have experience using social media in class assignments) all increased their agreement that social media can be an effective tool to enhance learning in higher education from pre-test to post-test, and the groups who were less experienced with using social media at the time the course began experienced larger percentage increases. These findings indicated that students who were more comfortable with social media (who reported that they accessed at least one social media site regularly or daily and/or had experience with using social media in class) started with a more positive outlook on whether social media could be an effective tool to enhance their learning than their peers who did not frequently access social media or had no experience using these platforms in class.

Most of the students (88.5%) who reported that they had previously used social media in class assignments reported that they believed it was an effective tool to enhance learning on the pre-test, meaning they had likely had a positive experience when they were exposed to this practice in a previous class environment. These findings are intuitive, as students with more knowledge of a tool might tend to feel more comfortable with it, and therefore report a more positive viewpoint. The tendency for students who are comfortable using social media to agree that it is valuable as a tool in an educational environment is supported by other researchers' findings regarding student attitudes toward using social media (Buzzetto-More, 2015; DiVall and Kirwin, 2012; Jones and Shao, 2011; Kassens-Noor, 2012; McCarthy, 2010; Minocha, 2009; Özmen and Atıcı, 2014). A fitting analogy for this situation is to think of asking 100 people if they thought that riding a bicycle to work was a good idea. If a subset of people in this group ride bicycles daily and consider this a regular means of transportation, we could reasonably expect that most or all of that subset would answer "yes." As discussed below in the Recommendations section, instructors can use these findings to shape the way they implement incorporating social media into their class assignments.

Only slight differences were observed between the responses on the pre and post-tests by traditional and non-traditional students. The pre-test data revealed similar percentages for traditional (69.6%) and non-traditional students (67.7%) who indicated that they believed social media outlets can/will be an effective learning tool to enhance learning in higher education. However, traditional students maintained the same percentage on the post-test while non-traditional students increased their "yes" responses by 24.2 percent. This finding suggested that both groups of students already had a positive outlook on the effectiveness of using social media for class assignments, but non-traditional students' perspectives shifted to nearly total agreement (91.9%) after the class ended, while traditional students' perspectives were unchanged. The researchers found the lack of difference of opinion between traditional and non-traditional students to be interesting, but not surprising, considering the increasingly age-inclusive landscape of social media users (Greenwood, Perrin, and Duggan, 2016).

The analysis of student comments on the pre and post-tests highlighted several themes that students expressed in various ways, including the following: (a) Social media is already a big part of students' lives, so universities should incorporate it into the learning environment where possible. (b) Information on social media can be helpful if the user is discerning. (c) Social media can be distracting for students. (d) Students found value in connecting with relevant industry professionals and learning how to apply that example to their own social media usage. Instructors who wish to incorporate assignments that involve social media can use these themes to support and shape the work they assign to students, as outlined in the Recommendations section.

From an instructor standpoint, a few informal observations were made by these researchers with regards to incorporating social media into class assignments. These assignments seemed to afford more active discussions when they provided an opportunity to apply concepts to real-world and real-time situations, particularly in online courses. The method was relatively easy to apply to courses in the social sciences, as students who were not regular social media users were not required to set up their own social media accounts to complete the assignments. While the original intent of this study did not focus on using the social media assignments as tools to help students understand and improve their online presence, this was a welcome unexpected benefit for students. The researchers also felt that incorporating social media into class assignments was a good way to try something new at no cost to the instructors or university.

Previous research revealed that incorporating social media assignments in college class assignments has increased student engagement (DiVall and Kirwin, 2012; Dixson, 2010; Junco, Heiberger, & Loken, 2011; Kurtz, 2014; Özmen & Atıcı, 2014; Prestridge, 2014; Veletsianos, Kimmons, & French, 2013), increased student to student interaction (Dixson, 2010; Fox & Varadarajan, 2011; Kassens-Noor, 2012;

Kurtz, 2014; McCarthy, 2010; Prestridge, 2014; Veletsianos, Kimmons, & French, 2013), increased student to instructor interaction (Kurtz, 2014; Özmen and Atıcı, 2014), and increased student to content interaction (Kurtz, 2014; Minocha, 2009; Prestridge, 2014). The current study further supports the practice of incorporating social media into class assignments by contributing data which verified that students maintain positive perceptions of the practice, especially once they experienced it.

Recommendations and Best Practices

When introducing new technology into an online course, instructors or instructional designers could benefit from following some guidelines as they select new tools to incorporate into their course. Social media offers diverse platforms with varying user populations and functionalities. The purposes and functions of social media platforms have evolved over time, but are still considered to be relatively new, with the oldest successful sites being only about a decade old.

The first, and perhaps the most important, consideration for instructors or instructional designers as they prepare to incorporate social media into a course is to determine the specific learner objective or facilitative role of using a social media platform in the course. These platforms can serve many functions including aggregating information, tracking trends on a subject, sharing images, providing a new way to facilitate discussion, networking, gathering news, studying, marketing, or offering new ways to complete specific assignments. Another important consideration when preparing to incorporate social media usage into course curriculum is the instructor or instructional designer's personal comfort level with various social media sites. If an instructor has never used a social media site of any kind, then he or she will need to allow time to learn, experiment, and feel comfortable with the site that will be utilized in class. Instructors should also consider whether there are potential negative consequences of incorporating the platform selected, such as distraction or exposure to negative or inappropriate comments/feedback/arguments.

With proper planning, instructors can leverage the existing and emerging research on this topic to realize a benefit for their students by effectively incorporating social media usage into course curriculum. The recommendations and best practices listed here are intended to provide basic guidelines and considerations for those who wish to explore this modern concept with an open mind for new technologies in the online classroom.

CONCLUSION

The quantitative analysis in this study indicated that overall, students responded positively to using social media for class assignments, as 17.7% more students surveyed had a positive outlook on the potential for social media to be an effective learning tool in higher education after completing at least one assignment using social media during a course than they did before completing the assignment(s). Student comments largely echoed this sentiment, and patterns in their perceptions included themes such as social media being a natural fit in the learning environment since it is already a big part of students' lives, information on social media being helpful if the user is discerning, and finding value in connecting with relevant industry professionals and learning how to apply that example to students' own social media usage. However, some students continued to point out, even on the post-test, that they believed social media serves more as a distraction for students than an educational tool.

This study highlighted the generally positive student view of using social media in class assignments. These findings echo the findings of other researchers (Buzzetto-More, 2015; DiVall and Kirwin, 2012; Jones and Shao, 2011; Kassens-Noor, 2012; McCarthy, 2010; Minocha, 2009; Özmen and Atıcı, 2014) who also found that students maintain a positive view of using social media in class.

Future researchers may find value one or more of the following:

- Surveying larger groups of students and/or breaking the information down by major to determine if students in certain majors find more value in the practice than others.
- Conducting a meta-analysis of studies conducted on students' perceptions of the value of using social media in class assignments to recognize trends in the results.
- Conducting studies that allow for content analysis of the social media assignments as well as control group comparisons to examine the quality of learning outcomes achieved by the use of social media class assignments and further investigate the students' beliefs about social media in education.
- Conducting similar studies using survey instruments that collect more detailed information to provide insight into the nature and value of social media in higher education.
- Conducting a study in which the researcher narrows down whether a singular type of social media assignment is potentially better received than another (both in student perception and achievement of learning objectives) by making the assignments uniform in nature and comparing data over time.

REFERENCES

ALS Association. (2014). Your Ice Bucket Dollars at Work. Retrieved from http://www.alsa.org/fight-als/ibc-progress.html

Buzzetto-More, N. (2015). Student attitudes towards the integration of YouTube in online, hybrid, and web-assisted courses: An examination of the impact of course modality on perception. *Journal of Online Learning and Teaching / MERLOT*, *11*(1), 55–73. Retrieved from http://jolt.merlot.org/vol11no1/Buzzetto-More_0315.pdf

DiVall, M., & Kirwin, J. (2012). Using Facebook to facilitate course-related discussion between students and faculty members. *American Journal of Pharmaceutical Education*, *76*(20), 1–5. Retrieved from http://www.ajpe.org/doi/pdf/10.5688/ajpe76232 PMID:22438604

Dixson, M. (2010). Creating effective student engagement in online courses: What do students find engaging? *The Journal of Scholarship of Teaching and Learning*, *10*(2), 1–33. Retrieved from http://josotl.indiana.edu/article/view/1744/1742

Ebner, M., Lienhardt, C., Rohs, M., & Meyer, I. (2010). Microblogs in higher education: A chance to facilitate informal and process-oriented learning? *Computers & Education*, *55*(1), 92–100. doi:10.1016/j.compedu.2009.12.006

Facebook. (2017). Facebook Newsroom Company Info. Retrieved from https://newsroom.fb.com/company-info/

Fox, B. I., & Varadarajan, R. (2011). Use of Twitter to encourage interaction in a multi-campus pharmacy management course. *American Journal of Pharmaceutical Education, 75*(5), 88. doi:10.5688/ajpe75588 PMID:21829262

Greenwood, S., Perrin, A., & Duggan, M. (2016). Social Media Update 2016. *Pew Internet.* Retrieved from http://www.pewinternet.org/2016/11/11/social-media-update-2016/

Harris, P. (2015). The top three things that employers want to see in your social media profiles. Retrieved from http://www.workopolis.com/content/advice/article/the-three-things-that-employers-want-to-find-out-about-you-online/

Heath, A. (2017). Instagram's user base has doubled in the last 2 years to 700 million. *Business Insider.* Retrieved from http://www.businessinsider.com/instagram-number-of-users-700-million-2017-4

Jones, C., & Shao, B. (2011). *The net generation and digital natives: Implications for higher education.* York, UK: Higher Ed Academy.

Junco, G. R., Heiberger, E. G., & Loken, E. (2011). The effect of Twitter on college engagement and grades. *Journal of Computer Assisted Learning, 27*(2), 119–132. doi:10.1111/j.1365-2729.2010.00387.x

Kassens-Noor, E. (2012). Twitter as a teaching practice to enhance active and informal learning in higher education: The case of sustainable tweets. *Active Learning in Higher Education, 13*(1), 9–21. doi:10.1177/1469787411429190

Kurtz, G. (2014). Integrating a Facebook Group and a Course Website: The Effect on Participation and Perceptions on Learning. *American Journal of Distance Education, 28*(4), 253–263. doi:10.1080/08923647.2014.957952

McCarthy, J. (2010). Blended learning environments: Using social networking sites to enhance the first year experience. *Australasian Journal of Educational Technology, 26*(6), 729–740. doi:10.14742/ajet.1039

Meishar-Tal, H., Kurtz, G., & Pieterse, E. (2012). Facebook Groups as LMS: A Case Study. *The International Review of Research in Open and Distributed Learning, 13*(4), 33. Retrieved from http://www.irrodl.org/index.php/irrodl/article/view/1294/2295 doi:10.19173/irrodl.v13i4.1294

Minocha, S. (2009). Role of social software tools in education: A literature review. *Education + Training, 51*(5/6), 353–369. doi:10.1108/00400910910987174

Özmen, B., & Atıcı, B. (2014). Learners' Views Regarding the Use of Social Networking Sites in Distance Learning. *International Review of Research in Open and Distance Learning, 15*(4), 21–42. doi:10.19173/irrodl.v15i4.1790

Pinterest. (2017). 175 million people discovering new possibilities on Pinterest. Retrieved from https://business.pinterest.com/en/blog/175-million-people-discovering-new-possibilities-on-pinterest

Prestridge, S. (2014). A focus on students' use of Twitter – their interactions with each other, content and interface. *Active Learning in Higher Education, 2*(15), 101–115. doi:10.1177/1469787414527394

Twitter. (2017). Selected Company Metrics and Financials. Retrieved from https://investor.twitterinc.com/

Veletsianos, G., Kimmons, R., & French, K. (2013). Instructor experiences with a social networking site in a higher education setting: Expectations, frustrations, appropriation, and compartmentalization. *Educational Technology Research and Development, 61*(2), 255–278. doi:10.100711423-012-9284-z

YPulse. (2017). The 15 News Sources Millennials and Gen Z Turn to Most. Retrieved from https://www.ypulse.com/post/view/the-15-news-sources-millennials-gen-z-turn-to-most

This research was previously published in the International Journal of Web-Based Learning and Teaching Technologies (IJWLTT), 14(3); pages 1-14, copyright year 2019 by IGI Publishing (an imprint of IGI Global).

APPENDIX A: STUDENT SURVEY: PRE-TEST

1. Enter your first and last name. (Used to match your responses to this survey with your responses to a second survey to be given at the close of the semester.)
2. Which best describes the course in which you are currently enrolled related to this survey?
   a. online course
   b. face-to-face course
   c. hybrid course
3. Which best describes the course in which you are currently enrolled related to this survey?
   a. graduate b. undergraduate
4. Which best describes you?
   a. Traditional student (age 18 – 24; typically enrolled in school full-time)
   b. Non-traditional student (over the age of 24, typically enrolled in school part-time)
5. Are you male or female?
   a. male b. female
6. What is your country of birth?
7. How frequently do you access any social media accounts?
   a. I never access social media.
   b. I occasionally access social media (less than once a week).
   c. I frequently access social media (more than once a week).
   d. I access social media on a daily basis.
8. How frequently do you access Twitter?
   a. I never access Twitter.
   b. I occasionally access Twitter (less than once a week).
   c. I frequently access Twitter (more than once a week).
   d. I access Twitter on a daily basis.
9. Do you have previous experience with using social media as part of a learning experience in higher education?
   a. Yes, I have taken classes in which I used social media for course requirements.
   b. I have never been required to use social media for a class.
10. Do you believe that social media outlets can/will be an effective learning tool to enhance learning in higher education?
    a. Yes b. No

Briefly explain why or why not.

APPENDIX B: STUDENT SURVEY: POST-TEST

1. Enter your first and last name. (Used to match your responses to this survey with your responses to the previous survey, given at the beginning of the semester.)
2. Do you believe that social media usage enhanced learning in this course?
    a. yes
    b. no
        Explain.
3. Do you believe that social media outlets can/will be an effective learning tool to enhance learning in higher education in general?
    a. yes
    b. no
        Explain.

Chapter 4
The Impacts of Social Media in Higher Education Institutions:
How It Evolves Social Media in Universities

Verónica Gutiérrez
Escuela Superior Politécnica del Litoral, Ecuador

Ariana Daniela Del Pino
iD https://orcid.org/0000-0002-0629-2994
Escuela Superior Politécnica del Litoral, Ecuador

ABSTRACT

Today, social networks have become an important part of an individual's life. Most people use social networks to interact and communicate not only with people, but also with different companies or institutions in search of information. This includes higher education institutions. The role of social networks in a higher education institution is important; It helps show what the university does, what services it offers, the achievements of its students, what achievements they get, etc. Social networks, with the right strategies, can create a great impact on how students see the university and what to do, and also they become an admission tool to generate interest in future students.

INTRODUCTION

The purpose of this chapter is to highlight the importance of social networks in higher education institutions and how today is an essential tool to expose all their activities, achievements, among others, and stay connected with students (and the university community usually). To establish the content and define the strategies, which must be used in the social networks managed by the university; It is essential to know the profile of the users that exist in our social media community. This encompasses multiple audiences ranging from undergraduate students, alumni and future students to parents, teachers, collaborators, researchers and other institutions, the entire community.

DOI: 10.4018/978-1-6684-7123-4.ch004

This chapter also explores different tips for the correct use of social networks for higher education institutions. In addition, it provides advice on certain errors that should be avoided and that may cause a negative reaction from users. These reactions can increase and many users can begin to expose their discontent in an important way, through social networks, the situation can lead to a crisis. According to Maresh-Fuehrer and Smith "Social media has been recognized in crisis communication research as facilitating both the spread and mitigation of crises" (2015, p. 621). What is a social media crisis? How can it intensify if a quick response is not given? And how can it be managed? They are also part of the analysis that involves understanding the functioning of social networks.

Universities are not only managed under the brand scheme, but a global academic institutional identity scheme, showing all their strengths, advantages and including all the intellectual material created by academics and students as part of their contribution. Universities must disseminate and disseminate everything that is forged as ambassadors of knowledge, therefore, it must have a presence in different events, be they scientific, sports, educational, in newspapers, internet and social networks, where they demonstrate progress, inventions, academic achievements, congresses, conferences and other outreach events. Depending on the extension of the university where you show your careers, postgraduate degrees, faculties or school, you can use multiple pages, it can cause traffic in the cyber city for trend brands and move search analytics. As indicated by Castillo et al. (2013) "The most advantageous universities when it comes to transmitting their brand in the online environment pay attention to innovation as a variable that gives differential value in the coordinates in which higher education currently operates". (Castillo Diaz, Carillo Durán, & Tato Jiménez, 2013)

Two decades ago it was only planned to handle face-to-face classes, the new advantages of virtual classrooms change the focus on the way of teaching through portals, online games, digital resources such as social networks, videos or audios, adaptation of materials, digital materials hypertext, content on web pages, ICT skills, etc. (Barberá & Badía, 2004) We have edX, which is one of the virtual classrooms worldwide that has quite a lot of prestige and is endorsed by several of the best universities and institutes, it was founded by Harvard University and MIT in 2012, they seek to increase the level of virtual or face-to-face education in anywhere, it has 90 partners and they offer quality courses from the best universities in the world. (edX, 2012)

Social networks and especially in universities, academic social networks are a great tool to expose the information that you have generated with your team. Relations between institutions are managed through simultaneous digital communication media, there are more and more users, some of them allow you to share information, documents, among others, they are a good option to work as a team, where they can share comments in real time, topics of interest, experiences and hypotheses, among others. According to Merlo in their article on science 2.0: application of the social web to research, they comment that "social networks are excellent virtual laboratories, since they offer all the services that a research group demands: communication resources systems, communication systems, document warehouse and discussion forums" (Merlo Vega, 2010).

In addition, you can speak with the Academic Community Manager, who knows how to disseminate and disseminate research results and upcoming scientific publications, the person who will help the teaching researcher to know how to inform through social networks, academic and professional social networks the progress of your research, through the use of online resources that allow remote information to be shared with different researchers worldwide. (Del Pino, 2016)

BACKGROUND

Lau said "In today's society, social media have become an almost indispensable part of daily life, particularly among university students, who are generally heavy social media users" (Lau, 2016, p. 286).

For this reason, it is essential that a higher education institution has a presence on social networks and can connect with different users at any time of the day. This is due to the fact that, although publications on social networks are mainly carried out under a publication calendar design by the Community Manager (the person who manages an online community of the institution) of the University; Users can see them the moment they connect.

Achieving a strong university community in social networks is essential not only to attract the target audience to the university, but also to maintain them throughout life, with positive loyalty and word of mouth after completing all levels of education. Students' experiences and emotions can be improved through the social networks of higher education institutions, as well as through communication with former students and the development of the brand over time. In addition, it is a tool to identify the university and can help increase student engagement. (Nevzat, Amca, & Tanova, 2016, p. 551)

Even if a large part of the online university community are students, it is important to create content that may be of interest to other users, which reinforces the institutional image. Teachers and doctorates, for example, can attract students with results. It is also essential that the content of social networks generate engagement and interaction of the community in social networks, positive responses. By engagement, it refers to users who interact in the different social networks in which the university also has a presence.

MAIN FOCUS OF THE CHAPTER

The Importance of Social Media in Universities

The dissemination of information in digital media or spaces such as social networks or web pages allows your digital brand to become known, with relevant aspects, products or updates and with the purpose that your company has a place of digital recognition. Through the networks you can know everything that is said about the company, who our clients are, which allows us to achieve business intelligence and improve the strategy used, it is important to keep all innovations and everything that may be viral monitored, in the future in favor of the brand. The technologies developed for monitoring both social networks and web pages gather national and global statistics. Looking for all the mentions, impacts, interactions, popularity and opinions that the brand causes, it can also be of one or more products or services of the company.

There are some tools that allow us to keep up to date with Trends and analytics, many of them analyze more or less in depth, others offer services to manage the programmed content, it all depends on the needs of the company, transforming all this into data and relevant conclusions. Young people in general, this includes university students, who use social networks more and more frequently as a communication tool. This communication includes from issuing opinions on a specific topic, to making inquiries and requesting assistance in solving academic problems.

For these reasons, it is important that universities have a presence in social networks. It is not only a direct channel of communication with students, but also an opportunity to expose what the university is, what it does and show them not only to the students, but also to their community in general (teachers, alumni, collaborators, strategic partners, among others.) everything achieved. Using social media to highlight what the university offers also helps draw attention to future students, especially during the admission process. Trends are known for their creativity, empowerment of social aspects, and their capacity for massive reproduction, through trends, a great movement or change in the behavior of users is created. Universities have a large presence in social networks, creating trends, social media trends analyze behaviors or reactions to them, provide statistics and results with keywords, from which strategies can be created to improve the visibility of the brand, with this we can determine who are the influencers in various areas, people who contribute to our brand in a positive way and who have greater contact with our customers, who recommend the product or service, appearing something called, network of contacts and invisible circles scientists for academics. (Crane, 1972)

It is necessary and important to know the search statistics, who make up our interest groups, the keywords and the people who can disseminate information quickly. In part, contact networks allow the interaction of groups of people for a specific topic, theme or activity, it helps to spread profiles, knowledge and skills, through networks they can be social, academic or professional, the members who have a greater number of contacts, allow to have a nexus with each other, their main function is to share information, experiences, knowledge and disseminate information. (Palavecino, s.f.)

The invisible scientific circles arise within "the academic-scientific intellectual life is exercised primarily by a system of informal social circles called invisible universities" (Schlesinger, 1987). By contacting professors or researchers in the world, we achieve a small invisible thread, with benefits for editing or writing articles or books. We know that this system is managed under academic and scientific peers, this generates a network of academic contacts and this is where a professional social network also arises, widely used worldwide such as LinkedIn that allows you to share your professional achievements, skills, knowledge and more of the work or academic point of view. Another important point with social networks, the beginning of the influencers who have become the face of many products, including universities, through their students, so now, we can talk about academic influencers, professors, researchers or professors who share information, articles, books, statistics or classes through their blogs, social networks or academic social networks and who can hold a gathering of people for scientific events such as conferences or talks, among others. Also the so-called academic social networks such as ResearchGate or Academia.edu, where articles or books can be shared. Don't forget Google Scholar, which is a complete platform and automatically updates your information.

Developing the University Brand on Social Media

An interview with Ballouli and Hutchinson to Amy Martin entitled " Digital-Branding and Social-Media Strategies for Professional Athletes, Sports Teams, and Leagues: An Interview with Digital Royalty's Amy Martin " she said in a kind of analogy, that success in Social networks depend on the ability of the seller and the desire to live the brand, delivering value *"when, where and how fans want to receive it"* (2010, p. 396)

Before starting to develop strategies to be used in social networks, it is essential to know the brand, in this case the University. Regardless of publishing the different activities, events, congresses, among others, which take place weekly in the institution, strategies must be developed that allow users to learn about the life and culture of the campus; to show the online community what differentiates the University from others: with added value.

The effective university brand goes far beyond a logo, stamp, emblem, brand or key phrase. The brand is the story that tells about its institution, the soul that sells, the distillation of its most prominent values and characteristics and its identity as a place of learning throughout life. This is what prospects, students and graduates think when they hear the name of their university or find their content online, news or talking with others. (Full Frabric, s.f.)

The variety in the content of the publications is important. Making the same type of posts constantly will cause users to stop paying attention. It is advisable to focus on different areas that may generate interest in students and also attract the interest of future participants. For example:

- **News:** Activities of the university, its faculties and other academic units.
- **Notes or Reports**: About the University, its activities and achievements in the media.
- **Student Achievements:** Featured projects, academic awards, triumphs in competitions, international recognitions, etc.
- **Non-Academic Activities:** Student clubs, languages, sports practices, etc.
- **Academic Exchange:** Experiences of students who have participated in exchange programs with universities abroad.
- **Contribution to Society:** Linking programs and volunteering.
- Life and culture of the campus.
- Campus facilities and nature.
- **Alumni:** Success stories of the graduates of the university.
- **Research:** Project development, papers published by researchers and professors of the university

Most universities are made up of several faculties; The larger the university, the greater the number of faculties it will have. It is practically impossible for the social networks of the University to publish all the activities carried out by each of them. It is for this reason that they must manage their own social networks. For everyone to function as a hole, it is recommended that there be guidelines for shared content and that there is a brand unit in each of them, through a social media manual. In higher education institutions, faculties are often responsible for maintaining the same values, vision and mission as the university or higher institutions to which they belong, but they operate separately when they teach specific content. These faculties provide unique educational experiences, so allowing them to provide unique experiences on social networks seems correct, as long as they maintain the parameters set forth by the institution. (DMI Daily Digest, s.f.)

Set Your Content Schedule According to the Social Network

Once the different areas of the university that will be shown on social networks have been defined, it is important to establish in which of them the University will have a presence. There are several, but the most popular are: Facebook, Twitter and Instagram, YouTube is more for music.

There must be unity among all official social media accounts of the University, from the names, users, the description of the institution and, of course, the profile photos with their respective colors that are used according to the brand. (This also includes the social networks of the faculties).

Facebook

Facebook is the most popular social network that brings together millions of users worldwide. Through a fan page on Facebook, a university can reach many people. It is important to denote that a fan page is for companies / brands and that users, that is, different people, connect through a personal profile.

As George explains in a digital post "Unlike a personal Facebook profile, fan pages are visible to everybody on the Internet. Anyone on Facebook can connect to and receive updates from a page by becoming a fan (i.e. 'Liking' the page)". (George, 2012)

Among the advantages that Facebook has is that you can make publications with several photographs and you can also create albums. You can upload videos directly with different periods of time (although it is recommended to use short videos, because users do not always watch the video completely, especially when it is extensive and with a lot of information). Ideally, show the activities of the University through countless photographs and videos, something that works very well on Facebook.

Another very useful tool is live streaming. The event of the University can be transmitted directly from Facebook and also allows users to interact in the moment, give opinions, ask questions, comments, hearts, etc.

We can see the handling of the images in figure 1. The *Escuela Superior Politécnica del Litoral,* has about de 36 official Facebook accounts associated with its name. These are some examples that can be visualized of how this social network is managed.

Twitter

Twitter, like Facebook, is a social network, an online news site, through short messages called tweets. From these new networks, new words emerge, such as Tweet, which is to publish short messages, that anyone who follows you can see and be interesting to someone in your audience. (Gil, 2019)

Twitter features allow users to post different tweets in a row on a specific topic. It is especially practical when the activities of the University are shown at the same time they occur, which allows to reach the community in real time. In return, account followers can share information through RT (retweets) or I like it, which makes the content reach more users.

The use of hashtags on Twitter is common and helps users find and follow a thread on a specific topic. It is recommended that when a university event is tweeted, at the time it takes place, especially the most important ones, such as an anniversary ceremony, graduation, etc., and even a unique hashtag (including the name of the University). By using it in each of the tweets and with the help of RT, likes and responses from other users, the hashtag can become a topic of local, national or global trend, which means that a conversation has been built around the University event. "Also called TT or trend, these are the words, hashtags or phrases that are repeated more at a given time. In the case of Twitter, 10 stand out and these change according to their popularity". (Socialpubli, 2018)

The same example of image handling in figure 2 and 3. The *Escuela Superior Politécnica del Litoral*, has about 42 twitter accounts associated with its name. These are some examples that can be visualized of how this social network is managed.

Figure 1. Graduation ESPOL 2019
Source: Espol, 2019

Instagram

Instagram is a social network used to share photos and videos, that is, for visual content. Unlike Facebook, Instagram only allows up to 10 photos per post and the videos in the feed can only last up to a maximum of one minute; however, a publication may contain photographs and videos. For universities, it is a well-used social network that allows students and future students to visualize the campus; culture, student life and different events.

Instagram stories (photos or short videos in a 15-second vertical format that only remain published for 24 hours), allow the University to display its activities at the time they are happening and include many tools that can be added to the content such as filters, texts, emojis, etc.

Figure 2. Graduation ESPOL 2019 (first tweet prior the ceremony)
Source: ESPOL, 2019

Figure 3. Hashtag #GraduadosESPOL2019 was trending topic during the live coverage of the event
Source: Trendsmap, 2019

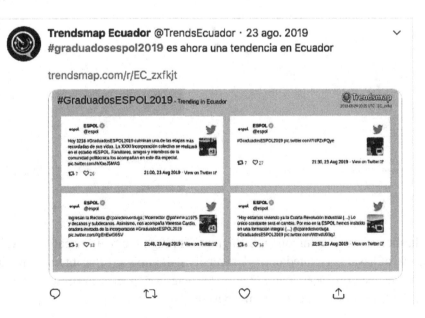

In a paragraph written by Higher Education Marketing said that:

Unlike the more stylized and virgin publications that dominate the rest of the site. Stories was designed as a way for Instagram users to share more spontaneous and less polished content. With that in mind, schools that want to use the feature should focus on creating fun and informal publications that capture daily events. Special events such as graduations, social activities for students, guest conferences and conferences can be particularly good sources of content. (Higher Education Marketing, 2019)

It is important to see Figure 4, an example of how through Instagram, students can be recruited.

Figure 4. Number of recruit students by instagram
Source: Hobsons, 2017

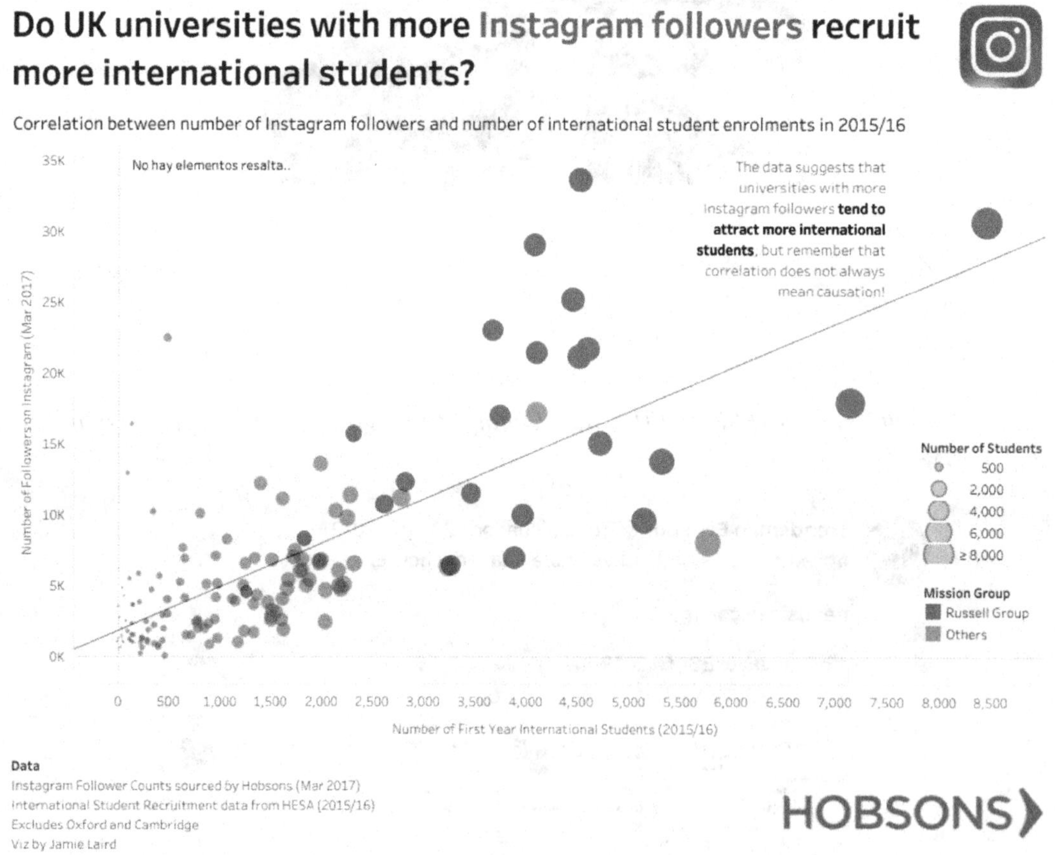

The use of hashtags is also common on Instagram; Through them, users can discover content while searching. The use of hashtags related to the University will allow greater interaction with the publications. It is also highly recommended to use popular hashtags for specific purposes. For example, publish an old photo of the University campus with the hashtag #tbt (setback on Thursday).

A schedule of content must be administered for each of the University's social networks; It must be done every month and establish what will be published week by week, day by day. This schedule must be constantly updated and flexible; In the case of universities, there are activities that can be carried out overnight, for example, the visit of some authority of another institution or university.

It is important to keep in mind that social networks are constantly evolving, that is, their platforms are constantly updated, as are certain tools for creating or editing publications. It is necessary to have identified blogs and web pages from which this information can be obtained and reviewed frequently.

The *Escuela Superior Politécnica del Litoral* has, about 12 Instagram accounts associated with its name. These are some examples that can be visualized of how this social network is managed, and in figure 5, we can see an example.

Figure 5. Anniversary 61th
Source: Espol, 2019

Ver estadísticas   Promocionar

Les gusta a **josejavierrol2** y **2888 más**

espol1 ¡Hoy ESPOL conmemora su Aniversario! Son ya 61 años formando integralmente profesionales que cooperan para mejorar la calidad de vida y promueven el desarrollo sostenible y equitativo del Ecuador y el mundo. ¡Celebremos juntos por lo que hemos sido, somos y seremos!
#ESPOL61años #aniversario #politecnica #desarrollo #sostenibilidad #somosespol

Ver los 15 comentarios

29 de octubre de 2019   **Ver traducción**

Built a Relationship With Your Audience

Having a presence in social networks is a daily commitment. It is very similar to maintaining a friendship. Friendships require constant attention and communication to stay strong. Social networks are no different. As in real life, if you only talk about yourself, people will soon get bored of that. If you ignore your fans or followers when they talk to you or publish on your profile, they will not continue talking to you, they are looking for an interaction. Constant communication in both directions is crucial to the success of social networks (Burkhardt, 2010). Interacting with its users is essential for the success of the university's social media management. More and more people seek information and make inquiries through social networks. The comments in the publications, and above all, through private messages that work on Facebook, Twitter and Instagram, students, future students, etc., seek to obtain answers on different topics that occur in the University, immediately.

In terms of social networks, we can now communicate with consumers instead of with them, everything becomes more personalized. The social term, in itself, speaks of the fact that it really is a place to communicate from person to person, instead of serving as a marketing channel, the brand and dealing with customers becomes more human. It is important to understand who is the user asking the question or query. The tone or way of responding depends on this. Although the majority of users are young people (students or people interested in studying at the University), they can also be parents or representatives of another institution. A kind and effective response may be the difference and may influence the decision to study at the University or not. Social networks are a form of brand exposure in which your presence must match relationships and followers. To build these relationships, you must be constantly listening to your audience and providing the information they are looking for. (Ballouli & Hutchinson, 2010, p. 397)

Frequently, users expect different situations or problems to be resolved through social networks. For example, a student may have trouble registering for a record. Although the registration cannot be done through a social network, there must always be a response and the will to help and guide the student towards the faculty, the academic unit or others, of the University, where they will be in charge of providing assistance to resolve the problem.

Trolls

Negative comments always exist on social networks. But there are cases in which users are recurring and, in different publications, where they express complaints and discontent on certain issues, even if the problem is not related to the publication. These types of users are called trolls. Trolling, another word created from the beginning of social networks, associated with the creation of discord on the Internet when starting disputes or disturbing people by publishing inflammatory, offensive or off-topic messages in an online community. Basically, a social media troll is someone who deliberately says something controversial, insulting or misplaced to encourage other users to do the same. (Hanson, 2017)

How to deal with this type of users? Respond with facts and generate positive actions. Although the troll probably will not find any satisfaction with the answer, because its purpose is only to annoy, the rest of users will notice it and will realize that the University is attentive and reads what they comment in their publications. In extreme cases where trolls resort to insults or aggressive comments, it is important to review the content policies of the different social networks. If the user is committing a violation of them, the situation can be reported to the social network and will be analyzed. It is recommended to have a crisis manual with answers for these cases.

Engagement and How to Measure It

Martin explain a very significant idea:

There are two important things to do when measuring your social-media efforts. The first is to establish key performance indicators, and the second is to remain consistent in tracking and measuring those indicators. We recommend that brands identify at least two key performance indicators each in the categories of volume, engagement, and conversion. Examples of volume indicators include the number of fans or followers you have following your brand and the number of original topic trends on your page. With regard to engagement, the kind of indicators we're looking for are metrics that speak to the amount of time a fan spends with your brand online. (Ballouli & Hutchinson, 2010)

When publishing content, it is necessary to know if it is reaching users and if it is to their liking. It is not about the quantity of publications that are made, nor of the "likes", but that they fulfill the objective of generating interest in the users and for this, it is important to measure the commitment of the publications.

How engagement works? It can be in different forms, taking into account the social network:

- **Facebook:** Making comments on the publications and sharing them.
- **Twitter:** Replying to tweets and retweets.
- **Instagram:** Through repost, saving the post or sending it to another user

And, of course, "like" so you can generate a post on different social networks like Facebook, Twitter and Instagram.

Creating interaction in social networks is not only based on answering user questions, but also calling for action to interact in specific publications or begin to share content. For example, if a photograph of the university campus is published on Instagram, a good strategy might be to invite them to share photos taken by them of the campus; You can make a publication with the selection of the best, giving credit to the students who took them. Another way to generate interaction is by publishing and writing a question related to it. For example, a publication in which some students give their opinion on a certain topic of the University, the idea is that users respond on the subject or give their opinion.

How to measure commitment? Facebook, Twitter and Instagram have their own analysis with which different metrics can be obtained in general (number of followers gained over a period of time) and more specific ones, such as the number of people reached by a publication and the commitment generate.

Social Media Crisis

According to Liebowitz explains that "a social media crisis is an event that can have a negative effect on a brand's, company's, or individual's reputation. It can be something that occurs offline and is then brought to social media channels, or it can begin on social media channels, and then spread" (Liebowitz, 2014). As mentioned earlier, the existence of negative comments through social networks will always exist. This situation is something that you have to keep in mind on social networks, regardless of the content, all brands are exposed to this; Social networks are an open platform for all types of users to comment. But when the University performs a specific action and triggers a series of negative comments about it that become viral, it is called the social media crisis. We will present a case study, where you can see a social media crisis.

Case of Study: Rebranding of Escuela Superior Politécnica del Litoral, ESPOL (Guayaquil, Ecuador)

On May 27, 2019, the *Escuela Superior Politécnica del Litoral*, ESPOL, unveiled its new logo and it was made known through its social media accounts. This University for many years had as an emblematic symbol a Galapagos Turtle (representing the vernacular of Ecuador, seen internationally in relation to the Galapagos Islands); the new logo did not include the Galapagos Turtle in its design. The response from the users was massive and a large percentage of react negatively in all institutional social networks.

Facebook

In the social network Facebook, users showed a rejection for about six months. In table 1, you can see the amount of person who accepted or rejected the new profile picture (new brand), the option of anger, laughter or sadness, is the one that has more. Clearly, the sense of belonging with the seal or emblem used so far, people felt part of the community and was recognized by everything. The rejection of the new brand was abysmal. What the users had not understood is that the Turtle was never the mark of the institution, it was always the seal or emblem, something that continued, while the new brand was created as such, to represent the institution in a way business, the negative comments stopped at six months, users have not fully accepted the new image.

Table 1. Reaction of the community in fan page.

Facebook	People Reached	Comments and Shares	Like / Love	Wow	Haha / Sad / Angry
Profile picture	163.933	1.944 / 1.136 times	1.143	274	3.555
Video (rebranding)	62.368	275 / 266 times	830	39	866
Video cover	16.861	64 / 85 times	184	10	411

Source: Fan Page Espol, May to Sept 2019

The Facebook profile picture generated an organic engagement of 163.933. Most of the reactions where: sad (more than 1.5000) and angry (more than 1.300). Also there where approximately 2000 comments, in the majority, negative. The majority expressed their discontent of the turtle not being part of the logo anymore, the data is shown in table 1.

Twitter

On May 27th 2019, the unveiling of the new logo of ESPOL was heavily discussed on Twitter. Words and hashtags related to the University became trending topic: (Trending Ecuador, 2019)

- #ESPOLyoteexijo (approximately 7 minutes)
- #DevuelvelaTortugaEspol (approximately 4 minutes)
- Polito, the name of the Galapagos turtle in the symbol (3:30 minutes)
- Espol (3:20 minutes)
- #ESPOL (1:35 minutes)

Table 2. Reaction of the community in Twitter

Twitter	Impressions	Retweets	Likes
Video (rebranding)	90.561	191	344
El Universo (newspaper) link	26.788	23	62

Source: Twitter Espol, May 27 and 28, 2019

Instagram

On Instagram, because of the collage feed, there were 7 posts published related to the new ESPOL logo. In every one of them, users wrote negative comments. They weren't massive like in Facebook, but specially in the last frame of the collage, the comments were approximately 250. The data shown in table 3 is from the launch video and a mosaic photo. (ESPOL, 2019)

Table 3. Reaction of the community in Instagram

Instagram	Engagement	Impressions	Likes
Video (rebranding)	7.512	11.611	610
Collage feed frame 1	5.628	7.631	151
Collage feed frame 2	5.285	7.019	123
Collage feed frame 3	5.210	6.795	128
Collage feed frame 4	4.991	6.795	142
Collage feed frame 5	5.852	8.327	154
Collage feed frame 6	10.690	18.090	482

Source: Instagram Espol, May 27 and 28, 2019

Timeline of the Social Media Crisis

Approximately one month before the presentation of the new logo, on April 30, 2019, during the welcome of the new students, the presentation of a character called *Polito* (a Galapagos turtle). The introduction of *Polito* was planned as a strategy so that, at the time of the revelation of the new logo (without the Galapagos turtle), it was assumed that the university community was in love with the character; The plan was for *Polito* to become the mascot of the university. Unfortunately, *Polito* was not well received. The design generated question marks and the strategy failed.

Other strategies were planned: a contingency plan was designed, where several scenarios that could occur were raised, such as the questions that would arise on social networks and the answer that would be given to users. These questions and answers were shared internally with the people responsible for managing the different social networks related to the University. In addition, the Rector of the University conducted an interview with one of the most recognized newspapers in Ecuador, explaining the reason why the logo was changed. This note was released the same day of the presentation.

But none of these preventive actions helped during the time of the crisis. Users showed rejection of the new logo in different ways: through memes, emojis (a turtle), expressing their opinion, some politely, others with insults. There was also the association of the new logo with other existing logos. Two days after the revelation of the logo, the University published a statement to try to stop the wave of comments on the subject. Little effect had. Users demanded that the symbol or emblem with the turtle be reinstated.

How Did the Social Media Crisis Develop on Facebook, Twitter and Instagram?

After the declaration, the university decided not to publish more information in the next 5 days. Publications were made about the regular activities and events of the Institution.

Instagram

In the photographs in which the logo was shown, users continued to comment on the turtle, but to a lesser extent than in the publications published during the presentation. This situation lasted approximately one month (until June 2019).

Finally, Instagram users stopped commenting on the matter, even in photographs containing the new logo. Example: a photo of the main building (showing the logo) with a sunset in the background.

Twitter

Because Twitter works differently from Facebook and Instagram, instead of comments on tweets generated by the University's Twitter account, users turned to tweets and mentions to give their opinion on the new logo. There were recurring users who created conversations on the subject (with other users). However, like Instagram, after June 2019, tweets and mentions decreased and practically disappeared.

Facebook

The situation on Facebook was totally different. It is important to clarify that the ESPOL account on Facebook is the oldest and has more followers.

Regardless of the content of the publication, several users began to perform the following actions:

- Use of Facebook reactions in posts: users begin to react massively to posts with angry emoji, a way to express their discontent over the new logo.
- Comments not related to the publication: especially in the publications that showed the new logo.
- Use of emojis, gifs and memes: users completed the comments with these visual illustrations, most of which showed a turtle.

This situation continued until August 23, 2019, the day the University launched a new statement through social networks. The authorities expressed that they had heard the opinion of the community and that the decision had been made to restore the symbol with the turtle to accompany the current logo on diplomas and different institutional events (for example, commemoration of graduation and anniversary).

SOLUTIONS AND RECOMMENDATIONS

In social networks, administrators or community manager, who can use social networks to monitor the environment of the created pages of universities dynamically, adaptively and prepare completely for the occurrence of crisis events. When a crisis occurs, mostly through the Internet, universities can understand and understand in time the various publications that they must make, through Microblog and other platforms on crises, and react quickly, to avoid increasing what happened. In addition, through the comment function, public opinion can be understood. This will encourage universities to initiate crisis early warning measures and take the necessary crisis management measures, which can improve the efficiency of dealing with crisis events. (Wenting, 2019)

A crisis in social networks can occur unexpectedly; A unique event can go viral in minutes when enough users start a conversation about it. The University must have a communication plan and a crisis team always ready to deal with these types of situations. When a crisis arises, an emergency meeting should be established to analyze what is happening and quickly decide the course of action to be taken.

Recommendations in case of a social crisis:

- **Give a Quick Response:** When a crisis event is unleashed, it is important to report it immediately so that the crisis team can make a quick decision about the actions that will be taken. The longer it takes to give an answer; Users will have the opportunity to make the conversation viral on social networks. On Twitter, for example, they can create a hashtag and turn it into a trend topic. A quick response will not necessarily mean that the crisis disappears, but it will indicate that the University is attentive to what is happening.
- **Have a Statement Prepared for an Eventuality:** In cases such as the presentation of a new logo, where comments and negative opinions are expected, a statement with the reasons and why the decision was made must be prepared and ready to be shared with the community.
- **Do not Block Users, or Hide or Delete Comments:** This will only cause users to make more comments and even, if blocked, will expose this situation to other users. This may even make the crisis increase or disrespectful comments contain with bad words, which may be the exception.
- **Stop Publications on Other Activities:** If a crisis breaks out and users are talking about a specific topic, making publications that are not related to the topic gives the interpretation that the University does not care what is happening.
- **Evaluate and Learn:** After overcoming a crisis, the situation must be analyzed and conclusions drawn to help in the event that a new crisis arises in the future.

FUTURE RESEARCH DIRECTIONS

Future discussions raised contemplate the implementation of practical manuals of action for other users who have gone through a crisis in social networks and have not known how to handle it, other research on how to use social networks for universities and businesses to be useful.

CONCLUSION

Today's social networks are the most important platform to expose the different activities carried out by a university. Being a technological tool, it is important to know the constant changes and updates of the social media experience.

In case of eventualities, such as the explosion of a crisis, the University must be prepared and take the necessary measures. It is important to perform a detailed analysis after the crisis. During these types of events, publications may obtain more commitment than other publications during a normal period. This means that during a social media crisis, high participation in publications does not translate as something positive. It is important to keep this in mind when analyzing what happens during the crisis.

Having a presence in social networks is essential for a university. With the right strategies, it is an opportunity to strengthen your brand, involve your students in the different activities that are carried out, generate interest and attract future students and connect with your alumni and with the University community in general.

REFERENCES

Ballouli, K., & Hutchinson, M. (2010). Digital-Branding and Social-Media Strategies for Professional Athletes, Sports Teams, and Leagues: An Interview With Digital Royalty's Amy Martin. *International Journal of Sport Communication*, *3*(4), 395–401. doi:10.1123/ijsc.3.4.395

Burkhardt. (2010). Social media: A guide for college and. *College & Research Libraries*, 1-3.

Castillo Diaz, A., Carillo Durán, M. V., & Tato Jiménez, J. L. (2013, March). Branding online en las universidades españolas. Análisis de los valores funcionales y emocionales en sus websites corporativos. *Estudios sobre el Mensaje Periodístico*, 85–97.

Crane, D. (1972). *Invisible colleges: Diffusion of knowledge in scientific communities*. Chicago: University of Chicago Press.

Daily Digest, D. M. I. (n.d.). *The Importance Of Social Media In Higher Education*. Retrieved from DMI Daily Digest: https://digitalmarketinginstitute.com/blog/the-importance-of-social-media-in-higher-education

ESPOL. (2019). *Instagram ESPOL*. Retrieved from Instagram ESPOL: https://www.instagram.com/p/Bx-NRWMg-Mr/?utm_source=ig_web_copy_link

ESPOL. (2019a, August 23). *Fans Page ESPOL*. Retrieved from Fans Page ESPOL: https://www.facebook.com/espol/posts/10157363299348286?__tn__=-R

ESPOL. (2019b, August 23). *Twitter ESPOL*. Retrieved from Twitter ESPOL: https://twitter.com/espol/status/1165005799015505920?s=20

ESPOL. (2019c, August 23). *Twitter ESPOL*. Retrieved from Twitter ESPOL: https://twitter.com/TrendsEcuador/status/1165057527698132993?s=20

ESPOL. (2019d, October 29). *Instagram ESPOL*. Retrieved from Instagram ESPOL: https://www.instagram.com/p/B4NB2P7AoJz/

Full Frabric. (n.d.). *Five things to consider when developing your university's brand*. Retrieved from Full Frabric: https://blog.fullfabric.com/five-things-developing-university-brand

George, D. (2012, August 9). *What is a Fan Page on Facebook? You Need To Know This!* Retrieved from Heyo Blog: https://blog.heyo.com/what-is-a-fan-page/

Gil, P. (2019, Noviembre 9). *What Is Twitter & How Does It Work?* Retrieved from Lifewire: https://www.lifewire.com/what-exactly-is-twitter-2483331

Hanson, J. (2017, November). *Trolls and Their Impact on Social Media*. Retrieved from University of Nebraska-Lincoln: https://unlcms.unl.edu/engineering/james-hanson/trolls-and-their-impact-social-media

Higher Education Marketing. (2019, October 18). *Go-To Instagram Marketing Strategies For Higher Education*. Retrieved from Higher Education Marketing: https://www.higher-education-marketing.com/blog/essential-instagram-marketing-strategies-higher-education

Hobsons. (2017, March 18). *Do UK universities with more Instagram followers recruit*. Retrieved from QS Enrolment Solutions: https://public.tableau.com/profile/qsenrolments#!/vizhome/InstagramFollowersversusInternationalStudentRecruitment/InstagramFollowersversusInternationalStudentRecruitment

Lau, W. (2016). Effects of social media usage and social media multitasking on the academic performance of university students. *Computers in Human Behavior*, 286–291.

Liebowitz, M. (2014, January 17). *What the Heck Is a Social Media Crisis Anyway?* Retrieved from FALCON.IO: https://www.falcon.io/insights-hub/topics/customer-engagement/heck-social-media-crisis-anyway/

Maresh-Fuehrer, M., & Smith, R. (2015). Social media mapping innovations for crisis prevention, response, and evaluation. *Computers in Human Behavior*, 620–629.

Nevzat, R., Amca, Y., Tanova, C., & Amca, H. (2016). Role of social media community in strengthening trust and loyalty for a university. *Computers in Human Behavior*, *65*, 550–559. doi:10.1016/j.chb.2016.09.018

Palavecino, M. (n.d.). *El Valor de la Red de Contactos – Networking*. Retrieved Julio 04, 2016, from Proyecto Profesional: http://www.proyectoprofesional.com.ar/index.php/el-valor-de-la-red-de-contactos-networking/

Schlesinger, P. (1987). *Los intelectuales en la sociedad de la información*. Barcelona: Anthropos Editorial.

Socialpubli. (2018, Agust 14). *How To Be Trending Topic on Twitter*. Retrieved from Socialpubli: https://socialpubli.com/blog/how-to-be-trending-topic-on-twitter/

Trending Ecuador. (2019). *Trending Ecuador*. Retrieved from Trending Ecuador: https://www.trendinalia.com/twitter-trending-topics/ecuador/ecuador-190527.html

Wenting, X. (2019). Discussion on Strategies of Crisis Management in University Under the Background of Social Media. *Science Journal of Education*, 14-18.

KEY TERMS AND DEFINITIONS

Brand on Social Media: The brands, increasingly exposed, have life on the internet, so management must be adequate.

Hashtag: A word used to highlight an event or find a specific topic.

Rebranding: Redesign of the management or brand management, focused on a change or a new marketing strategy.

Social Media Crisis: A negative event that stars or develops in the social networks and can have a negative effect in the image of an institution or company.

Social Media for Recruitment: Means by which, people seek to know their brands and products, for their choice.

Social Networks: Internet social media sites that are used to connect with different people and can have different purposes like for social interaction or business.

Chapter 5
The Attitude Towards and the Use of Social Networking in European Higher Education:
An Exploratory Survey

Silvia Gaftandzhieva
University of Plovdiv "Paisii Hilendarski", Bulgaria

Rositsa Doneva
University of Plovdiv "Paisii Hilendarski", Bulgaria

ABSTRACT

Nowadays, social networking is becoming a more and more powerful tool for students for communication, sharing of information and discussions on various topics. The study presented in this article investigates the extent to which teachers from different European countries use social networking sites in their teaching practice for different purposes and what their attitude is towards the use of social networking in higher education in general. The study is intended to seek clarity on the issues, whether the use of social networks is related to teacher information about social networking sites; their participation in interest groups and research for the use of social networks in education; and whether the results obtained from the survey vary according to the country. For this purpose, the statistical software IBM SPSS Statistics is used. On the other hand, the study explores specific areas of the use of social networking in higher education, with an emphasis on their efficacy.

INTRODUCTION

Students in the 21st century are growing up constantly connected to the world around them through smart phones, tablets, and computers. The European Commission has adopted a Digital Education Action Plan (DEAP, 2018) which includes 11 initiatives to support technology-use and digital competence development in education. According to the Digital Economy and Social Index (DESI, 2018) there is an

DOI: 10.4018/978-1-6684-7123-4.ch005

urgent need to boost digital competences in Europe and to improve the uptake of technologies in education because 37% of the EU workforce has low digital skills (or none at all), less than half of students are in schools which are highly equipped digitally and only 20-25% of them are taught by teachers who are confident using technology in the classroom. In order to meet the unique learning needs of digital natives, teachers need to move away from traditional teaching methods that are disconnected from the way students learn today (Morgan, 2014; Aviles & Eastman, 2012). Students from the digital age thrive on creative and engaging activities, varied sources of information, and a more energetic environment. Teachers are faced with the challenge to understand how they learn, how they communicate and interact with the world in order to meet the needs of today's students and to teach more effectively.

Nowadays social networking is becoming a more and more powerful tool for communication, sharing of information and discussions on various topics. According to a worldwide survey, approximately 2 billion web surfers are using social networks today (Statista, 2018). The wide academic and research interest in the use of social networking for educational purposes in higher education is the natural result of the constantly growing popularity of social networking. In recent years there has been extensive academic and research interest in the use of social networking for educational purposes (Acharya, Patel & Jethava, 2013; Voorn & Kommers, 2013; Wang, Woo, Quek, Yang & Liu, 2011; Kropf, 2013; Arquero & Romero-Frías, 2013; Alam, 2018; Carapina, Bjelobrk & Duk, 2013; Ghanem, El-Gafy & Abdelrazig, 2014; Doneva & Gaftandzhieva, 2017; Abu-Shanab & Al-Tarawneh, 2015; edWeb, 2009; Faculty Focus, 2011) and the presentation of higher education institutions on social networks (Golubić & Lasić-Lazić, 2012; Golubić, 2017).

According to UK company Pearson (Seaman & Tinti-Kane, 2011), a learning company that promotes the effective use of technology, "A majority of faculty now use social media in a professional context (any aspect of their profession outside of teaching). Use of social media for teaching purposes has lagged even more, but like the other patterns of use, it has increased every year. The number of faculty who use social media in the classroom still does not represent a majority, but teaching use continues its steady year-to-year growth. Faculties are sophisticated consumers of social media. In general, they see considerable potential in the application of social media and technology to their teaching, but not without a number of serious barriers".

A number of surveys have been conducted worldwide on the use of social networks by teachers and students (Hendee, 2014; Faculty Focus, 2011; Zanamwe, Rupere & Kufandirimbwa, 2013; Mardikyan & Bozanta, 2017; Moran, Seaman & Tinti-Kane, 2011; Kolan & Dzandza, 2018; Abu-Shanab & Al-Tarawneh, 2015). The results of these surveys show that teachers do not use social networkinh sites for communication with their students (Ghanem, El-Gafy & Abdelrazig, 2014; Hendee, 2014; Faculty Focus, 2011) and during lessons (Hendee, 2014). Teachers use social networking sites to share information and resources with educators, to create professional learning communities and to connect with peers and colleagues (edWeb, 2009), to improve students' engagement in their course and their educational experience (Hendee, 2014; Mardikyan & Bozanta, 2017; Rutherford, 2010; Rodriguez, 2011; Junco, Elavsky & Heiberger, 2013).

Most of these surveys are held within a university or country (some of them are conducted in countries outside the Europe). Therefore, the summarised results of these surveys do not allow us to draw conclusions about the attitude of teachers towards the use of social networks in Europe.

The objective of the study is to investigate whether the extent of knowledge about social networking of teachers in tertiary education from European countries and their research interests on the use of social networking in education is related to which teachers use social networking in their academic practice.

The paper presents the method, organization of the study and thorough analyses of the results in accordance with the study objectives. Some general conclusions about the latest trends in the use of social networking in education are derived.

Survey Method

This section describes briefly the process for data collection and analysis, in order to contextualise the sections that follow.

The study´s method is based on an empirical approach – an exploratory survey using questionnaire for data collection, that has been used to study the attitude towards the use of social networking in Bulgarian higher education (Doneva & Gaftandzhieva, 2017).

The questionnaire contains 20 questions and statements divided into three sections. The questions in Section 1 (see Appendix 1) aim to determine the profile of respondents: gender, age, degree, title, university, country and the degree of awareness of participants about social networking. Section 2 includes a list of 8 statements with numbers 8-15 (see Appendix 1) asking the teachers about the use of social networking in their academic practice for difference purposes: formal use (for communication, consultation, discussions, organization, sharing of information, see Statements 8-10), during training (see Statements 11, 14, 15), for research (see Statements 12-13). Section 3 is a list of 3 statements about the use of social networking for educational purposes in general. Most of the statements in Section 2 and Section 3 are multiple choice. Respondents should state the extent of their agreement with formulated statements on the 5-point Likert-type scale in which 1 means Strongly Disagree (SD), 2 - Disagree (D), 3 - Neutral (N), 4 - Agree (A) and 5 - Strongly Agree (SA). There is an open-ended question for teachers at the end of these sections, which allows teachers to indicate how they use social networking in their teaching practice, as well as why they consider that the use of social networks in education has a negative effect (if so).

This study collected data from teachers working in higher educational institutions in Europe.

The questionnaire was sent by email. Due to the fact that the questionnaire was sent only by email without face-to-face communication, and participants are randomly selected according to the information available in websites of higher education institutions, it is difficult to take into consideration country contextual differences in the result analysis. Therefore, for most of the data analysis the participants are treated as a group, results are not analysed by country, and country contextual differences have not been taken into consideration in the results analysis. However, for the seven countries with the largest number of participants, an attempt for a deeper analysis has been made and differences of these countries have been taken into consideration in the results analysis.

Data analysis includes two stages. On the first stage, the summarized answers of all questions are presented in tables and figures (see Survey Result). On the second stage, the summarized results are compared with results of other surveys and answers of research questions are given (see Findings and Discussions).

The following research questions were formulated in line with the stated objective of the study:

- RQ1. Does the extent to which teachers use social networking sites depend on their information about them?

- RQ2. Does the extent to which teachers use social networking sites depend on their participation in groups interested in the use of social networking for educational purposes?
- RQ3. Does the extent to which teachers use social networking sites vary according to the country?

To give answers to the research questions and to determine whether the dependencies formulated there are in force a deeper analysis of data collected have been made and chi-square tests for independence have been conducted. The analyses made for RQ1 and RQ2 include calculation of the number/percentage of answers to other questions according to the answer given to Question 7 and Statement 12, as well as a comparison of average scores to statements of teachers who answered positively or negatively to Question 7 and Statement 12. The analyses made for RQ3 includes calculation of average scores of all statements (Statement 8-19)/sections (Section 2 and Section 3) given by teachers from the seven countries with the largest number of participants in the survey. Results of these analyses are presented in tables and figures. Chi-square test method is used to find out if there is a significant association between thee data collected and statements checking the opinion about or extent of use of the social networking for different purposes in the academic practice of the surveyed teachers and answers on:

- Question 7 (the teachers' degree of information about social networking) – to answer the RQ1;
- Statement 12 (the teachers' participation in groups interested in the use of social networking for educational purposes) – to answer the RQ2;
- Question 6 (the European country where teachers work) – to answer the RQ3.

Chi-square tests are used to determine whether the following hypotheses for independence are true:

- H1. There is no relation between the use of social networking for different educational purposes both in education in general, and the degree of information of the surveyed teachers about social networking.
- H2. There is no relation between the participation of the surveyed teachers in groups interested in the use of social networking for educational use and the use of social networking for different purposes in their academic practice.
- H3. There is no relation between the country where teachers work and their attitudes towards the use of social networking for different educational purposes in their academic practice and the use of social networking sites for educational purposes.

SURVEY Results

The analysis of the survey results is presented on the basis of valid responses of 5907 teachers from 37 European countries who participated in the survey (teachers from more than 75% of European countries took part in the survey). Figure 1 presents the number of participants from each country. Countries are ranked in descending order according to the number of respondents (indicated in brackets). 110 teachers did not answer the question about the country in which they work.

Figure 1. Number of participants by country (created with https://mapchart.net)

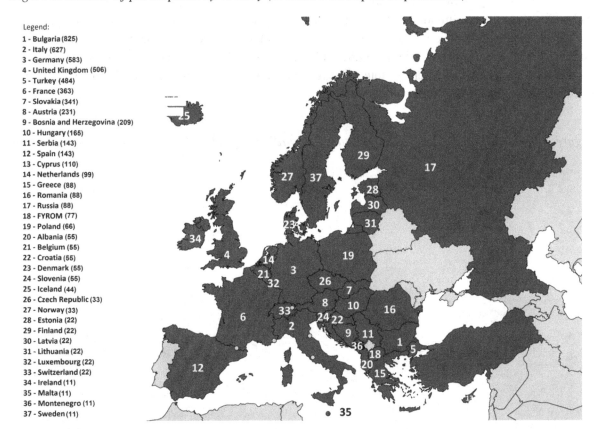

Out of the total number of teachers (537) 55.87% are male and 44.13% are female. The largest group of teachers (31.47%) is 45-54 years old, 26.82% of teachers are 35-44 years old and 22.53% of teachers are above 55 years old. The smallest groups of teachers are 25-34 years old (16.76%) and below 25 years old (2.42%). Most of the teachers have a Ph.D. degree (65.74%) and D.Sc. degree (6.52%). The largest part of the teachers are Associate Professors 24.02%, followed by Assistant Professors – 22.72%, Professors – 22.53%, others – 18.81% and Assistants – 11.92%.

Most surveyed teachers are familiar with social networking sites – 62.00% answered Yes and 32.00% Yes/No to the question "Are you well informed about social networking (e.g. Facebook, Twitter, Google+, Bebo, Myspace, LinkedIn, etc.)?" Figure 2 presents the percentage of answers given by their faculty position and age group. The results clearly show that the majority of teachers with experience (over 35 years old) are well informed about social networking – 93.09% of them are well informed about social networking (59.68% answered Yes and 33.41% answered Yes/ No to the Question 7).

A smaller part of surveyed teachers use the social networking sites to communicate with their students (47.86% answered SD or D, and 19.93% answered N to Statement 8) and participate in online social networking groups for information sharing, discussion and organization of courses (53.44% answered SD or D to Statement 9, and 57.17% answered SD or D to Statement 10). The percentage of teachers who believe that the use of social networking during the lesson increases the engagement of students is even smaller - only 13.69% (see answers to Statement 11). The number of teachers who participate in online groups interested in the use of social networking for educational purposes is also small - 30.54%.

56.70% of the surveyed teachers have a public profile in a social networking site to share research interests and to connect with like-minded people (Statement 13). Finally, when teachers are asked to agree that the use of social networking has a positive effect on student achievement and increases the involvement and interest of students in the training, 39.85% of teachers stated that they are SD or D with Statement 14 and 41.52% 39.85% of teachers stated that they are SD or D with Statement 15. Table 1 presents summarized results of Section 2.

Figure 2. Percentage of the answers to Question 7 according to teachers' faculty position and age group

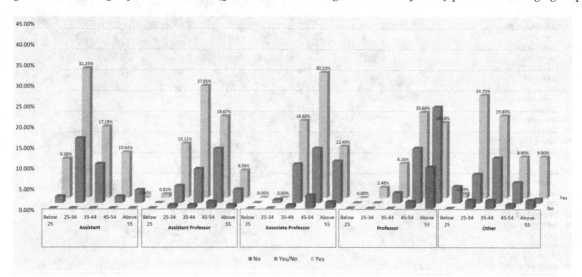

Table 1. Using of social networking sites in teachers' academic practice

Statement	1=SD	2=D	3=N	4=A	5=SA
8. You often use social networking sites for communication and consultation with your students.	1683 (28.49%)	1144 (19.37%)	1177 (19.93%)	1089 (18.44%)	814 (13.78%)
9. You participate in social networking group/groups with your students for information sharing and discussions on the courses.	2024 (34.26%)	1133 (19.18%)	1177 (19.93%)	1034 (17.50%)	539 (9.12%)
10. You participate in social networking group/groups with your students for organization of the courses.	2222 (37.62%)	1155 (19.55%)	1012 (17.13%)	990 (16.76%)	528 (8.94%)
11. You use social networking sites during the lesson in order to increase students' involvement and to keep track of their reactions.	2882 (49.16%)	1287 (21.95%)	891 (15.20%)	495 (8.44%)	308 (5.25%)
12. You participate in online group/groups interested in the use of social networking for educational purposes.	2024 (34.26%)	924 (15.64%)	1155 (19.55%)	1122 (18.99%)	682 (11.55%)
13. You have a public profile in some of social networking sites to share yours research interests and to connect with a wide range of people with similar preferences.	748 (12.69%)	726 (12.31%)	1078 (18.28%)	1628 (27.61%)	1716 (29.10%)
14. The use of social networking sites in your teaching practice has a positive effect on the student achievements.	1507 (25.51%)	847 (14.34%)	1892 (32.03%)	1078 (18.25%)	583 (9.87%)
15. The use of social networking sites in your teaching practice increases the involvement and interest of students in the training.	1584 (26.82%)	869 (14.71%)	1650 (27.93%)	1210 (20.48%)	594 (10.06%)

The majority of teachers (see Table 2) agree that the use of social networking in education can be useful - 21.42% answered SA to Statement 17 and 37.62% answered A. Significantly greater is the number of teachers who agree that the role of social networking in education will increase – 33.77% answered SA and 36.94 answered A to Statement 18. This shows that despite the relatively low rate of the current use of social networking, the majority of teachers tend to use social networks in the future. The answers given on Statement 19 show that the low rate of use of social networks at the moment is probably due also to the low level of participation of teachers in research on the use of social networking in education – only 1452 teachers (24.77%) stated participation in such research.

Table 2. Using social networking for educational purposes in general

Statement	1=SD	2=D	3=N	4=A	5=SA
17. Social networking sites are/can be useful in education.	286 (4.84%)	605 (10.24%)	1529 (25.88%)	2222 (37.62%)	1265 (21.42%)
18. The role of social networking sites will increase.	220 (3.73%)	374 (6.34%)	1133 (19.22%)	2178 (36.94%)	1991 (33.77%)
19. You participate in research related to the use of social networking sites in education.	2266 (38.65%)	1089 (18.57%)	1056 (18.01%)	792 (13.51%)	660 (11.26%)

Overall, the survey results show that teachers have a negative attitude towards the use of social networking in their academic practice (an average score 2.63 on the eight statements from Section 2 of the questionnaire). Although the surveyed teachers do not use social networking sites in their academic practice now, they believe that social networking sites can be useful for education in general and have a positive attitude towards the use of social networking for educational purposes (an average score 3.30 on the three statements from Section 3 of the questionnaire). Figure 3 presents the average scores on statements from Section 2 and Section 3 of the questionnaire given by the teachers.

Figure 3. Average scores on statements from Section 2 and Section 3

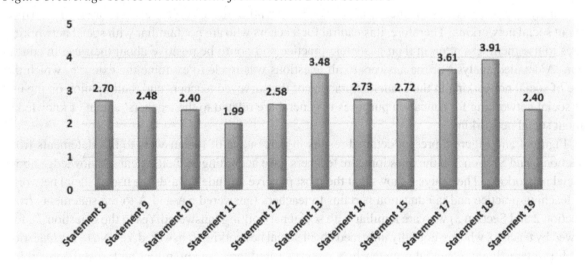

FINDINGS AND DISCUSSIONS

Most of the results from this survey are in line with the findings of other surveys on the use of social networking in education. For example, some surveys conducted among teachers (Ghanem, El-Gafy & Abdelrazig, 2014; Hendee, 2014; Faculty Focus, 2011) show that teachers do not use social networks for communication with their students and prefer to use conventional communication channels (email, phone calls, and text messaging respectively). The conclusion that a small number of teachers use social networking during lessons also confirms the results of another survey (Hendee, 2014). The finding that most teachers use social networking sites to share their research interests and to connect with a wide range of people with similar preferences confirms the results of the survey conducted by MMS Education (ed-Web, 2009). That survey concludes that teachers use social networking to share information and resources with educators, to create professional learning communities and to connect with peers and colleagues. Moreover, the positive attitude of the teachers towards the statements that social networking sites can be useful in education and their role in education will increase substantiates the teachers' expectation to increase their use of social media in the future (Faculty Focus, 2011). However, some of the findings from the current survey do not correspond to those of other studies. This study's conclusions that the use of social networks doesn't increase students' engagement and interest while studying their course differ from the conclusions of other studies, according to which the use of social networks does improve students' engagement in their course and their educational experience, on the one hand (Hendee, 2014; Mardikyan & Bozanta, 2017; Rutherford, 2010; Rodriguez, 2011; Junco, Elavsky & Heiberger, 2013), and peer interaction and students' interaction with faculty members, on the other (Zanamwe, Rupere & Kufandirimbwa, 2013; Mardikyan & Bozanta, 2017). The findings do not corroborate the results of another study (Kolan & Dzandza, 2018) conducted among the students, according to which the use of social networking increases their understanding of topics discussed in class and improves their scores. This persuasion contradicts the opinion of surveyed teachers that the use of social networking sites in their teaching practice does not have a positive effect on student achievements.

Analysis According to Extent of Knowledge About Social Networking (Answer to Research Question RQ1)

The analysis of the answers to Question 7 shows that not all of the surveyed teachers are well informed about social networking. Therefore, it is natural for teachers who are not familiar with social networking sites to use them less often in their academic practice and not to be positive about their use in education. A detailed analysis of the answers to all questions was made to examine the extent to which the use of social networking in the academic practice of the surveyed teachers and their opinion on the use of social networking for education purposes in general are related to the teachers' extent of knowledge about social networking.

Figure 4 and Figure 5 present detailed results in percentage of the answers to the statements from Section 2 and Section 3 in the questionnaire teachers gave according to their extent of knowledge about social networking. The analysis shows that the most positive attitude towards the use of social networks in teaching practice and in education pertains to teachers (answered SA and A to the statements from Section 2 and Section 3) who are familiar with social networking (answered Yes to the Question 7), followed by teachers who are not fully informed about social networking (answered Yes/No to the Question 7). It is interesting to note that even teachers who answered they are unfamiliar with social networking believe that social networking sites can be useful for education and they are convinced that the role of social networks in education will increase (see Figure 5).

Figure 4. Percentage of answers to Statement 8-15 according to degree of information about social networking

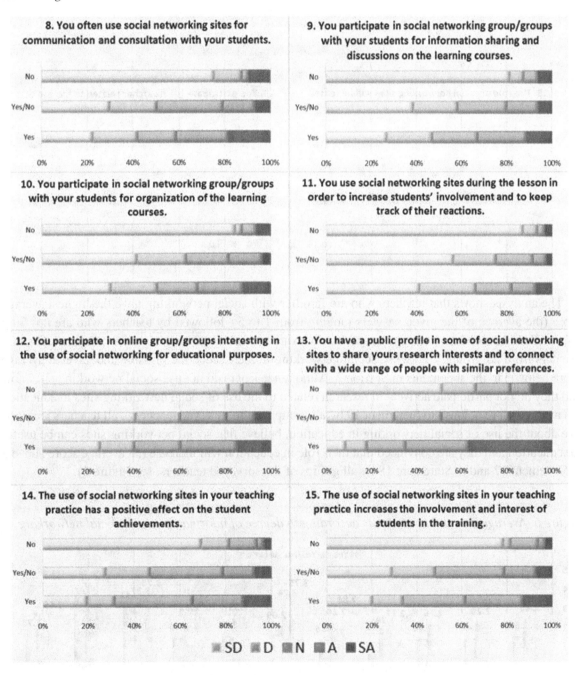

Figure 5. Percentage of answers to Statement 17-19 according to degree of information about social networking

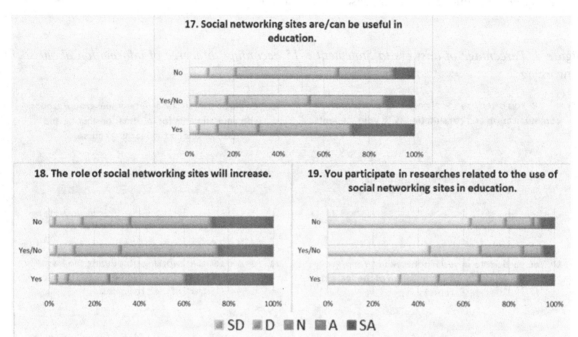

The analysis shows that teachers who are familiar with social networking gave the highest average score (the average of the given answers ranging from 1 to 5), followed by teachers who are not fully informed about social networking and teachers who are not familiar with social networks at all. Overall, teachers from all groups do not use social networking in their academic practice and gave an average score below 3 to the statements in Section 2. Although teachers do not use social networking sites now and they do not participate actively in research related to the use of social networking sites in education (an average score below 3 to Statement 19 by all groups of the surveyed teachers), all teachers are positive about the use of social networking in education, believe that social networking sites can be useful for education and they are convinced that their role in education will increase (an average score above 3 to Statement 17 and to Statement 18 by all groups of the surveyed teachers, see Figure 6).

Figure 6. Average scores on statements according to degree of information about social networking

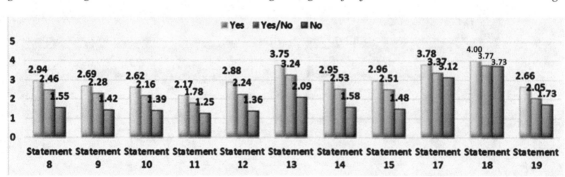

Statistical hypothesis H1. There is no relation between the use of social networking for different educational purposes both in education in general, and the degree of information of the surveyed teachers about social networking was checked to determine whether the use of social networking for different educational purposes depends on the surveyed teachers' extent of knowledge about social networking. Chi-Square Tests were conducted and Pearson's coefficients were calculated to verify the zero hypothesis that there is no relation between the use of social networking for educational purposes both in education and in general and the surveyed teachers' extent of knowledge about social networking.

The results of Chi-Square Tests show that since $p<0.05$ (in fact $p <0.001$) there is a dependence between teachers' knowledge about social networking (Statement 7) and the use of social networks for different educational purposes: for communication and consultation (Statement 8), for information sharing and discussions (Statement 9), for organization of the courses (Statement 10), during lesson (Statement 11), participation in online groups (Statement 12), for sharing research interests (Statement 13), to increase students' achievements (Statement 14), increase involvement and interest of students in the training (Statement 15).

The results show that the opinion of the surveyed teachers on the usefulness of the social networking sites (Statement 17) and their participation in research related to the use of social networking sites in education (Statement 19) also depends on teachers' extent of knowledge about social networking since $p < 0.05$ (in fact $p < 0.001$). The null hypothesis for independence of the teachers' opinion about the future role of social networking (Statement 18) and teachers' extent of knowledge about the social networking sites can't be rejected since $p = 0.062$.

Analysis According to the Teachers' Participation in Groups Interested in the Use of Social Networking for Educational Purposes (Answer To Research Question RQ2)

A small part of the surveyed teachers participate in groups interested in the use of social networking for educational purposes - only 1804 (30.55%) of the surveyed teachers answered A or SA to Statement 12. You participate in online group/groups interested in the use of social networking for educational purposes. Significantly higher is the number of teachers who do not participate in groups interested in the use social networks for educational purposes - 2948 of the surveyed teachers answered SD or D to Statement (49.90%).

Table 3 presents the number of answers given by teachers who do not participate in groups interested in the use of social networking for educational purposes. The results show that teachers who do not participate in such groups rarely use social networking sites in their teaching practice. The analysis of the answers shows that teachers are skeptical towards the use of social networking for communication and consultation with their students, discussions about the studied material and organization of training courses – only 14.18% answered A or SA to Statement 8, 13.18% answered A or SA to Statement 9 and 8.95% answered A or SA to Statement 10. Most teachers are strongly against the use of social networking sites during lessons – only 4.76% of teachers gave answers A or SA to Statement 11. Teachers are skeptical that the use of social networking sites has a positive effect on students' achievements and that it increases their involvement and interest in the university course – 9.33% of teachers gave answer A or SA to Statement 14 and 11.56% of teachers gave answer A or SA to Statement 15.

The teachers who participate in groups interested in the use of social networking for educational purposes are more positive and actively use social networks in their academic practice.

Table 3. Using of social networking sites in academic practice according to answers on Statement 12 (SD = 1 and D = 2)

Statement	SD=1	D=2	N=3	A=4	SA=5
8. You often use social networking sites for communication and consultation with your students.	1408 (47.76%)	737 (25.00%)	385 (13.06%)	220 (7.46%)	198 (6.72%)
9. You participate in social networking group/groups with your students for information sharing and discussions on the courses.	1661 (56.34%)	572 (19.40%)	308 (10.45%)	319 (10.82%)	88 (2.99%)
10. You participate in social networking group/ groups with your students for organization of the courses.	1793 (60.82%)	550 (18.66%)	341 (11.57%)	198 (6.71%)	66 (2.24%)
11. You use social networking sites during the lesson in order to increase students' involvement and to keep track of their reactions.	2200 (75.19%)	506 (17.29%)	110 (3.76%)	77 (2.63%)	33 (1.13%)
13. You have a public profile in some of social networking sites to share yours research interests and to connect with a wide range of people with similar preferences.	649 (22.02%)	396 (13.43%)	572 (19.40%)	682 (23.13%)	649 (22.02%)
14. The use of social networking sites in your teaching practice has a positive effect on the student achievements.	1320 (44.78%)	495 (16.79%)	858 (29.10%)	176 (5.97%)	99 (3.36%)
15. The use of social networking sites in your teaching practice increases the involvement and interest of students in the training.	1331 (45.15%)	550 (18.66%)	726 (24.63%)	231 (7.83%)	110 (3.73%)

Table 4. Using of social networking sites in academic practice according to answers on Statement 12 (A=4 and SA=5)

Statement	SD=1	D=2	N=3	A=4	SA=5
8. You often use social networking sites for communication and consultation with your students.	110 (6.10%)	187 (10.36%)	462 (25.61%)	572 (31.71%)	473 (26.22%)
9. You participate in social networking group/groups with your students for information sharing and discussions on the courses.	154 (8.54%)	319 (17.68%)	462 (25.61%)	506 (28.05%)	363 (20.12%)
10. You participate in social networking group/groups with your students for organization of the courses.	187 (10.37%)	418 (23.17%)	275 (15.24%)	517 (28.66%)	407 (22.56%)
11. You use social networking sites during the lesson in order to increase students' involvement and to keep track of their reactions.	374 (20.86%)	440 (24.54%)	396 (22.08%)	330 (18.41%)	253 (14.11%)
13. You have a public profile in some of social networking sites to share yours research interests and to connect with a wide range of people with similar preferences.	44 (2.45%)	132 (7.36%)	198 (11.05%)	605 (33.74%)	814 (45.40%)
14. The use of social networking sites in your teaching practice has a positive effect on the student achievements.	55 (3.05%)	165 (9.14%)	528 (29.27%)	627 (34.76%)	429 (23.78%)
15. The use of social networking sites in your teaching practice increases the involvement and interest of students in the training.	77 (4.27%)	198 (10.98%)	418 (23.17%)	737 (40.85%)	374 (20.73%)

Table 4 presents the number of responses from teachers participating in such groups. The analysis of answers shows that most of the surveyed teachers use social networking for communication and consultation with their students, discussions about the studied material and organisation of courses – 57.93%

answered SA or A to Statement 8, 48.17% answered A or SA to Statement 9 and 51.22% answered A or SA to Statement 10. Despite the positive attitude towards the use of social networking sites for communication, discussions and organization, most teachers are strongly against their use during lessons – only 32.52% of teachers answered A or SA to Statement 11. Most teachers believe that the use of social networking sites has a positive effect on students' achievements and that it increases their involvement and interest in the course – 58.54% of teachers answered A or SA to Statement 14 and 61.58% of teachers answered A or SA to Statement 15.

The analysis of the answers clearly shows (see Figure 7) that teachers who participate in groups interested in the use of social networking sites for educational purposes gave highest average scores of all statements in Section 2. These teachers gave an average score above 3 to the six statements in Section 2. Although they have a positive attitude towards social networking in general, a small part of them use social networking sites during lessons - an average score 2.80 on Statement 11.

Chi-Square Tests were conducted and Pearson's coefficients were calculated to verify the zero hypothesis H2. There is no relation between the participation of the surveyed teachers in groups interested in the use of social networking for educational use and the use of social networking for different purposes in their academic practice.

The results show that there is a relation between the participation of teachers in groups interested in the use of social networking for educational purposes and the extent to which they use social networking for different educational purposes (Statement 8-15) since $p < 0.05$ (in fact $p < 0.001$).

Figure 7. Average scores on statements from Section 2 according to answers on Statement 12

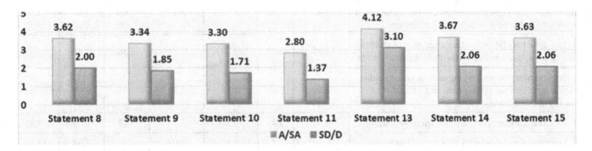

Analysis According to the Country Where Teachers Work (Answer to Research Question RQ3)

Table 5 presents the average scores given by teachers from the seven countries with the largest number of participants in the survey - over 300 participants per country. The analysis of the answers shows that the surveyed teachers from all countries do not use social networking sites in their academic practice as a whole (see average scores on Statement 8-15). Teachers from Bulgaria stated that they use social networking sites for communication and consultation with students (an average score 3.13 to Statement 8). Teachers from Turkey have the most positive attitude towards the statements that social networking sites increase the interest and involvement of students in the course and the use of social networking sites in education has a positive effect on student achievements (average scores above 3 to Statements 14 and 15). Also, they are the most active in groups interested in the use of social networking for educational purposes (an average score above 3 to Statements 12) and sharing of research interests (the highest average score to Statement 13). Teachers from all countries believe that the use of social networking in education can have a positive effect and their role in education will increase. They all gave average scores above 3 to Statement 17 and Statement 18. Although the answers given and teachers' conviction in positive effects and the role of social networking, only teachers from Turkey participate in research related to the use of social networking for educational purposes (an average score above 3 to Statement 19).

Table 5. Average answers by countries

Statement	Bulgaria	Italy	Germany	United Kingdom	Turkey	France	Slovakia
8. You often use social networking sites for communication and consultation with your students.	3.13	2.60	2.15	2.52	2.86	2.67	2.77
9. You participate in social networking group/groups with your students for information sharing and discussions on the courses.	2.87	2.26	2.15	2.41	2.91	2.21	2.42
10. You participate in social networking group/groups with your students for organization of the courses.	2.75	2.35	2.11	2.24	2.86	2.36	2.26
11. You use social networking sites during the lesson in order to increase students' involvement and to keep track of their reactions.	1.92	1.80	1.64	2.00	2.51	2.12	1.84
12. You participate in online group/groups interested in the use of social networking for educational purposes.	2.65	2.32	2.21	2.91	3.34	2.00	2.06
13. You have a public profile in some of social networking sites to share yours research interests and to connect with a wide range of people with similar preferences.	3.43	3.16	3.32	3.39	3.66	3.48	3.35
14. The use of social networking sites in your teaching practice has a positive effect on the student achievements.	2.95	2.46	2.30	2.74	3.36	2.45	2.97
15. The use of social networking sites in your teaching practice increases the involvement and interest of students in the training.	2.89	2.60	2.34	2.85	3.41	2.48	2.52
17. Social networking sites are/can be useful in education.	3.68	3.49	3.21	3.76	3.93	3.09	3.81
18. The role of social networking sites will increase.	3.85	3.74	3.57	3.98	4.32	3.64	4.10
19. You participate in research related to the use of social networking sites in education.	2.15	2.14	2.34	2.46	3.59	1.82	2.46

Figure 8 presents the average scores of all statements in Section 2 and Section 3 given by the surveyed teachers. The chart clearly shows that teachers do not use social networking sites in their practice now – only teachers from Turkey have a positive attitude towards the use of social networking sites in academic practice (an average score 3.12 on Section 2). Teachers from all of the seven countries with the largest number of participants in the survey think that in general the use of social networking sites can be useful for education and the educational role of the social networks will increase in the coming years. Only teachers from France gave an average score below 3 on Section 3, but this is mainly due to the fact that a small part of them participate in research related to the use of social networking sites for educational purposes (an average score 1.82 to Statement 19, see Table 5).

Figure 8. Average scores on statements according to country

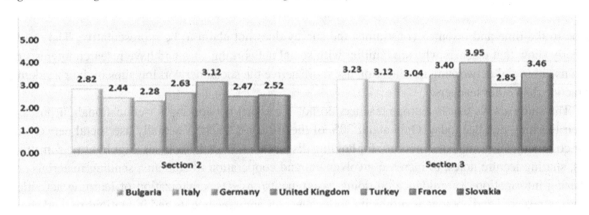

These average results are not in line with the official data about the digital competences of the population from the digital economy and society index of these countries (DESI, 2018). Germany and the United Kingdom have the most advanced digital economies in the Europe from these six countries (Turkey is outside the European Union, it is not included in the DESI and there is no comparable official data about the digital competencies of its population) followed by France and Slovakia. Italy and Bulgaria have the lowest scores in DESI. Despite the fact that Germany is the most advanced country, teachers from Germany are the most skeptical towards the use of social networking in education. On the other hand, Bulgaria is 27th in DESI (from 29 European countries), but Bulgarian teachers have more positive attitude towards the use of social networking in education in accordance with the more advanced countries. Teachers from the United Kingdom, Bulgaria and Slovakia, followed by teachers from France, Italy and Germany, were most positive towards the use of social networking in their practice and in education. Chi-Square Tests were conducted and Pearson's coefficients were calculated to verify the zero hypothesis H3. There is no relation between the country where teachers work and their attitudes towards the use of social networking for different educational purposes in their teaching practice and the use of social networking site for educational purposes. The results ($p < 0.05$) show that there is a dependence between the country where teachers work and their attitude towards the use of social networking in their teaching practice for the organization of courses (Statement 10), during lesson (Statement 11), for sharing research interests with colleagues (Statement 12), to increase the students' achievements (Statement 14) and interest of students in the course (Statement 15).

The hypotheses for independence between the country where teachers work and their attitude towards the use of social networking for communication and consultation (Statement 8), for information sharing and discussions (Statement 9) and for sharing of research interests (Statement 13) can't be rejected since $p >= 0.05$. The results show that the opinion of the surveyed teachers on the usefulness of the social networking sites (Statement 17), the future role of social networking in education (Statement 18) and their participation in research related to the use of social networking sites in education (Statement 19) also depends on the country where teachers work since $p < 0.05$.

CONCLUSION

Due to the time and resource constraints, the survey does not claim to be representative. The results clearly show that teachers who are familiar with social networking sites and have research interests on the use of social networking in education use more active the social networking sites in their academic practice than other teachers.

The study shows that in Europe teachers do not use social networking for educational purposes in their teaching practice today. Only about 30% of the surveyed teachers actually use social networking for communication and consultations, for holding discussions about the courses, highlighting some topics, sharing lecture notes, to increase involvement and cooperation of students, sending materials and sharing information, for guidance on doing assignments/projects, organization of learning activities, sharing research and communication with colleagues, for announcements and invitations to workshops and conferences, to contact alumni and former students, etc.

Although the surveyed teachers do not use social networking sites in their practice now, they agree that the educational role of the social networks will increase in the coming years. Teachers believe that in general social networking sites can be useful for education (an average score 3.30 on the three statements from Section 3 of the questionnaire). The answers of the open-ended question in the end of Section 3 show that most teachers today have a negative attitude towards the use of social networking for organizational/teaching activities for the following reasons: distraction of the students, lack of face-to-face communication, it requires time to manage it, danger of superficiality, lack of a reflective approach to learning, sharing mechanisms blur the boundary between private and public/academic public, plagiarism, lack of motivation, laziness of thought and analytical skills, severe drop in communication and presentation skills, issues connected to privacy and security, it can blur boundaries between students and instructors and devalue the role of academics and education, etc.

The negative attitude of teachers today is related to the fact that not all of them are well informed about social networking and a small part of them participate in research related to the opportunities for the use of social networking in education. Teachers who have a positive attitude to the use of social networking for educational purposes believe that their use is quite beneficial if the networking site is created for educational purposes only and if the students are properly targeted to the use of the social networks. They think that social networks make discussions between students, and between students and staff, much easier and more fluent. For these teachers, social networking can be a useful tool for creating a sense of community and for sharing resources, for organising and motivating students, for research networking and production. Furthermore, teachers stated that social networking can create interaction and increase the knowledge of students (especially in language teaching). Teachers who do not use social networking for organizational/teaching activities today think that all this possibly will change in the next years with new students (with new social media behaviour) coming in.

The presented study has some limitations. The study method includes only a questionnaire for data collection. All teachers were invited to participate via emails, and they were randomly selected according to the information available in websites of higher education institution. Many of the invited teachers did not fill out the questionnaire for different reasons. Due to the fact that the study did not involve teachers from many universities in the same country, the differences between the different educational systems have not been taken into consideration in the research design in full degree. Otherwise, the lack of face-to-face communication did not allow additional interviews to be conducted in order to gain deeper insights into the topics being examined.

A study underway aims to establish the attitude towards the use of social networking all over the world. Teachers from overseas universities are invited to participate in that study. Future studies should also be considered in terms of possibilities for the fully valued use of social networking in higher education.

\ACKNOWLEDGMENT

The paper is supported within the National Scientific Program "Young scientists and Post-doctoral students" in accordance with Appendix No. 11 of Council of Ministers Decision No. 577 of 17 August 2018.

REFERENCES

Abu-Shanab, E., & Al-Tarawneh, H. (2015). The influence of social networks on high school students' performance. *International Journal of Web-Based Learning and Teaching Technologies*, *10*(2), 49–59. doi:10.4018/IJWLTT.2015040104

Acharya, V., Patel, Ad., & Jethava, S. (2013). A Survey on Social Networking to Enhance the Teaching and Learning Process. *International Journal of Advanced Research in Computer Science and Software Engineering*, 3(6).

Alam, L. (2018). *Teaching with web 2.0 technologies: Twitter, wikis & blogs*. Retrieved from https://tv.unsw.edu.au/files//unswPDF/CS_Web2_LTTO.pdf

Arquero, J. L., & Romero-Frías, E. (2013). Using social network sites in Higher Education: An experience in business studies. *Innovations in Education and Teaching International*, *50*(3), 238–249. doi:10.1080/14703297.2012.760772

Aviles, M., & Eastman, J. K. (2012). Utilizing technology effectively to improve millennials' educational performance. *Journal of International Education in Business*, *5*(2), 96–113. doi:10.1108/18363261211281726

Carapina, M., Bjelobrk, D., & Duk, S. (2013). Web 2.0 tools in Croatian higher education: An overview. In Proceeding of Information & Communication Technology Electronics & Microelectronics (MIPRO 2013) (pp. 676-680).

DEAP. (2018). *Digital Education and Action Plan*, Retrieved from https://ec.europa.eu/education/sites/education/files/digital-education-action-plan.pdf

DESI. (2018). *Digital Economy and Society Index*, Retrieved from https://ec.europa.eu/digital-single-market/en/desi

Doneva, R., & Gaftandzhieva, S. (2017). Social Media in Bulgarian Higher Education: An Exploratory Survey, *International Journal of Human Capital and Information Technology Professionals*, 8(4), 67-83.

edWeb. (2009). *A Survey of K-12 Educators on Social Networking and Content-Sharing Tools*, Retrieved from https://www.edweb.net/fimages/op/K12Survey.pdf

Faculty Focus. (2011). *Social Media Usage Trends Among Higher Education Faculty*. Retrieved from https://www.facultyfocus.com/free-reports/social-media-usage-trends-among-higher-education-faculty/

Ghanem, A., El-Gafy, M., & Abdelrazig, Y. (2014). Survey of the Current Use of Social Networking in Construction Education. In *50th ASC Annual International Conference Proceedings*.

Golubić, K. (2017). *The Role of Social Networks in the Presentation of Croatian Higher Education Institutions* [PhD Thesis]. Retrieved from https://urn.nsk.hr/urn:nbn:hr:102:527811

Golubić, K; & Lasić-Lazić, J. (2012). Analysis of On-line Survey about Need for Presence of Higher Education Institutions on Social Networks: a Step towards Creation of Communication Strategy. *Journal of Computing and Information Technology, 20*(3), 189-194.

Hendee, C. (2014). *Teachers have mixed feelings on using social media in classrooms*. Retrieved https://www.bizjournals.com/denver/news/2014/02/11/teachers-have-mixed-feelings-on-using.html

Junco, R., Elavsky, C. M., & Heiberger, G. (2013). Putting twitter to the test: Assessing outcomes for student collaboration, engagement and success. *British Journal of Educational Technology, 44*(2), 273–287. doi:10.1111/j.1467-8535.2012.01284.x

Kolan, B., & Dzandza, P. (2018). Effect of Social Media on Academic Performance of Students in Ghanaian Universities: A Case Study of University of Ghana, Legon. *Library Philosophy and Practice*.

Kropf, D. C. (2013). Connectivism: 21st Century's New Learning Theory. *European Journal of Open, Distance and e-Learning. 16*(2), 13-24.

Mardikyan, S., & Bozanta, A. (2017). The effects of social media use on collaborative learning: a case of Turkey. *Turkish Online Journal of Distance Education, 18*(1), 96-110.

Moran, M., Seaman, J., & Tinti-Kane, H. (2011). *Teaching, Learning, and Sharing: How Today's Higher Education Faculty Use Social Media*. Pearson Learning Solutions and Babson Survey Research Group.

Morgan, H. (2014). Using digital story projects to help students improve in reading and writing. *Reading Improvement, 51*(1), 20–26.

Rodriguez, J. E. (2011). Social media use in higher education: Key areas to consider for educators. *MERLOT Journal of Online Learning and Teaching, 7*(4), 539–550.

Rutherford, C. (2010). Using online social media to support preservice student engagement. *MERLOT Journal of Online Learning and Teaching, 6*(4), 703–711.

Statista. (2018). *Most popular social networks worldwide as of January 2018, ranked by number of active users (in millions)*. Retrieved from https://www.statista.com/statistics/272014/global-social-networks-ranked-by-number-of-users/

Voorn, R. J., & Kommers, P. (2013). Social media and higher education: Introversion and collaborative learning from the student's perspective. *International Journal of Social Media and Interactive Learning Environments, 1*(1), 59–71. doi:10.1504/IJSMILE.2013.051650

Wang, Q., Woo, H. L., Quek, C. L., Yang, Y., & Liu, M. (2011). Using the Facebook group as learning management system: An exploratory study. *British Journal of Educational Technology*. doi:10.1111/j.1467-8535.2011.01195.x

Zanamwe, N., Rupere, T., & Kufandirimbwa, O. (2013). Use of Social Networking Technologies in Higher Education in Zimbabwe: A learners' perspective. *International Journal of Computer and Information Technology*, 2(1).

This research was previously published in the International Journal of Virtual and Personal Learning Environments (IJVPLE), 10(1); pages 51-69, copyright year 2020 by IGI Publishing (an imprint of IGI Global).

Appendix- Survey

Section 1. Personal Information for participant

1. What is your gender? ○ male ○ female
2. How old are you? ○ below 25 ○ 25-34 ○ 35-44 ○ 45-54 ○ above 55
3. What is your scientific degree? ○ PhD ○ D.Sc. ○Other
4. What is your academic position? ○Assistant ○Assistant Professor ○Associate Professor ○Professor ○Other
5. In which university/institute/academy are you working?
6. In which country are you working?
7. Are you well informed about social networking (e.g. Facebook, Twitter, Google+, Bebo, Myspace, LinkedIn, etc.)? ○Yes ○Yes/No ○No

Please, give your opinion on the statement from Section II and Section III by expressing your agreement / disagreement in the following five-point scale: 1. Strongly disagree; 2. Disagree; 3. Neutral; 4. Agree; 5. Strongly agree.

Section 2. Opinion on the use of social networks in teaching practice

8. You often use social networking sites for communication and consultation with your students.
   ○1. Strongly disagree ○2. Disagree ○3. Neutral ○4. Agree ○5. Strongly agree.
9. You participate in social networking group/groups with your students for information sharing and discussions on the courses.
   ○1. Strongly disagree ○2. Disagree ○3. Neutral ○4. Agree ○5. Strongly agree.
10. You participate in social networking group/groups with your students for organization of the courses.
    ○1. Strongly disagree ○2. Disagree ○3. Neutral ○4. Agree ○5. Strongly agree.
11. You use social networking sites during the lesson in order to increase students' involvement and to keep track of their reactions.
    ○1. Strongly disagree ○2. Disagree ○3. Neutral ○4. Agree ○5. Strongly agree.
12. You participate in online group/groups interested in the use of social networking for educational purposes.
    ○1. Strongly disagree ○2. Disagree ○3. Neutral ○4. Agree ○5. Strongly agree.
13. You have a public profile in some of social networking sites to share yours research interests and to connect with a wide range of people with similar preferences.
    ○1. Strongly disagree ○2. Disagree ○3. Neutral ○4. Agree ○5. Strongly agree.
14. The use of social networking sites in your teaching practice has a positive effect on the student achievements.
    ○1. Strongly disagree ○2. Disagree ○3. Neutral ○4. Agree ○5. Strongly agree.
15. The use of social networking sites in your teaching practice increases the involvement and interest of students in the training.
    ○1. Strongly disagree ○2. Disagree ○3. Neutral ○4. Agree ○5. Strongly agree.
16. You use social networking sites in your teaching practice in ways other than those stated above – please specify.

Section 3. Opinion on the use of social networking for educational purposes in general

17.   Social networking sites are/can be useful in education.
       ○1. Strongly disagree ○2. Disagree ○3. Neutral ○4. Agree ○5. Strongly agree.
18.   The role of social networking sites will increase.
       ○1. Strongly disagree ○2. Disagree ○3. Neutral ○4. Agree ○5. Strongly agree.
19.   You participate in researches related to the use of social networking sites in education.
       ○1. Strongly disagree ○2. Disagree ○3. Neutral ○4. Agree ○5. Strongly agree.
20.   You think that the use of social networking sites for educational purposes has a rather negative effect - specify.

Chapter 6
Rethinking Twitter:
Unique Characteristics of Twitter Render It an Instructional Asset

Armand A. Buzzelli
Robert Morris University, USA

Gregory Holdan
Robert Morris University, USA

Allen R. Lias
Robert Morris University, USA

Daniel R. Rota
Robert Morris University, USA

Trebor Z. Evans
Robert Morris University, USA

ABSTRACT

Despite being more widely known for its contributions to pop culture, and more recently political news and events, a growing body of literature exists about Twitter's use in education. This chapter presents a framework for using Twitter as an instructional review tool, leveraging its timely, unique, and efficient communication style while incorporating theories of memory and cognitive psychology that are more than two centuries old. The authors present applied practice study examples of how Twitter may be used as a means for distributed practice in learning concepts. While practitioners may be concerned about student adoption of Twitter, research presented in this chapter reports that Twitter is user-friendly and is most engaging for students when an instructor frequently participates.

DOI: 10.4018/978-1-6684-7123-4.ch006

INTRODUCTION

A typical study guide for an exam may include a list of key terms, concepts, or definitions that are tested for subject mastery. When a student gets the physical study guide, and reviews it in the day or days leading up to the exam in preparation, the phenomenon is referred to as "massed practice." This effect occurs when the material to be learned is presented repeatedly in a short period of time. Distributed or spaced practice as it is also called, is defined as "the effect of inter-study interval (ISI) upon learning, as measured on subsequent tests… and ISI is the interval separating different study episodes of the same materials (Cepeda, Pashler, Vul, Wixted, & Rohrer, 2006, p. 354). An example of the difference between spaced practiced and massed practice is essentially deciding to review exam material weekly and to cover the same key concepts five different times over the course of a month as opposed to reviewing those topics five different times one or two nights before an exam.

Twitter would appear to serve as an ideal tool for concept learning because it requires a user to create a succinct, 140-character or word string. In September 2017, Twitter increased the character limit to 280 characters; however, it is a reasonable assumption that this limit still forces the author to be concise. While the character limit may hinder detailed explanation, the social network offers a model platform for efficient examples and non-examples of concepts. Twitter can be easily spaced out over time, thus developing a customizable spaced practice regimen. This chapter will expand upon two studies: one by Buzzelli, Holdan, Rota, and McCarthy (2016) that attempted to determine if sending tweets with examples and non-examples related to predetermined major concepts would assist students in effectively learning concepts through distributed practice, and another by Evans (2017) that looked at engaging students in a higher education setting through the use of Twitter.

BACKGROUND

Studies that date back to over 130 years ago in the fields of psychology and education have examined the effects of spacing the study of concepts versus providing comprehensive information at one time. German psychologist Herman Ebbinghaus (1885) studied memory and practice effect by testing subjects on their recall of nonsense syllables. Chief among his conclusions was the formation of a concept called serial position effect, which included recency and primacy. The recency effect describes the increased recall of the most recent information because it is still in the short-term memory. The primacy effect causes better memory of the first items in a list due to increased rehearsal and commitment to long-term memory. While the definition of spaced versus massed practice is subjective, Underwood (1961) determined that spaced practice occurred when trial intervals are greater than fifteen seconds; massed practice (MP), when intervals are two to eight seconds.

Dempster (1989) found that "spacing effects can best be understood in terms of the 'accessibility' hypothesis, and that spaced repetitions have considerable potential for improving classroom learning" (p. 309). The accessibility hypothesis states that memory will be accurate when the ease of accessibility is correlated with memory behavior; however, if the ease of processing is not correlated with memory in a given task, then the judgments will not be accurate (Schwartz, 1994). The theory dates back to studies conducted by Tulving and Pearlstone (1966) that worked with cued recall. Their study demonstrated that subjects who were non-cued had information reach their memory stage but not their retrieval stage in contrast to those who received spaced cues.

Studies by Estes (1955), Glenberg (1979), Raaijmakers (2003), and Pavlik and Anderson (2005) found that by increasing the spacing of practice, subjects had improved recall. Likewise, Bahrick (1979) found that when spacing was moved closer together the recall of subjects worsened. This research suggests that the timing of reviews by instructors should be spaced increasingly further apart to improve performance.

The mobility and ability to pre-schedule content delivery through Twitter makes it a suitable tool to space information to learners and aid in concept learning. Bruner, Goodnow, and Austin (1967) defined concept attainment (concept learning) as "the search for and listing of attributes that can be used to distinguish exemplars from non-exemplars of various categories" (p.233). Seels and Glasgow (1990) described a process to help instructors identify important concepts for teaching by "defining what is to be learned, planning an intervention that will allow the learning to occur, and refining the instruction until the objectives are met" (p. 3).

In addition to providing examples of concepts during instruction, there has been conflicting research on providing non-examples to assist in concept learning. Tennyson (1973) identified several studies (Smoke, 1933; Morrisett & Hovland, 1959, Tennyson, Wooley & Merrill, 1972) where outcomes varied when using non-examples. For the purpose of the primary example being used in this text, non-examples of concepts were included in tweets shared with students.

Despite being founded by Jack Dorsey, Evan Williams, Noah Glass, and Biz Stone in 2006, a growing body of literature exists about Twitter's use in education. Twitter users organically created the concept of hash-tagging. By utilizing hashtags (#) before a keyword, the instructor found it simple to search for other flashcards from the class and organize them accordingly; Trueman and Miles (2011) found that Twitter could be used to create interactive flash cards that can be used for review. In their study, students developed five tweets per participant and they were consolidated into a master review board. Twitter is an apt forum for electronic flashcard development, because as students tweet flashcards in live time, they may serve to prompt ideas for flash cards from other students. Similarly, students are able to post each individual flashcard as they think of them, as opposed to emailing them all or posting them all at once on the learning management system Blackboard.

According to statistics from Twitter in August 2017, there are 328 million monthly active users, of which 80% are active on mobile devices. Twitter differs from Facebook and other social media networks because it serves as a micro-blogging tool (Kieslinger, Ebner, & Wiesenhofer, 2011). Twitter is unique in a number of ways. From a social relationship perspective, the most important difference is the ability to "re-tweet" a friend or followed user's tweet. A re-tweet promotes affirmation of other users' comments and serves as encouragement for a producer of Twitter content. Boyd, Golder, and, Lotan (2010) found that re-tweeting provided broader sharing of information and a method for attracting new followers to a given Twitter account. Several studies have tried to determine if Twitter can create more engagement in students when incorporated in the classroom. Welch and Bonnan-White (2012) found that students who reported enjoying using Twitter would perceive themselves as more engaged in class than those who did not enjoy Twitter. In a study conducted by Junco et al. (2011), students who used Twitter had a significantly greater increase in engagement than the control group, as well as higher semester grade point averages. Jacquemin, Smelser, and Bernot (2014) reported that students, as compared to faculty, who used social media more frequently in their personal lives, were more amenable to including social media in their academic lives.

Ricoy and Feliz (2016) found that the use of Twitter improved the learning of higher education students as they become more and more proficient with the technological tool. They also found that the restricted number of characters required by Twitter led students to synthesize complex ideas and improve their information selection skills. In a study conducted by Fernandez-Ferrer and Cano (2016) higher education students showed improved involvement, motivation, and satisfaction of the subject with the use of Twitter as a means of formative peer-assessment. However, they did not find improved learning, which indicates a need for more research on the integration of Twitter in the classroom.

With regard to K-12 education, Fox and Bird (2017) studied how teachers must deal with the personal and professional use of social media including Twitter. As schools and teacher unions develop appropriate use guidelines they conclude that teachers are aware of how they must use care in integrating social media tools to enhance student learning. They also found that more teachers believe Twitter offers a social media space more conducive to professional and personal uses than does Facebook. It is suggested that in order for basic education teachers to capitalize on the educational potential of social media tools like Twitter, they must be educated and reassured by administrators and professional organizations that their appropriate use of these technologies is encouraged.

TWITTER IN APPLIED INSTRUCTIONAL PRACTICE

This chapter will review two research studies that incorporated Twitter into the instructional environment. One focused on using Twitter to space practice in reviewing for an exam. The other was dedicated to exploring perceptions of student engagement through the use of Twitter.

Twitter as a Distributed Practice Concept Learning Tool

Buzzelli, Holdan, Rota, and McCarthy (2016) attempted to determine if the efficient 140-character per tweet communication style of Twitter could translate into an appropriate tool for reviewing class material. The character limit at the time of the study was 140 characters; this is now 280 characters, which still limits the length of tweets. They used examples and non-examples of major concepts in an attempt to aid students in effectively learning concepts through distributed practice.

Their research questions posed were as follows:

- **Research Question One:** Does utilizing Twitter as a distributed practice tool serve as a more effective review than a traditional end-of-unit study guide for concept learning?
- **Research Question Two:** Does Twitter create student engagement in the overall class discussion?

Overview of Methodology

Subjects were randomly placed into two groups, one treatment group that received tweets with characteristics, examples, and non-examples of primary concepts from their course material, and another that received the same information in a review worksheet. Immediately following the treatment, each group was tested for concept learning and scores from each group were compared. The concept test consisted of multiple choice questions developed by the host professor that covered the concepts reviewed in the study.

Once the experiment started, a tweet with characteristics, an example, and a non-example were created for each concept. Pre-scheduled tweets went out three times per day per concept. Tweets for two class concepts were tweeted on a typical day, and those tweets would typically be staggered by an hour in the morning, afternoon, and night. The same tweets for each concept were then tweeted out again later in the experiment to create a spacing effect. Each of the tweets was followed by a hashtag that was developed for the class.

Following the first exam in the study, the conditions of the study were reversed and the Twitter review group from the initial study became the new control group and the control group became the Twitter group for the following unit. The same methodology was used to provide the treatment group Tweets spaced out over a four-week unit for review, while the control group received a traditional worksheet review prior to the exam. Additionally, all students who were given a survey, which was used to determine their level of engagement in the class and their comfort level with Twitter, in addition to other demographic questions.

Throughout the two units, all instruction was provided in the same format from the same professor with the exception of Twitter use for the one randomly selected group of students. The dependent variable in this experiment was the post-test scores for students. The independent variable is the review method, which was distributed practice through Twitter for the treatment group and a traditional worksheet for the control group.

Students were surveyed at the completion of the experiment and provided feedback on their experiences using Twitter. Results were reported in aggregate and open-ended responses were coded and reported based on common findings.

Results

An independent-samples t-test was conducted to compare performance on the Twitter review and traditional worksheet review conditions. There was no significant difference in the scores for Twitter (M=12.30, SD=1.34) and traditional review (M=12.00, SD=1.41) conditions; $t(18) = .487, p = 0.632$. These results suggest that using Twitter for review in an introductory college history course may be as effective as a traditional end-of-unit review worksheet.

Summary of Test Results

While there is a lack of substantial quantitative data that shows the effect of applying Twitter as a review tool, the results are not surprising considering a study by Smith and Tirumala (2012) found that students who used Twitter did not have improved scores in questions that tested the memory of class content. Other researchers (Dunlap & Lowenthal, 2009; Paul & Ianitti, 2012; Trueman and Miles, 2011) have demonstrated that Twitter can be used as both an instructional tool and a way to provide supplementary communication with students.

Summary of Survey Findings

- Students self-reported that they both used Twitter (M = 2.88, SD = 1.89) and checked their Twitter feeds for class (M = 2.31, SD = 1.35) on average more than "1-5 times per week" based on their mean scores.
- The item with the highest score of the three student engagement questions asked students to compare Twitter's use as a collaborative tool with a Learning Management System (LMS).

- Overall students did not appear to be overly concerned by privacy issues as it relates to using social media. The highest reported concern students had related to prospective employees. Students appeared to be least concerned with their privacy as it related to their peers at their own institution.

Analysis of Open-Ended Responses

There were a total of seven open-ended questions within the survey. Creswell (2013) stated that data should be organized into themes in qualitative studies. In order to determine themes from the open-ended survey responses, the data was collected and coded in a manner that Saldana (2012) calls "generic coding," which includes a first cycle and second cycle phase of coding.

The open-ended questions that generated the most feedback referenced student recommendations for educators with respect to using social media. Table 1 displays a breakdown of responses to the question. While the question called for students to provide recommendations for social media use, the responses could be summarized in a few words. Respondents found social media to be easy to use and understand, helpful in terms of their memory, popular among students, and useful. One respondent recommended that the quality of information shared is most important for educators, and three others suggested using social media more often. Several respondents' answers could be classified in more than one category, with "usefulness" being the most commonly categorized response.

Table 1. Themes developed from student open-ended responses

Theme	Example Quotes from Students' Responses
Twitter is easy for students to use and is useful in classroom instruction.	"Use these; it is easier for our generation to understand." "It is a lot more useful to answer student questions."
Twitter is a popular social media platform for college students.	"Social media is very popular and students use it every day." "Finding the popular site students use (Twitter) is helpful because students can effortlessly be exposed to information."
Twitter helps students remember class material.	"Use it more. The Twitter helped me remember in class." "It helps students remember so I would recommend using it"

Summary of Study Findings by Research Question

Does utilizing Twitter as a distributed practice tool serve as a more effective review than a traditional end-of-unit study guide for concept learning?

Twenty students in an introductory college history course participated in this study. Ten students received daily review tweets over the course of a four-week unit and the remaining 10 students were provided with a traditional study guide prior to the exam that was a compilation of the information tweeted. There was no significant difference in the scores for Twitter and traditional review conditions. An additional test using the same groups but flipped conditions also showed that there was no significant difference in the scores for Twitter and traditional review conditions. These scores show that while many educators are leery of using social media in the classroom that Twitter may serve as an equally effective review tool as a traditional study guide for concept learning.

Does Twitter Create Student Engagement in the Overall Class Discussion?

One of the themes developed from student open-ended responses was that Twitter is a popular social media platform for college students. Despite that finding, students reported low scores in their frequency of communicating via Twitter for class, how frequently they checked their Twitter feed specifically for class, and their level of interaction with peers in the class.

These results may be explained by a number of factors described by the host faculty member interviewed following the study. He cited the nature of an introductory course with few history majors, the class time (immediately after lunch), and the privacy settings of the Twitter account as potential impediments to class engagement. Twitter was used in a very specific methodical way in this study that included a private account, and tweets that were only sent out as examples, non-examples, and characteristics of concepts from class.

Engaging Students Through Twitter

The following study by Evans (2017) took an in-depth look at the physical, social, emotional, behavioral, supportive and cognitive components of student engagement through Twitter.

Two research questions addressed in this study directly examined engagement in using Twitter in several undergraduate education classes.

- **Research Question One:** How does utilizing Twitter affect students' perception of their engagement in the classroom?
- **Research Question Two:** How does the use of Twitter affect students' perception of engagement outside the classroom?

Defining Student Engagement

Several definitions for the term engagement emerge from the literature. Hu and Kuh (2001) defined engagement as "the quality of effort students themselves devote to educationally purposeful activities that contribute directly to desired outcomes" (p. 3), while Krause and Coates (2008) offered "[engagement is] the extent to which students are engaging in activities that higher education research has shown to be linked with the high-quality learning outcomes" (p. 493). Welch and Bonnan-White (2012) offer that "student engagement is the time and effort students devote to activities that are empirically linked to desired outcomes of the college and what institutions do to induce students to participate in these activities" (p. 683). The breadth of engagement is further evidenced in work by Chickering and Gamson (1987), who offered a framework of seven key actions to encourage student engagement: student-faculty contact, cooperation among students, active learning, giving prompt feedback, emphasizing time on task, communicating high expectations, and respecting diverse talents and ways of learning.

Junco et al. (2011) used Chickering and Gamson's (1987) framework when they investigated Twitter as a method of actively engaging students. The engagement framework provided continuity for class discussions, "giving students a low-stress way to ask questions, have book discussions, post class reminders, display campus event reminders, and provide academic and personal support; this helped students connect with each other and instructors, organizing service learning projects, and organizing study groups" (Junco et al., 2011, p. 122).

Indicators of Student Engagement

There are varied indicators of student engagement, including time students spend on educationally purposeful activities, the quality of the work students put forth, the student's interest in the material, interactions between students that are educationally purposeful, and interactions between the student and instructor (Huh & Kuh, 2001; Krause & Coates, 2008; Kuh, 2009, Junco et al., 2011; Welch & Bonnan-White, 2012). However, these are not the only indicators of student engagement. They complement the framework of Chickering & Gamson (1987), which focused on student-faculty contact, cooperation among students, active learning, giving prompt feedback, emphasizing time on task, communicating high expectations, and respecting diverse talents and ways of learning. The NSSE (2013) groups elements of student engagement into participation in educationally purposeful activities, challenge of material, "perceptions of the college environment", educational and personal growth during the program, and "background and demographic information (para. 1). These elements are important; however, they do not give a holistic description of engagement.

Fredricks et al. (2011) further broke down the elements discussed thus far into psychometric categories of behavioral, emotional, and cognitive aspects of student engagement. For example, a student participating in class, having good attendance, and preparing for class are indicators of the behavioral aspect of engagement. Similarly, if a student expresses liking school, shows signs of enjoyment and interest, and has family support for his or her learning, these are indicators of the emotional aspect of engagement. Cognitive indicators include how the learner takes "ownership of his or her own learning," and how invested he or she is in his or her learning (Evans, 2017, p. 44). The indicators of student engagement discussed above are common elements found through the literature but are not meant to serve as a complete list of every possible indicator of student engagement. Table 2 organizes the common elements of student engagement in the literature.

Evans' (2017) study focused on select subsets of these dimensions that support the use of Twitter. Behavioral aspects of engagement focused on in his study included attention, participation, and effort. One emotional aspect was included: the student forming connections with peers and the instructor. Finally, cognitive aspects of students' learning and remembering the material were addressed by student and instructors self-reporting their perceptions of engagement.

Study Methodology and Results

Six college classes consisting of 45 undergraduate education majors from a suburban private university near Pittsburgh, Pennsylvania used Twitter as a mandatory portion of their coursework. Several studies suggest that a best practice for using Twitter in the classroom is to require the use of Twitter (Domizi, 2013; George & Dellasega, 2011; Junco et al., 2013; Prestridge, 2014; Wei et al., 2012; Wynn, 2013). This study was a descriptive study, meaning that the environment was intact (Office of Research Integrity, 2016). The instructors were asked to use Twitter in their class prior to each class beginning, but from the students' point of view, the environment was intact and did not change during the semester in relation to the use of Twitter. Instructors were given guidelines as to how to use Twitter, so that the actualization of Twitter usage would be the same across the classes. Use of Twitter did not replace assignments that prior session of each class had; rather, it added the element of challenging the students to concisely react to the week's material, interact with each other or the instructor, and provided a new avenue for critical thinking and analysis.

Table 2. Student engagement elements from the literature

Category	Element
Behavioral or Physical	• Adherence to classroom rules • Asking questions, raising hand in class • Attendance • Attention • Concentration • Effort (general effort put forth) • Participation in class • Participation in school activities • Persistence • Preparation for class • Risk behaviors such as skipping school
Cognitive	• Curiosity about the subject or material • Interest in the subject or material • Kinds of strategies used to learn, remember, and understand the material • Motivation to focus on and complete assignments; motivation to achieve • Self-regulation strategies used to achieve goals • Student takes ownership of his or her learning
Emotional	• Expressing feeling of belonging • Expressing interest and enjoyment in class • Feeling happy or anxious about class • Feeling safe • How does the student feel about class • Reporting fun and enjoyment about class • Student confidence, self-efficacy
Environmental and Supportive	• Academic challenge of the curriculum • Diversity of the classroom • Relevant and interesting choices of literacy activities • Relevant and interesting texts • Supportive campus climate • Supportive instructor, teacher involvement • Supportive family/home environment
Social	• Effort student puts forth in interaction with instructor • Effort student puts forth in interaction with peers • Level of interactions with peers outside the classroom (related to course materials) • Student discusses the current class in casual conversation with friends and family • Student involvement in educationally purposeful activities with other students

Source: (Evans, 2017)

After engaging in Twitter for one academic semester, students were surveyed using an instrument that included both Likert-scale items and open-ended questions regarding their feelings about Twitter, especially about how engaged they felt. Students in the study were given some initial instruction about Twitter and then Twitter was used as a class instructional technology for nearly 15 weeks for the six education classes that were involved. It was mandatory as a class requirement for students to use Twitter during this semester. Table 3 illustrates the percentages of positive and negative responses by engagement category and engagement element related to RQ1 (How does utilizing Twitter affect students' perception of their engagement in the classroom?) from survey participants.

Table 4 illustrates the percentages of positive and negative responses by engagement category and engagement element related to RQ2 (How does the use of Twitter affect students' perception of engagement outside the classroom?) from survey participants.

Table 3. Participant responses cross-referenced with engagement elements for RQ1

Engagement Category	Engagement Element	Positive Response	Negative Response
Emotional	Express Interest and Enjoyment	28.9%	71.1%
Emotional	Student Confidence, Self-Efficacy	42.3%	57.7%
Behavioral	Preparation for Class	60.0%	40.0%
Behavioral	Attention	13.3%	86.6%
Behavioral	Preparation for Class	26.6%	73.3%
Emotional	Student Confidence, Self-Efficacy	31.1%	68.8%
Social	Effort in Interaction with Peers	46.7%	53.4%
Social	Effort in Interaction with Instructor	31.1%	68.9%
Supportive	Supportive / Involved Instructor	82.7%	17.2%
Supportive	Supportive / Involved Instructor	62.6%	37.5%
Cognitive	Curiosity about Subject or Material	68.9%	31.1%

Note: Totals of positive and negative response in some categories equal 99.9% or 100.1% due to rounding.
Source: (Evans, 2017)

Table 4. Survey questions cross-referenced with engagement elements and responses for RQ2

Engagement Category	Engagement Element	Positive Response	Negative Response
Cognitive	Interest in Subject or Material	68.9%	31.1%
Cognitive	Interest in Subject or Material	77.8%	22.2%
Emotional	Happy about Class	33.3%	66.7%
Cognitive	Motivation to Complete Assignments / Achieve	20.0%	80.0%
Social	Student Discusses Current Class in Casual Conversation (Friends, Family)	48.8%	51.1%
Social	Level of Interaction with Peers Outside Classroom (Related to Course)	53.3%	46.7%
Cognitive	Strategies to Learn	66.6%	33.3%
Behavioral	Effort Put Forth for Class (General)	33.3%	66.7%
Emotional	How Student Feels about Class	20.0%	80.0%
Social	Effort in Interaction with Instructor	62.2%	15.5%

Note: Totals of positive and negative response in some categories equal 99.9% or 100.1% due to rounding.
Source: (Evans, 2017)

In addition to survey items, open-ended questions were developed and responses were coded and analyzed. Three themes arose from coding the open-ended questions on the student-participant surveys: Concerns, Neutral Experience, and Value of Using Twitter in Class. The themes in Table 5 are listed in order of prevalence, where thematic coding resulted in 100 instances of Value of Using Twitter for Class, 80 instances of Concerns, and 64 instances of Neutral Experience. Table 5 displays the initial coding categories and a sample quote from student-participant responses followed by a discussion on the initial coding categories.

Table 5. Student-participant qualitative survey initial and thematic coding categories

Theme	Initial Coding	Sample Quote
Value of Using Twitter for Class	Like Twitter as a Platform	"I liked the fact that it was a familiar format to me, so it was easy to construct my tweets"
	Out-of-Class Engagement	"I was able to learn a lot more outside the classroom in a quick and current way"
	Overcome Shyness or Hesitancy	"I liked exposing thoughts I wouldn't normally in class; so I shared my opinion in a way I felt more comfortable."
	Reflection	"I thought it was a useful and good way to reinforce what we were talking about in class."
	Sharing of Thoughts and Ideas	"I enjoyed using Twitter because it was a quick and easy way to share ideas and information"
	Student-Instructor Engagement	"It definitely allowed us to engage with our […] professor more."
	Student-Material Engagement	"The use of Twitter let me explore topics I liked more, so I was able to have enthusiasm over certain subject material."
	Student-Student Engagement	"I liked the interaction with my classmates."
	Supplemental Material	"I enjoyed the different resources that were made available; if I didn't have to tweet, I would not have discovered useful articles, videos, and activities I used within my student teaching."
Concerns	Alternate Platforms	"Prefer Reddit."
	Dislike Social Media	"I really dislike using and keeping up with social media."
	Dislike Twitter	"I don't know why I dislike Twitter so much, but I do; I dislike the limited characters because I feel like I need more room to discuss everything."
	Dislike Forced Usage	"I disliked the use [of Twitter] only because it was forced upon us rather than an option;"
	How Twitter was Actualized	"I found it [Twitter usage] more of a burden to have to tweet twice a week for multiple courses."
	Looked at Twitter Like an Assignment	"I saw tweeting more as an assignment, not something to make me actually engage; we have to tweet for a grade."
Neutral Experience	No Value Realized	"It didn't add or take away my interest in this class."
	Twitter for Personal vs. Academic	"I will use it more for a personal usage rather than academic."

Source: (Evans, 2017)

Summary of the Study Results

Student-participants did not like using Twitter, mostly because it was mandatory and used in more than one class in a student's schedule. Despite this negative reaction, student-participants did report gains in perceived engagement within certain elements of engagement. These were more prevalent in out-of-class engagement than in-class engagement, though both student-participants and instructor-participants shared positive experiences with the instructor-participants talking in class about tweets that the student-participants had made. Twitter helps bring supplemental materials into class, raising student-participants interest and curiosity. Instructor-participants raised concerns over the accuracy of the sources used, and noted that instructor workload increased. Twitter does have the potential to increase student engagement, but careful planning must be considered to avoid some of the caveats brought to light in this study.

Implications

Educators should do careful planning before implementing Twitter in their courses. Though not readily apparent in the literature, educators should be prepared for students not liking Twitter or other forms of social media at all, and the associated pushback that may therefore accompany mandatory usage. Solutions include allowing students to frame how Twitter will be used, and if needed, having an alternate assignment available. Allowing the students to help frame how Twitter is used may help to alleviate negative reactions to Twitter usage due to how it was actualized. The literature is clear on mandatory usage to achieve a successful Twitter implementation in class (Domizi, 2013; George & Dellasega, 2011; Junco et al., 2013; Prestridge, 2014; Wei et al., 2012; Wynn, 2013). Care must be given to the planning of Twitter across multiple classes, and even within just one class in relation to workload. This calls for communication between an educator and other instructors, and with academic management. Based on a review of the literature an instructor's workload is likely to increase when implementing Twitter, and this was realized in the studies presented in this text. Collaboration with peers may yield ways to combat this, such as a suggestion from the instructor-participant of this study that a rotating group of students per class be the only ones that have to tweet in a given week.

What students are expected to tweet is another item to plan carefully. Defining this expectation up front can be helpful, as evidenced in studies that gave clear expectations (Bissell, 2014; Buzzelli, 2014; George and Dellasega, 2011; Hirsh, 2012). Based on instructor-participant feedback in the present study, the researcher recommends that educators implementing Twitter in their courses clearly define their expectations such as tweeting about concepts that are relevant to the present week's material and focus rather than just generally applicable to the course. If the educator wishes to have only peer reviewed or otherwise academically acceptable sources used for supplemental materials, this too should be communicated as an expectation.

Finally, if an educator chooses the implementation of Twitter, it should be aligned with learning outcomes. This may lead to a much more positive reception by students, especially if the students understand the potential benefits of using Twitter, and are given the chance to help frame how to use Twitter to achieve the defined learning outcomes. In the present study, participants reported perceived increases in various elements of student engagement. Aligning Twitter usage closer to learning outcomes and involving students in framing may lead to further increases in perceived student engagement.

ISSUES, CONTROVERSIES, PROBLEMS

Much like in a traditional classroom setting, alpha personalities develop and inequities exist in Twitter communication. The top 10% of Twitter users make up 90% of the content produced on the site, with the median Twitter user only tweeting once (Heil & Piskorsky, 2009). A study from Heil and Piskorsky (2009) also found that the average man is twice as likely to follow another man and likewise a woman is 25% more likely to follow a man on Twitter, despite a similar number of users by gender. Heil and Piskorsky (2010) also found that women produced the majority of content on Twitter.

As stated previously in an example about reporting the news, communication on Twitter has a tendency to alternate between personal and professional, which often leads to distortion. Kieslinger, Ebner, and Wiesenhofer (2011) found that scientists in their study utilized personal communication of a private nature approximately 1/3 of the time while using Twitter as an e-learning supplement. Depending on the level of experience and maturity of potential participants, this number could increase drastically.

Among the issues that Dhir, Buragga, & Boreqqah (2013) found with Twitter as a classroom tool were that it could be addictive and distracting, while causing students to waste time that they could potentially be on task. One could argue that students may already be spending significant time on Twitter without any prompting by teachers to incorporate it into class. Another side effect of students utilizing the tool frequently is that they will inevitably become familiar with its functions and become more efficient at using it for whatever purpose they choose.

In a case study conducted by Lin, Hoffman, and Borengasser (2013), students initially utilized Twitter frequently as a supplemental communication tool, but tapered off as the semester continued. The missing component in this type of situation is the role of the instructor. It is essential that the instructor not only establishes a purpose for using Twitter, but also models the behavior that he or she would like to see the class exhibit. Scaffolding is not only done at the beginning of Twitter implementation, but it should be done intermittently when it is identified as necessary.

In a worst-case scenario, student privacy may be invaded or they may become prey for sexual predators while using social media. In a one year study conducted by the Crimes Against Children Research Center at the University of New Hampshire, an estimated 2,322 arrests were made for sex crimes against minors that were initiated using social networks (Wolak, Finkelhor, & Mitchell, 2010). That figure does not include the number of crimes that went unreported or undetected. Due to the lack of security inherent in any social network, it is important for a teacher to become familiar with privacy settings and to train their students accordingly.

Social Media and Education Law

There are well-documented cases that have reached the media of teachers jeopardizing their jobs due to improper social media use. In one case, a 24-year old Georgia public school teacher named Ashley Payne posted a photo holding a glass of wine in one hand and a beer in the other. This photo would eventually be the target of scrutiny by the administration at her school district, and prompt her principal to leave her with an ultimatum to resign or face immediate suspension (Eckes, 2013).

The principal encouraged her to resign in their discussion, stating that if she were to be suspended, she would likely lose her teaching license in the state of Georgia (Downey, 2011). Payne sought legal action against her school district after they eventually refused to reinstate her. Her attorney filed a writ of mandamus alleging that the Georgia Fair Dismissal Act entitled Payne to a hearing and appropriate compensation. The state court judge held that by resigning she was not protected under the act, and the case is now under appeal (Oppenheim, 2013 Payne v. Barrow County School District, 2009).

In Payne's case, she shared personal photos on her Facebook profile and an anonymous emailer tipped off the school towards her actions. Because the nature of her offense may be seen as harmless to many, it gained national media attention in 2009. Other similar cases have arisen and in some cases, the teachers involved haven't provided consent for the material posted. Despite the lack of consent in terms of material being posted on a social network, any controversial or inappropriate material posted on a teacher's behalf may put their job in jeopardy.

Acceptance of Technology by Varying Demographics

One's willingness to accept technology is influenced by several factors such as age, education, income, and race (Porter and Donthu,2006). Also, if someone has been exposed to a technology, they will be more likely to accept that technology. Porter and Donthu also found that a consumer's perceptions about ease of use and usefulness had a strong effect on acceptance. A study by Chung, Park, Wang, Fulk, and McLaughlin (2010) found that "baby boomers" perceived mobile data services as more useful, yet more difficult to use, than members of "generation X". Gender may also play a role in influencing a consumer's acceptance of technology as males seem to be more interested in the usefulness and practicality of technology, whereas females tend to be attracted by the of ease of use of technology (Venkatesh & Morris, 2000).

Income level is an important factor as far as access to technology is concerned. A Pew report (Zickuhr & Smith, 2012) found that only 62% of people in households making less than $30,000 a year used the Internet; for those making $50,000-74,999 approximately 90% of people used it. The report also points to smart phones as a possible bridge for the divide, as smart phones are able to provide Internet access to populations previously at a digital disadvantage. Furthermore, the Pew Report found that young adults, minorities, those with no college experience, and those with lower household income levels are more likely to access the internet primarily through their smart phones. As smart phones continue to make Internet access more realistic for low-income students, social media is another resource that could help bridge the digital divide.

SOLUTIONS AND RECOMMENDATIONS

Make Twitter Accessible

One of the major considerations for any instructor prior to implementing Twitter is determining how to ensure that students would be able to access and use Twitter effectively. The authors of this chapter suggest developing a "How-To" guide for new Twitter users and consulting with experienced faculty members for advice. The literature available suggests that students who grew up in the digital era find it easy to use Twitter and follow along for the course of the study. Adult and non-traditional students may need additional support or guidance. This guidebook in the Buzzelli, et. al. (2016) study turned out to be unnecessary when it was found that all students either had an account or knew how to navigate Twitter easily. The host faculty member also said that he received no technology or Twitter related questions or complaints from the students throughout the entire study.

In addition to the ease of use for the students, the collaboration between the faculty member and researcher in creating and distributing the tweets was made easy through readily available technology. The collaborative nature of easily accessible software such as Google Drive lends itself to sharing of social media resources between instructors. Tweets may be developed in a Google Doc and stored in Google Drive by one faculty and shared with another faculty member so that at any point prior to the tweet being published comments or corrections can easily be made. Hoot Suite, a social media management utility, is also a free an effective tool for scheduling tweets in advance. This will prevent the instructor from having to constantly update the Twitter feed with new material, while compiling a list of past tweets and future tweets that was easy to navigate.

The idea of easily compiling tweets in an archived list also brings up another point that should be investigated in future research. Twitter allows you to go back and search the lists of tweets by user, hashtag, or keyword. In the Buzzelli, et.al. (2016) study every concept had three spaced original tweets with a hashtag for the term as well as a class specific hashtag. Even a novice Twitter user could engage in both spaced and massed practice by simply reviewing the list of tweets that were created by the instructor account prior to the exam. This would give the Twitter users an inherent advantage over a traditional end of unit review.

Class Engagement

Twitter on its own does not enhance student engagement for the class based on a review of the literature. There may additional reasons for a lack of engagement including the time of the class, the ability level of the class, and the rationale for taking a class (i.e. graduation requirement for all traditional undergraduate students).

Another reason that there may not be as much engagement in the class as anticipated by an instructor is the privacy settings on the teacher account. If an account is made private to protect information, the viral nature of sharing or "re-tweeting" information may be rendered useless. While Twitter has been referred to as a "cocktail party" of conversations, the dialogue in studies such as Buzzelli, et.al. (2016) was completely one-sided and did not allow for student interaction.

Instructors need to engage in the conversation with their students. Limited research is available on the impact of informal Twitter interaction between students and instructors, but this type of communication should be considered. The more conversation between class constituents that occurs through Twitter, the more likely all users are to access it and engage.

Despite there being limited interaction during the studies presented in this chapter, these results only should be viewed in the context of how Twitter was utilized in each study. Twitter has been shown in other studies to create richer dialogue outside of the classroom (Grosseck & Holotescu, 2008), more interactive with faculty (Junco, et. al., 2011), and provided an opportunity for more introverted students to participate in class discussion (Paul & Ianitti, 2012). While the studies presented reported that Twitter did not increase student engagement, students still reported that Twitter was popular among their classmates and helped them remember facts from class.

Privacy and Public Speech

While many privacy issues exist in regards to social media usage, the students in the Buzzelli, et. al. study overwhelmingly did not to appear to be concerned. This goes against the literature that shows colleges have begun to monitor incoming and current students' social media activity more closely. A 2012 Kaplan (Schaffer & Wong) study found that college admissions officers' discovery of online material damaging to applicants nearly tripled from 2011-2012. Likewise, Barnes (2006) found that "a social exchange between friends has now become a way for universities to monitor student behavior."

There have also been a number of court cases that demonstrate the impact of negative student behavior on social media. In the 2007 Layshock v Hermitage School District case, a student made "vulgar, defamatory, and plainly offensive school-related speech (Cain & Fink, 2010)" about his principal, which prompted the school to suspend him and move him to an alternative school for 10 days. While the court later ruled the school had violated Layshock's right to freedom of speech, exercising caution on social media accounts should be an important lesson taught in schools.

Technology has continued to improve making information collection via social media more accessible. With the emerging mobile and wearable technology that uses artificial intelligence and machine learning becoming commonplace, social media continues to integrate into every aspect of life. This makes it essential for students to learn about the importance of a person's social media footprint and its potential career and reputation implications.

The authors of this chapter suggest incorporating a lesson devoted to educating students on their digital footprint. Students must learn about the scope 1st amendment right to freedom of speech and the limits of its protections in terms of employment. Organizations such as private universities and companies monitor social media usage of prospective employees and students. Learning the importance of privacy settings and maintaining professionalism on social media is key to overall student development in the digital age.

FUTURE RESEARCH DIRECTIONS

Twitter as a Spaced and Massed Practice Tool

Twitter has the potential to be used for both spaced and massed practice because of its ability to archive information. This is not something that can be done with a traditional paper review at the end of the chapter. If a faculty member could provide some additional up-front instruction on when to specifically look for tweets during a class unit, and demonstrate the archiving capabilities of Twitter to the students, they would be better prepared to study material on an ongoing basis as well as to conduct a massed practice session prior to their exam.

While hypothetically an instructor could cut out paper copies of concept definitions and distribute them regularly to the class to over the course of a unit, Twitter would appear to be a more efficient way of spacing review. The study presented in this chapter did not examine Twitter's additional ability to mass practice through archived lists of tweets. A future study that might compare Twitter as a massed and spaced practice tool versus a massed practice tool such as a study guide may provide some additional insights.

Twitter as a Tool for Learning Assessment

As stated previously, literature on spacing practice included ongoing assessment of learning through practice. The studies presented in this chapter did not provide ongoing assessment due to the desire of the researcher and faculty member to maintain equity of the information provided to each group and because of the limited time constraints of the study. In an interview with the host faculty member following the study conducted by Buzzelli, et.al. (2016), the instructor suggested using Twitter to quiz the students throughout the unit.

By using Twitter as an assessment tool, it may provide an opportunity to better utilize spaced practice as opposed to simply looking at spaced review. A study that analyzed interspersed Twitter quizzes throughout the unit or semester versus frequent paper quizzes might provide valuable insight into other uses for Twitter as an instructional tool. A researcher may want to consider whether those Twitter quizzes should be formal (graded) or informal to determine if they could boost class engagement and interaction.

CONCLUSION

It is clear that Twitter has evolved from a simple social media platform into a sophisticated tool for sharing information, for dispensing political dogma, for a news feed, and as a teaching/learning tool. The two research studies in this chapter provide evidence of the usefulness of Twitter in education. For the most part, Twitter is an engaging platform for learning for many students. We've just scratched the surface of the potential educational uses of Twitter.

REFERENCES

Bahrick, H. P. (1979). Maintenance of knowledge: Questions about memory we forgot to ask. *Journal of Experimental Psychology. General, 108*(3), 296–308. doi:10.1037/0096-3445.108.3.296

Barnes, S. (2006). *A privacy paradox: Social networking in the united states.* Retrieved from http://firstmonday.org/ojs/index.php/fm/article/view/1394/1312

Bissell, J. (2014). *Evaluation of student achievement on course concepts by augmenting content through twitter* (Order No. 3648352). Available from Dissertations & Theses @ Robert Morris University; ProQuest Dissertations & Theses Global. (1647758356). Retrieved from http://search.proquest.com/docview/1647758356?accountid=28365

Boyd, D., Golder, S., & Lotan, G. (2010, January). Tweet, tweet, retweet: Conversational aspects of retweeting on Twitter. In *System Sciences (HICSS), 2010 43rd Hawaii International Conference on* (pp. 1-10). IEEE.

Bruner, J., Goodnow, J. J., & Austin, G. A. (1967). *A study of thinking.* New York: Science Editions.

Buzzelli, A. A. (2014). *Twitter in the classroom: Determining the effectiveness of utilizing a microblog for distributed practice in concept learning* (Doctoral dissertation). Robert Morris University. Retrieved from http://search.proquest.com/docview/1647758207?accountid=28365

Cain, J., & Fink, J. III. (2010). Legal and ethical issues regarding social media and pharmacy education. *American Journal of Pharmaceutical Education, 74*(10), 184. doi:10.5688/aj7410184 PMID:21436925

Cepeda, N. J., Pashler, H., Vul, E., Wixted, J. T., & Rohrer, D. (2006). Distributed practice in verbal recall tasks: A review and quantitative synthesis. *Psychological Bulletin, 132*(3), 354–380. doi:10.1037/0033-2909.132.3.354 PMID:16719566

Chickering, A., & Gamson, Z. (1987). Seven principals for good practice in undergraduate education. *AAHE Bulletin, 40,* 3–7.

Chung, J. E., Park, N., Wang, H., Fulk, J., & McLaughlin, M. (2010). Age differences in perceptions of online community participation among non-users: An extension of the Technology Acceptance Model. *Computers in Human Behavior, 26*(6), 1674–1684. doi:10.1016/j.chb.2010.06.016

Cresswell, J. W. (2013). *Research design: Qualitative, quantitative, and mixed methods approaches.* Sage Publications, Incorporated. *Educational Psychology Review, 1*(4), 309-330.

Dhir, A., Buragga, K., & Boreqqah, A. A. (2013). Tweeters on campus: Twitter a learning tool in classroom. *Journal of Universal Computer Science, 19*(5), 672–691.

DiMarzo, G. (2012). Why can't we be friends? The banning of teacher-student communication via social media and the freedom of speech. *American University Law Review, 62*(123), 123-166. Retrieved from http://digitalcommons.wcl.american.edu/cgi/viewcontent.cgi?article=1680&context=aulr&sei-redir=1&referer=http://www.google.com/url?q=http%3A%2F%2Fdigitalcommons.wcl.american.edu%2Fcgi%2Fviewcontent.cgi%3Farticle%3D1680%26context%3Daulr&sa=D&sntz=1&usg=AFQjCNGWeVNe6CBOtbRu-E65-OPnfgC4BQ

Domizi, D. (2013). Microblogging to foster connections and community in a weekly graduate seminar course. *TechTrends, 57*(1), 43–51. doi:10.100711528-012-0630-0

Downey, M. (2011, October 11). Court rules against ashley payne in facebook case. but more to come. *Atlanta Journal Constitution.* Retrieved from http://blogs.ajc.com/get-schooled-blog/2011/10/10/court-rules-against-ashley-payne-in-facebook-case/

Dunlap, J. C., & Lowenthal, P. R. (2009). Tweeting the night away: Using Twitter to enhance social presence. *Journal of Information Systems Education, 20*(2), 129–135.

Ebbinghaus, H. (1885). Memory. New York: Teacher's College, Columbia University.

Eckes, S. (2013, September). Strippers, beer, and bachelorette parties: regulating teachers' out-of-school conduct. *Principal Leadership.* Retrieved from https://www.nassp.org/Content/158/PL_sept13_casesinpt.pdfhttps://www.nassp.org/Content/158/PL_sept13_casesinpt.pdf

Estes, W. K. (1955). Statistical theory of spontaneous recovery and regression. *Psychological Review, 62*(3), 145–154. doi:10.1037/h0048509 PMID:14371893

Evans, T. (2017). *Twitter in the Higher Education Classroom: Exploring Perceptions of Engagement* (Doctoral dissertation). Robert Morris University. Retrieved from http://search.proquest.com/docview/1647???????accountid=28365

Fernandez-Ferrer, M., & Cano, E. (2016). The influence of the internet for pedagogical innovation: Using twitter to promote online collaborative learning. *International Journal of Educational Technology in Higher Education, 13*(22), 1–15.

Fox, A., & Bird, T. (2017). The challenge to professionals of using social media: Teachers in England negotiating personal-professional identities. *Education and Information Technologies, 22*(2), 647–675. doi:10.100710639-015-9442-0

Fredricks, J. A., McColskey, W., Meli, J., Mordica, J., Montrosse, B., & Mooney, K. (2011). Measuring student engagement in upper elementary through high school: a description of 21 instruments. *Issues and Answers Report, 98*, 26-114. Retrieved from http://ies.ed.gov/ncee/edlabs

Fullmer, E. (2010). Privacy expectations and protections for teachers in the internet age. *Duke Law & Technology Review,* (14). Retrieved from http://scholarship.law.duke.edu/cgi/viewcontent.cgi?article=1209&context=dltr&sei-

George, D. R., & Dellasega, C. (2011). Use of social media in graduate-level medical humanities education: Two pilot studies from Penn State College of Medicine. *Medical Teacher, 33*(8), e429–e434. doi: 10.3109/0142159X.2011.586749 PMID:21774639

Glenberg, A. M. (1979). Component-levels theory of the effects of spacing of repetitions on recall and recognition. *Memory & Cognition, 7*(2), 95–112. doi:10.3758/BF03197590 PMID:459836

Grosseck, G., & Holotescu, C. (2008). Can we use Twitter for educational activities? In 4th international scientific conference, eLearning and software for education, Bucharest, Romania.

Heil, B., & Pikorski, M. (2009). New Twitter research: Men follow men and nobody tweets. *Harvard Business Review.*

Hirsh, O. (2012). *The relationship of Twitter use to students' engagement and academic performance in online classes at an urban community college* (Order No. 3545578). Available from ProQuest Dissertations & Theses Global. (1241616410)

Hu, S. & Kuh, G. (2001). *Being (dis)engaged in educationally purposeful activities: The influences of student and institutional characteristics.* Paper presented at the American Educational Research Association Annual Conference, Seattle, WA.

Jacquemin, S., Smelser, L. & Bernot, M. (2014). Twitter in the higher education classroom: A student and faculty assessment of use and perception. *Journal of College Science Teaching, 43*(6), 22-27.

Junco, R., Elavsky, C., & Heiberger, G. (2013). Putting Twitter to the test: Assessing outcomesfor student collaboration, engagement and success. *British Journal of Educational Technology*44(2), 273-287. doi:10.1111/j.1467-8535.2012.01284.x

Junco, R., Heiberger, G., & Loken, E. (2011). The effect of Twitter on college student engagement and grades. *Journal of Computer Assisted Learning, 27*(2), 119–132.

Kieslinger, B., Ebner, M., & Wiesenhofer, H. (2011). Microblogging practices of scientists in e-learning: A qualitative approach. *International Journal of Emerging Technologies in Learning, 6*(4), 31–39.

Kuh, G. (2009). What student affairs professionals need to know about student engagement. *Journal of College Student Development, 50*(6), 683–706. doi:10.1353/csd.0.0099

Lin, M., Hoffman, E., & Borengasser, C. (2013). Is social media too social for class? A case study of Twitter use. *TechTrends, 57*(2), 39–45. doi:10.100711528-013-0644-2

Lipka, S. (2008, December 04). Judge sides with university against student-teacher with 'drunken pirate' photo. *Chronicle of Higher Education.* Retrieved from http://chronicle.com/article/Judge- Sides-With-University/42066/

Morrisett, L. Jr, & Hovland, C. (1959). A comparison of three varieties of training in human problem solving. *Journal of Experimental Psychology, 58*(1), 52–55. doi:10.1037/h0044703 PMID:13664884

National Survey of Student Engagement (NSSE). (2013). *A Fresh Look at Student Engagement: Annual Results 2013*. Retrieved from: http://nsse.iub.edu/ NSSE_2013_Results/pdf/NSSE_2013_Annual_Results.pdf

Nunnally, J. C. (1978). *Psychometric theory* (2nd ed.). New York: McGraw-Hill.

Office of Research Integrity. (2016). Descriptive Studies. *U.S. Department of Health and Human Services*. Retrieved from: http://ori.hhs.gov/education/products/sdsu/res_des1.htm

Oppenheim, R. (2013, May 9). *High school teacher files an appeal in case of social media related resignation*. Retrieved from http://www.californiabusinesslitigation.com/2013/05/high_school_teacher_files_an_a.html

Paul, J. E., & Iannitti, N. (2012). On beyond clickers: Twitter as a classroom response system. *The Journal of Health Administration Education, 29*(4), 319–328.

Pavlik, P. Jr, & Anderson, J. (2005). Practice and forgetting effects on vocabulary memory: An activation-based model of the spacing effect. *Cognitive Science, 29*(4), 559–586. doi:10.120715516709cog0000_14 PMID:21702785

Porter, C., & Donthu, N. (2006). Using the technology acceptance model to explain how attitudes determine Internet usage: The role of perceived access barriers and demographics. *Journal of Business Research, 59*(9), 999–1007. doi:10.1016/j.jbusres.2006.06.003

Prestridge, S. (2014). A focus on students' use of Twitter: Their interactions with each other, content and interface. *Active Learning in Higher Education, 15*(2), 101–115. doi:10.1177/1469787414527394

Raaijmakers, J. (2003). Spacing and repetition effects in human memory: Application of the SAM model. *Cognitive Science, 27*(3), 431–452. doi:10.120715516709cog2703_5

Ricoy, M. C., & Feliz, T. (2016). Twitter as a learning community in higher education. *Journal of Educational Technology & Society, 19*(1), 237–248.

Saldaña, J. (2012). *The coding manual for qualitative researchers* (No. 14). Academic Press.

Schaffer, R., & Wong, C. (2012, October 04). *Kaplan test prep survey finds that college admissions officers' discovery of online material damaging to applicants nearly triples in a year*. Retrieved from http://press.kaptest.com/press-releases/kaplan-test-prep-survey-finds-that-college-admissions-officers-discovery-of-online-material-damaging-to-applicants-nearly-triples-in-a-year

Schwartz, B. L. (1994). Sources of information in metamemory: Judgments of learning and feelings of knowing. *Psychonomic Bulletin & Review, 1*(3), 357–375. doi:10.3758/BF03213977 PMID:24203520

Seels, B., & Glasgow, Z. (1990). *Exercises in instructional design*. Columbus, OH: Merrill Publishing Company.

Smith, J. E., & Tirumala, L. N. (2012). Twitter's Effects on Student Learning and Social Presence Perceptions. *Teaching Journalism and Mass Communication, 2*(1), 21–31.

Smoke, K. L. (1933). Negative instances in concept learning. *Journal of Experimental Psychology*, *16*(4), 583–588. doi:10.1037/h0073724

Tennyson, R. D. (1973). Effects of negative instances in concept acquisition using a verbal learning task. *Journal of Educational Psychology*, *64*(2), 247–260. doi:10.1037/h0034400

Tennyson, R. D., Woolley, F. R., & Merrill, M. D. (1972). Exemplar and nonexampler variables which produce correct concept classification behavior and specified classification errors. *Journal of Educational Psychology*, *63*(2), 144–152. doi:10.1037/h0032368

Trueman, M. S., & Miles, D. G. (2011). Twitter in the classroom: Twenty-first century flash cards. *Nurse Educator*, *36*(5), 183–186. doi:10.1097/NNE.0b013e3182297a07 PMID:21857333

Tulving, E., & Pearlstone, Z. (1966). Availability versus accessibility of information in memory for words. *Journal of Verbal Learning and Verbal Behavior*, *5*(4), 381–391. doi:10.1016/S0022-5371(66)80048-8

Underwood, B. J. (1961). Ten years of massed practice on distributed practice. *Psychological Review*, *68*(4), 229–247. doi:10.1037/h0047516

Venkatesh, V., & Morris, M. G. (2000). Why don't men ever stop to ask for directions? Gender, social influence, and their role in technology acceptance and usage behavior. *Management Information Systems Quarterly*, *24*(1), 115–139. doi:10.2307/3250981

Wei, C., Chen, N., & Kinshuk. (2012). A model for social presence in online classrooms. *Educational Technology Research and Development*, *60*(3), 529–545. doi:10.100711423-012-9234-9

Welch, B. K., & Bonnan-White, J. (2012). Twittering to increase student engagement in the university classroom. *Knowledge Management & E-Learning: An International Journal*, *4*, 325–345.

Wolak, J., Finkelhor, D., Mitchell, K. J., & Ybarra, M. L. (2010). Online "predators" and their victims. *Psychology of Violence*, *1*(S), 13–35. doi:10.1037/2152-0828.1.S.13

Wynn, M. (2013). Student perceptions of technology in the classroom: A faculty and student collaboration. *Researcher: An Interdisciplinary Journal*, *26*(3), 21–33.

Zickuhr, K., & Smith, A. (2012). *Digital differences*. Pew Internet & American Life Project. Pew Internet Research Project.

KEY TERMS AND DEFINITIONS

Concept Learning: The search for and listing of attributes that can be used to distinguish exemplars from non-exemplars of various categories.

Distributed Practice (DP): The search for and listing of attributes that can be used to distinguish exemplars from non-exemplars of various categories. Used interchangeably with spaced practice.

Hashtag (#): The # symbol is used to mark keywords or topics in a Tweet. It was created organically by Twitter users.

Inter-Study Interval (ISI): The interval separating different study episodes of the same materials.

Massed Practice (MP): This effect occurs when the material to be learned is presented repeatedly in a short period of time.

Re-Tweet: A Tweet by another user, forwarded to you by someone you follow. Often used to spread news or share valuable findings on Twitter. Or the act of forwarding another user's Tweet to all of your followers.

Twitter: An information network made up of 140-character messages from all over the world.

This research was previously published in Advanced Online Education and Training Technologies; pages 163-184, copyright year 2019 by Information Science Reference (an imprint of IGI Global).

Chapter 7
Facebook in the International Classroom

Inna Piven
Unitec Institute of Technology, New Zealand

ABSTRACT

The case explores international students' learning experiences with Facebook-based activities within the eight-week study term known as the intensive mode of course delivery. By implementing participant observation and two asynchronous Facebook focus groups, the study investigates the potential values of Facebook for learning from international students' perspective. In addition, the case looks at the challenges faced by students and discusses key factors that may impact international students' experiences with courses that incorporate Facebook as a learning tool. The research is framed in the context of New Zealand tertiary education and intended as a contribution to the emerging body of educational research on social media.

INTRODUCTION

The world that is fast emerging from the clash of new values and technologies, new life-styles and modes of communication, demands wholly new ideas and concepts. (Toffler, 1980, p. 2)

During the last decade there has been a noticeable interest among educators towards social media and the changes they have brought about to teaching and learning. For many universities and institutions, emerging online learning environment is a novel situation. Matters are complicated further by the fact that tertiary student profiles, demands of the employment market as well as the learners' expectations, personal goals, learning habits and behavior have also changed. In addition, taking into consideration a constantly growing number of international students coming to New Zealand, tertiary education authorities have pointed out a necessity to develop new models of course delivery with a strong focus on communication and social connections.

DOI: 10.4018/978-1-6684-7123-4.ch007

Given the above issues, the concern here is to explore not just new social contexts for learning that tertiary educators suddenly have been provided with, but first and foremost learners' experiences with these contexts. Although teachers and learning designers have been using social media in course design and delivery for a while, academic researchers have only recently begun to acknowledge the importance of looking at social media in the tertiary education context.

In this regard, research questions, typically, have ranged from affordances of social media in contract with learning management systems, to social media for students' self-regulated leaning, and teachers' views on benefits and challenges associated with social media. Absent in current research are insights into international learners' experiences with social media. As has already been mentioned, due to the internationalization of tertiary education, there is a need for new, well-functioning models that could respond to "the demands of more diverse learners", and a "changing society" (New Zealand Productivity Commission, 2017). The motivation behind this study is informed by several gaps identified through the literature review as set out below.

Firstly, the literature review reveals that there is a lack of empirical data and evidence related to international students' learning experiences with social media as a learning tool, specifically in the context of intensive courses that are defined as "compressed, concentrated, or short-term learning" (Serdyukov, 2008, p. 37). Secondly, despite the growing use of social media in delivering courses, the research into what kind of factors may impact students' learning experiences remains limited. Finally, the existing research still focuses on a homogeneous rather than diverse student population, suggesting that insights are required into international students' learning experiences with social media.

This study aims at exploring international students' learning experiences with Facebook-based activities incorporated in two undergraduate intensive business courses: Event Planning and Management and Entrepreneurship at Otago Polytechnic Auckland International Campus, New Zealand (OPAIC). Therefore, the research question is: What are the educational values of Facebook for international students enrolled in the intensive courses?

The study has been guided by the following supporting questions:

1. What are international students' views on the intensive courses that incorporate Facebook closed groups as a learning tool?
2. What are international students' views on Facebook as a learning tool in comparison with learning management systems such as Moodle?
3. What are the factors that may impact international students' learning experiences with courses incorporating Facebook?

The chapter starts with a theoretical background by looking at some key questions and concepts associated with social media, international students' experiences, and the intensive mode of course delivery. It also details the gaps in the existing research and explains the research methodology and design. Drawing on research data, the next section discusses international students' learning experiences with Facebook. The chapter concludes with solutions and recommendations followed by an outline of prospects for future research.

BACKGROUND

For nearly a decade, there has been a growing interest towards social media in educational research that covers a wide range of topics from practical issues of knowledge sharing to risks linked to online learning environments. To develop a more strategic view on social media use in education, it is important to work through some key definitions and useful concepts related to social media.

Kaplan and Haenlein (2010) argue that "there is no systematic way in which different social media applications can be categorized" (Kaplan & Haenlein, 2010, p. 61). However, some forms of social media have been identified based on its core activities and the degree of the user's social presence. Hence, scholars recognize that social media include different types of online applications, for example social networks or social media (Facebook and Twitter), blogs, virtual game communities (the Second Life), and content communities, such as Wikipedia and YouTube.

Research by Hoffman and Novak (2011) states that social media allows users to be orientated toward "higher-order goals: connect, create, consume and control" (p. 4). Beer and Burrows (2010) add to that understanding, highlighting the participatory culture of social media. In a similar vein, Fischer and Reuber (2010, p. 5), using the example of Twitter, state "social media appears to be giving rise to new types of social interactions". This is also a central argument in Shao's study, which suggests that social media is useful for different social activities, including "participation in social interaction and community development" (as cited in Heinonen, 2011, p. 358). Heinrichs, Lim and Lim (2011) believe that social media is "an interaction tool used by individuals to discover and share content, opinions, and information" (p. 347). Overall, scholars tend to view social media as: a) a computer-generated environment; b) real time online communications; c) media for collaboration, group activities and sharing; and d) user-generated content.

Even though the advent of social media has prompted a significant amount of new research in the educational context, the studies on social media use in the international classroom are limited. Meanwhile conventional modes of course design, content areas, and learning and teaching models are continuously being challenged due to an increased number of international students (Ho & Piven, 2015). According to the New Zealand Productivity Commission Report (2017), "in contrast to domestic students, the number of international students enrolled with New Zealand tertiary providers has steadily increased" (p.36). Available data on enrolments in New Zealand tertiary education shows that "international students made up to 15 percent of all tertiary education students in 2015, up from 13 percent in 2014" (International students enrolled in tertiary education, 2017). Moreover, a new high has been predicted for 2018 due to students coming from China and Latin America (Gerritsen, 2017).

In scholarly discussions about international students' experiences, some of the following topics typically rise to the surface:

- There are many challenges faced by international students that are linked to unfamiliar pedagogy and teaching practices. As Sherry, Thomas and Hong Chui (2010) point out "problems may occur in adjusting to a new culture [in terms of] experiencing academic difference" (p. 34). Taking into consideration the diversity of international students, it is important to explore if social media can help students from different cultural backgrounds to adapt to a new learning environment.
- It has been suggested that social media can serve as a social support mechanism for international students' cultural adaptation (Ryan, Magro & Sharp, 2011). However, the conclusions presented in research around this topic are mainly literature based and lack empirical evidence.

- The term "international student experience has now become a catch-all phrase", and "has almost lost its meaning and direction" (Welikala, 2015). While universities put a lot of effort into understanding the key factors that may affect international students' learning, the discussion is still limited to cultural differences or differences in learning styles.
- There is no common understanding of the alternative ways of learning or of how to make effective use of new technologies including social media "to address the unique needs of international students" and not to "leave these students feeling disappointed, unfulfilled, and even exploited" (Sherry, Thomas & Chui, 2010, p. 34).

In general, researchers and educators recognize that international students have to "deal with academic challenges, social isolation, and cultural adjustment" (Wu, Garza & Guzman, 2014, p. 1). Over the years, it has become clear that "the tertiary education system is not well-placed to respond to uncertain future trends and demands of more diverse learners" (New Zealand Productivity Commission Report, 2017) and new strategies responsive to a changing student profile are much needed.

The changing student profile can be seen in relation not only to internalization of tertiary education, but also to ongoing technological developments. A report "The social revolution" by Hootsuite, a well-known platform for managing social media, describes today's students as "truly digital natives" (2017). Baird and Fisher (2006) characterized the new generation of learners as "always-on", and as those who "expect to utilize technology in their learning" and connect "to their peers, professors, and course content through... social networks..." (p. 10). Interestingly enough, despite a variety of learning management systems currently available for educators, such as Moodle, Echo360, Blackboard, there has been a noticeable gravitation towards social media. It seems that pressure on tertiary education providers to meet new situations signalled by both a "changing society and world of work" ("New Zealand Productivity Commission Report", 2017) has become stronger and stronger. However, according to Hootsuite's report based on the analysis of 128 Australian universities and institutions, tertiary education has been "struggling with the transition to digital campuses, where social media has the potential to connect and deliver a revolutionized student experience" (Hootsuite, 2017).

Understanding the challenges and barriers to international students' learning, a project "The International Student Experience" undertaken by Education New Zealand and Study Auckland pointed to a need to design courses that are "student-centered", "focus beyond the on-campus experience", and enable students "[to] grow as individuals" ("Journey to transformational student experience", 2017). The project has put forward a strategy that aims at creating "the ecosystem surrounding international students" based on collaboration, social connectivity and communication ("International Student Experience Project", 2017). Trying to redress the situation faced by international students, some scholars have been emphasizing the importance of Facebook-like channels in constructing the institution-learner relationships. According to Roblyer, McDaniel, Webb, Herman and Witty (2010), "faculty who see teaching as establishing a relationship with students may view [deploying] Facebook-like technologies as an efficient, even business-like way to accomplish that connection" (p. 135). Ryan, Magro and Sharp (2011), in their study on first semester international Ph.D. students, have carefully analyzed the impact of Facebook groups on students' adaptation to a Ph.D. program and a new culture. They have come to the conclusion that the social network enabled "various types of knowledge exchange" and helped "students alleviate apprehension by the sharing of a variety of experiences" (p. 13). According to Sleeman, Lang and Lemon (2016), "social media facilitates important communication, acculturation, and educational [process] and "can assist educators in developing more inclusive learning environments" (p.

402). Similarly, Zhao (2016) sets educational providers the task of embracing the accessibility of social media to "maintain connection with international students beyond the classroom to offer better support for students in their everyday lives" (p. 6).

While some educators agree that social media can positively contribute to students' learning, others think that using social media "is as much of a challenge for many students as it may be for most educators" (Gray, Lucas, & Kennedy, 2010, p. 971). Very interesting insights into social media use in the international classroom have been introduced by Alfarhoud, Alahmad, Alqahtani and Alhassan (2016). Their findings reveal that "many international students see that using social media during the class is a distraction factor…" Having said that, the authors retain the belief that social media offers very helpful tools if they are well integrated with the learning environment.

In addition, research publications draw attention to the educational potential of social media. It has been established that social media can effectively be used for learning purposes. For example, Lofgren suggested "social media in education settings has a positive impact on students' comprehension of class material" (as cited in Alfarhoud et al., 2016, p. 45). A New Zealand based study by Rahman (2014) concludes that social media should not only be allowed in class, but also be actively integrated in academic programs as international students can then use them for independent learning.

To meet "the global context of education" and "the character and composition of students" (Davies, 2006, p. 1) some tertiary education providers have been offering intensive courses characterized as "semester- or quarter-equivalent classes offered in compressed, accelerated, or condensed formats" in which the number of weeks per semester is reduced while the number of hours per class may increase (Scott, 2003, p. 29). Definitions of intensive courses range from "intensive, compressed, concentrated, or short-term learning" (Serdyukov, 2008, p. 37) to "multi-sensory, brain-compatible teaching and learning methodology" (McKeon, 1995, p. 64). Wlodkowski and Kasworm (2003) believe that intensive learning first of all is "the active learning method of teaching" that allows flexibility and acknowledges students' existing knowledge and experiences (p. 94). However, it is not surprising that some scholars hold quite a negative view of intensive courses. Critics typically point out a lack of time allocated for scaffolding students' learning and reflections on what is being learned (Wlodkowski, 2003). In this respect, the advocates of intensive courses feel pressured to demonstrate the effectiveness of such an educational approach (Swenson, 2003).

The major challenge faced by universities and other institutions offering the intensive mode of course delivery is organizing the learning processes in a way that enables students to take charge of their learning and achieve academic results equivalent to traditional semester courses. While some educators agree that the intensive courses offer more flexible study options, others argue that the intensive learning can be difficult for international students due to the high-paced nature of course delivery, time-constrained projects and a necessity to quickly adapt to a new learning environment. However, a study by Ho and Piven (2015) found that international students prefer the intensive mode of course delivery to a traditional semester due to a timesaving course schedule and more opportunities for feedback and interaction with a lecturer. Moreover, students found themselves more efficient and productive due to having more time for independent leaning.

Even though, intensive courses are gaining popularity among international students, there has been a lack of relevant studies on, and interest in social media as one of the possible solutions that can help international students to overcome challenges associated with the intensive mode of course delivery and to overall enhance their learning experiences.

In closing, being confronted with a need to develop more effective learning environments for international students, tertiary education tends to accept that technology in general and social media may potentially change traditional teaching practices. And the message is clear - there is an obvious gap between educational approaches and the world of international learners. This chapter is intended as a contribution to the research on international students' learning experiences focusing on the intensive courses delivered in a blended format which is through class-based tutorials, Moodle, and closed groups on Facebook. Emerging from the point of view and experiences of international students, the study enriches the conversation on the applicability of social media in the international classroom and presents useful examples for educators who wish to incorporate social media in their courses.

Instrumental Case Study Design and Methodology

In this instrumental study, defined in line with Yin (2003) as "an empirical inquiry that investigates a contemporary phenomenon within its real-life context" (p. 13), Facebook closed groups were set up for two undergraduate courses at Otago Polytechnic Auckland International Campus (OPAIC). OPAIC offers courses for international students only and follows the intensive mode of course delivery that is five terms each year instead of two traditional semesters. OPAIC classes are relatively small - the average class size varies from 12 to 30 students. Each term is comprised of eight weeks of teaching, followed by a two-week break. Such schedule allows students to concentrate on fewer courses at one time (two versus four).

The decision to set up Facebook closed groups for the Event Planning and Entrepreneurship courses was largely motivated by two interrelated factors: the rapid integration of social networks into students' everyday lives and the educational need for international learners to take an active part in determining their study paths and meet the challenges associated with the intensive mode of course delivery. The decision was also encouraged by the current research on social media in education which claims that social media has the potential to help students "not only to improve their teamwork, but also their learning skills" (Bicen & Uzunboylu, 2012, p. 658).

The undergraduate students involved in the study were enrolled in Event Planning and Entrepreneurship courses (level 7). There were 15, 3.5 hour face-to-face tutorials during the term. Both courses were delivered in a blended format including traditional classroom-based teaching, Moodle, and Facebook. In general, Moodle served as a point of departure and course navigation system for students while Facebook was used for real-time conversations and activities. The mode of course delivery and frequency of communication with students on Facebook were the same for both courses. The following Facebook based activities were implemented during both courses delivery:

- **Content Distribution:** A course outline, assessments' instructions, exemplars, guest speakers' presentations, and additional resources such as articles were provided on Facebook under the "Files" menu option throughout the courses.
- **Course Announcements:** Facebook was used as an online information board that kept students informed about guest speakers, field trips, and extra tutorials. Once students subscribed to the class notifications, they automatically received timely updates. Students were also reminded about assessment due dates and notified when the tutor issued the assessment grades.

- **"Before, During and After Class" Activities:** Facebook was used to shift courses towards a flipped classroom. In-class activities were intertwined with Facebook. Students continued working on projects introduced in class or were asked to complete some tasks prior to the next class and post results on Facebook. For example, Entrepreneurship students were asked to post their favorite Kickstarter or Pledge Me project on Facebook and justify their choices. The idea was to check students' understanding of the concept of innovation and use their posts as an opening activity in the next class.

Figure 1. Course announcements on Facebook: Closed group of the entrepreneurship course, level 6

- **Team Projects:** Facebook was used as a collaborative platform for group-based assessments and self-regulated group work. Facebook was adapted for meetings, group discussions, sharing information, exchanging ideas, raising important issues, and keeping teams updated.
- **Reflections on Learning:** Students regularly shared their notes/images/videos and links relevant to topics covered in class. They also reflected on different class activities such as field trips or events.
- **Questions/Answers Sessions:** Facebook was used to test students' understanding and progress before summative assessments as well as to encourage follow up discussions and peer feedback. Facebook served as a 24/7 support allowing students to ask questions or seek assistance from a lecturer or other students outside the class hours.
- **Summative Assessments:** Facebook was incorporated into project-based summative assessments for both courses. For example, Entrepreneurship students were expected to create a Facebook page for their business ideas. Event Planning students ran a promo campaign for an event they were organizing.

- **Content Creation:** Facebook was used for student-generated original content that included business pages for start-up businesses (Entrepreneurship course), events (Event Planning course), images, posters, videos, and stories. Content creation was one of the most important elements of the Event Planning course as students were expected to run a social media campaign.
- **Inter-Institutional Collaborations:** Facebook was used to extend course projects beyond Facebook closed groups, focusing on collaboration at the institutional level. For example, Entrepreneurship students' start-up ideas and Event Planning students' event proposals were displayed on the OPAIC Facebook page for voting upon.

Figure 2. Inter-institutional collaboration on Facebook: Startup idea group project. The Entrepreneurship course, level 6

A total of 25 Event Planning students and 13 Entrepreneurship students were engaged with the Facebook closed groups during the course delivery. All observation and focus group participants were OPAIC students, mainly from China and India, aged between 21 to 33. A total of seven Event Planning students and seven Entrepreneurship students participated in the focus groups on Facebook after their completion of the courses. The study employed a qualitative instrumental case study methodology in which online participant observation of the Event Planning and Entrepreneurship courses had been implemented in triangulation with two asynchronous Facebook focus groups. The choice of methodology was motivated by the exploratory nature of the research question and the characteristics of Facebook, which has a dual function in this study: as the research context and the tool for data collection.

The data was collected in two stages: 1) participant observation on the Event Planning and Entrepreneurship Facebook closed groups between March 2015 and March 2016; 2) two asynchronous Facebook focus groups in April 2016. Evidence from observational data (stage 1) was used as stimuli during the focus groups (stage 2). Such an approach allowed the tutor/researcher to capture international students' activities, reactions and behavior through the participant observation on Facebook, and then to use observational evidence to develop and facilitate a focus group discussion.

Table 1. Data collection

Stage	Method of Data Collection	Source of Data
1	Participant observation (Event Planning and Entrepreneurship Facebook closed groups)	International students' narratives/ images/ links/ questions/ comments/ reactions/generated content/ frequency of participation/ group conversations
2	Two asynchronous focus groups on Facebook	International students' reflection on their learning experiences with Facebook closed groups

The choice of an asynchronous focus group on Facebook was motivated by the idea that "asynchronous communication…allows participants to construct more considered narratives, providing a depth that might be absent in uttered data" (Stewart & Williams, 2005, p. 413). Mann and Stewart point out that an online focus group "is an efficient and highly-cost-effective mechanism for gathering detailed data, in large quantities" (as cited in Kozinets, 2010, p. 48). It is also important to emphasize that this method is not time restricted. In this respect, an asynchronous online focus group has some obvious advantages over the face-to-face approach. Furthermore, the asynchronous focus group opens up the possibility of increasing the duration of group discussions, which is a big plus if there is a need to cross-test the preliminary research findings.

STUDY RESULTS AND DISCUSSION

The next sections introduce study results related to the following research question: What are the educational values of Facebook for international students enrolled in the intensive courses? The discussion and much of the pedagogical concepts used in the analysis link in one way or another to several guiding questions provided earlier in this chapter. They are as follows:

1. What are international students' views on the intensive courses that incorporate Facebook closed groups as a learning tool?
2. What are international students' views on Facebook as a learning tool in comparison with learning management systems such as Moodle?
3. What are the factors that may impact international students' learning experiences with courses incorporating Facebook?

What is presented further does not claim to be a definitive guide for social media use in the international classroom, and should be seen merely as ideas and suggestions that can help learning designers and teachers to begin incorporating social media into teaching and learning. Based on the guiding research questions above, the discussion breaks down all students' learning experiences into the categories shown in Table 2.

Table 2. Discussion structure

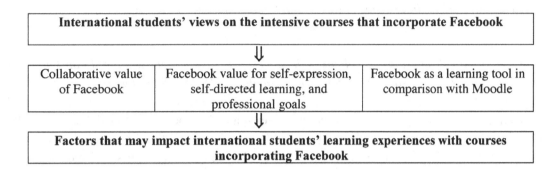

International Students' Views on the Intensive Courses That Incorporate Facebook

I really enjoyed every aspect of the course. I thought it was challenging, meaningful. – Facebook focus group participant (Entrepreneurship course)

The study results indicate that the majority of the research participants welcomed learning opportunities presented on Facebook. Based on the data analysis, international students enrolled in the two intensive business courses recognized a number of Facebook values for learning. This study results have been grouped around two broad categories. First, participants' experiences with Facebook were social and collaborative. These experiences took place in the form of team projects, information search, problem solving, timely feedback, discussions, and shared resources. Second, participants saw a value of Facebook as providing for self-expression, self-directed learning and professional goals. What seems to emerge here is that course-related communications and activities on Facebook boosted international students' confidence and creativity, and enabled them to develop new skills.

Collaborative Value of Facebook

The educational industry's interest in collaborative learning has been motivated by what Smith and MacGregor (1992) call "rich contexts" that "challenge students to practice and develop higher order reasoning and problem-solving skills" (p. 12). According to the authors, "collaborative learning is socially and intellectually involving. It invites students to build closer connections to other students, to their faculty, to their courses, and to their learning" (Smith & MacGregor, 1992, p. 13). In this regard, social media holds out a promise to provide different scenarios for collaboration and triggers "specific learning mechanisms" while students are involved in a "situation in which particular forms of interaction...are expected to occur (Dillenbourg, 2007, p. 4).

Research results show that in general, participants thought that Facebook allows for organizing team projects more effectively. Thus, Facebook greatly contributed to team communications by providing the easiest and fastest way to keep team members updated, share ideas and resources:

Sharing links, new ideas and tips for creating businesses...are useful. It also allows the class to discuss the idea in detail. It [Facebook] allowed communicating with each other outside class and learning collectively. (Entrepreneurship class participant)

Everyone can join the discussion...Facebook is the fastest way to announce what we [team] have done, if there is a problem or suggestions they can reply immediately (Event Planning participant).

This result is consistent with previous research. For example, Rambe (2012) found that Facebook can "complement classroom practices by creating student learning communities for knowledge generation" (p. 309). From students' perspectives, Facebook appeared to be useful for course-related communications outside the class:

It was an amazing team to work with and everyone put in their best...It was different from Moodle and most of all it was very interactive.

Participants also acknowledged Facebook as having the collaborative value that is associated with easy access to resources and information:

Websites like Facebook have people sharing useful links, which can be informational and educational. I access Facebook once or twice daily for 10 to 15 minutes (Entrepreneurship course participant)

Figure 3. Team projects on Facebook: Closed group of the Event Planning course, level 6

What should be emphasized here is that although participants in both Event Planning and Entrepreneurship focus groups pointed out a collaborative value of Facebook, this, however, is not supported by the observational data of the Entrepreneurship course. While the majority of Event Planning participants regularly interacted with each other by commenting, posting, and liking, Entrepreneurship participants were less active and mainly communicated with the lecturer. Contrary to expectations, peer-to-peer communications are not evident in the observational data. Entrepreneurship participants saw the lecturer as the main point of contact, not their peers. To some extent this was also reflected in some focus group data:

You can create study groups, audio or video lessons, send pictures, graph & facilitate real time communication between a lecturer & students (Entrepreneurship course participant).

It should be noted that some findings on Facebook's collaboration qualities are mixed and differ from previous research which says that Facebook can "encourage discussions" or improve "learning outcomes by facilitating discussions with peers" (Salmon, Ross, Pechenkina, & Chase, 2015, p.6). It seems fair to say that putting students into a collaborative situation on Facebook does not necessarily mean that interactions and collaborative learning automatically occur. Facebook collaborative values perceived by some participants could not be solely related to student-to-student interactions and teamwork. For instance, the lecturer's proximity and engagement on Facebook played the most important role in learning experiences of international students enrolled in the Entrepreneurship course. In contrast, Event Planning participants saw the collaborative value of Facebook for networking, and not only in class settings, but also at the institutional level and far beyond that:

Facebook can be the strongest and best marketing tool for event planning... It [Facebook] helps to make good connection with people. We can use Facebook to generate ideas for event by asking people's opinions before and after the event (Event Planning course participant).

Such results suggest that there is a need to identify what kind of teaching approaches may increase the probability that collaborative learning that involves students with different cultural backgrounds occurs on Facebook. Unfortunately, the study did not produce enough evidence to develop this argument. However, based on Dillenbourg's research (2007) on collaborative learning, it can be suggested that: 1) Facebook based collaboration should be carefully designed with a strong focus on activities and knowledge that "cannot be solved solely with one type of knowledge"; 2) Facebook based collaboration requires specific and clear interaction rules to scaffold effective team communications; 3) Facebook based collaboration needs a regular teacher's input and "minimal pedagogical interventions in order to redirect the group work in a productive direction or to monitor which members are left out of the interaction" (p. 6).

Several other principles for teaching in the international classroom have been put forward by Rovai (2007) who has studied synchronous online discussions that involved culturally diverse students. The author points out that "basic communication rules that may bring success in an intra-cultural context may not be sufficient for a successful inter-cultural interaction" and strongly encourages teachers to help students to get to know each other and learn about each other's cultural background and personal goals (p.84).

Some participants acknowledged the benefits of collaborative learning on Facebook for their personal experiences, cultural adaptation in particular:

I have learned a lot about New Zealand culture through Facebook. For example, I never knew what Anzac day is but then I read an article about Anzac day on Facebook...All these are part of my learning from social media. It is indeed important now for me...it helps me a lot, and in the end I know where I stand with the information I have on a particular subject (Event Planning course participant).

This finding is in line with previous research by Arkiodies et al. (2013), which states that Facebook "may contribute to a more positive international study experience by creating opportunities for overseas students to make digitally mediated points of connection with the host culture" (as cited in Sleeman et al., 2016, p. 401).

Figure 4. Students' feedback on Facebook based activities: Closed group of the Event Planning course, level 6

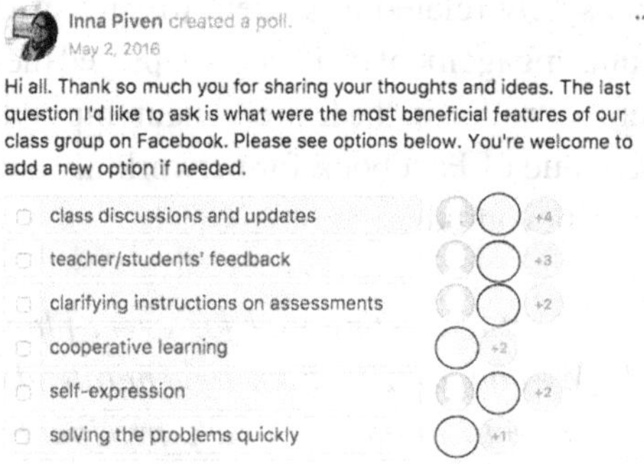

Facebook Value for Self-Expression, Self-Directed Learning, and Professional Goals

Based on the observational data from both courses, the study assumes that some participants' learning experiences were often activated by a need for self-expression. It is particularly evident in the Event Planning course where participants regularly posted photos taken during field trips or class activities. Interestingly, those experiences were also linked to participants' professional interests or goals. For example, participants with a background and career prospects in photography took the initiative to capture the class events and share them with their peers on Facebook. The same can be said about course content generated by participants: being provided with a number of collaborative scenarios, participants were able to embrace their professional skills and express themselves through creation of content (e.g. videos, posters) relevant to their professional or personal interests. Surprisingly, some participants continued posting in groups after the course completion. As one Entrepreneurship participant concluded, "*we got a chance to express ourselves*".

Interestingly, in Bangert's seven principles framework to online teaching, it is stressed that in order to create a unique experience for each learner, there is a need to recognize and acknowledge "a diverse range of academic talents, preferences, and experiences" students bring to the educational environment (2006, p. 230). What does it mean in practice? Teachers should create a wide range of activities, which suit international students' learning needs, styles and interests, and offer "multiple opportunities for demonstrating knowledge and skill proficiencies" (Rovai, 2007, p. 84). It is therefore about empowerment and allowing students to make informed decisions and progress towards their personal learning and professional goals.

When designing a course incorporating social media, it is also important to consider international students' future employment opportunities. In comparison with domestic students, international students are faced with a much more difficult time finding a job. The project "The International Student

Experience" by Education New Zealand and Study Auckland mentioned earlier, found that "many international students are unaware of what it takes to fit with New Zealand employers" and "the gap between expectations from employers and international students is much greater than we had realized" ("International Student Experience Project", 2017). As said earlier, some research data suggest that students may considerably benefit from social media activities and resources that are associated with their future workplace and industry. More examples related to international students' view on social media as an enabler of employability skills will be presented further when comparing Facebook to Moodle.

Facebook can be used as a learning tool. You gain knowledge from different pages you liked on Facebook for different topics (Event Planning course participant).

Figure 5. Students' reflections on a field trip: Closed group of the Event Planning course, level 6

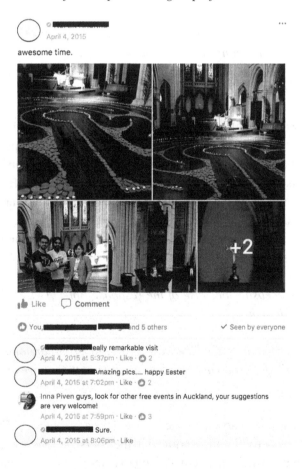

In addition, some observational data demonstrate that a number of participants were willing not just to engage with course-related activities on Facebook, but to become an opinion leader by regularly sharing content that they thought might be useful for the class. While the study did not come to a clear conclusion about specific reasons behind such behavior, it can be assumed that through interacting with peers, active posting and sharing on Facebook, participants were able to communicate or shape their self-identity and to some extent satisfy their needs for self-expression. As proposed by Schmidt (2007), "social media facilitate three social cognitive processes: information management, identity management, and relationship management…that result in a change of self-representation…" (as cited in Dabbagh & Kitsantas, 2012, p.4). Although, physiological needs have been well researched in the educational context, the studies on intentional student's self-representation and self-expression in the social media context remain rather silent.

Facebook as a Learning Tool in Comparison With Moodle

Even though there was agreement amongst research participants that Facebook can potentially serve as a learning tool, it was also noted that not all learning activities should be implemented on the social media. The majority of participants believed that Moodle is the best fit for self-directed learning in comparison with Facebook.

I …prefer Moodle over Facebook…reason being Facebook is more distracting as compared to Moodle. For me Moodle is better if I am learning something new individually…also when I am studying I don't want my notification to popup saying someone liked my picture or something like that…that's what I mean by distracting (Event Planning course participant).

Research results appear to contradict some earlier studies on social media that reported that "Facebook's closed groups are more popular among students than Moodle" (Osepashvili, 2014, p. 378). For example, one of the focus group participants views Facebook "for group announcements and off-class discussion" while Moodle is considered to be "a platform for self-learning". But what participants really gained from Facebook in comparison with Moodle are immediate feedback and the availability of real-time information and communication. By sharing the same platform with different industries, businesses, relevant academic journals and resources, participants were able to direct their learning towards career goals and professional interests.

Facebook is better than any websites because of the response time…I visit Moodle only twice a week (Event Planning course participant).

Facebook can be great for group activities like we did. All our group announcements were over Facebook…None of us used Moodle for group activities, as we are not that active on Moodle (Event Planning course participant).

It is interesting to note that some participants recognized the advantages of Facebook over Moodle for new skills building. Facebook activities incorporated in the course assessments encouraged participants to learn and apply, for example, social media marketing to team projects. Social storytelling and content creation were two key skills students recognized the most. They also found their hands-on experiences with Facebook to be useful for professional development and future employment.

We got to know how to advertise an event through social media, how we can contact a larger audience in just one post. It [Facebook] taught us how to write the right content at the right time (Event Planning course participant).

I use a lot of social networking sites for professional purposes. I follow certain financial consultants and Financial companies like EY, Deloitte, PWC, KPMG, Concentrix, Accenture etc.

It gives me job alerts as I have posted my profile over there so certain employers have contacted me... (Entrepreneurship course participant).

In addition, participants noted that Facebook could be an ideal platform for courses that have more room for creativity, such as marketing, management and entrepreneurship. In general, the study results confirm the previous research on social media that identified the benefits of using social media in creating personal learning environments "that help learners aggregate and share the results of learning achievements, participate in collective knowledge generation, and manage their own meaning making" (Dabbagh & Kitsantas, 2012, p. 2). In this respect, research is needed to analyze the position of self-directed learning in international students' experiences.

Factors That May Impact International Students' Learning Experiences With Courses Incorporating Facebook

The research found it interesting that Event Planning and Entrepreneurship participants responded differently to the same mode of course delivery, types of activities and assessments, and communication style on Facebook. The study reveals that such factors as students' cultural background, class size, type of class activities, other students' engagement, and familiarity with the platform may impact international students' learning experiences with courses delivered on Facebook. For example, one of the research participants noted that the class size and the level of other students' engagement with the course on Facebook might stop some students from being active:

The size of the class, having too many people can lead to less interaction and active participation by all... [...and other students] social media presence. Do they access Facebook regularly or not?

Research results also show that some cultural differences may impact on international students' learning with Facebook. For instance, for Chinese students, it took longer to adapt Facebook for their studies due to a lack of experience, as the network has been blocked in China since 2009. Facebook can be a big "no" for students coming from traditional religious families, for example, for Muslim females. One of the Entrepreneurship class Muslim students could not participate on Facebook because of her family norms and beliefs. To make this student feel included and less isolated, all Facebook based activities were introduced and discussed in class.

It should be noted that students' adjustment to the Facebook classroom did not happen rapidly. At the beginning it was a chaotic experience due to some students' unfamiliarity with the platform and a lack of understanding of reasons why Facebook was incorporated in the course. One participant from the Entrepreneurship course expressed the view that he does not see the learning value of Facebook:

I didn't find any changes in my learning. If you are going to choose other platform such as LinkedIn then it will be more valuable than Facebook (Entrepreneurship course participant).

As mentioned earlier, the intensive course delivery can be challenging for international students as they are expected to learn and apply multiple new concepts within a short space of time. More importantly, the intensive method of teaching may be new to students. That is why it was critical to organize the learning process in a way that enables students to meet challenges presented by the intensive studies. Despite a lack of evidence on the intensive mode of teaching and learning as a contributing factor to participants' experience with Facebook, some observational data show that one of the most common practices the participants were regularly engaged with was asking a lecturer for instructions, clarifications on assessment' requirements, and key dates for release of results.

It was a good idea to convey the message in an easiest way (Entrepreneurship course participant).

It seems that participants recognized the advantages of using Facebook over Moodle for intensive studies, as it offers more opportunities for feedback and interaction with the lecturer.

SOLUTIONS AND RECOMMENDATIONS

Tertiary institutions in the last five years have exhibited a noticeable drift towards innovative forms of teaching in which social media has become a trending topic. Within this context, some directions for social media use in tertiary education with a strong focus on the changing student profile and ongoing technological developments can be identified.

- More focus is needed on self-regulated learning via information/resources search, networking, and well-designed collaborative projects on social media.
- Implementing social media based cross-disciplinary projects would allow international students to adapt better to a new cultural, social and educational environment.
- It is important to link the assessment strategies to collaborative learning with the use of social media.
- There is a need to recognize and take into consideration students' prior knowledge, their current competences, careers goals and professional interests that can be used as triggers for collaborative learning on social media.

FUTURE RESEARCH DIRECTIONS

Despite a growing awareness of the benefits associated with the courses delivered in a blended format with the use of social media, little coherence exists in education research whether such courses can deliver good results. Hence, empirical evidence focusing on relationships between students' use of social media for learning and their academic performance are much needed. As Irwin, Ball, Desbrow and Leveritt (2012) noted "it is unclear if and how Facebook can enhance student learning outcomes" (p. 1230).

The scarcity of exploratory studies on international students' learning experiences in the context of tertiary education also welcomes further research as well as critical discussion on the educational value of social media. First of all, even though a variety of social media activities has been developed and implemented, students' learning experiences within a relatively new and highly social context of education have not been characterized and conceptualized. As many articles published around students' self-regulated learning and personal learning environments are mainly literature-based, research is needed from the perspectives of actual learners. To understand what self-regulated learning as an educational approach implies in a social media context, future studies should be grounded in concrete learning situations, as learning is always behavior-in-context.

This chapter also encourages dialog on the applicability of social media to the intensive mode of course delivery. Even though the existing research concludes that there is no significant difference between students' performances enrolled in short or full-semester courses (Daniel, 2000), more research is required on international students' experiences of intensive learning with the use of social media.

CONCLUSION

This chapter has presented the results of an instrumental case study undertaken within a four-month period while teaching the Event Planning and Entrepreneurship undergraduate courses at Otago Polytechnic Auckland International Campus, New Zealand. Both courses were delivered in a blended format through class-based teaching, Moodle and Facebook.

To develop a more strategic view on international student learning, the study deployed the instrumental case study methodology and used two methods of data collection (participant observation on Facebook and two asynchronous focus groups) in triangulation. Emerging from the points of view and experiences of international students, the study enriches the conversation on the applicability of social media in the international classroom and produces interesting insights into the educational values of Facebook for collaboration, self-directed learning and professional goals.

One of the most interesting findings is that the majority of research participants tended to prefer Moodle to Facebook for self-directed learning, while Facebook was viewed as a platform for group projects and course announcements. The study also identified some contributing factors that may impact international students' experiences with courses incorporating Facebook including students' cultural background, social media habits, familiarity with the social media platform, as well as class size and level of engagement with course activities.

The study did not find a significant connection between the intensive mode of teaching with the use of Facebook and international students' learning experiences. It seems reasonable to assume that if social media based activities are well-planned and successfully integrated into an institution's learning environment, the mode of course delivery, either intensive or traditional, is not central to students' learning.

The importance of this study can be appreciated in the context of ongoing discussions about new models of delivering education in response to changes in technology and the continuing internationalization of tertiary education.

REFERENCES

Alfarhoud, Y. T., Alahmad, B., Alqahtani, L., & Alhassan, A. (2016). The experience of international students using social media during classes. *International Journal of Education*, 8(2), 32–47. doi:10.5296/ije.v8i2.9224

Baird, D. E., & Fisher, M. (2005-2006). Neomillennial user experience design strategies: Utilizing social networking media to support "always on" learning styles. *Journal of Educational Technology Systems*, *34*(1), 5–32. doi:10.2190/6WMW-47L0-M81Q-12G1

Bangert, A. W. (2006). The development of an instrument for assessing online teaching effectiveness. *Journal of Educational Computing Research*, *35*(3), 227–244. doi:10.2190/B3XP-5K61-7Q07-U443

Beer, D., & Burrows, R. (2010). Consumption, prosumption and participatory web cultures. *Journal of Consumer Culture*, *10*(3), 3–12. doi:10.1177/1469540509354009

Bicen, H., & Uzunboylu, H. (2013). The use of social networking sites in education: A case study of Facebook. *Journal of Universal Computer Science*, *19*(5), 658–671.

Dabbagh, N., & Kitsantas, A. (2011). Personal learning environments, social media, and self-regulated learning: A natural formula for connecting formal and informal learning. *Internet and Higher Education*, *15*(1), 3–8. doi:10.1016/j.iheduc.2011.06.002

Davies, W. M. (2006). Intensive teaching formats: A review. *Issues in Educational Research*, *16*(1), 1–20.

Dillenbourg, P. (1999). What do you mean by collaborative learning? In P. Dillenbourg (Ed.), *Collaborative learning: Cognitive and computational approaches* (pp. 1–19). Oxford, UK: Elsevier.

Fischer, E., & Reuber, A. R. (2011). Social interaction via new social media: (How) can interactions on Twitter affect thinking and behavior? *Journal of Business Venturing*, *26*(1), 1–18. doi:10.1016/j.jbusvent.2010.09.002

Gerritsen, J. (2017). *Foreign student numbers jump*. Retrieved from http://www.radionz.co.nz/news/national/329800/foreign-student-numbers-jump

Gray, K., Lucas, A., & Kennedy, G. (2010). Medical students' use of Facebook to support learning: Insights from four case studies. *Medical Teacher*, *32*(12), 971–976. doi:10.3109/0142159X.2010.497826 PMID:21090950

Guess, A. (2008). *Facebook, meet Blackboard*. Retrieved from https://www.insidehighered.com/news/2008/05/14/sync

Heinonen, K. (2011). Consumer activity in social media: Managerial approaches to consumers' social media behavior. *Journal of Consumer Behaviour*, *10*(6), 356–364. doi:10.1002/cb.376

Heinrichs, J. H., Lim, J.-S., & Lim, K.-S. (2011). Influence of social networking site and user access method on social media evaluation. *Journal of Consumer Behaviour*, *10*(6), 347–355. doi:10.1002/cb.377

Ho, H. W. L., & Piven, I. (2015, May). *Perceptions of international students on intensive learning at a tertiary institution in New Zealand*. Paper presented at the Sixth Annual Scholarship of Teaching and Learning Academy Conference at the University of Findlay.

Hoffman, D. L., & Novak, T. P. (2012, January 17). *Why do people use social media? Empirical findings and a new theoretical framework for social media goal pursuit*. Retrieved from Social Science Research Network http://papers.ssrn.com/sol3/papers.cfm?abstract_id=1989586

Hootsuite. (2017). *The social revolution: Redefining the student experience in Australian higher education institutions*. Retrieved from https://hootsuite.com/resources/the-social-revolution-australia-higher-education#

International Student Experience Project. (2017). *ATEED & Education New Zealand*. Retrieved from https://intellilab.enz.govt.nz/document/270-2017-international-student-experience-project

International students enrolled in tertiary education. (2017). Retrieved from https://www.education-counts.govt.nz/statistics/indicators/main/student-engagement-participation/international_students_enrolled_in_formal_tertiary_education

Irwin, C., Ball, L., Desbrow, B., & Leveritt, M. (2012). Students' perceptions of using Facebook as an interactive learning resource at university. *Australasian Journal of Educational Technology*, *28*(7), 1221–1232. doi:10.14742/ajet.798

Jih-Hsuan, L., Kim, W. P., Kim, M., Kim, S. Y., & LaRose, R. (2012). Social networking and adjustments among international students. *New Media & Society*, *14*(3), 421–440. doi:10.1177/1461444811418627

Journey to transformational student experience. (2017). Retrieved from https://enz.govt.nz/news-and-research/ed-news/journey-to-transformational-student-experience-2/

Kaplan, A. M., & Haenlein, M. (2010). Users of the world, unite! The challenges and opportunities of Social Media. *Business Horizons*, *53*(1), 59–68. doi:10.1016/j.bushor.2009.09.003

Kozinets, R. V. (2010). *Netnography: Doing ethnographic research online*. Los Angeles, CA: Sage.

McKeon, K. J. (1995). What is this thing called accelerated learning? *Training & Development*, *49*(6), 64–66.

New Zealand Productivity Commission Report. (2017). *New models of tertiary education: Final Report*. Retrieved from https://www.productivity.govt.nz/sites/default/files/New%20models%20of%20tertiary%20education%20FINAL_3.pdf

Osepashvili, D. (2014). The using of social media platform in modern journalism education. In *Proceedings of the European Conference on Social Media* (pp. 378-387). Brighton, UK: University of Brighton.

Rahman, N. (2014). The usage and online behavior of social networking sites among international students in New Zealand. *The Journal of Social Media in Society*, *3*(2), 65–81.

Rambe, P. (2012). Critical discourse analysis of collaborative engagement in Facebook postings. *Australasian Journal of Educational Technology*, *28*(2), 295–314. doi:10.14742/ajet.875

Roblyer, M. D., McDaniel, M., Webb, M., Herman, J., & Witty, J. V. (2010). Findings on Facebook in higher education: A comparison of college faculty and student uses and perceptions of social networking sites. *Internet and Higher Education*, *13*(3), 134–140. doi:10.1016/j.iheduc.2010.03.002

Rovai, A. P. (2007). Facilitating online discussions effectively. *The Internet and Higher Education*, *10*(1), 77–88. doi:10.1016/j.iheduc.2006.10.001

Ryan, S., Magro, M., & Sharp, J. (2011). Exploring educational and cultural adaptation through social networking sites. *Journal of Information Technology Education: Innovations in Practice*, *10*, 1–16.

Salmon, G., Ross, B., Pechenkina, E., & Chase, A. (2015). The space for social media in structured online learning. *Research in Learning Technology, 23*(1), 28507. doi:10.3402/rlt.v23.28507

Scott, P. A. (2003). Attributes of high-quality intensive courses. *New Directions for Adult and Continuing Education, 97*(97), 29–38. doi:10.1002/ace.86

Seo, H., Harn, R., Ebrahim, H., & Aldana, J. (2016). International students' social media use and social adjustment. *First Monday, 21*(11), 11–17. doi:10.5210/fm.v21i11.6880

Serdyukov, P. (2008). Accelerated learning: What is it? *Journal of Research in Innovative Teaching, 1*(1), 35–59.

Sherry, M., Thomas, P., & Chui, W. H. (2010). International students: A vulnerable students population. *Higher Education, 60*(1), 33–46. doi:10.100710734-009-9284-z

Sleeman, J., Lang, C., & Lemon, N. (2016). Social media challenges and affordances for international students: Bridges, boundaries, and hybrid spaces. *Journal of Studies in International Education, 20*(5), 391–415. doi:10.1177/1028315316662975

Smith, B. L., & MacGregor, J. T. (1992). What is collaborative learning? In A. S. Goodsell (Ed.), *Collaborative learning: A sourcebook for higher education* (pp. 10–30). University Park, PA: National Center on Postsecondary Teaching, Learning, and Assessment.

Stewart, K., & Williams, M. (2005). Researching online populations: The use of online focus groups for social research. *Qualitative Research, 5*(4), 395–416. doi:10.1177/1468794105056916

Swenson, G. (2003). Accelerated and traditional formats: Using learning as a criterion for quality. *New Directions for Adult and Continuing Education, 97*(97), 83–93. doi:10.1002/ace.91

Toffler, A. (1980). *The third wave* (1st ed.). New York: Bantam Books.

Welikala, T. (2015). *Universities don't understand how international students learn.* Retrieved from https://www.theguardian.com/higher-education-network/2015/jul/03/universities-dont-understand-how-international-students-learn

Wlodkowski, R. J. (2003). Accelerated learning for adults. *New Directions for Adult and Continuing Education, 97*, 5–15. doi:10.1002/ace.84

Wlodkowski, R. J., & Kasworm, C. E. (2003). Accelerated learning: Future roles and influences. *New Directions for Adult and Continuing Education, 97*(97), 93–97. doi:10.1002/ace.92

Wu, H. P., Garza, E., & Guzman, N. (2015). International student's challenge and adjustment to college. *Education Research International, 2015*, 1–9. doi:10.1155/2015/202753

Yin, R. K. (2003). *Case study research: Design and methods* (3rd ed.). Thousand Oaks, CA: Sage.

Zhao, X. (2016). *Social media and the international student experience.* International Education Association of Australia. Retrieved from https://www.ieaa.org.au/documents/item

KEY TERMS AND DEFINITIONS

Blended Learning: The process of gaining and applying knowledge, skills, and experiences through the combination of traditional classroom based activities and digital media tools.

Collaborative Learning: An educational approach that focuses on social contexts of learning. This approach allows students to undertake complex projects and tasks working in teams.

Facebook Closed Group: A type of private group in which all group members have to be approved an administrator prior to joining the group, and only group members can see posted content.

Flipped Classroom: A teaching method where students' learning of a new subject begins prior to in-class tutorials via reading or implementing some activities, and class time is used to develop a deeper understanding of the subject through research, analysis and application of knowledge.

Intensive Mode of Course Delivery: A course delivery option that offers a different timetabling scheduling that allows learners to complete the course in a shorter time frame.

Inter-Institutional Collaborations: A type of collaborative learning that involves communication and networking at the institutional level and engages staff and students from all departments. The purpose of such collaboration is to enhance students' learning through designing, implementing and managing higher-level team projects and showcasing their skills.

International Students: Non-New Zealand students studying at a university or other tertiary education institutions.

Learning Experiences: The process of gaining knowledge and skills through systematic study, practice, and reflections.

Learning Management Systems: Web-based applications used to plan, create, deliver, and document course content and activities.

Moodle: A learning management system that allows organizing and managing course contents, resources, activities, and administrative matters.

Online Learning Environments: Ubiquitous learning settings created through digital devices and social media that enable learning at any time, and provide interactive forms of course activities, resources, and delivery of content.

Project-Based Assessments: A type of assessment based on a project or series of projects that require students to apply diverse knowledge, skills, and strategies to real-world scenarios, problems, or tasks for an extended period of time.

Self-Regulated/Self-Directed or Independent Learning: A process in which students take control of their own learning by understanding their learning needs and goals, identifying appropriate resources and tools, and ways of learning.

Social Media as a Learning Tool: The use of social media in course design and delivery, including content areas, resources, learning activities, and assessments.

Student-Centered Course Design: An approach to course design in which students' learning needs and goals, current knowledge, and skills are central to course content, learning outcomes, resources, activities, and assessments.

Summative Assessments: A type of assessment that evaluates students' academic achievements against learning outcomes related to knowledge and skill acquisition outlined in the course description. Summative assessments are typically scheduled at the end of semester, study block, or unit, and are formally graded and carry weighting toward a student's final grade.

This research was previously published in Global Perspectives on Social Media in Tertiary Learning and Teaching; pages 20-50, copyright year 2018 by Information Science Reference (an imprint of IGI Global).

Section 2
Development and Design Methodologies

Chapter 8
Bridging Activities:
Social Media for Connecting Language Learners' in-School and Out-of-School Literacy Practices

Ellen Yeh
Columbia College Chicago, USA

Svetlana Mitric
University of Illinois at Chicago, USA

ABSTRACT

This study applied pedagogically-focused project design by using Instagram as a platform to investigate how the use of social media such as Instagram in a multimodal digital storytelling model could bridge the skills English language learners (ELLs) learn in the classroom to out-of-school literacy practices. The study applied the five learning objectives of the bridging-activities framework to investigate to what extent ELLs achieve these objectives. There were forty-two participants (female: n= 22; male: n= 17), international arts and media students. The study collected their main Instagram posts, questionnaires were given with a five-point Likert scale and open-ended questions, and individual follow-up interviews for content analysis. A cross-tabulation was conducted to investigate the relationships between ELLs' Instagram use and how they perceive Instagram as a meaningful way of communication for professional purposes. The findings revealed pedagogical practices of using Instagram as a tool for professional purposes and how ELLs achieved the bridging-activities learning outcomes.

INTRODUCTION

Digital technologies have drastically changed language learners' use of the target language, understanding of genres, and recognition of different purposes of writing (Zheng & Warschauer, 2017). English as a second language (ESL) classrooms are no longer the dominant learning environments, as English language learners (ELLs) are exposed to a wider range of technology-mediated literacy practices outside

DOI: 10.4018/978-1-6684-7123-4.ch008

of school. These practices often require formal and informal communicative skills through texting, blogging, emailing, participating in social media, remixing online content, or playing online games. These out-of-school literacy practices offer opportunities for ELLs to engage in dialogues on topics they are interested in within multimodal contexts and require certain knowledge of genres in reading and writing (Reinhardt & Thorne, 2011). Although out-of-school literacy has become more crucial for ELLs to prepare for not only interpersonal communication but also their future professional lives outside of the classroom, a wide gap still remains between their out-of-school and in-school literacy practices (Zheng & Warschauer, 2017).

Previous studies suggested that limited empirical research has focused on advanced foreign language proficiency students' internet communication and use of information tools in technology-mediated language education (Byrnes, 2007; Thorne & Reinhardt, 2008). While many curricula in upper-level language classrooms emphasize literature, educators neglect the importance of pragmatic practices in both professional and interpersonal contexts of communication. Thorne and Reinhardt (2008) argue that there is a need for linguistic and genre-specific activities for advanced language learners so that they can acquire the knowledge required to use the target language through social practices in digital environments.

In order to help ELLs and instructors understand ways to integrate and connect out-of-school and in-school literacy practices in the rapidly evolving digital wilds (Thorne, Sauro, & Smith, 2015), the current study drew on a pedagogical framework of bridging activities (Thorne & Reinhardt, 2008) to demonstrate the use of social media as a multimodal digital storytelling tool in ESL curriculum. This model implemented structured approaches for ELLs to enhance critical awareness of social media practices and obtain the ability to connect the literacy practices they learn in-class to out-of-school environments (Thorne, Sauro, & Smith, 2015). The bridging activities framework has been introduced and discussed in several research articles (e.g., Thorne & Smith, 2011; Thorne, Sauro, & Smith, 2015; Zheng & Warschauer, 2017); however, more empirical studies are needed to explore ways this framework could effectively influence ELLs' language learning. Therefore, the present study further examined to what extent this model helped ELLs achieve the five learning objectives proposed in the bridging-activities framework.

THEORETICAL FRAMEWORKS

Bridging-Activities Framework

Bridging activities, an instructional framework proposed by Thorne and Reinhardt (2008) derived from multiliteracies pedagogy (New London Group, 1996) and language awareness-based pedagogy (Carter, 1998), aims to foster technology-mediated second language (L2) teaching and learning. While language learners bridge their daily experiences and practices with their schooling, their language proficiency and awareness could increase by being exposed to more meaning-making practices through social and cultural interaction. Through these practices, language learners are able to develop their language awareness of the grammatical and lexical use in the target language and critically consider ways to use the language appropriately in various interpersonal, social, and cultural contexts (Halliday & Matthiesen, 2004). Further, raising L2 learners' critical awareness fosters their cyberpragmatics ("the analysis of how information is produced and interpreted within the Internet environment;" Yus, 2011, p. 13) and allows them to analyze conventions to bridge in-class activities with their technology-mediated language use in the "real world" (Thorne & Reinhardt, 2008).

Pedagogical Integration of Bridging Activities

The current study applied the five learning objectives proposed by Thorne and Reinhardt (2008) to integrate bridging activities into the curriculum to encourage the development of language awareness in social media contexts. The skills that were taught in class and were expected to be practiced outside of the classroom included how ELLs can communicate meaningfully with other professionals in their art fields, exchange and access useful information, build networks with other artists online, and achieve the five bridging-activities learning outcomes listed in the theoretical framework below.

Instagram was the platform that ELLs used for this project because it meets the criteria of the bridging activities model: providing content that is relevant to communicative practices that ELLs are already familiar with or are willing to engage at the interpersonal and professional levels in their everyday life. The learning objectives for bridging activities, and for this project, were as follows:

1. To improve understanding of both conventional and internet-mediated text genres, emphasizing the concept that specific linguistic choices are associated with desired social-communicative actions;
2. To raise awareness of genre specificity (why certain text types work well for specific purposes) and context-appropriate language use;
3. To build metalinguistic, metacommunicative, and analytic skills that enable lifelong learning in the support of participation in existing and future genres of plurilingual and transcultural language use;
4. To bridge toward relevance to students' communicative lives outside of the classroom;
5. To increase student agency in relation to the choice, content and stylistic specifics of the texts contributing to the language learning process (Thorne & Reinhardt, 2008, p. 566).

In addition, the present study incorporated a three-phase cycle of activities into the project so that participants focus their assignment procedure on "observation and collection, guided exploration and analysis, and creation and participation" (Thorne & Reinhardt, 2008, p.566).

LITERATURE REVIEW

Instagram for Digital Storytelling in ESL Curricula

Digital storytelling, as a multimodal tool, serves as one scaffolding approach in the ESL context that allows writers opportunities for personal expression in an authentic language learning environment. When engaged in creating digital stories, ELLs can draw on a variety of new literacy practices and competencies, as well as their sociocultural identities (Skinner & Hagood, 2008). Furthermore, by sharing their writing and digital stories, ELLs can reach authentic audiences and take part in broader digital, global communities of ELLs with the same interests and backgrounds (Skinner & Hagood, 2008). Moreover, digital storytelling technologies give voice to struggling writers and readers, as well as to quiet students who would not otherwise be able to find a powerful, authentic way to express themselves (Bull & Kajder, 2005).

Many students use Instagram on a daily basis, and there is some evidence of this social media tool being used for educational purposes. The existing literature suggests that Instagram can increase students' motivation and engagement (Mansor & Rahim, 2017). It can also boost students' confidence in writing and encourage them to express ideas in a digital environment (Salomon, 2013).

While Instagram is primarily known as a visual tool for sharing photographs, several studies have investigated it as a tool for multimodal writing. Anggraeni (2017) investigated students' perspectives on Instagram as part of English writing assignments and revealed benefits and challenges using this social media platform. Some of the benefits included improved writing skills, enhanced confidence to share writing in public, and useful feedback from instructors, followers, and friends. Prasetyawati's study (2018) further claimed that outside-the-classroom writing on Instagram increases student engagement because students, as creators of the content, find their target audiences and thus are able to communicate their writing to their specific groups of interest.

As described above, most current research on Instagram for educational purposes focuses on students' overall communication and interaction with their peers. However, there is limited research that investigates the pedagogical practices integrating social media in ways relevant to ELLs' professional fields, particularly for arts and media students using Instagram in higher education in the United States.

Instagram for Professional Purposes

Social media networks, and Instagram in particular, have been used for multiple purposes other than just connecting with friends. While at an individual level Instagram has been commonly used for posting personal content for an audience of friends, to date, this platform has gained its popularity and use for professional purposes (Garifova, 2016; Raice & Ante, 2012). Artists and celebrities use Instagram for many different reasons, such as interacting with their fans, promoting their artwork and shows, and advertising fashion brands (Garifova, 2016). As Instagram became the fastest growing social media network, companies and brands saw a great marketing opportunity in this application (Garifova, 2016; Raice & Ante, 2012). Companies began hiring "influencers" who are considered micro-celebrities to promote their products or services. One study examining the relevance of these micro-celebrities found that beauty, fashion, travel, lifestyle, and entertainment were the most preferred fields of the influencers participants follow (Jurij, 2019). Another study investigated Instagram users' perceptions and found that these influencers were perceived trustworthy by their audience (Eroglu & Bayraktar Kose, 2019). With the wide use of Instagram, limited research examines how language learners' use Instagram for building their professional career. The current study integrated this platform into a project aiming to encourage ELL artists to use Instagram not only for personal use but for promoting their artwork to the public and reaching out to other art professionals.

This Study

This project was developed at a liberal arts college specializing in arts and media disciplines in an urban setting. The multimodal digital storytelling model was designed to explore ways Instagram could foster ELLs in-class literacy practices and apply them to out-of-school literacy practices, especially in ways relevant to their creative industry professional fields. According to Anders Petterson, an author of the Hiscox Online Art Trade Report, "Instagram has become the leading social media tool for discovering, showing, and following art, particularly for people below the age of 35" (Reyburn, 2017). Not all artists prefer using social media, but the platforms allow more opportunities and space for young artists to express themselves and tell their own stories. Through the use of Instagram, this multimodal digital storytelling project encourages ELLs to acquire communicative skills in promoting their artwork and telling stories by branching out to the context outside of their everyday classrooms. The research questions for this study are:

1. What are the relationships between ELLs' Instagram use and how they perceive Instagram as a meaningful way of communication for professional purposes?
2. How does using Instagram as a multimodal digital storytelling tool help ELLs achieve the learning objectives of the bridging-activities framework?

METHODOLOGY

Participants

Forty-two international undergraduate students aged 18 to 22 studying at an arts and media college in downtown Chicago. All participants were advanced and high-intermediate level ELLs with iBT TOEFL scores between 80-110. There were seventeen male and twenty-five female participants, from countries including Brazil (n=5), China (n=16), Ecuador (n=1), Japan (n=1), Netherlands (n=1), Panama (n=2), Peru (n=2), Philippine (n=1), South Korea (n=5), Russia (n=1), Taiwan (n=3), and Thailand (n=2), Ukraine (n=1), Vietnam (n=1). The majority of the students in this college are artists who major in creative-industry fields such as acting, arts management, cinema art and science, dance performance, directing, fashion design, filmmaking, graphic design, journalism, musical theatre, and photography. Participants were recruited because they enrolled in a speaking class in the English as an Additional Language (EAL) program in the college. One instructor taught one section of the course and the other instructor taught two sections of the course. Each course contained 14 international students. The two researchers were the instructors of the EAL program, and one was also director of the program. In order to prevent students from worrying about feelings of coercion, participants were anonymous, and their data results were dis-identified before starting the analysis process. The researchers did not start analyzing and coding the data until students' final grades were submitted. In addition, the classroom-instructors conducted interviews and coded data from participants that were not in their own classrooms. For the interview data collection, researchers invited students who were not in their own class to participate in the interview. Students attended the interview voluntarily, and its schedule was dependent on students' availability outside of the class.

As the project's aim was to obtain a deeper insight into participants' use of Instagram to achieve bridging activities' learning objectives, we decided to focus on three cases based on their particularity and the complexity of the content in their Instagram posts. The criteria for selecting these participants included submitting all four Instagram tasks, utilizing different types of genre-specific writing styles across the four tasks, and demonstrating specific linguistic choices in multimodal writing associated with social-communicative actions. We gave these participants the pseudonyms "Maria," "Han," and "Emma." Their demographics are further described in the results section.

Procedures

In the project that lasted for six weeks, students engaged in four Instagram tasks. In the first part of the project, the class instructor conducted a workshop where students completed a questionnaire investigating students' knowledge of social media. Students then examined several Instagram accounts that represented different creative industries. Examining those accounts, students were required to make observations about the purpose of the account, types of posts, and intended audience. They then were asked to identify the common keywords people use for a hashtag (#) in the given creative industry. At the end of the workshop, students were asked to create Instagram accounts separate from their personal accounts to protect their privacy, submit their usernames to the instructor, and choose the creative industry their account would be dedicated to. Students were suggested to select themes and issues that are relevant to their future careers.

Having completed the workshop, for their first task students were asked to use the hashtag indexing function to connect to other artists, research what other relevant content can be found on Instagram and discover users who have been working in similar fields. Students identified one artist or post that is in the same creative industry field. Then, they took screenshots of the posts they found and reposted them on their account with a 50-word paragraph to describe to their audience why this artist's work is appealing or inspiring, and how the post is related to their own creative industry work (see Figure 1). On the due date of the assignment, students discussed and analyzed their posts in class and provided feedback to each other in small groups.

For their second task, students were asked to explore neighborhoods and events in Chicago related to their topics and document these data through Instagram. They then submitted one image or video with short paragraph to tell their audience stories behind the image and how it connected with the creative industry they chose (see Figure 2). As with the previous task, students brought their posts to class to share and discuss with others.

Figure 1. Task 1: Review and repost other artist's work on Instagram

This is a screenshot from Johnpeters. He is a photographer and a sociologist. He always post things about society issues. This picture talks about an issue that old people still need to work hard to survive in Nigeria. I'm major in Documentary, and I wish to solve problems like that through documentaries in the future.

Figure 2. Task 2: Explore Chicago neighborhood about art history

The Chicago Water Tower is considered a landmark of Chicago now. Built in 1869, it helped to meet an increasing need for water supply when there was a severe growth of population. However, the city was overwhelmed by a fierce fire in 1871, after which the whole city nearly lay in ruins. Luckily, the Chicago Water Tower remained and became the only survivor of all the public architectures. The tower no longer serves for water supplies today. With some old pictures stored inside, it attracts people from all over the nation, sharing them with the history and evolution of the city. Plus, some visitors come here solely intending to appreciating the Gothic Architecture style in the 13th Century Europe. As an arts management major, I would say it is a wonderful arts product containing practicability, history, tourism

3 likes

SEPTEMBER 26

Add a comment...

Developing a survey and conducting an interview were included in the third task of this digital storytelling project. Students were instructed to select a person who belonged to the creative industry they chose, then create a list of interview questions. The interviewees were other artists, colleagues, professors in the relevant field, people that work in that particular creative industry, or participants in art events. These interviews were recorded and posted on students' Instagram accounts as videos, images, and short paragraphs to describe the artist interviewed (see Figure 3). Upon task completion, students shared and discussed their experiences with the interviews they conducted in the next class meeting.

For the final task, students were asked to post an image of their own artwork (e.g., performance, work in progress, studio, equipment, film settings) and a short paragraph to introduce their work (see Figure 4). In class, students talked in small groups about their work and posts. During this class, the instructor also introduced the guidelines for the final presentation of students' digital storytelling projects. Demonstrating example Instagram posts that resembled students' four tasks, the instructor explained expectations for the final presentations.

Next class, each student presented their final project by using their Instagram posts to tell their stories as an artist and about their artwork. Following the presentation, students completed a survey to capture their experience with the project. Finally, follow-up interviews with three students who volunteered to participate were completed.

Figure 3. Task 3: Interview other artists in the same creative industry field

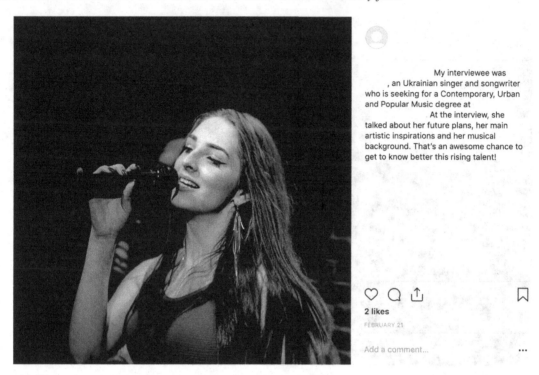

My interviewee was , an Ukrainian singer and songwriter who is seeking for a Contemporary, Urban and Popular Music degree at . At the interview, she talked about her future plans, her main artistic inspirations and her musical background. That's an awesome chance to get to know better this rising talent!

2 likes

FEBRUARY 21

Add a comment...

Figure 4. Task 4: Students' work majoring in contemporary, urban, and popular music program

I'm majoring in a program that includes music theory,music production,performance techniques etc.For me as for a musician and a singer it is important to participate in the whole process and to be in control of it.Making music and recording it is a very exciting but at the same time challenging thing.There are always a lot of nuances in arranging and voice techniques that you have to work on.Specifically this picture was taken in the studio in West Town where I was recording my first song. (graduated from ,audio design major) composed and produced the whole track.I wrote a lyrics for this song.We were listening,experimenting with it and just having fun because it's all music is about #musicproduction #studio #recording

11 likes

FEBRUARY 22

Data Collection and Analysis

Two sets of questionnaires were conducted in this study, with both using single-item 5-point Likert scale questions with open-ended follow-up questions to offer insight into participants' perspectives. The first questionnaire was completed before participants conducted the Instagram project, and the second questionnaire was distributed after the project was completed. It was distributed to students via an email with a Google Form link to the questionnaire. They were given 30 minutes before they began their first task. The first questionnaire sought demographic information on participants' comfort level in communicating on social media platforms like Instagram. Likert scale questions were coded strongly disagree (1), disagree (2), neutral (3), agree (4), and strongly agree (5). It also included multiple choice questions about participants' habits using social media, such as "How often do you check Instagram in a typical day?" (see Table 1).

The second questionnaire was also electronically distributed by their instructor via Google Forms. Students were given 30 minutes for completion questionnaire after they completed the last task of the Instagram project. This questionnaire was constructed based on the instructional framework of bridging activities to examine participants' perspectives on their experiences in obtaining the five learning objectives throughout the project. The first variable was measured by asking a question on how participants perceived Instagram as a meaningful communication platform, intending to examine participants' awareness of specific linguistic choices and genre specificity in relation to the online social and cultural context (see Table 1 for survey questions). Another variable was measured by asking a question on how participants will use Instagram for professional purposes in the future, intending to understand participants' willingness to use this platform outside of school in their future professional art careers. A five-point Likert scale was used to ask general questions about how participants perceived this project, and open-ended questions were used to elaborate on their perspectives. The first stage of data analysis used the Likert scale questions coded from strongly disagree (1) to strongly agree (5), with some variation based on the nature of the question (i.e., very unlikely to very likely, or very uncomfortable to very comfortable). Researchers then examined the open-ended questions that corresponded to selected Likert scale responses for further analysis of whether participants will use this platform for more meaningful communication and for professional purposes in the out-of-school settings. Cross-tabulation was also performed to compare responses from different groups based on demographic data in the first part of the questionnaire. The cross-tabulation was analyzed by using SPSS software to further understand the relationships between the previous experiences of using Instagram and ELLs' perspectives on (1) how this platform can foster meaningful communication and (2) expanding the purpose of using it to a broader context as in their professional fields. The first variable was selected in the first survey about "the frequency of using Instagram on a typical day". The four categories were coded as "I do not check social media most days", "once a day", "2-4 times a day", and "5 or more times a day". The other two variables were selected in the second survey asking questions, such as "Do you think this project is a meaningful way to use English to communicate with others?" and "Do you think you will continue to read and post comments on Instagram for your professional purpose (creative industries) in the future?" Each of these items were coded as 5-point Likert scale (from strongly disagree coded as 1 to strongly agree coded as 5).

Four participants volunteered to participate in a 30-minute follow-up individual interview: "Han," an Arts Management major from China; "Maria," Journalism major from Russia; "Juan," a filmmaking major from Ecuador; and "Jin," a Cinema Art and Science major from China. The interview questions and the protocol were based on the content participants posted on Instagram and the comments they wrote on their post-task questionnaire. Participants were asked to describe their language use (i.e., choice, content and stylistic specifics of the texts and images) in their Instagram posts, their awareness of genre specificity while interacting on Instagram, and how the relevance of this project to their communicative lives outside of the classroom. Participants were asked to read the content they wrote and to elaborate on their experience working on this model.

Regarding the qualitative data, interview transcriptions and open-ended responses from questionnaire were further analyzed and coded. Two researchers analyzed and coded the data separately, then later discussed emerging themes together, establishing patterns (Miles, Huberman, & Saldaña, 2014). To develop more detailed naturalistic generalizations (Creswell, 2007) about the three selected case studies, content analysis of participants' Instagram posts was further conducted. While coding the Instagram data, a priori coding based on the five bridging-activities learning objectives was applied in content analysis. This guide was established to define codes to ensure both researchers were consistent throughout the coding process. Posts of selected cases were independently coded by each of two researchers, and then discrepancies were discussed together.

RESULTS AND DISCUSSION

RQ1: Instagram as a Meaningful Way of Communication for Professional Purposes

To answer the first question regarding the relationships between ELLs' Instagram use with how they perceive Instagram as a meaningful way of communication for professional purposes, cross-tabulation was performed to compare responses from different groups based on the two questionnaires participants completed before and after the project. The question "How often do you check Instagram in a typical day?" from the first set of the questionnaire and two variables from Likert scale questions retrieved from the second part of the questionnaire were used for the cross-tabulation analysis (see descriptive statistics in Table 1). The following sections first analyze data from the post-task questionnaire, then present findings from the cross-tabulation.

Frequency of Using Instagram and ELLs' Perceptions of Meaningful Communication

While the descriptive statistics showed overwhelmingly positive perspectives, a cross-tabulation of these factors was further analyzed to examine other insights that could be gained. The first comparison investigated the relationship between the frequency of using Instagram and participants' perceptions of the platform as a meaningful communicative tool in out-of-school literacy practices. Participants evaluated whether the use of Instagram had a positive or negative impact, or no impact at all. Figure 5 illustrates that there was no linear correlation between the frequency of Instagram use and participants' perspectives of the platform as a meaningful communicative tool across all four groups. However, there was a majority of positive views across all four groups. Among the four groups, only "I don't check social

Table 1. Descriptive statistics

Questions	n	%
How often do you check Instagram in a typical day?		
I do not check social media most days	8	19.05%
Once a day	8	19.05%
2-4 times a day	7	16.67%
5 or more times a day	19	45.23%
Do you think this project (posting and responding comments/images on Instagram) is a meaningful way to use English to communicate with others?		
Disagree strongly	2	4.76%
Disagree	1	2.39%
Neutral	7	16.67%
Agree	13	30.95%
Agree strongly	19	45.23%
Do you think you will continue to read and post comments on Instagram for your professional purpose (creative industries) in the future?		
Disagree strongly	1	2.39%
Disagree	5	11.90%
Neutral	8	19.05%
Agree	9	21.43%
Agree strongly	19	45.23%

Note. N=42.

media most days" and "5 or more times" groups had negative responses. Compared to 5.26% negative views in "5 or more times" group, "I don't check social media most days" group had 25% negative views. With the highest negative views from the group that uses Instagram the least, these results indicate that when ELLs have limited prior online experience of a platform or encounter a new technology, there may be resistance and learning curves during the process. Instructors should be aware that social media platforms that many students rely on daily are "complex and require decoding," and that there are many new approaches to represent language, data, knowledge, and forms of communication that require learner training in order to use them in meaningful ways (Kessler, 2013, p. 308).

The study also examined data from open-ended questions and interviews to better understand participants' explanations. Participants with positive responses stated that the power of multimodal communicative platforms allowed them to use not only written texts but also images and sounds to express themselves and their art. Jin stated in the interview that Instagram has become a fundamental device to showcase her documentaries and photographs. It also offers a platform for her to connect with people and is particularly useful for language learners because, in her words, "if someone didn't get what I mean, they can see the pictures or art I posted. It helps them imagine the situation better. Sometimes images are louder than words in this type of social media." For students who responded negatively, the open-ended questionnaire data revealed that some students were skeptical of interaction on digital platforms like Instagram replacing face-to-face communication and networking. According to one participant, "While an efficient form of communication, Instagram cannot replace personal interaction and speech as communication." Participants felt this platform was simply a tool for self-advertisement and building networks but should not become a main method for communication.

The overall results indicate that the more experience ELLs have using Instagram and engaging in Instagram activities, the more likely they have positive and successful learning experiences on this project. The findings support the previous literature that ELLs' prior online experiences positively influence their language socialization and help them become active participants in the target language community (Thorne, 2003, 2005; Thorne, Black, & Sykes, 2009), as well as numerous research findings that suggest previous learning experience with technology has a strong impact on participation in online or computer-assisted language learning curricula (Liu, Chen, Sun, Wible, & Kuo, 2010; Reed & Oughton, 1997; Reed, Oughton, Ayersman, Ervin, & Giessler, 2000). Therefore, language instructors should provide more opportunities for this type of meaningful communicative practice so that ELLs can develop critical awareness of out-of-school literacy practices, such as the knowledge of how to build their online portfolio, effectively use hashtags to branch out to new networks, communicate with other artists in their field, and access the latest news about art events and exhibitions. Instructors should also be sure to provide adequate learner training before using social media tools like Instagram, and provide scaffolded practice and exploration opportunities so that less experienced users can build up familiarity with the tool before being expected to fully participate in such new environments.

Figure 5. ELLs' perceptions of meaningful communication on Instagram

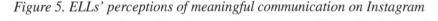
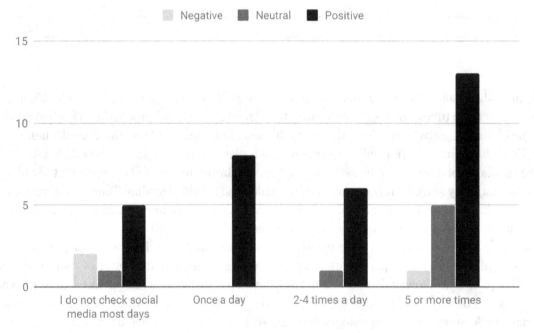

Frequency of Using Instagram and ELLs' Perceptions of Using it for Professional Purposes

The second comparison investigated the relationship between the frequency of using Instagram and participants' perceptions of using it for professional purposes in the future. Figure 6 shows that there is no positive linear correlation between the frequency of Instagram use and participants' perspectives of using Instagram for professional purposes in the future across all four groups. Most of the groups had a majority of positive responses except the "once a day" group, where positive and neutral responses were even and negative responses were close behind. Negative responses were present across all four groups; however, compared to the other three groups, the "5 or more times" group had the lowest percentage of 10.53% negative views. The findings revealed the students who had positive responses in the more experienced user groups, "2-4 times a day" and "5 or more times," were able to articulate in the open-ended responses that they use Instagram for building networks and interact with other artists in their fields.

The study further analyzed the qualitative data from the open-ended questionnaire and interviews and found reasons participants would use Instagram for future professional purposes included the affordances of being able to access to other artists' work and follow the latest gallery exhibitions or film screening events. Many participants were inspired by being able to reach out to other artists and talk about their work. Participants viewed this platform as a self-promotion and marketing tool they could use to build a portfolio for their future creative industry career. However, many participants were concerned about privacy and were hesitant to share their art and ideas online. Further, some ELLs cannot use Instagram in their home country; for instance, Han stated in the interview, "If I want to build networks with other artists, I will not choose Instagram because I cannot use it in China. I prefer using WeChat so after I graduate and go back home, I can still access it." A minority of participants like Han experienced decreased motivation in using this tool because they viewed it as not relevant to their future careers. Future studies could avoid this by allowing students to choose the platforms they see as relevant, but that would remove the benefit of sharing a common platform and easily accessing other participants' contributions.

The results of this first research question support the previous literature in that the more experienced users of technology were able to use the Instagram platform for multiple purposes that could potentially lead to better outcomes than merely use it for a single purpose such as viewing it as only a tool for entertainment (DiMaggio & Hargittai, 2001; Warschauer, 2003). For instance, experienced users may use technology to seek better job opportunities by building professional networks and online portfolios on social media, exchanging viewpoints in social and political issues, and engaging in meaningful communication such as participating in civic engagement and social justice issues (Warschauer, 2003).

In contrast, students who did not use the platform frequently struggled with anxiety and lack of confidence in interacting with other users. One participant in the "once a day" group reported that he found it frustrating to navigate the platform and was very anxious about how other people would comment on his posts. This student was not a frequent user of this platform but was very conscious of his performance and tried to improve it throughout the project. This finding supports previous literature that students seeking active participation in online target language platforms could benefit from more exposure to such environments through learner training that integrates these platforms into the curriculum (Hubbard & Levy, 2006; Prensky, 2007). The group that "does not check social media most days" had higher positive responses than the "once a day" group, potentially because participants in this group were mostly novice users and reported in the post-task questionnaire that they had very limited knowledge of this platform. Whether people reacted positively or negatively on their posts did not bother them because they regarded Instagram as an informal platform, or in the words of one student a "new toy" that was not seen as a formal school assignment.

Figure 6. ELLs' perceptions of using Instagram for professional purposes in the future

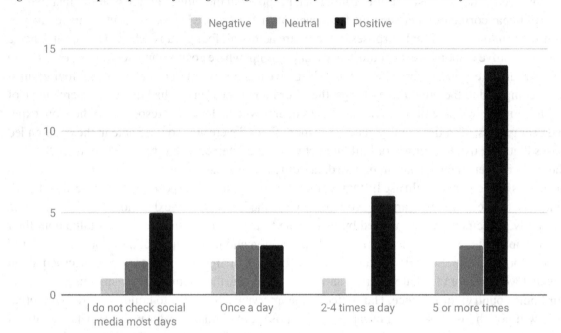

RQ2: Five Learning Objectives in the Bridging-Activities Framework

To answer the second research question on how the multimodal digital storytelling model helps ELLs achieve the learning objectives of bridging-activities framework, the following sections present the stories of Maria, Han, and Emma, with the goal of illustrating the ways in which they negotiate and connect in-school and out-of-school literacy practices, especially branching out of the ESL classroom to their professional creative industry fields. Based on the five learning objectives in the bridging-activities framework, researchers analyzed the qualitative data including participants' Instagram posts, post-task questionnaires, and individual follow-up interviews to gain an in-depth understanding of the extent to which these three ELLs achieved the learning objectives through the multimodal digital storytelling project. The selection of these three case studies was based on the complexity and richness of these participants' Instagram posts. Thematic content analysis of Instagram posts, open-ended questionnaire, and reflections in the individual interviews was used to determine whether ELLs were able to successfully carry the skills that they have learned in class to environments outside the classroom (i.e., the five learning objectives). The following Table 2 provided information of ELLs' perspectives of the skills they learned through this model and how they demonstrate achievement of the bridging-activities learning outcomes. The emerging themes were collected and coded from interview and open-ended data.

Table 2. ELLs' perspectives of the skills they learned through this model and how they demonstrate achievement of the bridging-activities learning outcomes

Bridging-Activities Learning Outcomes	Emerging Themes From Students' Perspectives of the Skills They Obtained Through This Project
Understand specific linguistic choices associated with desired social-communicative actions.	Identifying who the target audience is and who would be interested in the post by effectively using hashtags (i.e., selecting the right keywords) to communicate with other users. Connecting the Instagram content students post to a broader social justice issue to raise awareness of their artwork.
Become more aware of genre specificity.	Writing in different genres that students will use in their future career; for instance, students in journalism majors practicing writing news blurbs on Instagram. Using specific genre and writing style in multimodal forms to promote their art and relate art to people's daily lives.
Participate in existing and future genres of plurilingual and transcultural language use.	Relating one's own culture to other people's culture and advocating for their rights. Using Instagram posts as a message to introduce their own heritage and cultural norms to other users' from different cultural backgrounds.
Bridge toward relevance to students' communicative lives outside of the classroom.	Seeing multiple purposes for the use of social media; for instance, use it to look for job opportunities, make connections with potential employers, meet future collaborators, and build online portfolios. Being able to not only critically evaluate and access useful information but also use social media to exchange and communicate with other users outside of the classroom.
Increase student agency in relation to the choice, content, and stylistic specifics of the texts contributing to the language learning process.	Understanding how the use of language and word choice on Instagram could affect other users' responses. Connecting with the target audience by using genre and stylistic specifics of the texts.

Case Study of Maria

Maria was from a metropolitan city in Russia and had been in Chicago for a year before she participated in this project. Her previous school and work experience in the U.S. were her first real opportunity to communicate in the target language. Since there were not a lot of Russian students at school, she had to speak English the majority of the time. Maria was confident in her oral language proficiency and actively participated in class discussions. However, she was struggling with her writing, especially in the writing genre of her professional field of journalism.

A trajectory of growth in Maria's critical awareness of social media practices and context-appropriate language use was apparent through her posts and interview data. In Maria's first post observing other journalists' work on Instagram, she wrote her description using a first-person narrative. She briefly described the image and the news of her post but failed to recognize the potential target audience that might be interested in the image. The use of language was formal but contained redundant content and lack of key words and effective use of hashtags. Maria was not aware of the specific internet-mediated text genres while posting her assignment, which required more practices of social-communicative actions to understand the concept of specific language choices. Maria discussed in the interview that she used formal language in her first assignment posting and tried to be careful in selecting keywords but was not sure what type of words can effectively catch the attention of a wider audience, so she used very general terms for hashtags. This ended up attracting several unrelated comments.

Every week, the class discussed students' posts in small groups for reflection and feedback from the instructor and peers. This was an important practice because students were able to reflect on their postings. In the second assignment about exploring students' selected creative industry in Chicago, Maria decided to put some meaning into her project. "Chicago is a very liberal city compared to many regions in the U.S. and also my home country so I am very interested in exploring issues related to social justice and interview protesters," she wrote. She chose to write her content as a journalist, which was what she was working towards becoming. This result showcases how she was developing the literacy skills (e.g., multimodal writing skills, media literacy, and genre specificity) that she will need in her future professional career outside of the classroom. She was able to achieve enhanced agency in relation to the choice and content specifics of the texts, contributing to not only her language learning development but also her communicative life outside of the classroom.

Maria continued the theme of social justice in her third assignment and interviewed a filmmaker for a feature film called "May I Be at Peace." The film advocates for the social support of patients with eating disorders by telling the story of a seventeen-year-old girl suffering with the disease. In this assignment, Maria showed that her critical awareness of social media practices had increased because she was able to consider who her readers were and how certain texts worked well for specific purposes. For instance, she tried to help promote and advertise this film, but her ultimate goal was to advocate for patients with eating disorders. Maria stated in her interview that she became more aware that the benefits of using Instagram are not only for entertainment but also more meaningful communication and reaching out to more people.

The last assignment was to showcase participants' artwork in their creative industry field. Maria posted about a project where she was invited to a local talk show and worked with the professional camera crew and audio board team. Compared to the first assignment post, which was also a first-person narration, Maria became more mature and aware of how platforms like Instagram powerful tools and how certain texts could be worked for specific purposes to influence the target audience in various ways. "I need to be aware of the way I write and how I present myself in the text and images, especially if I become a journalist one day." The multimodal digital storytelling project seemed to contribute to Maria's learning process by allowing her to participate in genres within digital contexts and enhancing her critical awareness of social literacy practices, both in-school and out-of-school.

Case Study of Han

Han was a freshman who had never studied in the U.S. before this project; however, she was very motivated and tried to actively participate in class discussions. Han took each assignment very seriously, which showed in her writing, postings, and final presentation. In the interview, Han revealed that she took her Instagram posting project to the Tutoring Center to work on her writing. She also practiced more than 20 times for her presentation. She was not very confident in her language skills; however, due to her effort, she always achieved high academic performance.

Differing from Maria, Han was very intentional and conscious of language use in her posts in the very beginning of the project. She chose to use very formal language that was rarely seen on Instagram. She carefully proofread each post and ensured the content was fruitful and relevant to the target audience. For instance, in the first task introducing an artist's work posted on Instagram, Han had already understood the importance of social communicative action in this type of platform. She introduced a painting by Li Jin which depicted China's Mogao Grottoes. Rather than solely introduce the painting like the majority of her classmates, she drew readers' attention to the wider issue of protecting Chinese World Heritage sites. She described the art piece objectively and stated that her her mission as an Art Management major was to bring awareness of the World Heritage art pieces to the general public. Her text and image showed that she took into consideration who would be interested in this issue, so she carefully considered the use of hashtags throughout the whole text. Although the use of hashtags was not able to attract many users, it successfully narrowed the potential audience to people who were actually eager to learn more about the piece.

In the second task Han introduced another historical landmark, the Chicago Water Tower, and introduced the history of the Chicago fire and the Gothic architecture design. Han was aware of the specific genre and writing style, which was a type of writing she learned from her Art Management class: introducing, critiquing, analyzing, and connecting art to people's daily lives. This project showcased her ability to apply skills that she learned at school into her professional field to communicate with people who were less familiar with the topic.

During the weekly peer feedback and discussion with peers, Han was a little confused about the formal way she approached this project. "It seems like I am the only few people who wrote very long texts and used very serious tones," said Han. She was then skeptical about her postings and didn't think people had time to read her long texts. She was conflicted because she had been very intentional in her linguistic choices associated with desired social-communicative actions. Han still wanted to use this platform to convey messages about art history and World Heritage, but she realized that instead of introducing too much detailed information she should highlight the main points she wanted to express. In the third and fourth tasks, Han tended to use fewer professional terms so the text was easier to read and be understood by the general public. This change from focusing on a more specific audience to wanting more of the general public to relate to her work indicated Han was able to understand how certain texts and genres work well for specific purposes, and that she was learning how to apply this to her future career.

Case Study of Emma

As a filmmaking major, Emma was very fond of creative works such as photography, movies, and poetry. This project provided a creative space for her to express herself through her photographs and poems.

Deliberately choosing poetry as a specific genre and consistently using it to express her thoughts, Emma attempted to raise awareness of genre specificity and context-appropriate language use. Although students were asked to write short descriptions of their posts, Emma opted to write poetry instead. Despite poetry being a more demanding genre requiring higher order language skills, Emma firmly decided to raise her voice through her poetry. Each of her poems vividly describe the sentiments of the people in the photographs. Not only did she choose poetry as a writing genre, but she intentionally chose the genre of black and white photography. The example of her purposeful selection of these writing and photography genres showed her awareness of choosing specific styles and content relevant to her language learning process, interests, and future career. It appears that Emma was intending to increase her agency, presence, and connection to the specific photography community that appreciated poetry and black and white photographs. Additionally, unlike Han and Maria, Emma did not use first person perspective to communicate to her audience. She was talking from the perspective of the person in the photo, as seen in the example in Figure 7.

Emma did not fully adhere to the assignment guidelines, but decided to choose a specific genre to connect to the audience and community she was interested in. This poses a question and a challenge for an instructor: whether to acknowledge students' contributions in any form or require specific guidelines to be followed consistently throughout the project. Since one of the ultimate goals of digital storytelling is to allow students greater agency and autonomy, it may be beneficial to allow students flexibility in how strictly they adhere to the assignment guidelines in some cases, rather than forcing them to be confined by rigid rules. However, if students' creativity is keeping them from achieving the learning objectives, they may need to be redirected toward the assignment guidelines.

Figure 7. Example of Emma's post

Pedagogical Implications

Despite the fact that many ELLs have been using social media platforms such as Instagram on a daily basis, the findings showed that more time is needed to develop cyberpragmatics of internet-mediated text genres. The case studies of both Maria and Han indicated they became more aware of language use in different genres and adjusted their linguistic choices associated with their social-communicative actions over time. Maria learned to become a more sophisticated writer within her journalism field, gaining understanding of how certain text types work well for specific purposes and certain audience. Meanwhile, Han had been very aware of genre specificity and context-appropriate language use during the whole process of the project but learned to bridge her language use toward relevance to her communicative lives outside of the classroom in her arts management field.

Implications of this study also suggest that language instructors should understand the power of multimodal communicative platforms in how they allow ELLs to use multiple ways to express themselves and further connect to others. Furthermore, creating meaningful communicative curricula and practices like the multimodal digital storytelling model to enhance ELLs' critical awareness and connect in-school and out-of-school literacy practices could help students develop skills to be more comfortable and confident when participating in real-world interaction. However, language instructors should keep in mind that regardless of how frequent ELLs use social media, many of them still prefer face-to-face communicative practices. While social media platforms like Instagram could potentially foster understanding of internet-mediated text genres and awareness of context-appropriate language use, it is a tool for facilitating the language learning development but should not replace the face-to-face interaction.

While implementing this model, learning objectives should be established and explained at the beginning of the course so that students understand the assignment guidelines. Instructors should also be explicit regarding how much freedom students have while posting in the digital wilds. As seen from Emma's case, she did not follow the task guideline but decided to post what she believed would communicate with her audience. Instructors could also provide options for students to choose whether they prefer using their existing personal account or create a new account for this project. In the present study, many students reported that it is more authentic to use their original accounts so that they can connect with more people.

LIMITATIONS AND FUTURE STUDIES

While this project yielded insights into the implementation of Instagram as a tool used in an ESL classroom, future studies can strengthen the findings in several ways. Although the participants were heterogeneous in terms of language proficiency levels, disciplines, and cultural backgrounds, the sample size was too small to divide participants into groups for further comparison and generalization. Therefore, future studies with larger sample sizes of learners from diverse backgrounds could further investigate how differences in language proficiency, cultural background, gender, and age may result in different learning experiences.

Another limitation of this study is that it asked students to think about their future digital practices but did not examine data on their actual practices outside of the classroom; however, future longitudinal studies could further examine the effectiveness of how students actually use the skills they learned in their real-life professional fields. Future studies should also consider tracking ELLs' trajectory of engagement in their language learning while using Instagram over a longer period of time. This project only examined ELLs' posts over six weeks. However, a follow-up study tracking students' engagement on Instagram to establish trends and more valid conclusions is needed. Since our project only included four interviews, we suggest future studies consider more follow-up interviews or focus group interviews with all participants to gain a more in-depth understanding of their learning experience. This could also provide more opportunities for ELLs to experience the three-phase cycle of activities.

CONCLUSION

This study uses a digital tool to help ELLs bridge in-school literacy practices with their professional fields. By using multimodal forms, the project encourages ELLs to express their artwork through images and texts, allowing them to seek more opportunities to connect with other artists in similar fields. While this project uses Instagram and art, it is just one example of how instructors can combine digital tools and students' personal interests to help language learners connect what they do in class with their everyday lives, leading to more sustained changes in their literacy practices.

REFERENCES

Anggraeni, C. W. (2017). Students Perspectives toward the Use of Instagram in Writing Class. In *Proceedings from the 2017 English Language and Literature International Conference (ELLiC)* (Vol. 1, pp. 68–74). Academic Press.

Bull, G., & Kajder, S. (2005). Digital storytelling in the language arts classroom. *Learning and Leading with Technology, 32*(4), 46–49.

Byrnes, H. (2007). Locating the advanced learner in theory, research, and educational practice: An introduction. In H. Byrnes, H. Weger-Guntharp, & K. Sprang (Eds.), Educating for advanced foreign language capacities: Constructs, curriculum, instruction, assessment. Academic Press.

Carter, R. (1998). Orders of reality: CANCODE, communication, and culture. *ELT Journal, 52*(1), 43–56. doi:10.1093/elt/52.1.43

Creswell, J. W. (2007). *Qualitative inquiry and research method: Choosing among five approaches.* Thousand Oaks, CA: Sage Publications.

DiMaggio, P., & Hargittai, E. (2001). From the 'digital divide' to 'digital inequality': Studying Internet use as penetration increases. Princeton: Center for Arts and Cultural Policy Studies.

Eroglu, F., & Bayraktar Kose, E. (2019). Utilization of online influencers as an experiential marketing tool: A case of Instagram micro-celebrities. *Journal of International Social Research, 12*(63), 1057–1067. doi:10.17719/jisr.2019.3297

Garifova, L. F. (2016). Realization of small businesses economic interests on Instagram. *Journal of Economics and Economic Education Research, 17*(Special Issue), 133–139.

Halliday, M. A. K., & Matthiesen, C. (2004). *An introduction to functional grammar.* London: Arnold.

Hubbard, P., & Levy, M. (Eds.). (2006). *Teacher Education in CALL.* Amsterdam: John Benjamins. doi:10.1075/lllt.14

Jurij, A. (2019). Insta-story for personal branding and product promotion. *MASTERCOM-Politehnica Graduate Student Journal of Communication, 4*(1).

Kessler, G. (2013). Collaborative language learning in co-constructed participatory culture. *CALICO, 30*(3), 307–322. doi:10.11139/cj.30.3.307-322

Liu, I., Chen, M. C., Sun, Y. S., Wible, D., & Kuo, C. (2010). Extending the TAM model to explore the factors that affect Intention to Use an Online Learning Community. *Computers & Education, 54*(2), 600–610. doi:10.1016/j.compedu.2009.09.009

Mansor, N., & Rahim, N. A. (2017). Instagram in ESL classroom. *Man in India, 97*(20), 107–114.

Miles, M. B., Huberman, A. M., & Saldaña, J. (2014). *Qualitative data analysis: A methods sourcebook* (4th ed.). Thousand Oaks, CA: Sage.

New London Group. (1996). A pedagogy of multiliteracies. *Harvard Educational Review, 66*(1), 60–92. doi:10.17763/haer.66.1.17370n67v22j160u

Prasetyawati, O. A. (2018). *The use of Instagram to promote student engagement in basic writing class* [Doctoral dissertation]. Sanata Dharma University. Retrieved from https://core.ac.uk/download/pdf/157574463.pdf

Prensky, M. (2007). *Digital game-based learning*. St. Paul, MN: Paragon House.

Raice, S., & Ante, S. E. (2012, April 10). Insta-rich: $1 billion for Instagram. *The Wall Street Journal Europe Ed.* Retrieved from: https://www.wsj.com/articles/SB10001424052702303815404577333840377381670

Reed, W. M., & Oughton, J. M. (1997). Computer experience and interval-based hypermedia navigation. *Journal of Research on Computing in Education, 30*(1), 38–52. doi:10.1080/08886504.1997.10782212

Reed, W. M., Oughton, J. M., Ayersman, D. J., Ervin, J. R. Jr, & Giessler, S. F. (2000). Computer experience, learning style, and hypermedia navigation. *Computers in Human Behavior, 16*(6), 619–628. doi:10.1016/S0747-5632(00)00026-1

Reinhardt, J., & Thorne, S. (2011). Beyond comparisons: Frameworks for developing digital L2 literacies. In N. Arnold, & L. Ducate (Eds.), Present and future promises of CALL: From theory and research to new directions in language teaching (pp. 257–280). CALICO.

Reinhardt, J., & Zander, V. (2011). Social networking in an intensive English program classroom: A language socialization perspective. *CALICO Journal, 28*(2), 326–344. doi:10.11139/cj.28.2.326-344

Reyburn, S. (2017, January 20). Art market mines gold on Instagram. *The New York Times*. Retrieved from https://www.nytimes.com/2017/01/20/arts/art-auction-instagram.html

Salomon, D. (2013). Moving on from Facebook Using Instagram to connect with undergraduates and engage in teaching and learning. *College & Research Libraries News, 74*(8), 408–412. doi:10.5860/crln.74.8.8991

Skinner, E. N., & Hagood, M. C. (2008). Developing literate identities with English language learners through digital storytelling. *Reading Matrix: An International Online Journal, 8*(2), 12–38.

Thorne, S. L. (2003). Artifacts and cultures-of-use in intercultural communication. *Language Learning & Technology, 7*(2), 38–67.

Thorne, S. L. (2005). Epistemology, politics, and ethics in sociocultural theory. *Modern Language Journal, 89*(3), 393–409. doi:10.1111/j.1540-4781.2005.00313.x

Thorne, S. L., Black, R. W., & Sykes, J. (2009). Second language use, socialization, and learning in internet interest communities and online games. *Modern Language Journal, 93*, 802–821. doi:10.1111/j.1540-4781.2009.00974.x

Thorne, S. L., & Reinhardt, J. (2008). Bridging activities, new media literacies, and advanced foreign language proficiency. *CALICO Journal, 25*(3), 558–572. doi:10.1558/cj.v25i3.558-572

Thorne, S. L., Sauro, S., & Smith, B. (2015). Technologies, identities, and expressive activity. *Annual Review of Applied Linguistics, 35*, 215–233. doi:10.1017/S0267190514000257

Thorne, S. L., & Smith, B. (2011). Second language development theories and technology-mediated language learning. *CALICO Journal*, *28*(2), 268–277. doi:10.11139/cj.28.2.268-277

Warschauer, M. (2003). *Technology and social inclusion: Rethinking the digital divide*. Cambridge, MA: The MIT Press.

Yus, F. (2011). *Cyberpragmatics: Internet-mediated communication in context*. Amsterdam, Philadelphia: John Benjamins Publishing Company. doi:10.1075/pbns.213

Zheng, B., & Warschauer, M. (2017). Epilogue: Second language writing in the age of computer-mediated communication. *Journal of Second Language Writing*, *36*, 61–67. doi:10.1016/j.jslw.2017.05.014

This research was previously published in the International Journal of Computer-Assisted Language Learning and Teaching (IJCALLT), 10(3); pages 48-66, copyright year 2020 by IGI Publishing (an imprint of IGI Global).

Chapter 9
Using Social Media for Dynamic Information Dissemination in the 21st Century

Fredrick Olatunji Ajegbomogun
(iD) https://orcid.org/0000-0001-8471-7794
Olusegun Agagu University of Science and Technology, Nigeria

ABSTRACT

The implementation and usage of information and communication technology (ICT) in library functions and facilities has revolutionized the way people use information and librarians perform their work. As a result of the advent of social media, the world's knowledge outlook has changed significantly, resulting in the sharing of thoughts, emotions, images, and videos as resources. A library is worth considering; it is a key to learning, a foundation for long-term mastery of information, and it promotes independent decision-making. The use of social media in library activities has enticed a significant number of users, but it has also challenged libraries to modernize their service delivery. Facebook, Twitter, Wikis, WhatsApp, MySpace, and LinkedIn facilitate community courses, collaboration, and information sharing. As a consequence, it is vital for libraries to consider and prioritize their users' needs.

INTRODUCTION

The advent and application of information and communication technology (ICT) in library functions and services has brought about a revolution in the use of information and librarians' job performance. Hence, the information outlook of the world has changed drastically as a result of this invention of social media, further resulting in the exchange of ideas, feelings, pictures, and videos as tools for knowledge acquisition. Among the present innovations in Information and Communication Technology (ICT) are the social media, which stands out among the best in the group of internet-based applications and is built on the ideological and technological foundations of Web 2.0 which allows the creation of user-generated content (Kaplan & Haenlein 2010). The Media and MediaLive International Conference that was held

DOI: 10.4018/978-1-6684-7123-4.ch009

in San Francisco, October 2004, Tim O'Reilly and his colleagues presented Web 2.0 and its features as a forum for information interaction. In 2016, Lim Berners Lee proposed Web 3.0 that features reading, writing, and knowledge application in the social realm.

The main goal of Web 3.0 technology is to make it easier for web users to contribute information in a way that computers can understand, process, and share. These advancements in Web technology would enable Web applications to perform time-saving tasks such as collating data from various sources and assisting users inefficiently searching for specific information based on their needs. The rapid increase in the number of semantic markups available on the Web, the number of organizations beginning to conduct research and development activities in the field, and the number of Web 3.0 applications that now exist in recent years has prompted rising interest in the new generation of Web. Technologies have changed the traditional way of education to the modern way of learning, like artificial intelligence (Di Vaio et al. 2020). This merger is primarily concerned with the development and upkeep of world models that allow reasoning about themselves and their associated data (Lassila & Hendler, 2017). Web 3.0 provides an opportunity for knowledge connection and use. Since then, the growing dimension and the use of social media among students and researchers have been overwhelming.

As of March 31, 2019, Facebook registered 2.38 billion monthly active users and 1.56 billion daily active users (Facebook 2019). In 2022, the total number of social media users is expected to reach 3.29 billion, accounting for 42.3 percent of the global population (eMarketer 2018). Given the enormous potential audience that spends several hours a day on social media across multiple channels. Social media has also been adopted by academics, with a large body of work on social media marketing and related topics. People can now be reached more easily. Social media "gives people the power to build community and bring the world closer together. Use Facebook to stay connected with friends and family, to discover what's going on in the world, and to share and express what matters to them "(Facebook 2019).

Social media is a multi-dimensional instrument that enables knowledge sharing through discussions, communication, and collaboration with other scholars in the social space. For example, social media has been discovered to pervade some scholars' lives as well as to be used in specific goal-oriented ways (Matikiti, Kruger, and Saayman (2019). When researchers use social media to create and disseminate information, we see a wide variety of activities to help them achieve their goals. The use of social media has enhanced the re-engineering of library service delivery in conformity with users' new ways of using library resources. Thus, this makes it possible for students, teachers, professionals, and other interested users to search and access information in various databases that are capable of meeting their information needs. Through social media, researchers all over the world are involved in the conversation and sharing of their research work. This interaction and how information is presented depend on the varied perspectives as people share information freely, discuss and interact with each other. Social media tools are widely accessible and utilized by various categories of people, ranging from researchers to students. It plays a crucial role in the creation of a user's social media network. A user's engagement in social media may be motivated by more than just information. Social networking digital content is often produced and posted to elicit reactions.

Social media facilitates collaborative and interactive learning in schools, thereby offering unique opportunities to students and promoting socialization among members in the institutional environment. This, in turn, leads to the accomplishment of the institutional goals. It is therefore imperative for users to be acquainted with the various social media tools available. They should be able to access information and judiciously utilize it when conducting any research, because most users in the online space prefer chatting with friends, sharing knowledge, and engaging in various social activities.

The study is premised on the theory and its application in enhancing the use of social media for dynamic information dissemination in the 21st century. The Media System Dependency (MSD) theory was initially introduced by Sandra Ball-Rokeach and Melvin Defleur in 1976. The theory is aimed at studying the effects of the media on the audience, individual and social environment as they depend on one another. Similarly, each element relies on the other segments by depending on common resources to fulfill their goals. Specific consideration is given to the resources of media systems in modern society while an increase or decrease in individuals' reliance on the media systems determines their use. Essentially, the Media Systems Dependency theory is the ability of a medium to satisfy the needs of individuals as much as possible, thus making an individual depend more on such a medium as long as it can meet their needs.

BACKGROUND AND LITERATURE REVIEW

The Media Systems Dependency theory, as stated by Baran (2010), as cited in Eke, Omekwu, and Odoh (2014), states that the more a person relies on a specific medium to meet his or her needs, the more important the role of the media in such individual's life, and thus the greater the impact of the media on the individual. People turn to the media to communicate, interact and make them aware of happenings in their environment. The more an individual depends on the media for the sharing of thoughts, ideas, and opinions, the more impact the media has on the individual. Again, the more we rely on social media, the more our attitudes, cognition, our emotional states or behavior are influenced by social media. By implication, researchers and scholars will use a particular social media site if such a site is capable of meeting their research and information needs. Thus, the media system dependency theory also incorporates collaborative learning and this is commonly illustrated when groups of people work together to seek understanding, meaning, or solution or a product of their learning, which includes group projects, joint problem solving, and other activities. It is through interacting that learning occurs and development is guaranteed.

People develop dependency relationships with the media or media that appear to be the most supportive in the pursuit of their goals because they expect the media system to assist them in achieving their goals and meeting their research and information needs. The strength of this theory and its relevance to this work lies in the acceptance of social media technology by library users, with emphasis on social media interactions to meet individual needs. Having a positive attitude towards technology use encourages greater achievement in the area of research publications. According to Chua and Goh (2010), there are different ways technologies are adopted, used, and applied in various sectors of life. By describing these differences, scholars have not only been able to understand the access rates of certain social media tools in some regions but have also acquired insight into the potential environmental and contextual factors shaping the use or non-use of these applications. In addition, people should get acquainted with the use of the social networking tools they feel at ease with which will assist them in accomplishing their scholarly research.

In recent times, researchers on social media and university libraries have focused on the ability of librarians to promote services to remain relevant to the users and achieve a new level of interactivity between library personnel and users. According to Scale and Quan-Haase (2012), social media tools, such as Facebook, WhatsApp, Twitter, Blogs, and Wikis, have been viewed as good ways to disseminate information. Over the years, social networking has become more popular among students. It is a way of connecting students not only on campus but with friends outside their domain. Social media sites are tools that enable people to feel as if they belong to a community because of their collaborative, interactive, and participatory features (Owusu-Acheaw & Larson, 2015). Social media does not merely allow knowledge transfer but also facilitates students' collaborative learning to create understanding among students, discussion with peers, lecturers, increase knowledge sharing and improve students' research skills (Redecker et al., 2010).

The current generation primarily use social media tools for social purposes and entertainment but may be less familiar with information-seeking skills on the Web or the methods to use and access digital resources. Therefore, it is the responsibility of libraries to direct their operations towards this new technological development. A lot of studies have been done by researchers on the general usability of social media among students in tertiary institutions. Findings from these studies revealed that the adoption of social technologies is not an easy and straightforward process, but it is immensely helpful in their research exercise which has to be undergone by every student before completing their program in such institutions of learning. According to Matikiti, Kruger, and Saayman (2019), social media has evolved into a virtual portal that enables individuals to communicate with one another and create communities to quickly exchange information. Several earlier studies have shown evidence that efforts should be made by researchers and postgraduate students to start utilizing social media for educational activities.

Adewojo and Adebara (2018) believe that the advent of ICTs and associated resources such as social media has changed the data distribution mode concerning libraries. Jones and Harvey (2019) said social media is the best method for interacting with future library patrons. Furthermore, successful library customers may use social media to advertise their libraries in a flexible virtual environment. Social media is the all-time greatest revaluation of the knowledge age. The most effective cybernetic platform for promoting library programs is social media (Chai and Harper, 2019). Hence, lecturers and supervisors looking to incorporate social media in their instructional methods should make sure that the social media type used is aligned with the learning outcomes to improve academic performance.

The impact of social media on the reading culture of Tamale Technical University students in Ghana was investigated by Kojo, Agyekum, and Arthur (2020). The data was collected and analyzed using a quantitative method. Additionally, the results showed that the use of social media by students has a statistically important effect on their reading culture. However, the study found that students' frequent access to social media sites has a detrimental impact on them. Mbamalu and Onyido (2019) examined the impact of undergraduates' social networking dependence on their reading habits. The study claims, based on documentary sources, that reading is still indispensable. However, the increased involvement of students in social networking can hurt undergraduate reading habits.

Scholars' preferences for specific resources are undeniably diverse. Although Bowman's research indicates that faculty members use social media for professional purposes at rates ranging from 70% (Facebook) to 50% (Google Plus). A survey of 1,600 education scholars conducted by researchers at Michigan State University (Bergland, 2014) found that the use of social media for professional purposes is much lower for Twitter (15%), YouTube (20%), and Facebook (39%). Furthermore, adopters' approaches to using social media platforms differ. Hence, social media use should be purposeful and it should be employed in circumstances that are suitable for learning, where researchers and students understand (Liu, 2011).

ISSUES AND PROBLEMS

The challenge of librarians not being adequately acquainted with social networking tools in developing countries is a serious threat to knowledge development. Even the few that are aware are still struggling to use these sites for effective library services. Nevertheless, many challenges are being encountered in the process of establishing and use of social media.

Limited Bandwidth: One of the constraints to accessing social networking is associated with limited bandwidth in most institutions in developing countries. Poor connectivity can frustrate effective online participation. Where available, it is almost always operated at low speed and nothing tangible is achieved. The African Tertiary Institutions Connectivity Survey (ATICS) indicates that universities in Africa, on average, pay about US $40.50 per kilobit per second (kbps) per month while some institutions pay as much as the US $36 kbps for bandwidth. These figures are extremely high compared to users in North America who are on megabit and Gigabit speeds and pay much less, which is $10 per month for a 3 Mbps Digital Subscribers Line (DSL) link (Aluoch, 2006). Most African institutions' internet bandwidth connection is inadequate for social and online academic activities. Poor connectivity can frustrate effective online participation.

Lack of Maintenance Culture: Sustainable technological development is a Herculean task in most institutions in developing countries because they lack maintenance culture. Even, the few available technologies are in moribund conditions that may not support remote access to information. According to Obaseki, Maidabino, and Makama (2012), most of the print and non-print materials that are found in academic libraries have deteriorated to the extent that users find it difficult to consult or use them. This is due largely to high pressure on the materials coupled with inadequate preparation for the maintenance of these technologies.

Unreliable Power Supply: The low level of electricity supply discourages people from participating in the online forum. This has been a serious problem in developing countries because most of our leaders have not seen it as a priority that constitutes a blocking problem in nation-building. Most internet cafes and computer networks are run using generators which significantly increase the cost of internet access. Ossai-Ugbah (2018) claims that these power outages increase the general overhead and running costs, thus harming the use of social media for marketing library and information services in Nigerian university libraries. Providing a reliable power supply has to be part of the planning and development of network infrastructure.

Inadequate Training of Staff: Tion, Ilo, and Beetesh (2019) investigated some of the issues associated with the use of social media in university libraries, such as poor internet, a lack of qualified staff, a lack of proper skills, and the willingness of library staff to adopt social media in their respective libraries to improve their services. The new age calls for professionals to reposition their view on the new roles they are expected to offer. They need to attune themselves to the use of these new technologies, particularly the internet. There should be more emphasis on capacity building through training on the use of ICT in the library. In addition, libraries must constantly update their knowledge concerning social media networking.

Lack of Government Intervention: there is little or no intervention on the part of the government in the area of ICT development and the provision of social facilities. Social facilities like roads, railways, telecommunication networks, electricity supply systems, and water supply systems are all described as infrastructure that could sustain effective work activities in institutions, such as libraries, but are still dead in most African countries. Policies related to the management of library functions are also not fully encouraged in most developing countries.

Copyright Issues: Copyright is a legal right that protects the creator and his intellectual property and artistic work from being exploited without consideration for the interest of the originator of the work. Free access to information where people copy, paste, and edit without acknowledging the authority is a serious challenge to copyright management. Copyright infringement has been a major issue in Africa's tertiary institutional environment. Students and researchers copy each other's work without due acknowledgment of the owner, thus leading to infringement. Tosun (2018) comments that in today's digital environment, more and more of our personal information exists online, available and vulnerable to anyone with prying eyes and access to a computer. However, as technology continues to develop, images and sound, as well as video/computer games, can now be incorporated into the materials that can be copyrighted.

SOLUTIONS

The term social media has become an increasingly familiar instrument employed by university libraries to promote library services to users. Some universities in Nigeria use social media as a platform for them to communicate with their users, consisting of students, staff, and the community. Social media can be seen as a device or platform where the library can use the network to communicate, share information, build, or networked form groups. The university libraries in Nigeria majorly emphasize the importance and the need of a library to users, especially students. Social media apps are not foreign to librarians, especially for libraries in international schools.

Social media has become the latest platform in the library to interact and service users. The use of social media within university libraries is very widespread. Research in this area focuses on the use of Web 2.0 or Library 2.0 tools, such as Facebook, WhatsApp, LinkedIn, Twitter, and YouTube. The main opportunities associated with libraries using social networking tools as observed by Taylor & Francis Group (2017) are seen to be related to its low cost, its ability to take the library services to users in their preferred spaces, the opportunity to build a sense of community between the library and the users, to support co-development of collections and help librarians updated on industry news and initiatives.

Chi (2020) agreed that social media is a flexible virtual platform for libraries to reach their targeted customers and fulfill their needed services. Rachman and Putri (2018) agreed that libraries are taking benefit from social media to market their sources and services. In addition, social networking sites are playing their parts and making a massive impact on library sources and services.

The main goal of creating social media is to provide timely and useful information about services, resources, and community outreach events and projects in the library. It aims to start a conversation with our users and synthesize what the library can do, such as exposing library services, projecting library image and e-reputation, forming discussion groups and collaborative work, and reaching out to a new audience of potential users. For instance, sites like Facebook, Linkedin, Hi5, and MySpace allow users to build and customize their profile and communicate with friends such as, "Ask a Librarian". This augments library service delivery based on: how to use the library; finding information on your research assignment and thesis writing and also how to get information from library databases; Library services are also supplemented by providing access to electronic databases as well as a library guide that creates a hyperlink to library knowledge storage.

Social networking services could enable librarians and users to not only interact but share and exchange resources dynamically in an electronic environment. Users can create accounts with a library network service and be attuned to all necessary information regarding their needs. Social media networking tools allow for updating and publishing instantly. For instance, using blogs or micro-blogs is an opportunity for librarians to update related new services. Users can be well informed about the activities taking place in the library, the events that are occurring, what collections are available and selective dissemination of information about the things they are interested in.

University libraries have chosen a 21st-century facility to market their services (Choi, & Baek, 2019). Additionally, libraries always need a change and accept the new changes as a demand of the data era. Furthermore, libraries are using social media effectively regarding their service and sources of promotion. Baishya (2020) said that social media supports libraries to apply social media tools and systems to reinforce library services. In addition, for several decades, social media has taken a huge spot within the libraries to market library services. Chi (2020) said that social media is the vital resource that helps libraries to meet their potential, specific and targeted library customers. Furthermore, social media platforms such as Facebook, Whatsapp, Twitter, LinkedIn, Wechat, Wikis, Instagram, and YouTube make it easier for library users to obtain services by utilizing the tools and techniques that libraries have adopted.

Essentially, institution libraries must remain proactive, current and be aware of emerging technologies to sustain user interest. According to Chu & Du (2019), social networking tools have added more value to libraries and their services in many ways, such as increasing the library's relevance to users and improving the library's image. They have allowed interactive study, timely, convenient services to improve service level and quality, and a broader range of services increased users' participation and increased interactions and communication with users. They have broadened librarians' perspective and facilitated obtaining users' feedback and following readers' interest trends, drawing on collective knowledge to better serve clientele, enhanced librarian communication and expedited information dissemination to the users; facilitated instant problem solving with the benefit of traceable services, and improved knowledge sharing and collaboration.

Furthermore, social media helps librarians to share information with users and students in the easiest way in a digital library environment. The application of social media in the library and information management can be categorized into three broad activities, namely information communication, knowledge distribution, and knowledge organization.

INFORMATION COMMUNICATION

Instagram

The name Instagram is derived from two words: 'instant' and 'telegram,' and the idea was founded on a passion for photography. Instagram allows users to share their lives with their friends through a series of photos. "It's very simple; all you need is a fast mobile photo and a digital memory that will last a lifetime."Instagram now has a user base of over 150 million people (Facebook 2019). Research shows that Instagram has a 25% higher brand engagement rate than all other social media platforms. Instagram has the power to transform your pictures into vibrant, pleasant images that entice viewers to act.

Facebook

A free social networking site created by Mark Zuckerberg in 2004. The site was developed basically for Harvard University students. However, it is now open to anyone with an electronic mail account. In January 2018, over 2.2 billion users visited Facebook and the current internet users are about 3 trillion users worldwide (BloggingBasics101 2018). Facebook has an average of 1.65 billion active users, 989 million average mobile active users. 84.2% of daily users are outside the US and Canada (Facebook, 2016). Facebook users have a total of over 1.50 million friend connections and upload more than 350 million photos to Facebook each day. Through Facebook, people message their friends, family or groups, provide news feeds, people and post updates. People can now be reached more easily and family members cn be located. Facebook's mission statement was "to give people the power to create community and bring the world closer together. Using Facebook makes you stay connected with friends and family, to discover what's going on in the world, and to share and communicate what matters to them "when it was created in 2004. (Facebook 2019).

Facebook is rated among the networking tools and seen as librarian-friendly, which encourages access to applications of JSTOR search, World Cat, and much more. Libraries also link some of these specialized library applications on Facebook. Vidyakala and Nithyakala (2019) investigated the level of use of social networking sites among college students. According to the findings, college students used social networking sites for educational and social purposes, such as sharing academic reading materials and encouraging interactive discussion. In line with this, Anyanwu, Ossai-Onah, and Iroeze (2019) found that Facebook ranked first (89.2%) in the list of social media tools used by undergraduates.

WhatsApp

It allows users to create a virtual world. The virtual environment allows players to respond to multiple users simultaneously over the network, including the creation of their own identity through Avatars. The most popular virtual 3D game for libraries is Second Life (SL). It is an immersive 3D environment that can be used for entertainment and educational purposes. Due to increasing interest in digital services, some libraries have established virtual services on Second Life where users can interact with services in a practical way, such as walking around a virtual library, attending library training, and requesting reference services. According to Chow, Baity, Samarripa, Chappell, Rachlin & Vinson (2012), Second Life is one of the most well-known and largest adult interactive virtual environments, with anywhere from 35–50,000 avatars online at any given time in the libraries and encourages meeting and collaborating with librarians from around the world. The virtual world is created for game playing, as well as for collaborative work, learning activities, and information sharing.

LinkedIn

LinkedIn is increasing its popularity and has become the most used social networking platform for professional activities, even almost exceeding the popularity of Facebook. LinkedIn is used by libraries to create professional connections as well as market library services among other professionals working in different libraries in the world. Through LinkedIn, libraries can also project their ideas and professional experiences while library patrons can connect with subject specialists in their field of interest. Library professionals can use this platform to render specialized services such as Selective Dissemination of

Information (SDI). LinkedIn also facilitates and creates professional connections among library professionals. It can also be an effective marketing channel with proper planning and implementation.

Twitter

Twitter is a virtual social network that allows users to write short messages (of up to 140 characters), called tweets, that can be read by anyone with access to their page. It is an Internet social network and micro-blogging platform with interpersonal communication features for sharing (Chen, 2011; Buigues-García & Giménes-Chornet, 2012). The concept of juxtaposing the prospects and reputation of a company like Twitter is expected to generate $3.72 billion in sales. According to a Forbes survey, it earned 42 billion visits in 2019. This equates to 115 million visits a day. It has contributed significantly to the Nigerian economy in terms of job growth, technology transfer, and telecommunications. Twitter is the second most popular Web 2.0 platform. Library staff and patrons can be updated on the library's daily activities. Users can utilize this platform to type in short messages or status updates. Library service alerts can be created on Twitter (Eseani & Igwesi, 2017). The library could set up searches for its Twitter account to save and retrieve them quickly, just like setting up a search on the name of a library or setting up a geographical search. Carscaddon and Chapman (2013) extensively discussed Twitter as a marketing tool for libraries, including tips, best practices, evaluation, and assessment of a Twitter account.Twitter is an online real-time news and social networking platform where users post and interact with messages. The ease of posting, interacting, and sharing of information on this platform has made it a very vital platform for librarians to reach and interact with library users (Waddell and Barnes, 2018). Information on the go with users' responses can be tweeted at everybody's convenience. Waddell and Barnes (2018) note that the ease of posting and sharing information on Twitter makes it an essential tool for libraries to reach their users. It has made significant contributions to the Nigerian economy in terms of job creation, technology transfer, and taxation. Twitter has already indicated its readiness to immediately fill several roles in product and engineering to design, marketing, and communication base.

On moral value, in 2014, suggests that an increasing number of Nigerian children are getting exposed to internet porn. In fact, since the COVID-19 pandemic and subsequent lockdown, many young Nigerians have taken to all sorts of unusual tendencies to provide for themselves and their families.

Blogs

A Blog is an important social media that enables librarians to market and promote their library activities and services. Blog pages are social media web platforms where a writer or group of writers and readers or viewers share their views on a subject or topic, even news as it may apply (FirstSiteGuide, 2018). Ekoja (2011) says that blogs are extremely helpful in promoting library services like new acquisitions, opening hours, library events and programs, online discussions, and so on. Blogs are popularly used in libraries to broadcast library news and market other library resources. University librarians and faculty members can also develop blogs as subject guides. Several librarians have already introduced this Web 2.0 feature into library websites as information dissemination spaces provide information services to the users. Few librarians have also created specific subject blogs for users with interesting subjects, such as Catalogue blog, Bib-Blog, Cataloguer 2.0. Some provide news and library services through blogs, for instance, information Literacy Weblog, Community Virtual Library, and Librarian Blog.

Libraries are using Blogs to bring their users together and freely interact with the users and update them with current events in the library. Blogs permit librarians to occasionally post messages, share information on a particular subject matter and allow users to comment or contribute to the subject matter that is being discussed and expect instant feedback (Ezeani and Igwesi, 2017).

Wikis

A wiki is a "freely expandable network of interconnected web pages and hypertext mechanism for storing and modifying information" that first appeared in the mid-1990s. In other words, wikis are quick, interactive web-based environments that allow users to add and edit content collectively. It enables multiple users to upload, design, and create content as we speak. Wikis are referred to as a collection of web pages that allow users to add and edit content collectively. It is a free online encyclopedia that gives information on background knowledge and expressly discusses subject contents. It offers a platform whereby users can access information, edit and contribute to the content. Libraries use Wikis to facilitate personal learning and reflection, support group-level knowledge sharing, and help users to locate the knowledge. The wiki structure and the contributing processes require users' high-level participation and ability to critically evaluate information, synthesize information objects with different formats, and work independently and collectively with peer contribution (Moskaliuk, et al 2008).

INFORMATION DISTRIBUTION

YouTube

YouTube is another of the world's leading social media sites and the fourth most popular Web site in Canada (Alexa 2012). It was created in 2005 and specifically to share videos and allows people around the world to communicate and interact, making it a distribution point for user-created content through YouTube and allowing participatory culture on the web. It is a successful tool for reaching out to patrons because it is easily accessible without requiring frequent updates once a video has been uploaded, unlike Facebook or Twitter, which requires regular updates to maintain user interest (Collins & Quan-Haase, 2014).

Obadara and Olaopa (2018) studied the relationship between social media use, study habits, and academic performance of undergraduate students at the University of Education in Nigeria. They discovered that undergraduate students used social media via a variety of devices, including Android Phones, Laptops, Tablets, and other devices, resulting in a high level of social media use and knowledge sharing. University libraries primarily use YouTube to promote services, host lectures, and provide information literacy demonstrations for highlighting best practices for conducting research and navigating through specific databases. The high level of usage of the library's YouTube channel since inception suggests that the level of interaction between the library and its users would also increase.

Flickr

Flickr is a photo-sharing website that allows users to store, sort, search and post photographs and to create discussion groups. It provides an alternative form of content provision, with emphasis on virtual information. Flickr can be used by university libraries to display historic photographs of a library or university facilities, record annual events, social functions, services offered, and document original exhibitions held at the library. Librarians can use this tool to project images of libraries in areas such as collection displays of new arrivals of both books and journals, which can also be shared with users via Flickr. It can also be used to enlighten users on topical issues such as the different pictures of the past political gladiators in developing countries. The library can share a photo collection of workshops, conferences, and different programs that are organized within the campus.

Slideshare

Slideshare is a platform for slide holding services. It allows users to upload files privately or publicly which can be viewed by users. Slideshare has been playing a vital role in the field of education and e-learning, sharing ideas, conducting research, connecting with others who are skillful at the use of Slideshare. Individuals have the opportunity to present topics of interest to the audience, download them and reuse them for their purpose. Presenting a prepared slide that contains information about library products and services will notify every user who visits and shares them.

KNOWLEDGE ORGANIZATION

Library Thing

Library Thing is a tool that augments the Library Online Public Access Catalogue (OPAC). OPAC is electronic bibliography information stored in digital format. Once an account is created, a list of books with International Standard Book Number (ISBN) is sent to Library Thing, which sends back a piece of code that is pasted into the footer of the Library OPAC. This can be used by librarians to inform users of the current list of newly acquired materials. It enables users to catalog their books and view what other users share in those books. Brief descriptions, reviews, and tags can be constructed. Reading others' books will enable them to communicate asynchronously, blog, and "tag" their books.

Skype

The current Skype facilities could be expanded for use in reference work. As it provides a free, multifaceted seamless user experience. It could be worthwhile to investigate its use as a virtual reference service. Chorasia (2019) defines social media as machine tools that enable individuals or businesses to create, deliver, or exchange data, professional interests, opinions, pictures/recordings, and virtual organizations. Social media on the Internet offers a plethora of administrations.

The use of Skype enables librarians to identify with library patrons in social cyberspace and proactively provide the type of information that would normally result from a reference service. Voice over Internet Protocol (VoIP) like Skype could be used to achieve a successful and sustainable reference service by engaging in online face-to-face interaction. This is particularly useful for distance learners who seek information from different locations of the country with reference queries.

TikTok

TikTok is a video-based social media site like Instagram. Users create an account and choose whether they want to be content consumers (watching other people's videos), content creators (creating their videos), or both. The app makes it simple and enjoyable to make videos, which are usually 15 to 60 seconds long and include music, special effects, text, and stickers. The topics covered range from amusing, outrageous, or coarse to serious issues, social commentary, education, book reviews, politics, and activism. One of the most influential aspects of our library program has been its social media presence, especially in terms of generating support and interaction from our community. TikTok accounts assist the library in creating a virtual "common room" of communication that stretches beyond the physical school or library walls. It enables the library to remain a constructive and supportive force in students' lives after the school day has ended. TikTok has a fantastic sub-community called # booktok that can help with readers' advisory and collection development.

RECOMMENDATIONS

Scholars have observed that social media brought about changes and a significant impact on the daily life and activities of youths, not only changing the way people stay connected but also presenting considerable opportunities and challenges for librarians and educators. The use of social media by tertiary institutions is a captivating portion of research by students, researchers, and scientists. It describes the introduction of contents and focuses on how to share, interact, collaborate and socialize with its users. It enhances communication among and between scholars in virtual cities and must be sustained.

Social media and networking sites are aimed at building online metropolitan areas among people with common interests or activities and thereby provide tools that help them achieve this. The benefit of social networking, according to Muneja & Abungu (2012), includes reaching a vast audience in the virtual sphere that wouldn't be possible at a physical location. Furthermore, using social media and networking tools can encourage online discussion among students outside the classroom environment that is beyond the traditional classroom setting. For instance, studies indicated that postgraduate students use social media than undergraduate students because their activities require more research work which has to do with exploring the environment, invention, and innovation of new ideas, It has been argued by researchers Owusu-Acheaw & Lawson (2015) that the incorporation of social media will assist in the teaching and learning process. Thus, it is widely encouraged, especially concerning improving research work.

According to research, social media sites can guide students entering an unfamiliar social environment as well as meet their informational needs in terms of establishing and maintaining interpersonal connections. Social media networks have also been found useful in offering unique opportunities to promote socialization among students in the institution's environment as well as to meet their educational needs. They also support collaborative learning, creation, and dissemination of knowledge. It is therefore not surprising that scholars often explore the use of social media for academic purposes, and specifically focus on academic community development through blogs, online comments to articles, social bookmarking sites, wikis, and websites to post slides, text or videos, and so on (Nandez & Borrego, 2013).

Social media inspires spontaneous and collective learning, creation, and sharing as it is capable of providing local and current information. They also serve as outlets for viewpoints and voices that are not typically conveyed by traditional or dominant media outlets like the newspaper, flyers, handbills, etc. (Miller, 2006). With the popularity of social networking websites on the rise, our social interaction is influenced in numerous ways as we acclimatize to our increasingly technological world. The way web users collaborate and interact with each other has changed and keeps on evolving. These users now socialize through the internet. Social media and networking sites have affected our social interaction by changing the way we relate face-to-face with our colleagues, how we receive information, and the dynamics of our social groups and friendships (Asur and Huberman, 2010) cited in (Owusu-Acheaw & Lawson, 2015).

It is believed that social media sites have a noticeable impact on the work of researchers, as there are lots of social media sites accessible to them. For a user to effectively utilize social media sites, there is the need for them to create their profile and register with a particular social media site of interest to them so that its content will be accessible to such users. Profile implies the recording and organization of behaviors. The user's profile can contain information such as the user's name, age, gender, locality, pictures, hobbies, and so on. The profile is digitally self-presenting machinery to the users. Social media tools such as Facebook, Myspace, and Twitter have certain elements that assist users with video, share, and interact fully on the websites by allowing users to have access to the internet.

Social media accessibility is how an individual can access, create and publish his content as long as internet connectivity is available. Through social media, researchers can organize and showcase their research, collaborate with their colleagues in the social space and discover the latest information relating to their research. According to Al-Rahmi and Othman, (2013), there are four major advantages of social media use in tertiary institutions. These include enhancing relationships, improving learning motivation, offering customized course materials, and developing collaborative abilities. This means that social networking activities have the likelihood of improving student contact and help to improve their participation and involvement in-class activities, particularly where introverted students are involved. Students can function in online group learning, with less or no anxiety about needing to raise questions before their colleagues in school.

In addition to this, social media networks are designed to foster collaboration among individuals, institutions, and countries of the world with such joint effort going to realize important improvement through the sharing of ideas and resources (Zavazana, 2012). Most importantly, students in Nigerian tertiary institutions of learning can collaborate with their counterparts in other countries to meet the intellectual, economic, and social demands of the twenty-first century. Nowadays, students are digitally conscious and are accustomed to learning in an active, interactive, and collaborative e-learning environment beyond traditional learning systems. Under this scenario, learning is a recipe for cognitive, constructive, and social processes. Social software involves wider shared participation in the creation of information, encouragement of more active learning, and support of better group interaction. Therefore, it combines the advantages of traditional learning and social software to build an interactive and collaborative e-learning platform.

Collaborative learning and networking tools encourage a feedback mechanism, because of its two-way transparent communication, connecting people with a shared interest and getting opinions and ideas from one another. It is becoming a very popular means of both interpersonal and public communication in Nigeria and the world at large. This is because of its ease of use, accessibility, speed, and reach. As described by Kumar (2019), the adoption of social media in libraries is very high and librarians are eager to adopt the power of the 21st century.

Public perceptions of brands and social media are becoming more negative in response to growing privacy concerns. Consumers are deleting their social media accounts, with almost 40% of digitally linked people admitting to deleting at least one social media account due to concerns about their data being misused, according to a study (Cadwalladr & Graham-Harrison, 2018). This is a negative trend not only for social media platforms. Personal information, intellectual property, and information security are three major issues that are eroding customer confidence on social media sites and brands (Appel, Grewel, Hadi, & Stephen, 2020). Considering each of these concerns, concrete steps and measures must be taken to address each these concerns.

FUTURE RESEARCH SUGGESTIONS

A library is worth considering; a gateway to learning, a base for persistent mastering of knowledge that encourages independent decision-making. The adoption of social media for library activities has encouraged a large number of users but has also put pressure on libraries to modernize their service delivery.

Using social networking tools such as Facebook, Twitter, Wikis, WhatsApp, MySpace, and LinkedIn encourages collaborative studies, communication, and knowledge exchange. Accordingly, it is essential for libraries to know their users' needs and prioritize them. Studies have revealed that social media inspires spontaneous and collective learning, creation, and sharing as they are capable of providing local and current information. They also serve as outlets for viewpoints and voices that are not typically conveyed by the traditional or dominant media outlet. In their research, Ezeji and Ezeji (2018) discovered that social media use was common among Alvan Ikoku Federal College of Education students and had a significant impact on their academic achievement.

The advent of internet web technology has also restructured the way people communicate, interact, acquire, share knowledge, search, investigate and participate in the creation and re-use of content. When Web 1.0 was created, the platform did not have features and facilities for users to interact with. Web 1.0 began as a platform for businesses and organizations to reach out to people. In the Web 1.0 environment, users read what others wrote as a source of information, but now, Web 2.0 facilitates users to express their views and publish them online through services like Blogs and Wikis. The transition from Web 1.0 to Web 2.0 and then to Web 3.0 is characterized by a shift from a "read-only" web to a "read-and-write" web and then to a read-write-execute web.

The phrase Web 2.0 has become popular and led to the evolution of concepts like Business 2.0, Travel 2.0, Library 2.0, Librarian 2.0, and so on. The term Library 2.0 was first conceived by Michael Casey in 2006 on his blog Library Crunch, which refers to several social and technological changes that are having an impact upon libraries, their staff, and their patrons, and how they could interact. Library 2.0 can be defined as a model for a modernized form of library services that reflects a transition within the library world in the way library services are delivered to users. Library 2.0 is constantly updated and re-evaluated on how best to serve the library users. It is a concept that encourages a new generation of library services geared towards the needs and expectations of today's library users.

This evolution encourages Web 2.0 to be a dynamic, interactive, and collaborative platform that facilitates the exchange of information and knowledge amongst users. Web 2.0 or Library 2.0 is the label attached to new capabilities and services offered by the second-generation World Wide Web (WWW) that facilitates online collaboration and sharing among users. Web 3.0 or Library 3.0 tools are Internet-based services that include collaborative learning and publishing sites such as Wikis, Wikinut, Web Blogs; RSS (really simple syndicate) Feeds; Starpages; Social bookmarking like Furl, Del.icio. us, Simpy, Blinklist, CiteULike (articles), Connotea (articles), Reddit, Flickr (images), FreeGovInfo

(EPA government documents), LibraryThing (books), PennTags (library catalog records), Podcast.com (podcasts), Scribd (documents), Slideshare (PowerPoint presentations); photo sharing sites: Youtube, Flickr, Vimeo, and Photobucket; social networking tools such as, Facebook, Linkedin, Hi5, Flixter, Orktu, Ning and Bebo; Personal search agent; Instant messaging; resource discovery tools, mapping services, web annotation and so on.

CONCLUSION

Social media usage is essential in public university libraries because it allows librarians to stay up to date on new ideas in their field and helps them provide services that meet the varying needs of their patrons. Librarians must acquire the necessary skills to stay relevant in the socially networked environment and meet the growing needs of their users. Libraries, therefore, need to proactively embrace the new technologies to meet the challenging demands of social networking sites for better service delivery. This need has resulted in struggles over the years to reposition libraries through the application of ICTs. The current trends of social collaboration and knowledge sharing have yet to produce the desired results due to several challenges such as high infrastructure and maintenance costs, epileptic power supply, and a lack of skilled human resources. The exploitation of social media networking tools will strengthen information development in developing countries. It will go a long way in providing access and use of the world's knowledge. For marketers, this will reduce the need for call centers and agents, reducing points of friction in service and increasing the convenience for customers (Kaplan and Haenlein 2017).

REFERENCES

Adewojo, A. A., & Mayowa-Adebara, O. (2018). Social media usage by library staff in academic libraries: The case of Yaba College of Technology, Lagos State, Nigeria. Information and Knowledge Management, 6(1),43-49.

Al-Rahmi, W.M., & Othman, M.S. (n.d.). The impact of social media uses on academic performance among university students. *Journal of Information Systems, Research, and Innovation*, 1-10.

Alexa. (2012). *Top sites in Canada*. Retrieved 15 July 2018 from https://www.alexa.com/

Alonge, A. J. (2012). Social media in library and centers. In Library and Information Science in developing countries: Contemporary issues. IGI Global Publication.

Aluoch, A. A. (2006). The search for affordable quality Internet connectivity for African universities. *AAU Newsletter*, *12*(3), 8–15.

Anyanwu, E. W., Ossai-Onah, V. O., & Iroeze, P. (2013). Use of social media tools among Nigerian undergraduates in three selected tertiary institutions in Imo State, Nigeria. *Journal of Information and Knowledge Management*, *4*(2), 46–51.

Appel, G., Grewel, L., Hadi, R., & Stephen, A. T. (2020). The future of social media in marketing. *Journal of the Academy Marketing*, *48*, 79–95.

Asur, S., & Huberman, B. A. (2010). Predicting the future with social media. Social Computing Lab: HP Labs.

Baishya, R. (2020). A study on the attitude of library users of colleges towards the social media usage for promoting library services. *Library Philosophy and Practice*, 1-83.

Ball-Rokeach, S. J., & Defleur, M. L. (1976). A dependency model of mass media effects. *Communication Research*, (3), 3–21. Retrieved May 17, 2018, from http://www.uky.edu/~drlane/capstone/mass/dependency.htm

Baran, S. J. (2010). *Introduction to mass communication: media literacy and culture* (6th ed.). McGraw-Hill.

BloggerBasics101. (n.d.). www.bloggerbasics1010.com

Buigues-García, M., & Giménez-Chornet, V. (2012). Impact of Web 2.0 on national libraries. *International Journal of Information Management*, *32*(1), 3–10.

Cadwalladr, C., & Graham-Harrison, E. (2018). Revealed: 50 million Facebook profiles harvested for Cambridge Analytica in a major data breach. *The Guardian*. Available at: www.theguardian.com/news/2018/mar/17/cambridge-analytica-facebook-influence-us-election

Carscaddon, L., & Chapman, K. (2013). *Twitter as a marketing tool for libraries: Marketing with social media*. A LITA Guide.

Chi, D. T. P. (2020). Developing the use of social media in libraries. *International Journal of Library and Information Studies.*, *10*(2), 2231–4911.

Chorasia, T. (2019). Roles of social media in a social audit. *International Journal of Advanced Research*, *4*(10), 1408–1411.

Chow, A. S., Baity, C. C., Zamarripa, M., Chappell, P., David Rachlin, D., & Source, C. V. (2012). The information needs of virtual users: A study of second life libraries. *The Library Quarterly*, *82*(4), 477–510.

Chu, S. K. W., & Du, H. S. (2019). Social networking tools for academic libraries. *Journal of Librarianship and Information Science*, *45*(1), 64–75.

Chua, A. Y. K., & Goh, D. (2010). A study of Web 2.0 applications in library Websites. *Library & Information Science Research*, (32), 203–211.

Chua, A.Y.K. & Goh, D.H. (2012). Social networking tools for university library services. *Journal of Librarianship Information Science*, *45*(1), 64-75.

Collins, G., & Quan-Haase, A. (2014). Are social media ubiquitous in academic libraries? A longitudinal study of adoption and usage patterns. *Journal of Web Librarianship*, *8*(1), 48–68.

Cooper, J. D., & Alan, M. (2015). Library 2.0 at a small campus library. *Technical Services Quarterly*, *26*(2), 89–97.

Di Vaio, A., Boccia, F., Landriani, L., & Palladino, R. (2020). Artificial intelligence in the agri-food system: Rethinking sustainable business models in the COVID-19 scenario. *Sustainability*, *12*(12), 4851. https://doi.org/10.3390/su12124851

Dickson, A., & Holley, R. R. (2012). Social networking in academic libraries: the possibilities and the concerns. *School of Library and Information Science Faculty Research Publications*, Paper 33.

Eke, H.N., Omekwu, C.O., & Odoh, J. N. (2014). The use of social networking sites among the undergraduate students of the University of Nigeria, Nsukka. *Library Philosophy and Practice*, 1-28.

Ekoja, I. I. (2011). Modern ICT tools: Online electronic resources sharing using web 2.0 and its implications for library and information practice in Nigeria. *Samaru Journal of Information Studies*, *11*(1&2), 53–58.

eMarketer. (2018). *Social network users and penetration in worldwide*. Retrieved from https://tinyurl.com/ycr2d3v9

Ezeani, C. N., & Igwesi, U. (2017). Using social media for dynamic library service delivery: The Nigeria experience. *Library Philosophy and Practice*. Retrieved fromhttp://digitalcommons.unl.edu/cgi/viewcontent.cgi?article=2011&context=libphilprac

Ezeji, P. O., & Ezeji, K. E. (2018). Effect of social media on the study habits of students of Alvan Ikoku Federal College of Education, Owerri. *International Journal of Educational and Pedagogical Sciences*, *12*(1), 220–224.

Facebook. (2014). *Facebook First Quarter 2016 results conference call*. Retrieved from https://s21.q4cdn.com/399680738/files/doc_financeials/2016/FB_Q116_Transcri.pdf

Facebook. (2019). *Company Info*. Retrieved from https://tinyurl.com/n544jrt

Fewkes, A. M., & McCabe, M. (2012). Facebook: Learning tool or distraction? *Journal of Digital Learning in Teacher Education*, *28*(3), 92–98.

Hurt, N. E., Moss, G. S., Bradley, C. L., Larson, L. R., Lovelace, M. D., Prevost, L. B., Joe, S., Choi, N., & Baek, T. H. (2019). Library marketing via social media. *Online Information Review*, *42*(6), 940–955.

Jones, M. J., & Harvey, M. (2019). Library 2.0: The effectiveness of social media as a marketing tool for libraries in educational institutions. *Journal of Librarianship and Information Science*, *51*(1), 3–19.

Joosten, T. (2012). *Social media for educators: Strategies and best practices*. Academic Press.

Junco, R., Heiberger, G., & Loken, E. (2011). The effect of Twitter on college student's engagement and grades. *Journal of Computer Assisted Learning*, *27*(2), 119–132.

Kaitlin, C. (2010). Social Media Changing Social Interactions. *Student Journal of Media Literacy Education*, *1*(1), 1–11.

Kaplan, A., & Haenlein, M. (2017). Users of the world unite The challenges and opportunities of social media. *Business Horizons*, *53*(1), 59–68.

Khan, S. A., & Bhatti, R. (2012). A review of problems and challenges of library professionals in developing countries including Pakistan. *Library Philosophy & Practice*. https://www.webpages.uidaho.edu/~mbolin/khan-bhatti2.htm

Kojo, D. B., Agyekum, B. O., & Arthur, B. (2020). Exploring the effects of social media on the reading culture of students in Tamale Technical University. *Journal of Education and Practice*, *9*(7), 11–26.

Kumar Gireesh, T. K. (2013). Marketing of library services and products through social media: an evaluation. In *Proceeding of paper presented in National Conference on Inspiring Library Services (NCILS-2013)*. Sree Siddhartha Pre University College.

Lassila, O., & Hendler, J. (2017). Embracing "Web 3.0". *IEEE Internet Computing*, 90–92.

Lenhart, A., Purcell, K., Smith, A., & Zickuhr, K. (2010). *Social media and mobile Internet use among teens and young adults*. Retrieved 10 June 2018 from https://pewinternet.org/~/media//Files/Reports/2010/

Liu, Y. (2011). Social media tools as a learning resource. *Journal of Educational Technology Development and Exchange*, *3*(1), 101–114.

Matikiti, R., Kruger, M., & Saayman, M. (2019). The usage of social media as a marketing tool in two Southern African countries. *Development Southern Africa*, *33*, 1–16.

Maxim. (2018). *Every Selena Gomez Instagram post for puma is worth $3.4 million*. Retrieved from https://tinyurl.com/ybr6nzok

Mbamalu, B. O., & Onyido, J. O. (2019). A critical analysis of social networking and its influence on undergraduates' reading habits. *International Journal of Scholarly and Educational Research in Africa*, *12*(5), 7–16.

Mon, L. M. (2015). *Social media and library services*. Morgan & Claypool.

Moskaliuk, J., Kimmerle, J., & Cress, U. (2008). Learning and knowledge building with Wikis: The impact of incongruity between people's knowledge and a Wiki's information. In *Proceedings of the International Conference for the Learning Sciences*, (vol. 2, pp. 99-106). Utrecht, The Netherlands: International Society of the Learning Sciences.

Motia, E., & Sabque, M. (2017). *Next Generation Semantic Web 0.2 Applications*. Springer-Verlag Berlin.

Muneja, P., & Abungu, A. (2012). Application of Web 2.0 tools in delivering library services: a case of selected libraries in Tanzania. *Proceedings of SCECSAL XXth Conference*. Retrieved from http://http//www.scecsal.viel.co.ke/images/e/e3/Application

Nandez, G., & Borrego, A. (2013). Use of Social media for academic purposes: A case study. *The Electronic Library*, *31*(6), 781–791.

O'Reilly, T., & Musser, J. (2006). *Web 2.0: Principles and best practices*. O'Reilly Media Inc.

Obadara, O. E., & Olaopa, S. O. (2018). Social media utilization, study habit and undergraduate students' academic performance in a University of Education in Nigeria. *Library Philosophy and Practice*.

Obaseki, T. I., Maidabino, A. A., & Makama, F. H. (2012). The development and challenges of virtual library services in Nigerian Colleges of Education. *Trends in Information Management*, *8*(1), 1–8.

Owusu-Acheaw, M., & Larson, A. G. (2015). Use of social media and its impact on academic performance of tertial institution students. A study of students of Koforidu Polytechnic. *Journal of Education and Practice, 6*(6), 1–9.

Owusu-Acheaw, M., & Larson, A. G. (2015). Use of social media and its impact on academic performance of tertiary institution students: A Study of Students of Koforidu polytechnic. *Journal of Education and Practice, 6*(9), 1–9.

Rachman, Y. B., & Putri, D. A. (2018). Social media application in Indonesian academic libraries. *Webology, 15*(1), 25–48.

Redecker, C., Ala-Mutka, K., & Punie, Y. (2010). *Learning 2.0-The impact of social media on learning in Europe.* Policy brief. JRC Scientific and Technical Report. EUR JRC56958 EN. Retrieved from http//bit. ly/cljlpq

Roblyer, M. D., McDaniel, M., Webb, M., Herman, J., & Witty, J. V. (2010). Findings on Facebook in Higher Education: A Comparison of College Faculty and Student Uses and Perceptions of Social Networking Sites. *Internet and Higher Education, 13*(3), 134–140.

Scale, M-S., & Quan-Haase, A. (2012). *Categorizing Blogs as information sources: implications for collection development policies of libraries.* Paper presented at influence 12, Dalhousie University.

Sewell, R. (2013). Who is following us? Data mining a library's Twitter followers. *Library Hi-Tech Trends, 31*(1), 160–170.

Shakeel, A. K., & Rubina, B. (2012). Application of social media in marketing of library and information services: A case study from Pakistan. *Webology, 9*(1). Retrieved from https://www.webology.org/2012/v9ni/a93.html

Sheikh, A., Syed, K. A., & Naseer, M. M. (2016). Use of social media tools by reputed university libraries of the world: A comparative study. *Pakistan Library and Information Science Journal, 47*(2), 45–55.

Taylor & Francis Group. (2014). *Use of social media by the library: Current practices and future opportunities.* Retrieved from http://www.tandf.co.uk/journals/access/white-paper-social-media.pdf

Tion, S. D., Ilo, H. M., & Beetseh, K. (2019). Evaluation of the uses of social media in library operation in university libraries in Benue state. *Library Philosophy and Practice,* 1-13.

Tosun, L. R. (2018). Motives for Facebook use and expressing "true self" on the Internet. *Computers in Human Behavior, 28*, 1510–1517.

Vidyakala, K., & Nithyakala, K. (2017). An analysis on purpose and usage of social networking sites among college students in Coimbatore. *International Journal of Research in Finance and Marketing, 7*(3), 34–41.

Waddell, D.C., Barnes, M. & Khan-Kernaham. (2019). Tapping into the power of Twitter: A look at its potential in Canadian Health Libraries. Partnership: the Canadian *Journal of Library and Information Practice and Research, 7*(2).

Zavazana, C. (2012). *ICT for sustainable development: Projects and initiatives.* Connect Arab Summit.

KEY TERMS AND DEFINITIONS

Developing Countries: Developing countries are those that have not yet attained a substantial level of industrialization concerning their populations and having a low standard of living.

Information Communication: Includes the internet, cellular networks, mobile phones, computers, middleware, videoconferencing, social networking, and other media applications and services.

Information Distribution: Individuals, organizations, or various organizational units transmit data and knowledge through the process of information exchange.

Knowledge Organization: A knowledge organization is a management term that defines an organization in which people create, transform, manage, and use knowledge through business processes.

Librarians: A librarian is a professional who works in a library, providing users with access to information

Library Users: People who seek and use the information to meet their information needs are referred to as library users.

Media System Dependency (MSD) Theory: The study of the influence of mass media on consumers and the relationships between media, audiences, and social structures.

Social Media: Social media is a computer-based application that allows people to share ideas, thoughts, and knowledge.

Social Networking: This is the use of Internet-based social media platforms to keep in contact with friends, families, colleagues, customers, or clients.

University Libraries: University libraries are built to promote learning, teaching, and research.

This research was previously published in the Handbook of Research on Knowledge and Organization Systems in Library and Information Science; pages 231-250, copyright year 2021 by Information Science Reference (an imprint of IGI Global).

Chapter 10
Feature–Based Analysis of Social Networking and Collaboration in MOOC

Jyoti Chauhan

Department of Computer Science, University of Delhi, New Delhi, India

Anita Goel

Dyal Singh College, University of Delhi, New Delhi, India

ABSTRACT

The aim of this article is to get insight into the features of social networking and collaboration in a massive open online course (MOOC) platform. We performed a feature-based analysis of twelve popular MOOC platforms – seven proprietary and five open-source platforms. Our study reveals that there are: (1) Two ways to include social networking – in-course and external; and (2) Two ways to incorporate collaboration functionality – built-in tools and third-party tools. The functionality provided by third-party tools differs; so, the selection of the tool is a challenge. For a built-in tool of MOOC, there is a need to re-identify the features for including it in any other MOOC platform; (3) Different ways to integrate the same tool in platforms; and (4) Different features of the same tool supported by various platforms. The proposed feature list helps future MOOC providers and developers to include social networking and collaboration functionality by selection, in contrast to specifying them afresh; and prospective educators can compare and select platforms, accordingly.

INTRODUCTION

Massive Open Online Course (MOOC) is a popular way to deliver online education, globally. The courses offered as MOOC are open for unlimited (logically) participation and can be accessed from anywhere via the Internet. MOOC courses are delivered via MOOC platforms that are specially designed software with the required functionality to deliver the courses. There are proprietary platforms like Coursera and Udacity, and open-source platforms like, Open edX. Also, some popular Learning Management System

DOI: 10.4018/978-1-6684-7123-4.ch010

(LMS) has been enhanced to offer MOOC, also called LMS-MOOC like, Sakai, Moodle, BlackBoard, and Canvas.

Due to the open and massive nature of MOOC, the learners belong to diverse profiles. Learners are from different countries and cultures, and, have different social, communication and domain-specific skills. There is a need to bridge the social gap among the learners. According to several researchers, (Khalil & Ebner, 2014; Muilenburg & Berge, 2005; Shah et al., 2018), the learners in MOOC face the problem of social isolation and limited interactivity. This results in loss of the learner's engagement and lead to dropouts. In general, courses delivered as MOOC have a predefined structure defined by the course instructor. These courses follow the instructional based strategy, offering the learning material in the form of readings (text), video lectures, and the assessment activity. There is a need for the mechanism that can facilitates collaboration among the learners to shift their role from passive to active user, where they can collaborate with others, contribute new ideas and participate in knowledge generation.

MOOC supports the social-constructivist pedagogy of learning. For this, MOOC provides integrated technological support for social and collaborative learning. Several studies (Alario-Hoyos et al., 2013; Blom et al., 2013; Butcher et al., 2013; Hrastinski, 2008; Imran et al., 2016; Kayode, 2018) have stressed over the importance of social, connections (networking), and collaboration in online learning (MOOC), and, suggest benefits like, better learning outcomes and positive encouragement.

The social networking and collaboration functionality in MOOCs facilitates interaction among participants (instructor, learner) and helps them to learn in a collaborative environment. Here, the information is created by different activities of the learner, like, commenting, responding, updating and sharing. Such informal way of learning complements the traditional and structured way of learning. The inclusion of social networking and collaboration in MOOC changes the passive role of the learner from information consumer to an active user, by providing them the opportunity to create learning resource by active participation in the learning activities. It has resulted in a shift from teacher-centered learning to learner-centered learning, facilitating a more collaborative way to learn, considering interest, abilities and learning styles of the individual learner for the process of learning.

The social networking allows the learners to connect with other learners and build a network. Facebook[1] and Twitter[2] are commonly used social networks, used by learners to express their thoughts, opinions, and help them to connect. Here, learning emerges from connections among learners in a spontaneous way. The other benefit of forming connections is providing impetus and motivation for learners to persist in their learning (Kamel Boulos & Wheeler, 2007). Collaborative learning supports online learning goals by promoting creativity and critical thinking skills, sharing and reflecting knowledge and decision-making (Palloff & Pratt, 2003; Zygouris-Coe, 2019). Collaboration in MOOC helps the learner to establish online learning communities and bring the learners together to support peer learning. It facilitates the learners to work mutually on a single project to achieve a common learning goal. The learners enrolled in a course assist their peers, and enrich the course with discussions and interactions, such as, argumentation (Baker, 1994), knowledge building (Bereiter & Scardamalia, 2003), mutual regulation (Blaye & Light, 1990), and positive conflict resolution (Doise & Mugny, 1984). Also, collaboration provides a way to the learner to interact with the instructor.

The social networking and collaboration functionality can be incorporated in MOOC by adapting already existing tools like, Google Hangout[3] for video conferencing and WordPress[4] for blogging, to suit the need of a MOOC platform. Sometimes, a new tool may be written to include social media functionality and is integrated into the platform as well. Also, links may be provided to already existing networking platforms or new networking facility is created.

A lot of research has been carried out on social networking and collaboration focusing on particular platforms such as, edX (Chen et al., 2015), FutureLearn (Manathunga et al., 2017); specific tools such as, Blog (Mak et al., 2010), Forum (Chen et al., 2015; Mak et al., 2010), Twitter (Shen & Kuo, 2015); use of these tools, and on analyzing their impact on learning-related factors. However, there is no mention of the features of tools to be included or the technical support required, for providing social media functionality in MOOC. The inclusion of a tool and its features contribute to the learning as well. There is an absence of the feature specification document for social media in MOOC, even academically. As a result, when developing a new MOOC platform, the task of feature identification is required to be repeated every time, a new, whenever needed. Also, since MOOC provider may have little or limited knowledge about the features available for social networking and collaboration, the required features listed may not be complete. In cases where existing tools are used for integration, the absence of feature specification makes updating of the software tedious. Although, the support pages of existing tools or platforms describe the features provided by them, there is no mention of the feature specification for the social networking and collaboration functionality provided in MOOC.

In this article, the focus is on analyzing the features of social networking and collaboration functionality in MOOC. It helps during the development, in choosing and specifying the features for social networking and collaboration to be included in MOOC.

Here, we present a feature list for the functionality of social networking and collaboration in MOOC. The feature list is divided into two categories – (1) Social networking, and (2) Collaboration. For each category, the feature list is presented hierarchically at three levels – (i) Component, (ii) Operation, and (iii) Parameter. The feature list for social networking is presented for In-course network and External Network. The tools used for collaboration in MOOC are categorized based on their availability (common, selective) and integration (third-party, built-in) in MOOC, and also on the scope (platform, course, and user) of their use. The feature list for popular collaboration tool is presented here. Additionally, we also present the ways in which social networking and collaboration functionality are included in MOOC.

For understanding the social networking and collaboration functionality in MOOC, a study of *twelve* MOOC platforms was conducted. It includes seven popular proprietary MOOC platforms, namely, Coursera, edX, Udacity, FutureLearn, NovoEd, iversity, and Swayam; and five open-source platforms, namely, Open edX, Canvas Network, Sakai, Learn Moodle, and MooKIT. Since the platforms selected for our study are diverse in nature, these are supposed to cover the maximum possible aspects including features and ways of offering the functionality of social networking and collaboration functionality in a MOOC platform. So, our findings using these platforms as a basis may apply to all MOOC platforms.

The proposed feature list may also be used to improvise the design and implementation of the MOOC software. Instead of providing in-built features and functionality for social networking and collaboration, like for discussion forum; independent tools can be updated using the proposed feature list and integrated into the MOOC software as plug and play tool. This will provide flexibility to the developer to select a tool and integrate it into the MOOC software, in contrast, to modify the in-built tool.

The feature list is for MOOC providers and developers, to select the features from the list, in contrast to, specify afresh. The list is also of use for the platform providers and the educational practitioners to assist in comparing and selecting a platform or tool, based on the features provided and the level of support it offers for social networking and collaboration. It also helps in identifying and selecting the features for developing a new tool or enhancing the existing ones available. The feature list presented here can be easily updated to include new features. All or part of the functionality may be selected from the list.

The rest of the paper is organized as follows. Section 2 provides a theoretical background of this work, focusing specifically on the understanding of social networking and collaboration in MOOC. In Section 3 we present related work done in the area. Section 4 describes the research methodology used. Section 5 describes our analysis in detail. Section 6 presents our findings and discussion on the analysis presented. Section 7 enumerates the benefits of our analysis. The limitation of our work and the future direction is discussed in Section 8. Finally, Section 9 presents the conclusion.

THEORETICAL BACKGROUND

Social networking and collaboration focus on building connections for community-based learning. MOOC offers a range of social media tools that are integrated into the platform itself. This facilitates the learners to connect with their peers within the closed MOOC platform, thereby, addressing the privacy and personal security concern of the learner that may be an issue when connecting from outside the platform (Alario-Hoyos et al., 2013; Kop et al., 2011).

Social networking in MOOC helps the learners to find others having similar interest, registered in the same course, member of same team or group; express their thoughts, opinions, and connect to form a network. It also allows the learners to connect with their connections, which they have already built on various social networking platforms such as Facebook, Google Plus[5], Twitter, and LinkedIn[6]. Since MOOC is a centralized environment, so accessing of social networking platforms is done from within the MOOC, without any requirement of accessing it explicitly, outside of the platform. MOOC platform provides link between MOOC and the social networking platforms that facilitates the learners to access some features from the MOOC itself. MOOC allows accessing limited features of existing social networking platforms, from within. Generally, MOOC learners use social networking functionality to share course information, showcase their achievements, provide feedback, and connect with other learners in their network. Facebook is one of the most commonly used social networking platforms in MOOC.

Collaboration in MOOC facilitates the user (instructor, learner) to interact with others, work mutually on a project, create better learning resources, and achieve common learning goals. The learners registered in a MOOC course assist their peers, share their ideas, and enrich the course with discussions and related content as a way of crowdsourcing (Mackness et al., 2010). For interaction among learners and with the instructor, MOOC provides a collection of asynchronous (e.g. message) and synchronous (e.g. forum, video conference) tools. Forum and message tools are popularly used for communication between instructor and learner, while for interaction among themselves learner uses mostly forum with the social media integration (e.g. Facebook, Twitter) (Ortega et al., 2014). To go beyond the text-based communication, Google Hangout and Skype[7] are also used by the learners for face to face real-time interaction. Forum (discussion forum) is referred to as "an essential ingredient of an effective online course" (Mak et al., 2010), and it is currently the most commonly used tool in MOOC. Sometimes, the platform provider may also provide alternative tools that are external to the platform in order to extend the collaborative competencies for a specific course or platform.

RELATED WORK

Traditionally, much work has been carried out to understand the contribution of social networking and collaboration in learning. Bonk and Zhang (2006), Garrison and Kanuka (2004), and Muilenburg and Berge (2005) focus on analyzing learning-related factors like learner's performance, satisfaction, engagement, and learning outcomes. However, these studies do not particularly focus on MOOC.

Much research has been done to identify the impact of social networking and collaboration tools on learning in MOOC. Alario-Hoyos et al. (2013), analyzes the way a learner uses social tools and its impact on learner's performance and motivation. They analyze five social media tools including forum, Facebook and Twitter. Filvà, Guerrero, and Forment (2014) present a study on the effect of massiveness on leaner's participation and interaction happening using social networking and collaboration tools. Núñez, Gené, and Blanco (2014) show a positive result of using virtual communities with social networks in promoting knowledge and completion rate. Imran et al. (2016) have conducted a survey to understand the impact of social networking and collaboration tools on the learning activity, in both LMS and MOOC platforms. As an outcome of their survey, they found that the tools are contributing to the learning process and are significantly popular among learners. In another study by Liu et al. (2016), it was found that the additional social space provided by Facebook and Twitter was beneficial to the MOOC learners for the learning.

Recent work focuses on identifying new possibilities of using social networking and collaboration tools in MOOC. Mak et al. (2010), demonstrate the use of a blog for personal learning relations, and the use of the forum for fast-paced interactions. Núñez et al. (2014), show an increase in completion rate with the use of cooperative MOOC model that supports virtual communities with social networks. Filvà et al. (2014) study the effects of massiveness in social participation, by collecting statistics from the communication, ports, and discussion enclosed inside MOOC. Butcher et al. (2013) focus on the role of educational resources in social learning using forum community. Kellogg, Booth, and Oliver (2014) demonstrate that with the discussion forum, MOOCs can be leveraged to foster networks and facilitate peer-supported learning. These researches help the provider in designing a MOOC platform as well as course activities.

Researchers have also performed studies focusing on the kind of tools to be used for social networking and collaboration in MOOC. Alario et al. (2013), Kop et al. (2011), and MoocGuide (2011) discuss the process for the selection of tools. Alario-Hoyos et al. (2013) analyze five different tools including the forum, Facebook, and Twitter by collecting their qualitative and quantitative data. According to their analysis, the forum is preferred by learners for interaction and discussions. Kop et al. (2011) suggest considering different aspects such as, the role of facilitator, pedagogical approach and structure constraints when providing the facility for building connections and collaborations. The research also advocates the presence of facilitator and use of discussion forum over Facebook, with an outside group, in MOOC. MoocGuide (2011) recommends the selection of tools depending on the audience. For known learners the tools already used by them are chosen, otherwise, most accessible tools are selected. Also, since a tool serves a specific purpose, multiple tools may be provided by the MOOC platform.

There are several studies (Gillani & Eynon, 2014; García-Peñalvo et al., 2015; Zhang et al., 2016) that focus on analysis of the data generated from use of the social networking and collaboration tools in MOOC. Gillani and Eynon (2014) analyze patterns of learners in discussion forum. García-Peñalvo et al. (2015) track the conversations and participation in Twitter and Google Plus. Zhang et al. (2016)

identify the communication preferences of learners. This helps to understand the requirement of the learners and cater to them.

Though several papers exist that focus on different aspects of using social networking and collaboration in MOOC, we could not find any work related to their feature specification. Generally, the MOOC platforms provide connectivity for social networking (e.g. Facebook) and tools (e.g. discussion forum) for collaboration. They may also use third-party tools. However, MOOC provider has little or limited knowledge about the possible features that can be provided for social networking and collaboration. For the developer, the absence of a feature specification hardens the task of developing a new tool as well as updating existing tools. Thus, a specification of features is required for easier integration of social networking and collaboration in MOOC.

METHODOLOGY

Our analysis is based on the features and functionalities supported by different MOOC platforms for social networking, and for collaboration. In our view, the MOOC users like, instructor and learner, can choose the features that are offered to them by the platform. Thus, we performed a study of different MOOC platforms for the feature and functionality of social networking and collaboration offered by the platforms. For the study, we considered different aspects, like, integration mechanism, technology, features and type of support offered. Moreover, these may vary even for the same MOOC provider, among different courses, based on the subject area, need of the course and instructor preferences.

For the purpose of this study, we decided to identify platforms based on their popularity, license availability (open-source, proprietary), and reported use for offering MOOC. We have considered 12 MOOC platforms. Out of these, seven are popular proprietary platforms, namely, Coursera, edX, Udacity, FutureLearn, NovoEd, iversity, and Swayam; and five are open-source platforms, namely, Open edX, Canvas Network, Sakai, Learn Moodle, and MooKIT.

The selection of the proprietary platforms is based on the review reports of D. Shah (2018) and MoocLab (2017, 2018) ranking. The report of D.Shah is based on the number of courses offered by the platform and their enrollments. MoocLab uses several additional parameters, such as, social tools and features, interface usability, partner institutions, and certificates. From the reports of D. Shah (2018) and MoocLab (2018) ranking, the top five platforms are - Coursera, edX, Udacity, FutureLearn, and iversity. MoocLab (2017) includes NovoEd platform based on their social tool and features, which includes team-based learning. Swayam is a popular Indian platform having more than 2.1 million registered users, ranking six in the MoocLab (2018) on the basis of offered courses (~750 courses). Moreover, Coursera is the largest and most popular platform, followed by edX. Both together, deliver more than half (6000) of about 11400 total MOOC courses offered worldwide, serving 55 million out of 101 million MOOC users (D. Shah, 2018). In the open-source category, Open edX is the first platform released open in 2013 and drives edX, which is one of the most popular MOOC platforms. Canvas Network, Sakai, and Learn Moodle are MOOC platforms upgraded from the LMS. Canvas Network is among the top five platforms based on the number of offered courses (MoocLab, 2017). Sakai is among the top two open-source learning platform (Kats, 2013; Monarch Media, 2010) serving over 4 million users globally. Various elite institutions, including IITK and University of Amsterdam, use Sakai for offering MOOC courses (Kats, 2013). Learn Moodle is used by millions of users worldwide. MooKIT is a lightweight Indian platform built entirely using open-source technologies and trusted by more than 200K learners and teachers.

A descriptive and quantitative methodology was applied to the MOOC platforms to study social networking and collaboration functionality. For proprietary platforms, we enrolled in about 100 courses offered on different platforms. To consider the diversity of social networking and collaboration offered in different courses, we identified courses in different and popular subject areas- art and humanities, engineering, literature, data science, programming, business, and management. We also considered the course offerings - self-paced and scheduled courses; course levels - beginner, intermediate and advance; and, course certification - degree and certificate courses. Also, the courses were selected based on course duration - short and long; course type – lesson-based and project-based; and course user base size - small and large, delivered in English language only. Table 1 shows details of the selected courses. The study of open-source MOOC platform was performed in three ways – (1) Source code, release document, user guide, and published resource, (2) Demo sites, and (3) Sandbox sites. The demo site is already populated with courses, activities, and users; and sandbox provides an empty space to create courses and experience features of the platform. Table 2 shows the details for mode of study of open-source platforms.

During the study of platforms, we noticed there are certain tools that have been discontinued by the MOOC platforms, though they are available in the older, archived, or self-paced courses. Some of these tools are wiki, chat, and e-portfolio. From study of LMS-MOOC platforms (Canvas Network, Sakai, Learn Moodle), we observed, the platform continues to support some features and tools like, chat; which may not be useful for MOOC. A study done on the chat tool for MOOC suggests that "most students derive no benefit from the tool" (Coetzee et al., 2014). The chat tool is mostly used for sharing emotions rather than for learning (Bouchet et al., 2017). We have considered the tools that are currently being used in MOOC platforms.

The selection of a range of platforms and, a variety of courses from diverse subject areas offered by various institutes and instructors, helped us to capture the diverse tools and features of social networking and collaboration offered in MOOCs. The features were further analyzed, categorized, and compared to arrive at a feature list for different tools.

Table 1. Proprietary platforms: Selected courses

Sr. No.	Platforms	No. of Subjects		Subject - No. of Courses	No. of Courses Selected
		Offered	Selected		
1.	Coursera	11	5	Arts & Humanities-4, Computer Science-3, Data Science-5, IT-3, Language Learning-2	17
2.	edX	31	11	Biology -1, Business & Management-3, Chemistry-1, Computer Science-8, Design-1, Data Science & Statistics-3, Education & Teacher Training-4, Health & Safety-1, Language-2, Literature-1, Physics-1	26
3.	Udacity	6	5	AI -2, Business-1, Career-1, Data Science-3, Programming & Development -6	13
4.	Future Learn	13	8	Business & Management-3, Health & Psychology-1, Language & Culture-1, Science Engineering & Math-2, Study Skills -1, Teaching-1, Tech & Coding -1, Creative Art & Media-1	11
5.	NovoEd	-	-	All Course available	7
6.	iversity	22	10	Economics-1, Education-1, Engineering-1, Environmental Science-1, Health-1, Interdisciplinary-3, Management-2, Philosophy-1, Political Science-1, Social Science-1	13
7.	Swayam	8	6	Teaching Refresher Program -2, Arts & Recreation-2, Engineering.-2, General-3, Education-3, Math-1	13
	Total	**91**	**45**		**100**

Table 2. Open-source platforms: Mode of study

Sr. No	Platforms	Mode of Study		
		Code	Demo Sites	Sandbox Sites
1.	MooKIT	✓	www.mooconmooc.org	-
2.	Canvas Network	✓	www.canvaslms.com/try-canvas	-
3.	Open edX	✓	demo.edunext.io/	sandbox.edunext.io
			-	amc-app.appsembler.com
4.	Sakai	✓	trysakai.longsight.com	-
			cle.edia.nl/portal	-
5.	Learn Moodle	✓	school.demo.moodle.net	demo.moodle.net/

ANALYSIS

The social networking and collaboration functionality are incorporated in MOOCs in different ways like, provisions to connect, tools available in the platform and third-party tools. As a result, features provided to the learner vary with the way the functionality is incorporated.

The features of social networking and collaboration is classified hierarchically into - components, operations, and parameters. The components are the building blocks like, profile, connection, and post. Each identified component is further divided into operations that can be performed by the learner. The operations are supported by a list of parameters that are provided in the form of options or controls to be used by the learner to avail features of social networking and collaboration.

The features of social networking and collaboration provided by the MOOC platform are identified for learners. The identified features are presented in the feature list for social networking and collaboration, separately.

Social Networking in MOOC

The social networking functionality is incorporated in MOOC by providing provisions to the learner for connecting with their community of learners. A learner can connect with the participants that reside inside the learning environment or with their social connections in the social networking platform, external to the platform. Thus, the network supported by social networking in MOOC is divided into (1) in-course network, the network of learners within MOOC, and (2) external network, the network of learners created using the social networking platform outside MOOC. The list of features is formulated, depicting identified components, operations, and parameters for social networking in MOOC.

Each learner in the in-course network maintains a profile that contains basic information about the individuals. The visibility of this information can be controlled by the learner. Some courses allow learners to import their profile from existing accounts. A learner can also view activities of the network and of self, like, contributions (post, comment, reply) in a forum, blog. Also, learners can view people already in the contact list and/or add a new contact by requesting others.

A learner uses external network linked with the social media accounts for various course-related activities like, to get notified about new updates, share course link with friends, endorse a course by liking, tweeting, and share achievement in the form of certificates or final grades. For each of these purposes, ready-made options are provided like, 'vote', 'like', 'endorse', 'tweet.' A learner can log in to a course using their social media account like, Facebook, Google Plus, which gets automatically linked with the learner's account. A learner can also link or unlink these accounts manually from their course account. A learner is allowed by some MOOC platforms to share the help, FAQ or discussion forum posts with their external network connections. Some MOOC courses allow the learner to view information about their referrals shared as course link with their friends. For example, the total number of referrals sent and how many of them enrolled in the courses. Table 3 list the features provided for in-course and external network for social networking in MOOC. It also shows the presence (✓) and absence (-) of features supported by the platforms.

For in-course network, the platforms provide all functionality required for social networking within the platform. They provide provisions to create a network, maintain network and other related activities. In contrast, for the external network, the platforms provide provisions to facilitate sharing of course-related information and achievements with their social connections in other social networking platforms, directly, from within the MOOC. In general, MOOC providers do not have their own tools for external social networking, but they simply link the platform using provisions, with the existing social networking platforms (e.g. Facebook, Twitter).

Table 3. The feature list of social networking of the platforms

	Components	Operations	Parameters	Proprietary							Open-Source				
				C	E	U	F	N	I	W	M	O	V	S	L
In-Course Network	Profile	View	User Info, Team, Course Enroll	✓	✓	✓	✓	✓	✓	✓	✓	✓	✓	✓	✓
		Edit/ Delete	User Info of own profile	✓	✓	✓	✓	✓	✓	✓	✓	✓	✓	✓	✓
		Import	From Social Media Account	-	-	-	-	✓	✓	-	-	-	-	-	-
		Visibility Control	Public, Contact, Local, Group	-	-	-	✓	✓	-	-	-	✓	✓	✓	✓
	Activity	View Network	Contribution, Stats, Submission	-	-	-	✓	-	-	-	✓	-	-	-	✓
		View Self	Contribution, Submission	-	-	✓	-	✓	-	-	✓	-	✓	-	✓
	Contact/ Team	View	Name, Role, Group	-	-	-	-	✓	-	✓	-	-	✓	✓	✓
		Add	Send Request to Add	-	-	-	-	✓	-	-	-	-	✓	✓	✓
External Network	Course	Notify	Course, Feature, News	✓	✓	✓	✓	✓	-	-	✓	✓	✓	-	✓
		Endorse	Like, Tweet	-	-	-	-	✓	✓	-	-	-	✓	-	-
		Share	Course Link	✓	✓	✓	✓	✓	✓	-	-	✓	-	-	✓
		Share Attainment	Web Certificates	✓	✓	✓	✓	✓	-	-	-	✓	-	-	✓
			Final Grades	✓	✓	-	-	-	✓	-	-	-	-	-	-
	Account	Login	via Social media account	✓	✓	✓	✓	✓	-	✓	✓	✓	-	✓	✓
		Link/Unlink	Link/ Unlink social account	✓	✓	✓	-	-	✓	-	✓	✓	✓	✓	✓
	Post	Share	Help, FAQ, Forum Post	-	-	✓	-	✓	✓	-	-	-	-	-	-
	Connection	Refer (Invite)	Share-Link, Twitter, Email	-	-	✓	-	-	✓	-	-	-	-	-	-
		View Referral	Stats, #Enrollment in course	-	-	-	-	-	✓	-	-	-	-	-	-

C - Coursera, E - edX, U - Udacity, F- FutureLearn, N- NovoEd, I- iversity, W-Swayam, M - MooKIT, O - Open edX, V - Canvas Network, S - Sakai, L - Learn Moodle

Collaboration in MOOC

The collaboration functionality in MOOC is incorporated using various tools, like, discussion forum, video conference, and message. The collaboration tools are either developed by providers or already existing third-party tools are integrated. MOOC platforms incorporate the tools, mainly, in two ways- (1) third-party tools and (2) built-in tools. Third-party tools for video conference and blog are generally incorporated in MOOC. The discussion forum, journal, team creation, message, and blog are provided as built-in tools in MOOC. The provider may choose to enable or disable built-in tools. Additionally, some tools like blog, may be provided as third-party tools or built-in tools.

Moreover, from our analysis, it was found that all tools do not have global scope or common scope, but the scope or reach of the tools vary. The tool can be associated with a user (learner), course or platform. For example, an instance of message tool is provided to each learner, that will not change according to the courses enrolled or any other factor; the instance of a journal tool is associated with a specific course that may or may not be available to other courses even by the same provider; and a single instance of blog tool is provided for the full platform. Table 4 summarizes the collaboration tools and their scope currently supported in MOOC platforms.

Table 4. The list of collaboration tools offered in studied MOOC platforms

Tools	Scope
Blog	Platform
Video Conference	Course, User
Discussion Forum, Journal, Team creation	Course
Message	User

During our study, it was found that some collaboration tools are included in most of the platforms, and some tools are specific to certain platforms. So, based on the presence of tools in MOOC platforms, we categorize collaboration tools into two categories: (1) common tools, and (2) selective tools.

Common Tools

From the study of the selected platform, we found that discussion forum, video conference, and blog tools are included in most platforms. A feature list specifying the components, operations, and parameters is formulated, for these common collaboration tools.

A learner uses discussion forum for sharing their view, interacting with peers, asking peers for help, and to work mutually on a common problem. All discussions are centralized at one place and allow the learners to view them in the form of lists or categories, which may further have several filtering options, like trending, followed, and pinned. The learner can either view an individual contribution or view all discussion at once in the discussion list. The learner can publish their problems in a discussion forum by simply adding a post. On each post, the participants can provide their response. Only, author of the post/response/comment (contribution) is allowed to edit, update or delete their contribution. Various controls are offered to the learner for performing actions like, voting, marking as read /unread, and star.

Moreover, some posts are graded where it is mandatory for the learner to review the post and participate in the discussion. The participants are graded based on their contribution to the post. Table 5 lists the features of discussion forum provided in MOOC, showing their presence (✓) and absence (-) in platforms.

Generally, *video conferencing* functionality is provided using third-party tools, in MOOC. Two open-source tools - *Google Hangout and BigBlueButton*[8]; and a proprietary tool *WebEx*[9], are used in MOOC. The features of two open-source tools are summarized in Table 6. The learners view information about video conference, like, title, description, status whether it is still live or ended, on a single page as conference page. The instructor sets up a *general conference* for communicating with the learners, course-wide. Also, learners can set up a *personal conference* to interact with a group of learners' specific for a course unit. The participant use the conference interface to participate in a conference, interact with others, and manage interaction using controls provided for airing of video/audio and sharing of files, presentations or other resources. In Chauhan and Goel (2015), the features of a video interface are listed for MOOC.

A learner in MOOC uses the blog tool to share course information, ideas, suggestions, or comments on a topic. To provide the functionality of the blog, MOOC platforms either use third-party tools like, WordPress, Tumblr[10], or create their own tool. Features of blog for a web application are discussed by Gupta and Goel (2012), which may be used for MOOC as well.

Selective Tools

The *journal*, *team creation*, and *message* tools are found in a few selected MOOC platforms. For these tools, the list is formulated for their features provided as components, operations, and parameters; however, MOOC platforms are not compared for these selective tools. Table 7 shows the features of the journal, team creation, and message tool.

Journal provides a space for the learners to reflect their ideas and communicate privately with the instructor. The information in journal is maintained in the form of entries, and it can be kept private or made public. People can add entries to their own journal or just follow the journal of others. Sometimes, the followers can comment on entries of the journals. Moreover, the journal is sometimes added as a graded activity for the learners, where participation is compulsory.

Team creation facilitates a learner to gather and manage the community of learners in a group or team, which, in general is done by the course instructor. The participants can view or join the already existing team, or they can create their own team or group. Each team is given a private team space with facilities of communication, file exchange, and schedule meetings. To include such features, various third-party tools like Google Meet[11], Google Calendar[12], and Google Hangout, is provided by the author (learner/instructor) of a team. Apart from interaction and sharing of the content between the members, a team author can ask for mentor's feedback on specific course content. Some platforms restrict the learner to be a member of one team at a time in one course, while others allow becoming part of multiple teams.

Message is used as an internal message transfer system for exchanging messages with individuals and/or group of users, by their role and course category. In addition to composing a message, users can edit, delete, reply (one/all), forward, and search the message. By default, each course site provides a message center that records messages in different categories like, sent, received and deleted. Also, a user is allowed to create a folder to store messages.

Some MOOC platforms also provide additional tools for collaboration from third-party providers. For example, Google Docs[13], Google Drive[14], and Google Calendar are provided as third-party tools. The tools allow multiple users to work on a task as a group.

Table 5. The feature list of discussion forum tool

Components	Operations	Parameters	Proprietary							Open-Source				
			C	E	U	F	N	I	W	M	O	V	S	L
Discussion List	View List	Detail {Title, Type, Date, Unread Message}	✓	✓	✓	✓	✓	✓	✓	✓	✓	✓	✓	✓
		Filter {Liked, Followed, Commented, etc.}	✓	✓	✓	-	✓	✓	-	-	✓	✓	-	✓
		Identifier {Pinned, Followed, User Type}	✓	✓	✓	✓	✓	-	✓	✓	✓	✓	-	✓
		Sort {Recent, Most Voted, etc.}	✓	✓	✓		✓	✓	-		✓	✓	✓	-
		Status {Read, Subscribed, Graded, Total, etc.}	✓	✓	-	-	-	✓	✓	✓	✓	✓	-	✓
	View Category	By Topic, Followed/ Pinned, List, Trending	✓	✓	✓	✓	✓	✓	✓	✓	✓	✓	✓	✓
		By Filter {Same as in View list}	-	✓	✓	-	✓	✓	-	-	✓	✓	✓	✓
		By User name, Pinned, Liked, Recent, Date, etc.	✓	✓	-	✓	✓	✓	-	-	✓	✓	✓	✓
	Search	Topic, Post, Text	✓	✓	✓	-	✓	✓	✓	-	✓	✓	-	✓
	Keep Updated	Unread, New	-	✓	✓	-	✓	✓	-	-	✓	✓	-	-
		Notify via Podcast, Email	✓	✓	✓	✓	✓	✓	✓	✓	✓	✓	✓	✓
Post	View	Detail{Title, Author, etc.}, Read & Reply (#)	✓	✓	✓	✓	✓	✓	✓	✓	✓	✓	✓	✓
	Add & Edit	Select Topic	-	✓	✓	-	✓	✓	✓	-	✓	-	-	-
		Title, Content, Type, File, Post Setting	✓	✓	✓	-	✓	✓	✓	✓	✓	✓	✓	✓
		Follow, Preview, Reply, Post & see Reply	✓	✓	✓	-	✓	✓	-	-	✓	✓	-	✓
	Delete	Confirmation	✓	✓	✓	-	✓	✓	✓	-	✓	✓	✓	✓
	Feedback	Like, Vote, Follow, Answer, Report	✓	✓	✓	✓	✓	✓	-	✓	✓	✓	-	✓
	Control	Vote, Follow, Report, Mark, Print, Sort	✓	✓	✓	✓	✓	✓	✓	✓	✓	✓	✓	✓
Graded Post	View List	List Detail {Title, Topic, Date, Content, etc.}	✓	-	-	-	-	-	-	-	-	✓	-	-
		Post Detail {Title, Points, etc.}, Review	✓	-	-	-	-	-	-	-	-	✓	-	✓
	View Post	Post Detail, Identifier	✓	-	-	-	-	-	-	-	-	✓	-	✓
		Discussion, View Rubric, Add Comment	✓	-	-	-	-	-	-	-	-	✓	-	-
	Feedback	As Text, File From Peers	-	-	-	-	-	-	-	-	-	✓	-	-
Response	View	Post Detail, Identifier	✓	✓	✓	✓	✓	✓	✓	✓	-	✓	✓	✓
		Comment, Mark, Goto First, Reply Initial	✓	✓	✓	✓	✓	✓	-	✓	✓	✓	✓	✓
	Add & Edit	Content, Add File, Add Original text	✓	✓	✓	✓	✓	✓	✓	✓	✓	✓	✓	✓
		Preview	✓	✓	✓	-	-	✓	-	-	✓	-	-	-
	Delete	Confirmation	✓	✓	✓	-	✓	✓	✓	✓	✓	✓	✓	✓
	Feedback	Like, Vote, Spam, Abusive, Inappropriate	✓	✓	✓	✓	✓	✓	-	✓	✓	✓	✓	✓
	Control	Vote, Report, Reply, Copy Link, Bookmark	✓	✓	✓	✓	✓	✓	✓	✓	✓	✓	✓	✓
Comment	View	Original Comment, Author, Date	✓	✓	✓	✓	✓	-	✓	-	✓	✓	✓	✓
	Add & Edit	Comment, Add Attachment	✓	✓	✓	✓	✓	-	✓	-	✓	✓	✓	✓
		Preview	✓	✓	✓	-	-	-	-	-	✓	-	✓	✓
	Delete	Confirmation	✓	✓	✓	-	✓	-	✓	-	✓	✓	✓	✓
	Feedback	Like, Vote, Spam, Abusive	✓	✓	✓	✓	✓	-	-	-	✓	✓	✓	✓
	Control	Report, Bookmark, Share Link	✓	✓	✓	✓	✓	-	✓	-	✓	✓	✓	✓

C - Coursera, E - edX, U - Udacity, F- FutureLearn, N- NovoEd, I- iversity, W-Swayam, M - MooKIT, O - Open edX, V - Canvas Network, S - Sakai, L - Learn Moodle

Table 6. The feature list of video conferencing tools

Components	Operations	Parameters	GH	B3
Conference Page	View	Detail, Status {New, Ended}, Scope {Course, Unit}	✓	✓
Interface	Control	Display, View, Advance, Help	✓	✓
	Setting	Record, Type {Moderator/ Presenter}, Control {Lock, Mute}	✓	✓
General Conference	Join/Start	View Interface Options to interact	✓	✓
	Setting	Microphone (on/off), Browser, Plug-in, Other	✓	✓
Personal Conference	Create, Update	Detail, Status, Recording (on/off), Time Limit, Invite	-	✓
	Setting	Microphone (on/off), Browser, Plug-in	-	✓

GH- Google Hangout, B3- BigBlueButton

Table 7. The feature list of journal, team creation, and message tool

Tools	Components	Operations	Parameters
Journal	All Entries	View Entries	Detail {Title, Content, Comments}, Status {Followed}, Filter
	People	View, Search	Name, Follow/Following
		Control	See full journal, Follow
	Own Entry	Add, Update	Title, Content, Permission, Comment, Preview, Publish
		View	Title, Content, Comments, Followers, Publish Status
		Share	Using Social Media Accounts
	Comment	Add, Update	Add/ Edit/ Delete {Comment}, Preview
Team Creation	Team	View List	Team Name, Logo, Creator's Name, Members (#)
		View Team	Team Name, Tagline, Members List, Recent Activity
		Create	Detail {Name, Logo, etc.}, Author/Member Control {Invite, Leave, etc.}
		Join/ Follow	View Team, Join, Send Request to Join / Follow
		Search	Team Name, Search only Open Team {Select, Deselect}
		Support	Ask for mentor's feedback, Option {Mark all as Read, Reply}
	Default Team	View List	Name (Learner, Team), Picture, Country, Last Activity Time
		Search	Name, Location, Language, Who have a team, Group interest
	Group	View	Name, Type {Closed, Open}, Members (#)
		Create, Edit	Name, Tagline, Logo, Privacy (Open, Close, Member Control)
		Update	Post, Comment
Message	Message	View List	All/Course, Mark, Category {Inbox, etc.}, Control {Previous/ Next}
		View	Details {Author, File}, All/specific, Control {Reply, Mark Star}
		Create, Reply, Forward	Fields {Course, To, Subject, Message, Add Media}, Set {Bcc, cc, Label}, Ctrl {Preview, Save Draft}
		Move	To {Sent, Deleted, Draft, Archived}
		Search	Recipient, Conversation
		Control User	Block User, Report {Abusive, Spam}
	Folder	Update	Folder - Create, Add, Rename, Delete

FINDINGS AND DISCUSSION

The findings of social networking in MOOC are discussed here for both, in-course network and external network. For the in-course network, the maximum features, about 85%, are provided by NovoEd and Learn Moodle; and minimum about 14% of features are offered by edX. We find that only one component 'profile' with operations edit, view, and delete is supported by all platforms. The import of 'profile' from social media account, view of 'activity' in a network, and sending the request to add member in 'contact' are least popular, since they are supported by very few platforms. For the external network, the highest percentage of features (~77%) is offered by Coursera, and lowest percentage (~11%) is supported by Swayam. The notification of course and sharing of course link and web certificates is popular among the platforms. Almost all platforms support the component 'account' login and linking. However, the components 'connection' and 'post' are present in very few platforms. Also, for the component 'course', endorsing and final grade attainment is supported by three platforms only.

The analysis of discussion forum for collaboration reveals that all components except 'graded post' are supported by all platforms. The 'graded post' component is supported by only three platforms. We find that operations for different components of discussion forum are less supported by Future Learn, Swayam, and MooKIT. The video conferencing tools, Google Hangout allows interaction with a maximum of 10 users at a time, but BigBlueButton allows interaction with 50 users. A key difference between the two tools is, about the 'personal conference'. This feature is provided only by BigBlueButton.

Figure 1 displays the percentage of features supported by different platforms for social networking and collaboration. Some of our key observations are as follows:

- For social networking- NovoEd provides maximum functionality about 75% followed by Learn Moodle. Less than 40% of the features are provided by Swayam, MooKIT, and Sakai;
- The discussion forum functionality is best supported by Canvas Network, about 92%. Coursera, edX, Udacity, NovoEd, Open edX, and Learn Moodle provide more than 80% functionality. The least features are supported by MooKIT, about 46%.

Figure 1. Graph showing percentage of features supported by the platforms

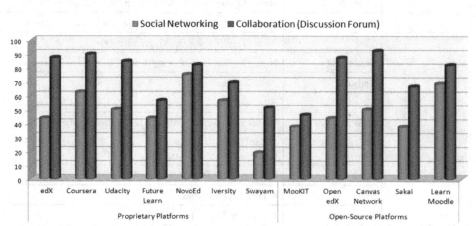

It is also noted that LMS-MOOC platforms (Canvas Network, Sakai, and Learn Moodle) provide more features for in-course social networking in contrast to external networking. This might be because of the closed nature of LMS, where learners connect with their peers inside the learning environment only. LMS-MOOC still supports in-course features and has been enhanced to include external networking features.

To encourage the use of open-source technology in delivering education, our finding from the comparative analysis of open-source platforms is as follows:

- Learn Moodle provides all components but supports few operations and parameters;
- Open edX supports maximum features of discussion forum components but does not include a component 'graded post';
- The maximum features are supported by Learn Moodle followed by Canvas Network, Open edX, MooKIT, and Sakai, for social networking;
- For collaboration, maximum features are supported by Canvas Network followed by Open edX, Learn Moodle, Sakai, and MooKIT.

From our findings, we suggest the selection of the platform on the basis of their social networking and collaboration features, as follows:

- EdX, Coursera, Udacity, NovoEd, and iversity, are the proprietary platforms offering 75% or more features for discussion forum and 40% and more for social networking;
- Canvas Network, Open edX, and Learn Moodle are the three open-source platforms providing maximum features for combined social networking and collaboration in MOOC.

From our analysis of the features and functionality of social networking and collaboration, we list some suggestions for improvement of the platforms:

- Proprietary platforms can add more components for in-course networking;
- Open-source platforms can be updated to include external social networking;
- Discussion form tool can be enhanced to include 'graded post' component;
- Platforms can be updated to include specific operations (view referral, endorse, import profile) and parameters (preview, bookmark).

BENEFITS OF THE ANALYSIS

The feature lists presented here is exhaustive, for including the social networking and collaboration functionality in MOOC platform. It has been derived after analyzing the most popular MOOC platforms.

For social networking, our analysis helps in deciding whether to support the in-course network, external network, or both. For collaboration in MOOC, it aids in deciding whether to include a third-party tool or create a built-in tool. Also, our feature comparison can be used for selecting the open-source third-party tool. In addition to common collaboration tools like, discussion forum, video conference, and blog; the features of specific tools (journal, team creation, and message) presented here, can be used to include them in MOOC platform. Moreover, the comparative analysis of platforms presented is of use during the selection of a platform, based on their level of support for social networking and collaboration.

LIMITATION AND FUTURE RESEARCH DIRECTION

For arriving at the feature list, for social networking and collaboration, the most popular MOOC platforms have been studied. There may be some functionality that are provided by other proprietary platforms and not included in the selected platforms. Also, other open-source MOOC platforms, which have not been studied, may have some extra features not included in our study. This is a limitation of our work. Another limitation of the feature list arises when the list is used for the purpose of creating standalone social networking and/or collaboration tools. This feature list may not be sufficient for such purposes. Standalone social networking functionality and collaboration tools may require more features, which does not lie in the scope of this paper.

In future, the authors aim to develop a structural design for social networking and collaboration software in MOOC. The authors intend to categorize the feature list into basic, advanced, and optional, so that the developer and the provider can choose from among the advanced and optional features based on their needs. A tool for the purposes of selection among the features is also proposed. Also, we aim to provide an estimation mechanism to compare different platforms for social networking and collaboration functionality supported by them.

CONCLUSION

This paper gives a holistic view of the social networking and collaboration functionality incorporated in MOOC. In this paper, we present a feature list for social networking and collaboration in MOOC. It benefits the MOOC providers and developers to select features from the list, in contrast to, specify afresh. The list can also be used to include the features in the platform. Our analysis also helps the platform providers and educational practitioners in selecting a platform as well as tools, based on the features list presented here. All or part of the functionality may be selected from the list. The proposed feature list is extensible and can be easily updated to include new functionality or feature.

REFERENCES

Alario-Hoyos, C., Pérez-Sanagustín, M., Delgado-Kloos, C., Muñoz-Organero, M., & Rodríguez-de-las-Heras, A. (2013). Analysing the impact of built-in and external social tools in a MOOC on educational technologies. *Proceedings of the European Conference on Technology Enhanced Learning* (pp. 5-18). Berlin: Springer. 10.1007/978-3-642-40814-4_2

Baker, M. J. (1994). A Model for Negotiation in Teaching-Learning Dialogues. *Journal of Artificial Intelligence in Education*, 5(2), 199–254.

Bereiter, C., & Scardamalia, M. (2003). Learning to work creatively with knowledge.

Blaye, A., & Light, P. (1990). Computer-based learning: The social dimensions. In H. C. Foot, M. J. Morgan, & R. H. Shute (Eds.), *Children helping children* (pp. 135–150). Chichester: Wiley.

Blom, J., Verma, H., Li, N., Skevi, A., & Dillenbourg, P. (2013). MOOCs are more social than you believe. eLearning Papers.

Bonk, C. J., & Zhang, K. (2006). Introducing the R2D2 model: Online learning for the diverse learners of this world. *Distance Education, 27*(2), 249–264. doi:10.1080/01587910600789670

Bouchet, F., Labarthe, H., Bachelet, R., & Yacef, K. (2017). Who wants to chat on a MOOC? Lessons from a peer recommender system. *Proceedings of the European Conference on Massive Open Online Courses* (pp. 150-159). Cham: Springer. 10.1007/978-3-319-59044-8_17

Butcher, N., Wilson-Strydom, M., Uvalic-Trumbic, S., & Daniel, J. (2013). *A Guide to Quality in Online Learning*. Academic Partnerships.

Chauhan, J., & Goel, A. (2015, May). An Analysis of Video Lecture in MOOC. In ICTERI (pp. 35-50).

Chen, Y. R., Lin, Y. C., Chu, L., Chiou, Y., & Shih, T. K. (2015, August). Team formation for collaborative learning with social network consideration based on edX's online discussion board. *Proceedings of the 2015 8th International Conference on Ubi-Media Computing (UMEDIA)* (pp. 146-151). IEEE. 10.1109/UMEDIA.2015.7297445

Coetzee, D., Fox, A., Hearst, M. A., & Hartmann, B. (2014). Chatrooms in MOOCs: all talk and no action. *Proceedings of the first ACM conference on Learning@ scale conference* (pp. 127-136). ACM. 10.1145/2556325.2566242

Doise, W., & Mugny, W. (1984). *The Social Development of the Intellect*. Oxford: Pergamon Press.

Filvà, D. A., Guerrero, M. J. C., & Forment, M. A. (2014). The effects of massiveness on the participation in social technologies: a MOOC in secondary education. *Proceedings of the Second International Conference on Technological Ecosystems for Enhancing Multiculturality* (pp. 397-402). ACM. 10.1145/2669711.2669930

García-Peñalvo, F. J., Cruz-Benito, J., Borrás-Gené, O., & Blanco, Á. F. (2015). Evolution of the Conversation and Knowledge Acquisition in Social Networks related to a MOOC Course. *Proceedings of the International Conference on Learning and Collaboration Technologies* (pp. 470-481). Springer International Publishing. 10.1007/978-3-319-20609-7_44

Garrison, D. R., & Kanuka, H. (2004). Blended learning: Uncovering its transformative potential in higher education. *The Internet and Higher Education, 7*(2), 95–105. doi:10.1016/j.iheduc.2004.02.001

Gillani, N., & Eynon, R. (2014). Communication patterns in massively open online courses. *The Internet and Higher Education, 23*, 18–26. doi:10.1016/j.iheduc.2014.05.004

Gupta, K., & Goel, A. (2012). Requirement checklist for blog in web application. *International Journal of System Assurance Engineering and Management, 3*(2), 100–110. doi:10.100713198-012-0116-7

Hrastinski, S. (2008). The potential of synchronous communication to enhance participation in online discussions: A case study of two e-learning courses. *Journal of International Management, 45*, 499–506.

Imran, A. S., Pireva, K., Dalipi, F., & Kastrati, Z. (2016). An analysis of social collaboration and networking tools in eLearning. *Proceedings of the International Conference on Learning and Collaboration Technologies* (pp. 332-343). Cham: Springer . 10.1007/978-3-319-39483-1_31

Kamel Boulos, M. N., & Wheeler, S. (2007). The emerging Web 2.0 social software: An enabling suite of sociable technologies in health and health care education 1. *Health Information and Libraries Journal*, *24*(1), 2–23. doi:10.1111/j.1471-1842.2007.00701.x PMID:17331140

Kats, Y. (Ed.). (2013). Learning management systems and instructional design: best practices in online education. Hershey, PA: IGI Global. doi:10.4018/978-1-4666-3930-0

Kayode, B. K. (2018). Effect of Communication Management on Distance Learners' Cognitive Engagement in Malaysian Institutions of Higher Learning. *The International Review of Research in Open and Distributed Learning*, *19*(4). doi:10.19173/irrodl.v19i4.3672

Kellogg, S., Booth, S., & Oliver, K. (2014). A social network perspective on peer supported learning in MOOCs for educators. *The International Review of Research in Open and Distributed Learning*, *15*(5). doi:10.19173/irrodl.v15i5.1852

Khalil, H., & Ebner, M. (2014). MOOCs completion rates and possible methods to improve retention-A literature review. *Proceedings of the World Conference on Educational Multimedia, Hypermedia and Telecommunications* (Vol. 1, pp. 1305-1313). Academic Press.

Kop, R., Fournier, H., & Mak, J. S. F. (2011). A pedagogy of abundance or a pedagogy to support human beings? Participant support on massive open online courses. *The International Review Of Research In Open And Distributed Learning*, *12*(7), 74–93. doi:10.19173/irrodl.v12i7.1041

Liu, M., McKelroy, E., Kang, J., Harron, J., & Liu, S. (2016). Examining the use of Facebook and Twitter as an additional social space in a MOOC. *American Journal of Distance Education*, *30*(1), 14–26. doi:10.1080/08923647.2016.1120584

Mackness, J., Mak, S., & Williams, R. (2010). The ideals and reality of participating in a MOOC. *Proceedings of the 7th international conference on networked learning*, University of Lancaster. Academic Press.

Mak, S., Williams, R., & Mackness, J. (2010). Blogs and forums as communication and learning tools in a MOOC. *Proceedings of the 7th International Conference on Networked Learning*, University of Lancaster. Academic Press.

Manathunga, K., Hernández-Leo, D., & Sharples, M. (2017). A social learning space grid for MOOCs: Exploring a FutureLearn case. *Proceedings of the European Conference on Massive Open Online Courses* (pp. 243-253). Cham: Springer. 10.1007/978-3-319-59044-8_29

Monarch Media. (2010). Open-source learning management systems: Sakai and Moodle. In *White Papers*. Santa Cruz, CA: Monarch Media, Inc.

MoocGuide. (2011). 4. Designing a MOOC using social media tools. Retrieved from http://moocguide. wikispaces.com/4

MoocLab. (2017). MOOC Platform Comparison Table - 2017. Retrieved from http://www.mooclab. club/pages/mooc_platform_comparison

MoocLab. (2018). MOOC Platform Comparison Table. Retrieved from https://www.mooclab.club/pages/mooc_comparison_2018/

Muilenburg, L. Y., & Berge, Z. L. (2005). Student barriers to online learning: A factor analytic study. *Distance Education, 26*(1), 29–48. doi:10.1080/01587910500081269

Núñez, M. M., Gené, O. B., & Blanco, Á. F. (2014). Social community in MOOCs: practical implications and outcomes. *Proceedings of the Second International Conference on Technological Ecosystems for Enhancing Multiculturality* (pp. 147-154). ACM.

Ortega, S., Brouns, F., Fueyo Gutiérrez, A., Fano, S., Tomasini, A., Silva, A., ... & López, E. (2014). D2.1 Analysis of existing MOOC platforms and services.

Palloff, R. M., & Pratt, K. (2003). *The virtual student: A profile and guide to working with online learners*. John Wiley & Sons.

Shah, D. (2018). Class Central MOOC Report. *By The Numbers: MOOCs in 2018*. Retrieved from https://www.classcentral.com/report/mooc-stats-2018/

Shah, V., Banerjee, G., Murthy, S., & Iyer, S. (2018, December). Learner-centric MOOC for teachers on effective ICT integration: Perceptions and experiences. *Proceedings of the 2018 IEEE Tenth International Conference on Technology for Education (T4E)* (pp. 77-84). IEEE. 10.1109/T4E.2018.00023

Shen, C. W., & Kuo, C. J. (2015). Learning in massive open online courses: Evidence from social media mining. *Computers in Human Behavior, 51*, 568–577. doi:10.1016/j.chb.2015.02.066

Zhang, Q., Peck, K. L., Hristova, A., Jablokow, K. W., Hoffman, V., Park, E., & Bayeck, R. Y. (2016). Exploring the communication preferences of MOOC learners and the value of preference-based groups: Is grouping enough? *Educational Technology Research and Development, 64*(4), 809–837. doi:10.100711423-016-9439-4

Zygouris-Coe, V. I. (2019). Benefits and Challenges of Collaborative Learning in Online Teacher Education. In Handbook of Research on Emerging Practices and Methods for K-12 Online and Blended Learning (pp. 33-56). Hershey, PA: IGI Global. doi:10.4018/978-1-5225-8009-6.ch002

ENDNOTES

[1]   www.facebook.com
[2]   www.twitter.com
[3]   https://handout.google.com
[4]   https://wordpress.com/
[5]   https://plus.google.com/s
[6]   https://in.linkedin.com/
[7]   https://www.skype.com/
[8]   https://bigbluebutton.org/
[9]   https://www.webex.co.in/
[10]   https://www.tumblr.com/

[11]   https://meet.google.com/
[12]   https://www.google.com/calendar
[13]   https://www.google.co.in/docs/about/
[14]   https://www.google.com/drive/

This research was previously published in the International Journal of Distance Education Technologies (IJDET), 18(2); pages 34-51, copyright year 2020 by IGI Publishing (an imprint of IGI Global).

Chapter 11
Social Media Content Analysis and Classification Using Data Mining and ML

Sambhaji D. Rane

DKTE Society's Textile and Engineering Institute, India

ABSTRACT

Students' natural conversations on social media such as Twitter and Whatsapp are useful to understand their learning experiences feelings. Collecting and analyzing data from such media can be a difficult task. However, the large scale of data is required for automatic data analysis techniques to classify Twitter data. The proposed new system is a combination of qualitative analysis and large-scale data mining and ML techniques. This system focuses on engineering students' Twitter posts, which are collected from engineering colleges, to understand issues and problems in their learning. The authors first conduct a qualitative analysis using ML studio on tweets collected from engineering colleges using term #DStudentsproblems, engineeringProblem, Aluminisuggestions, and ladyEngineer. Collected tweets are related to engineering students' college lives. In the proposed system, a multi-label classification algorithm to classify tweets reflecting students' problems such as soft skill issues, heavy study load, lack of social engagement, and sleep problems is used.

1. INTRODUCTION

Social media site Twitter and Whatsapp become important venue for the young generation to communicate and exchange information about their learning process and real time on going thinking process. On various social media sites, such as Twitter, Whatsapp and Facebook students discuss and share their everyday problems in an informal manner. Students' written tweets provide implicit knowledge and a whole new view for educational analysts to understand students' learning experiences outside the controlled classroom environment. This understanding can inform institutional decision-making on interventions for at-risk students, improvement of education quality in college and thus enhance student recruitment, retention ratio and placement in companies (G.Siemens ,2011).

DOI: 10.4018/978-1-6684-7123-4.ch011

The learning analytics and educational data mining fields have focused on data obtained from classroom technology usage, or controlled online learning environments to inform educational decision-making. Traditionally, educational analysts use methods to collect data for analysis such as surveys using offline forms, interviews with students, conduct various classroom activities to collect data related to students' learning experiences (M. Clark,2008). These methods usually require more time. The scale of such studies is usually limited. Twitter is a well liked social media site. Its content is mostly public and very short. Twitter provides free APIs for data stream. Therefore, in proposed system used Twitter for chose to start from analyzing students' posts.

Here more focus is given on engineering students' Twitter posts to find the problems in their educational experiences. Engineering colleges and departments have been struggling with students' recruitment, retention and placement issues. Based on understanding of issues and problems in students' life, policymakers can make decisions on services that can help students to overcome such problems and issues. Many issues such as study problems, lack of social engagement and soft skill issues clearly come out.

2. PROPOSED SYSTEM

A proposed system is focuses on engineering students' Twitter posts to understand issues and problems in their educational experiences. The proposed scheme is made up of Twitter data extraction, tweets data cleaning. Classification of tweet data and web module .The proposed scheme performs various operations on tweets as shown in Figure 1

Figure 1. Architecture of Proposed System for Mining Twitter Data using ML.

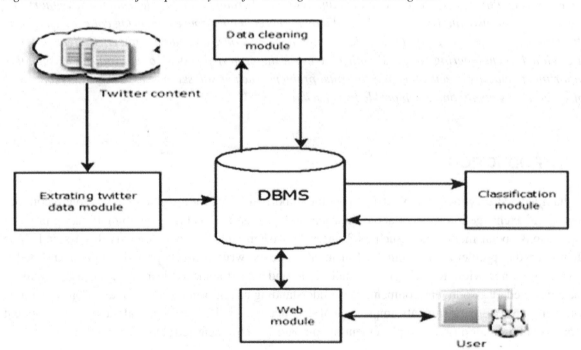

In the first phase user extract tweets from twitter using twitter standard API . Tweet processing operation performed in second phase. Then, tweet classification is perform using Naïve Bayes algorithm, tweets are classified into heavy study load, lack of social engagement, negative emotions, sleep problems, soft-skill issues and other. In data cleaning phase perform various operation on tweet to remove noise from it.

2.1 Extracting Twitter Data

Tweets searching started using possible terms such as engineer, students, college, class, homework, but the data set still contained more noise, also collected very small relevant tweets count. Found that, more relevant Twitter tweets are extracted using input query terms such as engineeringProblem, DStudentsproblems, Aluminisuggestions and ladyEngineer with use of Twitter. The authentication of API requests on Twitter is carried out using OAuth. Detailed steps for making an API call from a Twitter application using OAuth is given below.

1. Applications are required to register themselves with twitter. Through this process the application is issued a consumer key and secret.
2. The application uses the consumer key and secret to create a unique Twitter link to which a user is directed for authentication. Twitter verifies the user's identity and issues an OAuth verifier.
3. The application uses the PIN to request an Access Token and Access Secret unique to the user.
4. Using the Access Token and Access Secret, the application authenticates the user on Twitter and issues API call.

The tweets extraction algorithm is given in Algorithm 1. In this algorithm used query term such as engineeringProblem, DStudentsproblems, Aluminisuggestions and ladyEngineer as input for extract tweets from Twitter. The algorithm repeats itself recursively until there are no more tweets to be discovered. As a result, the output of algorithm tweets extraction is a set of tweets. These tweets are stored into database for further processing.

Algorithm 1: Tweets extraction.

```
1 Algorithm TweetExtraction (term)
2 Input: query term
3 Output: Tweets
4 // Extract tweets from the Twitter. Return true if successful.
5 begin
6 // Build connection with Twitter for tweets Extraction.
7 twitter: = TwitterFactory(cb.build()).getInstance()
8 while result for query not null do
9 result := twitter.search(query)
10 tweets := result.getTweets() return true
11 for each tweet do
12 insert tweets in to database
13 end for
```

```
14 end while
15 end
```

2.2 Tweet Data Cleaning and Text Pre-Processing

In this module pre-processed the texts and find useful text before training the classifier. Take input as tweets which are collect using Extracting Twitter Data module. Perform cleaning operation on tweets because there is noise present in to collected tweets so there to Pre-processing the tweets before training the classifier.

Use MySQL5.5 database for store collected and processed tweets. First database "social_data_mine" is created using create database social_data_mine command in sql. Under the "social_data_mine" database create various tables which are required for store data. Tables are tweet, search_topic and processing_tweet .Tweet table is used to store the collected tweets. Un-processed tweets are store in to tweet table. Search_topic table is used to store search topic name (query term) and topic id and processing_tweet table is used to store processed tweet.

Pre-processed the texts includes removed all the #engineeringProblems, #DStudentsproblems, #Aluminisuggestions and #ladyEngineer hashtags. For other co-occurring hashtags, only removed the # sign, and kept the hashtag texts. Remove all words from the tweets that contain non-letter symbols and punctuation. Tweets preprocessing done with help of remove special characters, stop words and stemming. After removing unnecessary symbols from collected tweet all the data is inserted in to processing_tweet table for further processing.

1. Remove HTTP Link: There is no use of http link for tweet classification, so remove the http link from the collected tweets. Perform splitting operation on processed tweet message. After splitting scan the every word from processed tweet. If the word not starts with http then add into the result and return the tweet without http link.

2. Remove Special Characters: Remove all the #engineeringProblems hashtags. For other co-occurring hashtags, Only removed the # sign, and kept the hashtag texts, Removed all words that contain non-letter (Chen, 2014; Clark et al., 2008; Davidov et al., 2010; Gaffney, 2010; Go et al., 2009; Goffman, 1959; Hong et al., 2011; Rost et al., 2013; Siemens & Long, 2011) symbols and punctuation, such as # ,:$,% ,?,/,>,=,!,|,(etc. Scan the processed tweet-I message, if the any special character found in the tweet message then it replace with the blank and return the tweet without special character.

3. Stemming: Stemming means reducing a word to its base (or stem).Stemming is useful when doing any kind of text analysis concerned about the content of a the different times of verbs and the different ending for singular and plural, make it difficult to discern the importance of specific words with in text when treat each word as it is .Use a dictionary that lists all words together with their stems. Wordnet dictionary is large lexical database of English Nouns, Verb, Adjectives and Adverbs. It is free and publicly available for download. For actually stemming dictionary and a morphological processor is used. If it returns null then word not present in wordnet dictionary. Find the word match do with help of LookupBaseForm().Get the wordstem form index word, index word used for organize the word in wordnet dictionary.

4. Remove Stopwords: Remove the words that are very commonly used in a given language because to focus on the importance words. Tweet text contain stop words such as hi, etc, be, as and many more words. Keep the words such as all, always, much, more because tweet used these words frequently.

Performing splitting operation on the processed tweet message, split tweet message in to separate word and scan the every word , if a word is not found in stopword list then it add into the result and return the tweet without stopwords. After processing all tweets, it store into processing_tweet table.

2.3 Tweets Classification

Categories Development : There were no pre-defined categories of the data so need to explore what students were saying in the tweets. It is very challenging task to develop categories for classification model. For categories development, online Azure Machine Learning (AML) studio is used. Model for find the topics from tweets is built using AML. Following processes is followed for topic modelling.

1. Create project for topic modelling
2. Upload the tweet data set
3. Choose the text analytics algorithm LDA for topic modelling
    Latent Dirichlet Allocation (LDA):

LDA represent tweets as mixture of topic that spit out words with probability.LDA algorithm has automatically detected the topics that tweets contain. It is used for topic modeling.LDA algorithm take input as topic count and n-gram term for classification tweets into topics number.

For topic name and qualitative result perform content analysis on topic result generated by text analytics algorithm such as Latent Dirichlet Allocation (LDA). Content analysis is to identify what are the major worries concerns and issues that engineering student encounter in their study and life. Prominent categories are identified after analysing result of AML studio tool are heavy study load, lack of social engagement, negative emotions, sleep problems, soft-skill issues and other.

Found that many tweets could belong to more than one category. For example, "Why I am not in art school? Hate being in engineering school. Too many stuff, No enjoyment" falls in to heavy study load, negative emotions at the same time. For that required to use multi-label classification.

The prominent categories are
1. **Heavy Study load:** Analysis shows that classes, homework, exams and lab dominate the student life. Libraries lab and the engineering building are most frequently visited places. Some illustrative tweets are "Study over 20 hours for test-I", "so much homework, so little time".
2. **Lack of social engagement:** Analysis shows that students need to sacrifice the time for social engagement in order to home work and to prepare for classes and examination. For example, "I feel like I am hidden from the world-life of engineering student".
3. **Negative emotions:** Only categories tweets as negative emotion when it specially express negative emotions such as hatred, anger, stress, sickness, depression, disappointment and despair. Students are mostly stressed with schoolwork. For example, "is it bad that before I started studying for my test today that i considered throwing myself in front of a moving car?"
4. **Sleep problems**: Sleep problems are widely common among engineering students. Student frequently suffer from lack of sleep and nightmares due to heavy study load and stress. For example, "I wake up from nightmares where I didn't finish my physical lab on time".

5. **Soft-skill issues:** Soft skill issues are widely common among rural engineering students. Student frequently suffer lack of confidence, lack of communication skill. For example, "required more training to improve communication skill".

6. **Other:** Tweet from this categories are do not have a clear meaning, do reflect various issues that engineering student have, but very small volume. For finding topics from this category AML studio is used. LDA algorithm is applied only on other category tweets, then gets tweets category related to curriculum problems, physical health problems, lack of gender diversity, lack of motivation, nerdy culture, identity crisis but count of tweets related to this categories are very small so, treated all this category as other. Tweet other than above five categories falls in to other category.

7. **Tweets Classification:** This model is used to classified tweets based on categories. Used multi label Naïve Bayes classifier to classified tweets based on categories. Take input as processed tweets. Apply classification algorithm on processed tweets for categories wise classification of tweets. Tweets are classifieds into prominent categories such as heavy study load, lack of social engagement, negative emotions, sleep problems, soft-skill issues and other. Algorithm result is stored into naivebayes table.

8. **Naïve Bayes (NB) Multi-Label Classifier:** Naïve Bayes is easy and fast to predict class of test dataset. It also performs well in multiclass prediction. When assumption of independence holds NB classifier perform better to other models (Chen, 2014). It performs well in case of categorical input. Naïve Bayes classifier used for tweets classification. Basic procedure for multi-label classifier follows. Each tweet is considered as document, there are a total number of N words in the learning dataset tweets collection $W=\{w_1, w_2,...., w_N\}$ and total number of L categories $C=\{c_1, c_2,.......c_L\}$.

Suppose there total number of M tweets in the training set and A of them are in category c. Then the prior probability of category c is

$P(c)= \dfrac{A}{M}$. And prior probability of other category is

$p(c')= \dfrac{M-A}{M}$. If a word w_n appears in category c for m_{wnc} and categories other than c for $m_{wnc'}$ times, then based on maximum likelihood estimation, the probability of this word in a specific category c is

$$p\left(w_n \mid c\right) = \dfrac{m_{w_n c}}{\displaystyle\sum_{n=1}^{n} m_{w_n c}}$$

word in this tweet, any word w_{ik} condition on c or c' follows multinomial distribution. Therefore the probability of tweet d_i belongs to category c is

$$p\left(c\middle|d_i\right) = \frac{p\left(d_i\middle|c\right) \cdot p\left(c\right)}{p\left(d_i\right)} \propto \prod_{k=1}^{K} p\left(w_{ik}\middle|c\right) \cdot p\left(c\right),$$

Posterior probability $P(c| d_i) = P(c)$ *(likelihood probability of words from tweet)

If $P(c| d_i)$ is larger than the probability threshold t, then *di* fit into category c, otherwise, *di* does fit into category c'. Other is only category if posterior probabilities of all categories are less than threshold value. Result of Naive Bayes (NB) classifier is stored in to naivebayes table.

The NB classifier algorithm is given in Algorithm 2. In this algorithm used collected tweets and categories as input for tweets classification. As a result, the output of algorithm NB classifier is classification of tweets into heavy study load (HSL), lack of social engagement (LOSE), negative emotions (NE), sleep problems (SP), soft-skill issues (SI) and other categories.

Algorithm 2: NB classifiers

```
1 Algorithm NBclassifier (tweet, category)
2 Input: processed Tweets and categories
3 Output: Categories wise classification Tweets
4 // Total number of M tweets in the training set and A of them in category c.
5 // d_i is tweet, P(c) is prior probability, P (W_n/c) is likelihood probabil-
ity.
6 // P (c| d_i ) is posterior probability
7 begin
8 categories C: = {c_1, c2 ….c_L}
9 for each category do
10 P(c) =A/M
11 end for
12 for each tweet do
13 divide d_i into sub words {w_1, w_2,….,w_N}
14 for each word do
15 P (W_n/c) = count of word/ total count of words in category c
16 end for
17 P (c| d_i) = P(c) * P(W_n/c)
18 if P (c| d_i) > probability threshold then
19 d_i does s fit into category c
20 end if
21 else
22 d_i does fit into category c'
23 end else
24 end for
25 end
```

3. RESULTS AND PERFORMANCE MEASURES

3.1 Performance Measures

To evaluate performance of system accuracy, precision, recall and f1-measure of four processes are used. There is a usually used Label based measure. Label based measures are calculated based on each category and then average over all category .

3.2 Label Based Evaluation Measures

Label based measures are calculated and average over each category. Create matrix in Table 1 for corresponding category c (Heavy study load).Similarly consider following matrix for each category.

Table 1. Contingency table for Heavy study load

	Tweet select by system	Tweet not select by system
Expected Tweet	True Positive(TRP) (actual heavy study load category tweets were correctly classified as heavy study load tweets)	False Negative(FAN) (heavy study load tweets s that were incorrectly marked as other category)
Not Expected Tweet	False Positive(FAP) (non- heavy study load tweets that were incorrectly classified as heavy study load)	True Negative(TRN) (all the remaining tweets are , correctly classified as non-Heavy study load tweets)

The sum of TRP, FAN, FAP and TRN is equal to total number of documents. Various metrics such as accuracy, precision, recall and F1 are used to measures the performance of classification algorithm. Then for one category c,

$$\text{Accuracy a} = \frac{TRP + TRN}{TRP + TRN + FAP + FAN}. \tag{1}$$

$$\text{Precision p} = \frac{TRP}{TRP + FAP}. \tag{2}$$

$$\text{Recall r} = \frac{TRP}{TRP + FAN}. \tag{3}$$

$$\text{F1} = \frac{2TRP}{2TRP + FAP + FAN}. \tag{4}$$

3.3 Twitter data Extraction Result

Twitter tweets are collected using input query terms such as engineeringProblem, DStudentsproblems, Aluminisuggestions and ladyEngineer. Using twitter API streamed tweets containing this query terms from January 2015 to July 2017.In total collected 16600 tweets. Table 2 shows summary of collected tweets.

Table 2. Tweets collection

Sr.no	Query term	count
1	engineeringProblem	12600
2	DStudentsproblems	2300
3	Aluminisuggestions	600
4	ladyEngineer	1100

3.4 Categories Development Result

For categories development online Azure Machine Learning (AML) studio is used. From this studio choose LDA topic modeling algorithm. This algorithm applies on tweet dataset for to generate topics based on tweets content. Result of LDA algorithm for some tweets using 7 topic and 2-grams. It only generates topics. For topic name, collect topic wise tweets together using probability values greater than 0.4. For correct topic name and qualitative result perform content analysis on topic result generated by text analytics algorithm LDA. Tweets are categories in to heavy study load, lack of social engagement, negative emotions, sleep problems, soft-skill issues and other.

3.5 Classification Result

From content analysis stage, a total of 600 #engineeringProblems, #Aluminisuggestions, and DStudent-sproblems tweets annotated with 6 categories. Uses this tweets for training and testing. Observation shows that when the probability threshold value is 0.004 the performance is better than other threshold values. Table 3 shows the categories wise tweets count.

Table 3. Number of tweets in each category for threshold value 0.004

Category	Number of tweets
Heavy study load	114
Lack of social engagement	69
Negative emotion	69
Sleep problems	73
Soft skill issues	69
Other	344

Performance measures are calculated using equation 1, 2, 3 and 4. Table 4 shows category wise percentage for each measure. Found that accuracy for all categories is above 93% for threshold value 0.004 using Naïve Bayes classifier.

Table 4. Category wise performance measure percentage

Category	Label a.	Label p.	Label r.	Label F1.
Heavy study load	93.24	68..42	95.12	79.59
Lack of social engagement	97.29	84.05	92.06	87.87
Negative emotion	97.29	86.95	86.95	88.23
Sleep problems	96.79	82.19	90.9	86.33
Soft skill issues	97.29	86.96	89.55	88.23
Other	96.45	75.00	75.16	75.00

3.6 Detect Student Problems From Offline Dataset

Naïve Bayes multi-label classifier is used to detect engineering student problems from offline dataset. There were 16000 tweets in offline dataset. Keep same threshold value for classifier for offline dataset. Table 5 shows number of tweets in each category for threshold value 0.004. So there is no extra human effort is needed when used classifier for classification.

Table 5. Categories wise result of offline dataset for threshold value 0.004

Category	Number of tweets
Heavy study load	1309
Lack of social engagement	528
Negative emotion	316
Sleep problems	375
Soft skill issues	205

4. CONCLUSION

A proposed system works for twitter data extraction, tweets data preprocessing and tweets classification. Query terms engineeringProblem, DStudentsproblems, Aluminisuggestions and ladyEngineer are very useful to collect relevant tweets. For category development topic modeling algorithm from ML studio is used. It gives categories wise tweets result. Content analysis is performed on ML studio result for category names and quality result. Naive Bayes multi label classifier algorithm performed on processed tweets for tweets classification. It gives the result in terms of accuracy above 93%, precision 85% and recall above 85%. In this workflow main problem of rural area engineering students such as soft skill issues is addressed. This proposed system result is very useful for educational policy makers to gain understanding of engineering students colleges' problems. It also provides a workflow for analyze Twitter data for educational purposes that overcomes the major limitations of traditional methods.

REFERENCES

Chen, X. (2014). *Mining social media data for understanding students learning experience*. IEEE Transactions.

Clark, M., Sheppard, S., Atman, C., Fleming, L., Miller, R., Stevens, R., Streveler, R., & Smith, K. (2008). Academic Pathways Study: Processes and Realities. *Proc. Am. Soc. Eng. Education Ann. Conf. Exposition*.

Davidov, D., Tsur, O., & Rappoport, A. (2010). Enhanced sentiment learning using twitter hashtags and smileys. *Proceedings of the 23rd International Conference on Computational Linguistics: Posters*, 241–249.

Gaffney. (2010). #iranElection: Quantifying Online Activism. *Proc. Extending the Frontier of Society On-Line (WebSci10)*.

Go, A., Bhayani, R., & Huang, L. (2009). Twitter sentiment classification using distant supervision. CS224N Project Report.

Goffman, E. (1959). *The Presentation of Self in Everyday Life*. Lightning Source Inc.

Hong, L., Dan, O., & Davison, B. D. (2011). Predicting popular messages in twitter. *Proceedings of the 20th international conference companion on World Wide Web*, 57–58. 10.1145/1963192.1963222

Rost, M., Barkhuus, L., Cramer, H., & Brown, B. (2013). Representation and communication: challenges in interpreting large social media datasets. *Proceedings of the 2013 conference on Computer supported cooperative work*, 357–362. 10.1145/2441776.2441817

Siemens, G., & Long, P. (2011). Penetrating the fog; Analysis in learning and education. *EDUCAUSE Review*, *48*(5), 30–32.

This research was previously published in the International Journal of Data Analytics (IJDA), 2(2); pages 75-84, copyright year 2021 by IGI Publishing (an imprint of IGI Global).

Chapter 12

Learner-Initiated Language Learning Through Social Media Sites (SMSs)

Rashad Ali Ahmed
Miami University, USA

ABSTRACT

Social media sites have become an essential part of communication and interaction all over the globe. They have also offered numerous opportunities to language learners across geographic borders, paralleled by a new research interest in their potential. The present study joins this relatively new line of research as it adds data from a sample of Yemeni English language learners about their uses and perceived benefits of using social media sites in English beyond formal education. The study came up with a conclusion that Yemeni EFL learners were actively participating in social media sites and were aware of their language-related benefits. The participants reported that social media sites were helpful for building various aspects of their English proficiency but found them most useful for their writing and reading skills, expanding their vocabulary, having access to authentic materials, and communicating with English speaking friends, both native and non-native speakers. They ranked their usefulness in the following order: Facebook, WhatsApp, and Twitter.

INTRODUCTION

Over the past two decades, the Internet, particularly Web 2.0 applications, has created new channels of human communication and learning. It is now easy to access enormous and ever-expanding bodies of information online. Meanwhile, Social Media Sites (hereafter SMSs) such as Facebook, WeChat, Instagram, Twitter, Snapchat, and WhatsApp enable millions of people across the globe to communicate and maintain connections with their friends and relatives (Al-Kadi, 2018; Bakeer, 2018, Greenhow & Lewin, 2016; Kasuma, 2017; Vivian, 2011). Some SMS users cultivate an audience comprised of people of different ages, nationalities, religions, and cultures, who follow and interact with them by commenting

DOI: 10.4018/978-1-6684-7123-4.ch012

on or sharing posts or even interacting virtually via face-to-face interplay. Many educational institutions, bedsides owning official pages on SMSs, are now offering learning opportunities. Students around the world spend a large portion of time present on social networking sites, performing different activities: chatting, gaming, gambling, etc. In 2008, TNS Global, a market research company, published a study on the use of digital technologies by adults from 16 industrialized nations. The study concluded that adults, on average, spend one third of their leisure time online. Most of the participants showed very high use of social networking, and over a third described social networking as 'fun' while over a quarter described it as 'interesting'.

Rationale

In the past, teachers have been generally regarded to be the primary sources of knowledge, and students depended entirely on their teachers as their exclusive providers of knowledge. With digital technology, today's language students have found new sources and resources to learn independently from parents, teachers, and other formal authorities. This trend is supported by a broader paradigm shift from teacher-dominance to learner-centered approach. Lee and McLoughlin (2008) argued that "outmoded didactic models, which place emphasis on the delivery of information by an instructor and/or from a textbook, may need to be replaced in order for student-centered learning to come to fruition" (p. 641). Now that computers and mobile technology are permeating students' lives, they spend substantial time using the Internet, seeking out new friends, playing games, watching videos, etc. (Feng, Wong, Wong, & Hossain, 2019). However, the efficiency of time that the EFL learners spend browsing social media to enhance language skills remains questionable. Feng et al. (2019) investigated how the use of Facebook and the Internet affect students' academic performance. The study found that using SMSs (e.g., Facebook) regularly for entertainment is a distraction for students and is negatively affecting their academic performance. The popularity of SMSs, specifically Facebook, demonstrates the appeal of online and virtual communities across generations, geographic locations, and cultures, but it also shows that these sites are particularly attractive to teenagers, homemakers, and students: demographics that may frequently feel isolated or lonely in their day to day lives (TNS Global, 2008).

Since TNS Global study was conducted, the use of social media has grown increasingly, especially among college students (Ha, Joa, Gabay, & Kim, 2018). As the importance of digital technology in today's world grows, so does the need to integrate these new technologies into the educational system. Thiele, Mai, and Post (2014) postulated that technology can "enhance learning by making the classroom more active and student-centered" (p. 80). Technology also offers access to authentic materials as well as opportunities for autonomous learning. Moreover, it allows language learners to communicate with native and non-native speakers from different parts of the world. Overall, the rise of modern technology among learners of English has received the attention of scholars in the field of English language teaching and substantial research exists on this issue (Al-kadi, 2018; Alsaleem, 2013; Bakeer, 2018; Chartrand, 2012; Manca & Ranieri, 2016). However, the specific language benefits of SMSs in informal settings have not been sufficiently explored. This omission serves as the primary rationale for this chapter.

LITERATURE REVIEW

Notwithstanding dozens of social networking sites, popular SMSs in the Middle East include Facebook, Twitter, WhatsApp, Instagram, WeChat, among many others. The personal utilization of these sites has become commonplace in academia. Empirical evidence in support of the beneficial effects of SMSs on students' learning and engagement remains both insufficient and inconclusive (Junco, Heiberger, & Loken, 2011). This dearth of evidence looms larger when one examines studies related to the potential benefits of SMSs for seamless informal language learning. Consequently, the literature review in this chapter is limited to the relatively small body of related studies with reference to three common SMSs: Facebook, Twitter, and WhatsApp.

Some studies have investigated the impact of social networking on education in general and on language learning in particular. The majority of these studies focused on formal language instruction (Manca & Ranieri, 2016; Kasuma, 2017; Rios & Campos, 2015). Other studies, though relatively few, found that technology has created new engaging environments for students to learn more easily and effectively outside formal institutions (Al-Kadi, 2018; Kurata, 2011; Trinder, 2017). Kurata (2011), Promnitz-Hayashi (2011), and Chartrand (2012) narrowed the focus from technology in general to the role of SMSs in language learning. The authors observed that SMSs have created new opportunities for language learners to access authentic language materials, which were difficult to find in the past. Through SMSs, learners of English can communicate with speakers from English speaking countries and non-native speakers from various countries in the world. On account of their ease to use and the emotional payoff of interacting with people that students may otherwise fail to encounter, SMSs also facilitate autonomous learning within a social environment. Similarly, Stanciu, Mihai, and Aleca (2012) conducted a study to analyze the impact of social networks on the educational process in Romanian higher education. The authors used a model for educational use of social networking adapted from Mazman and Usluel (2010). The model served to develop the usefulness of SMSs for teaching and learning in terms of six components: communication, collaboration, sharing resources, usefulness in the educational process, flexible technologies, and frequency of access. The results revealed that SMSs were very common among young people in Romania. Only 16% of the participants did not maintain SMS accounts. The study concluded that Facebook was the most common site with 87% of the participants reporting that they had Facebook accounts. Furthermore, the study found SMSs to be popular among teachers, with 56% of the participants already registered on SMSs, 44% of whom had Facebook accounts.

The following section outlines the main features of the SMSs in focus and the findings of studies that have investigated their roles in language learning. Firstly, Facebook has become one of the most frequently used social networks in the world. Statista.com reports that as of April 2019, Facebook claimed the largest number of active accounts ("2.32 billion monthly active users") and is therefore considered the most popular SMS all over the world. Facebook has many interactive features that enable users to post photos, videos, comments, add friends, and subscribe to groups. Promnitz-Hayashi (2011) observed how simple activities on Facebook helped students of a lower language proficiency class to develop various language skills. For instance, the learners who took part in the study became more comfortable while participating in online discussions, sharing opinions, and forging closer relationships with their classmates. The study reported that the incorporation of Facebook-based activities helped many of the more introverted students to be motivated to talk with their classmates. They began to express their opinions and provide extended reasoning in both face-to-face interactions and within their written classwork. In another study about Facebook as a medium of English language learning,

Kabilan, Ahmad, and Jafre (2010) investigated whether students of Sains Malaysia University (USM) considered Facebook a useful learning tool that would help them learn English with greater proficiency. The researchers collected the data through a survey distributed to 300 undergraduate students at USM (81 males and 219 females). The results showed that 137 of the participants (47 male and 116 female) had Facebook accounts, whereas the remainder did not. 33% of the participants were active Facebook users, logging onto Facebook at least once a day and 52% logging on at least once a month. The study concluded that Facebook could be an effective online learning environment to facilitate learning English in terms of students' improvement of language skills and students' motivation, confidence, and attitudes towards learning English. According to the authors, "the technologies that support FB [Facebook] and features that characterize FB are able to engage students in meaningful language-based activities, even though their initial intention of joining FB is to socialize" (p. 185).

Secondly, the microblogging service Twitter enables users to text about any topic using up to 280 characters per tweet. According to Statista.com (2019), Twitter has 269 million users, and by 2020, the number is estimated to reach 275 million. Studies on Twitter have mainly examined the use of Twitter in general education or analyzed properties of the network, but few studies have focused on the role of Twitter for informal language learning. One study that investigated the usefulness of Twitter in second language learning was conducted by Borau, Ullrich, Feng, and Shen in 2009. The researchers incorporated the use of Twitter into their classrooms and made students' participation in Twitter as a part of their final grade; and this is one method of linking Twitter-based activities with formal learning. The participants were bilingual in Chinese and English and were required to provide a certain number of responses on Twitter, which yielded a total of 5574 messages. After the experiment, the students completed a questionnaire about their Twitter usage and expressed their opinions about it. The study concluded that 70% of the students found it easier to communicate in English after using Twitter, 24% had a neutral opinion, and 4.88% opposed the requirement. The informants in general had a positive view on the effects of Twitter in terms of developing English communication and cultural competence. Likewise, Junco, Heiberger, and Loken (2011) investigated whether using Twitter in the field of education had any impact on college students' engagement and grades. 125 participants between 17 to 20 years of age were divided into two groups: 70 in the experimental group and 55 in the control group. The experimental group used Twitter as part of the class, whereas the control group did not. All students answered a survey adapted from the National Survey of Student Engagement (NSSE). The results provided additional evidence that students and faculty were both highly engaged in the learning process through communication via Twitter. This suggested that using Twitter in educationally-relevant ways could increase student engagement and improve grades. Consequently, the researchers concluded that online social media could be used as an educational tool to help students reach desired college outcomes.

Thirdly, WhatsApp is an application that supports different message types, from simple text to pictures, audio files, and videos. According to WhatsApp.com (2019), more than 1 billion people in over 180 countries are active WhatsApp users at present. Alsaleem (2013) investigated the effects of WhatsApp on English writing vocabulary, word choice, and the voice or perspective of the writer. The sample included 30 undergraduate Saudi students learning English as a foreign language (EFL). The researcher used a pre-test-post-test design. The pre-test and post-test topics were similar in terms of level of difficulty and interest. The treatment involved different message writing tasks on WhatsApp. The study showed that the participants promoted their writing skills after the treatment. This improvement was particularly observed in relation to the use of vocabulary and the expression of a personal voice or perspective.

The studies presented so far share positive learning benefits from the use of SMSs for users' overall communication skills, writing and reading skills, vocabulary knowledge, and ability to express a point of view. However, there are studies that discussed negative effects of SMSs on students' learning and social life. Reporting from a state university in Turkey, Turan, Tinmaz, and Goktas's (2013) study suggested that SMSs may be a waste of time and may eventually lead to addiction to such services. The study focused particularly on Facebook. It employed qualitative research methods in the process of data collection and analysis. The researchers examined underlying reasons for the non-use of SMSs among students and found that the majority of participants did not find Facebook to be a useful learning tool. Instead, they considered it, for the most part, a waste of time, and were unable to perceive its potential benefits.

Although most of the previous empirical research related to SMSs and their use for language learning purposes mainly focused on SMSs in formal settings, this review has revealed an overall positive trend. The majority of studies have reported benefits for the users in terms of improving their communication skills, writing and reading skills, building vocabulary knowledge, and confidence in expressing their voice or point of view (Alsaleem, 2013; Borau, Ullrich, Feng, & Shen, 2009; Chartrand, 2012; Junco, Heiberger, & Loken, 2011; Kabilan, Ahmad, & Jafre, 2010; Promnitz-Hayashi, 2011). Besides these benefits, some findings have suggested more critical views of SMSs and their educational potential, pointing to the fact that they can be addictive and therefore lead to destructive behavior or are otherwise waste students' time (Greenhow & Lewin, 2016; Turan, Tinmaz, & Goktas, 2013). All SMS studies (e.g. Kabilan, Ahmad, & Jafre, 2010; Kumar, & Kumar, 2013; Rios & Campos, 2015) unanimously show that Facebook is not only the world's largest SMS but also the most popular platform for online social networking among university students. However, the bulk of prior research put emphasis on formal learning; informal language learning through these websites has been inadequately explored. More pointedly, studies on informal language learning stemming from technology-based language activities remains an obvious rarity.

Thus, this study advances research in this area by providing evidence of informal uses of SMSs to enhance formal English instruction in a context where English is not commonly used in daily situations, but serves as the medium of operating such digital technologies. This amounts to a great deal of English learning opportunities beyond the physical confinement of the classroom. The study delves into an unexplored area in the existing body of empirical literature. It outlines particular language-learning benefits gained from informal uses of SMSs, with a particular focus on Yemeni learners of English who has been underrepresented in previous studies. The study examines how this cohort of learners used SMSs informally and whether or not these sites were helpful to promote their formal English learning. The current study aims to address the following research questions:

1. What are the most useful social networking sites that help Yemeni EFL learners learn English independently from formal agencies (teachers, tutors, lab assistants, etc.)?
2. How do Yemeni EFL learners perceive the overall usefulness of social networks in relation to improving their language skills?

METHODOLOGY

This study is part of a larger quantitative and qualitative research project that thoroughly investigated the use of SMSs and gender differences impacting English learning. An online survey was sent to 100 college students at two universities in Yemen. The survey consisted of 23 questions, 20 of which were Likert scale questions and 3 were mixed-type, open-ended questions. Of the 100 potential informants, 60 responded to the survey (37 female and 23 male), yielding a response rate of 60%, which according to Nardi (2006) is a good response rate. All the participants were undergraduates, aged between 19 and 33. The overall mean age of the participants was 22 years. The rationale of selecting this body of learners was that Yemeni EFL undergraduates constituted a population of young people who tend to use online resources and networks, like the majority of young people across the World. This assumption was proven correct by the demographic data, which showed that 72% of the participants used SMSs on a daily basis, 20% used them two to three times a week, 2% used them once a week, 3.3% used them twice a month, and 3.3% rarely used them.

Reliability and Validity

The questions were designed in such a way to prevent ambiguity, redundancy, and complexity. Detailed instructions were given to the participants along with a link to the survey. Some of the questions were adapted from the research instruments of Almaghrabi (2012) and Stevenson and Liu (2010). Both reported that they had ensured the instrument's validity and reliability. Additionally, the instrument was judged by a committee of three specialists in the field of Applied Linguistics at a Midwestern University in the U.S. Their feedback and input were taken into consideration to improve the reliability and validity of the instrument. Upon data collection, Cronbach's alpha test was performed to check for the internal consistency of the survey items related to the usefulness of SMSs in participants' independent learning of English. These items were measured on a Likert scale and were thus appropriate for internal consistency analysis (George & Mallery, 2009). The results are summarized in Table 1. According to George and Mallery, a value of *alpha* = or higher than .8 shows good internal consistency. In the present study, the Cronbach *alpha* = .858 could be interpreted to mean that the 13 usefulness questions were consistently measuring participants' perceptions of the usefulness of SMSs.

Table 1. Reliability statistics

Survey section	Cronbach's Alpha	Cronbach's Alpha based on standardized items	No. of items
Usefulness Items	.858	.861	13

Data Analysis

Descriptive statistics and frequency analyses were used to find out how frequently the participants used these networks on their own and how useful they found them for improving their English skills. The open-ended questions were subjected to content analysis to identify common themes and categories of responses. These were grouped, tabulated, and illustrated with quotes from the data.

RESULTS AND DISCUSSION

The first research question revolves around the frequency of using SMSs by Yemeni EFL learners. It aimed to examine the occurrences of SMSs uses, namely Twitter, Facebook, and WhatsApp that help students to learn English independently from their formal agencies (teachers, tutors, lab assistants, etc.). The participants were given six options to rate their SMS usage: (a) daily, (b) 2-3 times a week, (c) once a week, (d) 1-2 times a month, (e) rarely, and (f) never. The data were analyzed through frequencies and percentages of usage. The results are summarized in Table 2. As can be seen in the table, Facebook appeared to be the most commonly used SMS among the informants. Specifically, 50% of participants used Facebook on a *daily* basis, and 23.3% used it more than *2 to 3 times a week*. The second in frequency of use was WhatsApp with 36.7% of the participants using this application on a *daily* basis and 18.3% using it *2 to 3 times a week*. The third most common SMS was Twitter which was used *daily* by only 5% of the participants. Hence, Twitter was the least-used SMS among the participants, with 83.3% having *never* used it before. In addition to frequency of using SMSs in English, the participants were also asked to report how useful they found each one of the five SMSs for developing specific language skills in English. These results are presented in the following section.

Table 2. Frequency of use of online social networking sites in English

SNS	N	Daily	2-3 times a week	Once a week	1-2 times a month	Rarely	Never
Facebook	60	30 (50%)	14 (23.3%)	8 (13.3%)	3 (5%)	4 (6.7%)	1 (1.7%)
WhatsApp	60	22 (36.7%)	11 (18.3%)	3 (5%)	4 (6.7%)	7 (11.7%)	13 (21.7%)
Twitter	60	3 (5%)	1 (1.7%)	0 (0%)	2 (3.3%)	4 (6.7%)	50 (83.3%)

Using Facebook in English

Among the three SMSs, Facebook–based on the frequency data– was the most commonly used among learners, with over 90% of the participants reporting that they had used it in English. This finding corroborated previous research that Facebook ranks first among all other SMSs (e.g. Stanciu, Mihai, & Aleca, 2012). Regarding the language benefits of using Facebook in English, participants' responses elicited the following language skills ranked in order of usefulness: writing, reading, vocabulary, grammar, listening, and speaking. The results are summarized in Table 3 where the skills are ordered from the ones that elicited the highest means of usefulness to the lowest means of usefulness. The scales 5 and 4 (*very helpful* and *helpful*) are discussed as one category '*helpful*'. The means ranged from 4.43 for writing benefits to 3.52 for speaking benefits on a five-point scale. These results supported the conclusions of Kabilan, Ahmad, and Jafre's (2010) study, which concluded that Facebook could be very useful for students in improving their language skills as well as their attitude toward English.

Table 3. Participants' perceptions of usefulness of Facebook for learning English

Purpose	5 very helpful	4 helpful	3 somewhat helpful	2 unhelpful	1 very unhelpful	Ss who answered	Mean	SD
Writing	31 (51.7%)	19 (31.7%)	5 (8.3%)	1 (1.7%)	0 (0%)	56 93.4%	4.43	.735
Reading	26 (43.3%)	17 (28.3%)	10 (16.7%)	1 (1.7%)	0 (0%)	54 90%	4.26	.828
Vocabulary	26 (43.3%)	17 (28.3%)	11 (18.3%)	2 (3.3%)	0 (0%)	56 93.4%	4.20	.883
Grammar	17 (28.3%)	18 (30%)	12 (20%)	9 (15%)	0 (0%)	56 93.4%	3.77	3.77
Listening	19 (31.7%)	11 (18.3%)	10 (16.7%)	15 (25%)	0 (0%)	55 91.7	3.62	1.22
Speaking	15 (25%)	12 (20%)	16 (26.7%)	13 (21.7%)	1 (1.7%)	56 93.4%	3.52	1.12

As is evident from Table 3, the writing skill was believed to be the most facilitated by the use of Facebook in English. Specifically, 50 out of 56 students reported that Facebook was *helpful* for improving their writing in English. Five participants reported that using Facebook was *somewhat helpful*, and only one participant believed that using Facebook was *unhelpful*. The next skill's usefulness reported was reading, as 43 participants indicated that using Facebook was *helpful*, 10 reported that it was *somewhat helpful*, and 15 reported that it was *unhelpful*. The third most useful skill was vocabulary learning as 43 students reported that Facebook was *helpful*, 11 believed it was *somewhat helpful*, and 2 thought it *unhelpful*. For grammar, 35 participants reported that using Facebook was *helpful*, 12 reported that it was *somewhat helpful*, and 9 reported that Facebook was *unhelpful*. For listening, 29 participants reported that using Facebook was *helpful*, 10 believed it was *somewhat helpful*, and 15 thought it was *unhelpful*. The least useful was reported in relation to speaking in English. Specifically, 27 students reported that Facebook was *helpful* for them to improve their speaking in English, 16 reported that it was *somewhat helpful*, and 14 believed that using Facebook was *unhelpful*. On a broader level, these findings supported Promnitz-Hayashi's (2011) findings that Facebook has become a good environment for students to take part in discussions and share their opinions, not only about daily issues, but also about issues related to their classwork.

Using WhatsApp in English

The second most frequently used application was WhatsApp, as over 76% of the participants reported using WhatsApp in English. This percentage of participants stated that they found WhatsApp useful for developing their language skills and for building their vocabulary and grammar. The informants' scores yielded the following ranking in terms of usefulness: writing, reading, vocabulary, grammar, speaking, and listening, with a mean score ranging from 4.19 for writing to 3.13 for listening. Specifically, 37 out of 47 reported that WhatsApp was *helpful* for improving their writing in English, 4 reported that using WhatsApp was *somewhat helpful*, and 6 believed that using WhatsApp was *unhelpful*.

Table 4. Participants' perceptions of the usefulness of WhatsApp for learning English

Purpose	5 very helpful	4 helpful	3 somewhat helpful	2 unhelpful	1 very unhelpful	SS who answered	Mean	SD
Writing	26 (43.3%)	11 (18.3%)	4 (6.7%)	5 (8.3%)	1 (1.7%)	47 78.3%	4.19	1.11
Reading	18 (30%)	12 (20%)	11 (18.3%)	4 (6.7%)	1 (1.7%)	46 76.7%	3.93	1.12
Vocabulary	15 (25%)	15 (25%)	11 (18.3%)	5 (8.3%)	1 (1.7%)	47 78.3%	3.83	1.11
Grammar	11 (18.3%)	10 (16.7%)	17 (28.3%)	7 (11.7%)	2 (3.3%)	47 78.3%	3.45	1.13
Speaking	13 (21.7%)	4 (6.7%)	13 (21.7%)	15 (25%)	2 (3.3%)	47 78.3%	3.13	1.34
Listening	11 (18.3%)	6 (10%)	9 (15%)	19 (31.7%)	2 (3.3%)	47 78.3%	3.13	1.32

For reading, 30 participants reported that using WhatsApp was *helpful*, 11 reported that it was *somewhat helpful* and 5 reported that it was *unhelpful*. For vocabulary, 30 students reported that WhatsApp was *helpful*, 11 believed it was *somewhat helpful*, and 6 thought it *unhelpful*. For grammar, 21 participants reported that using WhatsApp was *helpful*, 17 reported that it was *somewhat helpful*, and 9 reported that it was *unhelpful*. For speaking in English, 17 students reported that WhatsApp was *helpful*, 13 reported that it was *somewhat helpful*, and 17 believed that it was *unhelpful*. For listening, 17 participants reported that using WhatsApp was *helpful* to improve their listening in English, 9 believed it was *somewhat helpful*, and 21 thought it was *unhelpful*. Looking at Table 4, it is observed that WhatsApp helped students the most in improving their writing, with a mean score of 4.19 and a Standard Deviation of 1.11. Listening and speaking in English had the lowest mean score of 3.13. The perceived large benefits for developing learners' writing skills in English corroborated the results of Alsaleem (2013) who found that participants who used WhatsApp showed improvement in their writing skills, especially word choice.

Using Twitter in English

As mentioned in Table 2, Twitter was less popular among Yemeni students, with 83.3% of participants reporting that they had *never* used Twitter. Therefore, it ranked third in use as only 10 of the participants (16.7%) indicated that they had used Twitter in English. Table 5 summarizes the responses to the question of how *helpful* the students found Twitter in the various English skills examined. The scales 5 and 4 (*very helpful* and *helpful*) are discussed as one category '*helpful*'. For reading, 13 participants reported that using Twitter was *helpful*, and 1 reported that it was *somewhat helpful*. For vocabulary, 12 students reported that Twitter was *helpful*, and 2 believed it was *somewhat helpful*. Out of 14, 12 students reported that Twitter was *helpful* for improving their writing in English, and 2 reported that it was *somewhat helpful*. For grammar, 7 participants reported that using Twitter helped them learn English grammar, and 7 reported that it was *somewhat helpful*. None of the participants reported that Twitter was *unhelpful* for writing, reading, vocabulary, or grammar. For listening, 7 participants reported that using Twitter was *helpful*, 5 believed it was *somewhat helpful*, and 2 thought it was *unhelpful*. For improving English speaking skills, 5 students reported that Twitter was *helpful*, 5 that it was *somewhat helpful*, and 4 that it was unhelpful. Overall, the 14 participants who reported using Twitter in English found it to be most helpful for improving their reading skills in English (Mean= 4.36, SD= .633) and to be least helpful for improving their English-speaking skills (Mean= 3.21, SD= 1.25).

Table 5. Participants' perceptions of the usefulness of Twitter for learning English

purpose	5 very helpful	4 helpful	3 somewhat helpful	2 unhelpful	1 very unhelpful	ss who answered	Mean	SD
Reading	6 (10%)	7 (11.7%)	1 (1.7%)	0 (0%)	0 (0%)	14 23.3%	4.36	.633
Vocabulary	5 (8.3%)	7 (11.7%)	2 (3.3%)	0 (0%)	0 (0%)	14 23.3%	4.21	.699
Writing	2 (3.3%)	10 (16.7%)	2 (3.3%)	0 (0%)	0 (0%)	14 23.3%	4.00	.555
Grammar	4 (6.7%)	3 (5%)	7 (11.7%)	0 (0%)	0 (0%)	14 23.3%	3.79	.893
Listening	5 (8.3%)	2 (3.3%)	5 (8.3%)	2 (3.3%)	0 (0%)	14 23.3%	3.71	1.13
Speaking	3 (5%)	2 (3.3%)	5 (8.3%)	3 (5%)	1 (1.7%)	14 23.3%	3.21	1.25

These findings corroborate the observation of Stanciu, Mihai, and Aleca (2012), who found that Twitter was less popular among students from the Bucharest Academy of Economic Studies. In addition, these results agreed with Junco, Heiberger, and Loken's (2011) finding that Twitter could be used as an educational tool to help students engage and eventually lead to better learning outcomes.

The second research question is related to learners' perceptions on the overall usefulness of social networks in relation to improving their different language skills. After having examined the usefulness of each of the three SMSs separately, this study will examine how Yemeni students viewed the overall usefulness of these SMSs in their learning of the English language. Thirteen Likert scale questions were used to elicit participants' perceptions. The scale had three levels: 1= *unhelpful*, 2= *somewhat helpful*, and 3= *helpful*. The data were analyzed through descriptive statistics, which showed that mean scores of usefulness on all 13 items ranged from 2.17 to 2.75, indicating that the participants perceived the overall usefulness of SMSs to be from somewhat helpful to helpful. These mean scores are summarized in Table 6 in descending order, from highest to lowest mean. Table 6 clearly illustrates that the participants found the SMSs to be most helpful for improving their reading skills (Mean = 2.75). The skill of writing comes after reading in the overall usefulness with a mean score of 2.72. The third most useful aspect of SMSs was reported for learning specialized vocabulary, such as words related to sports, fashion, music, politics, etc. (Mean= 2.70). The following two useful aspects of SMSs were related to staying in touch with English-speaking friends and learning things about different cultures. They yielded the same mean values (2.67).

Table 6. Overall usefulness of SMSs

Statements	N	Min.	Max.	M	SD
1) Improve my reading skills in **English**	60	1	3	2.75	.474
2) Improve my writing skills in **English**	60	1	3	2.72	.524
3) Learn specialized vocabulary, such as words related to 4) *sports, fashion, music, politics, etc.*	60	1	3	2.70	.530
5) Stay in touch with **English-speaking friends**	60	1	3	2.67	.542
6) Learn things about **different cultures**	60	1	3	2.67	.542
7) Make friends with **native speakers of English**	60	1	3	2.63	.610
8) Make friends with **non-native speakers of English**	60	1	3	2.62	.555
9) Learn things about **US culture**	60	1	3	2.60	.588
10) Learn everyday **English words**, including slang such as "cool", "awesome"	60	1	3	2.58	.561
11) Learn things about **British culture**	60	1	3	2.52	.596
12) Improve my listening skills in **English**	60	1	3	2.42	.787
13) Improve my **English grammar**	60	1	3	2.37	.688
14) Improve my speaking skills in **English**	60	1	3	2.17	.740

The participants also reported SMSs as 'useful' for making friends, both with native and non-native speakers. The two statements yielded close results; the former had a mean score of 2.63 and the latter of 2.62. Since the learners were exposed to British and American English only, they reported that SMSs helped them learn about the cultures of the U.S. and U.K. The mean score for learning about US culture was higher, Mean = 2.60, compared to a mean score of 2.52 for learning about British culture. The usefulness of SMSs for learning everyday English words, including slang such as "cool" or "awesome" was also rated quite highly with a mean score of 2.58. Following this was the usefulness for developing listening skills in English, which resulted in a mean score of 2.42. The highest usefulness score for developing participants' English grammar was 2.37, and the lowest was reported for developing speaking skills in English with a mean score of 2.17. Thus, SMSs were reported to be the most useful for developing participants' reading skills in English and to be the least useful for developing their speaking skills in English.

These findings support previous studies (e.g. Promnitz-Hayashi, 2011; Stanciu, Mihai, & Aleca, 2012) that have reported SMSs as helpful tools to create effective environments for students to learn a language. In a similar vein, social networking sites, by their nature, offer opportunities for practice beyond the formal classroom instruction and thereby enhances the overall language learning (Al-kadi, 2018; Greenhow & Lewin, 2016; Vivian, 2011).

The quantitative results about the usefulness of SMSs were further corroborated by the participants' narrative comments. In their answers to the question, *do you think that by using English on social networks you can develop your English skills?* The majority of the participants (83.3%) chose '*Yes*', 13.3% selected '*to some extent*', and only 3.3% chose '*No.*'

Figure 1. Participants' perceptions on social networks to develop English skills

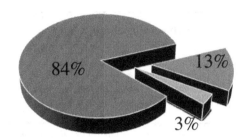

As summarized in Table 7, the narrative comments described particular benefits of SMSs. The commenters reported that although using SMSs helped them improve some language skills, these platforms were not helpful enough with other language skills. The students mentioned that when using SMSs in English, they felt they were mostly 'readers and writers' and rarely spoke or listened. Another skeptical view was expressed in relation to building learners' English grammar. The participants recognized that SMSs created an informal setting for communication and, therefore, grammar rules were often flouted.

The results of the current study, for the most part, support the positive view of SMS as a platform for self-determining language learning practices. Research on the potential of SMSs as language learning resources has provided controversial results. Some studies (e.g. Lee & McLoughlin, 2008; Promnitz-Hayashi, 2011; Chartrand, 2012) have found that SMSs encourage autonomous learning and offer language learners access to authentic language materials. In contrast, other studies (e.g. Turan, Tinmaz, & Goktas, 2013) have described SMSs as leading to addictive behavior with no learning benefits whatsoever. In the study at hand, these two rather opposing trends were revealed through the triangulation of the quantitative and qualitative data. However, it should be noted that the positive views were prevalent, whereas the skeptical ones were fewer and mainly concerned the usefulness of SMSs for developing grammatical accuracy and fluency in spoken skills. Moreover, the results of this study strengthen previous research findings that SMSs have been used as a means of communication and educational tools that promote autonomous learning within a social environment (Kabilan, Ahmad, & Jafre, 2010; Lee & McLoughlin, 2008; Promnitz-Hayashi, 2011; Stanciu, Mihai, & Aleca, 2012).

Regarding the current uses of SMSs, 77% of informants reported that their instructors either did not employ such platforms at all in the classroom or used them 'to some extent but not very much.' The primary rationales were of a socio-political and economic nature. Given the political climate in Yemen, which is a developing country undergoing many socio-political changes, these reasons were well-founded. Some universities still lack Internet service on campus, and classrooms are not uniformly equipped with the necessary technology. This was apparent in the comments of Participant 3 (Male) who observed that given the "circumstances in my country we barely could use social media. I just use all the theoretical type of learning. Hopefully by the very soon future, I would be able to do so."

Table 7. Using English on OSNSs to develop English skills

Themes	Illustrations (participants' actual quotes)	participants who contributed to a theme
Yes Category		
Improve vocabulary knowledge and language skills	*"I read many articles and messages, which help me to develop my reading skill, and providing me with many new vocabularies. It also help me to develop my skill of writing"*	40 participants out of 50 (80%)
Develop communication skills in English	*"Yes we can develop our English by being in touch with speakers of English either native speaker or non-_native speaker that we can practice English a lot"*	20 participants out of 50 (40%)
Opportunities for autonomous learning	*"It allows us more space to use English language outside the classroom through chatting with freinds via these websites either some or all."*	9 participants out of 50 (18%)
Access to information	*"Using English on social networking make me able to get the recent knowledge. And it enable me to improve all English skills."*	8 participants out of 50 (16%)
Somewhat Category		
Useful, but not for all language skills	*"to some extent cz i personally believe that not all the skills can be improved. In social networks i am just a reader and a writer. I neither speak no listen (at least for me)."*	6 participants out of 8 (75%)
Useful, but for grammar	*"I always use them for fun and chatting. When I use them, I do not care about grammar."*	2 participants out of 8 (25%)

CONCLUSION

The present study found that SMSs has been used to help students to develop their English language skills informally. In a bid to connect these informal uses of ICT tool with formal teaching, teachers need to embrace the potentials of SMSs in ways that are relevant to their students' learning. These sites serve as productive venues for exposure to authentic English. Learners present on SMSs may befriend native speakers to promote not only their linguistic abilities but also acculturation and awareness of worldwide issues. By promoting linguistic and cultural aspects, learners, belonging to preservative background, can get out of their shrinks and partake actively in the worldwide arenas. Taken together, the results of the current study added supporting evidence that Yemeni college students are not an exception to the general trend of using SMSs in learning English. Based on the findings, it is implied that informal uses of SMSs can be supplementary to the usual classroom procedures, mainly in providing authentic contexts for learning, alternative assessment, and facilitating communication between students and teachers.

Despite the viable findings this study concludes, some limitations are to be acknowledged. A major limitation is related to survey-based research for the most part, where participants were asked to select from predetermined options. Another limitation was the relatively small sample size, as surveys with larger numbers of participants are more representative of the whole population than surveys with smaller samples. The sample also had unbalanced distribution of male and female participants. In addition, the study focused on the use of and language benefits of using SMSs in English, and the results should not be generalized to other languages, not to other SMSs other than Facebook, Twitter and WhatsApp. All together, these limitations might be addressed in further research studies that might build on the findings this study establishes. Further research may integrate a corpus of SMSs electronic traces on these sites and measure the relevance of that to users' linguistic abilities.

ACKNOWLEDGMENT

My deep appreciation goes to Dr. Abdu Al-Kadi for his endless support, sage advice, insightful criticism, and patient encouragement that aided the writing of this chapter in innumerable ways. My thanks also go to the students who enthusiastically participated in this study, diligently answered all questions, and provided insightful responses to the open-ended questions.

REFERENCES

Al-Kadi, A. (2018). A review of technology integration in ELT: From CALL to MALL. *Language Teaching and Educational Research*, *1*(1), 1–12.

Almaghrabi, B. K. (2012). *Saudi college students' independent language learning strategies through multimedia resources: Perceptions of benefits and implications for language* (Unpublished master's thesis). Southern Illinois University.

Alsaleem, B. I. (2013). The effect of "WhatsApp" electronic dialogue journaling on improving writing vocabulary word choice and voice of EFL undergraduate Saudi students. *Arab World English Journal*, *4*(3), 213–225.

Bakeer, A. (2018). Effects of information and communication technology and social media in developing students' writing skill: A case of Al-Quds Open University. *International Journal of Humanities and Social Science*, *8*(5). doi:10.30845/ijhss.v8n5a5

Borau, K., Ullrich, C., Feng, J., & Shen, R. (2009). Microblogging for language learning: Using Twitter to train communicative and cultural competence. *Lecture Notes in Computer Science*, *5686*, 78–87. doi:10.1007/978-3-642-03426-8_10

Chartrand, R. (2012). Social networking for language learners: Creating meaningful output with web 2.0 tools. *Knowledge Management & E-Learning: An International Journal*, *4*(1), 97–101.

Feng, S., Wong, Y. K., Wong, L. Y., & Hossain, L. (2019). The Internet and Facebook Usage on Academic Distraction of College Students. *Computers & Education*, *134*, 41–49. doi:10.1016/j.compedu.2019.02.005

George, D., & Mallery, P. (2009). *SPSS for windows step by step: A simple guide reference 16.0 update*. Boston, MA: Pearson.

Global, T. N. S. (2008). *Digital world, digital life: Snapshots of our online behaviour and perspectives around the world*. Retrieved from http://www.wpp.com/~///marketing%20insights/tns_market_research_digital_world_digital_life.pdf

Greenhow, C., & Lewin, C. (2016). Social media and education: Reconceptualizing the boundaries of formal and informal learning. *Learning, Media and Technology, 41*(1), 6–30. doi:10.1080/17439884.2015.1064954

Ha, L., Joa, C. Y., Gabay, I., & Kim, K. (2018). Does college students' social media use affect school e-mail avoidance and campus involvement? *Internet Research, 28*(1), 213–231. doi:10.1108/IntR-11-2016-0346

Junco, R. R., Heiberger, G. G., & Loken, E. E. (2011). The effect of Twitter on college student engagement and grades. *Journal of Computer Assisted Learning, 27*(2), 119–132. doi:10.1111/j.1365-2729.2010.00387.x

Kabilan, M., Ahmad, N., & Jafre, M. Z. A. (2010). Facebook: An online environment for learning of English in institutions of higher education? *Internet and Higher Education, 13*(4), 179–187. doi:10.1016/j.iheduc.2010.07.003

Kasuma, A. A. (2017). Four Characteristics of Facebook activities for English language learning: A study of Malaysian university students' needs and preferences. *Advances in Language and Literary Studies, 8*(3).

Kumar, A., & Kumar, R. (2013). Use of social networking sites (OSNSs): A study of Maharishi Dayanand University, Rohtak, India. *Library Philosophy and Practice*. Retrieved from http://digitalcommons.unl.edu/cgi/viewcontent.cgi?article=2415&context=libphilprac

Kurata, N. (2011). *Foreign language learning and use: Interaction in informal social networks*. Continuum International Publishing Group.

Manca, S., & Ranieri, M. (2016). Is Facebook still a suitable technology-enhanced learning environment? An updated critical review of the literature from 2012 to 2015. *Journal of Computer Assisted Learning, 32*(1), 503–528.

Mazman, S., & Usluel, Y. (2011). Gender differences in using social networks. *Turkish Online Journal of Educational Technology, 10*(2), 133–139.

McLoughlin, C., & Lee, M. J. W. (2008). Mapping the digital terrain: New media and social software as catalysts for pedagogical change. In *Hello! Where are you in the landscape of educational technology? Proceedings ASCILITE Melbourne 2008*. Retrieved from http://www.ascilite.org.au/conferences/melbourne08/procs/mcloughlin.pdf

Most famous social network sites. (2019). Retrieved from https://www.statista.com/statistics/272014/global-social-networks-ranked-by-number-of-users/

Nardi, P. M. (2006). *Doing survey research: A guide to quantitative methods*. Boston: Pearson.

Promnitz-Hayashi, L. (2011). A learning success story using Facebook. *Studies in Self-Access Learning Journal, 2*(4), 309–316.

Rios, J. A., & Espinoza Campos, J. L. (2015). The role of Facebook in foreign language learning. *Revista de Lenguas Modernas, 23*, 253–262.

Stanciu, A., Mihai, F., & Aleca, O. (2012). Social networking as an alternative environment for education. *Accounting & Management Information Systems*, *11*(1), 56–75.

Stevenson, M. P., & Liu, M. (2010). Learning a language with web 2.0: Exploring the use of social networking features of foreign language learning websites. *CALICO Journal*, *27*(2), 233–259. doi:10.11139/cj.27.2.233-259

Thiele, A. K., Mai, J. A., & Post, S. (2014). The student-centered classroom of the 21st century: Integrating web 2.0 applications and other technology to actively engage students. *Journal, Physical Therapy Education*, *28*(1), 80–93. doi:10.1097/00001416-201410000-00014

Trinder, R. (2017). Informal and deliberate learning with new technology. *ELT Journal*, *71*(4), 401–412. doi:10.1093/elt/ccw117

Turan, Z., Tinmaz, H., & Goktas, Y. (2013). The reasons for non-use of social networking websites by university students. *Comunicar*, *21*(41), 137–145. doi:10.3916/C41-2013-13

Twitter: number of users worldwide 2020. (2019). Retrieved from https://www.statista.com/statistics/303681/twitter-users-worldwide/

Vivian, R. (2011). University students' informal learning practices using Facebook: Help or hindrance? In R. Kwan, C., McNaught, P., Tsang, F. Wang & K. C. Li (Eds.), Enhancing learning through technology (pp. 254-267). Berlin: Springer.

WhatsApp. (2019). Retrieved from https://www.whatsapp.com/about/

This research was previously published in Enhancements and Limitations to ICT-Based Informal Language Learning; pages 69-88, copyright year 2020 by Information Science Reference (an imprint of IGI Global).

Chapter 13
Moving Towards CLIL 2.0:
A Proposal for Social Media Integration in Content- and Language-Integrated Learning

Francisco Javier Palacios Hidalgo
ⓘ https://orcid.org/0000-0002-4326-209X
University of Córdoba, Spain

ABSTRACT

The 21st century has evolved when it comes to the presence of technology. Internet development has entailed a revolution in human life, especially in the field of interaction. The world has moved from the first Web 1.0 to Web 5.0, which not only allows users to access information but also to interact with millions of other users from every part of the planet. This global connection has led to the increasing necessity of being communicatively and interculturally competent. In this context, European countries develop bilingual education programs based on CLIL, whose main objective is to promote proficiency in non-linguistic and linguistic subjects and foster plurilingualism and intercultural awareness among citizens. Bearing in mind the social and educational implications of the increasing power of technology and the Internet, this chapter revises the progressive transformation of the World Wide Web from a social perspective since its origins until today, and it explains why integrating social media tools in the CLIL classroom could serve as a way to improve the results of bilingual programs.

INTRODUCTION

The 21st century has experienced a profound evolution when it comes to the use and presence of technology. In this sense, the development of the Internet has supposed a revolution in human life, especially in the field of interaction (Tavakoli & Wijesinghe, 2019). The world has evolved from the first Web 1.0, characterised by the consumption of online content, into Web 2.0, 3.0, 4.0 and 5.0, moving from its origins in the 1950s, to its initial versions of the Internet implemented in universities and research

DOI: 10.4018/978-1-6684-7123-4.ch013

centres during the 1960s and 1970s, to a later new commercial stage in the 1980s, and to its current social phase in the 2010s (Cohen-Almagor, 2011).

Over the last decades, the influence of the Internet on our daily routines has drastically grown. At this juncture, online social media has become the main platform of information dissemination, and Internet-enhanced activities such as online shopping or e-mail have become routines for citizens all over the world (Filsinger & Freitag, 2019). People can now obtain instant information from a variety of social platforms as well as share their texts, pictures and videos (e.g., Facebook, Twitter, Instagram, …). Although it is unequivocal that these technologies can contribute to the world's progress at different scales (not only social but also political, economic and cultural), they are also challenging in some ways (Nedelkoska & Quintini, 2018; Sorbe, Gal, Nicoletti, & Timiliotis, 2019): they can both help create new professional opportunities and destroy certain employment as a result of task automatization (Gal, Nicoletti, Renault, Sorbe, & Timiliotis, 2019). As Sorbe, Gal, Nicoletti and Timiliotis (2019) point out, "new technologies make it possible to automate an increasing share of tasks, and a key challenge is to enable the transition of displaced workers to new tasks, jobs, firms and sometimes industries" (p. 19). In this context, it could be said that the 21st-century society (known as the Information/Network Society) demands knowledge and new skills for citizens to be competent enough to participate in the world of today. Among such demands, linguistic, communicative and intercultural abilities arise as the main requirements for individuals to acquire and develop. For this reason, many European countries develop bilingual/multilingual education programs in order to promote proficiency both in non-linguistic and linguistic subjects and to foster plurilingualism and intercultural awareness among citizens (Council of Europe, 2001). These programs, based on Canadian language immersion plans and the Indian Bangalore project, follow the CLIL approach, which seeks learning a foreign language (FL) and contents in a simultaneous way by teaching non-linguistic areas in the FL (Coyle, Hood, & Marsh, 2010; Gómez, 2017; Roldán, 2012). In Europe, CLIL development has increased considerably over the last twenty years as a response to European Commission's guidelines seeking the promotion of FL learning among citizens (European Commission, 1995) based on the increasing internationalization and mobility which highlights the importance of languages. In words of Nikula, Dalton-Puffer and Llinares:

CLIL has received ample political support in the European Union, as it is seen as a means to achieve the 1+2 policy aim put forward in the 1995 White Paper on Education and Training by the European Commission (Teaching and Learning — Towards the Learning Society), i.e. that all EU citizens should master two community languages in addition to their mother tongue. At the same time, societal changes have resulted in increasing internationalization and mobility, which have highlighted the important role of languages in modern societies, with versatile language repertoires forming a social and economical asset for both individuals and societies. (2013, pp. 70–71)

Traditional methodologies do not work anymore as the world is becoming highly influenced by technology. For this reason, teachers in particular and educational institutions in general need to consider the potential of social media and take advantage of them. In words of Ulbrich, Jahnke and Mårtensson:

Members of the net generation use the web differently, they network differently, and they learn differently. When they start at university, traditional values on how to develop knowledge collide with their values. Many of the teaching techniques that have worked for decades do not work anymore because new students learn differently too. The net generation is used to networking; its members work collaboratively, they execute several tasks simultaneously, and they use the web to acquire knowledge. (2011, p. i)

Bearing in mind the social and educational implications of the increasing power of technology and the Internet, this chapter revises the progressive transformation of the World Wide Web from a social perspective since its origins until today, and it explains why the integration of social media tools in the CLIL classroom could serve as a way to improve the results of bilingual/multilingual programs.

EVOLUTION OF THE WORLD WIDE WEB: FROM WEB 0.5 TO WEB 5.0

As commonly thought, the words 'Internet' and 'World Wide Web' (or Web) are not interchangeably but different concepts. On the one hand, the Internet, which emerged in the 1960s as a result of United States' attempts to expand their influence in the world and surpass the Soviet Union, can be defined as global network consisting of millions computers connected together; on the other, the Web transfers information in the form of text, images, audio, video and a mixture of them by using Internet-based protocols (Cohen-Almagor, 2011; Tavakoli & Wijesinghe, 2019).

Several stages of the Web have been developing over the years; these, which are represented by version numbers from oldest to most recent, include Web 0.5, 1.0, 1.5, 2.0, 2.5, 3.0, 3.5, 4.0 (Weber & Rech, 2010) and 5.0 (Patel, 2013).

Web 0.5 started in the late 1980s and refers basically to the origins of the Web as we know it (Weber & Rech, 2010). Later, Web 1.0 was developed by Tim Berners-Lee in 1989 as a passive and read-only web of information connections with little possibility for interaction (Patel, 2013). The Web entered a new phase in the late 1990s, evolving into a more commercial stage which has been labelled as Web 1.5; during this period, webpages became more dynamic as well as complicated with the introduction of content management systems (Tavakoli & Wijesinghe, 2019).

The increase of mobile and smartphones' use during the last decade has had an effect on the evolution of the Web. In this context, the Web 2.5, also known as the mobile web (Pileggi, Fernandez-Llatas, & Traver, 2012), has arisen with a huge variety of mobile applications that benefit users in multiple ways as they can be used in almost every sphere of society. In words of Bernal:

A new form of symbiosis is developing on the Web. The current e-commerce model, which relies heavily on the supply of 'free' content, has made individuals and commercial enterprises mutually dependent: enterprises have built business models reliant on a currency of personal data, while individuals expect free access to services supplied by search engines, email systems and social networking sites and media services such as YouTube and Hulu. These 'free' services use personal data to generate revenues through targeted advertising, profile building, and the direct brokering of personal data. The symbiosis is essentially benign—it lies behind many recent positive developments. Both users and the businesses that provide online services benefit. (2010, p. 25)

The Semantic Web or Web 3.0 was introduced in 2006 in order to improve the quality of services and processes by providing users with personalized recommendations in their searches (Patel, 2013; Vieira & Isaías, 2015); online and virtual shopping and smart search are examples of Semantic Web (Tavakoli & Wijesinghe, 2019). Web 3.0 has evolved into Web 3.5, in which services are "pervasive, interactive, and autonomous agents considering the personal context based on advanced semantic technologies supporting reasoning and basic A[rtificial] I[ntelligence] that might bring the virtual and real world closer together" (Weber & Rech, 2010, p. 6), like, for instance, 3D and augmented reality social networks.

Web 4.0 can be referred to as an "Ultra-Intelligent Electronic Agent", a "Symbiotic Web" or a "Ubiquitous Web" (Patel, 2013, p. 416), consisting of "autonomous, proactive, content-exploring, self-learning, collaborative, and content-generating agents based on fully matured semantic and reasoning technologies as well as Artificial Intelligence" (Weber & Rech, 2010, p. 7). Basically, in Web 4.0 machines will be as powerful as the human brain, being capable of "reading the contents of the web, and react[ing] in the form of executing and deciding what to execute first to load the websites fast with superior quality" (Patel, 2013, p. 416). The Ubiquitous Web is acquiring great importance in the tourism industry as Web 4.0 technologies can help with travel issues (Soava, 2015).

The following figure (Figure 1) provides a graphical clarification of all World Wide Web stages aforementioned:

Figure 1. Theoretical vs. real Web evolution
Source: Pileggi, Fernandez-Llatas, & Traver, 2012, p. 853

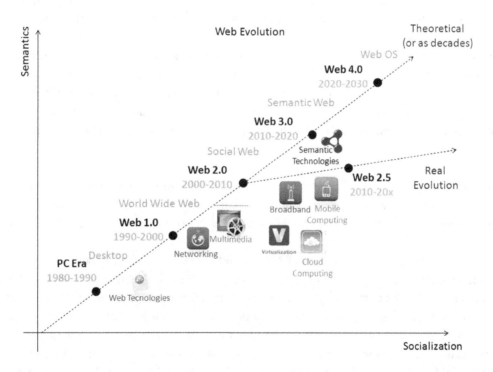

Web 5.0, known as the "sensory and emotive Web" (Benito-Osorio, Peris-Ortiz, Rueda, & Colino, 2013, p. 274), is the latest version of the World Wide Web. At this stage, human-machine interaction is enhanced by including the emotional dimension, such as face recognition followed by an emotional reaction, and sensorial emotions in virtual interactions between humans and virtual humans (Llargues et al., 2014; Parvathi & Mariselvi, 2017; Tavakoli & Wijesinghe, 2019).

In simple words, Web 1.0 was considered the web of cognition, web 2.0, the web of communication, web 3.0, the web of co-operation, web 4.0, the web of integration, and Web 5.0, the web of sensory-emotion (Aghaei, Nematbakhsh, & Farsani, 2012; Tavakoli & Wijesinghe, 2019).

THE WORLD WIDE WEB IN EDUCATION

The world of education has also been affected by the evolution of the World Wide Web and its progressive integration in every field of human life. The Web has favoured the democratization of learning and teaching as it provides opportunities to develop new learning experiences to which students could not access in any other way (Alexander, 1995; Khan, 1997). Since the beginning of the 21st century, research has suggested the great potential of the Internet and the Web for improving teaching and learning (Barrbera, 2004; Lee & Tsai, 2005; McCrory, 2004; Mendler, Simon, & Broome, 2002; Neo, 2003; Tsai & Tsai, 2003; Woo & Kimmick, 2000).

Concepts like *Web-based instruction* had already appeared at the very end of the 20th century with the arrival of the Web 0.5 and 1.0, an early technology-enhanced form of education including multimedia and Internet components and a variety of features such as global accessibility, online support, and cross-cultural interaction, among many others (Khan, 1997); this does not differ much from more modern Web-based learning approaches.

In the 21st century, new technology-based educational theories have been proposed; among them, *Technological Pedagogical and Content Knowledge* (TPACK), a model designed by Mishra and Koehler (2006), stands out as it analyses the role of teachers in order to achieve a good use of ICT in educational settings, giving importance to educators' digital competence and methodological knowledge. This model reveals the importance of teacher digital competence, a key aspect to take into consideration in every field of education. As the European Commission states:

The teaching professions face rapidly changing demands, which require a new, broader and more sophisticated set of competences than before. The ubiquity of digital devices and applications, in particular, requires educators to develop their digital competence. (European Commission, 2016, para. 1)

Figure 2 shows a graphical explanation of Mishra and Koehler's TPACK model:

However, we could say that the stages of the evolution of the Webs which revolutionized education were Web 2.0 and 2.5. The participative and mobile webs offer great possibilities for language learning; in fact, many technology-based educational approaches are being developed in this respect, such as *Technology-Enhanced Language Learning* (TELL), *Computer-Assisted Language Learning* (CALL) and *Mobile-Assisted Language Learning* (MALL), and all of them have been demonstrated to have multidimensional benefits in the FL learning process (Ghanizadeh, Razavi, & Hosseini, 2018; Palacios & Espejo, 2019; Tafazoli, Huertas, & Gómez, 2019).

Table 1 shows the evolution of the World Wide Web applied to education and the main features of the five main stages:

Figure 2. TPACK model
Source: Mishra & Koehler, 2012

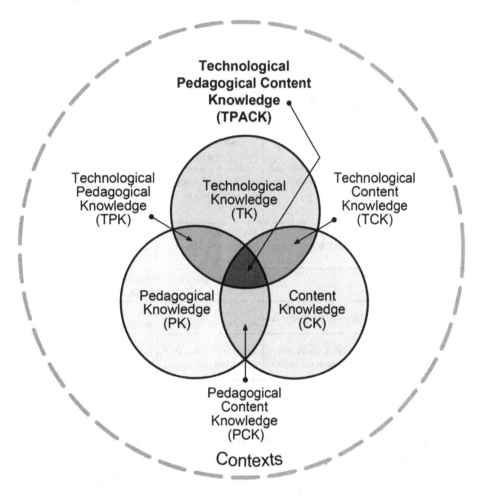

Web-Based Learning and Social Media in Language Education

The benefits of integrating the World Wide Web into the teaching of English as an FL have been extensively discussed by many researchers and practitioners in different parts of the world (Bikowski & Vithanage, 2016; Hajebi, Taheri, Fahandezh, & Salari, 2018; Soomro, Zai, & Jafri, 2015; Teo, Sang, Mei, & Hoi, 2019). In this respect, the last decade has been marked by the growth of social media. These received a great boost during the 2000s transforming the interaction of individuals with common interests (Edosomwan, Prakasan, Kouame, Watson, & Seymour, 2011). However, what is understood by social media? There is actually confusion in the scientific literature when providing a clear definition and examples of social media (Azab, Abdelsalam, & Gamal, 2013). As Chawinga points out, there is no consensus between researchers when classifying online services like Twitter and Facebook as Web 2.0 technologies or as social media due to the fact that "Web 2.0 and social media complement each other in affording end-users in cyberspace an opportunity to create, modify and publish content in a participatory and collaborative way" (2017, p. 2).

Table 1. Education 1.0 – 5.0 spectrum

	Web 1.0	Web 2.0	Web 3.0	Web 4.0	Web 5.0
Content is...	Dictated	Socially constructed	Socially constructed and contextually reinvented	Socially constructed and contextually reinvented in a constant way	Socially constructed and contextually reinvented in a constant way
Technology is...	Hardly used in the classroom (digital refugees)	Cautiously used (digital immigrants)	Everywhere (digital natives and migrants in the digital universe)	Everywhere (digital natives)	Everywhere (digital natives)
Teaching is done by...	Teacher to student	Teacher to student and student to student	Teacher to student, student to student, student to teacher, people to technology and technology to people	Teacher to student, student to student, student to teacher, people to technology and technology to people	Teacher to student, student to student, student to teacher, people to technology and technology to people
Schools are located...	In a building	In a building or online	Everywhere (thoroughly infused into society)	Everywhere (thoroughly infused into society)	Everywhere (thoroughly infused into society)
Parents view schools as...	Daycare	Daycare	A place for them to learn, too	A place for them to learn, too	A place for them to learn, too
Teachers are...	Licensed professionals	Licensed professionals	Everybody, everywhere	Everybody, everywhere	Everybody, everywhere
Hardware and software in schools...	Are purchased at great cost and ignored	Are open source and available at lower cost	Are available and used purposively	Are available and used purposively	Are available and used purposively

Source: (Adapted from Moravec, 2008)

The most common social media technologies can be classified into: (i) media sharing sites, such as YouTube, Instagram, Pinterest and Tumblr; (ii) social networking sites, such as Facebook, Twitter, and LinkedIn; (iii) wikis and blogs; and (iv) Rich Site Summary (RSS) feeds which offer a mixture of content (Chawinga & Zinn, 2016; Dzvapatsva, Mitrovic, & Dietrich, 2014; Gikas & Grant, 2013)

Edosomwan et al. (2011) develop a clear description of the benefits social media entails in the business world; however, these can easily be applied to education:

- They promote open communication between students and teachers and among students.
- They enable learners to share and communicate their ideas, knowledge and experiences.
- They effectively enhance collaborative and cooperative work, allowing rapid feedback from classmates and teachers.
- They promote better content based on students' interests through the use of multimedia items.
- They encourage learners to become both members of a community and responsible for their own learning process.
- They encompass a great venue for discussions.

Several studies have analyzed the integration of social media into the classroom, revealing the improvement of communication possibilities as their principal advantage; the main considered typologies are: blogs and wikis (Ballidag, 2018; Huang, 2015; Yim & Warschauer, 2017), podcasts (Elekaei, Tabrizi, &

Chalak, 2019; Fouz-González, 2019; Yoestara & Putri, 2018), language MOOCs or LMOOCs (Fuchs, 2019; Jitpaisarnwattana, Reinders, & Darasawang, 2019; Rinatovna, Vladimirovna, Bizyanova, & Haidar, 2017), and Language Learning Social Network Sites (LLSNS) (Greenhow & Askari, 2017; Lomicka & Lord, 2016; Rosell-Aguilar, 2018). Focusing on LLSNS, the revision carried out by Reinhardt (2019) is an illuminating example of the merits of social-media-enhanced language learning: the author analyses the formal and informal use of social media in the FL classroom revealing that these tools can improve the development of intercultural awareness, language learner identity, and FL literacy/proficiency. Similarly, Lin, Warschauer and Blake point that "LLSNSs offer the promise of bringing together tutorial software and opportunities to learn from interaction with native speakers" despite revealing "possible problems, including lack of long-term persistence and failure to contribute to learner accuracy" (2016, p. 143).

Lomicka and Lord (2016) provide a series of examples of social networking sites which, applied to the language classroom, can help improve the learning and teaching environment; they classify them into three categories according to the benefits they entail: written discourse enhancers, oral discourse enhancers, and picture-sharing sites. Table 2 displays some of the most representative LLSNS:

Table 2. Representative LLSNS

Name	Category	Description	URL
Edmodo	Written discourse enhancer	Education-oriented site that provides a safe environment for learners to connect and collaborate, share content with others, and access classroom material.	www.edmodo.com
Facebook	Written discourse enhancer	Social networking site originally designed for university students but currently extended to the general public.	www.facebook.com
HiNative	Oral and written discourse enhancer	Question-and-answer platform that allows users to post a question in the form of text or audio, which will be answered by native speakers with text and/or audio	www.hinative.com
Instagram	Picture sharing site	Online photo- and video-sharing social network that enables users to take and upload pictures (applying photo filters is also possible), and interact with others' in the form of text writing.	www.instagram.com
Plotagon	Written discourse enhancer	Online tool that enables users to create their own animated stories (plot and characters are designed by the user).	www.plotagon.com
PodOmatic	Oral discourse enhancer	Website that allows users easily find, create and share audio and video content.	www.podomatic.com
Snapchat	Picture sharing site	Mobile app that allows users to take and send pictures and short videos (applying photo filters is also possible) to other users deciding how long it will be visible once opened.	www.snapchat.com
Tumblr	Written discourse enhancer and picture sharing site	Blog-like social networking site that allows users to upload or reblog multimedia content to their dashboard. It also allows for private messaging.	www.tumblr.com
Twitter	Written discourse enhancer	Social networking site, more commonly referred as a *microblogging* site, that allows users to write and read messages up to 280 characters.	www.twitter.com
Voice Thread	Oral discourse enhancer	Interactive collaboration/sharing tool that allows users to add their own images, videos or documents, and to modify other users' multimedia content.	www.voicethread.com

Source: (Adapted from Lomicka & Lord, 2016, p. 261)

Despite the simplicity of the sites presented, these LLSNS can contribute to a greater extent to the improvement of learners' intercultural, linguistic and communicative competences. To this respect, Lomicka and Lord point the following:

[...] tools that tend to focus on written discourse can be used at beginning or intermediate levels to create self-descriptions and to engage in self-expression tasks [...] Other aspects of these tools may lend themselves nicely to longer, blog-type posts, which can be used for the development and interpretation of extended discourse. As learner proficiency increases, the same sites and tools can be maximized to promote meta-linguistic awareness of language structures and sociocultural aspects of language use [...] these sites offer learners the opportunity to observe native spoken language. They can use these sites to develop their comprehension skills, as well as to improve their own spoken speech. (2016, p. 262)

However, when implementing LLSNS in the classroom, teachers need to take into account a series of considerations to guarantee a quality and safe use of these tools. In this sense, Rodríguez (2011) suggests four key fields to consider: ownership and intellectual property, privacy and security, access, accessibility and compliance, and stability. Lomicka and Lord (2016) explain these considerations in simple words: teachers need to establish codes of conduct so that students' good behaviour is ensured; learners also need to be properly trained regarding privacy issues and the disadvantages of online environments –they should keep in mind the need for separating educational and personal environments in order to avoid complications and privacy problems. Furthermore, special needs when accessing these tools need to be considered and, if necessary, adaptations need to be made.

Barretta (2014) presents an interesting series of guidelines (classified into 4Cs and 5Rs) that teachers should follow when promoting LLSNS use in their classroom (although the author references Twitter, these ideas can be applied to any other site); these are: credibility, consistency, correctness, creativity, relevancy, reactivity, responsibility, respect, and reliability.

Considering all the aforementioned, the applicability of Web tools and social media in the FL classroom seems clear; however, it is necessary to reflect on their potential in bilingual education approaches such as, for example, CLIL.

BILINGUAL EDUCATION PROGRAMS: TAKING ADVANTAGE OF TECHNOLOGY

As mentioned in previous sections, globalization has led to an increasing necessity for individuals to be linguistically, communicatively and interculturally competent in such an interconnected world. This situation explains why educational systems' attempts to develop bilingual education programs –even multilingual in many cases, such as Cambodia (Benson & Wong, 2019) and Kenya (Kevogo, Kitonga, & Adika, 2015)– with the objective of promoting proficiency in non-linguisitc and linguistic subjects and fostering plurilingualism and intercultural awareness (Council of Europe, 2001).

In the case of Europe, the most used approach is CLIL, whose development has exponentially increased in the last two decades. CLIL integrates a great diversity of educational ideas that make it a deeply innovative and effective approach in terms of improving FL linguistic/communicative competence and content learning. Among its multiple benefits, CLIL promotes students' cooperation, critical learning, autonomy, interculture (Juan-Garau & Salazar-Noguera, 2015; Klimova, 2012; Nchindila, 2017), and even emotional competence (Nieto, 2012).

Although CLIL has been traditionally described as a "dual-focused approach" (Mehisto, Marsh, & Frigols, 2008, p. 8), i.e., it pays attention to both linguistic and non-linguistic areas, it could be better to refer to it as a *multiple-focused* approach, due to the fact that the majority of these models "can be seen to take into account learning goals related not only to content learning and language learning, but also to intercultural competence and the development of cognitive skills" (O'Dowd, 2018, p. 233).

The usefulness of ICT for learning is unquestionable today. In the particular case of CLIL, it is obvious that new technologies must be present in the classroom. As Huertas (2017) points out, ICT offer great potential in the development of educational materials. In this sense, as aforementioned, several technology-based language learning/teaching approaches have been developed, namely TELL and, more specifically, CALL and MALL, which, applied to bilingual settings, can also be beneficial for learners. The literature is profuse in this respect, with many studies highlighting how technology can enhance learning in CLIL: general ICT use in the Primary (Navarro-Pablo, López-Gándara, & García-Jimenez, 2019; Nga, Lan, & Nam, 2018) and the Secondary Education CLIL classroom (Fitria & Susilawati, 2019; Molina & Sampietro, 2015), and also CLIL teacher training (Arau, Morgado, Gaspar, & Régio, 2019; Díaz-Martín, 2017). In this respect, it has been demonstrated during the last decade that the use of technology-enhanced activities and methods has positive results as technological "communication tools can provide valuable support to a number of different teaching strategies" (Gimeno, 2009, p. 81). Similarly, virtual exchange and telecollaboration have been proved to help improve students' motivation and academic success; in this sense, O'Dowd states the following:

Students involved in online exchange projects carry out tasks with their international partners. They agree on collaborative projects related to their class subject matter. They engage in research in their local classroom or community and they share their results in the virtual exchange. Students also communicate together online to establish relationships with their international partners and to complete their project work, moving the emphasis of classwork away from teacher-controlled language practice. (2018, p. 234)

In this manner, it seems that the presence of technology in CLIL settings is not only clear but a necessary part of an up-to-date and innovative educational approach whose main aim is to make learners fully prepared for the context where they live. As for it, online collaboration initiatives can help achieve the goals of CLIL and, for this reason, CLIL educators should take advantage of online learning networks and communities in order to provide their students with the best learning opportunities.

INTEGRATION OF SOCIAL MEDIA INTO CLIL

As mentioned before, since the 2000s, social media has experienced a great boost transforming the interaction of individuals with common interests (Edosomwan et al., 2011). Basically, "social media employ mobile and web-based technologies to create highly interactive platforms via which individuals and communities share, co-create, discuss, and modify user-generated content" (Kietzmann, Hermkens, Mccarthy, & Silvestre, 2011, p. 241). In other words, thanks to social media and the advances of technology in the 21st century, Internet use (and, consequently, the access to information and knowledge) has evolved from a one-way broadcast delivery system controlled by web content providers to a user-focused and user-determined environment. This situation benefits students taking part in CLIL programs, which, by definition, are learner-centred (Arnaiz-Castro, 2017; Rumlich, 2017), by creating a setting where pupils become the centre of attention and are allowed to get the most out of their social competence by interacting with others with similar interests in a productive way.

It seems possible then to apply social media in CLIL environments and get better results. In fact, several studies have revealed that social media can promote immediate connectivity by providing access to authentic materials in the target language which basically allow learners to have direct contact with language learners from other parts of the world (Jenks, 2018; Lopriore, 2018; Sung, Ng, & Choi, 2018; Tess, 2013). However, it is required for educators to analyse the practical integration of social media within the course objectives and to have proper knowledge about the implications of using these tools based on a theoretical framework for using technology as a teaching and learning resource (Merchant, 2012).

Experts have come to the conclusion that three interrelated concepts should motivate the educational use of social media: (i) the changing nature of the student who may shift from interests; (ii) the changing relationship that learners have with the consumption and construction of knowledge; and (iii) the growing emphasis given by institutions to learner-centred education (Selwyn, 2010). Similarly, if we take Vygotski's social constructivism (1978) into consideration, learning, which has a conversational essence, can be enhanced by social media due to their conversational and collaborative nature, as well as for their possibilities to foster active participation and student-centred learning process (McLoughlin & Lee, 2010).

However, these are not the only theories that support the integration of social media in the classroom. For instance, other authors, such as Hung & Yuen (2010), consider that, if learning must occur in a social and participatory way, using social media in order to build a learning community seems to be something logical to take into account –because creating a sense of community among learners and educators is essential to foster successful learning.

It has been seen that the necessity of using ICT in the CLIL classroom is imperative. In this sense, and bearing in mind the fact that CLIL is a communicative approach based on real-life interactions and situations for learning along with the social media's benefits stated by Edosomwan et al. (2011), these web-based tools have too much to offer to bilingual programs. Furthermore, as one of the key aims of CLIL is fostering FL learning and, ultimately, proficiency, social media can promote open communication not only between the student and the teachers but also among students.

Going back to Table 1, it appears to be sure that Webs 3.0, 4.0 and 5.0 entail the best benefits for education and thus they should be applied to CLIL settings. For instance, content is socially constructed and contextually dependant, which implies that CLIL students will receive updated content and information in their learning process. Furthermore, considering that technology is everywhere, learners would be presumably prepared to use ICT as they had been born in a digital universe. Finally, in Education 3.0, 4.0 and 5.0, teaching is no longer teacher-centred but done by the teacher to the student, among students, by the student to the teacher, by people to technology and by technology itself to the people who use it (Moravec, 2008).

It must be taken into account that CLIL or non-CLIL students will not be able to get the most out of technology and social media if teachers themselves are not able to properly integrate them in their classrooms. As it has been presented in previous sections, much has been published on the power and possibilities that ICT offer to education and, indeed, it has been illustrated that they have turned into a reality in every stage of education. Nevertheless, universities and teacher-training centres should put their efforts into how to help both in-training and in-service teachers become fully digitally competent so that they are able to integrate social media in their teaching practice and, ultimately, train 21st-century students to use technology in a safe way. In this sense, the TPACK model proposed by Mishra and Koehler (2006,

2012; see Figure 2) provides a good base for fostering teachers' digital competence and methodological knowledge so as to address efficient social media use in the classroom.

It seems clear that social media is a revolution in education and, obviously, not all comments about it are positive. In that way, some experts point the possible barriers and pitfalls of applying social media in the classroom on the basis of different arguments such as technical issues (e.g., low connection speed and temporary failure of access to Internet) and institutional lack of support (Lee, 2011; Porter & Graham, 2016; Woo, Chu, Ho, & Li, 2011). In the following subsections, both specific merits and barriers of integrating social media in CLIL will be highlighted.

Merits of Social Media Implementation in CLIL

Although they have been already discussed in previous sections, Web tools and social media can have the following benefits in the language classroom (and, consequently, in CLIL settings):

- They promote affective learning through enhancing student motivation, interest and engagement (Hortigüela-Alcalá, Sánchez-Santamaría, Pérez-Pueyo, & Abella-García, 2019; Liu & Lan, 2016; Lomicka & Lord, 2016) which can facilitate both language and content acquisition in a more accessible way.
- They enhance collaborative learning as these tools provide learners with a naturalistic environment where they can practice and improve their language skills (Cortés, 2019; Rao, Wang, & Bender, 2016; Yim & Warschauer, 2017; Zou, Wang, & Xing, 2016); furthermore, this type of learning provides students with scaffolding whenever they need support for the learning of concepts of the non-linguistic areas.
- They foster the creation of learning communities and networks as Web tools help students with common interests (not only content-related but also linked to certain aspects of language learning, e.g., cultural issues) get in touch and practice the FL and the non-linguistic content at the same time they interact with each other on multiple topics and areas of knowledge (Luo, 2013; Mills, 2011).
- They help augment language performance, especially in the areas of writing (Bikowski & Vithanage, 2016; Levak & Son, 2017) and speaking skills (Cong-Lem, 2018; Sun & Yang, 2015), as well as cultural and intercultural competences (Lázár, 2015; Stockwell, 2016).
- They support metacognitive learning as they allow learners to reflect upon and self-regulate their own learning, thus improving their autonomy and making the learning process of both the target language and the content more meaningful (Broadbent & Poon, 2015; Cappellini, Lewis, & Rivens, 2017).

Barriers to Social Media Implementation in CLIL

In the same way that studies analyze the benefits of social media implementation in CLIL, there are several research projects focused on the barriers they pose to both language and content learning. According to Marzulina et al. (2018), the fact that the scientific literature presents the positive and negative perceptions on the use of LLSNS both from learners and teachers reveals that not everyone is in favor of social media integration into the learning and teaching process. Some of the most significant barriers to this extent are the following:

- Teachers show defensive behaviors about LLSNS integration in their teaching activities, feelings of potential privacy violations and lack of control the platforms (Herrington & Parker, 2013; Ng'ambi, 2013).
- Both teachers and students claim their lack of knowledge makes it difficult for them to use LLSNS, which may be consequently translated into a lack of digital and media competences (Murire & Cilliers, 2017; Prasojo et al., 2017).
- Institutional lack of support (in the form of economic investment or material provision) is another field of debate, since some educational bodies may not provide teachers and students with the necessary tools for integrating and using LLSNS. Additionally, the lack of institutional guidelines for effective integration and insufficient training may be another barrier for educators (Ng'ambi, 2013).

Despite the fact that the benefits of social media integration into CLIL are much more than the pitfalls, it is imperative to reflect on potential solutions to avoid such barriers in order to enable language teachers and learners to get the most out of LLSNS and, ultimately, prevent the phenomenon of the digital gap that "affects mainly the developing countries that lack the technical and financial means necessary to ensure access to information and communication technologies (ICTs) to all citizens" (Abascal, Barbosa, Nicolle, & Zaphiris, 2016, p. 180) and, consequently, the language gap (Johnson & Zentella, 2017).

CONCLUSION

This chapter has revised the progressive transformation of the World Wide Web from a social perspective since its origins as Web 0.5 and 1.0 until the Web 5.0 of today. Moreover, it has attempted to explain why the integration of social media tools in the CLIL classroom could serve as a way to improve the results of bilingual/multilingual programs, all of it bearing in mind the social and educational implications of the increase of power that technology and the Internet have nowadays. It has been shown how, according to the scientific literature on the topic, the social web and mobile devices have become the most important technologies in education –as, in fact, has been stated in several Horizon Reports since 2004; to mention some: Adams, Brown, Dahlstrom, Cummins, & Díaz, 2018; Johnson, Adams, Cummins, & Estrada, 2012; Johnson, Brown, & Adams, 2014; Johnson, Brown, Adams, Cummins, & Díaz, 2016; Johnson, Laurence, Levine, & Smith, 2007, 2009; Johnson, Laurence, Levine, Smith, & Stone, 2010; Johnson & Laurence, 2004.

Firstly, the different stages in which the Web have evolved into throughout the decades have been presented, focusing on the Web 2.0 or participative web, the Web 2.5 or mobile web, the Web 3.0, the symbiotic 4.0 web and the sensory and emotive 5.0 web (Benito-Osorio, Peris-Ortiz, Rueda, & Colino, 2013). Later, the presence of the Web in education has been revised, unveiling how it has favoured the improvement and democratization of learning and teaching thanks to its great potential (Barrbera, 2004; Khan, 1997; Lee & Tsai, 2005).

On another stage, the concept of CLIL has been introduced, as well as its close link to the use of ICT, whose usefulness and potential for learning and educational materials development are no longer questioned. Furthermore, some examples of research pointing out how technology can enhance learning in CLIL (in Primary, Secondary and Higher Education) contexts have been addressed.

Finally, some keys on the importance of social media integration in the CLIL classroom, its benefits and barriers have been offered, all in an attempt to clarify how and why these tools have the potential of improving students' performance in the FL and the outcomes of bilingual/multilingual programs. It has been also pointed out the need for teacher training and institutional support in order to guarantee an effective implementation of educational social media, and the dangers linked to this issue, which can contribute to expanding the digital, and consequently, the language gap.

However, although only the concept of social media has been considered in this study, it cannot be denied the rapid emergence of other promising technologies in the educational panorama. Such is the case of augmented reality and artificial intelligence, which, despite still being in their initial stages of use in education, are becoming more important as it is revealed by the growing literature analysing their impact in certain contexts, especially in language learning (Dizon, 2017; Johnson, 2010). In this sense, it could be interesting to analyse the pertinence and usefulness of applying these two methodologies to CLIL in future studies.

REFERENCES

Abascal, J., Barbosa, S. D. J., Nicolle, C., & Zaphiris, P. (2016). Rethinking Universal Accessibility: A Broader Approach Considering the Digital Gap. *Universal Access in the Information Society, 15*(2), 179–182. doi:10.100710209-015-0416-1

Adams, S., Brown, M., Dahlstrom, E., Cummins, M., & Díaz, V. (2018). *The 2018 Horizon Report Higher Education Edition*. Austin, TX: The New Media Consortium; Retrieved from https://bit.ly/2wrocSO

Aghaei, S., Nematbakhsh, M. A., & Farsani, H. K. (2012). Evolution of the World Wide Web: From Web 1.0 to Web 4.0. [IJWesT]. *International Journal of Web & Semantic Technology, 3*(1), 1–10. doi:10.5121/ijwest.2012.3101

Alexander, S. (1995). Teaching and Learning on the World Wide Web. In R. Debreceny, & A. J. Ellis (Eds.), *AusWeb95, Innovation, and Diversity: the World Wide Web in Australia* (pp. 94–99). Ballina, Australia: Southern Cross University; Retrieved from https://bit.ly/2OwKyue

Arau, M. C., Morgado, M., Gaspar, M., & Régio, M. (2019). Teacher Training for CLIL in Higher Education Through Blended Learning. In M. L. Carrió-Pastor (Ed.), *Teaching Language and Teaching Literature in Virtual Environments* (pp. 203–225). Singapore: Springer; doi:10.1007/978-981-13-1358-5_11

Arnaiz-Castro, P. (2017). An insight into CLIL in the Canary Islands Autonomous Community: key aspects and students' achievements. In M. E. Gómez, & R. Johnstone (Eds.), *Educación bilingüe: tendencias educativas y conceptos claves = Bilingual Education: Trends and Key Concepts* (pp. 235–247). Madrid, Spain: Ministerio de Educación, Cultura y Deporte; doi:10.4438/030-17-133-4

Azab, N., Abdelsalam, H. M., & Gamal, S. (2013). Use of Web 2.0 Collaboration Technologies in Egyptian Public Universities: An Exploratory Study. In Z. Mahmood (Ed.), *E-Government Implementation and Practice in Developing Countries* (pp. 99–127). Hershey, PA: IGI Global; doi:10.4018/978-1-4666-4090-0.ch005

Ballidag, S. (2018). Using Wikis to Increase Writing Skills in Writing Classes. *International Journal of Educational Research, 9*(1), 12–17.

Barrbera, E. (2004). Quality in Virtual Education Environments. *British Journal of Educational Technology, 35*(1), 13–20. doi:10.1111/j.1467-8535.2004.00364.x

Barretta, A. G. (2014, September 24). 9 Rules of Etiquette for Academic Twitter Use [Blog post]. Retrieved from https://bit.ly/2YP0z2S

Benito-Osorio, D., Peris-Ortiz, M., Rueda, C., & Colino, A. (2013). Web 5.0: The Future of Emotional Competences in Higher Education. *Global Business Perspectives, 1*(3), 274–287. doi:10.100740196-013-0016-5

Benson, C., & Wong, K. M. (2019). Effectiveness of Policy Development and Implementation of L1-Based Multilingual Education in Cambodia. *International Journal of Bilingual Education and Bilingualism, 22*(2), 250–265. doi:10.1080/13670050.2017.1313191

Bernal, P. A. (2010). Web 2.5: The Symbiotic Web. *International Review of Law Computers & Technology, 24*(1), 25–37. doi:10.1080/13600860903570145

Bikowski, D., & Vithanage, R. (2016). Effects of Web-Based Collaborative Writing on Individual L2 Writing Development. *Language Learning & Technology, 20*(1), 79–99. Retrieved from https://bit.ly/2NWddMr

Broadbent, J., & Poon, W. L. (2015). Self-Regulated Learning Strategies & Academic Achievement in Online Higher Education Learning Environments: A Systematic Review. *Internet and Higher Education, 27*, 1–13. doi:10.1016/j.iheduc.2015.04.007

Cappellini, M., Lewis, T., & Rivens, A. (Eds.). (2017). *Learner Autonomy and Web 2.0. Advances in CALL Research and Practice*. Sheffield, UK: Equinox; Retrieved from https://bit.ly/2xZ1wdn

Chawinga, W. D. (2017). Taking Social Media to A University Classroom: Teaching and Learning Using Twitter and Blogs. *An International Journal of Educational Technology in Higher Education, 14*(3), 1–19. doi: . doi:10.1186/s41239-017-0041-6

Chawinga, W. D., & Zinn, S. (2016). Use of Web 2.0 by Students in the Faculty of Information Science and Communications at Mzuzu University, Malawi. *South African Journal of Information Management, 18*(1), 1–12. doi:10.4102ajim.v18i1.694

Cohen-Almagor, R. (2011). Internet History. [IJT]. *International Journal of Technoethics, 2*(2), 45–64. doi:10.4018/jte.2011040104

Cong-Lem, N. (2018). Web-Based Language Learning (WBLL) for Enhancing L2 Speaking Performance: A Review. *Advances in Language and Literary Studies, 9*(4), 143–152. doi:10.7575/aiac.alls.v.9n.4p.143

Cortés, L. C. (2019). El aprendizaje en línea – una motivación. *Revista Iberoamericana de Producción Académica y Gestión Educativa, 6*(11), 1–8. Retrieved from https://bit.ly/2GmF7N7

Council of Europe. (2001). *Common European Framework of Reference for Languages: Learning, Teaching, Assessment*. Strasbourg, France: Council for Cultural Cooperation, Education Committee, Language Policy Division. Retrieved from https://bit.ly/2CRb2mh

Coyle, D., Hood, P., & Marsh, D. (2010). *CLIL: Content and Language Integrated Learning* (3rd ed.). Cambridge, UK: Cambridge University Press.

Díaz-Martín, C. (2017). El uso del vídeo para la formación inicial de docentes en AICLE. In M. E. Gómez, & R. Johnstone (Eds.), *Educación bilingüe: tendencias educativas y conceptos claves = Bilingual Education: Trends and Key Concepts* (pp. 23–32). Madrid, Spain: Ministerio de Educación, Cultura y Deporte; doi:10.4438/030-17-133-4

Dizon, G. (2017). Using Intelligent Personal Assistants for Second Language Learning: A Case Study of Alexa. *TESOL Journal*, *8*(4), 811–830. doi:10.1002/tesj.353

Dzvapatsva, G. P., Mitrovic, Z., & Dietrich, A. D. (2014). Use of Social Media Platforms for Improving Academic Performance at Further Education and Training Colleges. *South African Journal of Information Management*, *16*(1), 1–7. doi:10.4102ajim.v16i1.604

Edosomwan, S., Prakasan, S. K., Kouame, D., Watson, J., & Seymour, T. (2011). The History of Social Media and its Impact on Business. *The Journal of Applied Management and Entrepreneurship*, *16*(3), 79–91. Retrieved from https://bit.ly/2Nibu05

Elekaei, A., Tabrizi, H. H., & Chalak, A. (2019). The Influence of Autonomy on Iranian EFL Learners' Vocabulary Podcasting Tasks, Gain and Retention. *International Journal of Foreign Language Teaching & Research*, *7*(25), 127–141. Retrieved from https://bit.ly/2XbC0wO

European Commission. (1995). *White Paper on Education and Training – Teaching and Learning – Towards the Learning Society*. Brussels, Belgium: Commission of the European Communities. Retrieved from https://bit.ly/1Jq0nbT

Filsinger, M., & Freitag, M. (2019). Internet Use and Volunteering: Relationships and Differences Across Age and Applications. *Voluntas*, *30*(1), 87–97. doi:10.100711266-018-0045-4

Fitria, V. N., & Susilawati, S. (2019). Video Sharing in Content and Language Integrated Learning (CLIL) Context: Fostering Junior High School Students' Productive Skills. In A. G. Abdullah, A. A. Danuwijaya, N. Haristiani, R. Dallyono, Y. Wirza, & D. Yuliana (Eds.), *Proceedings of the Second Conference on Language, Literature, Education, and Culture (ICOLLITE 2018)* (Vol. 257, pp. 282–286). Indonesia. doi:10.2991/icollite-18.2019.62

Fouz-González, J. (2019). Podcast-Based Pronunciation Training: Enhancing FL Learners' Perception and Production of Fossilised Segmental Features. *ReCALL*, *31*(2), 150–169. doi:10.1017/S0958344018000174

Fuchs, C. (2019). The Structural and Dialogic Aspects of Language Massive Open Online Courses (LMOOCs): A Case Study. In Information Resources Management Association (Ed.), Computer-Assisted Language Learning: Concepts, Methodologies, Tools, and Applications (pp. 1540–1562). Hershey, PA: IGI Global. doi:10.4018/978-1-5225-0177-0.ch002

Gal, P., Nicoletti, G., Renault, T., Sorbe, S., & Timiliotis, C. (2019). Digitalisation and Productivity. In *Search of the Holy Grail – Firm-Level Empirical Evidence from EU Countries (OECD Economics Department Working Papers No. 1533)*. Paris, France: OECD Publishing; Retrieved from https://bit.ly/2EfPCQ6

Ghanizadeh, A., Razavi, A., & Hosseini, A. (2018). TELL (Technology-Enhanced Language Learning) in Iranian High Schools: A Panacea for Emotional and Motivational Detriments. *International Journal of Applied Linguistics and English Literature, 7*(4), 92–100. doi:10.7575/aiac.ijalel.v.7n.4p.92

Gikas, J., & Grant, M. M. (2013). Mobile Computing Devices in Higher Education: Student Perspectives on Learning with Cellphones, Smartphones and Social Media. *The Internet and Higher Education, 19*, 18–26. doi:10.1016/j.iheduc.2013.06.002

Gimeno, A. M. (2009). How Can CLIL Benefit from the Integration of Information and Communication Technologies? In M. L. Carrió-Pastor (Ed.), *Content and Language Integrated Learning: Cultural Diversity* (pp. 77–102). Bern, Switzerland: Peter Lang.

Gómez, M. E. (2017). Evaluación de los resultados de la educación bilingüe. In M. I. Amor, R. Serrano, & E. Pérez (Eds.), *La Educación Bilingüe desde una visión integrada e integradora* (pp. 195–202). Madrid, Spain: Síntesis.

Greenhow, C., & Askari, E. (2017). Learning and Teaching with Social Network Sites: A Decade of Research in K-12 Related Education. *Education and Information Technologies, 22*(2), 623–645. doi:10.100710639-015-9446-9

Hajebi, M., Taheri, S., Fahandezh, F., & Salari, H. (2018). The Role of Web-based Language Teaching on Vocabulary Retention of Adult Pre-intermediate EFL Learners. *Journal of Language Teaching and Research, 9*(2), 372–378. doi:10.17507/jltr.0902.20

Herrington, J., & Parker, J. (2013). Emerging Technologies as Cognitive Tools for Authentic Learning. *British Journal of Educational Technology, 44*(4), 607–615. doi:10.1111/bjet.12048

Hortigüela-Alcalá, D., Sánchez-Santamaría, J., Pérez-Pueyo, Á., & Abella-García, V. (2019). Social Networks to Promote Motivation and Learning in Higher Education from the Students' Perspective. *Innovations in Education and Teaching International, 56*(4), 412–422. doi:10.1080/14703297.2019.1579665

Huang, H. (2015). From Web-Based Readers to Voice Bloggers: EFL Learners' Perspectives. *Computer Assisted Language Learning, 28*(2), 145–170. doi:10.1080/09588221.2013.803983

Huertas, C. A. (2017). The Role of Technology in the Development of Materials for Bilingual Education. In M. E. Gómez, & R. Johnstone (Eds.), *Educación bilingüe: tendencias educativas y conceptos claves = Bilingual Education: Trends and Key Concepts* (pp. 209–220). Madrid, Spain: Ministerio de Educación, Cultura y Deporte; doi:10.4438/030-17-133-4

Hung, H. T., & Yuen, S. C. Y. (2010). Educational Use of Social Networking Technology in Higher Education. *Teaching in Higher Education, 15*(6), 703–714. doi:10.1080/13562517.2010.507307

Jenks, C. (2018). Learning Through Social Media. In A. Burns, & J. C. Richards (Eds.), *The Cambridge Guide to Learning English as a Second Language* (pp. 335–342)., Retrieved from https://bit.ly/2I7raCZ

Jitpaisarnwattana, N., Reinders, H., & Darasawang, P. (2019). Language MOOCs: An Expanding Field. *Technology in Language Teaching & Learning, 1*(1), 21–32. doi:10.29140/tltl.v1n1.142

Johnson, E. J., & Zentella, A. C. (2017). Introducing the Language Gap. *International Multilingual Research Journal, 11*(1), 1–4. doi:10.1080/19313152.2016.1258184

Johnson, L., Adams, S., Cummins, M., & Estrada, V. (2012). *Technology Outlook for STEM+ Education 2012-2017: An NMC Horizon Report Sector Analysis*. Austin, TX: The New Media Consortium; Retrieved from https://bit.ly/2LSN6mZ

Johnson, L., Brown, M., & Adams, S. (2014). *The 2014 Horizon Report Higher Education Edition*. Austin, TX: The New Media Consortium; Retrieved from https://bit.ly/1n3Xvq7

Johnson, L., Brown, M., Adams, S., Cummins, M., & Díaz, V. (2016). *The 2016 Horizon Report Higher Education Edition*. Austin, TX: The New Media Consortium; Retrieved from https://bit.ly/1ok1VzX

Johnson, L., & Laurence, F. (2004). *The 2004 Horizon Report Higher Education Edition*. Austin, TX: The New Media Consortium; Retrieved from https://bit.ly/32smu20

Johnson, L., Laurence, F., Levine, A., & Smith, R. (2007). *The 2007 Horizon Report Higher Education Edition*. Austin, TX: The New Media Consortium.

Johnson, L., Laurence, F., Levine, A., & Smith, R. (2009). *The 2009 Horizon Report K- (12th ed.)*. Austin, TX: The New Media Consortium; Retrieved from https://bit.ly/2UiQIn5

Johnson, L., Laurence, F., Levine, A., Smith, R., & Stone, S. (2010). *The 2010 Horizon Report K- (12th ed.)*. Austin, TX: The New Media Consortium; Retrieved from https://bit.ly/2LjIxTt

Johnson, W. L. (2010). Serious Use of a Serious Game for Language Learning. *International Journal of Artificial Intelligence in Education*, 20(2), 175–195. doi:10.3233/JAI-2010-0006

Juan-Garau, M., & Salazar-Noguera, J. (2015). Learning English and Learning through English: Insights from Secondary Education. In M. Juan-Garau, & J. Salazar-Noguera (Eds.), *Content-based Language Learning in Multilingual Educational Environments* (pp. 105–121). Berlin, Germany: Springer; doi:10.1007/978-3-319-11496-5_7

Kevogo, A. U., Kitonga, N. N., & Adika, S. K. (2015). Multilingualism and Language Use Patterns: Students Attitude towards Kiswahili in Garissa Town, Kenya. *Research on Humanities and Social Sciences, 5*(4), 185–193. Retrieved from https://bit.ly/2XSFAuE

Khan, B. H. (1997). Web-Based Instruction (WBI): What Is It and Why Is It? In B. H. Khan (Ed.), *Web-Based Instruction* (pp. 5–18). Englewood Cliffs, NJ: Educational Technology Publications.

Kietzmann, J. H., Hermkens, K., Mccarthy, I. P., & Silvestre, B. S. (2011). Social Media? Get Serious! Understanding the Functional Building Blocks of Social Media. *Business Horizons, 54*(3), 241–251. doi:10.1016/j.bushor.2011.01.005

Klimova, B. F. (2012). CLIL and the Teaching of Foreign Languages. *Procedia: Social and Behavioral Sciences, 47*, 572–576. doi:10.1016/j.sbspro.2012.06.698

Lázár, I. (2015). EFL Learners' Intercultural Competence Development in an International Web Collaboration Project. *Language Learning Journal, 43*(2), 208–221. doi:10.1080/09571736.2013.869941

Lee, L. (2011). Blogging: Promoting Learner Autonomy and Intercultural Competence through Study Abroad. *Language Learning & Technology, 15*(3), 87–109.

Lee, M.-H., & Tsai, C.-C. (2005). Exploring High School Students' and Teachers' Preferences Toward the Constructivist Internet-Based Learning Environments in Taiwan. *Educational Studies*, *31*(2), 149–167. doi:10.1080/03055690500095522

Levak, N., & Son, J.-B. (2017). Facilitating Second Language Learners' Listening Comprehension with Second Life and Skype. *ReCALL*, *29*(2), 200–218. doi:10.1017/S0958344016000215

Lin, C.-H., Warschauer, M., & Blake, R. (2016). Language Learning through Social Networks: Perceptions and Reality. *Language Learning & Technology*, *20*(1), 124–147.

Liu, S. H.-J., & Lan, Y.-J. (2016). Social Constructivist Approach to Web-Based EFL Learning: Collaboration, Motivation, and Perception on the Use of Google Docs. *Journal of Educational Technology & Society*, *19*(1), 171–186. doi:10.2307/jeductechsoci.19.1.171

Llargues, J. M., Peralta, J., Arrabales, R., Gonzalez, M., Cortez, P., & López, A. (2014). Artificial Intelligence Approaches for the Generation and Assessment of Believable Human-like Behaviour in Virtual Characters. *Expert Systems with Applications*, *4*(16), 7281–7290. doi:10.1016/j.eswa.2014.05.004

Lomicka, L., & Lord, G. (2016). Social Networking and Language Learning. In F. Farr, & L. Murray (Eds.), *The Routledge Handbook of Language Learning and Technology* (pp. 255–268). New York, NY: Routledge; Retrieved from https://bit.ly/2Ln3Gw4

Lopriore, L. (2018). Reframing Teaching Knowledge in Content and Language Integrated Learning (CLIL): A European Perspective. *Language Teaching Research*, 1–11. doi:10.1177/1362168818777518

Luo, T. (2013). Web 2.0 for Language Learning: Benefits and Challenges for Educators. [IJCALLT]. *International Journal of Computer-Assisted Language Learning and Teaching*, *3*(3), 1–17. doi:10.4018/ijcallt.2013070101

Marzulina, L., Habibi, A., Mukminin, A., Desvitasari, D., Yaakob, M. F. M., & Ropawandi, D. (2018). The Integration of Social Networking Services in Higher Education: Benefits and Barriers in Teaching English. *International Journal of Virtual and Personal Learning Environments*, *8*(2), 46–62. doi:10.4018/IJVPLE.2018070104

McCrory, R. (2004). A Framework for Understanding Teaching With the Internet. *American Educational Research Journal*, *41*(2), 447–488. doi:10.3102/00028312041002447

McLoughlin, C., & Lee, M. J. W. (2010). Personalised and Self-Regulated Learning in the Web 2.0 Era: International Exemplars of Innovative Pedagogy Using Social Software. *Australasian Journal of Educational Technology*, *26*(1), 28–43. doi:10.14742/ajet.1100

Mehisto, P., Marsh, D., & Frigols, M. J. (2008). *Uncovering CLIL. Content and language Integrated Learning in Bilingual and Multilingual Education*. Oxford, UK: MacMillan.

Mendler, J., Simon, D., & Broome, P. (2002). Virtual Development and Virtual Geographies: Using the Internet to Teach Interactive Distance Courses in the Global South. *Journal of Geography in Higher Education*, *26*(3), 313–325. doi:10.1080/0309826022000019891

Merchant, G. (2012). Mobile Practices in Everyday Life: Popular Digital Technologies and Schooling Revisited. *British Journal of Educational Technology*, *43*(5), 770–782. doi:10.1111/j.1467-8535.2012.01352.x

Mills, N. (2011). Situated Learning through Social Networking Communities: The Development of Joint Enterprise, Mutual Engagement, and a Shared Repertoire. *CALICO Journal, 28*(2), 345–368. doi:10.11139/cj.28.2.345-368

Mishra, P., & Koehler, M. J. (2006). Technological Pedagogical Content Knowledge: A Framework for Teacher Knowledge. *Teachers College Record, 108*(6), 1017–1054. doi:10.1111/j.1467-9620.2006.00684.x

Mishra, P., & Koehler, M. J. (2012). *Technological Pedagogical and Content Knowledge (TPACK).* Retrieved from https://bit.ly/2bBZwM1

Molina, M., & Sampietro, A. (2015). Propuestas didácticas para el uso de Internet y de la pizarra digital en contextos de educación bilingüe. *Digital Education Review, 28*, 1–18.

Moravec, J. (2008). Moving beyond Education 2.0. Retrieved from https://bit.ly/2HL1Mna

Murire, O. T., & Cilliers, L. (2017). Social Media Adoption among Lecturers at a Traditional University in Eastern Cape Province of South Africa. *South African Journal of Information Management, 19*(1), 1–6. doi:10.4102ajim.v19i1.834

Navarro-Pablo, M., López-Gándara, Y., & García-Jimenez, E. (2019). The Use of Digital Resources and Materials In and Outside the Bilingual Classroom. *Comunicar, 28*(59), 83–92. doi:10.3916/C59-2019-08

Nchindila, B. (2017). Investigating Benefits of Mother Tongue Instruction in Multilingual Africa: The Role of Content and Language Integrated Learning. *Tydskrif vir Taalonderrig, 51*(2), 11–33. doi:10.4314/jlt.v51i2.1

Nedelkoska, L., & Quintini, G. (2018). *Automation, Skills Use, and Training* (OECD Social, Employment and Migration Working Papers No. 202). Paris, France. doi:10.1787/1815199X

Neo, M. (2003). Developing a Collaborative Learning Environment Using a Web-Based Design. *Journal of Computer Assisted Learning, 19*(4), 462–473. doi:10.1046/j.0266-4909.2003.00050.x

Ng'ambi, D. (2013). Effective and Ineffective Uses of Emerging Technologies: Towards a Transformative Pedagogical Model. *British Journal of Educational Technology, 44*(4), 652–661. doi:10.1111/bjet.12053

Nga, H. T., Lan, T. T., & Nam, N. H. (2018). Teaching English for 5th Grade Student in Primary School via Science Topics on Approach of STEM Education: A Case Study of Learning Outside School Activities. *HNUE Journal of Science, 63*(9), 61–69. doi:10.18173/2354-1075.2018-0169

Nieto, E. (2012). CLIL and Development of Emotional Competence. *Miscelánea: A Journal of English and American Studies, 45*, 57–73. Retrieved from https://bit.ly/2HPlbmL

Nikula, T., Dalton-Puffer, C., & Llinares, A. (2013). CLIL Classroom Discourse: Research from Europe. *Journal of Immersion and Content-Based Language Education, 1*(1), 70–100. doi:10.1075/jicb.1.1.04nik

O'Dowd, R. (2018). Innovations and Challenges in Using Online Communication Technologies in CLIL. *Theory into Practice, 57*(3), 232–240. doi:10.1080/00405841.2018.1484039

Palacios, F. J., & Espejo, R. (2019). Webs y aprendizaje de lenguas: Análisis de actividades de reading y listening para el hablante no nativo de inglés; el caso de la BBC. *EDMETIC. Revista de Educación Mediática y TIC, 8*(1), 72–87. doi:10.21071/edmetic.v8i1.11089

Parvathi, M., & Mariselvi, R. (2017). A Bird's Eye on the Evolution – Web 1.0 to Web 5.0 : Lib 1.0 to Lib 5.0. [IJARTET]. *International Journal of Advanced Research Trends in Engineering and Technology*, *4*(4), 167–176. Retrieved from https://bit.ly/2HQTVDL

Patel, K. D. (2013). Incremental Journey for World Wide Web: Introduced with Web 1.0 to Recent Web 5.0. A Survey Paper. *International Journal of Advanced Research in Computer Science and Software Engineering*, *3*(10), 410–417. Retrieved from https://bit.ly/2UYstYa

Pileggi, S. F., Fernandez-Llatas, C., & Traver, V. (2012). When the Social Meets the Semantic: Social Semantic Web or Web 2.5. *Future Internet*, *4*(3), 852–864. doi:10.3390/fi4030852

Porter, W. W., & Graham, C. R. (2016). Institutional Drivers and Barriers to Faculty Adoption of Blended Learning in Higher Education. *British Journal of Educational Technology*, *47*(4), 748–762. doi:10.1111/bjet.12269

Prasojo, L. D., Habibi, A., & Mukminin, A. (2017). Managing Digital Learning Environments: Student Teachers' Perception on the Social Networking Services Use in Writing Courses in Teacher Education. *Turkish Online Journal of Educational Technology-TOJET*, *16*(4), 42–55.

Prasojo, L. D., Habibi, A., Mukminin, A., Taridi, M., & Saudagar, F. (2017). Managing Digital Learning Environments: Student Teachers' Perception on the Social Networking Services Use in Writing Courses in Teacher Education. *Turkish Online Journal of Educational Technology, 16*(4), 42–55. Retrieved from https://bit.ly/30wIYgz

Rao, Y., Wang, C., & Bender, J. (2016). French-Chinese Dialogical Interaction via Web Collaborative Blog-Writing: Code-Switching to Extend Online Tandem Language Learning. In C. Wang, & L. Winstead (Eds.), *Handbook of Research on Foreign Language Education in the Digital Age* (pp. 208–234). Hershey, PA: IGI Global. doi:10.4018/978-1-5225-0177-0.ch010

Redecker, C. (2016). *Digital Competence Framework for Educators (DigCompEdu)*. Luxembourg: Publications Office of the European Union. doi:10.2760/178382

Reinhardt, J. (2019). Social Media in Second and Foreign Language Teaching and Learning: Blogs, Wikis, and Social Networking. *Language Teaching*, *52*(1), 1–39. doi:10.1017/S0261444818000356

Rinatovna, G., Vladimirovna, E., Bizyanova, F., & Haidar, I. (2017). Moosle-ee: Massive Open Online Social Learning Environment for English eLearning System. *Revista San Gregorio*, *20*, 6–13.

Rodriguez, J. E. (2011). Social Media Use in Higher Education: Key Areas to Consider for Educators. *MERLOT Journal of Online Learning and Teaching, 7*(4), 539–550. Retrieved from https://bit.ly/32v7lNp

Roldán, A. R. (2012). The Shaping of Spanish CLIL. *Encuentro: Revista de Investigación e Innovación En La Clase de Idiomas*, *21*, 71–79.

Rosell-Aguilar, F. (2018). Twitter as a Formal and Informal Language Learning Tool: from Potential to Evidence. In F. Rosell-Aguilar, T. Beaven, & M. Fuertes (Eds.), Innovative Language Teaching and Learning at University: Integrating Informal Learning into Formal Language Education (pp. 99–106). Voillans, France: Research-publishing.net. doi:10.14705/rpnet.2018.22.780

Rumlich, D. (2017). CLIL Theory and Empirical Reality – Two Sides of the Same Coin? *Journal of Immersion and Content-Based Language Education, 5*(1), 110–134. doi:10.1075/jicb.5.1.05rum

Selwyn, N. (2010). Looking Beyond Learning: Notes Towards the Critical Study of Educational Technology. *Journal of Computer Assisted Learning, 26*(1), 65–73. doi:10.1111/j.1365-2729.2009.00338.x

Soava, G. (2015). Development Prospects of the Tourism Industry in the Digital Age. *Revista Tinerilor Economisti, 1*(25), 101–116. Retrieved from https://bit.ly/2JSP3Am

Soomro, K. A., Zai, S. Y., & Jafri, I. H. (2015). Competence and Usage of Web 2.0 Technologies by Higher Education Faculty. *Educational Media International, 52*(4), 284–295. doi:10.1080/09523987.2015.1095522

Sorbe, S., Gal, P., Nicoletti, G., & Timiliotis, C. (2019). *Digital Dividend: Policies to Harness the Productivity Potential of Digital Technologies (OECD Economics Department Working Papers No. 1533)*. Paris, France: OECD Publishing; Retrieved from https://bit.ly/2EfPL66

Stockwell, E. (2016). Using Web-Based Exploratory Tasks to Develop Intercultural Competence in a Homogeneous Cultural Environment. *Innovations in Education and Teaching International, 53*(6), 649–659. doi:10.1080/14703297.2015.1049642

Sun, Y.-C., & Yang, F.-Y. (2015). I Help, Therefore, I Learn: Service Learning on Web 2.0 in an EFL Speaking Class. *Computer Assisted Language Learning, 28*(3), 202–219. doi:10.1080/09588221.2013.818555

Sung, W., Ng, J. Y., & Choi, A. L. (2018). Integrating Corporate Social Media Communication into the English Language Curricula. *International Conference on Open and Innovative Education (ICOIE 2018) — The Open University of Hong Kong*, 121–133. Retrieved from https://bit.ly/2OyTgYZ

Tafazoli, D., Huertas, C. A., & Gómez, M. E. (2019). Technology-Based Review on Computer-Assisted Language Learning: A Chronological Perspective. *Pixel-Bit. Revista de Medios y Educación*, (54), 29–43. doi: . doi:10.12795/pixelbit.2019.i54.02

Tavakoli, R., & Wijesinghe, S. N. R. (2019). The Evolution of the Web and Netnography in Tourism: A Systematic Review. *Tourism Management Perspectives, 29*, 48–55. doi:10.1016/j.tmp.2018.10.008

Teo, T., Sang, G., Mei, B., & Hoi, C. K. W. (2019). Investigating Pre-Service Teachers' Acceptance of Web 2.0 Technologies in their Future Teaching: A Chinese Perspective. *Interactive Learning Environments, 27*(4), 530–546. doi:10.1080/10494820.2018.1489290

Tess, P. A. (2013). The Role of Social Media in Higher Education Classes (Real and Virtual) – A Literature Review. *Computers in Human Behavior, 29*(5), A60–A68. doi:10.1016/j.chb.2012.12.032

Tsai, M.-J., & Tsai, C.-C. (2003). Information Searching Strategies in Web-Based Science Learning: The Role of Internet Self-Efficacy. *Innovations in Education and Teaching International, 40*(1), 43–50. doi:10.1080/1355800032000038822

Ulbrich, F., Jahnke, I., & Mårtensson, P. (2011). Special Issue on Knowledge Development and the Net Generation. *International Journal of Sociotechnology and Knowledge Development, 2*(4), 1-2.

Vieira, J., & Isaías, P. (2015). Web 3.0 in Web Development. In T. Issa, & P. Isaías (Eds.), *Artificial Intelligence Technologies and the Evolution of Web 3.0* (pp. 209–228). Hershey, PA: IGI Global. doi:10.4018/978-1-4666-8147-7.ch010

Vygotski, L. S. (1978). *Mind in Society: Development of Higher Psychological Processes*. Cambridge, MA: Harvard University Press.

Weber, S., & Rech, J. (2010). An Overview and Differentiation of the Evolutionary Steps of the Web X.Y Movement: The Web Before and Beyond 2.0. In S. Murugesan (Ed.), *Handbook of Research on Web 2.0, 3.0, and X.0: Technologies, Business, and Social Applications* (pp. 12–39). Hershey, PA: IGI Global. doi:10.4018/978-1-60566-384-5.ch002

Woo, M., Chu, S., Ho, A., & Li, X. (2011). Using a Wiki to Scaffold Primary-School Students' Collaborative Writing. *Journal of Educational Technology & Society*, *14*(1), 43–54.

Woo, M. A., & Kimmick, J. V. (2000). Comparison of Internet versus Lecture Instructional Methods for Teaching Nursing Research. *Journal of Professional Nursing*, *16*(3), 132–139. doi:10.1053/PN.2000.5919 PMID:10860311

Yim, S., & Warschauer, M. (2017). Web-Based Collaborative Writing in L2 Contexts: Methodological Insights from Text Mining. *Language Learning & Technology*, *21*(1), 146–165. Retrieved from https://bit.ly/2GdVyJR

Yoestara, M., & Putri, Z. (2018). PODCAST: An Alternative Way to Improve EFL Students' Listening and Speaking Performance. *Englisia Journal of Language, Education, and Humanities*, *6*(1), 15–26. doi:10.22373/ej.v6i1.3805

Zou, B., Wang, D., & Xing, M. (2016). Collaborative Tasks in Wiki-Based Environment in EFL Learning. *Computer Assisted Language Learning*, *29*(5), 1001–1018. doi:10.1080/09588221.2015.1121878

ADDITIONAL READING

Burston, J. (2015). The Future of Foreign Language Instructional Technology: BYOD MALL. *The EuroCALL Review*, *23*(2), 3–9. doi:10.4995/eurocall.2016.4431

Dizon, G. (2016). Facebook vs. Paper-and-Pencil Writing: Comparing Japanese EFL Students' Opinions of the Writing Mediums. *Computer Assisted Language Learning*, *29*(8), 1249–1258. Retrieved from https://bit.ly/2LllZ4F. doi:10.1080/09588221.2016.1266369

Fernández-Fontecha, A. (2012). CLIL in the Foreign Language Classroom: Proposal of a Framework for ICT Materials Design in Language-Oriented Versions of Content and Language Integrated Learning. *Alicante Journal of English Studies*, *25*, 317–334. doi:10.14198/raei.2012.25.22

Kang, T. (2019). The Effectiveness of Multiple Media Tools in L2 Listening: A Meta-Analysis. In Information Resources Management Association (Ed.), Computer-Assisted Language Learning: Concepts, Methodologies, Tools, and Applications (pp. 585–616). Hershey, PE: IGI Global. doi:10.4018/978-1-5225-7663-1.ch028

Manzano, I., & Hunt-Gómez, C. I. (2018). Música, TIC y comunicación en el aula de lengua inglesa y contextos bilingües: mejora de las destrezas de escucha de la percepción del proceso de aprendizaje con Lyrics Traning. In M. E. Gómez & R. Johnstone (Eds.), *Nuevas Perspectivas en Educación Bilingüe: Investigación e Innovación* (pp. 133–136). Granada, Spain: Editorial Universidad de Granada.

Tian, L., & Franklin, T. (2015). Tweeting and Blogging: Moving Towards Education 2.0. *International Journal on E-Learning: Corporate, Government, Healthcare, and Higher Education, 14*(2), 235–258. doi:10.1111/j.1365-2729.2008.00306.x

Tseng, J.-J., Cheng, Y.-S., & Yeh, H.-N. (2019). How Pre-Service English Teachers Enact TPACK in the Context of Web-Conferencing Teaching: A Design Thinking Approach. *Computers & Education, 128*, 171–182. doi:10.1016/j.compedu.2018.09.022

Wang, S., & Vásquez, C. (2012). Web 2.0 and Second Language Learning: What Does the Research Tell Us? *CALICO Journal, 29*(3), 412–430. doi:10.11139/cj.29.3.412-430

KEY TERMS AND DEFINITIONS

CLIL: Content and Language Integrated Learning.

Digital Competence: The set of knowledge, strategies and skills that helps an individual to function in the digital world, solving digital problems by using a digital support.

Information/Network Society: Society where information creation, distribution and manipulation is a key economic, social, political and cultural activity.

Language Learning Social Networking Sites or LLSNS: Computer- or mobile-mediated technologies directed to language learning which help users create and share content via virtual communities and networks.

Media Competence: The set of knowledge, strategies and skills that allows an individual to efficiently face the media environment of today.

Social Media: A set of applications and websites that enables individuals to create and share information, ideas, and multiples ways of expression via virtual communities and networks.

World Wide Web or Web: An online information system where content and resources, commonly interlinked by hypertext, are freely accessible via Internet.

This research was previously published in the Handbook of Research on Bilingual and Intercultural Education; pages 359-382, copyright year 2020 by Information Science Reference (an imprint of IGI Global).

Chapter 14
Social Networking Sites Classroom Framework using Operant Conditioning of Learning

Yousuf Anwar Al Sandi
Salalah College of Technology, Salalah, Oman

Bernard Haber Ugalde
Salalah College of Technology, Salalah, Oman

ABSTRACT

In this information age, educational institutions have innovated to take the teaching and learning process to the next level. They are now infusing social media and social networks with traditional teaching as a method of instruction inside the classroom. Various studies have been carried out to find and suggest what social network is the best fit to adopt to education in general. However, there are no known standards on how to implement learning in social networks particularly in monitoring and responding to student behavior. This research is premised on the fact that positive response should be reinforced, and negative behavior is punished. Thus, this article presents how to use operant conditioning of learning inside a social network, particularly in managing a student's behavior. It was observed that there is an impact on the performance of students who used the developed classroom framework as compared to who did not. The result confirms that a monitored and guided social network approach can benefit students.

INTRODUCTION

In the recent era of technology, educational institutions have been trying to innovate itself to find new ways to enrich the whole teaching and learning process. It is seen that social network is having a pervasive impact and promising future in education. The educational institution then should no longer be asking if schools and universities will use the social network. Instead, they should be asking if social

DOI: 10.4018/978-1-6684-7123-4.ch014

networks are being utilized and adequately managed across the academe. Part of these monitoring and implementation steps is by looking into how students respond and behave inside these social networks. Student behavior should be managed so not to disturb other learners inside the social network and to ensure the smooth administration and delivery of the courses.

One classic learning theory in classroom management is operant conditioning. It is a learning process that uses both positive and negative reinforcements to encourage good and wanted behavior while deterring bad and unwanted behavior. Psychologists have observed that every action has a consequence, and if this is great, the person is more likely to do it again in the future. However, if the consequence is not so good, the individual will likely avoid doing it in a similar situation next time around.

Along with this thought, this paper discusses how to apply operant conditioning of learning when integrating social network into the classroom. It then analyzes the impact of integrating this learning theory to social network and classroom learning by measuring its impact on the academic performance of the learners. It also suggests ways and means how to leverage social networks to its full potentials. The result in this study will help to bring students and teachers to a new level of the learning experience.

Review of Related Literature

Below discusses the impact, advantages, and disadvantages of social networks in education. A brief note about the operant condition of learning is also presented on the succeeding sections.

Social Network in Education

The positive impact of social networks in education is now widely accepted. Thus, more and more efforts are conducted to analyze the effects of social networks in academic institutions. The study of Stanciu, Mihai and Aleca (2012) for instance claimed the significant impact of social networks on the educational process in Romanian higher education. The researchers also proposed a model for implementing Facebook usage in higher education learning processes.

In Oman, several studies have been conducted to find the relationship of social networks and its effect on the learning process of students. The study of Al-Mukhaini, Al-Qayoudhi and Al-Badi (2017) for example was to discover the motives of using social networks by higher education students in Oman. It was also aimed to recognize the impact of social networking tools in learning and education in general. It also analyzed the problems that students encountered while using social networks and determined whether the traditional learning methods needed to change. The study highlighted the benefits of using social networks as tools for developing a unique style of learning and presented the negative impacts that can influence the process of learning, all of which is geared to justify the use of social networks in higher education. Al-Harrasi and Al-Badi (2014) on the other hand, investigated the impact of social networking on college students. They found out that: (1) college students spend a long time on social networking sites; (2) college students are facing problems in trusting, filtering, and selecting different information accessed from social networking sites; and (3) social networks affect students in both positive and negative ways. Similar findings have shared by the research conducted by Mehmood and Taswir (2013) who investigated the pedagogical impacts of social networking sites of undergraduate students at the College of Applied Sciences, Nizwa, Oman.

All of these researches try to establish the impact of social networking in education which primarily aimed to helps create better student learning strategies and shape student culture of better academic performance. However, academic institutions still suffer from the deficiency of guiding learning theories for effective implementation (Tinmaz, 2017). Thus, research which focused on how to integrate social network effectively in education applying those learning theories in education.

Advantages of Social Networking Sites

Nowadays, academic institutions find it very essential to engage in social networks actively because of the known advantages of integrating social networks in classrooms. In the survey conducted by Eco (2017), showed that 67% of online adults use social networks. This data describes the fact that social networks can be used to improve the education of adults and students since these social networks already have a particular influence on the learners. It is quite apparent then that there are certain advantages of social networks to learners, here are some of them:

1. Worldwide connectivity. This is one of the most significant benefits of the social networking site. It creates an avenue where students and teachers can gain knowledge and share experiences. The social network goes beyond a specific group of people since it is accessible around the world (Sawyer, 2011). People of different ages, races, background, and culture can connect through a social network (Prakash Software, 2017). The use of social network in education provides students with the ability to get more useful information, to connect with learning groups and other educational systems that make learning convenient (Al-Zedjali, Al-Harrasi & Al-Badi, 2014).

2. It is free. Anyone who is interested in learning can gain knowledge and educate himself without paying money through the social network. Once information has been posted on the social network, it will be accessible to everyone for free (Thompson, 2015).

3. News and information updates. Students can update themselves with the latest information and news around the world quickly. Social networks are reshaping how information spread (Anderson & Caumont, 2014). It is now fast, participative by engaging their audiences and liken to storytelling. Thus, more information can be gained especially for students who are doing research or investigative projects.

4. Promotion. Students and teachers can promote their ideas through social networking sites. Anyone can advertise and build a brand through a social network (Meyer, 2017). Word-of-mouth recommendation and conversations can make or break anyone who ventures in the social network.

5. Overcoming limited resources. According to a study conducted by Ellison, Vitak, Gray, and Lampe (2014), a social network like Facebook is full of different resources. It may come in various forms like videos, pictures, animations, text, publications and more. Students and teachers can utilize and explore these resources as learning materials or aids in education.

6. Collaboration. Social media has been used by academic institutions to encourage collaborative learning and social interaction which leads to the better academic performance of learners (Rahmi & Zeki, 2017).

7. Feedback. Educational institutions can also gain valuable knowledge such as analytics on usage and insights on various issues of learners on social networks.

Disadvantages of Social Networking Sites

There are also some limitations that these social networking sites pose. The following enumerates the disadvantages of social networking sites:

1. Hacking. Privacy and personal data are vulnerable in the social network because it is easily hacked. According to Bishop (2013), while social network has changed how we interact with friends and associates, it is also high risk for security and threats. It can lead to damage to someone's personal life and career.
2. Addiction. This part of social networking is horrible since it may disturb an individual's life. More and more are persuaded to embrace social network since it is very accessible. Teenagers are the most affected by addiction, and it is a bigger problem than we think (Elgan, 2015).
3. Higher risks of fraud and scams. Fraud and scams are everywhere in the social network. Sometimes, as Rijnetu (2018) wrote, even experts cannot validate the legitimacy and authenticity of information posted in the social sites. Many users can face scamming problems, especially kids who are unaware of such risk.
4. Health issues. The more amount of time using social networking sites can also have a negative impact on health. Most users become lazy and they prefer to remain in their comfort zone. Their routine will change which may cause some health issues. Most common health problems is overuse injuries of the hand, obesity, muscle, and joint issues, eyestrain and some behavioral problems including aggressive behavior according to Walton (2017).
5. Reputation. Users can put themselves in danger if they share too much of personal information about themselves. People who can access any account can ruin other's life by creating the wrong story about them thus damaging reputation. To add, Cohen (2014) mentioned that inappropriate photos display a lousy image, attempt to be relevant could backfire, words can come back, and personal profiles could leak onto professional ones.

Operant Conditioning of Learning Framework

Operant conditioning theory otherwise known as instrumental conditioning is a learning process through which the strength of behavior is modified by reward or punishment (McLeod, 2015). An association is made between a behavior and a consequence for that behavior (Cherry, 2018).

The theory was developed by B. F. Skinner who was named to be the most influential psychologist of the twentieth century (Cherry, 2017). He is an American psychologist best known for his influence on behaviorism.

His theory is based on the idea that learning is a function of the change in overt behavior. He believed that all human actions were the direct result of conditioning. He said that the consequences of behavior determine the probability that the behavior will occur again. Changes in behavior are the result of an individual's response to events that occur in the environment. A response produces a consequence such as defining a word, hitting a ball, or solving a math problem. When a particular stimulus-response pattern is reinforced, the individual is conditioned to respond. The distinctive characteristic of operant conditioning relative to previous forms of behaviorism is that the organism can emit responses instead of only eliciting response due to an external stimulus. Figure 1 illustrates the concepts behind the theory.

Figure 1. Operant Conditioning

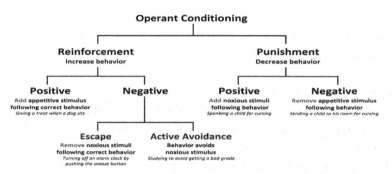

METHODOLOGY

The classroom framework on social networking sites using operant conditioning of learning was basically designed based on the literature review and repeatedly redrawn to incorporate suggestions of the teachers who were expert in educational management.

The framework was tested in Salalah College of Technology particularly in two groups of Fundamentals of Multimedia classes with a total population of 32 students. It was ideal since the course is a practical subject. The lecturer identified one particular topic were both groups of students took. However, one group was controlled. The first group is composed of 16 students who went through the topic based on the normal classroom management procedure.

On the other hand, the second group of 16 students used YouTube as social media and were managed using the operant conditioning of learning. The lecturer created tutorial videos and uploaded in YouTube. Then he asked all the students to subscribe to the channel. Students' behaviors were observed. Students who went through the videos and provided positive comments were given extra one mark as reinforcement of the behavior.

On the other hand, those who gave negative comments were either suspended to access the videos for one week or warned by personally talking to the students to avoid such unruly behavior. Additionally, those students who did not go through the exercise were either given additional work outside YouTube or were forced to unsubscribe to the channel. Both groups took the assessment and marks were recorded.

Some statistical measurements were used to determine the impact of incorporating operant conditioning in classroom management. T-test was used to compare means of the two groups for two independent samples. Statistical test for equality of means for two groups based on their scores was also done.

RESULTS

The following discussion presents the approach to the development of the framework and the implementation performed to determine the impact of the framework on the academic performance of students. It also discusses how to use the social network in education.

The Framework

By nature of social network to be opened and uncontrolled that the researchers propose the operant conditioning of learning as the learning model to be employed in the class when using social networking sites as illustrated in Figure 2. It is with the researcher's belief that students still need to observe proper etiquette and decorum inside this medium.

Figure 2. Proposed operant conditioning in networking site

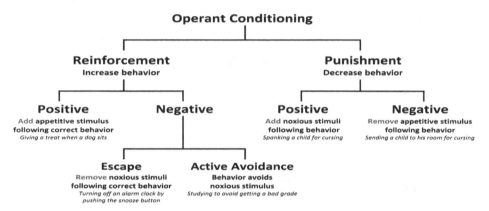

The researchers noted that rewards could reinforce student learning behavior on social networks. The basic principle is that extra points can be awarded to a student for a positive act. Mader (2009) and Johnson, Rice, Edgington and Williams (2005) have utilized this basic reinforcement in classroom management and they found effective. They even encourage the teachers to establish various levels of points associated with such rewards.

On the other hand, it is more likely that the teacher will act to restore order if students begin to misbehave. As a consequence of the negative action, teachers can temporality suspend student's access to the social network (Jin, Chen, Wang, Hui, & Vasilakos, 2013). This corrective action is usually the first defense of social network administrators to manage social network (Bosworth, Marlette, Putnam, & Wable, 2012).

At the same time, teachers can develop their voice assertively communicate their behavioral expectations on the usage of the social network. Teacher voice can be used to correct misbehaviors of students (Canter, 2010). Thus, this can be used as part of the active avoidance of behavior.

Additional learning activity is usually viewed by students as punishment. Consequently, introducing this in the learning process will definitely leave an impact on altered behavior from observed consequences and can be an effective positive punishment (Bandura, 1978).

As the worst case for non-participative and unruly students, they can be blocked in the social network forever.

Expanding the personalized learning devised by Gray (2014) the learning paradigm using operant conditioning of learning in social networks can be viewed in Figure 3. The research views social networks as one of the valuable media in classroom instruction and management. The learning paradigm is centered on student full and personalized learning. This is supported by the usual education pillars which are essential to the learning and delivery of knowledge such as learning strategy, assessment, teaching strategy, curriculum planning, and monitoring and support. Infusion of operant conditioning in the classroom management will surely help following the proposed framework.

Figure 3. Learning paradigm using the operant conditioning in networking site

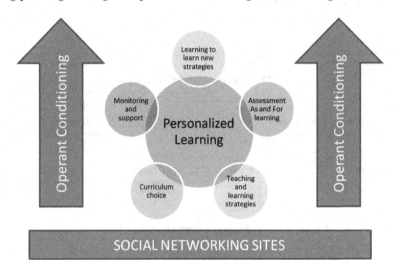

Testing of the Framework

The following discussions present the result of testing the framework.

Table 1 presents the summary of the behavior of students in the controlled group. Among the 16 students, eight were given extra one mark, and three were suspended to access the channel. The lecturer spoke to 2 students to correct negative behavior, two were given additional activity outside YouTube, and one was totally blocked in the networking site. It was observed that there are more students who took the activity. This can confirm that student sees the value of the social network in acquiring information thereby actively engaging themselves in watching the tutorial videos on YouTube.

It was also observed that the mean score of students who watch the videos got better marks compared to those who did not (Tables 2 and 3). This observation aligns the research results of Stanciu, Mihai, and Aleca (2012).

Table 1. Behavior of student in the controlled group

Watched the Videos in YouTube			Did Not Watch the Videos on YouTube	
Positive Comment	Negative Comment		Gave Additional Activity (outside of YouTube)	Blocked in YouTube
Gave Extra Point	Suspended Account for 1 week	Spoke to the Student for the Unruly Behavior		
8	3	2	2	1
Mean Average of Marks: 11.62			Mean Average of Marks: 7.67	

Table 2. Group statistics for normal group (1) vs. control group (2)

Group Statistics					
	Group	N	Mean	Std. Deviation	Std. Error Mean
Score	Goup1(Normal Class)	16	8.50	2.633	.658
	Group2 (Operant Conditioning)	16	10.88	2.335	.584

Table 3. Statistical test for equality of means for two groups based from their scores

Independent Samples Test										
		Levene's Test for Equality of Variances		t-test for Equality of Means						
		F	Sig.	t	df	Sig. (2-tailed)	Mean Difference	Std. Error Difference	95% Confidence Interval of the Difference	
									Lower	Upper
Score	Equal variances assumed	.044	.834	-2.700	30	.011	-2.375	.880	-4.172	-.578
	Equal variances not assumed			-2.700	29.576	.011	-2.375	.880	-4.173	-.577

Levene's test for equality of variance showed that the test for significance yielded (0.834) > 0.05 at 95% confidence interval; the score variance is approximately equal (Table 1) which showed that standard deviations did not vary significantly. Significance test for equality of means showed that t(0.011) is less than that at 0.05 level at 95% confidence interval which showed that the means of the two groups vary (i.e., mean of group 1 was significantly different from the mean of group 2). The result indicated that group 2 was better than group 1 as per scores comparison.

It was observed that students who were engaged in the social network have higher marks in the assessment as compared to those who did not engage in the activity. The result confirms that monitored and guided social network approach can bring benefit to the student's academic performance.

Leveraging YouTube

It has been noted that judiciously chosen videos may help students to engage more deeply in their courses according to Ferlazzo (2014). It helps students comprehend and understand the subject matter. This is because in general, most learners are visual and auditory in nature (Franz, 2017). They learn more if they are able to see and hear. Additionally, the new generation of learners finds it more appealing if presentations are made in the flashy and entertaining way thus videos are very useful.

Below are some points on how to blend in YouTube in the classroom or in the social networking site.

1. Downloading short videos and sharing them in the classrooms. Most of the presentation nowadays use videos as a way to call the attention of learners. Presenting a short clip can stimulate and encourage students to think and interact in the classroom or in any social network.

2. Create YouTube playlists as student assignments or as recommended extra resources. As mentioned by Whelan (2012), some people learn better by watching than reading, so providing video alternatives to the reading homework could really pay off for some students. Teachers can create playlists, either to supplement the discussion or as an alternative to the learning topic. A playlist puts it all into an easy, well-organized format for student's consumption.

3. Record the class lessons or lectures save them for future viewing. YouTube can work as a repository from which teachers can create, save and share whatever they record in the classroom. Once a video is recorded, YouTube can make it so easy for the teacher to share. Some students may miss the class, so they can go back to these videos on YouTube at any point in time. Students can use these videos as a reference for their future studies.

4. Take it to the next level. Teachers can use some applications to edit videos. Editing videos can help teachers to highlight important topics. It also allows teachers to incorporate some checkpoint like quizzes from which they can track student's level and understanding.

CONCLUSION

Since students are already using social networks outside the classrooms, integrating it into the classrooms will give students a new twist on a learning experience. There are dozens of advantages of social networking sites as presented in this paper which makes it very favorable for educational institutions to integrate it in the teaching-learning process. What is only left is for these institutions to develop strategies and monitor its implementation inside the classroom.

Thus, this paper presented a framework to help teachers infuse social networking inside the classroom. The researchers advocate appropriate management to infuse social network into the learning process effectively. Thus, the framework comes into its importance and can be a big help for teachers to manage and control student behavior inside the social networking site.

Furthermore, the paper presented the impact of the said framework to the academic performance of students. The result of the study proves the significant impact of integrating social network and operant conditioning of learning to the academic performance of students.

Lastly, the paper included some points on how to blend in social network particularly YouTube in the classroom.

ACKNOWLEDGMENT

The researchers would like to acknowledge Salalah College of Technology for the continuous support to such undertaking.

REFERENCES

Al-Harrasi, A., & Al-Badi, A. (2014). The impact of social networking: A study of the influence of smartphones on college students. *Contemporary Issues in Education Research, 7*(2), 129. doi:10.19030/cier.v7i2.8483

Al-Mukhaini, E., Al-Qayoudhi, W., & Al-Badi, A. (2017). Adoption of social networking in education: A study of the use of social networks by higher education students in Oman. *Journal of International Education Research, 10*(2).

Al-Rahmi, W., & Zeki, A. (2017). A model of using social media for collaborative learning to enhance learners' performance on learning. Journal Of King Saud University - Computer And. *Information Sciences, 29*(4), 526–535. doi:10.1016/j.jksuci.2016.09.002

Al-Zedjali, K., Al-Harrasi, A., & Al-Badi, A. (2014). Motivations for using social networking sites by college students for educational purposes. *International Journal of Social, Management, Economics And Business Engineering, 8*(8).

Anderson, M., & Caumont, A. (2014). How social media is reshaping news. *Pew Research Center.* Retrieved from http://www.pewresearch.org/fact-tank/2014/09/24/how-social-media-is-reshaping-news/

Bandura, A. (1978). Social learning theory of aggression. *Journal of Communication, 28*(3), 12–29. doi:10.1111/j.1460-2466.1978.tb01621.x PMID:690254

Bishop, E. (2013). 5 threats to your security when using social media. *Adweek.* Retrieved from http://www.adweek.com/digital/5-social-media-threats/

Bosworth, A., Marlette, S., Putnam, C., & Wable, A. (2012). U.S. Patent No. 8,296,373. Washington, DC: U.S. Patent and Trademark Office.

Canter, L. (2010). *Assertive discipline: Positive behavior management for today's classroom.* Solution Tree Press.

Cherry, K. (2017). B. F. Skinner Biography (1904-1990). *Verywell Mind.* Retrieved from https://www.verywellmind.com/b-f-skinner-biography-1904-1990-2795543

Cherry, K. (2018). What is operant conditioning and how does it work? *Verywell Mind.* Retrieved from https://www.verywellmind.com/operant-conditioning-a2-2794863

Cohen, P. (2014). 4 ways social media can ruin your reputation. *Social Media Today.* Retrieved from https://www.socialmediatoday.com/content/4-ways-social-media-can-ruin-your-reputation

Eco, S. (2017). Advantages and disadvantages of social networks information technology. *Mydigitalmedia123.* Retrieved from http://mydigitalmedia123.blogspot.com/2016/05/advantages-and-disadvantages-of-social.html

Elgan, M. (2015). Social media addiction is a bigger problem than you think. *Computerworld.* Retrieved from https://www.computerworld.com/article/3014439/internet/social-media-addiction-is-a-bigger-problem-than-you-think.html

Ellison, N., Vitak, J., Gray, R., & Lampe, C. (2014). Cultivating social resources on social network sites: Facebook relationship maintenance behaviors and their role in social capital processes.

Ferlazzo, L. (2014). The best ways to engage students in learning. *Education Week*. Retrieved from http://blogs.edweek.org/teachers/classroom_qa_with_larry_ferlazzo/2014/12/response_the_best_ways_to_engage_students_in_learning.html

Franz, J. (2017). Consider yourself a 'visual' or 'auditory' learner? Turns out, there's not much science behind learning styles. *Public Radio International*. Retrieved from https://www.pri.org/stories/2017-09-17/consider-yourself-visual-or-auditory-learner-turns-out-there-s-not-much-science

Gray, T. (2014). Personalizing learning: A strategy for review. *Virtual Learning Network*. Retrieved from https://vln.school.nz/discussion/view/892472

Jin, L., Chen, Y., Wang, T., Hui, P., & Vasilakos, A. V. (2013). Understanding user behavior in online social networks: A survey. *IEEE Communications Magazine*, *51*(9), 144–150. doi:10.1109/MCOM.2013.6588663

Johnson, D. D., Rice, M. P., Edgington, W. D., & Williams, P. (2005). For the uninitiated: How to succeed in classroom. *Kappa Delta Pi Record*, *42*(1), 28–32. doi:10.1080/00228958.2005.10532082

Mader, C. E. (2009). "I will never teach the old way again": Classroom management and external incentives. *Theory into Practice*, *48*(2), 147–155. doi:10.1080/00405840902776483

McLeod, S. (2015). Skinner - operant conditioning. Simplypsychology.org. Retrieved from https://www.simplypsychology.org/operant-conditioning.html

Mehmood, S., & Taswir, T. (2013). The effects of social networking sites on the academic performance of students in College of Applied Sciences, Nizwa, Oman. *International Journal Of Arts And Commerce*, *2*(1).

Meyer, E. (2017). How to leverage social media to build brand loyalty. *Forbes*. Retrieved from https://www.forbes.com/sites/forbesagencycouncil/2017/04/05/how-to-leverage-social-media-to-build-brand-loyalty/#204c85a02354

Prakash Software. (2017). The advantages of social network sites. Retrieved from http://www.prakash-infotech.com/the-advantages-of-social-network-sites

Rijnetu, I. (2018). Top online scams used by cybercriminals to trick you. *Heimdal Security Blog*. Retrieved from https://heimdalsecurity.com/blog/top-online-scams/

Sawyer, R. (2011). The impact of new social media on intercultural adaptation. *University of Rhode Island*. Retrieved from http://digitalcommons.uri.edu/cgi/viewcontent.cgi?article=1230&context=srhonorsprog

Stanciu, A., Mihai, F., & Aleca, O. (2012). Social networking as an alternative environment for education. *Accounting and management information systems*, *11*(1).

Thompson, C. (2015). What you really sign up for when you use social media. *CNBC*. Retrieved from https://www.cnbc.com/2015/05/20/what-you-really-sign-up-for-when-you-use-social-media.html

Tinmaz, H. (2017). Social networking websites as an innovative framework for connectivism. *Contemporary Educational Technology, 3*(3).

Walton, A. (2017). 6 ways social media affects our mental health. *Forbes.* Retrieved from https://www.forbes.com/sites/alicegwalton/2017/06/30/a-run-down-of-social-medias-effects-on-our-mental-health/#14a0ecde2e5a

Whelan, H. (2012). Why is it easier for some to learn from videos than from reading? *Quora.* Retrieved from https://www.quora.com/Why-is-it-easier-for-some-to-learn-from-videos-than-from-reading

This research was previously published in the International Journal of Smart Education and Urban Society (IJSEUS), 10(4); pages 30-39, copyright year 2019 by IGI Publishing (an imprint of IGI Global).

Chapter 15

A Framework Model for Integrating Social Media, the Web, and Proprietary Services Into YouTube Video Classification Process

Mohamad Hammam Alsafrjalani
University of Miami, Miami, USA

ABSTRACT

Online video streaming has gained ubiquity in disparate educational, governmental, and corporate environments. The ubiquity of these videos elicits new challenges in video classification that is used to promote relative videos and block unwanted content. These challenges include the incorporation of contextual information, rapid development of the ad-hoc query modules, and keeping pace with contemporary contextual information. In this article, the authors present a framework model for incorporating contextual information into video classification information. To illustrate the model, the authors propose a framework which comprises video classification, web search engines, social media platforms, and third-party classification modules. The modules enable the framework's flexibility and adaptivity to different contextual environment—educational, governmental, and corporate. Additionally, the model emphasizes standardized module interface to enable the framework's extensibility and rapid development of future modules.

1. INTRODUCTION

The importance of video classification has increased in the last decade due to the ubiquity and exponential growth of crowd-generated videos—more than 80% of the internet traffic will be for video streaming (Cisco, 2017). Demands for classifying videos are elicited by various corporate, government, and educational policies that require identification of harmful videos (e.g., phishing and spam), hate-

DOI: 10.4018/978-1-6684-7123-4.ch015

and crime-promoting content, pornography, and/or cyber bullying, which can be spread through online video streaming platforms. Alternatively, the classification information can be used to promote relative content, generate targeted advertisement, and retain more users (Duverger & Steffes, 2012; Xu, Zhang, et al., 2008).

To classify YouTube videos, machine learning algorithms (e.g. Convolutional Neural Networks (CNN) (Karpathy et al., 2014)) are used to extract key features from the videos' frames (e.g., (Roach, Mason, & Pawlewski, 2001)), text (e.g., (Brezeale & Cook, 2006)), audio (e.g., (Z. Liu, Wang, & Chen, 1998)), or a combination of these data (e.g., (Qi, Gu, Jiang, Chen, & Zhang, 2000)). This information is used to train the models offline using a set of pre-downloaded videos. After the models are trained, they are used to predict the class of new, unknown videos. However, the drawbacks of these approaches include lengthy training time and high computation complexity, and a priori access to training videos.

To reduce time and computation complexity, other research targeted key frames and segments (Lu, Drew, & Au, 2001), the video's texts (Huang, Fu, & Chen, 2010), such as the title, description, and/ or comments. However, these approaches can only predict classification of new videos using training on pre-determined features that were available during training time, and they did not consider new, unprecedented classes (e.g., a new online challenge). Furthermore, the exponential growth of the number of video creators on social media—over 1 million YouTube channels (YouTube, 2017) and 8 billion Facebook videos watched per day (Tang et al., 2017), the number of new, subjective video classes will increase beyond what a single model can determine. Furthermore, the subjectivity of the information technology's (IT) policies deployed at different entities—government agencies, corporate office, and education institution, exacerbate the relativity of the classification information. Since these policies are focused on the entity's demands, the policies require adaptivity to the contextual environment in which the video is being streamed.

A generic video classification information (sport, news, entertainment, …) must be accompanied with contextual information. Whereas the generic classification information provides valid information, awareness of the contextual environment will impact the IT decision about these videos. For instance, a video that was classified into commercial advertisement, as a result of pre-trained classification model, could be also classified as an online challenge based on recent events in the online and social media. Since the recent events, and possibly the category itself, were unavailable during the module training period, the trained module would fail to predict the online challenge as a category of the video. If the recent events, contextual information, is obtained as part of a classification framework, the IT policies can provide more accurate decisions.

To keep up with the correct usage of the video classification information, the contextual information must be captured in relatively short time by querying information available on platforms other than the video streaming platforms—such as news platforms, law and legislation bills, technical specifications, etc. Furthermore, since not all the platforms are always relative to query, querying the information should be an ad-hoc process that provides only the necessary information for the decision-making policy. Based on this information we deduce that the next challenges in video classification include not only video analysis, but also the contextual environment in which the classification is being used. Incorporation of contextual information, rapid development of the ad-hoc query modules, and keeping pace with contemporary contextual information must be addressed to meet future challenges in video classification.

In this paper we propose a framework model that enables rapid development of modules that perform contextual-information retrieval in conjunction with video classification information. We illustrate our model by developing a modular framework. The framework's modules obtain classification information from the video streaming platform and contextual information from social media, web content and third-party domain classification services. To enable flexibility, the modules work independently to make fine-grained, per-module classifications and collaboratively to make coarse-grained, final classifications decisions. Additionally, to enable rapid adjustment to disparate environment, the modules can be used in ad-hoc fashion. Furthermore, to enable the framework's extensibility, the modules have a standardized interface and communication protocols so that future modules can be easily integrated into the framework.

To evaluate our proposed framework, we classified 25 randomly selected YouTube videos and tested the accuracy of these classifications against human verification. Furthermore, we evaluate the framework modules in educational, governmental, and corporate environment and calculated the classification accuracies under different classification requirements. Our results revealed that our framework classified the videos with up to 90% accuracy, and classifications process completed in 1.5 seconds, on average. Additionally, our results demonstrate the flexibility of our framework under disparate classification requirements. Our framework's modules could be easily deployed in ad-hoc fashion to meet educational, governmental, and corporate video classification requirements.

2. PRIOR WORKS

Much prior work provided insights on video analysis and classification. With the exponential growth of online videos, other prior work focused solely on YouTube videos classification. Furthermore, to reduce video classification time, much prior works proposed frameworks that classified videos using less computational-intensive method such as textual information. In this section we present a selection of prior works that most closely correlate to our proposed model.

2.1. Video Classification

To classify videos, prior work extracted features from the videos directly form the compressed MPEG file (Kobla, DeMenthon, & Doermann, 1999). However, this process is infeasible for long and large number of videos. To speed up key feature extraction, (Snoek & Worring, 2005) used a platform that leveraged a unifying and multimodal framework that analyzed the video from the perspective of the video's author.

Alternative to analyzing MPEG videos, other prior work used machine learning algorithms to train classification modules using convolutional neural networks (CNN) (Karpathy et al., 2014), extracted key features from the videos' frames (Roach et al., 2001), or deduced information about the video using the video's caption (T. Liu, Zhang, & Qi, 2003), description (Brezeale & Cook, 2006), audio (e.g., (Z. Liu et al., 1998)), or a combination of audio-text-video (Qi et al., 2000). This extracted information was used to train the classification models, which were then used to predict the class of a new video. The classification of these works achieved 80% accuracy, however, the training process of these algorithms required long time and/or heavy computation energy that was not suitable for energy-efficient devices (Trestian, Moldovan, Ormond, & Muntean, 2012).

To alleviate the computation energy overhead, other work proposed analyzing segments of the video (Haubold & Naphade, 2007; Lin & Hauptmann, 2002; Lu et al., 2001). Whereas these classification methods sped up the computation process, these methods required a priori knowledge of the video (offline analysis), which did not scale with the exponential growth of the online-generated videos.

2.1. YouTube Video Classification

Huang et al. (Huang et al., 2010) provided a framework to classify YouTube videos using user generated text. The video's title, description, and comments comprised the text-data that the framework analyzed. The framework extracted lexical, syntactic, and content features from the text. The framework classified the videos using support vector machine (SVM) and Bayes techniques, and resulted in up to 87.2% accuracy.

To speed up the classification process, Agrawal et al. (Agarwal, Gupta, Singh, & Saxena, 2017) used a two-level text-based classification approach. The approach classified the videos first into a broad class, and second into a specific subclass. The dual-step approach sped up the classification process while maintaining accuracy between 26.6% and 100%. However, the framework focused on general classes centered around harassment categories only and was not extensible to other categories. In addition to the video's description, title, etc., Aggarwal et al. (Aggarwal, Agrawal, & Sureka, 2014) proposed a framework that considers the video's popularity and duration to predict the video class. The approached classified the videos with up to 80% accuracy.

To speed up the YouTube video classification process, other work classified nonvideo content on YouTube. Madden et al. (Madden, Ruthven, & McMenemy, 2013) classified the comments created by YouTube users to study commenting as a method of communication among the users. Siersdorfer (Siersdorfer, Chelaru, Nejdl, & San Pedro, 2010) studied the relationship between rated and unrated comments on YouTube. Koch et al. (Koch, Lode, Stohr, Rizk, & Steinmetz, 2018) used facial recognition to identify common content-creators across different YouTube channels. The authors used this information to detect collaboration and similarities between the channels.

Whereas these prior works contributed to YouTube video, comments, and channel classifications, these works did not consider the contextual environment and the future compatibility of the proposed frameworks.

2.3. Classification Frameworks

Duan et al., (Duan, Xu, Tian, Xu, & Jin, 2005) proposed a framework that employed supervised learning to perform a top-down video shot classification, which focused on high-level semantic analysis. Additionally, the framework focused on mid-level representations instead of exhaustive low-level features, which helped speeding up the video classification process. Alternative to semantic analysis, other frameworks analyzed the features in the videos. Wang et al., (Wu, Wang, Jiang, Ye, & Xue, 2015) provided a hybrid deep learning framework that modeled static spatial information and short-term motion clues in the videos. The features of the static spatial and short-term clues are then combined in a fusion network to predict the video classification.

To obtain contextual information about the videos, other frameworks leveraged non-video information in the classification process. Xu et al., (Xu, Wang, Lu, & Zhang, 2008) proposed a novel framework for sport-videos semantic annotation. Instead of analyzing the audio and video features alone, the framework incorporated web-casting text into the sport video analysis. Furthermore, the authors (Xu, Zhang, et al., 2008) built up on the previous model to retrieve summarized sports videos. The new framework analyzed webcast text that was broadcast along with video events. Analyzing the webcast text, the framework deduced which of the broadcasted videos was about sports. Wang et al., (Wang, Kwon, Choi, Wang, & Liu, 2013), sped up relative video retrieval using information available on social media. The authors presented a framework that leveraged the information about the social media interactions to predict relative videos. The framework learnt information about the videos shared on social media through the user interactions. Videos that were shared among the users were prefetched to the user mobile devices, speeding up the relative video retrieval.

Whereas these frameworks provided significant advancement in video classification and retrieval, each framework relied mainly on video analysis and feature extraction, targeted a specific video category, or provided contextual information within limited parameter.

3. THE FRAMEWORK DEVELOPMENT APPROACH

To alleviate computation complexity of the classification process, the framework comprises parsing modules that leverage the pre-determined information associated with the video. This information contains details about the video content, tags, description, etc., which is typically provided by the video-streaming platform. To enhance the framework's flexibility, each parsing module can parse one area of information (e.g., a description module, and a tag module). Given the specificity of each modules, the framework is capable to provide fine- and coarse-grained classification information outcomes.

To obtain classification relative to the contextual environment, the modules interface with web search engines, social media platforms, and third-party classification servers. This functionality enables the framework to work with independent sources of information in an ad-hoc fashion. Similar to the parsing modules, the searching modules can provide fine- and coarse-grained classification information about the video:

$$\sum_{x=1}^{n} combination \begin{pmatrix} n \\ x \end{pmatrix} = 2^n \qquad (1)$$

If the total number of modules in the framework is n, then there exists up to possible classification decisions, wherein x is the number of modules selected (deployed) during the classification decision process. Given the exponential growth of the classification decisions, it is imperative to control the number of decision-making modules in the framework.

To obtain a classification decision within controlled contextual parameters, our approach divides the framework modules into two categories, parsing and searching modules that work interdependently to provide the fine-grained, per-module classification, and collectively to provide the coarse-grain, final classification.

Whereas our model is applicable to any number of modules, and given the plethora of available video-streaming provides, web-based search engines, and social media platforms, we provide a proof of concept framework that focuses primarily on YouTube videos, Google and Twitter social media platforms, and one 3rd party service.

4. FRAMEWORK MODULES

Parsing modules collect data about the video under test (VUT) from YouTube and perform per-module classification. The collected information is tokenized and passed to the search modules for a second classification. Searching modules use the parsed information to mine the web, social media, and third-party database to classify the videos. Each module classifies the VUT into one, per-module class within the framework. The modules work interdependently to provide a final classification is using weighted-voting mechanism (Section 4.3).

4.1. Parsing Modules

The parsing modules traverse the targeted video information (title, video description, tags, related videos, channel description, etc.) to obtain keywords. The searching modules uses the keywords obtained from the parsing modules to mine the web (search engines, social media, 3rd party's server, etc.). Whereas our approach is expandable to any number of parsing modules, we illustrate our parsing modules with four modules. Figure 1 (a), (b), (c), and (d) depict our text-tag-title (3TM), description (DM), related videos (RVM), and channel (CM) parsing modules.

4.1.1. Text-Tag-Title Module

The 3MT module takes as input the URL of the VUT, which is provided by the framework's main entry or the other parsing modules. The module then queries YouTube for information about the title and tags of the VUT (if available). The 3TM parses the textual information and uses a natural language parser (NLP) to determine the subject and adjective in the VUT's title. 3TM module tokenizes and communicates this information to other modules in the framework.

3TM queries a local text repository that contains a list of keywords for each class. The module calculates a distance vector of the tokens from the classes in the text repository. Then, the module selects the class with the shortest distance as the class for the VUT. Since the keywords are not mutually exclusive to the classes (e.g., keyword basketball in sports and entertainment classes), it is possible to have multiple classes with the same distance for the same VUT. In this case 3TM randomly classifies the VUT into one of these classes. Additionally, our framework provides a maintenance interface to maintain and update the keyword repository.

4.1.2. Description, Related Videos, and Channel Modules

We designated a module for each textual component of the VUT; description (DM), related-videos (RVM), and channel (CM) modules. All these modules extract textual information from the VUT and obtain text tokens to pass to the 3TM and searching modules, and/or URL to pass to the searching modules.

The DM queries YouTube for the VUT's description, artist, and licensing agreement. The DM uses NLP to extract subject from the description, converts the subjects to text-tokens and pass these tokens to the 3TM and search modules. Additionally, the DM searches the VUT's description for embedded URLs; common practice to cross-reference other videos by the same channel. If DM determines valid URLs, the DM sends the URLs to the GSM and PM for classification (Section 4.2). To make a classification decision, the DM reads back the classification decisions from the 3TM, GSM, and PM modules and votes for the DM class.

Figure 1. The (a) 3TM, (b) DM, (c) RVM, and (d) CM parsing modules

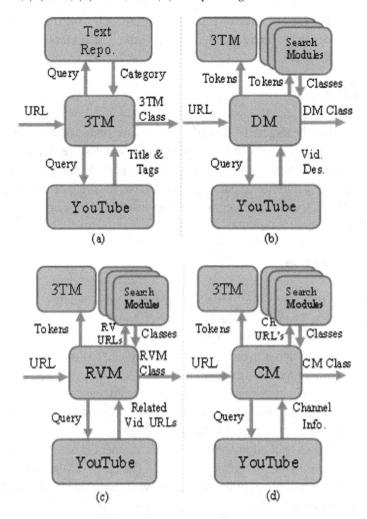

The RVM queries YouTube to obtain the VUT's related videos' titles and URLs. To provide a configurable balance between execution time and accuracy, we set the number of related videos as a variable, wherein $0 < r < all$. Classifying all of the related videos theoretically takes infinite time, given the number of videos on YouTube and the recursive nature of the suggested videos in the related videos section. Alternatively, classifying zero related videos could result in localized classification of the VUTs. However, we allow r to be a configurable parameter available to the end-user during the classification process.

Similar to the DM, using NLP, RVM extracts keywords from the titles and pass those keywords as tokens to the 3TM for classification. Additionally, RVM passes the URLs of the related videos to the GSM for classification. Finally, RVM uses the classification information returned by 3TM and GSM modules to vote for the RVM class.

CM queries YouTube to obtain the channel's name, about, author, ratings, and the titles of the videos in the channel. Similar to the DM and RVM, the CM passes the textual information to 3TM and the URLs in the channel information to GSM. Using the classification information returned by the 3TM and GSM, CM votes for the CM class.

Figure 2. The (a) Google, (b) Twitter, and (c) FortiGuard® search modules

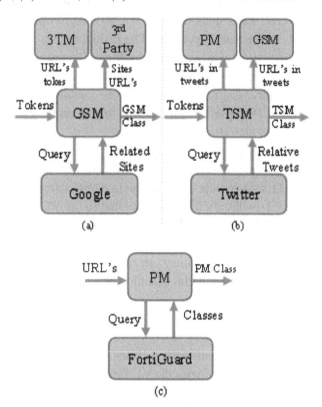

4.2. Searching Modules

To classify the VUT within the right contextual environment the searching modules search the web, social media, and 3rd party classification providers for some of the VUT's information. Our approach is applicable to any number of web search engines (Google, Bing, Yahoo, etc.), social media platforms (Facebook, Twitter, Pinterest, etc.), and 3rd party/proprietary classifiers (FortiGuard, Cisco Umbrella, etc.). However, we select one search engine, one social media, and one proprietary (third-party) server to illustrate the extensibility of our framework.

Figure 2 (a), (b), and (c) depict our Google, Twitter, and FortiGuard® search modules, respectively. These modules use the generated textual tokens and URLs of the VUT and query the information of these tokens on the respective media to retrieve data from the web and social media. Each of these modules returns a per-module VUT classification.

The Google search module (GSM) receives textual tokens from the parsing modules and queries Google search engine to retrieve relative URL for these tokens. The module then passes the page's title of the URL to the 3TM to obtain the 3TM classification, and the URLs' links to a 3rd-party server to retrieve a second/specific classification. The GSM performs a majority voting on the classifications received from 3TM and PM modules to provide the GSM class for the VUT. Since Google returns multiple links to the searched tokens, the number of classified URLs must be specified. To keep our framework flexible, we parameterized g, the number of links the GSM classifies. The default value of g is 1, classifying the top link of the token Googled.

The Twitter search module (TSM), receives textual tokens from the parsing modules and queries Twitter to obtain relative tweets. TSM does not accept URLs from other modules, since Twitter is searched by hashed keywords rather than hyperlinks. The textual tokens are converted into a hashtags or Twitter handles to search for tweets with the same hashtags. To enable flexible Twitter search, we enabled classification of t top Twitter hits, with default value of $t = 1$. The top Twitter hits are processed and passed to the 3TM module for classification. If the tweets contain URLs, TSM forwards the URLs to the proprietary module (PM). TSM performs a majority voting on the classification decision of the 3TM and PM to produce the TSM classification.

To enable integrability with corporate servers and to retrieve a specific classification, the PM provides an HTML interface for a corporate server to communicate with our framework. Furthermore, to obtain classification of the VUT with respect to the contextual environment on the world wide web, the proprietary classification is used to classify the URL's related to the VUT and not the VUT itself. The PM receives the URLs from the RVM, CM, GSM, and TSM and queries the 3rd-party server for a classification for each of the URLs. The majority of the URLs classes provide the PM class for the VUT.

Once the modules classify the VUT, the framework calculates the final classification decision, logs the per-module decisions, and saves the final classification in a local VUT Class database.

4.3. Modules Communications

Figure 3 depicts the framework's components and modules' communications. The framework accepts any number of VUTs' URLs, parses and classifies the VUTs information using the parsing and searching modules, and returns a final classification of the VUT.

The framework accepts a URL of the VUT from a graphical user interface (GUI) or a web-scraping library such as jaunt API (JAUNT, 2018). To increase the throughput of the framework, the VUT URLs are buffered and handled by a message broker, RabbitMQ (RabbitMQ, 2018). The message broker sends a VUT message, a VUT tag that contains the VUT's URL and unique identification value to the module manager. The tag is used by all of the modules and framework components to handle the VUT's classification information. Although the videos URL are unique, a tag is required to collect the classification and token information of the child URL's (those spawned off the parsing and searching modules), and to prevent a VUT from being classified in infinite loop among the modules. When a module classifies the VUT, the module updates the VUT tag and sends a message to the module manager.

The module manager requests and processes one VUT message from the message broker, one at a time. The module manager handles the communications and messaging between the parsing and searching modules. When the tag has been updated by all of the modules, the module manager sends the VUT's packet that contains the VUT's tag and a ready-to-classify information to a weighted voting process to calculate the final classification decision.

The weighted voting decision takes in as an input the per-module classification decisions, stored in the decision log, and votes to classify the VUT for each category present in the VUT tags. For each of the predefined classes c, the weighted voting decision process passes or fails the class if the vote exceeds a quota defined as:

$$q_c: m_1 + m_2 + ... + m_n \tag{2}$$

Figure 3. The framework's communication flow and dynamics

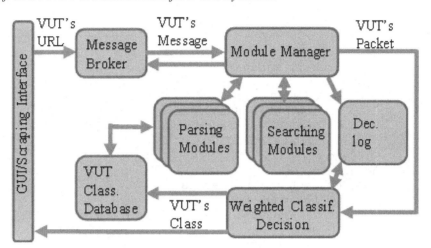

wherein m is the weight of the module, q_c is the minimum quota needed for the classification to pass, and each q_c is:

$$q = \frac{1}{2} \times \sum_{1}^{n} m_n \qquad (3)$$

The default weights for all m are equal across all modules, and each VUT can be classified into 1, and up to c classes.

To provide flexibility, the weight parameters are changeable. To reclassify a VUT with different weights, the decision process can leverage the existing classification information in the decision log. The weighted voting decision process requests the individual classifications of the VUT from the decisions log, using the VUT tag, and recalculates the final decision using the new weights.

The final classification decision is returned to the GUI/scraping interface and stored in a VUT classification database. Future requests to classify a video that has been already classified will simply be looked up in the framework's database.

4.4. Framework's Flow

Figure 4 depicts the process flow of the framework. The classification process begins and repeats if there are URLs in the queue (lines 1 to 2). The framework initializes the parsing and searching modules, the message broker, and the module manager (lines 3 to 4). Once initialized, the message broker processes each URL sequentially. It logs the VUT's URL, creates the VUT tag, sends the message to the module manager, and updates the queue status (lines 5 to 10).

Similarly, the module manager handles each broker message sequentially. For each broker message, and for each module in the framework, the module manager requests a classification (lines 11 to 14). The manager passes the VUT_tag to the requested module for classification (line 15). After the VUT_tag has been updated by all modules in the framework, the module manager updates the log with the per-class classification information (line 16).

Figure 4. The pseudo code for the framework classification process

```
1    Begin
2    whil(queue)
3        Init modules
4        init(broker, manager)
5        Broker
6            for each VUT request
7                log VUT's URL in message broker
8                Send VUT info to module manager
9                update queue
10           end
11       Manager
12           for each broker request
13               for each module
14                   request_classfication (module, VUT_Tag)
15               end
16               log_update (VUT_Tag)
17           end
18       frame_class(VUT_Tag)
19       Update_database
20   end
```

Finally, the framework initiates a frame_class process that takes in the VUT tag as an input (line 17). The process reads the per-class classification information and calculate the holistic (frame) class for that video. The classification information is updated in the framework's data base (line 19).

5. EXPERIMENT SETUP

We used java to construct the the parsing modules, decision log, and VUT class database. We imported YouTube API (YouTube, 2018) into the parsing and searching modules to query YouTube server for the VUT information. In addition to these API's, the searching also uses web-scraping API jaunt (JAUNT, 2018) and Twitter API (Twitter, 2017). To complement our scraping interface, we used HTML to provide a graphical user interface to accept manual video classification request. Finally, the message broker is implemented with RabbitMQ (RabbitMQ, 2018) and the database management system in the open source object relational database system PostgreSQL (PostgreSQL, 2018).

To provide realistic results, we selected 17 classes based on the FortiGuard ® (Fortinet, 2018) web filter, including abortion, advertising, advocacy, alcohol, believes/religion, armed forces, arts and culture, cartoon, entertainment, gaming, marijuana, music, news and media, political organization, sex education, sports, and tobacco. Each of these classes is identified with 15 to 30 keywords, stored in the framework's text repository. We set $t = 1$, $g = 1$, $r = 1$, measured the execution time between the request and final classification, and used human verification to check the final classification decision for correctness. To obtain 3rd party classification, we designated the PM to work with FortiGuard® web filter. FortiGuard® can classify a URL into one of the six general classes including security, general interest-business, general interest-personal; or into one of the sixty+ specific classes, including advertising, gaming, political organization, web hosting, etc.

To test our framework's flexibility, we evaluated the framework's modules independently and collectively using 25 distinct YouTube videos. We randomly selected videos from the YouTube suggestion list, trending videos, recently uploaded, topic specific, and top channels. We iterate that our approach focuses on the incorporation of contextual information and using large video classification benchmarks are out of the scope of this paper. To provide a pessimistic analysis, videos that were classified as *NA* (modules were unable to classify the VUT) are considered incorrect classification. We calculated the accuracy of the classifications against a human verification.

To test the contextual environment impact, we varied the Twitter, Google, and related video parameters from 1 to 10 and measured the impact of these values on the accuracy of the framework classification. Furthermore, to measure the framework's adaptivity to various contextual environment, we simulated educational, governmental and corporate policies. We used these policies in conjunction with the framework's final classification and evaluated the applicability of individual modules for each environment using the classification information and permission rules of the IT policies of these environments. Modules that were required to maintain high accuracy classification were considered applicable to the environment.

Table 1. Classification accuracy per module

Module	Accuracy	Module	Accuracy	Module	Accuracy
3TM	90%	CM	78%	PM	85%
DM	28%	TSM	48%		
RVM	75%	GSM	80%		

6. RESULTS AND ANALYSIS

6.1. Individual Module Analysis

Table 1 depicts the per module accuracy results of the framework. 3MT, DM, RVM, CM, GSM, TSM, and PM returned 90%, 28%, 75%, 78%, 80%, 48%, and 85%, accurate classification, respectively.

The 3TM module resulted in the highest accuracy result since the module uses the VUT's title and tags to make classification decisions. The title and tags are the most representative information about the VUT class, due to the direct description of the video by the author. Furthermore, since the 3TM used the VUT's title and tag, 3TM did not deviate from the VUT direct information, which resulted in a high accuracy of the classification decision.

The GSM resulted in 80% classification accuracy. The GSM used Google to search for the title of, and any embedded URL in the VUT on the web. The first web-link generally returned the YouTube link to the same VUT, which resulted in the same classification of the VUT. Hence, the GSM classified the VUT very similarly to 3TM. However, the URL's classification request from the other modules resulted in GSM classifying the VUT into class(es) which are different from the 3TM's.

The RVM resulted in 75% accuracy since the related videos did not necessary contain similar contextual information as the VUT. Furthermore, the results revealed that further related videos deviated from the VUT, which resulted in less accurate RVM classification. For instance, a YouTube video about top-ten horror movies triggered two types of related videos, top-ten (e.g., top-ten first person shooter (FPS) games, top-ten classic movies, etc.), and more horror videos type. RVM classified the top-ten FPS games as gaming videos, and classic movies as educational. Additionally, increasing the RVM threshold to r to 10 reduced the accuracy of the RVM classification to 55%. This result suggests that smaller value of r will speed up the RVM classification process while maintaining a modules classification accuracy within > 75%. Similar to the RVM, CM resulted in 78% accuracy. Since CM parsed the channel's information that contained similar videos to the VUT, the classification was close to the VUT's.

The TSM and DM modules resulted in the least accurate classifications with 48% and 28%, respectively. Since the Twitter module classified information found on the top hit of Twitter regarding the video's title and tags, the classification deviated from the main video's title/information. Furthermore, the top Twitter hit returned textual information that was classified very differently by the 3TM. Alternatively, the Twitter hits that contained URLs resulted in more accurate classification by the GSM. The description module had the lowest accuracy since many VUT's had blank description, which resulted in a *NA* classification by the DM.

The proprietary module resulted in 85% classification accuracy. Since YouTube URLs are always classified as streaming media by the PM, we excluded the VUT's URL from the PM accuracy calculation (otherwise 100% accurate). However, embedded links in the VUT provided classification of the VUT with 85% accuracy, on average. Embedded links typically provided connection to a company or external source that is directly related to the VUT, which resulted in the PM classification similar to the 3TM's. For instance, a video classified as education by the 3TM contained a URL to an online education institution, which as lo was classified as educational.

Table 2. Classification time per module in milliseconds

Module	Time (ms)	Module	Time (ms)	Module	Time (ms)
3TM	500	CM	1000	PM	2300
DM	1000	TSM	1600		
RVM	1000	GSM	1500		

6.2. Framework Classification and Performance

The final classification of the framework was as high as 90%. Since the modules have equal weights in the classification decision making, there was no veto or dictator module's weight that skewed the results in favor of higher classification accuracy. Since a single module cannot force a final classification in a voting mechanism, any VUT that had less than q value for a class, the VUT was not classified and the final classification returned *NA* for that VUT, which resulted in final classification average accuracy of 71%.

Since our experiment evaluates the framework's flexibility, we measure the execution times of the individual classification processes and present the raw values of these time measurements. Table 2 depicts the per-module execution time in milliseconds. 3TM, DM, RVM, CM, GSM, TSM, and PM required 500, 1000, 1000, 1000, 1500, 1600, and 2300 milliseconds (ms), rounded to the nearest 100 milliseconds, on average, to calculate the VUT's class. The 3TM required the least time of 500 ms, since the module access a local repository to perform the classification. Alternatively, the PM required the longest time of 2300 ms, since the module needed to access a remote server to obtain the URL classification of the VUT.

The RVM, CM and DM modules took 2X time as compared to the 3TM. Since the RVM, CM, and DM parsed the VUT's information and passed this information to the 3TM for classification, the 3TM 500 ms is part of the processing time. In theory, parsing the related videos', channels', and descriptions' information required as much time as classifying the information using the 3TM (500ms). However, the average total time to parse and classify the related video and description information was 1000 ms.

Similarly, the GSM and TSM required 1500 and 1600 ms, respectively. Since both modules query online servers, the modules produced delay overhead due to remote access to the Google and Twitter servers. Additionally, since GSM and TSM communicate with the 3TM to obtain classification information, GSM and TSM theoretically have 1000 and 1100 ms processing time; 500 ms accounted for by the 3TM. Reducing this processing time can be achieved by caching Google and Twitter search hits in a local database. To optimize the GSM and TSM, the size, refresh rate, and validate-purge policy of the local cache database can be adjusted to meet performance requirement. This will be part of our future work for the framework.

6.3. Contextual Environment Impact

Figure 5 depicts the accuracy percentage for different values of the searching threshold parameters t, g, and r, for the TSM, GSM, and RVM, respectively. The parameter sizes are selected from 1 to 10, individually, while holding the other two parameters constant at 1. In general, larger values of the parameters resulted in less accurate classification outcome. The RVM classified related videos accurately up to the 9th video suggested by YouTube, on average. Although YouTube suggest videos of the same category, YouTube also suggest videos by the same actors, however, about a different subject/category (e.g., a standup comedian take on religion).

For $g > 3$, the GSM deviated from accurate classification, since the first 1 to 3 links, on average were paid advertisement for the product/service solicited in the video. for $3 < g < 8$, GSM classified URLs to news, finance, and Wikipedia about the product/service solicited in the VUT. Since most products and services can relate to news and finance, the classification maintained 50% accuracy. However, the accuracy only degraded, for values of $g > 7$.

Similar to RVM and GSM, larger t values resulted in lower accuracy of TSM classification. However, since Twitter ordered tweets using popularity and date criteria, some tweets that referred to the VUT were 9th and 10th in rank.

Additionally, to measure the flexibility and applicability of the framework for different contextual environments, we simulated environments with different requirement, and evaluated our framework's modules for each environment. Table 3 summarizes the classes relative to the educational institutions, government agencies, and corporate offices environments. We select these classes based on common themes found in similar environments. We note that these classes are not comprehensive but can sufficiently illustrate our framework's adaptivity to different contextual environment. The classes in Table 3 are whitelisted in the IT policy of that environment; i.e., only Arts and culture, Cartoon, News, Religion, Sex Ed, and Sport classes are whitelisted in the educational environment.

Table 3. Sample classes that are relative to educational institution, government agencies, and corporate offices

Education	Government	Corporate
Arts/Cult.	Abortion	Abortion
Cartoon	Advertising	Advertising
News	Armed Forces	Advocasy
Religion	Marijuana	Alcohol
Sex Ed	News/Media	Armed forces
Sports	Politics	Arts/Cult
	Religion	Cartoon
	Sports	Entertainment
	Tobacco	News/Media
		Religion
		Sports
		Tobacco

Figure 5. The percentage of classification accuracy against variable sizes of t, g, and r constraints for the TSM, GSM, and RVM, respectively

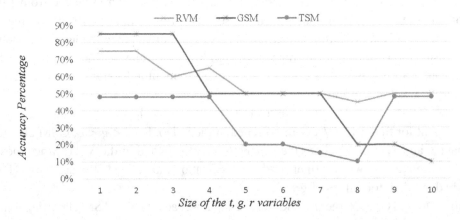

Our results revealed that not all modules are required to achieve high classification accuracy at each environment. For the educational environment only the 3TM, TSM and GSM were used to classify, with up to 90% accuracy, the VUTs into one of the whitelisted classes. In addition to these three modules, the governmental environment required the PM to achieve classification accuracy of 87%. The corporate environment required all but the RVM and CM to achieve 82% classification accuracy. This result suggests that for larger video classes, more modules are needed to maintain classification accuracy over 80%. The result also demonstrates that our framework model can quickly adapt, in ad-hoc fashion, to changing deployment and contextual environment.

7. CONCLUSION AND FUTURE WORK

In this paper we presented a framework model for integrating social media, the web, and proprietary services into YouTube video classification processes. We illustrated our model using our proposed framework that comprised independent and interconnected modules. The framework provides per-class, fine-grained and collaborative, coarse-grained video classification decisions, under several contextual environments. To alleviate the computation and energy requirements for classifying the videos, our framework leveraged the classification information provided by the video streaming platform. The individual modules and collective classification processes resulted in up to 90% and on average of 71%, classification accuracy for the VUTs. Furthermore, the framework took as little as 0.5 seconds to complete the classification processes.

Additionally, we demonstrated our model capability for rapid adaptation for various contextual environment. The framework's modules can be used in ad-hoc fashion for educational, governmental, and corporate environment. Our results revealed that environments with a small and large number of classification requirement benefited from few and many modules in the framework, respectively.

To enhance social media classification accuracy, future work includes an extensive classification implementation for the Twitter and description modules. Additionally, to enhance performance requirement, future work will add an optimized cache-database with adjustable size, refresh rate, and validate-purge policy.

REFERENCES

Agarwal, N., Gupta, R., Singh, S. K., & Saxena, V. (2017). Metadata based multi-labelling of YouTube videos. *Paper presented at the 2017 7th International Conference on Cloud Computing, Data Science & Engineering-Confluence*. Academic Press. 10.1109/CONFLUENCE.2017.7943219

Aggarwal, N., Agrawal, S., & Sureka, A. (2014). Mining YouTube metadata for detecting privacy invading harassment and misdemeanor videos. *Paper presented at the 2014 Twelfth Annual International Conference on Privacy, Security and Trust*. Academic Press. 10.1109/PST.2014.6890927

Brezeale, D., & Cook, D. J. (2006). Using closed captions and visual features to classify movies by genre. *Paper presented at the poster session of the seventh international workshop on Multimedia Data Mining (MDM/KDD2006)*. Academic Press.

Cisco. (2017). Cisco Visual Networking Index: Forecast and Methodology.

Duan, L.-Y., Xu, M., Tian, Q., Xu, C.-S., & Jin, J. S. (2005). A unified framework for semantic shot classification in sports video. *IEEE Transactions on Multimedia*, 7(6), 1066–1083. doi:10.1109/TMM.2005.858395

Duverger, P., & Steffes, E. M. (2012). Using YouTube Videos as a Primer to Affect Academic Content Retention. *Metropolitan Universities*, 23(2), 51–66.

Fortinet. (2018). FortiGuard Web Filtering. Retrieved from https://fortiguard.com/webfilter

Haubold, A., & Naphade, M. (2007). Classification of video events using 4-dimensional time-compressed motion features. *Paper presented at the Proceedings of the 6th ACM international conference on Image and video retrieval.* Academic Press. 10.1145/1282280.1282311

Huang, C., Fu, T., & Chen, H. (2010). Text-based video content classification for online video-sharing sites. *Journal of the American Society for Information Science and Technology, 61*(5), 891–906. doi:10.1002/asi.21291

JAUNT. (2018). JAUNT API. Retrieved from https://jaunt-api.com

Karpathy, A., Toderici, G., Shetty, S., Leung, T., Sukthankar, R., & Fei-Fei, L. (2014). Large-scale video classification with convolutional neural networks. *Paper presented at the IEEE conference on Computer Vision and Pattern Recognition.* IEEE. 10.1109/CVPR.2014.223

Kobla, V., DeMenthon, D., & Doermann, D. S. (1999). Identifying sports videos using replay, text, and camera motion features. *Paper presented at the Storage and Retrieval for Media Databases 2000.* Academic Press. 10.1117/12.373565

Koch, C., Lode, M., Stohr, D., Rizk, A., & Steinmetz, R. (2018). Collaborations on YouTube: From Unsupervised Detection to the Impact on Video and Channel Popularity. *ACM Transactions on Multimedia Computing Communications and Applications, 14*(4), 89. doi:10.1145/3241054

Lin, W.-H., & Hauptmann, A. (2002). News video classification using SVM-based multimodal classifiers and combination strategies. *Paper presented at the tenth ACM international conference on Multimedia.* 10.1145/641007.641075

Liu, T., Zhang, H.-J., & Qi, F. (2003). A novel video key-frame-extraction algorithm based on perceived motion energy model. *IEEE Transactions on Circuits and Systems for Video Technology, 13*(10), 1006–1013. doi:10.1109/TCSVT.2003.816521

Liu, Z., Wang, Y., & Chen, T. (1998). Audio feature extraction and analysis for scene segmentation and classification. *Journal of VLSI Signal Processing Systems for Signal, Image, and Video Technology, 20*(1-2), 61–79. doi:10.1023/A:1008066223044

Lu, C., Drew, M. S., & Au, J. (2001). Classification of summarized videos using hidden Markov models on compressed chromaticity signatures. *Paper presented at the ninth ACM international conference on Multimedia.* ACM. 10.1145/500141.500217

Madden, A., Ruthven, I., & McMenemy, D. (2013). A classification scheme for content analyses of YouTube video comments. *The Journal of Documentation, 69*(5), 693–714. doi:10.1108/JD-06-2012-0078

Postgre, S. Q. L. (2018). PostgreSQL Database Management System. Retrieved from https://www.postgresql.org/download/

Qi, W., Gu, L., Jiang, H., Chen, X.-R., & Zhang, H.-J. (2000). Integrating visual, audio and text analysis for news video. *Paper presented at the 2000 International Conference on Image Processing.* Academic Press.

Rabbit M.Q. (2018). RabbitMQ Message Broker Software. Retrieved from https://www.rabbitmq.com

Roach, M., Mason, J. S., & Pawlewski, M. (2001). Motion-based classification of cartoons. *Paper presented at the 2001 International Symposium on Intelligent Multimedia, Video and Speech Processing. ISIMP 2001.* IEEE. 10.1109/ISIMP.2001.925353

Siersdorfer, S., Chelaru, S., Nejdl, W., & San Pedro, J. (2010). How useful are your comments?: analyzing and predicting youtube comments and comment ratings. *Paper presented at the 19th international conference on World wide web.* Academic Press. 10.1145/1772690.1772781

Snoek, C. G., & Worring, M. (2005). Multimodal video indexing: A review of the state-of-the-art. *Multimedia Tools and Applications*, *25*(1), 5–35. doi:10.1023/B:MTAP.0000046380.27575.a5

Tang, L., Huang, Q., Puntambekar, A., Vigfusson, Y., Lloyd, W., & Li, K. (2017). Popularity prediction of facebook videos for higher quality streaming. *Paper presented at the 2017 USENIX Annual Technical Conference USENIX 17.* Academic Press.

Trestian, R., Moldovan, A.-N., Ormond, O., & Muntean, G.-M. (2012). Energy consumption analysis of video streaming to android mobile devices. *Paper presented at the 2012 IEEE Network Operations and Management Symposium.* IEEE. 10.1109/NOMS.2012.6211929

Twitter. (2017). Twitter API. Retrieved from https://developer.twitter.com/en/docs.html

Wang, X., Kwon, T., Choi, Y., Wang, H., & Liu, J. (2013). Cloud-assisted adaptive video streaming and social-aware video prefetching for mobile users. *IEEE Wireless Communications*, *20*(3), 72–79. doi:10.1109/MWC.2013.6549285

Wu, Z., Wang, X., Jiang, Y.-G., Ye, H., & Xue, X. (2015). Modeling spatial-temporal clues in a hybrid deep learning framework for video classification. *Paper presented at the Proceedings of the 23rd ACM international conference on Multimedia.* ACM. 10.1145/2733373.2806222

Xu, C., Wang, J., Lu, H., & Zhang, Y. (2008). A novel framework for semantic annotation and personalized retrieval of sports video. *IEEE Transactions on Multimedia*, *10*(3), 421–436. doi:10.1109/TMM.2008.917346

Xu, C., Zhang, Y.-F., Zhu, G., Rui, Y., Lu, H., & Huang, Q. (2008). Using webcast text for semantic event detection in broadcast sports video. *IEEE Transactions on Multimedia*, *10*(7), 1342–1355. doi:10.1109/TMM.2008.2004912

YouTube. (2017). YouTube Statistics. Retrieved from https://www.youtube.com/intl/en-GB/yt/about/press/

YouTube. (2018). YouTube API. Retrieved from https://developers.google.com/youtube/

This research was previously published in the International Journal of Multimedia Data Engineering and Management (IJM-DEM), 10(2); pages 21-36, copyright year 2019 by IGI Publishing (an imprint of IGI Global).

Chapter 16
Foreign Language Learning Through Instagram:
A Flipped Learning Approach

Alberto Andujar
https://orcid.org/0000-0002-8865-9509
University of Almeria, Spain

Fidel Çakmak
https://orcid.org/0000-0002-3285-7661
Alanya Alaaddin Keykubat University, Turkey

ABSTRACT

This chapter explores the use of a flipped learning approach through the application Instagram in an English as Foreign Language (EFL) class. A case study involving 53 participants at a high school is presented. A mixed methods approach using quantitative and qualitative information is carried out where 4 different data collection instruments collected information about students' perceptions of the flipped learning model as well as the use of Instagram. Findings emphasized the app and the flipped learning methodology as motivational and useful elements to develop language learning processes. However, learner feedback indicated that the flipped learning model used in this research was not viewed as superior to traditional lecture-based instruction. This chapter concludes with a discussion of the implications of implementing flipped learning models that utilize mobile devices in EFL education.

INTRODUCTION

The use of social networking platforms in classroom environments with the aim of developing different learning purposes has been a common practice since their appearance (Mao, 2014). From the use of wikis and blogs (Seaman & Tinti-Kane, 2013) to the use of the latest social networking platforms such as Facebook, Twitter, WhatsApp or Instagram (e.g., Andujar & Salaberri-Ramiro, 2019; Çakmak, 2019), researchers have attempted to exploit the possibilities of these platforms to facilitate language learning

DOI: 10.4018/978-1-6684-7123-4.ch016

processes. Among these possibilities, the different modes of communication within these virtual platforms (Mazer, Murphy, & Simonds, 2007) have allowed various types of interaction, whether written, spoken or through video and image-sharing. Likewise, these contexts have been found to be particularly promising for the development of blended learning models through which language educators can extend in-class time and provide a higher amount of input to their second or foreign language learners.

Apart from the different possibilities offered by social networking platforms for language development, at a university level it also seems necessary to leverage the latest educational resources in order to transform learning environments into contexts where in-class tuition and online learning processes coexist. In this sense, the combination of in-class tuition with online environments has given rise to blended learning models (Arbaugh, 2014) which are more flexible and autonomous contexts for language development than many conventional language classrooms. These new online environments have normally been investigated in the computer-assisted language learning (CALL) and mobile-assisted language learning (MALL) literature in which the impact of blended learning models for language development has been analysed (e.g., Chen Hsieh, Wu, & Marek, 2017; Hung, 2015). Among the different findings in blended learning studies investigating language development, it is worth mentioning factors such as higher participation and motivation levels, an increase in students' autonomy and a facilitation of the language learning process (Ball & Lindsay, 2012; Law, Geng, & Li, 2019; Miyazoe & Anderson, 2010).

In this context, social networking platforms such as Instagram, Facebook or WhatsApp allow teachers to facilitate language learning processes while students are involved in social interaction. For this research study, the application Instagram was selected due to the following factors: the widespread popularity of the application which reached 1 billion monthly active users and 600 million daily active users (Stout, 2019) as of September 2019; the possibilities of sharing and viewing video content through the social network that enables researchers to implement a flipped learning methodology; theoretical consideration such as the fact that students do not normally use technology they consider intrusive (Kukulska-Hulme & Shield, 2007); and the ubiquitous characteristics of mobile devices. Given this context, this study examines the growing literature on social networks and language learning and investigates the use of a blended learning model involving Instagram.

SOCIAL NETWORKS AND LANGUAGE LEARNING

Online social networking platforms, which are normally used for socializing, sharing information such as videos or pictures, or meetings (Boyd, 2014), are visited mostly by young people (Counts & Fisher, 2010; Dunn, 2013). Moreover, although the majority of these platforms provide web and mobile versions, social media usage is shifting towards mobile devices (Statista, 2019), which may lead to an increase in users' engagement levels as a consequence of a higher degree of accessibility. Thus, educators attempting to enhance learning through the use of social networks need to consider factors such as the type of learners and their accessibility to online contexts in order to develop successful learning environments. In this context, recent studies in the field, such as for example Andujar and Salaberri-Ramiro (2019), have demonstrated differences between the use of social networking tools in language learning from mobile and stationary devices.

With regard to the use of social networks, since their appearance, a great number of social networking tools have been used for different learning purposes (Mao, 2014). In the language learning field, it is worth mentioning the possibilities that this type of platform offers for interaction and communication through different channels (Mazer et al., 2007), which allow students to communicate by either texting, speaking, or simply through videos and pictures. Although the greater number of communication modes provides different possibilities from the second language learning perspective, not every social networking tool can be exploited in the same way. In this sense, social networks such as Twitter or Pinterest are bound to certain types of communication – written and visual respectively – whether others like WhatsApp or Instagram also allow voice recording and video sharing. These online environments have been found to be fertile ground to foster language interaction, group work and students' linguistic competence (Blattner & Fiori, 2011; Farr & Murray, 2016). Similarly, previous research making use of social networks to foster language development (e.g., Andujar & Salaberri-Ramiro, 2019; Andújar-Vaca & Cruz-Martínez, 2017; Lomicka & Lord, 2016) has emphasized the importance of social interaction for language learning. The interaction between native and non-native speakers or between non-native speakers has been found to foster an environment where language-related episodes (LREs) can occur (Swain & Lapkin, 1998). These LREs may be conducive to language learning as students reflect on the different language usage in the social network as well as on the language used by their peers. Furthermore, other factors such as students' observation and collaborative work appear to be increased during social interaction in these virtual platforms (Ryberg & Christiansen, 2008).

However, negative factors resulting from the use of social networks have also been identified in the literature. These include an increase in teachers' workload (Shih, 2011) owing to the fact that it is necessary to control the language and contents used in the platform, the type of language register that normally contains abbreviations, misspellings as well as great number of medium specific adaptations (Kabilan, Ahmad, & Abidin, 2010), privacy issues due to the necessary information exchange between peers and between students and teachers (Gettman & Cortijo, 2015; Teclehaimanot & Hickman, 2011) and the distracting nature of the medium often associated with informal learning (Rambe, 2012). Thus, it seems necessary to overcome these negative aspects as well as shed light on the different possibilities of certain social networks for language development in order to design successful learning environments.

Flipped Learning in EFL

The volume of research implementing blended learning environments in different educational contexts has grown rapidly in recent years (Yang, Sun, & Liu, 2017). In the field of blended learning, the growing popularity of flipped learning is noteworthy (Bergmann & Sams, 2012). This methodology, which involves the use of video lectures before the start of the class, practice problems as homework, and group-based activities during the in-class time (Bishop & Verleger, 2013), has been investigated in the EFL field as shown by the numerous articles published in high-ranked international journals (Yang, 2017; Chen Hsieh et al., 2017). The literature on flipped learning in the EFL field reported positive effects of this type of methodology on the development of various language skills.

In this context, studies have investigated the potential of the above methodology to develop EFL competences. Chen Hsieh et al. (2017) made use of the application Line to foster English idioms in a flipped learning context. An experimental design ($N = 48$) with a control group in which students received traditional lecture-based classes and an experimental group in which the above application was used, showed significant differences between students' idiomatic knowledge in favour of the latter. A questionnaire exploring learning experiences also yielded positive results. Moreover, the flipped model was found to be successful in achieving the instructional goals of the course. Apart from idiomatic expressions, other flipped learning studies in EFL such as Wu, Chen Hsieh and Yang's research (2017) investigated the potential of the flipped learning model to foster students' oral proficiency in the L2. Pre and post-tests on oral reading comprehension and structured interviews were used to assess 50 Taiwanese students of EFL. Results showed a significant improvement in students' oral proficiency and it was found that the flipped learning methodology motivated the participants and enhanced engagement. In the same vein, speaking skills were also investigated by Amiryousefi (2019) who used the mobile instant messaging application Telegram to implement a flipped learning model with 67 learners of EFL. Three different groups were created and different types of teaching were followed in each group: traditional lecture-based instruction, semi-flipped learning and flipped learning. An experimental design involving pre- and post-tests were administered to explore significant differences between the groups under investigation. In line with previous studies exploring flipped learning in EFL, results emphasized significant differences in the speaking skills of those who experienced the flipped learning model. Apart from the aforementioned studies, researchers have also made use of other platforms to develop flipped learning models in EFL such as Blackboard (e.g., Kang, 2015; Alsowat, 2016) or Moodle (e.g., Jeong, 2017; Webb, Doman, & Pusey, 2014) among others. However, either in an educational or EFL context, there is an absence of research exploring the potential of the application Instagram as a blended learning environment.

Instagram

Although the amount of research investigating the potential of Instagram in the language learning field is limited, there are a growing number of studies investigating the use of the application in other contexts. Likewise, there are also studies describing the different possibilities of the application to foster language development (e.g., Handayani, 2016). The remarkable popularity of this application among young people has elicited an increase in the amount of research exploring its potential. However, with regard to language learning purposes, only a small number of studies have been identified in the literature. One of these is Al-Ali's (2014) investigation into the use of the Instagram to develop different classroom activities. Forty female students had to first find a picture in the app, write a story about that picture and later upload a short video related to the photograph. A questionnaire measuring the overall experience in the platform yielded positive results and students were satisfied with the use of the app. However, some negative aspects were also reported regarded issues such as privacy or students' reluctance to upload their homework into the platform. Further recent research such as Akhiar, Mydin & Kasuma's (2017) study, investigated the potential of this app to develop students' writing abilities. In this research, participants ($N = 101$) had to comment on pictures taken by themselves in the app. Students were later asked about the learning experience and perception of the use of Instagram to foster writing in the L2. Positive results were reported with regard to the perceived improvement in students' writing abilities and the overall experience. However, as in the aforementioned research, some negative aspects were also identified such as the distracting nature of the application or a certain degree of fear of feeling judged when using the L2. Writing abilities were also explored by Yadegarfar and Simin (2016) who investigated the effects of Instagram on learning grammatical accuracy of word classes. Through the use of an experimental design, students were divided into a control ($N = 46$) and experimental group ($N = 46$). Word classes were taught through the application in the experimental group and through traditional lectures in the control group. Findings indicated that the experimental group outperformed the control with regard to learning grammatical accuracy of word classes. Likewise, participants reported a positive attitude towards the use of the application.

Regarding listening comprehension skills, Liliia and Gulnara (2016) investigated the potential of this tool with advanced level students of English as a foreign language. Participants ($N = 50$) watched three different videos per week through the app where they had to put into practice their listening skills and carry out a series of tasks and exercises. A mixed methods approach was used to collect qualitative and quantitative data and pre- and post-tests were also administered to assess participants' listening skills development. Results indicated positive findings with regard to the use of the app as an online educational environment for the improvement of listening skills. The video functionalities of the application were also investigated by Mansor and Rahim (2017) who required students to upload presentations that were subsequently commented on by their peers. Participants ($N = 20$) indicated feeling more motivated towards learning and highlighted a high degree of interaction with their peers. Results with regard to students' participation were also remarkable. Finally, Çakmak (2019) made use of the application to assess students' oral communication skills. Results emphasized that the use of the application facilitated students' oral performance and that personality traits were not predictors of students' performance in the application.

As observed in the above literature review, although the amount of relevant research regarding Instagram and language learning is growing, it appears necessary to further investigate which areas of EFL could be fostered through the use of this application. Thus, this chapter attempts to extend the existing literature in the field by conducting a case study in which the application was used to develop a flipped learning model in a second language class. In order to address this aim, the present study attempts to explore the following research question:

What are students' perceptions regarding the learning experience provided by Instagram in a course that utilises flipped learning?

THE STUDY

The case study in this investigation was implemented at a secondary school where students were learners of English as a foreign language. A total of 53 Spanish students – 30 female and 23 male – with ages ranging from 14 to 16 participated in the experiment in which a flipped classroom model was utilized involving the use of Instagram over a period of two months. Participants received regular classes and met for 3 hours per week. The material and contents provided in the course followed the didactic units of an English book for secondary education which met the parameters established by the *Common European Framework for Reference* (CEFR) for a B1 level. Short clips of the grammar contents that were going to be put into practice during the class were provided to students through the platform. The teacher of the group recorded the educational explanation and uploaded the videos to the wall of the account created for the class. The Instagram TV feature of the app was used for this purpose. Figure 1 presents a screenshot of the Instagram account students had to follow to view the videos.

Following the flipped classroom model (Bergman & Sams, 2012), students had to view the videos before the start of the lecture. An initial evaluation was carried out in order to evaluate the contents explained in the video and practice sessions were subsequently organized. Participants had to follow the teacher account in the social network and 'Instagram stories' were used to inform students that a new video was going to be released. In order to indicate that they had viewed the video, students had to press the 'like' button in the app. This allowed the teacher to track views of the video. All the students owned a mobile device to access the contents in the app and knew how to use the application as they

Figure 1. Account used by the teacher to upload the video contents

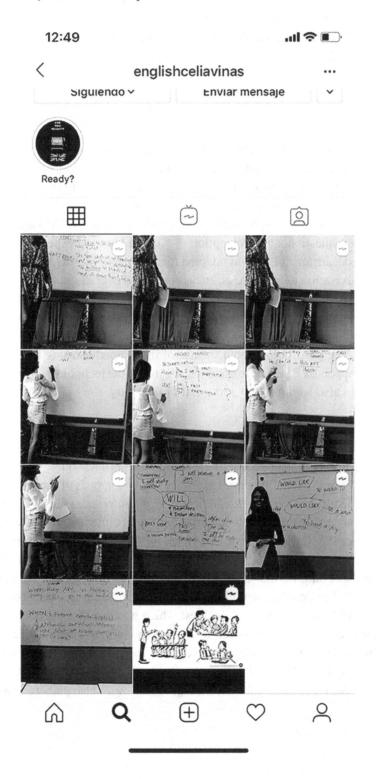

all had an Instagram account. Participants identities remained disguised during the data collection and analysis. Regarding analysis of the data, the teacher of the group was not the same as the researcher who evaluated the results of the study. In order to increase the reliability of the analysis, interrater reliability was calculated using two different raters. Agreement between the two raters was 98% indicating a strong agreement in the analysis carried out.

Methodology

This investigation followed a mixed methods methodology (Onwegbuzie & Teddlie, 2003) in which qualitative and quantitative data were analysed. In this sense, different data collection instruments were used. First, a log was used to collect the information regarding the tracking of the students in the platform such as the user name of the students in the app, the number of views per video or the amount of likes in each of the videos. In order to explore students' perceptions regarding the flipped learning model in the app, a 5-point Likert questionnaire 'Perception of flipped learning experience' (Chen Hsieh et al., 2017) regarding flipped learning in Line was adapted for this investigation (Appendix A). Four different constructs including motivation, effectiveness, engagement and overall satisfaction were evaluated. This questionnaire, which had already obtained expert validity and was based on relevant flipped learning literature, was analysed statistically after the data collection process in order to guarantee that items were appropriately and uniformly understood ($\alpha = .89$). Apart from this perception scale, in order to better understand students' perceptions about the use of the flipped learning model in the app, a semi-structured interview (Appendix B) was also conducted. Finally, the technology acceptance model (TAM) scale (Appendix C) was also administered at the end of the study.

Analysis

In order to analyse the information collected in the learning experience questionnaire and the TAM, the statistical software SPPS was used. Inferential statistics and an analysis of the frequencies were carried out. This branch of statistics allowed the researchers to make inferences about the sample under investigation as well as evaluate if participants tended more towards either end of the scale. The one-sample Wilcoxon rank test (Siegel & Castellan, 1956) was used for this purpose. This statistical test for ordinal variables also allowed the calculation of the effect size r for each of the constructs under investigation. Due to the fact that depending on the sample size almost everything could achieve significance, the effect size was calculated in combination with p value in order to further understand the relevance of the results obtained. In addition to this statistical test which was used for the questionnaire, descriptive measures and frequencies were also calculated for the two quantitative data collection instruments. As for the analysis of the semi-structured interview, a content analysis methodology was followed, coding relevant sections of the transcripts and identifying patterns in participants' responses. Examples of participants' responses in the focus groups for each the questions were also gathered and will be presented in the results section.

RESULTS

Quantitative Findings

The results obtained from the first data collection instrument, in this case the log used to track students' behavior in the application, are presented in Figure 2.

Figure 2. Audience of the Instagram TV videos

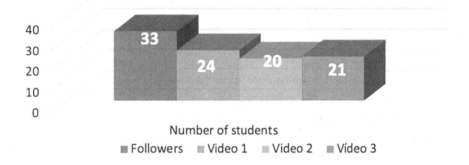

Number of students

■ Followers   ■ Video 1   ■ Video 2   ■ Vídeo 3

As can be observed in Figure 2, out of 53 students, only 33 followed the Instagram account created by the teacher for the class. In this context, it is worth mentioning that the total number of views of the videos did not live up to researcher expectations. The qualitative data obtained in the interview provides a more in-depth explanation of these findings and will be discussed at a later stage of this chapter.

The second research instrument explored students' perceptions about the flipped learning model in the app. Table 1 presents the results of the information collected in the questionnaire.

The Wilcoxon signed-rank test was used to explore significant differences between the different items. Item 1 explored students' perception of the flipped learning experience as a better way of learning in comparison with traditional language classes. Results yielded significant differences in favour of the implementation of a flipped learning approach ($Z = 2.5$, $p < .05$), although the effect size was low ($r = .34$). Similarly, results with regard to students' degree of enjoyment (item 2) were positive ($Z = 3.03$, $p < .05$) and the effect size was moderate ($r = .43$). These findings were later confirmed in subsequent items of the perception questionnaire such as item 7 or item 9 where students indicated that they considered the flipped learning method worthwhile and expressed their preference over traditional lecture-based classrooms. Results indicated significant differences in favour of the flipped learning model ($Z = 3.04$, $p < .05$ and $Z = 2.54$, $p < .05$ respectively) with moderate ($r = .43$) and low effect sizes respectively ($r = .36$). Finally, item 14 explored the overall satisfaction with the flipped learning experience. Positive responses gave rise to significant differences ($Z = 3.50$, $p < .05$) with a moderate effect size ($r = .50$) confirming previous findings in the questionnaire. Thus, the results emphasized that although students enjoyed the flipped learning experience, there was still room for improvement.

Table 1. Descriptive statistics of the "Flipped learning experience" questionnaire (Chen Hsieh et al., 2017)

	N	Mean	SD
1. A flipped classroom model is a better way of learning.	48	3.44*	1.25
2. I enjoyed the Flipped classroom teaching approach more.	48	3.56*	1.23
3. I think the flipped classroom is a more effective and efficient way to learn.	48	3.33	1.27
4. I feel more motivated in a flipped classroom.	48	3.27	1.10
5. I participated and engaged myself more in learning in the flipped classroom.	48	3.04	1.01
6. I became a more active learner in the flipped classroom.	48	3.08	1.25
7. I thought the time and effort I spent in the flipped classroom was worthwhile.	48	3.54*	1.09
8. I learned more and better in the flipped classroom.	48	3.17	1.17
9. I prefer the flipped classroom to a lecture-based classroom.	48	3.56*	1.35
10. I think the flipped classroom learning guided me toward better understanding of the course topics.	48	3.13	1.08
11. I experienced pleasure in the flipped classroom.	48	3.63*	1.08
12. I devoted myself more to the instructional/class activities in the flipped classroom.	48	3.27	1.08
13. I spent more time and effort than usual on my flipped classroom learning activities.	48	2.92	1.04
14. Generally, I am happy and satisfied with this flipped learning experience.	48	3.65*	1.15

*Statistically significant difference p < .05

The third research instrument developed for this investigation was the technology acceptance model which attempted to explore the overall learning perception of the use of Instagram in the course. The information collected in this scale was again analysed quantitatively through the use of inferential statistics. Descriptive measures of this scale are presented in Table 2.

Table 2. Descriptive measures of the TAM

Construct	N	Min	Max	Mean	SD
System characteristics	45	1	4	3.16	.85
Material characteristics	45	1	4	3.53	.69
Perceived ease of use	45	2	5	3.87	.91
Perceived usefulness	45	1	4	3.09	.90
Attitude about use	45	1	4	3.31	.84
Behavioral intention	45	1	4	3.16	.85

The TAM is divided in six different subconstructs in order to fully ascertain participants' overall perception of the use of Instagram. The first construct evaluated students' perceptions regarding the system characteristics ($M = 3.16$). Results yielded a positive perception with regard to the use of Instagram as a stimulating and realistic environment for learning English and students highlighted feeling comfortable while visualizing the videos. The second construct evaluated the materials provided to students through the app ($M = 3.53$). Students' responses regarding the comprehension, usefulness, and support provided through the materials and contents used in the videos were quite positive. Although suggestions were given in the qualitative analysis section of this chapter to improve the materials, students' degree of satisfaction was high.

The third construct investigated the perceived ease of use of the application. Participants already knew how to use the app as all of them had the social network already installed in their devices. Thus, students did not have many problems visualizing the contents or using the app ($M = 3.87$) throughout the flipped classes. With regard to the fourth construct, students found the use of the app beneficial in fostering their language abilities and their eagerness to learn was also increased ($M = 3.09$). However, these results were not noteworthy as the average of responses is close to 3 which was considered as neutral response.

The fifth construct explored whether students enjoyed using Instagram for language learning and whether they had a positive attitude towards the use of the app. Results indicated that students welcomed the platform as a language learning resource ($M = 3.31$) and found the app potentially interesting for language learning. The last construct in the TAM explored whether students would like to continue using Instagram for learning English as well as for participating in conversations in the platform. Students responded positively ($M = 3.16$), a finding that suggests further research in this area is warranted. In answer to the research question, data show that students were satisfied with the use of Instagram for learning the target language and found the environment to be comfortable and motivating.

Qualitative Findings

In order to obtain the qualitative data, interviews with 5 different focus groups which consisted of 6 participants were carried out. Nine different questions about the flipped learning experience through Instagram were asked to participants. Question 1 explored students' perspectives regarding the methodology. Most of the students highlighted the use of this methodology as a good idea and common reasons already pointed out in the flipped learning literature such as the possibility of pausing, rewinding and watching the lecture several times were emphasized. Furthermore, other reasons related to the use of the application were also pointed out by participants such as the possibility of writing comments to the videos or asking questions about in the app. Participants also highlighted feeling closer to the teacher during the flipped classes. The following are examples of these learners' comments:

If there are different levels in class, each person can watch the explanations at his/her own pace. (Focus group 1)

You can watch the videos whenever you want. (Focus group 1)

You are not distracted with your classmates while watching the videos. (Focus group 3)

If you don´t attend the classes, you can watch the lessons instead. (Focus group 4)

As you have your teacher in Instagram, the relationship is closer. (Focus group 4)

You can write comments in order to ask questions. (Focus group 5)

Among the adjectives used by students when answering this question, words like motivational, curious, interesting, comfortable, different, innovative, entertaining or useful came up. Some negative opinions were also found in the focus groups such as the distracting nature of the application, wifi connectivity, the length of the videos, the difficulty in remembering the content of the videos or the impossibility of asking questions directly to the teacher. The following comments highlight these issues:

You get distracted with other things in your mobile phone and you never end up watching the full video. (Focus group 1)

Sometimes we do not have an available wifi network. (Focus group 2)

Videos are sometimes too long. (Focus group 3)

In my opinion, I don´t like it because I have doubts and I cannot ask questions. (Focus group 4)

Sometimes, I don´t remember the explanation in the video so it's difficult for me to follow the class. (Focus group 5)

The second interview question explored whether students considered useful the implementation of the flipped learning model. Two focus groups unanimously responded positively to this question. Some exceptions were found in other focus groups were students indicated the absence of the teacher and a high number of distractions as problematic.

No, because I get distracted. (Focus group 3)

The teacher is not there so if you don´t understand the language, it's difficult. (Focus group 5)

The third question in the structured interview evaluated the accessibility of the videos in the platform. Most of the students in the focus groups highlighted the easy access to the videos. However, a small number of students also indicated some problems such as the lack of the required updates, or the amount of time required to load them. Learner feedback is presented below:

I did not have the updates so I couldn´t watch the videos. (Focus group 2)

The loading of the videos was very slow. (Focus group 4)

I was punished without my phone. (Focus group 5)

Question four of the structured interview evaluated students' perceptions regarding the content of the videos. The majority of the students in the focus groups indicated that the contents provided in the videos were clear and comprehensible. Furthermore, positive answers with regard to the inclusion of extra content, the organization of the videos or the corrections to some of the in-class tasks were given. Students' responses are presented below:

Everything is well-explained and, in addition, there are things that do not appear in the book. (Focus group 1)

I like the division of the contents in three short videos. (Focus group 2)

I pay more attention to the video than to the class. (Focus group 4)

A small number of negative opinions were also expressed regarding the content, mainly regarding the lack of understanding in some cases, the quality or the need to join and sum up the videos:

I did not understand the language so it was difficult for me to understand the contents. (Focus group 3)

The audio quality was average. (Focus group 4)

I believe that is better to summarize everything in one video because many times I don't realize there are more videos and I don´t watch all the contents. (Focus group 5)

The fifth question of the structured interview explored whether students had experienced difficulties understanding the videos. Most of the students in the focus groups responded negatively, which suggests that the contents of the videos were appropriate for the language level of the participants. However, some discrepancies were found particularly in those students with a low English level or those who complained about the quality of the audio. The following comments are examples of the aforementioned discrepancies.

Yes, mainly because my English level is very bad. (Focus group 1)

I found difficult to understand certain words. (Focus group 2)

The audio was not great. (Focus group 5)

The sixth question of the structured interview analysed students' opinions about the flipped learning model and traditional learning. In this question, a disparity of opinions was found depending among the participants. Approximately half of the participants indicated their preference towards the flipped learning model over traditional learning. The rest preferred traditional learning except for a small number of students who indicated their preference towards a mixed model that combined flipped and traditional learning. The following comments present some examples of these preferences.

I would choose the flipped learning model but using Kahoot. (Focus group 3)

I would learn better with the flipped learning model as I can play the video several times. (Focus group 4)

I prefer in-class teaching but in a dynamic and innovative way. (Focus group 5)

I would learn more with videos but in the class. (Focus group 1)

Question number seven of the structured interview analysed the advantages students perceived of using the flipped learning methodology. As mentioned previously, the possibility of watching the videos several times is the most frequent answer among participants. Other participants also suggest factors such as: the possibility of carrying out different activities at the same time; the motivational component of Instagram; the absence of classmates that could distract them; the use of Instagram; the possibility of watching the videos in different locations; and the entertaining characteristics of the flipped learning methodology.

I find Instagram motivating. (Focus group 1)

I can do other things while I watch the video"/ "It's more entertaining. (Focus group 2)

You have more in-class time to practice. (Focus group 3)

You don´t get disturbed by people in the class. (Focus group 4)

You can see the lecture everywhere and through a social network. (Focus group 5)

Question eight tackled the disadvantages perceived by students. The most frequent responses by participants included factors such as the distracting nature of mobile phones and the audio quality. Other factors such as the lack of instant teacher feedback were also pointed out.

You can get distracted with the chat conversations in your mobile phone or watching other Instagram posts. (Focus group 1)

The quality of the audio was poor at times. (Focus group 2)

Sometimes you forget the doubts you had when you watched the video and you cannot ask the teacher in class. (Focus group 4)

Further disadvantages found in a smaller proportion of responses were the length of the videos, the difficulty in understanding the contents, updates in the app or the data plans in some of the devices used by participants. The last question of the structured interview explored possible recommendations regarding the improvement of the videos for subsequent implementations. Factors such as adding subtitles, reducing the length, improving the audio quality and uploading videos more frequently were the most common responses provided by participants.

Uploading the videos with Spanish subtitles. (Focus group 1)

Making the videos shorter and uploading them more frequently. (Focus group 2)

Using Kahoot to evaluate the explanations in the videos. (Focus group 3)

Improving the audio quality of the video. (Focus group 4)

Stop the video in certain parts in order to see the whole explanation. (Focus group 5)

Thus, answering the research question of this investigation, the quantitative and qualitative analyses conducted provide a detailed and largely positive account of students' perceptions. These perceptions will be further discussed and compared with similar studies in the following discussion.

CONCLUSION

The questionnaire yielded positive findings with regard to students' satisfaction with the methodology in line with similar research involving use of a flipped learning approach in the EFL class (e.g., Chen Hsieh et al., 2017; Nouri, 2016). However, students did not feel that the use of this methodology improved their linguistic competence and language skills in comparison with lecture-based classes. This finding contradicts results from similar studies conducted in EFL (e.g., Chen Hsieh et al., 2017) or second language learning contexts (Lim, Kim, & Lee, 2016), and suggests that a flipped classroom model did not imply more effective language teaching or a higher degree of language learning. Owing to the fact that this type of methodology is relatively new, it appears essential to train teachers appropriately to carry out this type of activity. This may contribute to changing students' perceptions with regard to the possibilities of this methodology for language learning as previous studies have already shown the positive effects of flipped learning in terms of motivation and engagement (e.g., Hao, 2016; Yilmaz, 2017).

With regard to the flipped learning model, the advantages of this methodology over traditional lecture-based classes in EFL contexts are also highlighted by the findings of this research. Factors such as the possibility of watching the videos several times, greater autonomy and more in-class practice time (Bergman & Sams, 2012) appear beneficial in supporting learning. Apart from these advantages which are common to any flipped learning context, the ubiquitous characteristics of mobile devices together with the inclusion of a social element provide more opportunities to foster students' engagement. Nevertheless, the characteristics of mobile devices also highlight several potential disadvantages that need to be considered when implementing blended learning models. Factors such as internet connectivity, the distracting nature of mobile devices or poor audio quality may also have an impact on the implementation and development of a flipped learning model. Further specific elements of foreign learning contexts also need to be considered such as the use of subtitles in order to improve the understanding of the L2, in an effort to reduce distractions. Similarly, adjusting the videos to the linguistic competence of the students through stops, emphasis and repetitions also seems a relevant factor, given the impossibility of answering students' questions while they watch the explanations.

Regarding the results of the TAM, the use of Instagram was found to be positive, and motivational as students were already familiar with this app. These findings also correlate with previous studies involving use of Instagram (e.g., Çakmak, 2019, Mansor & Rahim, 2017) which highlighted the potential of the app to foster students' motivation and engagement. However, it also seems necessary to control the distracting nature of this application, which at times gave rise to situations where students stopped watching the videos to explore other posts and videos. Although the results found in this data collection instrument could also be reported in other platforms where flipped learning is viable such as Facebook or Youtube, it is worth emphasizing that Instagram is mainly used through mobile devices which led to ubiquitous access to the contents and explanations. At the same time, the tremendous popularity of the application among students also became a relevant factor in selecting this app as the flipped learning platform in an attempt to improve participants' engagement during the project.

Overall, the implementation of new pedagogical perspectives such as blended learning models in language learning is still a field that requires further investigation. Likewise, research exploring the potential of Instagram to foster language development is very limited. Thus, this chapter attempts to combine these two elements in order to further understand their potential for language development and how to effectively facilitate learning using them. In this context, the information collected in this investigation could be used as a stepping stone towards more in-depth analyses of the learning gains of this type of language instruction. Further lines of research could also investigate the impact of a ubiquitous flipped learning methodology like the one presented in this chapter on students' linguistic competence. Use of an experimental design, control and experimental groups may provide relevant data regarding the differences between flipped and traditional lecture-based instruction. However, in order to effectively implement these approaches, researchers would be well advised to consider the factors identified in this investigation.

REFERENCES

Akhiar, A., Mydin, A., & Kasuma, S. A. A. (2017). Students' perceptions and attitudes towards the use of Instagram in English language writing. *Malaysian Journal of Learning and Instruction (MJLI), Special issue on Graduate Students Research on Education*, 47-72.

Al-Ali, S. (2014). Embracing the selfie craze: Exploring the possible use of Instagram as a language mlearning tool. *Issues and Trends in Educational Technology*, 2(2), 1–16.

Alsowat, H. (2016). An EFL flipped classroom teaching model: Effects on English language higher-order thinking skills, student engagement and satisfaction. *Journal of Education and Practice*, 7(9), 108–121.

Amiryousefi, M. (2019). The incorporation of flipped learning into conventional classes to enhance EFL learners' L2 speaking, L2 listening, and engagement. *Innovation in Language Learning and Teaching*, 13(2), 147–161.

Andujar, A., & Salaberri-Ramiro, M. S. (2019). Exploring chat-based communication in the EFL class: Computer and mobile environments. *Computer Assisted Language Learning*, 1–28.

Andújar-Vaca, A., & Cruz-Martínez, M. S. (2017). Mobile instant messaging: WhatsApp and its potential to develop oral skills. *Comunicar*, 25(50), 43–52.

Arbaugh, J. B. (2014). What might online delivery teach us about blended management education? Prior perspectives and future directions. *Journal of Management Education*, 38(6), 784–817.

Ball, P., & Lindsay, D. (2013). Language demands and support for English-medium instruction in tertiary education: Learning from a specific context. In A. Doiz, D. Lasagabaster, & J. M. Sierra (Eds.), English-medium instruction at universities: Global challenges (pp. 44-62). Bristol, Blue Ridge Summit: Multilingual Matters.

Bergmann, J., & Sams, A. (2012). Flip your classroom: Reach every student in every class every day. International Society for Technology in Education: Alexandria, VA.

Bishop, J. L., & Verleger, M. A. (2013). *The flipped classroom: A survey of the research*. Paper presented at the 120th American Society for Engineering Education Annual Conference and Exposition, Atlanta, GA.

Blattner, G., & Fiori, M. (2011). Virtual social network communities: An investigation of language learners' development of sociopragmatic awareness and multiliteracy skills. *CALICO Journal, 29*(1), 24–43.

Boyd, D. (2014). *It's complicated: The social lives of networked teens*. London, UK: Yale University Press.

Çakmak, F. (2019). Social networking and language learning: Use of Instagram (IG) for evaluating oral communication skill. In A. Andujar (Ed.), *Recent tools for computer- and mobile-assisted foreign language learning* (pp. 103–131). Hershey, PA: IGI Global.

CEFR. (2018). *Common European Framework of Reference for Languages: Learning, Teaching, Assessment (CEFR)*. Retrieved from https://www.coe.int/en/web/common-european-framework-reference-languages

Chen Hsieh, J. S., Wu, W. C. V., & Marek, M. W. (2017). Using the flipped classroom to enhance EFL learning. *Computer Assisted Language Learning, 30*(1-2), 1–21.

Counts, S., & Fisher, K. E. (2010). Mobile social networking as information ground: A case study. *Library & Information Science Research, 32*(2), 98–115.

Dunn, L. (2013, April 19). Teaching in higher education: can social media enhance the learning experience? In *6th Annual University of Glasgow Learning and Teaching Conference*. Glasgow, UK.

Farr, F., & Murray, L. (Eds.). (2016). *The Routledge handbook of language learning and technology*. New York: Routledge.

Gettman, H. J., & Cortijo, V. (2015). "Leave me and my Facebook alone!" Understanding college students' relationship with Facebook and its use for academic purposes. *International Journal for the Scholarship of Teaching and Learning, 9*(1), 1–16.

Handayani, F. (2016). Instagram as a teaching tool? Really? *Proceedings of ISELT FBS Universitas Negeri Padang, 4*(1), 320–327.

Hao, Y. (2016). Exploring undergraduates' perspectives and flipped learning readiness in their flipped classrooms. *Computers in Human Behavior, 59*, 82–92.

Hung, H. T. (2015). Flipping the classroom for English language learners to foster active learning. *Computer Assisted Language Learning, 28*(1), 81–96.

Jeong, K. O. (2017). The use of Moodle to enrich flipped learning for English as a foreign language education. *Journal of Theoretical & Applied Information Technology, 95*(18), 4845–4852.

Kabilan, M. K., Ahmad, N., & Abidin, M. J. Z. (2010). Facebook: An online environment for learning of English in institutions of higher education? *The Internet and higher education, 13*(4), 179–187.

Kang, N. (2015). The comparison between regular and flipped classrooms for EFL Korean adult learners. *Multimedia-Assisted Language Learning, 18*(3), 41–72.

Kukulska-Hulme, A., & Shield, L. (2007). An overview of mobile assisted language learning: Can mobile devices support collaborative practice in speaking and listening. *ReCALL, 20*(3), 1–20.

Law, K. M., Geng, S., & Li, T. (2019). Student enrollment, motivation and learning performance in a blended learning environment: The mediating effects of social, teaching, and cognitive presence. *Computers & Education, 136*, 1–12.

Liliia, K., & Gulnara, G. (2016). Mobile technologies in teaching English as a foreign language in higher education: A case study of using mobile application Instagram. *Proceedings 9th International Conference of Education, Research, and Innovation* (pp. 6155-6161). Seville, Spain. Academic Press.

Lim, C., Kim, S., & Lee, J. (2016). Designing the flipped classroom in higher education. In J. M. Spector, D. Ifenthaler, D. G. Sampson, & P. Isaias (Eds.), *Competencies in teaching, learning and educational leadership in the digital age* (pp. 245–258). Cham, Switzerland: Springer.

Lomicka, L., & Lord, G. (2016). Social networking and language learning. In F. Farr, & L. Murray (Eds.), The Routledge handbook of language learning and technology (pp. 255–268). Routledge, NY. Academic Press.

Mansor, N., & Rahim, N. A. (2017). Instagram in ESL classroom. *Man in India, 97*(20), 107–114.

Mao, J. (2014). Social media for learning: A mixed methods study on high school students' technology affordances and perspectives. *Computers in Human Behavior, 33*, 213–223.

Mazer, J. P., Murphy, R. E., & Simonds, C. J. (2007). I'll see you on "Facebook": The effects of computer-mediated teacher self-disclosure on student motivation, affective learning, and classroom climate. *Communication Education, 56*(1), 1–17.

Miyazoe, T., & Anderson, T. (2010). Learning outcomes and students' perceptions of online writing: Simultaneous implementation of a forum, blog, and wiki in an EFL blended learning setting. *System, 38*(2), 185–199.

Nouri, J. (2016). The flipped classroom: For active, effective and increased learning-especially for low achievers. *International Journal of Educational Technology in Higher Education, 13*(1), 1–10.

Rambe, P. (2012). Constructive disruptions for effective collaborative learning: Navigating the affordances of social media for meaningful engagement. *Electronic Journal of e-Learning, 10*(1), 132-146.

Ryberg, T., & Christiansen, E. (2008). Community and social network sites as technology enhanced learning environments. *Technology, Pedagogy, and Education, 17*(3), 207–219.

Seaman, J., & Tinti-Kane, H. (2013). *Social media for teaching and learning*. London, UK: Pearson Learning Systems.

Shih, R. C. (2011). Can Web 2.0 technology assist college students in learning English writing? Integrating Facebook and peer assessment with blended learning. *Australasian Journal of Educational Technology, 27*(5), 829–845.

Siegel, S., & Castellan, N. J. (1956). *Nonparametric statistics for the behavioral sciences* (Vol. 7). New York: McGraw-Hill.

Statista. (2019). Global mobile social network penetration rate as of January 2019, by región. Retrieved from https://www.statista.com/statistics/412257/mobile-social-penetration-rate-region/

Stout, D. (2019). Social Media Statistics 2019: Top networks by the numbers. Retrieved from https://dustinstout.com/social-media-statistics/#whatsapp-stats

Swain, M., & Lapkin, S. (1998). Interaction and second language learning: Two adolescent French immersion students working together. *Modern Language Journal*, *82*, 320–337.

Teclehaimanot, B., & Hickman, T. (2011). Student-teacher interaction on Facebook: What students find appropriate. *TechTrends*, *55*(3), 19. doi:10.100711528-011-0494-8

Webb, M., Doman, E., & Pusey, K. (2014). Flipping a Chinese university EFL course: What students and teachers think of the model. *The Journal of Asia TEFL*, *11*(4), 53–87.

Wu, W. C. V., Chen Hsieh, J. S., & Yang, J. C. (2017). Creating an online learning community in a flipped classroom to enhance EFL learners' oral proficiency. *Journal of Educational Technology & Society*, *20*(2), 142–157.

Yadegarfar, H., & Simin, S. (2016). Effects of using Instagram on learning grammatical accuracy of word classes among Iranian undergraduate TEFL students. *International Journal of Research Studies in Educational Technology*, *5*(2), 49–60.

Yang, C. C. R. (2017). An investigation of the use of the 'flipped classroom' pedagogy in secondary English language classrooms. *Journal of Information Technology Education: Innovations in Practice*, *16*(1), 1–20.

Yang, L., Sun, T., & Liu, Y. (2017). A Bibliometric Investigation of Flipped Classroom Research during 2000-2015. *International Journal of Emerging Technologies in Learning*, *12*(6), 178–186.

Yilmaz, R. (2017). Exploring the role of e-learning readiness on student satisfaction and motivation in flipped classroom. *Computers in Human Behavior*, *70*, 251–260.

ADDITIONAL READING

Aloraini, N. (2018). Investigating Instagram as an EFL Learning Tool. *Arab World English Journal (AWEJ). Special Issue on CALL*, *9*(4), 174–184.

Donmus, V. (2010). The use of social networks in educational computer-game based foreign language learning. *Procedia: Social and Behavioral Sciences*, *9*, 1497–1503.

Gonulal, T. (2019). The use of Instagram as a mobile-assisted language learning tool. *Contemporary Educational Technology*, *10*(3), 309–323.

Harrison, R., & Thomas, M. (2009). Identity in online communities: Social networking sites and language learning. *International Journal of Emerging Technologies and Society*, *7*(2), 109–124.

Lin, C. H., Warschauer, M., & Blake, R. (2016). Language learning through social networks: Perceptions and reality. *Language Learning & Technology*, *20*(1), 124–147. http://dx.doi.org/10125/44449

Mondahl, M., & Razmerita, L. (2014). Social media, collaboration and social learning: A case-study of foreign language learning. *Electronic Journal of E-learning, 12*(4), 339–352.

Purnama, A. D. (2017). Incorporating memes and Instagram to enhance student's participation. *LLT Journal: A Journal on Language and Language Teaching, 20*(1), 1-14.

KEY TERMS AND DEFINITIONS

Blended Learning: Style of learning in which students learn through computer and electronic devices as well as through traditional classroom sessions.

Flipped Learning: Type of blended learning methodology that involves viewing teacher's explanations from a computer or mobile device before the class. In-class time is devoted to the evaluation and practice of the contents explained in the videos.

Instagram TV: Functionality of the social networking tool "Instagram" that allows user to record long duration videos that can be subsequently uploaded to users' profiles.

MALL: Mobile-assisted language learning (MALL) is a field of study that investigates the use of mobile devices to foster second language development.

Social Media: Online environments that allow users to share content or participate in social activities through the web.

TAM: The technology acceptance model (TAM) is a scale which is used to explain students' use and behavior towards technological devices and applications.

This research was previously published in New Technological Applications for Foreign and Second Language Learning and Teaching; pages 135-156, copyright year 2020 by Information Science Reference (an imprint of IGI Global).

APPENDIX A (Chen Hsieh, Wu & Marek, 2017)

Please circle the following items.
1 = Strongly disagree; 2 = Disagree; 3 = Neutral; 4 = Agree; 5 = Strongly Agree

1. A flipped classroom model is a better way of learning.
2. I enjoyed the Flipped classroom teaching approach more.
3. I think the flipped classroom is a more effective and efficient way to learn.
4. I feel more motivated in a flipped classroom.
5. I participated and engaged myself more in learning in the flipped classroom.
6. I became a more active learner in the flipped classroom.
7. I thought the time and effort I spent in the flipped classroom was worthwhile.
8. I learned more and better in the flipped classroom.
9. I prefer the flipped classroom to a lecture-based classroom.
10. I think the flipped classroom learning guided me toward better understanding of the course topics.
11. I experienced pleasure in the flipped classroom.
12. I devoted myself more to the instructional/class activities in the flipped classroom.
13. I spent more time and effort than usual on my flipped classroom learning activities.
14. Generally, I am happy and satisfied with this flipped learning experience.

APPENDIX B: STRUCTURED INTERVIEW

What's your opinion about this methodology?

Do you consider this methodology useful?

Did you have any problem when accessing the videos?

What do you think about the contents of the videos?

Did you have any difficulty with understanding the videos?

Do you think you would learn better with the flipped learning model or with traditional lecture-based instruction?

Advantages of using this methodology.

Disadvantages of using this methodology.

Any recommendation on how to improve the videos to use them in a flipped learning model?

APPENDIX C: TECHNOLOGY ACCEPTANCE MODEL

Please circle the following items.
1 = Strongly disagree; 2 = Disagree; 3 = Neutral; 4 = Agree; 5 = Strongly Agree

System Characteristics

The use of Instagram provided a realistic learning environment to learn English.

The use of Instagram provided a stimulating learning environment.

I felt comfortable using Instagram to view the theoretical explanations compared to face-to-face tuition.

I could use Instagram to improve my learning due to the teacher's explanations.

Material Characteristics

The audio/video materials made by the teacher led to a better comprehension of the course contents.

The audio/video materials made by the teacher helped me immerse myself in the learning atmosphere of the class.

The audio/video materials made by the teacher were useful to learn the class contents.

The audio/video materials made by the teacher helped learn the most important aspects of the different units.

I believe that the audio/video materials made by the teacher were useful for improving my English level.

Perceived Ease of Use

I received clear guidance about how to use Instagram and view the videos.

Using Instagram did not require much time.

Learning how to use Instagram for the in-class activities was easy.

The visualization of the videos through Instagram was adequate and not stressful.

Perceived Usefulness

Learning through Instagram improved my English skills.

Learning through Instagram enhanced my desire to use the contents learnt.

Learning through Instagram provided a beneficial outcome to this class.

The videos made by the teacher were useful to improve my class work.

Attitude About Use

I like using Instagram to learn English.

I have a positive attitude towards the use of Instagram in this class.

I believe that using Instagram to learn English was a good idea.

I looked forward to using Instagram in this class.

Behavioural Intention

When I use Instagram, I will continue writing in English and following English accounts apart from Spanish ones.

I will continue using Instagram to improve my English level.

I will be happy to use the contents I have learnt when using Instagram.

When I use Instagram, I will have confidence when I participate in conversations in English.

Chapter 17
Influence of Age Groups and School Types on Informal Learning Through the Use of Social Networking Sites

Siew Ming Thang
HELP University, Malaysia

Lay Shi Ng
Universiti Kebangsaan Malaysia, Malaysia

ABSTRACT

The use of Social Networking Sites (SNSs) as a learning tool is increasingly popular nowadays. This chapter investigates perceptions of 799 secondary-school Malaysian secondary school students of two age-groups, and three school-types (urban, suburban, and rural) towards the use of the SNSs for informal learning purposes. For this chapter, learning that takes place outside the classroom is classified as "informal learning". Data were analysed quantitatively and comparisons across age-groups and school-types were made. The findings revealed that there was a general acceptance of SNSs as an alternative learning mode and that difference in usage between age groups was not significant. However, the findings across school-types were significant. Suburban and rural students appeared to use the SNSs more frequently for informal learning than urban students. This strongly suggested the need for Government to intensify its efforts in improving ICT infrastructure and facilities in rural areas.

INTRODUCTION

The popularity of social networking sites (SNSs) has rapidly increased over the past few years in Malaysia. GlobalWebIndex (2015) revealed that Malaysia has the second highest penetration of social networking usage among Internet users in Asia. It was further reported that on average a Malaysian with a social networking account spends 2.8 hours per day on SNSs. Now with the widespread use of smartphones, it

DOI: 10.4018/978-1-6684-7123-4.ch017

is believed that the time spent on SNSs will continue to rise. SNSs such as Facebook, Instagram, WhatsApp and WeChat are the most commonly used Internet-based social spaces in Malaysia, particularly among young individuals.

Boyd and Ellison (2007) defined a social networking system as a web-based service that allows individuals to do the following: i) build public or semi-public profile in a system, (ii) share a connection, and (iii) view and cross-list their relationship with others in the system. Such systems enable easy and rapid connection with friends, families, classmates, customers and clients. In addition, SNSs are also seen as media that allows people to come together around an idea or topic of interest. In fact, SNSs are increasingly being leveraged as a learning tool, especially for today's tech-savvy students. According to Lai et al. (2013), many students are immersed in out-of-school online activities. When using digital media, students engage in a new learning culture which is very different from what they have been enculturated in traditional schools. Many studies have indicated the potential of using social networking for learning purposes (Selwyn, 2009; Griffith & Liyanage, 2008). However, it is not possible to use it as a tool for learning in Malaysian secondary schools due to the constraint of not allowing students to bring their cell phones to schools. Thus, it would be interesting to find out to what extent students use SNSs for learning purposes outside the classroom which has been defined as "informal learning" in this study. This definition is in line with that of Livingstone (1999) and Marsick and Watkins (2001). Livingstone (1999) described informal learning as any activity involving the pursuit of understanding, knowledge or skill which occurs outside the curricula of educational institutions, or the courses or workshops offered by educational or social agencies. Marsick and Watkins (2001) further described it as intentional but unstructured, contextualized learning.

This study extends on these studies in its attempt to investigate how differences in age and school-types affect students' usage of SNSs for informal learning purposes. Findings of this study will add to the current body of research, conducted on the effects of social networking on Malaysian secondary school students.

The following research questions specifically seek to investigate whether there are differences in usage for the following categories of students: (a) between students of two different age-groups and (b) between students from three school-types (namely urban, suburban and rural):

1. What types of SNSs usage patterns are displayed among the different categories of Malaysian secondary school students?
2. How much time do these different categories of students spend on SNSs?
3. To what extent do these different categories of students use SNSs for learning and what types of learning do they focus on?
4. What are the differences in usage of SNSs for informal learning purposes of the different categories of students?

RELATED LITERATURE

Social Networking Sites

Social networking was introduced 15 to 20 years ago. Since then it has grown from a niche to a mass online activity, in which millions of Internet users (from different ages, cultures and education levels) are engaged in during their leisure time and at their workplace (Misra et al., 2015; Mazman and Usluel, 2011).Its impact cannot be overstated. Social networking is the most popular online activity worldwide accounting for nearly 1 in every 5 minutes spent online in October 2011, and reaches 82 percent of the world's Internet population, representing 1.2 billion users around the globe (ComScore, 2011). According to a study by Lenhart et al. (2010), young people were much more likely than older adults to use social networks. Several studies conducted in the U.S. found that 80% of online teens used social network sites, Facebook being the most popular, with 93% of those teens reporting its use (Manago et al., 2008). Likewise, it was reported that Malaysians were spending more than three hours on their smartphones each day, where 40% of users' time were spent on social networking and chatting (Vserv, 2015).

Differences in SNSs' Usage According to Age

Surveys have found substantial differences in social media use according to age. According to a report published by Pew Research Center, in 2018, 88% of the Americans between the ages of 18-29 used SNSs. However, the social media adoption rate of Americans between 30-49 was 78%, while older age group (50-64) was 64%. Women were more likely than men to use social media. The report also indicated that a majority of Americans used Facebook and YouTube, but young adults (especially those age 18-24) were especially heavy users of Snapchat and Instagram.

In USA, the age group between 35-44 displayed dominant use of SNSs across the social web (Briansolis.com, 2010). According to a survey by Sproutsocial (2017), more than 60% of Americans age above 34 preferred to use Facebook, while only 33% of Millennials preferred Facebook and 25% of younger Millennials (ages 18-24) identified Instagram as their favourite social media network. In Malaysia, over 90% of Internet users used SNSs. Older age group reported a lower rate of Internet use compared to younger group. Only 7.5% of Malaysians age 50-64 used Internet (MCMC, 2017). Hence, it is obvious that the usage of social media is higher among young Malaysians than the older age group.

Differences in SNSs' Usage According to the Urban-Rural Divide

Hosseini, Niknami, and Chizari (2009) reported that rural communities in Malaysia faced several challenges in the implementation and use of ICT. These include lack of interest and expertise in using ICT, concerns about the risks of using ICT, low quality of the services provided by the service centres, and the lack of interest by the private sector to participate in the rural development of ICT. According to Zulkhairi, Azizah, Abdul Razak, and Rafidah (2010), the rate of literacy and the rate of broadband penetration in rural areas still remained at a low level of less than one percent. Umar and Jalil (2012) further revealed that that there was a significant difference between urban school students and rural school students in terms of ICT skills. This clearly indicated that the ICT infrastructure in the rural areas had to be improved to rectify this situation. To overcome this the Government had assigned of RM12 billion to enhance ICT development strategy in rural areas through the National Broadband Initiative (NBI). Through this initiative, the Ministry of Information Communication and Culture aimed to increase broadband facilities and extend the coverage of internet access in rural areas, and hopefully this would lead to increase in ICT literacy rate.

Despite these efforts, Internet penetration in Malaysia is still very much an urban experience with ICT development in rural community lagging far behind (Wok and Mohamed, 2017). Government statistics compiled by Malaysian Communication and Multimedia Commission (2018) further confirmed this.

It indicated that majority of the Internet users were from the urban areas (70.0%) and only 30% were from the rural areas. Way back in 2008, Donner (2008) had proclaimed that the portability, simplicity and affordability of mobile devices would make them naturally suitable for educational activities and this statement proved to be true as mobile devices are widely used nowadays for education purposes in a variety of settings but its use in rural areas in Malaysia is still very limited due to poor internet coverage.

Regarding attitude towards ICT in rural areas, Halili and Sulaiman's (2018) study on 450 secondary school students from more than 10 rural districts in Malaysia revealed that on the whole the students had moderately positive attitudes toward ICT use for educational purposes. However, they further discovered that facilitating conditions were the most influential determinant of ICT use among rural students. In other words, the main contributing factor towards lack of ICT use was inadequate infrastructure and ICT facilities.

In January 2019, it was reported that 78% of the Malaysian population were active social media users (Statista.com, 2019) and majority of these users were teenagers. It was also earlier mentioned that those living in urban areas had better access to internet facilities than those living in rural areas. This seems to suggest that the use of SNSs for learning purposes would be higher among urban students than rural students. However, this cannot be confirmed without scientific inquiry and as far as I am aware of no study has explored this issue. Thus, to fill this gap in knowledge, one of the primary objectives of this study is to investigate to what extent students from different demographic background (urban vs rural) use SNS for learning informal learning purposes.

SNSs and Informal Learning

Many studies have dealt with the uses of SNSs in learning and learners' opinions toward the use of SNSs for learning. According to Pempek, Yermolayeva, and Calvert (2009), SNSs exposed students to an extensive range of discourse functions and online writing that enhanced critical literacy and language skills, and launched creative deployment of language play. Lai et al., (2013) stated that using technologies in informal settings could be more motivating and engaging than using technologies in school settings as informal learning often engaged students in real life problems and used community resources. Students with a collaborative learning preference had been found to use SNSs more frequently for informal learning (Vivian & Barnes, 2010). Boyd (2008) revealed that high school students used SNSs to connect with other students for homework and group projects. SNSs could also actively encourage online community building, hence, extending learning beyond the boundaries of the classroom (Smith, 2009; Brady, Holcomb and Smith, 2010). According to Tiene (2000), written communication on cyberspace enabled students to take part in discussions at a time convenient to them and articulate their ideas in more carefully thought-out and structured ways. Deng and Tavares (2013) added that web-based discussions could contribute to the development of students' reflective ability and critical thinking skills.

Learning online as well as through SNSs can be considered as an informal way of learning. According to Laskaris (2015) informal learning could give the highest level of learning with the deepest cognitive impact. In the Malaysian context, Hamat, Embi and Abu Hassan (2012) found that university students made use of social media for informal learning. Studies also revealed that students of different age-groups and school-types participate in informal learning activities for different personal reasons. According to Farrah and Melati (2013), Malaysian teenagers had the tendency to use SNSs to gather specific information for the purpose of completing assignments given by their teachers in schools. On the other hand, older age group used SNSs to access information and issues related to challenges associated with later life such as retirement, aging, and health, family and finances (Nimrod, 2013). They further found that when people of different age-groups were exposed to different types of knowledge they would decide on what to believe and practise in a systematic manner. There is still a lack of studies in the Malaysian context that explore the use of SNSs as an informal learning tool. Hence this study will add new knowledge to this area of research.

METHOD

Participants

A convenience sampling approach was used to recruit 799 students from three types of schools located in the Klang Valley and Selangor in Malaysia, i.e. an urban school, a sub-urban school and a rural school. The reason for choosing the three types of schools was to give a convincing representation of the different types of schools found in Malaysia. However, the choice of actual schools depended on the willingness of the principals to allow their students to participate in the study. A brief description of each type of school is given below:

The urban school is situated about 17 km from Kuala Lumpur. It is a secondary co-education school where the medium of instruction for all subjects except English and Bahasa Malaysia is in Mandarin. All of the students come from National Type Chinese School (with Mandarin as the medium of instruction). The performance of students in this school for the PT3/ UPSR (Primary Three/Primary Six) examinations is generally mixed with high and average performing students.

The suburban school is about 30 km from Kuala Lumpur. The students are Malay male and female students who come from national primary schools. The medium of instruction for all subjects except English is in Malay. The performance of students for the PT3/UPSR examinations in this school is mixed ranging from good to below average. Their proficiency in English is generally average. Students in this school generally speak Malay at home, come from middle income families where most of their parents are civil servants, and they live around Putrajaya.

The rural co-education school is about 30 km from Kuala Lumpur. It is a normal type of Malaysian school where students are drawn from the surrounding areas. The medium of instruction for all subjects except English is in Malay. However, the students in this school come from mixed primary school background. Some would have studied their primary education in a National Type Chinese school (with Mandarin as the medium of instruction, some in National Type Tamil schools (with Tamil as the medium of instruction) and some in National school (with Malay as the medium of instruction). The performance of students in this school for the PT3/UPSR examinations is mixed with more low performing students than high performing students.

In addition to that, only Form Two (14 years old) and Form Four (16 years old) students from the three different types of schools were utilised for this study. This was due to the fact that it was not possible to obtain permission from the Ministry of Education to conduct the research on examination classes (i.e. Form Three and Form Five students). Form Two students represented lower secondary school students who were generally assumed to be less exposed to technology than the Form 4 students who represented upper secondary school students. The truth of this assumption would also be investigated in this study.

The sample of this study consists of 50.9% female and 49.1% male, and they were secondary school students of age 14 and age 16 from the three different types of school mentioned above. Table 1 gives a breakdown of students according to the age-groups,, gender and school-types. As shown in the Table the number of suburban and rural students are almost equal for both age-groups whereas the number of urban students are almost one-third less for both age-groups. However, this difference will not affect the validity and reliability of the data since both descriptive and inferential statistical tools were utilised.

Table 1. Breakdown of students from the three different types of school

School	Students Age 14						Students Age 16						Overall Total	Overall %
	F	%	M	%	Total	(%)	F	%	M	%	Total	(%)		
Urban	42	21.8	48	24.7	90	23.3	53	24.8	60	30.3	113	27.4	203	25.4
Suburban	67	34.7	82	42.3	149	38.5	69	32.2	80	40.4	149	36.2	298	37.3
Rural	84	43.5	64	33.0	148	38.2	92	43.0	58	29.3	150	36.4	298	37.3
Total	193	100	194	100	387	100	214	100	198	100	412	100	799	100

Key: F=Female; M=Male

Instrument

In this study, the role of SNSs in teenagers' informal language learning experiences was measured through a questionnaire survey that consists of two sections:

1. Section A elicits demographic information of the students.
2. Section B elicits information from the students regarding their use of SNSs for informal language learning purposes This section consists of 14 items with a four-point likert scale comprising responses that varied from 1 (Never) to 4 (all the time).

Research Procedure

An e-mail was sent to the person-in-charge of each school to ask for permission to conduct the questionnaire survey during school hours. The participants were given approximately 15 minutes to complete the questionnaire survey. Participants were assured of their anonymity and were informed that participation was voluntary and that they would receive a small gift as a token of appreciation for participating in this study. The questionnaire was only distributed to Form Two (14 years old) and Form Four (16 years old) students from the three different types of schools.

Data Analysis

The questionnaire data were analysed using SPSS (Statistical Package for the Social Sciences) version 17. Descriptive and inferential statistical tools were used. The descriptive data analysis involved comparing of mean scores and ranking of items. Inferential statistics analysis involved the use of ANOVA to measure the significance of the difference in mean scores between the students from different school-types.

RESULTS

Analysis of Baseline Data According to Age-Groups and School-Types

Table 2 showed that the four most popular SNSs among the age 14 students are Facebook, WhatsApp, Instagram and WeChat with rankings that vary slightly with school-types.

Table 2. SNSs that age 14 students are members to according to school-types

SNSs frequented by students	Age 14										
	Urban	%	R	Suburban	%	R	Rural	%	R	T	%
Facebook	86	22.7	1	108	17.9	3	125	23	1	319	20.9
WhatsApp	68	17.9	2	132	21.9	1	98	18	3	298	19.5
Twitter	24	6.3	7	64	10.6	5	39	7.2	5	127	8.3
Instagram	53	14	4	110	18.2	2	84	15.4	4	247	16.2
WeChat	68	17.9	2	96	15.9	4	113	21	2	277	18.1
Line	36	9.5	5	26	4.3	7	30	5.5	7	92	6
Tumblr	8	2.1	8	18	3	8	13	2.4	8	39	2.6
Pinterest	8	2.1	8	7	1.2	9	10	1.8	9	25	1.6
Skype	28	7.4	6	43	7.1	6	32	5.9	6	103	6.7
Total no. of respondents to Qs*	379			604			544			1527	

Key: R = Rank; T=Total; Qs=Questionnaires

As shown in Table 3, the SNSs that are most favoured by the age 16 students are WhatApps, Facebook, Instagram, WeChat and Twitter with some variation in ranking according to school-types. Thus, there seems to be not much difference between the preference of the age 14 and age 16 students except that Twitter features more highly in the age 16 group.

For this study, spending less than 5 hours on SNSs per day is considered as spending a reasonable amount of time on social networking and spending more than 5 hours on SNSs is considered as "excessive use". This is calculated based on the assumption that students need 8 hours of sleep per night and 7 hours to attend school leaving them with 9 hours for other activities. If more than 5 hours (i.e.55%) of this remaining time is used for SN, then they are left with only 4 hours (i.e. 45%) for important activities such as taking their meals, doing their homework, other recreational activities and relaxation.

Table 4 revealed that out of the three groups, rural students spend the least among of time on SNSs with 69.6% of them spending less than 5 hours on SNSs whereas the amount of time urban and suburban students spend on SNSs is almost the same (urban 57.3% and suburban 55.8%). We should be concerned with this pattern as we can expect higher usage in future particularly in the case of urban and suburban students where more than 40% of them are already spending more than 5 hours on SNSs.

Table 3. SNSs that age 16 students are members to according to school-types

SNSs frequented by students	Age 16										
	Urban	%	R	Suburban	%	R	Rural	%	R	T	%
Facebook	73	23.3	2	35	9	5	57	16.2	4	165	15.7
WhatsApp	86	27.5	1	99	25.6	2	100	28.5	1	285	27.1
Twitter	33	10.5	5	42	10.9	4	27	7.7	5	102	9.7
Instagram	39	12.5	3	102	26.4	1	74	21.1	2	215	20.5
WeChat	34	10.9	4	58	15	3	72	20.5	3	164	15.6
Line	13	4.2	6	6	1.6	9	6	1.7	7	25	2.4
Tumblr	7	2.2	8	17	4.4	7	2	0.6	8	26	2.5
Pinterest	10	3.2	7	8	2.1	8	2	0.6	8	20	1.9
Skype	18	5.8	5	20	5.2	6	11	3.1	6	49	4.7
Total no. of respondents to Qs*	313			387			351			1051	

Key: R = Rank; T=Total; Qs=Questionnaires

Table 4. Time spent on SNSs per day by the age 14 students according to school-types

Time spent SN	Types of schools							
	Urban	%	Suburban	%	Rural	%	Total	Total %
Less than 2 hours	20	22.5	34	23.1	45	30.4	99	25.8
2 to 5 hours	31	34.8	48	32.7	58	39.2	137	35.7
5+ to 8 hours	12	13.5	28	19.0	26	17.6	66	17.2
More than 8 hours	26	29.2	37	25.2	19	12.8	82	21.3
Total	89	100	147	100	148	100	384	100

With regard to the age 16 students, as shown in Table 5, the difference between the three groups of students are less apparent compared to the age 14 students. Between 69.8% to 65.8% spend less than 5 hours on SNSs which goes to show that for older students there is no rural-urban divide in the amount of time spent on SNSs. However, it noted that more than 30% of all three groups spend more than 5 hours on SNSs which is still something to be concerned about. A comparison across indicated that the age 16 groups spend more time on SNSs then the age 14 groups.

Table 5. Time spent on SNSs per day by the age 16 students according to school-types

Time spent SN	Types of schools							
	Urban	%	Suburban	%	Rural	%	Total	Total %
Less than 2 hours	23	20.5	36	24.2	31	21.1	90	22.1
2 to 5 hours	55	49.1	62	41.6	67	45.6	184	45.1
5+ to 8 hours	23	20.5	30	20.1	28	19.0	81	19.9
More than 8 hours	11	9.9	21	14.1	21	14.3	53	13
Total	112	100	149	100	147	100	408	100

Comparing the Differences in the Usage of SNSs for Informal Learning for Students of Different School-Types According to Age-Groups

Descriptive Statistics

For analysis of use of SNSs for the informal learning, both descriptive and inferential tools were used. For descriptive analysis, a mean score of 2.5 and above is taken as inclining to "often". The learning items showed in Table 6 demonstrated the different ways age 14 students use SNSs for informal learning. The Age 14 urban students have 3 out of 14 items (28.6%) that are inclined to "often". Out of these, only one of them (33.3.1%) are on learning of English. As for the suburban students, 9 out of 14 items (64.3%) are inclined to "often". Out of these items, 4 items (44.4%) are on the learning of English. Regarding the rural students, 8 out of 14 (57.1%) are inclined to "often" and 4 out of these (50%) are on the use SNSs for learning English.

Thus, the findings demonstrated that suburban and rural students are more inclined to use of SNSs for informal learning (around 60%) and out of these about 50% are inclined to use SNSs for learning English. The use of SNSs for informal learning in the case of urban students is rather low, only about 30%.

Table 6. The usage of SNSs for informal language learning purposes according to school-types (age 14) Key: 4 = "all the time", 3 = "often", 2 = "sometimes" and 1 = "never".

Student learning (age 14)	Urban			Suburban			Rural		
	N	Mean	R	N	Mean	R	N	Mean	R
1.Gain new knowledge	90	2.62	1	149	2.98	1	147	2.99	1
2.Learn from communicating with friends	90	2.31	5	149	2.87	2	147	2.63	3
3.Discuss lessons with friends	90	2.52	3	149	2.83	3	148	2.74	2
4.Give you a chance to communicate in English	90	2.57	2	149	2.82	4	147	2.67	4
5.Form a study group to discuss homework	90	1.89	10	149	2.72	5	146	1.85	14
6.Provide information related to your studies	90	2.28	7	149	2.70	6	148	2.57	6
7.Improve English through chatting with others	90	2.29	6	149	2.64	7	147	2.51	8
8.Improve English by reading articles or other people's writing	90	2.13	9	148	2.59	8	145	2.57	6
9.Learn new words in English	90	2.46	4	149	2.52	9	148	2.60	5
10.Use an online dictionary to find new words in English	90	2.24	8	149	2.18	10	147	2.37	9
11.Learn from communicating with teachers	90	1.82	11	149	2.07	11	146	2.03	11
12.Learn how to pronounce English words from an online dictionary	90	1.77	12	148	2.03	12	148	2.03	11
13.Form a group to chat in English	90	1.58	13	148	2.03	12	147	2.37	9
14.Learn words in foreign language	90	2.14	7	149	1.96	14	148	2.03	11

The learning items showed in Table 7 demonstrated the different ways age 16 students use SNSs for informal learning. The Age 16 urban students have 7 out of 14 items (50%) that are inclined to "often". Out of these, only 3 of them (33.3.1%) are on learning of English. As for the suburban students, 11 out of 14 items (78.6%) are inclined to "often". Out of these, five items (45.5%) are on the learning of English. With regard to the rural students, 10 out of 14 (71.4%) are inclined to "often" and 5 out of these (50%) are on the use SNSs for learning English.

The findings clearly demonstrated that over 70% suburban and rural students use SNSs for informal learning and about 50% are inclined to use SNSs for learning English, even higher than the age 14 groups. The use of SNSs for learning in the case of urban students is much lower, only about 50% for informal learning and about 30% for learning English. However, the percentage is much higher than for the age 14 group.

Table 7. The usage of SNSs for informal language learning purposes according to school-types (age 14)
Key: 4 = "all the time", 3 = "often", 2 = "sometimes" and 1 = "never".

Student learning (age 16)	Urban			Suburban			Rural		
	N	Mean	R	N	Mean	R	N	Mean	R
1.Gain new knowledge	113	2.91	1	147	3.15	1	150	3.15	1
2.Learn from communicating with friends	112	2.66	4	147	3.10	2	149	2.81	4
3.Discuss lessons with friends	113	2.80	3	147	3.08	3	149	2.85	3
4.Give you a chance to communicate in English	112	2.88	2	147	3.07	4	150	2.88	2
5.Form a study group to discuss homework	112	2.23	10	147	3.03	5	150	2.68	6
6.Provide information related to your studies	112	2.56	6	147	3.03	5	148	2.66	8
7.Improve English through chatting with others	112	2.50	7	147	2.88	7	149	2.68	6
8.Improve English by reading articles or other people's writing	112	2.46	8	145	2.76	8	145	2.59	9
9.Learn new words in English	112	2.65	5	147	2.71	9	149	2.72	5
10.Use an online dictionary to find new words in English	112	2.34	9	147	2.63	10	149	2.56	10
11.Learn from communicating with teachers	112	2.05	12	147	2.51	11	148	2.24	12
12.Learn how to pronounce English words from an online dictionary	112	1.96	13	145	2.38	12	149	2.36	11
13.Form a group to chat in English	112	1.74	14	147	2.27	13	147	2.03	14
14.Learn words in foreign language	112	2.09	11	145	2.17	14	149	2.05	13

Inferential Statistics

Inferential statistics were used to support or refute the findings from the descriptive analysis. Inferential statistical data analysis was undertaken using ANOVA to identify the statistically significant results. Most research studies use a cut-off of 5% (that is the p-value is less than 0.05). This is the p-value that is used for this research study. In view of that only significant findings were displayed and school-types with significantly higher mean scores were underlined.

Table 8. Comparison of mean scores across school-types for age 14 students

Students age 14	Urban			Suburban			Rural					
	N	Mean	SD	N	Mean	SD	N	Mean	SD	df	F	P-value
1.Gain new knowledge	90	2.62	.787	149	2.98	.881	147	2.99	.721	2	6.70	.001
2.Learn from communicating with friends	90	2.31	.956	149	2.87	.905	147	2.63	.907	2	10.27	.000
3.Discuss lessons with friends	90	2.52	.838	149	2.83	.926	148	2.74	.786	2	3.73	.025
5.Form a study group to discuss homework	90	1.89	.953	149	2.72	.959	147	2.37	.861	2	22.80	.000
6.Provide information related to your studies	90	2.28	.765	149	2.70	.794	148	2.57	.793	2	8.06	.000
7.Improve English through chatting with others	90	2.29	.902	149	2.64	.953	146	2.51	.832	2	4.24	.015
8. Improve English by reading articles and other's people writing	89	2.13	.894	148	2.59	.946	145	2.57	.941	2	7.82	.000
13. Form a group to chat in English	90	1.56	.823	148	2.03	.954	146	1.85	.897	2	7.63	.001

Table 9. Comparison of mean scores across school-types for age 16 students

Students age 16	Urban			Suburban			Rural					
	N	Mean	SD	N	Mean	SD	N	Mean	SD	df	F	P-value
2. Learn from communicating with friends	112	2.66	.855	147	3.10	.894	149	2.81	.852	2	8.62	.000
3. Discuss lessons with friends	113	2.80	.888	147	3.07	.892	149	2.85	.833	2	3.92	.021
5. Form a study group to discuss homework	112	2.23	.958	147	3.03*	.925	150	2.68	.936	2	23.22	.000
6. Provide information related to your studies	112	2.56	.720	147	3.08	.848	148	2.66	.822	2	16.16	.000
7. Improve English through chatting with others	112	2.50	.794	147	2.88	.872	149	2.68	.894	2	6.43	.002
8. Improve English by reading articles and other's people writing	112	2.46	.879	145	2.76	.907	145	2.59	.961	2	3.50	.031
10. Use an online dictionary to find new words in English	112	2.34	.812	147	2.63	.838	149	2.56	.954	2	3.59	.028
11. Learn from communicating with teachers	112	2.05	.858	147	2.51	.932	148	2.24	.770	2	9.37	.000
12. Learn how to pronounce English words from an online dictionary	112	1.96	.859	145	2.38	.958	149	2.36	.901	2	7.97	.000
13 Form a group to chat in English	112	1.74	.791	145	2.17	.986	147	2.03	.883	2	7.18	.001

* For item 5, mean scores of suburban students also significantly higher than that of rural students.

The inferential analysis for the Age 14 students as shown in Table 8 revealed that 8 items out of the 14 items displayed significant differences. 3 of these items are specifically on the learning of English. The mean scores of age 14 suburban students are significantly higher than the urban students for all 8 items and the mean scores of age 14 rural students are significantly higher than the urban students for 6 items. These findings confirmed that of the descriptive analysis in demonstrating that the use of SNSs for informal learning is clearly less in age 14 urban students compared to the other two groups.

The inferential analysis for the Age 16 students is more complex than the age 14 students. As shown in Table 9. 10 items out of the 14 items displayed significant differences. 5 of them are specifically on the learning of English. The mean scores of age 16 suburban students are significantly higher than the urban students for all 10 items. 5 of these items are on the learning of English. However, the mean scores of age 16 rural students are significantly higher than the urban students for only 3 items and two of these items are on the learning of English. The findings further revealed that the mean scores of the suburban students are significantly higher than the rural students for 4 items – all not on the learning of English. These findings supported the findings of the descriptive data in confirming that the use SNSs for informal learning is higher among suburban students and rural students than the urban students. Besides, it further revealed that rural students used SNSs for informal learning less than suburban students.

Ranking

With regard to the top five rankings, as shown in Table 6, the "gain new knowledge" item has the highest ranking for all age 14 groups suggesting that students see this as the most important thing they can gain from the SNSs. The next four items for the suburban group are all inclined towards learning through interaction with others suggesting that they view the social interaction online as very beneficial. With regard to the rural and urban students, their items 2 to 5 are also inclined to learning through interaction though not in the same order as the suburban students, except for one item i.e. item 9 which suggests that these two groups believe that using SNSs help them to learn new English words too.

With regard to the bottom five items, the three common items are items 11,12 and 13 with some slight variation in rankings. The overall pattern shows less preference for learning with teachers, group learning and also learning languages alone.

The pattern for age 16 students are somewhat similar to that of the age 14 students. The "gain new knowledge" item also has the highest ranking and the next four items for the suburban group are all also inclined towards learning through interaction. In addition to that items 2 to 5 items for the rural and urban students are also inclined to learning through interaction except for item 9.

With regard to the bottom five items, there are five common items for all age 16 groups except for one item in the case of urban students. On the whole the pattern indicates less preference for learning with teachers, group learning and also learning languages alone like in the case of age 14 students.

OVERALL DISCUSSION

This study investigated the use of SNSs for learning purposes by Malaysian secondary students of two different age-groups and three school-types. Four research questions were addressed in the study. First question looked into the SNSs patterns that Malaysian secondary school students preferred. The findings revealed that there is not much difference between the types of SNSs that are popular among students age 14 and students age 16 except for some variation in rankings. Generally, all students chose Facebook, WhatsApp, Instagram and WeChat as the first four choices except twitter features more prominently in the age 16 students. This is in line with the findings of GlobalWebIndex (2015) which suggests that there is no apparent difference in patterns of use between between students of different age-groups.

The second research question explored the amount of time the different categories of students spent on SNSs to get an idea of the extent of use. The study revealed that about 70% of the age 14 rural students spent less than 5 hours on SNSs whereas the percentage is between 55 to 58% in the case of the urban and suburban students. With regard to the age 16 students, the difference between the three groups of students are less apparent. This suggests that although accessibility to internet is less in the case of rural areas as pointed out by Wok and Mohamed (2017), older students in rural have more opportunity to access to internet. Despite lower usage among age 14 rural students, this pattern of usage in general is something to observe as it will lead to higher usage in future and this may have detrimental effects.

The third research question investigated to what extent the different categories of students use SNSs for informal learning and the types of learning they focus on. The findings revealed the used of SNSs for learning for informal learning is much higher in suburban students and rural students than urban students. In the case of age 14 the use of SNS for informal learning is highest among suburban students followed by rural students and the lowest among urban students. The pattern is somewhat similar in the case of age 16 students. In the case of learning of English it would also appear that suburban and rural students used the SNSs for that purpose more than urban students. These findings are very interesting and it is only possible to make some postulations regarding this at this stage. It is my conjecture that urban students are exposed to many opportunities to enhance their learning including attending tuition classes and out of the class learning activities. Hence, they do not utilise the SNSs much for learning and use it more for social communication purposes. In the case of the suburban students they are less exposed to learning opportunities and hence they depend on the SNSs to help them to learn. Likewise in the case of rural students but in this case to a lesser extent because they have less access to the internet. However further research needs to be undertaken to investigate the truth of this conjecture.

The last research question investigated whether there were any differences in usage of SNSs for informal learning between the students from the three school-types. The findings revealed almost similar findings. Generally all groups felt that using SNSs to gain new knowledge was most important followed by learning through interactions and learning new words in English. The least preferred types of learning for all groups were learning alone, learning through the help of a teacher and learning through a group chat. However, there seem to be less preference for activities that have to be performed alone or with the support of the teachers. These findings corroborated previous findings (Boyd, 2008; Smith, 2009; Brady, Holcomb and Smith, 2010) that show SNSs can be used for informal learning for a variety of purposes.

IMPLICATIONS AND CONCLUSION

In conclusion it is possible to say that Malaysian students age 14 and 16 from three school-types have used SNSs for informal learning to a reasonable extent and that their involvement in SNSs has beneficial effects. This study has identified the types of learning these students are involved in and they encompass a variety of learning activities: gaining new knowledge seem to be considered most important followed by search for knowledge and learning through interactions and learning new English words. However, the students show lower preference for activities that involve self-learning and teacher involvement.

The differences between students from different school-types seem not be obvious in terms of learning types and preferences

Social networking has become an essential part of life for most Malaysian secondary school students and that it serves not only as a primary tool for communication and socialization but also a tool in assisting students' education development outside the classroom. The findings of this research can help teachers and parents understand how lower secondary and upper secondary students from different types of schools learn after classes. The fact that suburban and rural students seem to use the SNSs more frequently for informal learning is encouraging. This strongly suggests that the government should intensify its efforts in improving ICT infrastructure in rural areas so that their opportunities to learn through ICT including SNSs can increase and help rural students improve their ICT skills which were found to be lacking (Umar and Jalil, 2012).

Findings from this research study can also help school teachers design meaningful activities involving the use of SNSs for learning purposes knowing what learning activities the students preferred. Apart from that, this research may also help to expand methods for teaching languages in classroom contexts since the findings show that informal online engagement leads to successful language learning. According to the Global Information Technology Report 2015 by Dutta et al. (2015), Malaysia was ranked 32nd out of 143 countries listed in the Networked Readiness Index 2015, and it is the only country in Asia that was featured in the top 60. The report also revealed that the internet access in schools was ranked 34th out of 143. This clearly indicates that it will not be difficult for Malaysian schools to harness social networking as an educational tool.

Although this research has successfully achieved its objectives, there are unavoidable limitations that need to be mentioned here. It has to be admitted that there is a possibility of sample selection bias in this study. The study has targeted a fairly narrow demographic segment, namely, secondary school students (age 14 and 16) from three schools located in the Klang Valley and Selangor. An earlier study (Ng et al. 2018) which explored patterns of use of SNSs for informal learning between male and female students of the same sample population did provide insights into their patterns of use but exploring other variables such as different ethnic origins and different social economic status will further enrich the findings. However, it is not possible to explore all of them within the scope of this study. It is possible that this narrow focus may have limited the generalisability of the results to Malaysian school population as a whole. Hence, for future research, it is recommended that a more extensive study covering more variables and wider demographic segments be undertaken.

ACKNOWLEDGMENT

This paper was part of a research project (Code SK-2015-003) funded by the Malaysian Communications and Multimedia Commission (MCMC).

REFERENCES_

Bond, B. J. (2009). He posted, she posted: Gender differences in self-disclosure on social networking sites. *Rocky Mountain Communication Review*, 6(2), 29–37.

Boyd, D. M. (2008). *Taken out of context: American teen sociality in networked publics. (Ph.D. Dissertation)*. Berkeley, CA: School of Information, University of California-Berkeley; Retrieved from https://www.danah.org/papers/TakenOutOfContext.pdf

Boyd, D. M., & Ellison, N. B. (2007). Social network sites: Definition, history, and scholarship. *Journal of Computer-Mediated Communication, 13*(1), 210–230. doi:10.1111/j.1083-6101.2007.00393.x

Brady, K., Holcomb, L., & Smith, B. (2010). The use of alternative social networking sites in higher educational settings: A case study of the e-learning benefits of Ning in education. *Journal of Interactive Online Learning, 9*(2), 151–170.

Briansolis. (2010). The age of social networks. Retrieved from https://www.briansolis.com/2010/03/the-age-of-social-networks/

Bruestle, P., Haubner, D., Schinzel, B., Holthaus, M., Remmele, B., Schirmer, D., & Reips, U. D. (2009). Doing E-learning/doing gender? Examining the relationship between students' gender concepts and E-learning technology. *Proceedings of the 5th European Symposium on Gender & ICT Digital Cultures: Participation - Empowerment – Diversity, University of Bremen.*

Chun, W. S. M. (2013). An exploration of gender differences in the use of social networking and knowledge management tools. *Journal of Information Technology Management, 24*(2), 20–31.

ComScore. (2011). It's a social world: Social networking leads as top online activity globally, accounting for 1 in every 5 online minutes. Retrieved from https://www.comscore.com/Insights/Press-Releases/2011/12/Social-Networking-Leads-as-Top-Online-Activity-Globally

Cuadrado-García, M., Ruiz-Molina, M. E., & Montoro-Pons, J. D. (2010). Are there gender differences in e-learning use and assessment? Evidence from an interuniversity online project in Europe. *Procedia: Social and Behavioral Sciences, 2*(2), 367–371. doi:10.1016/j.sbspro.2010.03.027

Deng, L., & Tavares, N. (2013). From moodle to Facebook: Exploring students' motivation and experiences in online communities. *Computer Educ, 68*, 167–176. doi:10.1016/j.compedu.2013.04.028

Donner, J. (2008). Research approaches to mobile use in the developing world: a review of the literature. *The Information Society, 24*(3), 140–159. doi:10.1080/01972240802019970

Dutta, S., Geiger, T., & Lanvin, B. (2015). The global information technology report 2015. Retrieved from http://www3.weforum.org/docs/WEF_Global_IT_Report_2015.pdf

Yusop, F. D., & Sumari, M. (2013). The use of social media technologies among Malaysian youth. *Procedia: Social and Behavioral Sciences, 103*, 1204–1209.

GlobalWebIndex. (2015). Quarterly report on the latest trends in social networking. Retrieved March 2018 from https://www.globalwebindex.net/hs-fs/hub/304927/file-2812772150 pdf/Reports/ GWI_Social_Summary_Report_Q1_2015.pdf

Griffith, S., & Liyanage, L. (2008). An introduction to the potential of social networking sitesin education. *Proceedings of the Second Emerging Technologies Conference 2008. Australia: Wollongong.*

Halili, S. H., & Sulaiman, H. (2018). (article in press). Factors influencing the rural students' acceptance of using ICT for educational purposes. *Kasetsart Journal of Social Sciences*, 1–6.

Hamat, A., Embi, M. A., & Abu Hassan, H. (2012). The use of social networking sites among Malaysian university students. *International Education Studies*, 5(3), 56–66. doi:10.5539/ies.v5n3p56

Hosseini, S. J. F., Niknami, M., & Chizari, M. (2009). To determine the challenges in the application of ICTs by the agricultural extension service in Iran. *Journal of Agricultural Extension and Rural Development, 1*(1), 292e299.

Joiner, R., Gavin, J., Brosnan, M., Cromby, J., Gregory, H., Guiller, J., ... Moon, A. (2012). Gender, internet experience, internet identification and internet anxiety: A ten year follow-up. *Cyberpsychology, Behavior, and Social Networking*, 15(7), 370–372. doi:10.1089/cyber.2012.0033 PMID:22690795

Kirkup, G. (2010). Academic blogging: Academic practice and academic identity. *London Review of Education*, 8(1), 75–84. doi:10.1080/14748460903557803

Kirkup, G., & von Prümmer, C. (1997). Distance education for European women: The treats and opportunities of new educational forms and media. *European Journal of Women's Studies*, 4(1), 39–62. doi:10.1177/135050689700400104

Lai, K.-W., Khaddage, F., & Knezek, G. (2013). Student technology experiences in formal and informal learning in WCCE 2013: Learning while we are connected. *Proceedings of the IFIP Computers in Education 2013 World Conference*, 290-290. Torun, Poland: Nicolaus Copernicus University Press.

Laskaris, J. (2015). 6 Benefits of informal learning. *Talentslms.com*. Retrieved from https://www.talentlms.com/blog/6-benefits-of-informal-learning/

Lenhart, A., Madden, M., & Hitlin, P. (2010). Social media and mobile internet use among teens and young adults. *Washington, D.C.: Pew Internet & American Life Project*. Retrieved from https://files.eric.ed.gov/fulltext/ED525056.pdf

Liu, C. Y., & Yu, C. P. (2013). Can Facebook use induce well-being? *Cyberpsychology, Behavior, and Social Networking*, 16(9), 674–678. doi:10.1089/cyber.2012.0301 PMID:24028138

Livingstone, D. W. (1999). Exploring the icebergs of adult learning: Findings of the first Canadian survey of informal learning practices. *Nall Working Paper No:10*. Centre for the Study of Education and Work, OISE/UT, Toronto. Retrieved from https://tspace.library.utoronto.ca/bitstream/1807/2724/2/10

Malaysian Communications and Multimedia Commission. (2017). Internet users survey 2017. Retrieved from https://www.mcmc.gov.my/skmmgovmy/media/General/pdf/MCMC-Internet-Users-Survey-2017.pdf

Malaysian Communications and Multimedia Commission. (2018). Internet users survey 2018. Retrieved from https://www.mcmc.gov.my/skmmgovmy/media/General/pdf/Internet-Users-Survey-2018.pdf

Manago, A. M., Taylor, T., & Greenfield, P. M. (2012). Me and my 400 friends: the anatomy of college students' Facebook networks, their communication patterns, and well-being. *Developmental Psychology*, 48(2), 369–380. doi:10.1037/a0026338 PMID:22288367

Marsick, V. J., & Watkins, K. E. (2001). Informal and incidental learning. *New Directions for Adult and Continuing Education*, *89*(89), 25–34. doi:10.1002/ace.5

Mazman, S. G., & Usluel, Y. K. (2011). Gender differences in using social networks. *The Turkish Online Journal of Educational Technology*, *10*(2), 133–139.

Misra, N., Dangi, S., & Patel, S. (2015). Gender differences in usage of social networking sites and perceived online social support on psychological well-being of youth. *The International Journal of Indian Psychology*, *3*(1), 63–74.

Ng, L. S., Thang, S. M., & Mohd, N. N. (2018). The usage of social networking sites for informal learning: a comparative study between Malaysia students of different gender and age group. [IJCALLT]. *International Journal of Computer-Assisted Language Learning and Teaching*, *8*(4), 76–88. doi:10.4018/IJCALLT.2018100106

Nimrod, G. (2013). Applying gerontographics in the study of older Internet users. *Journal of Audience & Perception Study*, *10*(2), 46–64.

Pempek, T. A., Yermolayeva, Y. A., & Calvert, S. L. (2009). College students' social networking experiences on Facebook. *Journal of Applied Developmental Psychology*, *30*(3), 227–238. doi:10.1016/j.appdev.2008.12.010

Pew Research Center. (2018). Social media use in 2018. Retrieved from http://www.pewinternet.org/2018/03/01/social-media-use-in-2018/

Selwyn, N. (2007). An investigation in undergraduates' academic use of the Internet. *Active Learning in Higher Education*, *9*(1), 11–22. doi:10.1177/1469787407086744

Selwyn, N. (2009). Faceworking: Exploring students' education-related use of "Facebook". *Learning, Media, and Technology*, *34*(2), 157–174. doi:10.1080/17439880902923622

Smith, B. V. (2009). *Use of online educational social networking in a school environment*. (Unpublished master's thesis). North Carolina State University, Raleigh, NC. Retrieved from http://www.ncolr.org/jiol/issues/pdf/9.2.4.pdf

Social Media Today. (2016). Gender-specific behaviors on social media and what they mean for online communications. Retrieved from https://www.socialmediatoday.com/social-networks/gender-specific-behaviors-social-media-and-what-they-mean-online-communications

Sproutsocial. (2017). The Q1 2017 Sprout social index-The social generations: Millennials ask, Gen X buys & Baby Boomers observe. Retrieved from https://sproutsocial.com/insights/data/q1-2017/

Statista.com. (2019) Retrieved from https://www.statista.com/statistics/883712/malaysia-social-media-penetration/

Tiene, C. D. (2000). Online discussions: A survey of advantages and disadvantages compared to face-to-face discussions. *Journal of Educational Multimedia and Hypermedia*, *9*(4), 371–384.

Umar, I. N., & Jalil, N. A. (2012). ICT skills, practices, and barriers of its use among secondary school students. *Procedia: Social and Behavioral Sciences*, *46*, 5672–5676. doi:10.1016/j.sbspro.2012.06.494

Vivian, R., & Barnes, A. (2010). Social networking: From living technology to learning technology? In C.H. Steel, M. J. Keppell, P. Gerbic, & S. Housego (Eds.), Curriculum, Technology, & Transformation for an unknown Future. Proceedings of Ascilite Sydney 2010, 1007–1019.

Vserv. (2015). Smartphone user Persona report (SUPR) 2015. Retrieved from https://www.vserv.com/vserv-unveils-first-smartphone-user-persona-report-supr-malaysia/

Wok, S., & Mohamed, S. (2017). Internet and social media in Malaysia: Development, challenges and potentials. *The Evolution of Media Communication*, 45-64.

Yusop, F. D., & Sumari, M. (2013). The use of social media technologies among Malaysian youth. *Procedia: Social and Behavioral Sciences, 103*, 1204–1209. doi:10.1016/j.sbspro.2013.10.448

Zulkhairi, M. D., Azizah, A., Abdul Razak, A., & Rafidah, A. R. (2010, November). Community informatics: Success factors at a rural community telecentre. *Proceedings of rural ICT development 3rd national conference on rural ICT development,* UUM Sintok, Malaysia. Retrieved from http:// www.moe.gov.my/userfiles/file/PPP/Preliminary-Blueprint-Eng.pdf

This research was previously published in Recent Developments in Technology-Enhanced and Computer-Assisted Language Learning; pages 30-47, copyright year 2020 by Information Science Reference (an imprint of IGI Global).

Chapter 18
The Use of Social Media in Facilitating Participatory Design:
A Case Study of Classroom Design

Fatimah Alsaif
Victoria University of Wellington, New Zealand

Brenda Vale
Victoria University of Wellington, New Zealand

ABSTRACT

This chapter examines the effectiveness of using social media as an aid to primary school students participating in the design of their classroom interior layout. It describes two different attempts to do this that achieved varying degrees of success. Where a blog and Facebook page were set up to provide a virtual space for classroom design to happen, and despite teachers' expressed enthusiasm for involving students in the design of their classroom layout, very few participants resulted. However, one school successfully used the virtual space to show the work of the children and this example is described in the chapter. Social media was of more use in a second example where it formed an additional channel of communication between the researcher in the role of architect and the students. However, here it built on face-to-face communication, suggesting social media can aid in participatory design but is not a substitute for the latter.

INTRODUCTION

Social media is fast spreading among individuals with the result that people all around the world in various environments are becoming connected. People in their home, work, on the move, and even walking along the streets are checking their social media accounts and communicating with others to get the latest news, work on unfinished jobs, get in touch with relatives and friends, or just for fun and entertainment. Officially this social media is defined as a set of applications permitted by the Internet that allow individuals to gather in virtual locations, communicate easily, and share material (Reyes &

DOI: 10.4018/978-1-6684-7123-4.ch018

Finken, 2012; Picaza-Vela et al 2016). Social media comes in different forms, such as mobile communication through Short Message Service (SMS) and picture messaging; social networking and media sharing sites as in Facebook, Flickr, and YouTube; or open blogging tools as in Wordpress and Tumbler (Hagen & Robertson, 2010). This chapter looks at how some of these applications can be used to enable users to become part of the building design process for learning environments—normally known as participatory design (DiSalvo et al, 2017).

At present, people do not need specialized knowledge to use the Internet, although they still need to become familiar with certain basic operations. This has parallels with the idea behind participatory design, where the end users become involved early in the design process and, in the case of a building, well before any construction starts on site. Just as instructions for using the Internet are normally given in the form of a manual or on-screen instructions that are easy to use, the use of online media in participatory design needs precise and sensibly designed tools that create environments that are attractive to their potential users. Another thing to consider in using social media in enabling participatory design is the openness of discussion within social media open forums (Näkki & Antikainen, 2008). The aim behind using social media for participatory design is to increase the quality of products or services through approaches where designers and developers can communicate with and involve the users (Johnson, 2013), and some of this may need to be confidential. This means careful setting up of social media situations.

In the research described in this chapter, participatory design was not just tested and observed in the design of primary schools and classrooms in New Zealand but social media in the form of a blog set up for the purpose was also evaluated to see if it was an aid to participatory design. The aim was to see whether having a blog would encourage more communication between school users, particularly children, and architects. This need for better communication came out of an earlier survey conducted to find out how teachers in New Zealand schools and local architects regarded participatory design (Alsaif, 2015). Both parties agreed teachers and children should be involved in classroom design but felt the need for better means of communication between school users and architects. This chapter describes the process of building on this knowledge and the attempts to involve the use of social media.

BACKGROUND

Participatory Design in Learning Environments

Ideally design should be a social process that involves communication, negotiation, and agreement, and the design process itself should be as important as the finished product (Clancy et al, 2015; Zhang and Zhang, 2010). As products, including buildings, are designed in order to be used by people, designing should involve both creating the product and setting the rules for how it could be used. As a result, the designer needs to understand the language of the product (materiality, tectonics), and the users should understand how to use it or give clear descriptions of what they need (Brandt, 2006).

There is little research into teacher involvement in the design of classrooms and schools. However, some teachers and educators have participated in designing their learning environments, ranging from a kindergarten to a high school. Helen West (2007) was a primary curriculum adviser at the Inner Western Region of The Catholic Education Office in Sydney, where a team of kindergarten teachers started a programme for establishing kindergartens in inner city schools in Sydney. One of the important factors they dealt with was designing appropriate learning spaces in these, given that potential child users would be from different cultural and linguistic backgrounds. Teachers were interested in adapting play based learning and using it as the basis for the design of the learning environments. Both the educators' team and the teachers involved wanted the spaces to be flexible, accessible to all, and reflect student needs. For example, partition walls were designed to be easily moveable, so as to make larger or smaller spaces as needed. The decision was made to remove a lot of the conventional furniture to create larger, furniture free spaces inside classrooms. Bookshelves were used as partitions or dividers between different activity corners. The aim was to design settings to support interaction between peers, quiet study, and reading and listening activities.

Participatory Design and Social Media

The variety of social media applications available for public use offer methods that could be integrated in participatory design (Lukyanenko et al, 2016). Reyes (2012) indicated how a traditional method for participatory design could be interpreted and used with Facebook. His project involved the design of a mobile app that would encourage the public to become active in stabilizing and developing heritage photographs, and making these available for comments from other people as well as additional contributions to the site. The project started with several meetings that involved Reyes, the project leader, a supervisor from the research facility, and a communication advisor. The main aims were first to establish a media site using Facebook, chosen because of its popularity and ease of access. There were 18 participants including the project owners, designers and users. The Facebook workshop had a number of different phases. The critique phase allowed participants to give their opinions about the heritage photo service and to suggest improvements. There was also a fantasy phase where participants were asked to imagine and describe their ideal service, and finally an implementation phase where the best ideas from the fantasy phase as selected by the participants were improved and developed into the final service design. The study found that using Facebook enhanced the traditional methods of participatory design, especially as Facebook was well known and consequently most participants did not have to spend time becoming familiarized with different media and methods. Social media in this case also allowed more people to participate as they could access the site from home, rather than in a meeting situation, such as in typical charette type participatory design (Hanington and Martin, 2012, p.58-9). With the appropriate design of the site participants could also remain anonymous. Not having to share opinions face to face, as in traditional participatory design methods, could also encourage people to participate. Additionally, through Facebook participants could receive feedback about their work and also easily be informed about the progress of the design process. The only disadvantage seemed to be that participants were not necessarily able to meet other participants, which could cause them to miss the feeling of being in a community involved in a process of change.

Another study involving online participatory design is the open web lab Owela. This is an online media site created to enable users, customers, developers, and stakeholders to complete the design of anything they collectively desire in a participatory manner. Owela is considered to be social media, as it offers interaction between members of a society regardless of time and place. It also provides a set of tools and methods to facilitate participatory design through discovering the needs and experiences of potential users. Over 40 different types of participatory design have used this web lab and examples of completed projects include user driven software development, a consumer study of cloud software, generating ideas and concept evaluation, and public codesign of a multicultural web community called Monimos. In these projects, consumers and citizens communicated and interacted with companies and researchers to create new products or services such as a city tourism service. Most of the examples focused on the early stages of the innovation process, such as collecting information about user needs, creating ideas, and assessing new product and service concepts. Users can participate from anywhere, as they only need Internet access and basic knowledge of using social software and this saves user time and effort. With Owela, designers and developers can reach large numbers of users quickly and easily. Owela also allows different degrees of involvement as the relationships and communication through the media site can be long or short term. However, Owela does not guarantee the production of successful designs, as this will depend on the aims of each project and the effectiveness of communication between participants. Users of Owela also found this particular social media site useful, as they had the chance to obtain feedback from users and developers without having to attend direct feedback sessions (Kaasinen et al., 2013).

Participatory Design in Schools using the Internet

There are two websites that encourage more user involvement in designing learning environments and that also give tips on redesigning learning spaces. The "Classroom Architect", provides tools to help teachers with this. The first is a set of tools with which to draw the floor plan of the classroom and arrange its furniture in different layouts to achieve the best use of space. The tools provided can only draw rectangular or square floor plans, which could be a disadvantage for classrooms of different shapes, such as the not uncommon L shape. Teachers can use the furniture from the template provided on the website or draw their own furniture. However, the shapes of furniture in the template are also limited to being square, rectangular or circular. The first section in the "Classroom Architect" also gives some instruction on using the tools.

The second section provides information on how learning environments affect learning outcomes. It explains there is no ultimate design for classrooms, as each should be designed according to its students' needs and nature. A group of elements for successful classroom design are mentioned, such as having neutral colours for walls (grey, off white, beige), preventing overcrowded corners as these can result in behaviour issues, and creating different zones that serve different learning styles, such as individual and group work. The third section provides examples of classroom floor plans to instruct teachers about layout possibilities, although this link was not working at the time of writing this chapter ("Classroom architect", 2008).

The other website is linked to the "Edutopia" website, which provides more general tips about what works for education. This is written by David Bill, a designer and educator. One of the topics gives eight tips and tricks for teachers when redesigning or reorganising their classrooms. The first is to involve the students, as they are the main users of the classroom environment. Bill (2014) suggests this could take different forms, such as seeking out visual inspiration by looking for photos of classrooms from magazines or on the Internet. As another suggestion for involving students is printing the existing classroom floor plan at large scale and then allowing students to comment on how they feel about everything in their classroom. His second tip is to use research and brainstorming methods in the redesigning process. These could involve subjects such as how to create collaborative space in the classroom. The third tip is to organize volunteers to help the teacher in the participatory design process, while the fourth is to remove all unnecessary items from the classroom, and the fifth to define any new materials and settings that are required before starting the classroom redesign. The sixth tip is to recycle and reuse any available materials. For example, plastic containers from the grocery store could be used as storage units. The seventh tip is organizing the learning tools in the classroom according to their frequency of use. Colours or labels on the storage units could be used to identify each set of tools by type and how often it is used. For the last tip, Bill provided a list of links to additional resources teachers could use in their process of classroom redesign. These resources included books, photos and information about selected educational projects, together with a number of guidelines for designing learning environments.

Children, as users of schools as well as teachers, also have the right to participate in designing learning environments. Researchers claim children have good potential for participating in design processes, and that this should be a recommendation (Nesset & Large, 2004). Child and developmental psychologists (De Winter et al., 1999) claim that children can face difficulties in completing the tasks and activities set them and argue that these difficulties are related to the children's environments, as these offer them insufficient room for learning and developing. They suggest some of these problems could be prevented by enabling children to participate in designing the environments they use for learning. They also state the social participation of children affects their mental health and involving children as active components of their environments in addition to letting them manage and arrange events in their lives could contribute towards giving them confidence and mastery over their lives and health. Long term use of dependent environments may lead children to develop problems in defining their abilities to complete actions responsibly. When children are involved in decision making, they learn, gain experience and end up with confidence and self respect. Children may also have thoughts that adults might not conceive because of the practical experience of the latter of living in many different environments but this also means that some of the ideas of children could be impossible to implement. Thus, the recommendation is to limit the expectations of children before they start to generate ideas, by providing a brief description of the project and the design process (Nesset & Large, 2004). Ignoring children's participation in designing and planning their built environments makes them feel that they have no control over their learning spaces, and consequently, they may not be able to move freely in their built environment. Thus the environment may limit their actions and potential (Said, 2007). Studies show that school designs that involve student participation, through using children's imaginations in the design process, end up with good, innovative ideas not considered by either architects or teachers (Bland, 2009). Architects and designers also need recognize the importance of children's experiences and thought processes in order to be able to design effective learning spaces. Designing is, in the end, all about the attitudes of users to built environments (Nair & Fielding, 2007).

Participatory Design in New Zealand schools: A Case for using Social Media

In New Zealand, there are almost no studies of classroom layouts. Rather, the New Zealand studies on learning environments have focused on environmental issues such as acoustics, natural lighting, fresh air, and temperature. Even the Ministry of Education's learning studios pilot project only dealt with the building shell and failed to focus on furnishing these environments and creating good internal layouts. In general, it seems there is less care about the internal layout in New Zealand classroom studies. From observations made in earlier research into learning environments in primary schools (Alsaif, 2011), teachers are supposed to be responsible for the classroom layout and furniture arrangements. So on the one hand learning environments in New Zealand are not studied enough, while on the other there is also a lack of concern about the role of users in designing learning environments.

For true participatory design, users of designed environments should work alongside the designers. In the case of primary school learning environments, designers and architects might find it hard to work with young users, in addition to the difficulty of having a large number of users to include. This led to the idea of setting up a situation where the effect of social media on the participation of users in the design process of learning environments could be studied. The aim was to see the extent to which social media might be useful in enabling the participation of students and teachers in the design of their learning environments, and to reveal problems that might be encountered.

METHOD

As this research aimed at finding the effectiveness of using social media as a means of user involvement, in design an experimental methodology was selected. The creation of a blog (see section The two case studies) was based on Groat and Wang (2002) and their description of designing experiments for architectural research. Their methodology includes studying the effect of identifiable variables in the research. These variables can be manipulated or controlled by the researcher in order to create a suitable experiment. In this study the variables are the work of students uploaded to the blog and their teachers' comments and posts. The work of the students was determined by the design based exercises provided in the blog. Thus, the exercises were carefully planned given that they were dealing with young minds. For this project, a large part of the background on how to research and work with young people was taken from Thomson (2008). The research also built on the experience of working with primary school age children from earlier Master's research, through observing and interviewing them and in drawing sessions (Alsaif, 2011).

Another part of the methodology based on Groat & Wang (2002), was identifying the units of the experiment and manipulating their management. In this study, the work of the students was grouped into categories based on the main ideas behind it. For example, the work might reflect what they liked or disliked about their existing environments, or it might be complaints about the furniture in the learning environments, or ideas about future learning environments and their furniture and fixtures. Managing the ideas was accomplished by defining problems with existing learning environments and finding suitable solutions from the ideas for future ones. It was felt the blog could also help in understanding the ideas and in sorting out the problems and solutions through the online discussions it offers. Generally, lab research is more likely to take causality for granted than research that involves the reactions or behaviour of people. Thus, studies about people's reactions and behaviour tend to focus on the conditions and limitations of a causal interpretation (Groat & Wang, 2002). In order to help define the limitations and conditions of this experiment, teachers were asked to attach information to each piece of student work. The information could include the age of the student, the type of existing learning environment (single cell or open plan), how much time the students spent on the work, and the environment in which the work was completed. The blog was thus set up to encourage teachers to set the exercises in limited conditions; for example, for the suggested target group of students aged from 9 to 11 years, the work was to be completed within one school day, and the environment within which the work was done was to be the same learning environment as dealt with in their work.

The Two Case Studies

In order to explore the use of social media in participatory design involving children two case studies were conducted. These were developed consecutively. The first involved the use of a blog and a facebook page. It used a series of exercises to help children understand the issues involved in planning a classroom and developing ideas for their ideal classroom. This case study is referred to as 'the blog'. The second and later case study used a blog in addition to face to face communication between children, teacher and architect. This case study is called 'the blog plus'. The aim was to see which better aided participatory design of learning environments. The two case studies are first described and the results compared and conclusions drawn.

The Blog

Figure 1. The structure of the blog "Designing my Classroom"

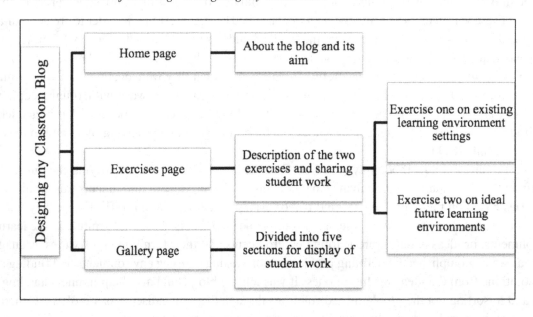

An experimental blog was set up supported by exercises for the students to encourage them to produce suitable ideas for designing learning environments. It included two exercises and teachers had control of using these with their students. Teachers also had to upload the ideas and thoughts about learning environments produced by their students. The blog was designed to allow students to look at the work of other children in different schools under the supervision of the teachers. Although at this stage architects were not involved, it was envisaged that in real projects architects and designers could easily access these ideas with a view to their possible integration into designs for learning environments. Alternatively, they could discuss the ideas with the users (teachers and supervised students) through the comments in the same blog. It was hoped this experimental methodology would save time and make communication between architects and students easier than setting up face to face meetings. The blog was intended as a private place, with only invited participants having access. The two set exercises helped teachers introduce the task to students in a series of well described steps. The first aimed to encourage students to produce ideas and thoughts about their current learning environments, while the second was about future and ideal learning environments. Figure 1 shows the blog's structure. The students' work could be in individual or group format and in any medium chosen by the students, such as writing, manual or digital drawings, and video or voice recordings. The blog also provided a tutorial on how to upload and post student work.

Difficulties With the Blog

Measuring the effectiveness of the blog could not be completed as originally envisaged because of the very low response rate. In June 2013, an invitation was sent to primary school teachers throughout New Zealand to participate in the first blog. Despite the enthusiasm of teachers for involving children in participatory design from the earlier survey, it was disappointing that only 16 teachers accepted the invitation and of these only 3 posted material on the blog. The posts from the participatory design blog were supposed to be discussed in a focus group in a later phase of the research, but this was not really possible for two reasons. The first was there were too few posts that really only represented the student users of one classroom. The second was the difficulty in finding school architects willing to take part in a focus group, with only one enthusiastic response received. This meant there were could be no discussions about the posts and the ideas on the blog and no analysis of these in terms of the problems with and solutions for a participatory design process. The absence of measured outcomes and the lack of discussion of these meant the blog experiment was incomplete. It seemed that using social media in the form of a blog would not help participatory design of primary school learning environments.

The second step was, therefore, to set up a Facebook page the hope it would be more popular than a blog. As a result, in September 2013, a Facebook group with the same aims and exercises as the blog was initiated and invitations were again sent to primary school teachers around New Zealand. This time 27 teachers accepted the invitation. However, none posted anything related to the exercise or any previous involvement in the design process of learning environments. Some members of both the Facebook group and the blog declared they were happy to participate in these social media events and were using the exercises with their students but nothing was posted. It seems that teachers, as they said in the survey, like the idea of getting involved in collaboration and using these social media but find they are too busy for actual involvement.

As the experiment could not be completed with so few posts, a case study method was used for analysis. The posts, including the students' work, formed the case study and the material was used to answer the question: How can participants to the blog contribute in a design process through using social media? The proposition is that teachers and students do have sufficient knowledge to be able to participate in the design process of their learning environments. The units of analysis include teachers, students, and their posts on the blog. The data was collected from these posts in the form of documentation. The findings from analysis of this case study are presented below but first the second step in the attempted use of social media is described.

The Blog Plus

In the second case study the use of social media was a small part of the participatory process rather than the main method. This case study involved two classrooms in two primary schools in Wellington city, New Zealand. The exercise was to rearrange the furniture of each classroom based a revised layout devised by the users (teacher and students). Here the researcher took the role of the architect coming to the classroom with the aim of helping the students and their teacher evolve a classroom furniture layout design without any budget implications.

The design process in both classrooms started with an exploration stage in which the researcher collected information about the classroom layout and dimensions. This stage was completed from a visit supplemented with information gained from an interview with each teacher. The second stage was a brainstorming session that involved discussing general information about architecture and classroom layouts. This stage was completed via observations and discussions with the whole class, including the teacher. The third stage was the students rearranging the classroom layout on paper and discussing the new designs with each other and the teacher. All students, in addition to the teacher, were involved in this stage with the researcher as observer. The fourth stage used whole class gatherings and discussions, including the teacher to decide on the final design. The final stage was getting feedback from the students via a short questionnaire. At the start a social media blog was set up for each classroom where students could post comments and share their ideas and work. This blog was active throughout all stages of the participatory design process and its aim was to provide extra communication between students and the researcher who was taking the role of architect. All ideas and drawings could be uploaded to each of the two separate classroom blogs. Students and teachers were introduced to the blogs and how they could access and use them. Each blog gave students the opportunity to see each other's posted work and comment on this. Students thus gave design feedback through the blogs. The researcher as architect could analyse the students' comments in the blog without wasting school time.

After the brainstorming session, students had the first chance to open the blogs and participate by posting their own comments about the existing layout of their classroom. There was no given time for this task and the teachers encouraged their students to complete it during any free time in the given week. The researcher analysed these comments (see section The blog plus results) and then discussed them with the students in a face-to-face classroom session. This session was also used to introduce the students to the exercise on designing a new classroom layout. Some students were amazed that they had the chance to express their ideas through using a video camera or voice recorder. However, later, they discovered that drawings were easier than creating videos or voice recordings. As a result, most students chose to draw their ideas for the new classroom layout. Students chose to work in groups of two or three.

In the final visit by the researcher related to the design process, the ideas and comments in the form of the drawings, written work, voice recording, and videos in both classrooms were first discussed in a whole classroom session that included the teacher. Following this a discussion about the final layouts in each classroom took place. For this a floor plan of each classroom with only the fixed furniture and features was provided, together with the movable classroom furniture cut out of pieces of cardboard. The discussion was in the form of a consultation, where the architect (the researcher) consulted the students and teacher about the location of each zone and piece of furniture and then placed the cardboard cut-outs to create a series of options. This was the point at which the issue of scale was discussed. Students became especially aware of this problem at this stage, because of the scale cardboard furniture cut-outs. As some students suggested ideas for the layout other students and the teachers voted for the ideas they liked. This part was important, as the researcher wanted to find a way of all users participating in a decision. The researcher as architect also gave opinions as an 'expert' on the design of spaces. The last part of this stage was moving the furniture cut-outs to create a final layout based on the whole class discussion.

For the last stage of this second case study, a final visit was made to each classroom after the furniture had been changed and the new layout put into place. A short presentation including photographs of students working on the classroom layout project was given and discussed with the students. Finally the students and the teachers were given a feedback sheet that asked for their opinions of the new layout. The feedback sheet for students consisted of a floor plan of the old furniture layout, a floor plan of the new one, three questions and a space for general comments.

RESULTS

The Posts in the Blog

In June 2013, the blog opened to participants. It has been previously introduced through the survey sent to all primary schools in New Zealand. In the survey 50 teachers responded positively to being part of the blog but as stated above only 16 accepted the invitation to join, and only 3 posted work.

In the first post (post 1), a teacher and her students completed exercise one. However, there were no drawings, sketches, or photographs submitted. They started the exercise with a brainstorming session about the current layout of their single cell classroom. It had one wall of windows, a front door, an art bay, and a door leading to the cloakroom bay. The teacher mentioned not having a veranda and expressed her feelings about that with a 'sad face'. The students then listed what they liked and did not like in the learning space. Likes included the interactive settings in the classroom, such as the interactive whiteboard, the computers, iPads, and a fishbowl with two fish. Students liked the fact that they changed seats every week. They also liked the natural light coming through the windows and the desks located by these. They liked some of the storage units, as they felt these provided a good place for classroom stuff such as the iPads, laptops, maths equipment, and classroom books. The teacher said that they liked the teacher's desk being in the art bay (in the cave area). Students liked the fact they could change their seats and did not have a fixed place for the whole school term. In addition, they liked having the option of sitting on cushions on the floor. In terms of their dislikes, they did not like the location of some settings, such as the bookshelf at right angles to the computer cupboard or having a shoe rack inside the classroom by the window. They also disliked the mess created by the cords by the computer tables. They would have liked to add to and change some of the existing furniture, and change the location of other pieces. However, there was no discussion of why they had these likes and dislikes, although some of this emerged in the students' drawings from the second exercise. They had, however, already changed from desks to tables, as they found the tables encouraged students not to be attached to one particular workspace (the student's desk). Instead, they had the choice of changing workspaces during activities. The teacher also claimed that the tables were easier to move than desks when they wanted to create a furniture free space for certain activities. They wanted to add more tables and storage boxes to the classroom, as unlike desks, the tables had nowhere to store books and pens. They wanted to move the jelly-bean shaped tables to the reading corner. They also mentioned changing the location of the interactive whiteboard, as when the sun entered the room it shone into their eyes when they looked at it.

In terms of participating in the classroom design the teacher said the students had the option to work in any setting inside the classroom such as at desks, at tables, on the floor, move around, or with laptops/iPads. However, the students would not normally choose the layout of the classroom furniture or the location of the settings inside the classroom.

The second post (post 2) was also about the first exercise on the existing learning space. The teacher and her students started by talking about the layout of their classroom. This was a fully carpeted room with a sink, shelving, wireless controller, "two work stations", high windows, individual desks grouped in fours, and an interactive whiteboard. The classroom had a door leading to a veranda with some seating, and the other door led to the cloakroom bay and toilets. They also listed what they liked and disliked about the classroom. Likes included the interactive board, the two workstations and the wireless service, as it enabled them to use the laptops at any time and in any place, and they liked the large area on the walls for display of things that help students to learn, such as the world map that showed where all the students' families were from. They liked that they had a fishing net hung from the ceiling and that they used it for learning purposes, such as catching the vocabulary words that were new to students. The teacher said that they liked having the books in desk trays. On the other hand, they disliked not having a proper wet area, as this made the sink area a mess, the fact there was not enough space in the mat area and that the colours of the classroom were dull (they would have liked bright colours). They also had an overheating problem, as not all windows had proper shading treatment, and this meant afternoon sun would heat up the classroom. The students claimed the desks were too low for some students and the chairs were uncomfortable.

In the third post (post 3), the teacher (the same teacher, students, and classroom of post 1) asked her students to redesign their existing classroom in a way they would like. The teacher gave them a floor plan as the basis for redesigning the existing internal layout. Not all the students of the classroom participated in this exercise. Students worked in pairs or individually and produced 11 redesigned floor plans (Figures 3 and 4). Students completed the exercise whilst inside their current classroom.

In the first drawing (Figure 2A) the student drew the existing layout of the classroom, as she liked it as it was. In this existing layout the cave area contained the teacher's desk in addition to the art bench that included a sink and tables were located in the centre of the classroom for group work. There were a number of storage units and a small furniture free area for mat time. Having this drawing was very useful, as the ideas of other children could be compared against the existing layout. This highlights the importance of having a drawing of the existing classroom layout at the start of any participatory design activity. In the second drawing (Figure 2B) the student kept the teacher's desk in the cave area. However, there was less furniture than in the existing classroom layout, which created a larger furniture free space for mat time or free movement of students. The desks and tables were arranged for students to work in groups. In the third drawing (Figure 2C) the cave was used for student activities rather than for housing the teacher's desk. In this layout, there were desks and tables for individual and group work. The fourth drawing (Figure 2D) divided the classroom into mini rooms for different activities, such as a reading room, play room, writing room, and a "treat" room. This layout had windows on all the classroom walls in order to light all these rooms. Some rooms have no furniture, which creates more space for students to move, learn, and play freely. In Figure 2E the cave was also converted to cater for student activities. The whiteboard and mat area were obvious in this layout in the top left corner. The students furnished the mat area with cushions and arranged the desks to serve both individual and group work. There were also furniture free spaces for free movement. In Figure 2F there was even less furniture to create more empty space for moving around. The students who completed this drawing included various design details, such as the lighting units and location of windows. Windows were located in all classroom walls for maximum natural light.

Figure 2. (A-F) student drawings from post 3 on the blog

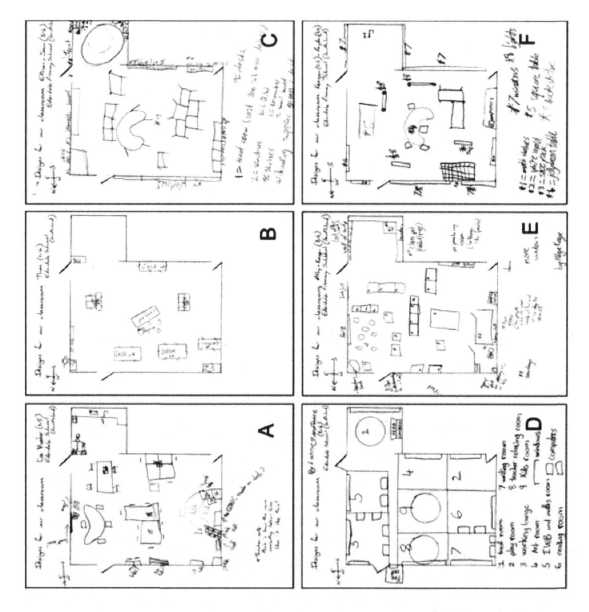

In Figure 3G the student made the cave into an area for student activities and moved the teacher's desk to another corner. Also included were various activity corners and settings around the classrooms. The main observation from this drawing was that the desks were arranged in the traditional way, with rows of individual desks facing one side of the classroom. In another design (Figure 3H) the students also suggested group tables for student group work and included activity corners around the classroom. Details covered the location of the heat pump. Figure 3I shows very similar ideas to the previous drawings, including having group-work tables and a number of activity corners. Noticeably, a couch was introduced in this layout. The last two drawings (Figures 3J and 3K) were also similar to the others, with group-work tables and activity areas. The teacher's desk was kept in the cave area in both these drawings.

Figure 3. (G-K) student drawings from post 3 on the blog

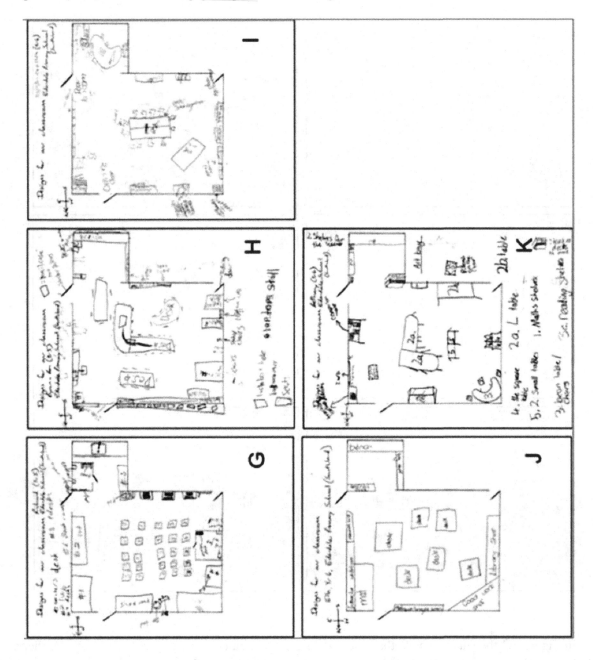

The Blog Plus Results

Students readily posted comments about their existing classrooms in the second case study. In one classroom these comments on could be put into three categories. The first contained comments on the desk arrangement and almost all comments in this category were about how crowded the desks were. Some students commented on the desk arrangement being boring. "They need [to be] dynamic," one student said. The second category was about the mat area. Although this was observed to be slightly crowded in use, some students commented it was too big. Others said they would like the location of the mat area changed. The third category was random comments. A student commented on the window treatments and the fact there are no curtains to block the sunlight when using the data projector. Other students suggested creating a bigger library/reading area. Some students suggested adding more soft settings such as beanbags.

Figure 4. Student's written work from one of the rearrangement case studies

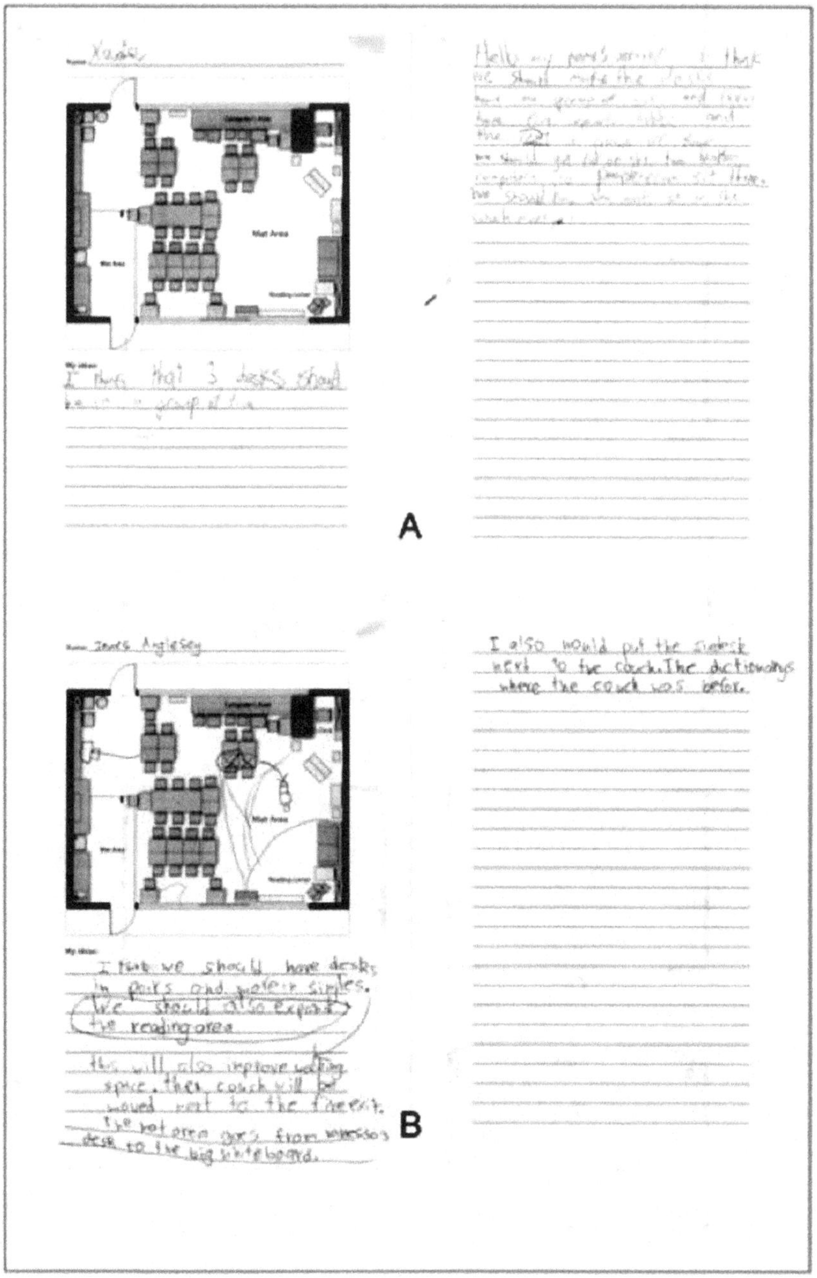

As a result of the exercise on redesigning the classroom layout the students produced two pieces of written work, one voice recording, two videos, and nine completed drawings (Figures 4 and 5). In the written work, students suggested changing the layout of the desks, getting rid of the broken computers, having a bigger reading area and more circulation space, as well as some changes in the overall layout (Figure 4).

Figure 5. Student drawings from one of the rearrangement case studies

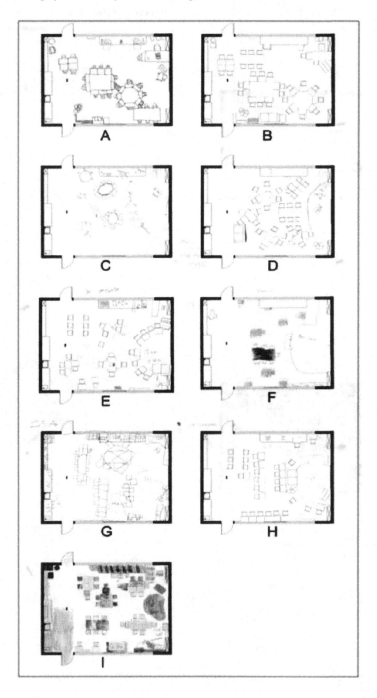

In the drawings, all students suggested changing the desk arrangement (Figure 5). They also wanted more space free of furniture than in the existing layout. However, students who used the paper furniture to test out their ideas had less furniture-free space in the revised work (Figure 5C & D). In Figure 5A the student drew the furniture at a similar scale to the actual furniture. So when he tested his work he achieved a similar layout to the existing (Figure 5B). Most drawings did not change much in terms of the overall locations for settings. Some drawings suggested changing the teacher's desk to another corner between two mat areas (Figure 5G). In general, the drawings focused on changing the desk arrangement. The voice recording and videos replicated the ideas in the drawings and written work of changing the desk arrangement and having more space for circulation.

Comparison of the Design Results

This discussion first considers the commonalities in the posts and drawings from both case studies and then the limitations of the exercises. The posts reveal common ideas when it comes to the likes and dislikes within the existing learning environments. Teachers and their students liked the use of technology inside the classroom, such as the interactive whiteboard and the laptops. It is also obvious children want to use laptops wherever they like in the classroom, including on the floor. What also emerges is that there are problems using IT equipment, both from glare and in terms of dealing with wires. Students also liked having some space free of furniture for various activities, and this is reflected in the drawings, as students drew less furniture than the existing and created new furniture free spaces. This liking for the latter could be because it gives young students more freedom to play, move around and be creative in completing their set activities, rather than being stuck in a chair. However, there was a problem with scale in all the students' drawings. Students found it difficult to understand and draw the true size of familiar classroom furniture items. This led to some students suggesting more furniture free space within the same furniture and settings. However, some students had created more empty space by putting fewer pieces of furniture in the classroom, which could indicate that these students preferred working and learning on the floor more than using furniture. The designs from blog plus perhaps have more realism because the researcher as architect was able to ensure the children understood about scale, and the use of furniture cut-outs was a simple way to do this.

Students created group-work stations in nearly all drawings in both case studies, which probably underlines how much they like working in groups, although it may also reflect what they already have in their existing classroom. In the third post from the first case study, some students converted the cave area, which was used for art and to house the teacher's desk, into a space only for student activities. This perhaps indicated a student preference for having a semi private corner for quiet activities such as thinking or reading. Students also showed in their drawings that they wanted natural light as they drew windows in walls even where these would not be possible (Figures 3D and 3F). This was also mentioned in one of the posts, where the teacher said that students like to sit by the windows. Only one student suggested a traditional desk arrangement (Figure 4G), which may indicate that the majority of students prefer modern layouts that involve different activity settings that cater for different teaching and learning styles. Children also picked up on details such as giving the heat pump a location (Figure 4H). This suggests children of this age are well able to participate in the design of their classrooms. In terms of what children want in their classrooms the simple answer is a variety of spaces for working and for most children having space that is free of furniture so they can easily move around and work on the floor.

The majority of students in both case studies liked classrooms with specialized corners. Additionally, having spaces for separate activities was also liked, and this could well represent how students like to learn in different ways and that they have different needs inside the classroom, as the theory of multiple intelligences argues (Armstrong, 2009).

In terms of limitations, students may have not been in other types of classroom, so their ideas were extensions of what their current or previous classrooms offered. The exception was the two students who divided the space into many separate rooms for different functions (Figure 3D). The schemes from blog plus are also more realistic and having the researcher as architect may have limited the imaginations of the children compared to the first blog case study. This is where social media could have another role, as suggested by Bill (2014), by putting together a gallery of different types of learning environments for students to look at before they did their own designs. In the drawings from the first blog case study, the teacher gave her students the outline of the classroom for them to draw their different layouts on and she said that this might be the reason that no student tried to change the classroom shape, although the students who proposed drawing 3D did change its architecture. In the blog plus case study the students had to use the same shaped classroom as the aim was to change the classroom layout. It is also notice-able that student ideas were expressed only in plan form and no student drew either a section or three dimensional representation of the classroom. This may be the fault of the exercises in both the blog and blog plus case studies in not suggesting both plan and section of the existing classroom should be the starting point for the student work.

Comparison of the Blog and Blog Plus Methods

Using social media in different situations will probably give different results. The first blog experiment in participatory classroom design did not work as planned. However, the blog in the blog plus case study where a real project was involved worked well, or at least better than in the first experiment. The first point to emerge from the comparison is that using social media worked where there was a clear goal, which was changing the internal layout of classrooms with zero budget implication and with the researcher acting in the role of the architect. Having an aim or problem to solve seemed to generate more practical ideas and solutions in comparison to discussing general ideas or imagining ideal classrooms. Users, especially children, have little or no experience in interior design or architecture but giving them a project where they could see the results of applying their design ideas to a classroom setting gave them the chance to learn more about designing their learning spaces.

The second issue from the comparison is that in both experiments social media and online commu-nication worked as a facilitator for saving time and effort for some activities. That said, participatory design using social media worked best where the researcher (as architect) was present in the classroom for almost all the stages in the experiment. The researcher could analyse the comments the students made on the blog but also had the chance to discuss issues with participants directly. The researcher also had the opportunity to change terms and words to simplify the tasks and discussion according to the students' abilities. Students and teachers could also chat with the researcher about many things, including some not directly related to the research. This built trust and made the communication friendlier than just giving instructions and orders. This changing of things as the design progressed was not possible when setting up the first blog and Facebook page, and it may be the communication about what was expected was not always clear. Although the researcher worked hard to simplify the tasks and exercises in the blog, there was no assurance that the teacher and students read them as intended.

The last point is that working with social media when the researcher acted as architect was only a small part of the study while in the first blog case study the whole work depended on the social media. It seems a mixture of social media and face-to-face communication worked much better. In the second blog plus study the students had a number of communication options. As well as social media they could engage in direct discussions, have hands on task sessions (such as physically rearranging the classroom layout), and use different media to express their ideas (videos, voice recording, writing, and drawing). Having these multiple communication options gave the classroom users a chance to participate in the way they liked. This again reflects the needs of students for multiple ways of learning in the classroom. Figure 6 summarises how social media was used in both methods.

Figure 6. The difference in using social media in the blog and blog plus case studies

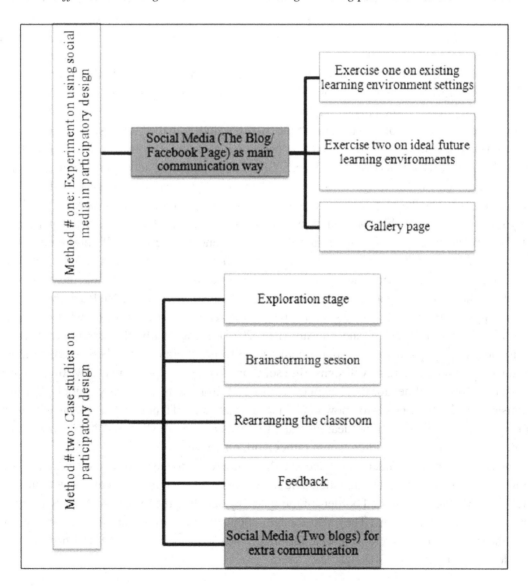

CONCLUSION

The main and perhaps most important comment is that the students produced, with the help of their teacher only in the first blog case study, architectural floor plans. For their age, these drawings indicate that students were ready to participate in the design process of learning environments. They understood what the classroom layout meant and could deliver their ideas for this, both in discussion sessions and through their drawings.

The fact that most students in the two classrooms chose to draw as a way to express their ideas may indicate that drawing is the easiest method for students. It also may indicate that students can express their design ideas through drawings better than in any other way. This is, after all, the way architects work.

The case studies showed how students like to be involved in a design process. Students learned many things about their learning environment by completing the design process of rearranging the furniture of their classrooms and perhaps the most important thing they learned was that they had the right to talk about their ideas. Students could deliver ideas in the ways they found best. The design process also had a positive effect on the students' attitudes toward designing learning environments. Students learned that their ideas could be applied in the real environment if they were suitable and other users agreed with them. Students learned how to think about their needs, how to design layouts that would meet these, and how to negotiate towards a final agreed layout.

When it comes to the use of social media in the two case studies in the blog case study it seems teachers did not have the time to get involved in these online social media sites in order to explore classroom design with children as a general learning topic. Given the contrasting success in giving student users control over their classroom design with the more hands-on approach, this suggests that using online social media may not be the best way to increase user involvement in the design process of New Zealand primary schools. However, this conclusion may be influenced by the fact the very few participants in this study were currently involved in a school building or renovation project. If children did, with the help of their teacher, rearrange their classroom layout at the start of every year or after a period of use (perhaps after the first half-term), then social media is a useful way of collecting together proposals and comments on these, providing again the teacher has time to analyse these and feedback the results. This will only happened if designing a classroom is part of the regular curriculum, and what students learn from doing this is seen as useful and relevant (Bill, 2014). Additionally, the results produced by the children (mostly drawings) in these two case studies would allow architects, teachers, and the Ministry of Education to use their ideas in new designs, find solutions to common problems in existing classrooms, or form a base for guidelines for the design of learning environments in primary schools. For instance the Ministry of Education needs to know that children want to use IT but find problems with its use in existing classrooms. The search for ideal furniture for primary schools (Watson, 2017) may be an inappropriate waste of money if children would rather work on the floor.

The posts completed by students revealed that they were ready to have a role in the design process of learning environments. Students can understand the elements of designing spaces. They thought about the shell, which is the architectural borders of the space, by deciding the locations of doors and windows and by creating different rooms. They also thought about the use of interiors for learning when they changed the space layout and removed some furniture. The use of social media was perhaps a small part of their design achievements.

REFERENCES

Alsaif, F. (2011). *Intelligence-friendly environments: A study of New Zealand primary school classroom design in relation to multiple intelligences theory* (Master's thesis). Victoria University of Wellington.

Alsaif, F. (2015). *New Zealand learning environments: The role of design and the design process* (PhD thesis). Victoria University of Wellington.

Armstrong, T. (2009). *Multiple intelligences in the classroom.* Alexandria, VA: ASCD.

Bill, D. (2014, August). *8 Tips and Tricks to Redesign Your Classroom.* Retrieved October 3, 2014 from: http://www.edutopia.org/blog/8-tips-and-tricksredesign-your-classroom

Bland, D. C. (2009). Re-imagining school through young people's drawings. *Proceedings of the 1st International Visual Methods Conference University of Leeds.*

Brandt, E. (2006, August). Designing exploratory design games: A framework for participation in participatory design? In *Proceedings of the ninth conference on Participatory design: Expanding boundaries in design* (vol. 1, pp. 57-66). Trento, Italy: Academic Press. 10.1145/1147261.1147271

Clancy, G., Fröling, M., & Peters, G. (2015). Ecolabels as drivers of clothing design. *Journal of Cleaner Production, 99*, 345–353. doi:10.1016/j.jclepro.2015.02.086

Classroom Architect. (2008). Retrieved October 3, 2014 from: http://classroom.4teachers.org/index.html

De Winter, M., Baerveldt, C., & Kooistra, J. (1999). Enabling children: Participation as a new perspective on child health promotion. *Child: Care, Health and Development, 25*(1), 15–23. doi:10.1046/j.1365-2214.1999.00073.x PMID:9921418

DiSalvo, B., Yip, J., Bonsignore, E., & DiSalvo, C. (2017). *Participatory Design for Learning.* New York: Routledge.

Groat, L., & Wang, D. (2002). *Architectural research methods.* New York: John Wiley &Sons, Inc.

Hagen, P., & Robertson, T. (2010). Social technologies: challenges and opportunities for participation. In *Proceedings of the 11th Biennial Participatory Design Conference* (pp. 31-40). ACM. 10.1145/1900441.1900447

Hanington, B., & Martin, B. (2012). *Universal Methods of Design: 100 Ways to Research Complex Problems, Develop Innovative Ideas, and Design Effective Solutions.* Beverly, MA: Rockport Publishers.

Johnson, M. (2013). *How social media changes user-centred design: Cumulative and strategic user involvement with respect to developer–user social distance.* Aalto University Publication Series. Retrieved September 17, 2014 from: http://inuse.fi/2013/03/15/johnson-2013-how-social-media-changes-user-centred-design/

Kaasinen, E., Koskela-Huotari, K., Ikonen, V., & Niemeléi, M. (2013). Three approaches to co-creating services with users. In J. C. Spohrer & L. E. Freund (Eds.), Advances in the Human Side of Service Engineering (pp. 286–295). Academic Press.

Lukyanenko, R., Parsons, J., Wiersma, Y. F., Sieber, R., & Maddah, M. (2016). Participatory design for user-generated content; Understanding the challenges and moving forward. *Scandinavian Journal of Information Systems, 28*(1), 37–70.

Nair, P., & Fielding, R. (2007). *The language of school design: Design patterns for 21st century schools.* Minneapolis, MN: Design Share.

Näkki, P., & Antikainen, M. (2008). Online tools for codesign: User involvement through the innovation process. *New Approaches to Requirements Elicitation,* (96), 92–97.

Nesset, V., & Large, A. (2004). Children in the information technology design process: A review of theories and their applications. *Library & Information Science Research, 26*(2), 140–161. doi:10.1016/j.lisr.2003.12.002

Picaza-Vela, S., Fernandez-Haddad, M., & Luna-Reyes, F. L. (2016). Opening the black box: Developing strategies to use social media in government. *Government Information Quarterly, 33*(4), 693–704. doi:10.1016/j.giq.2016.08.004

Reyes, L. F. M., & Finken, S. (2012, August). Social media as a platform for participatory design. In *Proceedings of the 12th Participatory Design Conference: Exploratory Papers, Workshop Descriptions, Industry Cases* (vol. 2, pp. 89-92). ACM. 10.1145/2348144.2348173

Said, I. (2007). Architecture for Children: Understanding Children [sic] Perception towards Built Environment. In *Proceedings of International Conference Challenges and Experiences in Developing Architectural education in Asia.* Islamic University of Indonesia. Retrieved March 1, 2012, from http://eprints.utm.my/3575/

Thomson, P. (2008). *Doing visual research with children and young people.* London: Routledge.

Watson, D. (2017). The seat of learning (quest for the ideal school chair) (Talking Point). *Times Educational Supplement,* (5232), 44-45.

Zhang, J., & Zhang, Z. (2010). The Knowledge Management of Furniture Product Design and Development. *Proceedings 3rd International Conference on Information Management, Innovation Management and Industrial Engineering, 1,* 464-467.

KEY TERMS AND DEFINITIONS

Cave Area: A small area inside a classroom originally created for quiet reading and study.

Interactive Whiteboard: An instructional tool that allows computer images to be displayed on a board using a digital projector; teachers or students then can manipulate the elements on the board digitally.

Mat Area: A furniture free area inside a classroom usually used for class gathering and whole class activities.

Multiple-Intelligences: A theory proposed by Howard Gardner that suggests the existence of eight types of intelligences that people use variously when they learn.

Wet Area: An area inside the classroom used for messy and wet work such as painting and working with clay.

This research was previously published in Optimizing E-Participation Initiatives Through Social Media; pages 209-235, copyright year 2018 by Information Science Reference (an imprint of IGI Global).

Chapter 19
Correlating Formal Assessment with Social Network Activity within a Personal Learning Environment

Eleni Koulocheri
Hellenic Open University, Patras, Greece

Michalis Xenos
University of Patras, Patras, Greece

ABSTRACT

Social networks have undoubtedly penetrated into our daily life, in such a degree that educational life could not avoid this effect, as proven by the many education-oriented social networks that have emerged. The education-oriented social network environment named HOU2LEARN, used by the Hellenic Open University, is one of these networks, providing a valuable source of data about students' networking behavior and their tensions. This article aims at contributing to the investigation of possible linkages between social network behavior and student performance as assessed within a formal learning environment. The article is focused on analyzing data and performing statistical correlations from two consecutive and recent academic years in a computer science course, attempting to reach robust conclusions. Although the research question remains the same: Is there a relationship between grades and social activity within the social network? This article is supported by increased sampling and data, providing concrete and intriguing answers, thus setting the pillars for further research goals regarding contemporary and smart learning environments.

DOI: 10.4018/978-1-6684-7123-4.ch019

INTRODUCTION

Social Network Analysis (SNA) is a research methodology that seeks to identify underlying patterns of social relations based on the way actors are connected with each other (Wasserman & Faust, 1994). Within the field of education, SNA is accepted as a valuable analytical tool for deeper understanding of the learning processes occurring in networked learning environments (de Laat, Lally, Lipponen, & Simons, 2007). Additionally, SNA can play the role of a useful instrument for decision makers to see how instructors and students act as a group.

Although, social networks have penetrated into every aspect of people's lives (Christakis & Fowler, 2009), when social networking analytics are applied in a dedicated field, such as learning, should always stay focused on the learning activity (Gašević, Dawson, & Siemens, 2015). This could mean that SNA in learning environments should additionally take into consideration the learning performance, hence leading to an enhanced social network monitoring beyond stereotypes. Bearing in mind that learning performance can be quantified through grading, this paper combines the typical learning performance metric –grading– with social network analytics. This work has been conducted in HOU2LEARN (H2L), an education-oriented social network environment, aiming at investigating valuable affiliations between learning performance and SNA, using both statistical and non-statistical approaches.

Data has been collected at the Hellenic Open University (HOU), a distance-learning university that encourages social networking among students through its own platform and thus can combine formal grades and SNA metrics. Analysis of H2L data is based on two axes: a) on analyzing the learners' social behavior based on activities that can be measured by metrics, such as introvert behavior, extrovert behavior etc., and b) on considering final exam students' performance on the final exams. The statistical analysis of the data collected from two consecutive academic years, aimed at revealing dependencies between social activities metrics and student performance. The validation of these dependencies has been tested on data from two consecutive academic years.

The rest of this article is organized as follows. The next section presents the research hypothesis and discusses similar approaches, followed by the section presenting H2L. Subsequently, the research data are presented, along with explanations of how SNS is applied to H2L and the presentation of a set of three SNA metrics that are applied in this work. Afterwards, the visualization of social connections that are developed among H2L users is graphically presented as well as the statistical analysis of the data. Finally, conclusions and future work are drawn.

FROM LEARNING ANALYTICS TO SOCIAL NETWORK ANALYSIS

Analytics is a term used in business and science to refer to computational support for capturing digital data to help assist in decision-making, while learning analytics (LA) is a relatively recent term (coined during the 1st International Conference on Learning Analytics and Knowledge, 2011) and refers to the collection and analysis of digital traces that every learner leaves. According to (Buckingham, 2012) LA appropriates the concept of analytics for education: "what should a digital nervous system look like when the focus is on learning outcomes, and to extend the metaphor, what kind of 'brain' or collective intelligence is needed to interpret the signals and adapt the system's behavior accordingly?"

Therefore, learning analytics is the measurement, collection, analysis and reporting of data about learners and their contexts, for purposes of understanding and optimizing learning and the environments in which it occurs (Fournier, Kop, & Sitlia, 2011). The goal is to return the analysis results to the learner as useful information, to improve the learning process and to enhance the outcomes (Siemens et al., 2011). This is achieved by collecting data of past learning events that can be used to make decisions about future ones. This procedure could potentially offer more solid results in case of longer data time-cycles (Clow, 2012) and could have impact on students' behavior, their performance indicators, or summative assessments (Shum & Ferguson, 2012). According to various researchers (Dawson, Heathcote, & Poole, 2010; Downes, 2010; Yuen & Yuen, 2008), most of the tools that measure learning engagement look at measurements of trivial variables such as logs, page access, geographical origin, etc. Considering these tools useful for a basic level of assessment, Downes (Downes, 2010) takes it one step further, believing that future learning analytic systems will analyze even the learners' contributions, which may enhance the provisioned quality. To this direction, a set of five axes that define LA has been proposed (Siemens & Long, 2011):

1. **Course Level:** Social network analysis, discourse analysis, learning trails.
2. **Educational Data Mining:** Pattern recognition and predictive modeling.
3. **Intelligent Curriculum:** Development of semantically defined curriculum resources.
4. **Adaptive Content:** Provision of adaptive content using recommendation procedures, based on learner behavior.
5. **Adaptive Learning:** Social interaction and learner support as an adaptive learner process.

A major difference of our work from previous studies is that within the scope of this paper, extracted analytics are applied at course level, since focus is concentrated on analytics derived from learning networks in the context of Personal Learning Environments (PLEs) (Soumplis, Chatzidaki, Koulocheri, & Xenos, 2011). To achieve this the Open Educational Platform H2L was used to trace the learners' social activity in the networks. Our research investigates the first axis, of the five mentioned above, referring to course level relating the research with SNA, learning trails and discourse measurements using activity metrics. The feedback does not return to the students in real time, but remains recorded for future analysis. As an extension to SNA, formal assessment through the students' grades is taken into consideration for those H2L members that also happened to be students of the Hellenic Open University and participated to final exams.

In this paper, SNA acts as a quantitative method of LA. Therefore, SNA uses network graphs to illustrate network connections. This visualization can reveal nodes they are in a more central position (Fournier et al., 2011) with increased impact to their connections (neighbors). It consists of two basic structure components: nodes (or vertices or agents) and edges (or connections). In our case, as in most cases of an education-oriented social network, nodes represent physical members of a network, such as learners and instructors. Edges denote the connection between two nodes and consist of lines that point from one node to another. Edges may be directed or undirected; directed edges, represented as arrows, have an origin and a destination and may represent "who is following who", "who influence who", etc. (Hansen, Shneiderman, & Smith, 2010).

In the setting of a PLE such as H2L, students have a wide range of activities that occur from the engagement and involvement in a course, as also presented in the following section. All these activities are involved in the term 'discourse' according to (Siemens & Long, 2011) five axes and can lead to highly interactive connections among them. Similar to our work, (Kamel Boulos & Wheeler, 2007; Stahl, 2005) investigate such educational environments from a social constructivist perspective and support that they can play the role of a venue in which learners can have both collective and individual gain. Our work focuses on the correlation of social activity with learning as measured by formal assessment. In our case, H2L as a PLE, supports both the abovementioned facets of a PLE (i.e. activities support and connectivity). It can also assist this informal communication among the learners of a B.Sc. course in which, at the same time, a formal grading system is applied. By informal communication, it is meant that, students communicate in a loose and natural way, without following standardized rules (Nascimbeni, Fischer, Cullen, & Kugemann, 2009; Van Harmelen, 2006).

Comparing our work to similar studies, (J. Hommes et al., 2012) use a similar research context, but not within an e-learning environment. A physical network of students was investigated, and its connections were based on questions and replies among them. This research highlighted that students' performance was related to the kind of friendship in this network. Other studies (Baldwin, Bedell, & Johnson, 1997; Juliette Hommes et al., 2014) have also found a strong linkage between SNA and academic performance. On the other hand, (Gašević, Zouaq, & Janzen, 2013) showed that higher number of social ties does not ensure a better learning performance. (Cho, Gay, Davidson, & Ingraffea, 2007) also discussed the impact of brokerage position on learning performance within a learners' network; (García-Saiz, Palazuelos, & Zorrilla, 2014) presented an e-learning data mining tool that also considers SNA theory for use over a learning management system (LMS); (Romero, López, Luna, & Ventura, 2013) discussed data mining approaches for improving prediction of students' final performance starting from participation indicators in both quantitative, qualitative social network forums; (Cela, Sicilia, & Sánchez, 2015) had compiled a number of 37 studies aiming to understand how SNA has contributed to the understanding of e-learning. All these works show that this field is in its infancy and can be a ground for valuable research in the direction our work is.

The research question of our work investigates if there is an affiliation or relationship between grades and social activity within a (informal) PLE that is used in the context of a (formal) B.Sc. course. The work is based on the initial research that has now been majorly extended, for validation purposes, by including also: new data from an additional academic year and, b) investigation of the statistical correlation between SNA metrics and formal grades for both years and comparison of results.

THE ENVIRONMENT: HOU2LEARN (H2L)

Contemporary learning environments are more social and collaborative than the traditional LMSs and provide great vital opportunities to create, maintain and redistribute content. They also incorporate strong social networking characteristics as well as a loosely structured collection of various widely used Web 2.0 tools such as fora, wikis, blogs, glossaries, etc. Such learning environments are based on the learning theory of the digital age, called connectivism. Connectivism is a hypothesis of learning, which emphasizes on the role of social and cultural context. In connectivism, the starting point for learning occurs when knowledge is actuated through the process of a learner connecting to and feeding information to a learning community (Siemens, 2014).

The Hellenic Open University (HOU) has always been interested in education trends and innovative technologies, has set up a PLE, named HOU2LEARN (H2L) which was launched in September 2010. H2L is a part of an ongoing research aiming at helping studies concerning the correlation among Learning 2.0 challenges, social networking activities and informal learning. Technically, H2L is based on the Elgg[1] framework, including functionalities and widgets such as file uploading and sharing, blogs, social bookmarks, personal pages, polls and status updates. The most important H2L functionality is social networking; Users are connected with each other with the well-known relationship "Follower-Following."

The way H2L has been set up, does not make it yet another traditional LMS. Of course, it supports the formal part of the course, by offering the educational material that is needed for the course, such as assignments, presentations, eBooks, etc., but it also encourages networking among students and tutors in an informal and loose way. To that extend, students by building their network of followers can create their own schema of sources that can help them while studying. Furthermore, students can communicate with and/or help their colleagues, thus increasing their impact on the network.

After a fine-tuning period, H2L has been promoted as the sole environment for the educational requirements of the postgraduate course "Special Issues on Software Engineering" (PLH42) of HOU for what is referred as 'Year 1' hereinafter. To that extend, a special group within H2L, named PLH42 had been established for the need of the course. Tutors or other members of H2L could also be accepted as group members under request. All PLH42 members were encouraged to get familiarized with the environment and actively collaborate with each other, as well as with tutors, co-students and external users. This encouragement was promoted during all five physical meetings per course. All supporting material was available only in H2L and not in Moodle or IBM Lotus Quickr (both were the official communication channels for HOU so far), aiming at further encouraging students in using only H2L.

Tutors also promoted the use of H2L when communicating with students with other means e.g. email. All questions were expressed and replied through H2L and all communication was accomplished through H2L using all provisioned functionalities that Elgg offers. To that extend, H2L could assist students about their peers' doubts and problems but could also inform tutors about their students' knowledge of the course contents. The same concept was applied the following academic year (hereinafter 'Year 2'), increasing the research sample. Classes of both years had the same tutors and the environment was still open to external users such as researchers, visitors etc.

Following a previous study (Koulocheri & Xenos, 2013) based only on 'Year 1' data, this paper extends the period covered, dealing with data covering two subsequent academic years aiming at reaching at more robust outcomes and proceeds with data correlation. Users under investigation are students of PLH42 that participated in the final exams, their tutors and all external H2L members (with no certification rights) that wished to join the PLH42 network. The total number of 170 users that are included in this study is distributed as follows: 74 students, 3 tutors and 3 external members for 'Year 1' and 87 students, 3 tutors (all common for both years) and 6 external members for 'Year 2' (3 common for both years). The two years' connections are combined into a sole graph and the differences between the two years' patterns are discussed beyond visualization and documented with numbers. Besides data visualization, the two years data were collected and used to perform a statistical analysis applying Least Squares Regression and Pearson Correlation, aiming at investigating any possible correlation existing between formal student performance and their social activity for each academic year.

RESEARCH DATA

Formal Grades

In PLH42, during both years, formal assessment was conducted using the grade a_i, i=1, 2, …, 6 of six formal written assignments that were due during the academic year, along with the grade of the final exams e at the end of the year. Assignments and exams were graded using the 0-10 scale. Students could participate in the exams, if:

$$\sum_{i=1}^{6} a_i > 30$$

The final grade g is calculated as following:

$$g = \begin{cases} 0.7 * e + 0.3 * \sum_{i=1}^{6} a_i, & if\ e \geq 5 \\ \text{non-pass}, & if\ e < 5 \end{cases}$$

For 'Year 1', the minimum g was 5.05 and the maximum g was 9.76 and for 'Year 2', 2.67 and 8.71 respectively. Students that didn't participate in the final exam have not been taken into consideration, since for this paper the final grade g (counting both written assignments and final exams grade) reflects the total student performance.

Social Network Analysis Metrics

As aforementioned, H2L is an open educational platform with social network features and this encourages the development of connections among members (students, tutors, researchers, others). To better visualize the members' connections, a SNA diagram (graph) is used to present the connections of members of H2L that follow the Group "PLH42", the examined case study course. Every graph node represents a group member and the member ID is also displayed. The connections among the members are represented by edges. This work focuses on the relationship "followings/followers", thus the edges have a direction, i.e. they have been pictured with arrows; an arrow from member A to member B means that A follows B. This leads to a "directed" graph.

Along with the basis of SNA that is connectivity, there is a number of metrics that allow researchers to systematically slice up the social world, quantizing how people come together and interact, creating a basis on which to compare networks and determine the relative position of individuals and groups within a network. There is a variety of SNA metrics with various levels of complexity used to cover the needs of various fields such as sociology, mathematics, etc. (Hansen et al., 2010; Wasserman & Faust, 1994). This paper, is focused on three SNA metrics, which are briefly presented:

- **Indegree Centrality:** Degree centrality measures the number of nodes that follow a specific node. It counts the number of edges (arrows) that point inward at a node or, in other words, the number of followers.
- **Outdegree Centrality:** Outdegree centrality has similar nature with indegree one, but it counts the number of edges (arrows) that point outward towards other nodes. It illustrates the number of members a member follows (i.e. followings).
- **Betweenness Centrality:** This is a more complex SNA metric that counts the brokering ability of a node. Popularity is important, but it is not enough; it is significant to quantize how much a node enables the transfer of an information (or content, or a virus, or a news, etc.) to its neighbors. According to (Hansen et al., 2010) betweenness centrality is a kind of 'bridge' score and measures the impact of removing a person in disrupting the connections between other nodes in the network.

VISUALISATION OF SOCIAL NETWORK CONNECTIONS

Final Grade as a Node Attribute

To effectively visualize the social network connections, NodeXL software was used. It is a Microsoft Excel extension that uses as input the node names/IDs and their connections (followers and followings) and generates as output the graphs and the SNA metric values.

The initial concept was to take final grades (hereinafter, grades) into consideration while social network analysis is performed. This was conducted through the nodes' size: The student with the higher final grade had the largest node's size. Considering the limitations: a) in NodeXL, nodes' size must be a number between 1 and 100, and b) since it was necessary that all grades be visible, but proportional to each other, the grades were normalized accordingly into a scale from 1 to 100. For example, the normalized value of the grade $g=5.06$ is normalized as 51.

Figure 1. Two years connections in a sole graph

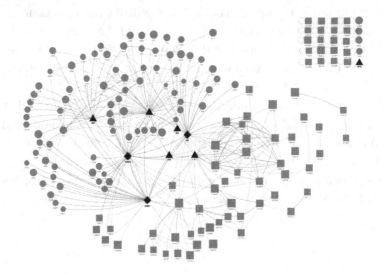

In Figure 1, the two years connections were illustrated in a sole graph. In this graph, 'Year 1' students (shown as grey squares) connected with their tutors (shown as solid black diamonds). The same tutors are also connected with 'Year 2' students (shown as grey disks). Node's size depicts the final grade g. As expected, there are no connections among students of different years. For PLH42 external members, i.e. not PLH42 students such as tutors, researchers, etc., a unified size of 25 was applied. External users are shown with a black solid triangle.

For all graphs shown in this paper, the Harel-Koren Fast Multiscale layout arrangement algorithm was applied (Harel & Koren, 2000). Respecting all privacy issues, all 170 members were represented with an internal ID (assigned randomly and not related to any student ID of any other form), thus avoiding names and usernames and anonymizing the graph. SNA was applied for each year separately and SNA metrics were calculated for these two cohorts separately. The graphs for each year were generated accordingly. Mainly in terms of comparison, but also for space saving purposes, these two groups were merged into one sole graph as the one shown in Figure 1. Tutors were common for both years; hence they appear to have connections with students of both classes.

SNA Metrics as a Node Attribute

SNA metric values, as generated by NodeXL, may vary from 0 to the total number of nodes for indegree and outdegree centrality and from 0 to more than 100 (depends on the position in the graph) for betweenness centrality. Aiming to create graphs in which the node size depends to the SNA metric values and considering the limitation of the NodeXL (node size should be from 0 to 100), SNA metric values had also to be normalized in values from 0 to 100. This was conducted by assigning the value 100 to the node with the highest SNA metric value and harmonizing the rest of the node sizes' respectively.

Figure 2. Two years connections in a sole graph. Node's size depicts the indegree centrality

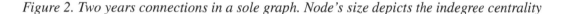
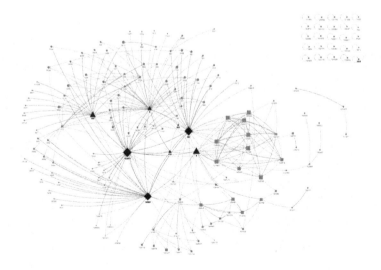

The indegree centrality using both 'Year 1' and 'Year 2' connections in a sole graph is shown in Figure 2. As in Figure 1, the 'Year 1' students (shown as grey squares) connected with their tutors (shown as solid black diamonds). The same tutors relate to the 'Year 2' students (shown as grey disks). Node's size depicts the indegree centrality.

Figure 3 illustrates the outdegree centrality for the two years while Figure 4 illustrates the betweenness centrality. For all Figures (2, 3, and 4) the same rules were also applied for non-PLH42 students such as tutors and external members and their nodes were also illustrated with a solid square and other users with a solid triangle.

Reviewing the graphs, some similarities and some differences between two academic years are revealed and discussed in the following subsection.

Figure 3. Two years connections in a sole graph. Node's size depicts the outdegree centrality

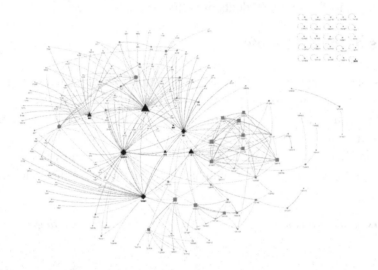

Figure 4. Two years connections in a sole graph. Node's size depicts the betweenness centrality

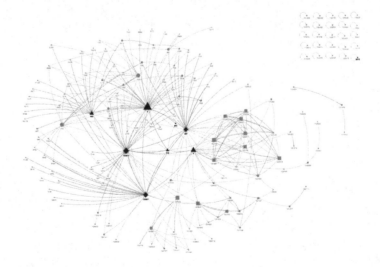

Discussion

As students in the two cohorts had no opportunities or incentives to work and learn together across the two implementations, the clear segregation of grey disks and squares is visible in all figures. It is important however to note, that students of both years received entirely the same instructions and guidance on how to get involved in H2L. Beyond this, these two classes present interesting differences regarding connectivity and performance:

1. The 20 out of the 74 students (27%) from 'Year 1' (shown as squares) preferred to be totally isolated since they had no connections even with their tutors, but only 4 of 87 students (4.6%) from the 'Year 2' (shown as disks) acted the same.
2. During 'Year 2', most students avoided to connect with each other and mostly connected with their tutors. This lead to low SNA metrics for them and small node sizes in Figures 2, 3 and 4. However, during 'Year 1', a small group of students created a sub-network with internal connections that increased their SNA metric values.
3. Because of 2), all SNA metrics average values have been decreased in the second year. More precisely, second year average indegree centrality (shown in Figure 2) was 14.47% lower, outdegree centrality (shown in Figure 3) was 40.87% lower and betweenness centrality (shown in Figure 4) was 62.52% lower than the respective average values for the first year.
4. The average final grade for 'Year 2' was also lower than that for Year 1 by 8,92%.

The results show that in 'Year 2', students were more willing to connect and be part of the network, since the percentage of isolated students was dramatically smaller than in 'Year 1'. But, SNA metrics in Year 2 had lower values than in Year 1 and the same happened to the average final grade of the same year.

Combining the findings, it appears that although in 'Year 2', students had lower tension to isolation, they weren't as cohesively connected (in terms of SNA metrics) as students in 'Year 1'. Considering also that 'Year 2' students had lower final grades, one could argue that low average SNA metrics values are related to low average final grades. Especially, betweenness centrality, related to the influence that every node has to the rest of the graph, which was dramatically lower in 'Year 2', seems to also have had an impact to the formal performance of the students (final grades). Therefore, SNA metric and in particular betweenness centrality can be used as a performance evaluator for students to predict lower grades.

DATA STATISTICAL ANALYSIS

Although visualization could offer useful feedback about the relative positions of members in the graph, it cannot help the researcher to investigate if formal course performance is related to the social network performance and how tight this relationship –if there is any– could be. Furthermore, even if in the case of the figures and for better illustrating and comparison purposes, the two classes (years) were merged into one graph, to proceed with the statistical analysis of the data, the classes are considered separately i.e. separate network and metrics for each year.

The analysis that follows, aims at measuring the correlation between formal grades and each of the social network metrics, presented in the previous section. Before proceeding, it is vital to clarify:

1. In this section, only students that participated in the final exam have been included in the statistical analysis, since tutors and external users obviously had no grade.

2. All data elaboration described in the previous section has been conducted for visualization purposes only, however, using that format in data correlation revealed a calculation inaccuracy risk. Hence, neither the grades nor the social network metrics have been normalized in this section. Grades are in their original format (scale 0-10) and the social network metrics are also in their original format as calculated by NodeXL when, separately, creating the networks for each year.

Hereinafter the Least Squared Regression (LSR) and the Pearson's correlation (PC) results are presented for the original (not normalized for visualization) data.

Least Squares Regression (LSR)

The method of Least Squared Regression (LSR) is applied, in order to identify whether higher social network analysis metric values during each academic year would result in higher grades in the final exams. To that extend, let each SNA metric be the independent variable X and the final grade be the dependent variable Y. The formula that was applied in order to calculate the regression of the final grade Y over each SNA metric X and for each year, follows:

$$\hat{b} = \frac{n \sum_{i=1}^{n} x_i y_i - \left(\sum_{i=1}^{n} x_i \right) \left(\sum_{i=1}^{n} y_i \right)}{n \sum_{i=1}^{n} x_i^2 - \left(\sum_{i=1}^{n} x_i \right)^2}$$

$$\hat{a} = \overline{y} - \hat{b}\overline{x}$$

where:

$$\overline{y} = \frac{1}{n} \sum_{i=0}^{n} y_i, \overline{x} = \frac{1}{n} \sum_{i=0}^{n} x_i$$

Table 1 summarizes the LSR results for each year separately:

Pearson Correlation

In order to identify any relationship between formal performance and social network activities, Pearson's correlation (PC) was applied in three pairs of data for each year: 'indegree centrality and grade', 'outdegree centrality and grade', and 'betweenness centrality and grade'.

The results are summarized in Table 2.

The nature of the research data (centralities have recurrent values) does not allow applying rank correlations such as Spearman's, Kendall's and Goodman and Kruskal's ones.

Table 1. Least Square Regression Results per Year and per Data Pair

Least Square Regression	Year 1 (n = 74)	Year 2 (n = 87)
Indegree (X) – Grade (Y)	a = 6.632 b = 0.128 SD_X = 2.000 SD_Y = 1.318	a = 6.315 b = -0.006 SD_X = 0.918 SD_Y = 1.267
Outdegree (X) – Grade (Y)	a = 6.607 b = 0.130 SD_X = 3.196 SD_Y = 1.318	a = 6.206 b = 0.069 SD_X = 2.015 SD_Y = 1.267
Betweeness (X) – Grade (Y)	a = 6.775 b = 0.003 SD_X = 109.08 SD_Y = 1.318	a = 6.278 b = 0.002 SD_X = 69.944 SD_Y = 1.267

Table 2. Pearson Correlation Results per Year and per Data Pair

Pearson Correlation	Year 1 (n = 74)	Year 2 (n = 87)
Indegree – Grade	0.23080405	-0.150422
Outdegree – Grade	0.31489971	0.10616477
Betweenness – Grade	0.26959704	0.08263165

Results Discussion

Regarding statistical correlation, LSR revealed that 'outdegree centrality and grade' and, 'betweenness centrality and grade' have had similar behavior in 'Year 1' and this has been validated in 'Year 2', although the standard deviation for the 'betweenness centrality' has shown diversity. In case of 'indegree centrality and grade', it has had negative value in 'Year 2', which shows that higher final grades have been linked to lower number of followers.

At the same time, statistical correlation applying PC method has revealed a weak positive linear relationship for every pair of data in 'Year 1', while having slightly stronger results in the 'outdegree centrality and grade' pair. This could mean that an extrovert student who liked following other students had higher grades. For 'Year 2', the state in the 'outdegree centrality and grade' pair is less clear. The correlation is closer to zero (0) and in the case of 'indegree centrality and grade' pair, it is negative, meaning that 'Year 2' results cannot be used as validation for the findings of 'Year 1', for the case of the 'indegree centrality and grade' pair.

Regarding the practical implications of these results, it is shown that outdegree centrality has a positive association with high grades and therefore could be a parameter educator should focus on and encourage in social networking in learning environments. In such networks, our study showed that one the one hand, having a high number of followings, or having higher brokering ability in the social network could lead to higher student performance. On the other hand, having a high number of followers cannot ensure high performance.

CONCLUSION AND FUTURE WORK

In this paper, an educational social platform, H2L, has been utilized as the sole environment for the teaching purposes of a B.Sc. in computer science course at the Hellenic Open University for two years. Data in terms of social networking behavior and formal grades of students have been collected and analyzed. This paper visualized the combined results from two consequent years and applied statistical correlation in each year's data separately, specifically, between SNA metrics and grades with two methods: Least Squares Regression and Pearson Correlation. A positive association between grades and outdegree centrality has been revealed for the first year, and was validated in the second year with LSR. The PC analysis revealed a similar association for these pairs, but weaker than in LSR. However, for the 'indegree centrality and grade' pair, the results of the second year do not confirm that, having a high number of followers means higher grades and this was shown by both methods of statistical analysis used. Furthermore, in terms of average values, the second year has shown lower average final grades and lower average SNA metric values than in the first year.

As a conclusion, this work and the way HOU2LEARN was applied in PLH42, has shown that having a high number of followings (the quality of followings could be another research topic) or having higher brokering ability in the social network could lead to higher student performance, as it was formally assessed by final grades. On the contrary, having a high number of followers cannot ensure high performance. Unquestionably, it would be more than interesting to apply the same analysis to a few more academic years, to formulate more robust conclusions.

Future research has two directions: a) to focus on a course and accumulate data for more academic years, investigating any behavior and performance patterns among each year students, and b) to focus on a class and accumulate data about its performance during its attendance to many different courses. In the first scenario, the conditions of teaching and syllabus stay the same, but students change each year. In the second scenario, the user group remains the same and its behavior, using H2L across different courses and syllabuses is investigated.

REFERENCES

Baldwin, T. T., Bedell, M. D., & Johnson, J. L. (1997). The social fabric of a team-based MBA program: Network effects on student satisfaction and performance. *Academy of Management Journal, 40*(6), 1369–1397. doi:10.2307/257037

Buckingham, S. (2012). *Learning Analytics Policy Brief.* UNESCO.

Cela, K. L., Sicilia, M. Á., & Sánchez, S. (2015). Social Network Analysis in E-Learning Environments: A Preliminary Systematic Review. *Educational Psychology Review, 27*(1), 219–246. doi:10.100710648-014-9276-0

Cho, H., Gay, G., Davidson, B., & Ingraffea, A. (2007). Social networks, communication styles, and learning performance in a CSCL community. *Computers & Education, 49*(2), 309–329. doi:10.1016/j.compedu.2005.07.003

Christakis, N. A., & Fowler, J. H. (2009). *Connected: The surprising power of our social networks and how they shape our lives.* Little, Brown.

Clow, D. (2012). The learning analytics cycle: closing the loop effectively. *Paper presented at the 2nd International Conference on Learning Analytics and Knowledge*, Vancouver, Canada. 10.1145/2330601.2330636

Dawson, S., Heathcote, L., & Poole, G. (2010). Harnessing ICT potential: The adoption and analysis of ICT systems for enhancing the student learning experience. *International Journal of Educational Management, 24*(2), 116–128. doi:10.1108/09513541011020936

de Laat, M., Lally, V., Lipponen, L., & Simons, R.-J. (2007). Investigating patterns of interaction in networked learning and computer-supported collaborative learning: A role for Social Network Analysis. *International Journal of Computer-Supported Collaborative Learning, 2*(1), 87–103. doi:10.100711412-007-9006-4

Downes, S. (2010). Collaboration, Analytics, and the LMS: A Conversation with Stephen Downes. *Campus Technology*, (Oct): 14.

Fournier, H., Kop, R., & Sitlia, H. (2011). The value of learning analytics to networked learning on a personal learning environment. *Paper presented at the 1st International Conference on Learning Analytics and Knowledge*. 10.1145/2090116.2090131

García-Saiz, D., Palazuelos, C., & Zorrilla, M. (2014). Data Mining and Social Network Analysis in the Educational Field: An Application for Non-Expert Users. In A. Peña-Ayala (Ed.), *Educational Data Mining: Applications and Trends* (pp. 411–439). Cham: Springer International Publishing. doi:10.1007/978-3-319-02738-8_15

Gašević, D., Dawson, S., & Siemens, G. (2015). Let's not forget: Learning analytics are about learning. *TechTrends, 59*(1), 64–71. doi:10.100711528-014-0822-x

Gašević, D., Zouaq, A., & Janzen, R. (2013). "Choose your classmates, your GPA is at stake!" The association of cross-class social ties and academic performance. *The American Behavioral Scientist, 57*(10), 1460–1479. doi:10.1177/0002764213479362

Hansen, D., Shneiderman, B., & Smith, M. A. (2010). *Analyzing social media networks with NodeXL: Insights from a connected world*. Morgan Kaufmann.

Harel, D., & Koren, Y. (2000). A fast multi-scale method for drawing large graphs. *Paper presented at the working conference on Advanced visual interfaces*, Palermo, Italy. 10.1145/345513.345353

Hommes, J., Arah, O. A., de Grave, W., Schuwirth, L. W., Scherpbier, A. J., & Bos, G. M. (2014). Medical students perceive better group learning processes when large classes are made to seem small. *PLoS One, 9*(4), e93328. doi:10.1371/journal.pone.0093328 PMID:24736272

Hommes, J., Rienties, B., de Grave, W., Bos, G., Schuwirth, L., & Scherpbier, A. (2012). Visualising the invisible: A network approach to reveal the informal social side of student learning. *Advances in Health Sciences Education: Theory and Practice, 17*(5), 743–757. doi:10.100710459-012-9349-0 PMID:22294429

Kamel Boulos, M. N., & Wheeler, S. (2007). The emerging Web 2.0 social software: An enabling suite of sociable technologies in health and health care education1. *Health Information and Libraries Journal, 24*(1), 2–23. doi:10.1111/j.1471-1842.2007.00701.x PMID:17331140

Koulocheri, E., & Xenos, M. (2013). Considering formal assessment in learning analytics within a PLE: the HOU2LEARN case. *Paper presented at the Third International Conference on Learning Analytics and Knowledge*, Leuven, Belgium. 10.1145/2460296.2460304

Nascimbeni, F., Fischer, T., Cullen, J., & Kugemann, W. (2009). *Informal learning in the era of Web 2.0. In ICT and lifelong learning for a creative and innovative Europe Findings, reflections and proposals from the Learnovation project*. Barcelona: PAU Education.

Romero, C., López, M.-I., Luna, J.-M., & Ventura, S. (2013). Predicting students' final performance from participation in on-line discussion forums. *Computers & Education*, *68*, 458–472. doi:10.1016/j.compedu.2013.06.009

Shum, S. B., & Ferguson, R. (2012). Social learning analytics. *Journal of Educational Technology & Society*, *15*(3), 3–26.

Siemens, G. (2014). *Connectivism: A learning theory for the digital age. International Journal of Instructional Technology and Distance Learning*. ITDL.

Siemens, G., Gasevic, D., Haythornthwaite, C., Dawson, S., Shum, S. B., Ferguson, R., . . . Baker, R. (2011). *Open Learning Analytics: an integrated & modularized platform* [Doctoral dissertation]. Open University Press.

Siemens, G., & Long, P. (2011). Penetrating the fog: Analytics in learning and education. *EDUCAUSE Review*, *46*(5), 30.

Soumplis, A., Chatzidaki, E., Koulocheri, E., & Xenos, M. (2011). Implementing an Open Personal Learning Environment. *Paper presented at the 15th Panhellenic Conference on Informatics, PCI2011*, Kastoria, Greece. 10.1109/PCI.2011.2

Stahl, G. (2005). Group cognition in computer-assisted collaborative learning. *Journal of Computer Assisted Learning*, *21*(2), 79–90. doi:10.1111/j.1365-2729.2005.00115.x

Van Harmelen, M. (2006). Personal Learning Environments. *Paper presented at the ICALT*. 10.1109/ICALT.2006.1652565

Wasserman, S., & Faust, K. (1994). *Social network analysis: Methods and applications* (Vol. 8). Cambridge university press. doi:10.1017/CBO9780511815478

Yuen, S. C.-Y., & Yuen, P. (2008). Social networks in education. *Paper presented at the E-Learn: World Conference on E-Learning in Corporate, Government, Healthcare, and Higher Education*.

ENDNOTES

[1]   http://www.elgg.org

This research was previously published in the International Journal of Web-Based Learning and Teaching Technologies (IJWLTT), 14(1); pages 17-31, copyright year 2019 by IGI Publishing (an imprint of IGI Global).

Chapter 20
Merging Social Networking With Learning Systems to Form New Personalized Learning Environments (PLE)

Steve Goschnick
Swinburne University of Technology, Australia

ABSTRACT

The future of learning environments lies with the merging of the better aspects of learning management systems (LMS), with those popularized in social networking platforms, to personalize the individual learning experience in a PLE (personal learning environment). After examining the details of a particularly flexible LMS, followed by the investigation of several key data structures behind the Facebook social networking platform, this chapter demonstrates how such a merging can be done at the conceptual schema level, and presents a list of novel features that it then enables.

INTRODUCTION

This paper investigates the fusion of *social networking* capabilities with those from a fine-grained Learning Management System (LMS), into a *personalised learning environment* (PLE), described largely in terms of a design expressed as a conceptual schema. The social network platform investigated is Facebook, which perhaps surprisingly, has several of the necessary generic structures already in place, should that company choose to pursue the emerging personalised learning environment marketplace. However, an LMS could equally be evolved, taking on some aspects popularised by social networking platforms, in new ways that personalise a learner's experience.

DOI: 10.4018/978-1-6684-7123-4.ch020

Some General Background

In situating the research in this chapter it is first worth noting that learning systems have advanced in parallel with similar strides in learning theory, and those in ICT (Information Communication Technology) in general. Although they are interrelated, we concentrate here on the technology side, with brief reference to some theory in learning, only when it is useful to the main research direction. We are primarily concerned with personalised learning environments (PLEs) – which are predicated on putting the student into a more central and active role in their own learning, both with regard to the design of learning materials, and the learning path or trajectory they take in using them. Such an underlying basis of PLEs makes them both more personalised and more adaptive than the typical LMS (Learning Management Systems – such as WebCT, Blackboard and Moodle, and many lesser-known platforms) that thousands of universities and schools have used for up to a decade now.

Tsolis et al (2011) state that '*A traditional LMS offers to all its users the same services and content, meaning that all learners taking an LMS-based course, regardless of their knowledge, goals and interests, receive access to the same educational content and the same set of tools, with no further personalized support.*' Some envisage PLEs as an approach that will replace (or at least speed-up the evolution of) the LMS (Downes, 2010; Trolis et al, 2011). According to Downes: '*the typical LMS is static, declarative, authority-based*' whereas '*a personal learning environment is learning through community; a PLE is a technological tool that allows us to do (that)*'. According to Trolis et al: they are '*extending the capabilities of a traditional open source LMS (Moodle), into (their) proposed OWLearn system ... an adaptive, personalized and open source e-Learning system*' – yet that paper is little more than a wish-list of the features they want to see realised in it, with little in the way of design or specification toward achieving it. Others see a merging of PLEs and LMS into something new beyond either (Mott, 2010). According to Mott: '*the LMS has become a symbol of the status quo that supports administrative functions more effectively than teaching and learning activities*'; and that '*PLEs offer an alternative ...but with their own limitations*' including security and reliability. Mott believes the two approaches should and can be mashed up into '*open learning networks*'. Mott presents a good comparison of the strengths and weaknesses of both the LMS and the PLE, as he sees them.

The concept of a PLE preceded the arrival of well-endowed tools to demonstrate it, and as such there is some variation around the edges of what a PLE is, or should be. Attwell (2007) believed that the tools were already available. He believed that the software applications many people use regularly, together with the services they call upon, could be aggregated to enact a PLE just by changing the mindset of both students and teachers toward personalised learning. His example application tools included: the word processor, Keynote (for presentations), Net Newsreader, Garage Band (for podcasts) and iMovie (for video editing). While his example range of existing services that could be folded in included: Skype, Delicio-us (for sharing bookmarks), Flickr (for sharing photos), and Joomla (for creating web sites). '*It was not a software application, instead it was more of a new approach to using technologies for learning... by the net-generation*'.

Downes (2005) was happy with the blogging tools of the day – e.g. Blogger and WordPress – but he saw a further need for some automation in the way that these *page islands* of output by creative, active learners could be interrelated. Initially, the RSS aggregator (of newsfeeds from blogs in RSS format) was Downes' early answer to that automation, in what Mott called '*the PLE (is) the educational manifestation of the webs "small pieces loosely joined"*' - incorporating a quote from Dave Winer, the inventor of RSS.

Some researchers took that early optimism about available tools and services, and put it upon their 'net-gen' students to *'put students in a more central position in the learning process by allowing them to design their own learning environment'* (Valtonen et al, 2012). They embedded this in the running of actual vocational courses in Finland, across a range of disciplines. Valtonen et al asked themselves *'what kinds of personal learning environments would (the) students produce'*. The feedback was mixed, with many students expressing the negative impact of the learning of the tools needed, against what they actually needed to learn in their respective subjects (i.e. catering services, international business, health care, computer science, engineering, massage therapy). Valtonen et al cite their experience in retrospect as *'romantic constructionism'*. One of their conclusions is that instead of focusing on technology *'the emphasis ought to be on the pedagogical demands of PLEs in education'*, and interestingly, that *'with adequate pedagogical support from teachers, students can potentially make use of PLEs for learning and thus develop their metacognitive and self-regulative skills'*.

Beyond the use of mundane (everyday) software applications and existing services by net-gen learners to spontaneously create or *mashup* effective PLEs, the two other approaches advanced in the research thus far to achieve a PLE are: to evolve an existing LMS towards a PLE; or thirdly, to create a new PLE unrelated to any founding LMS. A fourth approach is considered in this chapter: to examine what would be necessary to evolve an existing social network platform into a PLE.

So, what features set a PLE apart from an LMS? Personalised learning includes both personalisation to suit the individual learner – this often requires a much more detailed profile than in a typical LMS, with tagging (i.e. assigning *keywords*) to highlight an individual's interests and also a similar set of tags to represent their existing knowledge. Personalisation includes adaptability of the learning materials presented, and also allows or empowers the student to be more pro-active in creating learning material themselves, often in a collaborative way with participating peers. The adaptability achieved through techniques such as tagging, can be manual or automated in some manner. Some automation of the personalisation and any automation of the adjustable learning content, added to a PLE beyond adjustments in a more manual manner, either by the student or the teacher, are also increasingly possible.

Within learning technologies, the now well-used traditional LMS are generally characterised with features that do *not* lend themselves well to personalisation and adaptability to individual learners, such that those taking such a route are on a difficult path to achieve their goal - unless the LMS has more flexibility than most, or the necessary changes are coming via the LMS vendor. The open source LMS, Moodle, gains some such flexibility by way of the open source approach to its licensing, allowing others to add plugins to it in the form of apps, a route that a number of the researchers of papers cited in this chapter, have taken or are in the process of taking. There are other LMSs that have considerable flexibility in their initial design, such as the one described in following section.

In a significant contrast to the Valtonen et al (2012) approach of putting the onus on 'net-gen' students to come-up with their own novel PLEs, Limongelli et al (2011) take the third approach to having a PLE: creating a new one from technologies unrelated to a traditional LMS. Adding to the contrast, they put emphasis on helping the *teachers role* (by adding some smarts via some automation) in providing a PLE experience to students. The basic technology they do call upon in the absence of an LMS, is the use of planner technology based on *Linear Temporal Logic* (Mayer et al, 2007) from AI, and the way they use it serves as a useful illustration in applying a formulaic approach to adaptive learning:

From the adaptive learning perspective, *Lecomps5* (their system) is for creating *learning paths* through a sequence of *Learning Objects* (LO) that have metadata added to each, which they then call *Learning Components* (LC). Their system allows for two types of such sequences: one where the sequencing is performed at the beginning (by the planning software), and the second, an adaptive step-by-step sequencing, following the student during their path through the graph of Learning Components. Both types use quizzes to fuel the decision points in the planning software. The metadata is added to the Learning Objects by the teacher and includes two sets of tags (either from formal ontologies, or else any other terms): concept prerequisites are set as a series of *Required Knowledge* (RK) tags – just identifiers representing a set of concepts; and the concepts-to-be-acquired as a series of *Acquired Knowledge* (AK) tags. Each of those two series of tags represent a set of like *knowledge items* (*ki*).

As a learner moves through a course (a sequence of LCs), their Cognitive State (CS) is represented by a subset of *ki* from the pool of LCs (plus any ki's they had previously acquired as prerequisites relevant to the current course). The Lecomps5 system also provides for different learning styles (LS) of students (initially four styles: *intuitive-visual, intuitive-verbal, sensing-visual, sensing-verbal* – adapted from Felder & Silverman, 1988), by having four different versions of the LCs (specifically, variations of the instructional content within them). They then consider they have a relatively simple student model (SM): Cognitive State (CS) and the LS measure of the learner i.e. SM = CS + LS (Note: they allow the teacher to put weights against the four learning styles for the one student, as a vector that can be adjusted over time). A traditional LMS requires a significant amount of work on the part of the teacher to manually select and sequence the learning content and activities, so the Lecomps5 system is focused on lightening that load on the teacher considerably.

Their approach to adding smart technology into the learning process does put focus back on learning theory (which as already stated, is not the focus of this chapter). However, a learning framework by Luckin (2008) is specifically aimed at using technologies and other resources beyond the desktop, as a scaffold (meaning *tutorial assistance*) for learning. It is called *The Learner Centric Ecology of Resources*. It helps design learning experiences that matches up available resources to the needs of the learner. The underlying premise is that the learner needs to be in a collaborative environment, where a more abled participant can step in when need be, to occasionally guide the learner, who is otherwise advancing at their own pace. The aim of most smart learning technology is usually to be a part of that assistance, and/or facilitate it from other human participants. Luckin's framework sets about making that possible: "*For technology to provide software scaffolding the system needs a model of its learners*". The PLE developed by Limongelli et al (2011), as we have seen, has a simple Learner model (SM), one that includes their knowledge state and learning style. However Luckin's approach is much more detailed and based on well-accepted learning theory.

The PLE developed by Limongelli et al (2011) is described by them as providing '*automated production and adaption of personalized courses*', but it has no features that enhance collaboration or that enables learners to author their own content, nor any use of social software to make up for those gaps in a PLE feature set. Nonetheless, they inform the reader that in another research effort they are integrating their approach with Moodle – presumably for its administrative and other functions, including the feature that allows it to have plugins from the community around that particular open source LMS.

In a strong sense, the focus and tool development on automating *teacher tasks* by Limongelli et al, and the focus of Valtonen et al (2012) upon the *learner tasks* with the tools at hand, are near the two extremes of the envelope of features and focus that a PLE can have. Our research is looking toward a good balance somewhere in the middle.

What Follows in This Chapter

In the next section describes in detail a pioneering online education content and delivery system developed at the University of Melbourne (by a company then wholly owned by the University) in 1997-98 which foreshadowed the presentation of learning objects we now see in iBooks on the Apple iPad. It was more flexible and adaptive than most mainstream LMSs then and now. As well as describing the Creator LMS, we look at key structures in that system which lend themselves to similar usage in a PLE. It was also early in employing 'smart' technology in an LMS, in the form of intelligent software agents, to seek out a certain form of specific data across the web – again, a technique and tool that could be much more broadly applied in a PLE future.

In the section *Conceptual Models from a Social Networking Platform* we look at structures underpinning the Facebook social network platform, from research that infers a *conceptual data model* from the textual programming API (Graph API V2.0) that Facebook makes available to third party developers. We do this with the aim of uncovering aspects of a social network platform that will add user-friendly proactive content creation features to a smart PLE, where a student may create, curate, participate and share such content with peers and friends, regardless of context, mobile or otherwise.

In Section 4 we draw from the models and experience presented in Sections 2 and 3, with a view to putting some combination of them together in the one PLE system, in particular with an emphasis on what would be needed to turn the existing Facebook conceptual model into a Personal Learning Environment (PLE), as one such future possibility.

TECHNICAL PARALLEL BETWEEN AN OLD AND A NEW LEARNING SYSTEM

What first sparked this research was an observation of a direct parallel in the technologies used to deliver online course material to the browser within an earlier pioneering educational content creation and management system, with a much more recent need to deliver personalised educational content to tablets and large-format smartphones such as Apple iOS devices. This new need requires high fidelity presentation and fine-grained delivery of educational content down to the page level, and even multiple learning objects on such a tablet displayed page. The earlier system was called Melbourne IT Creator and was briefly introduced in Goschnick (1998).

The *authoring* tools in the Creator platform were delivered in a technology open to *most* teachers, academics and other content creators, including students using the premier cross-platform language of that time (the Java language on the desktop). We chose HTML V4, CSS V1 and the JavaScript language to *deliver the content* to students using almost any computers available (all those with a web browser). The HTML mark-up code allowed broad student access via all the major web-browsers, while the then lesser known CSS V1 was used to place *learning objects* (any presentation/interactive technology that could be presented on the screen upon a rectangular sub-area) within the HTML rendered page, at an absolute location (x,y, width, height) in the browser window. This choice of underlying technology gave content developers WYSIWYG (what-you-see-is-what-you-get) delivery, which was deemed particularly important by our designers and multimedia artists. The JavaScript language was used to retrieve and manipulate server-side stored content, and create the needed CSS and HTML code to render it as intended.

When investigating the iPad much more recently as the target device for personalised, dynamically configurable content, the *Page* was once again seen as the fundamental unit of both design and delivery to the learner. The iBook format – itself based on EPUB3 (V3) – was identified as an attractive format for the purpose. For example, Adobe *InDesign,* a page mark-up tool used by many page design professionals, can output in the EPUB3 format, as can a number of open-source tools, which can in turn be directly imported into iBookstore on the iPad. A significant goal in the later project was to find a good balance between: professionally designed and built learning objects, and professionally designed page renditions that house those objects; or alternatively, end-user developer pages and media content, and a smart personalised system that can dynamically select the particularly learning-objects most applicable for the individual learners' (and their peers') current circumstance. EPUB3 is basically *HTML5* (with a formal index-page structure) – which is a term generally used interchangeably with three closely integrated standards used in the web browser, namely: *HTML V5* mark-up, *CSS V3*, and *JavaScript* (W3C, 2014) – i.e. these are simply later versions of the same three technologies used to deliver Creator content in the web-browser, 15+ years earlier. That being the case, the design and conceptual data model behind Creator lent itself to further investigation, as an eminently suitable one for storage and retrieval of learning-objects in a newly envisaged personalised learning environment (PLE).

Description and Conceptual Model of Creator

The earlier online education system presented in this section was called *Melbourne IT Creator* (Goschnick, ibid). It was the culmination of a research and development project from mid-1997 until mid-1998 in the company Melbourne IT Pty Ltd, then a wholly-owned subsidiary of the University of Melbourne. Note: The company was *floated* – the *IPO* initial public offering - on the ASX (Australian Stock Exchange) in the year 1999, raising some $90 million for the university.

Creator was an integrated system that provided an end-to-end solution to authoring, management and presentation of web-based online learning materials, in the genre of what now is the LMS. It had three primary functions:

- Content Authoring
- Content Storage and Management
- Content Presentation and Delivery

The central concept introduced in Creator was the *learning object*, of which there are two categories: *simple* and *complex* (composite in nature). Creator also defined a number of *views* of the overall system, as seen by users with distinctly different *roles,* to help users navigate what had become a large and sophisticated system.

Simple Learning Objects

Simple learning objects can be one of the following: Plain Text (paragraphs); Tables (HTML <table>); Images; Audio; Video; Interactive Animation (e.g. Flash, Shockwave); Programmed Component (Javabeans, Java Applet, Microsoft COM objects); Question (Simple True/False; Multiple Choice; Mutually-exclusive Choices; Matching (2D matrix of choices); or, Free text entry).

Composite Learning Objects

Composite (also called complex) learning objects can be one of the following:

- **Page:** A HTML page that may contain numerous and any combination of the simple learning objects above.
- **Reference Work:** A hierarchy of sequentially linked *Pages*.
- **Learning Activity:** A complex web of *Pages* linked in a non-linear sequence (a network graph), with conditional paths based on student choices and progress.
- **Document:** An externally authored document in one of various formats including MS/WORD, Adobe Acrobat (PDF), and RTF.

Figure 1 is a conceptual data model of the learning objects, and how they are inter-related within the unifying model. This logical model can be easily detailed further into the physical model of the server-side database, which stores the current state of a Creator-hosted online learning system in a Relational DBMS server, a type of system that later became known as a Web 2.0 approach (2005).

Figure 1. Part 1 of the Conceptual Data Model that stores the Learning Objects in Creator

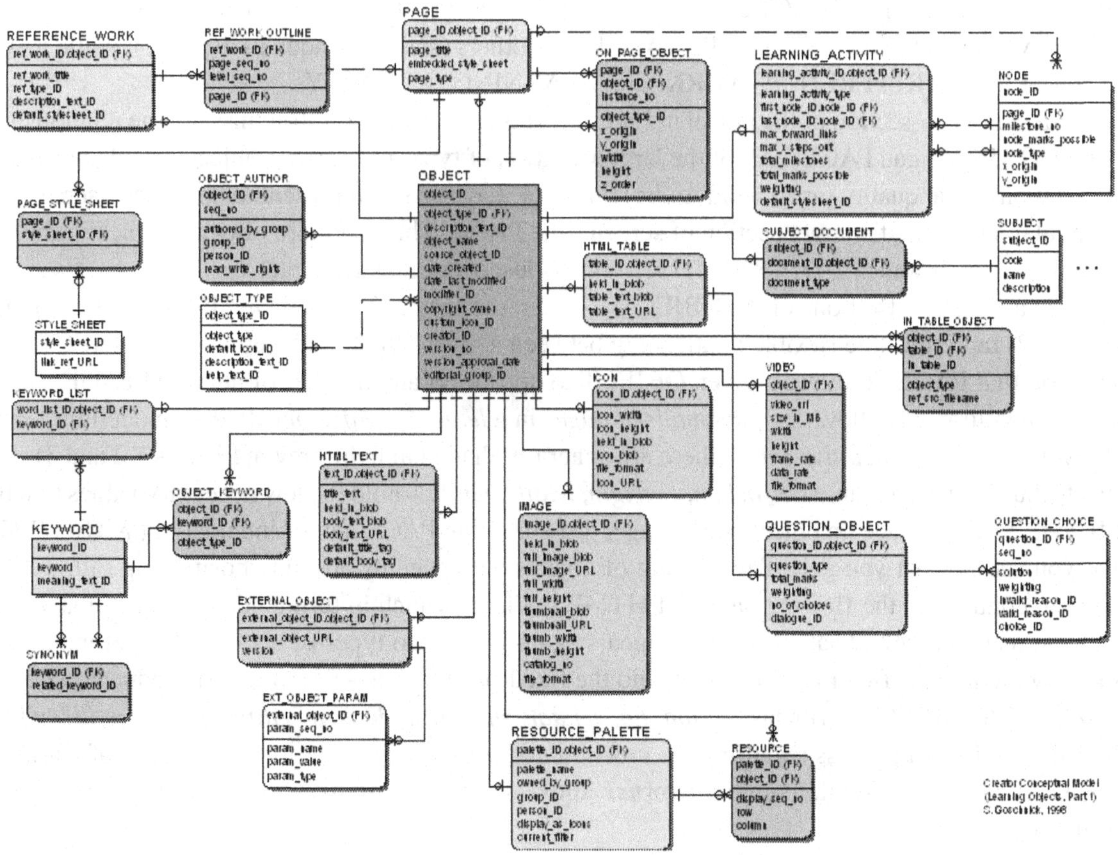

Note 1: Each of the main entities shaded in yellow in Figure 1 (REFERENCE_WORK, PAGE, LEARN-ING_ACTIVITY, QUESTION_OBJECT, KEYWORK/KEYWORK_LIST and RESOURCE_PALETTE) had a dedicated authoring tool written in the Java language. Figure 4 is an example of the interface of one of the authoring tools: the *Learning Activity Tool*.

Note 2: The entities shaded in grey are associative entities (which represent many-to-many relation-ships); those in light-blue are less-significant objects, such as icons and images, which do not need custom authoring tools; while those in white are simply less significant entities in the model, included for completeness.

The Page as Fundamental Unit in Course Delivery

Early in the life of the project, a one-week discussion between many stakeholders took place, regarding the prominent place of *objects* in the design *versus* the prominent place of *pages* in the design – with effectively two sides of roughly equal numbers of stakeholders, leaning each way. (In a sense, it was parallel to the self-dialogue in Downes (2005), where he effectively dismisses the 'atoms' that are learning-objects in an LMS, structured together into activities, subjects and courses; but then he outlines his alternative vision of the web-page (in blogs, etc), similarly aggregated together into a loose structure, of more personally suited content via RSS aggregation). The resulting conceptual schema in Creator places both *Pages* and *Objects* in the design, with each holding a significant foundational position in the underlying structure: the OBJECT entity is a so-called *super-type* to the simple learning objects, such as IMAGE, VIDEO, HTML_TXT, HTML_TABLE, and others (shaded in aqua in Figure 1); while PAGE can appear in both REFERENCE_WORKs and LEARNING_ACTIVITYs.

Figure 2 is a sub-section of the model in Figure 1, showing the central structure and the relationships between OBJECTs and PAGEs. All of the large variation of types of learning-objects listed above have the common visual quality (apart from *Audio*) that they may each be represented on a user's screen in a rectangular sub-area of a larger section of screen - the PAGE. This is a more obvious choice in the age of the iPad, than it was in 1997/98 as HTML V4 was just becoming available.

While a PAGE is itself one of the OBJECT_TYPEs, the structure named ON_PAGE_OBJECT (rhs in Figure 2) represents the flexible relationship between a given PAGE and a number of OBJECTs that appear on that PAGE. It allows a given OBJECT to appear on any number of authored PAGEs in the system, and ultimately allows for *personalised pages* in a *learning trajectory*. In data modelling termi-nology it is of type *associative entity* (these are generally shaded in light-grey in Figures 1,2 and 3). The data attributes within it named: *x_origin, y_origin, width, height* – hold the few necessary values that the CSS code needs to place an object on the page, just so, as the PAGE author intended it (WYSIWYG – what-you-see-is-what-you-get). This placing of objects on a page by absolute positioning (allowed by CSS) ran contrary to the flowing nature of HTML mark-up, which in turn tended to upset many page designers using HTML. That dichotomy appears again in the two types of ebooks allowed in Apple's iBookstore today: the flowing text format, and the fixed-page format - added in a subsequent version.

Note 1: The OBJECT attributes *version_no, version_approval_date* and *editorial_group_id* – which allowed for a formal process regarding the creation and subsequent evolution of all types of learning-objects in the system. While *copyright_owner* allowed for attributions right down at the individual learning object level.

Note 2: The OBJECT_AUTHOR entity allowed for the authorship of learning objects to be either by an individual or a group of authors.

Figure 2. Detail from Figure 1 showing the relationship between Objects, Pages and Reference_Works

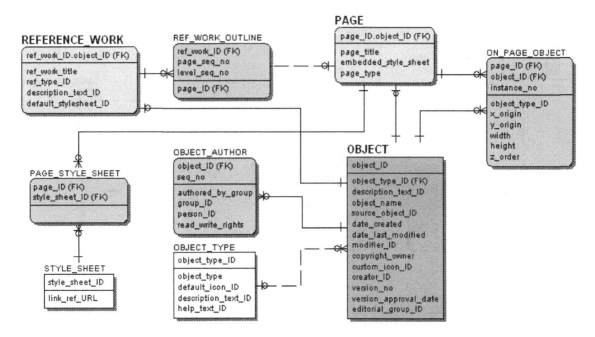

Figure 2 also shows the arrangement of a set of PAGEs into REFERENCE_WORKs. Clearly from its name, a Reference Work can be seen as an online ebook with interactivity, but what is less obvious is that the Reference Work may actually be customised down to the Page level, for individual learners, as we will see further down. That is, the PAGE was designed as the fundamental unit of course/subject delivery in the Creator system. The entity REF_WORK_OUTLINE is the structure that holds the data to build the Contents of a Reference Work. The authorship of the Page (and the complex learning objects) is not restricted to teachers and tutors – it is entirely in the hands of the administration rights in the Creator system (which are non-hierarchical), such that a PLE of a sort is possible with little change to the tools.

The Learning Activity Learning Object

The most complex learning-object in Creator is the *Learning Activity*. It also interacts with the *Question Object* – which appears on the Page as a question that a student answers. A Learning Activity here is a pre-designed series of PAGEs that a learner encounters, the order of which is dynamic and generally non-linear, depending on the learner's interaction with it; as opposed to the sequential movement through a Reference_Work.

As with a REFERENCE_WORK the PAGE is the fundamental unit of delivery for a LEARNING_ACTIVITY. The overall structure of a Learning Activity is that of a *network graph* (see Figure 4 for an example of a network graph of Pages within the authoring tool), as opposed to the hierarchical structure of a Reference Work or an ebook. The entities directly involved in a Learning Activity are portrayed in Figure 3. A *NODE* represents a Page in the network graph which includes a *milestone* manually set by the author of a particular Learning Activity.

Figure 3. Part 2 of the Conceptual Data Model that stores the Learning Objects in Creator, but also student responses as they move through a Learning Activity

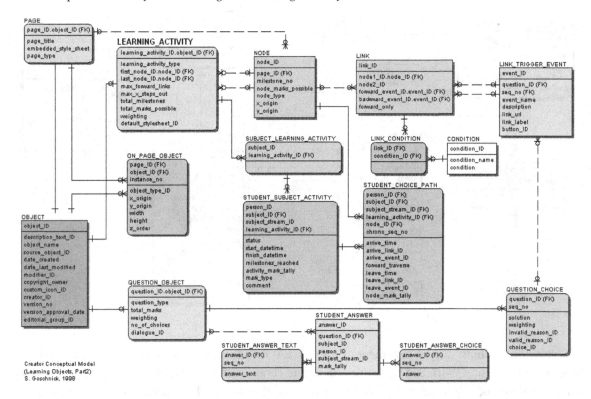

The *LINK* entity represents the *arc* between two NODEs, the IDs of which are stored in attributes *node1_ID* and *node2_ID*. LINKs can be either one or two-way, at the authors discretion. The learner can back-step if it is designated a two-way link. The transition of the learner from one NODE/PAGE to the next, depends on an *event* stored in the *LINK_TRIGGER_EVENT* entity. One such triggering event is a particular *QUESTION_CHOICE* that a learner has selected within a multiple-choice Question, as they negotiate the Learning Activity. This allows for a dynamic *path* through the network of PAGEs, based on the learning outcomes of an individual learner. E.g. if they pick the right answer it goes in one direction, if not, then it goes a different way, possibly a remedial learning path to make sure they achieve a particular learning milestone. Another trigger event type is the simple pressing of a particular button with *button_ID*. In addition to the trigger event, a number of filtering *Conditions* can be placed on the *Link*, for example, that a particular video was watched in-full by the learner.

An individual student's *personal learning trajectory* is recorded in the entity *STUDENT_CHOICE_PATH*. We take a deeper look at it in Section 4 where we press the concept and technique into finergrained *personalised learning trajectories*, taking the student's current context into consideration with respect to the types of events that can trigger a particular path through a Learning Activity.

What is not immediately clear in Figure 3 is that the concatenated primary-keys (the attributes above the dividing-line in an entity box) in the two entities STUDENT_SUBJECT_ACTIVITY and subsequently, STUDENT_CHOICE_PATH, include several foreign-keys (FK) from entities that don't appear in Figure 3, namely, *person_ID, subject_ID* and *subject_stream_ID*. Those identifiers come from entities left out of Figure 3 for clarity sake. We will revisit them down in Section 4. Enough to say here that there is a whole other Creator sub-model that deals with the *administration* of *subjects, students* and *subject-streams,* some of which necessarily appear down in Figure 9 (the white entities).

What can be gleaned from the details in Figure 3 is that the entity STUDENT_SUBJECT_ACTIV-ITY records an individual student's progress within a particular Learning Activity, via their enrolment in a particular SUBJECT_STREAM, storing the state of that progress in the appropriate data attributes: *start_datetime, finish_datetime, milestone_reached, activity_mark_tally* and *comment.*

Finer-grained detail of a student's navigation through a Learning Activity, node-by-node, is recorded in the STUDENT_CHOICE_PATH entity, in the data attributes: *arrive_time, arrive_event, arrive_link_ID, arrive_event, leave_time, leave_link_ID, leave_event_ID,* and *node_mark_tally.* Such data could be data-mined to identify general problems in a given Learning Activity.

Figure 4. The interface of (one of) the actual authoring tool for creating Learning Activities - clearly showing the network graph structure of such an activity

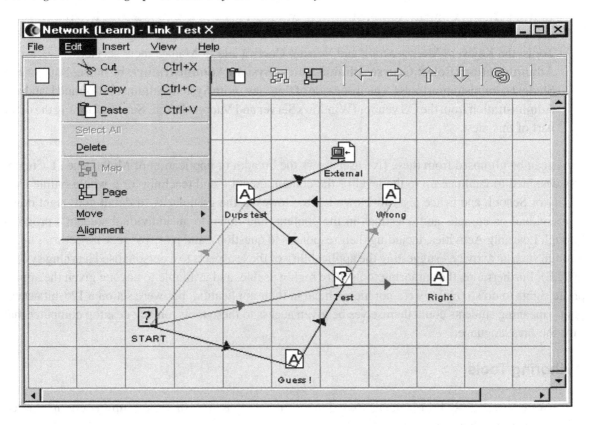

User Views and Roles, and the Tools That Service Them

User Views and User Roles

There are five *User Views* that facilitate the chunking of functionality in the Creator system, with respect to locating and using the right tool for the right task. Very briefly, these views are as follows:

1. **Authoring (Roles: Teacher/Author/Senior Tutor):** This view brings together the Authoring Tools, the Search Tools and Version Controls Services to facilitate the creation of subject and course content, down to the page level.
2. **Learning (Roles: Student/ Tutor):** This view brings together the Session Control interface, the Search Tools and the Communication Tools (see immediately below).
3. **Discussion (Roles: Teacher/Author/Tutor):** The Communication Tools represent the totality of this view. Note: Melbourne IT Creator used off-the-shelf tools for *email*, *newsgroups* and *conferencing* – namely Microsoft NetMeeting and Exchange Server, for expediency.
4. **Library (Roles: Content Administrator/IP Manager):** This view included the Reference Works accumulated in the system, external documents included in various Learning Activities, the Search Tools, the Keyword Manager tool, and Version Control and IP Management services.
5. **Administration (Roles: Course Administrator/ System Administrator):** bCourse, Subject and Student administration tools formed one side of this view, with System Administration and Database Administration from the OS vendor (Windows Server and Microsoft SQL Server) forming the other part of this view.

As can be glimpsed from these five user views the breadth of application of Melbourne IT Creator was designed to facilitate up to the level of the content creation and teaching for a whole online University or School, and hence is a full-blown LMS. However, the granularity of detail goes right down to individual paragraphs and questions in the content, and down to an individual student's progress through Learning Activities, including their responses to questions, and page-by-page trajectories taken through such an activity – suggesting the applicability of those aspects to a personalised learning system (a PLE). Furthermore, the authoring tools were highly usable, and available to anyone given the appropriate rights to do so (*rights* were not hierarchical in their application, but were set on a 128-bit access key) – meaning students could themselves be given access to these tools, on any desktop computer that runs the Java language.

Authoring Tools

There were five distinct Java-language based authoring applications, that made up the one integrated software tool, which were:

1. **Page Designer:** An innovative (for the time) WYSIWYG editor for creating pages in HTML with absolute positioning of learning-objects, using the CSS standard. A Page thus created, could be used in either: a Reference Work, and/or a Learning Activity.
2. **Page Linker:** Used to create the innovative Learning Activities as seen in Figure 4 and described above in Section 2.4.

3. **Resource Palette:** Used to amass a collection of learning-objects, both simple and complex, that may then be easily accessed and drag-and-dropped onto a Page within the Page Designer.
4. **The Outliner:** Used to create a Reference Work from pre-authored Pages.
5. **Keyword Manager:** Used to populate the keyword-related entities in Figure 1, namely: KEYWORD, SYNONYM, OBJECT_KEYWORD and KEYWORD_LIST – in turn used in keyword searches across the *internal* store of learning-objects. I.e. Within the other authoring tools, keyword searches can be done by an author to locate appropriate objects in the overall Creator system, during an authoring session.

Search and the FAME Agent

While the Keyword Manager built indexes against the learning-objects held *within* a Creator system, there was a need for external Internet-wide search, particularly with regard to research-paper citations, often needed by the authors of subject-based learning materials. To cater for this gap in Creator a research project was undertaken by researchers from the Intelligent Agent Lab within the Department of Computer Science & Software Engineering at the University of Melbourne, who had expertise in precisely this area (Cassin & Sterling, 1997; Loke, Davison, & Sterling, 1996; Goschnick & Cassin, 1997).

The intelligent software agent was thereafter known as the Finder and Minder Agent Engine (FAME Agents). The snippets of information from content authors lead to URLs that were then used to *seed* deep web-crawling searches of the site and its links on a regular basis. I won't expand any further in this chapter on the FAME Agent. However, the current field of *recommendation systems* use either software agents or other AI techniques in a similar way to FAME usage in Creator, suggesting many potential applications within PLEs with regard to the personalisation of learning content, and the alignment of collaborative tasks across individual learners.

CONCEPTUAL MODELS FROM A SOCIAL NETWORKING PLATFORM (FACEBOOK)

While Downes (2010), Mott (2010) and others saw benefits of social networking software within PLEs, they mainly saw them as linked informally by the student themselves in their daily learning, in the form of light-weight mashups. Functionally, that could be as simple as a learner having multiple windows from multiple apps on the one screen, or using an RSS aggregator to pull information in from such sites on the web. In more recent times there has been a growing body of research that directly investigates the use of social software (the terms used vary but have similar or overlapping meanings: social media, social semantic web, social networks, social software) with respect to learning, particularly personalised learning: Halimi et al (2014) investigate personalised *recommendations* based on similarity using the social semantic web; Leung (2015) investigates the use of social media against academic performance and perceived social support; Dabbagh & Kitsantas (2012) investigate the combination of social media and self-regulated learning with personalised learning environments (PLEs); while Archee (2012) suggests that the lure of Facebook as an external tool being embraced by educational institutions is 'mistaken' and that the proponents thereof (those that '*regard Facebook as a pedagogical model*' at least) are '*technological determinists*'. None of those studies looks at a specific social network platform from an *information system design* point-of-view, to investigate either: *how* the key features that attract people to social networking platforms such as *Facebook, LinkedIn, Twitter* and *Google+*, might be put into a PLE technology; or alternatively, how easily the vendor of such a platform could focus it into a PLE, should the vendor decide to point their respective considerable commercial focus toward the PLE marketplace.

We investigate these two scenarios in the next Section, but before doing so we need to outline the *why* and the *what* of social network platforms, that are of such interest and potential in the creation of PLEs.

The Why of Social Software in a PLE

Looking at the functionality of current-day social networking platforms, they generally eclipse the earlier use of email and newsgroups in the Creator LMS, regarding social functionality. Beyond communication and collaboration possibilities, the sheer ease that some simple content can be created and the speed that it can be uploaded and shared in the social media platforms, has set the precedence regarding usability and immediacy for a generation or two of what learners now expect in any current or forthcoming PLE.

The What of Social Software in an Advanced Smart PLE

While Facebook has a programming API available to third-party developers, they do not publish a formal or even a conceptual *data model* overview of what is clearly a structured data system behind the scenes. Recently, the author inferred a complete conceptual model of the Facebook platform (Goschnick, 2014), one that fits the data textual descriptions in the publicly available Facebook Graph API V2.0 (Facebook, 2017). The inferred conceptual model has 85 entities – a mid-range information system, in terms of conceptual scope.

The first point of note about the Facebook model is the number of entities – the Facebook platform is far from the light-weight service that the earlier cited PLE enthusiasts (e.g. Mott, 2010; Attwell, 2007) were considering for inclusion in their mashups. Despite its relatively easy to use desktop interface - and discarding the sheer scale and logistics of its physical model and infrastructure to cope with upwards of 2 billion users - underlying the Facebook platform is a sophisticated and extensive *conceptual data model*. As pointed out in (Goschnick, 2014), Facebook has gone to considerable lengths to deny an underlying logical structure, instead saying it is simply a realtime Graph, they call the '*People Graph*, akin to Google's *Search Graph*'. And yet they gather information that fits strict, limited pigeon holes that they themselves define and provide to users, unlike Google's search engine which must deal effectively with the unstructured or widely different structured data from hundreds of millions of independent content creators. That is, the Facebook platform has a definite structure, albeit an extensive one of enterprise system proportions.

However, Facebook has shown considerable innovation in making their enterprise-scale data model highly usable on smartphones and tablets, demonstrated with their more recently released apps: *Facebook Groups* (November, 2014) and *Messenger* (August, 2011 on Android; July, 2014 on iPad). Each app provides limited but focused slices of functionality from the enterprise-scale model, in a highly user-friendly manner on every-day devices. This is a usability strategy that many more enterprise-scale platforms could learn from.

In this chapter, in the next 5 sub-sections we will look in detail at five of the sub-models from the overall Facebook model - those we perceive as having some value to our cross PLE/Social network software comparison, in our goal for an improved smart PLE. They are: the part of the model that deals with *Posts* (which can give *context* to and about the learner's situation); the part that deals with *Groups* (which can replicate the sorts of groups represented in learning environments but also the wider social groups that a learner is a part of – even extending to a global community of traditional and other sub-groups, according to Zuckerberg (2017) more recently); the part that deals with *Events* (which can chart future events such as lectures, project meetings, reading group meetings, etc. - and facilitate all sorts of contextual dialog around them); and the part that deals with *Pages* - given the central place that *Pages* has in both LMS and envisaged PLEs, as discussed above; and *Apps* the part that can bring in unprecedented levels of personalisation through both self-written apps by a new code-savvy generation, and/or via an app store dedicated to learning.

The Facebook Posts Sub-Model

Goschnick (2014) begins with a general description of social networks, with particular reference to Facebook, saying that they "are about connecting people and collecting data; they are communication services upon which further services can be added and customised. The 'people' part leads to *groups* (of friends, family and associates), *sub-groups* and *events*. The 'communication' part leads to *posts, messages, comments* and *questions*. The 'collecting data' part leads to *links, photos, albums, videos, photo-tags, video-tags* and *check-ins* to particular *places* (including *locations* in the real world)".

A *User* has a set of *Friends* who each receives the user's *Posts* and vice-versa. The *Posts* may be a simple text message (status update), but it may be accompanied with a *Photo*, a *Video* or a *Link* (to some web page – often taking a graphic and a headline from that www page). Posts appear in a user's *Newsfeed* – which is effectively a *default home page*, of chronologically listed posts for one's social network (depending on various privacy settings). The Newsfeed is increasingly being peppered with news from outside one's personal social group. This is for both commercial reasons and also now claimed by Zuckerberg (2017) to help counter the problems associated with a 'filter bubble' and 'fake news'. There is a *timeline* version of the newsfeed, which is generally just the full list of a User's own Posts, each entry timestamped.

This simple mechanism can be supported by the *conceptual data model* in Figure 5. Note: the entities *Link, Video*, and *Photo* are sub-types of *Post* - itself a so-called super-type in ER modelling terminology. The *Profile* entity is a generalised way of representing a profile in Facebook of more than just people, which is discussed in the next section. The *With_Tags* entity (an associative entity) is a simple mechanism to store the presence of various friends or peers, with the user when they posted a Post – this is separate from the people 'tagged' in an actual photo which are stored down the bottom in the *Photo_Tags* entity. The *Media* and *Interest* entities are a simple method of storing the various books, music, movies, bands and other things from popular culture, that a user has flagged as of particular interest to them (Note: there is a more extensive way of flagging interests via *Pages*, covered further down). Facebook stores a variety of resolutions of a single image in the *Image* entity to deliver a version that is most appropriate (efficiency-wise) to the current device of the post-receiving user.

The *Users, Friends* and *Posts* are foundational to Facebook and go back to its early history. *FriendList* allows some basic grouping of one's Friends. The free-flowing newsfeed of content (which is conceptually and procedurally similar to a dynamically updated *report* coming from a database system of underlying data), by way of text, photos, video and links, provides a simple and quick content publishing system using a basic stylesheet, broadcast to one's social network. People in that social network may show their support via a *Like* (a one-button click/touch response), and/or a *Comment*, which can expand into an ongoing conversation, involving anyone who has access to that item in the newsfeed.

Figure 5. Users, Friends and their Posts, taken from (Goschnick, 2014 – Figure 3.1)

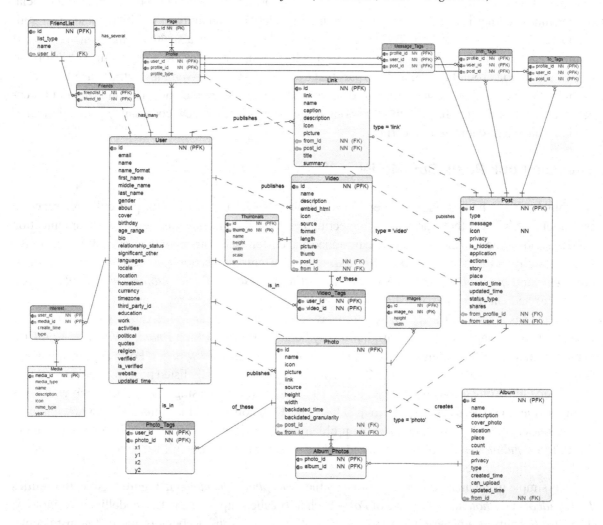

This simple, authoring and communication mechanism, with the immediacy of affirmation and feedback from friends and peers, is now the norm of a generation or two. The smartphone has placed access to it wherever the mobile user currently is. Images from the smartphone can be posted to one's social networks almost instantly and via a user-interface with indiscernible friction. (Note: the *Instagram* app is also now owned by Facebook).

Video requires somewhat more bandwidth, but the evolving telecommunication infrastructure and data plans, means that uploading video will soon be nearly as painless as uploading images for a large percentage of users.

That usability and the responsiveness of the communication is now what a PLE needs to use or to replicate, to meet learner expectations with regard to personalised authoring of content, broadcasting it, and communicating around it with peers, friends and others. Simple in its use, complex but efficient in its delivery infrastructure, and powerful regarding the consequences upon the emotional aspects of learning.

The Facebook Groups Sub-Model

Groups in Facebook are like a series of generalised *FriendLists* (see entity top-left in Figure 5), with extra capabilities and features. For example the *link* attribute in the *Group* entity in Figure 6, holds a *url* to the external Home Page website of the group, who may be a more traditional community. The members of a particular Group are all represented in the associative entity *Member*. A user may join an existing group or start a new one. The Group has a record in the *Profile* entity (together with the user_id of the *User* who first set-up or 'owns' the *Group*). This is a clever mechanism which allows a Group to have a newsfeed of *Posts* by members, just like an individual User has a newsfeed of Posts. All posts emanating from the group via its members, are referenced by records in the associative entity *Group_Feed*. The users get *alerts* when new *Posts* emanate from another group member.

Figure 6. Facebook Groups reproduced here from (Goschnick, 2014; Figure 4.1)

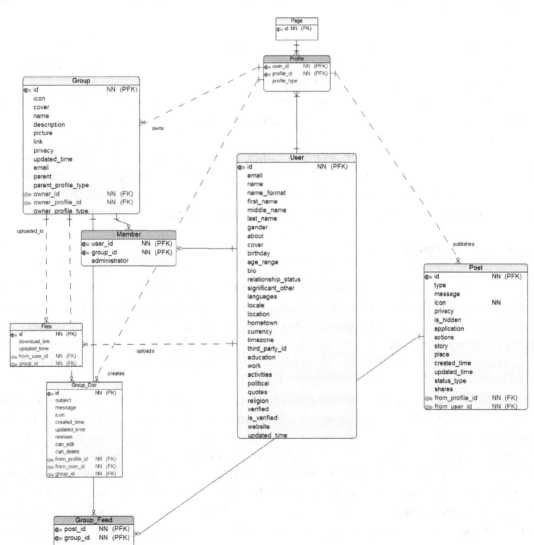

External files created by all sorts of external applications can be uploaded to the Group, as recorded in the *Files* entity. In addition to those, internal *Group_Doc* documents can be created within Facebook (using HTML formatting), and these can be jointly edited by the members of the group.

The attribute in the *Group* entity named *parent* represents the *id* of its parent (if it has one), while *parent_profile_type* can be either: a *Page*, an *App* or another *Group*. I.e. Groups can recursively own other Groups, creating a hierarchical structure of groups that is entirely similar to the *newsgroups* from earlier Internet times, and to *forums* in various wikis and most traditional LMS.

The Groups feature was only added to Facebook in 2010 and when it was introduced, it quickly became their most popular feature (Goschnick, 2014). A free smartphone app (named: *Facebook Groups*) dedicated to just those features in Groups was released by Facebook in 2014 - currently available from both: the Apple App Store for iOS devices, and the Google Play Store for Android OS devices. The features available through this app replicate most of those available through the web browser interface for Groups.

The Facebook Events Sub-Model

Events in either the virtual or real world can be organised, tracked and recorded in Facebook. The *What? When? Where? Who's invited? Who is coming? And who can't make it?* - are all captured and broadcast via the features of the Event part of the Facebook platform.

Furthermore, as with Groups (via the same *Profile* mechanism), *Events* have their own *newsfeed* of *Posts* coming from those users *posting* to the event. The *Event* entity has a *privacy* attribute (see Figure 7) which can be set to either: *Invite-Only*, *Public*, or *Friend-of-Guests* – which are self-descriptive in terms of who can see and join an *Event*. As noted earlier, a timetabled lecture, a project meeting, or a tutorial are each *events* forward in time - all ideal candidates for Facebook *Events*.

Another attribute of the *Event* entity of interest here is *venue_id*, which is the id of a *Page* (described in the next section), of either the: *place*, *location*, *organisation* or some other entity hosting the *event*.

The Facebook Pages Sub-Model

The Page, the fundamental unit of the www was introduced into Facebook as an entity separate from a User, in April 2010. It became the way that Facebook allowed corporate and other identities (e.g. celebrities by stage-name), into what had previously been a people-identity-only system – where everybody was supposedly going by their real names and identities. (Note: that has been a point of contention over the years, where a number of effectively anonymous trolls have seemed to continue on in Facebook with impunity).

The *Page* entity in the conceptual model is a super-type (see Figure 8) with numerous specialised sub-types across the top of the Figure: *Company_Organization, Brand_Product, Local_Business, Websites_Blogs, Other*. Each of the sub-types have a few extra attributes beyond what they have in common in the *Page* entity. They also each have a distinct stylesheet, evident when the different types are displayed in the browser. Facebook has scores of categories and sub-categories of the Page types, with little or no current variation across many of them with-respect-to the attributes available in the Graph API, so only five sub-types are currently necessary in the conceptual model. This aspect of Facebook renders it much like a content management system (CMS), where the default presentation of a *page* is provided by care-

Figure 7. Conceptual model of Facebook Events taken from (Goschnick, 2014; Figure 8.1)

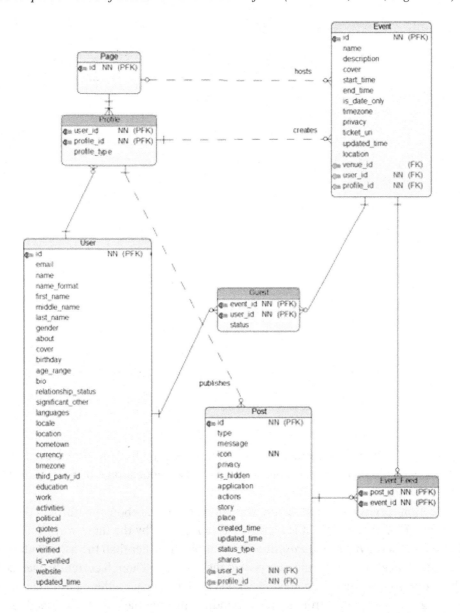

fully designed stylesheets. That also means that authoring such pages is inflexible, compared to an LMS or a CMS with WYSIWYG editing tools available to the content creator, such as Creator covered above.

In 2010 Facebook also added *Places* (see the *Place* and *Location* entities in Figure 8) to their platform, which have a one-to-one relationship with *Page*, but only with pages that represent *a place in the real world* – such as a store/shop, the head office of an organisation, or a park, and so on. This was Facebook's foray into location-based services (e.g. attributes in the *Place* entity include *parking* and the opening *hours*), whereby Facebook users can check-in and check-out of actual places in the real world (see the *Checkin* entity between Page and User), either by themselves or via their friends. Note that *Location* has a self-relationship such that hierarchies of locations (e.g. a store in a street, in a suburb, in a city, in

Figure 8. Pages, Places and Locations, from (Goschnick, 2014; Figure 9.1)

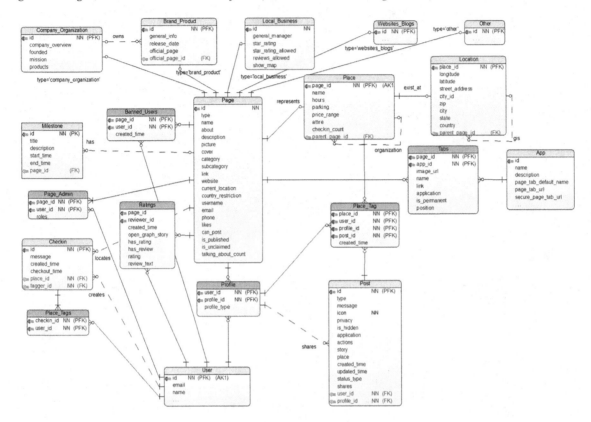

a state, in a country) can be represented, in a GIS-fashion (Geographical Information System). That is, the Page and Place entities can be used to tie in location-based educational or other facilities related to one's learning activities.

A second location-services inspired feature was added to the Facebook platform in the recent rendition of the Graph API in April 2014: it is represented in Figure 8 by the three-way *Place_Tag* associative entity between *Place, Profile* and *Post*. It allows for people other than the user sending the *post*, to also be tagged at a *Place*, at the time the user posted the *Post*. I.e. Though currently enacted by people, it technically allows for automatic recorded check-ins by GPS, or via other sensors as the Internet of Things (IoT) progresses, of people from a user's friendlist, placing them at the scene, at the time of the post. The privacy issues associated with such an automation are substantial.

Other entities from this model of specific interest to us here, include:

- **Ratings:** Ratings and user-stories about a Page can be accumulated via this associative entity. E.g. a Subject can have a Page, as can a finer-grained Learning Activity.
- **Banded_Users:** People who have offended the owner of a page in some non-resolved way, can be banned from viewing and interacting with a given page, by the page owner.
- **Milestone:** Milestones there-in are a special type of post that appears in the timeline of a Page, so that it is visibly flagged in the chronological history of the Page.

All these features and others could be put to very good use within an advanced PLE.

The Facebook Apps Sub-Model

On July 10, 2008 Apple released the App Store in the then new second version of iOS. It allowed third party app developers to write and sell apps for Apple smartphones for the first time. Google followed suit between 2009-2011, initially only allowing third party developers from the US and the UK for the first year. With the Apple App Store, Steve Jobs created another revolution in the software world: "Apps are the software artifacts that allowed the previously inert mobile/cell phone to take over the computing world, no less" Goschnick (2014). Facebook had long had apps (games mainly) that could run within a page on Facebook, including their own *Notes* app for writing longer stories with some basic HTML formatting. With the release of their Graph API V2, Facebook introduced functionality that allowed third party app developers who publish in the Apple, Google, web and Windows app stores, to integrate with Facebook at some level, rather than attempt to woo them into Facebook's own App Center (which then, as now, is nearly all *games*). In particular, by placing an advertisement for an app within a Facebook user's newsfeed, courtesy of Facebook's business model, when/if the user clicked on it, they could be taken to the app publishers web page, or to the link in the App Store or the Play Store for app installation.

Facebook correctly identified a marketing problem for indie app developers, centred on *app discoverability* as there was soon millions of apps to choose from in each of the two main stores. Instead of competing with Apple's App Store and Google's Play Store via their own App Center which houses Facebook games, they decided instead to leverage the marketing power of the social groupings within Facebook, as a solution to that discoverability of apps in the major app stores, and tap into a significant revenue stream coming from app advertising. While this chapter has no interest in the advertising side of Facebook, the structures related to apps within the Facebook Graph API V2, are of interest with a view to the potential of educational apps within possible future PLEs.

Of the 27 entities in Figure 9 the ones of most interest here, are within the column of entities second from the left, as it represents the relationships between the User and an App, or else between a particular Facebook Page and an App.

Of those entities the ones of specific interest here, include:

- **Tabs:** Is an associative entity between Page and Apps, such that user-selected Facebook apps can be installed-on/accessible-from a specific page (via a tab), making them directly clickable from that Page. Note: this is a bit analogous to the complex Learning Objects that can be placed on a Page in Creator – though less flexible in its placement on the page, it is potentially more powerful regarding a broad selection of third-party apps that might be installed on a Page (although most/ all apps currently in the Facebook App Center are games, of which there is no educational-games category).
- **Installed_App:** This simply records which apps a given user has. As an associative entity it can be used to list all users of a particular app, or alternatively, all apps that a particular user has installed.
- **App_Group:** This entity associates an app with a Group. The link here includes the profile of the user who is the administrator of that particular Group.
- **Subscriptions:** Used to enact subscriptions to an app, which may expire after a period of time. Used to post updates or to flag the need for a user to renew their subscription.

- **Review:** An associative entity such that a user can post reviews of many apps, and a app can receive many reviews.
- **Scores**: A simple score that a user has attained in an app.
- **Achievement:** For apps such as game that have leader boards, but within the Facebook environment if the inclusive attribute no_feed_story is set 'false' than the particular achievement a user reached will be broadcast to the newsfeeds of the users 'friends'.
- **Domain:** Represents a web site domain out on the greater Internet that has become known within the Graph API, for the purposes of Facebook Insights (a marketing dashboard). A third party developer/publisher can 'claim' a domain as their own, such that forward of the claim, traffic related to Facebook users to their web site will appear in their Insights statistics, which can be drilled down on various user demographics to aid their future marketing campaigns.

Figure 9. Apps and Related Entities, from (Goschnick, 2014; Figure 10.1)

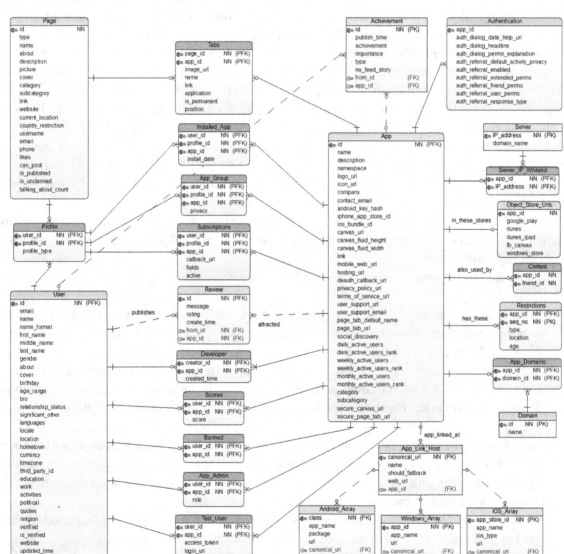

Each of these features could be put to some good use within an advanced PLE that allowed app plugins as such. Apps can bring in unprecedented levels of personalisation in learning.

A MERGING OF MODELS

There is some recent research regarding how students use existing social networking platforms with respect to their working patterns within current study routines, alongside the traditional learning technologies (Arndt & Guercio, 2012), but none we could find regarding how the social networking platforms could be enhanced to incorporate such working routines; or conversely, how an LMS or PLE platform could be modified to bring in the best features of the social network platforms. There is a paper outlining a planned set of features researchers would like in a conventional LMS, mirroring something of the features in social networking platforms, but when it comes to the specifics, there are vague ideas about how such features could be used to make learning more personalised and adaptive. For example, in Tsolis et al (2011), in which they propose modifying the Moodle LMS given its adaptability, they outline a brief plan to: expand the user profile page allowing the user to add tags (keywords) indicating their interests; have shared bookmarks; have shared galleries of digital content (this last proposal is like the shared *Resource Palette* in Creator covered earlier, though they make no mention of learning-objects).

In the section on the Conceptual Data Models from the Facebook platform, we investigated numerous aspects of them, with an open mind regarding two possible future directions that PLEs and social networking platforms might advance, regarding personalised learning, namely: what can be gained from such a case study with respect to folding similar social functionality into a PLE; and conversely, to gauge how accommodating is the current Facebook structural design, should that vendor choose to move their market focus in the personalised education direction. Interestingly, we can examine both those scenarios in the one design exercise: by folding appropriately selected aspects of the two models (those from Creator and those from Facebook) into the one model.

While the concept of *posts* to one's *friendlist* was a central early strength of social networking software, when looking across the models in Figures 6, 7, 8 and 9 five *generic* concepts stand out: *Groups*; *Events*; *Pages*; *Places* and *Apps* – all of which were added much later to the Facebook platform (mainly in 2010). The generic nature of the four makes them highly adaptable to other software application areas; not just applications in the small-feature *app* sense, but applications *at the platform level*, such as a personalised PLE, or an adaptive LMS.

Looking at Figure 8, the way that a number of Page *sub-entities* are *derived* from the generic *Page* super-type, is indicative of what can also be done by sub-typing GROUP in service of our aim, e.g.: *Class, Tutorial-Group, Study Group, Year-level, Reading Group, Project Team, Lab Group*, and so on for the more traditional groupings in an educational setting. Similarly, sub-types of EVENT could include: *Lecture, Lab Session, Workshop, Demonstration, Tutorial, Seminar, Research Seminar*, and so on. In other words, the *current* Facebook platform is already well endowed with generic structures and capabilities that could be specialised into an LMS of some capability, by the vendor should they choose such a path (note: not an infeasible decision given the Facebook company founder's large donations to public education in the US: $100M in New York in 2010, and $150M in the San Francisco Bay area public school system in 2014).

Figure 10. Merging models from Figures 3, 6 and 7

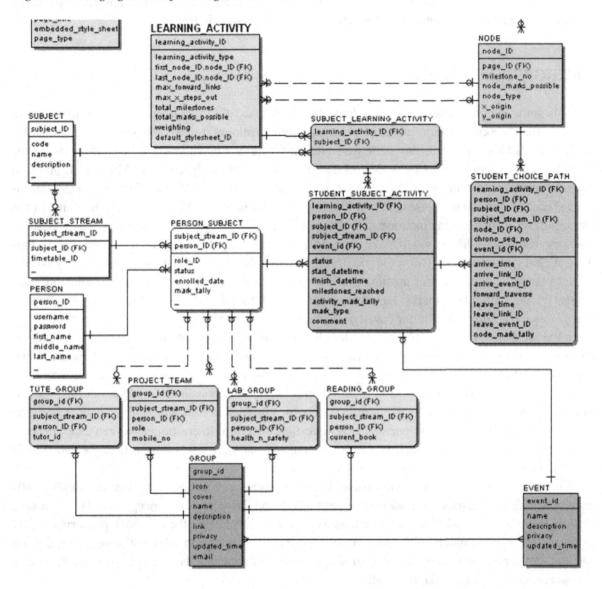

Furthermore, if we take a finer-grained view of learning down at a single *Learning Activity* level as demonstrated in Creator (i.e. where a *Learning Activity* which in that system may be as small as a single page with learning-objects on that page, that in turn may or may not also be a sub-section of a more traditional *Lab Session*, a *Workshop,* a *Tutorial* and so on), it can be very personalised in a PLE that incorporates social networking capabilities. As a *small* illustration, Figure 10 combines the *Learning Activity* concepts represented in Figure 3, with the generic entities from the Facebook Platform model in Figures 6 (*Groups*) and 7 (*Events*) – the rest of Figures 6 and 7 are assumed to be part of the merged model, without the need to re-present them and clutter-up the figure. Alternatively, *Groups* and *Events* are also generic entities (they may have different names) in many LMS and indeed other systems too, such as multi-agent systems, e.g. the ShaMAN multi-agent meta-model has them as *SocialWorlds* and *Events* (Goschnick, Sonenberg & Balbo, 2008).

Events are fine-grained via a possible relationship between *Event* and *Student_Subject_Activity*. We have also introduced four sub-entities of *Group*, namely - *Tute_Group, Project_Team, Lab_Group, Reading_Group* – each of which may have extra specific attributes. E.g. *tutor_id, mobile_no, health_n_safety*, and *current_book* respectively as simple examples. Furthermore, *Events* and *Groups* are related via a many-to-many relationship, as one is often related to the other.

The combined structure would enable new features such as:

- An automatic *posting* of the achievement of reaching a *milestone* in a single learning activity, to one's friends and family (those that have the right *privacy* setting);
- The many-to-many relationship means that some events can involve many groups, and some groups will be involved in many events – and which-are-which can easily be set and/or discovered;
- Those people reading the same *current_book* within and across different *reading groups* can be alerted to the possibility of fruitful discussions, if so sort out;
- Those learners that are up to the same *milestone* can be alerted to their common situation;
- A course administrator can quickly see if there are any lab groups that have no one that has yet completed the pre-requisite health-and-safety course – and post them on their mobiles about the observation (A 'smart' Lab, could check that all by itself – see next paragraph);
- And more;

To be implemented with straight-forward/light-weight procedural coding. And furthermore, if entities like many of those in Figures 8 and 9 were also merged in the combined structure:

- A location-based service across a university campus could likewise be interfaced model-wise, at the *Location* entity in Figure 8.
- An *app* from a library of subscribed-to or purchased educational apps, could be placed by the author (may be a student) at the individual *Page* level in the PLE, via the *Tab* entity in Figure 9.
- Both students and teachers could provide significant feedback at the individual Page level via the *Review* entity in Figure 8, *any time* rather than just at Quality-of-Teaching/Student-Experience survey time; and so on.
- The *Tabs* on a Facebook page is simply a parallel with Learning Objects in Creator – i.e. educational apps can be thought of as smart learning objects that could be plugins to a page in the PLE, down at the granularity of the individual learner for a highly customized personal learning experience.
- The *App_Group* structure in Facebook demonstrates how to make an app available to a specific group of learner in the PLE. To a: tutorial, lab, workshop, or other cohort of learners.
- App *Subscriptions* clearly would allow for a pay-as-you-go series of learning apps, where that is desired feature.
- The *Installed_App* would be useful to know who has got what installed from an administration point of view, down to the user level of granularity.
- While the app *Achievement* entity would allow for gamification in apps *within* learning activities, similar to the milestone feature *at* the learning activity level already mentioned.

CONCLUSION

The Merging of Models section above highlighted some of the key features evident in a social network platform like Facebook, that could be included in the blueprint of an advanced PLE platform. Also sketched out were *just a few* of the new features that could be built upon such a merged model.

Furthermore, in demonstrating aspects of that merged model, we have also shown how 'education-ready' the current Facebook platform is, given the number of generic structures such as *Groups* and *Events,* that have been folded into the Facebook platform in recent times. With relatively superficial technical modifications at the level of the foundational structures, and a changed or additional direction in the marketing focus of that company, Facebook Inc. could enter an emerging PLE marketplace, for better or for worse. Given Zuckerberg's (2017) more recent grander plan for "building a global society" which aims to also motivate the self-inclusion of "tradition groups" into Facebook in greater numbers, the personalized learning goals made possible in a PLE, is possibly subsumed in that grand Facebook plan.

Either way, an advanced PLE by whom ever, based on such a merged conceptual model would be capable of a significant degree of personalisation, adaptability and socialisation.

Another aspect of the Facebook platform touched upon, is their strategic slicing up of functionality into discrete apps (each simpler than their desktop/web interface), as a way to keep the usability high and the individual user focused on specific sub-sections or *views* (i.e. the *Facebook Groups* and *Messenger* apps) of their system. This works, despite the enterprise-system scale of their overall platform. Both LMSs and future PLEs could also benefit from such an approach, particularly the LMS given the typical enterprise nature of them.

FUTURE DIRECTIONS

We have touched on how the *Apps* part of the Facebook conceptual data model, when merged into a PLE, would afford certain features; however, our future research will focus more on how *educational apps* are brought into Personalised Learning Environments. I believe that apps can bring unprecedented levels of personalisation into learning through both an app store dedicated to learning accessible within the PLE; and, by allowing the incorporation of self-written apps by a new code-savvy generation in block-based and text-based programming languages. In a sense, the Scratch environment is a very rudimentary forerunner to the PLE proper – one simply dedicated to lessons on coding and story telling – that shows something of the personalised planned and unplanned collaborations that take place. It gives us a glimpse of the learner taking control of what they learn and how they learn. Similarly, the near universal ownership of a smartphone by students down to a certain age level (and the age is getting lower all the time), gives each student a remarkable sensing and recording device that can be folded into the PLE, through an array of innovative apps. Again, the potential for personalized learning with respect to smartphone apps and the sensors in the phone (and in the environment itself) offers unprecedented opportunities to empower learners and teachers, and the impact and outer usefulness of their mutual learning (See iNaturalist.org for an example use of the humble smartphone coupled with an entusiastic individual).

The future of learning environments lies with the merging of the better aspects of flexible Learning Management Systems with features popularised in Social Networking platforms, supplemented with the smartphone, to personalise and energise the individual learning experience in Personal Learning

Environments. I believe we have underlined such a possibility in this paper by demonstrating how that can be done at the conceptual schema level.

REFERENCES

Arndt, T., & Guercio, A. (2012). Social Networking and E-Learning: Towards a More Effective Online Learning Experience. *GSTF Journal on Computing*, *2*(2), 89–94. doi:10.5176/2010-2283_2.2.173

Attwell, G. (2007). The Personal Learning Environments – the future of eLearning? *eLearning Papers*, *2*(1).

Berners-Lee, T., Hendler, J. & Lassila, O. (2001). The Semantic Web. *Scientific America*, *284*(5), 34-43.

Cassin, A., & Goschnick, S. B. (1998). *FAME Agent System Design and Specifications. Internal Document, Melbourne IT Pty Ltd.* University of Melbourne.

Cassin, A., & Sterling, L. (1997). IndiansWatcher: Single Purpose Software Agent. *Proceedings of the Second International Conference on the Practical Application of Intelligent Agents and Multi-Agent Technology (PAAM 97)*, 529-538.

Chatti, M. A., Jarke, M., & Frosch-Wilke, D. (2007). The future of e-learning: A shift to knowledge networking and social software. *International Journal of Knowledge and Learning*, *3*(4/5), 404–420. doi:10.1504/IJKL.2007.016702

Dabbagh, N., & Kitsantas, A. (2012). Personal Learning Environments, social media, and self-regulated learning: A natural formula for connecting formal and informal learning. *Internet and Higher Education*, *15*(1), 3–8. doi:10.1016/j.iheduc.2011.06.002

Downes, S. (2005). E-learning 2.0. *eLearning Mag*. Retrieved from http://elearnmag.acm.org/featured.cfm?aid=1104968

Downes, S. (2010). *Elements of a Personal Learning Environment*. ITK Conference, Keynote address, Hameenlinna, Finland. Accessed here: http://www.downes.ca/files/Personal%20Learning%20Environments.pdf

Facebook. (2017). *Facebook's Graph API 2.0*. Accessed Nov 30, 2017 at: https://developers.facebook.com/docs/graph-api

Felder, R.M., & Silverman, I.K. (1988). Learning and teaching styles in engineering education. *Engineering Education*, *78*(7).

Goschnick, S. (1998). Design and Development of Melbourne IT Creator – a System for Authoring and Management of Online Education. Academic Press.

Goschnick, S. (2014). *Facebook from Five Thousand Feet: A Visual Mapping from Conceptual Model to Ground-level Graph API Data*. EbookDynasty.net.

Goschnick, S., Balbo, S., & Sonenberg, L. (2008). From Task Models to Agent-Oriented Meta-models, and Back Again. *Proceedings, TAMODIA-2008 the 7th Workshop on Task Models and Diagrams.* 10.1007/978-3-540-85992-5_4

Goschnick, S. B., & Cassin, A. (1997). *Requirements Document – Agents-in-cMILE V1.0. Internal Document, Melbourne IT Pty Ltd.* University of Melbourne.

Halimi, K., Seridi-Bouchelaghem, H., & Faron-Zucker, C. (2014). An enhanced personal learning environment using social semantic web technologies. *Interactive Learning Environments, 22*(2), 165–187. doi:10.1080/10494820.2013.788032

Leung, L. (2015). A Panel Study on the Effects of Social Media Use and Internet Connectedness on Academic Performance and Social Support. *International Journal of Cyber Behavior, Psychology and Learning, 5*(1), 1-16. doi:10.4018/ijcbpl.2015010101

Limongelli, C., Sciarrone, F., Temperini, M., & Vaste, G. (2011). The Lecomps5 framework for personaliszed web-based learning: A teacher's satisfaction perspective. *Computers in Human Behavior, 27*(4), 1301–1320. doi:10.1016/j.chb.2010.07.026

Loke, S. W. D., & Sterling, L. (1996). *CiFi: An Intelligent Agent for Citation Finding on the World-Wide Web.* Technical Report 96/4. Department of Computer Science, the University of Melbourne.

Luckin, R. (2008). The Learner Centric Ecology of Resources: A Framework for using Technology to Scaffold Learning. *Computers & Education, 50*(2), 449–462. doi:10.1016/j.compedu.2007.09.018

Mayer, C., Linongelli, C., Orlandini, A., & Poggioni, V. (2007). Linear temporal logic as an executable semantics for planning languages. *Journal of Logic Language and Information, 1*(16).

Mott, J. (2010). Envisioning the Post-LMS Era: The Open Learning Network. *Educause Review Online.* Accessed: http://www.educause.edu/ero/article/envisioning-post-lms-era-open-learning-network

Tsolis, D., Christia, P., Kampana, S., & Tsakalidis, A. (2011). OWLearn: An Open Source e-Learning Platform Supporting Adaptability, Personalization and Mobile Learning. *Proceedings of the International Conference on Information Technologies (InfoTech-2011),* 383-392.

Valtonen, T., Hacklin, S., Dillon, S., Vesisenaho, M., Kukkonen, J., & Hietanen, A. (2012). Perspectives on personal learning environments held by vocational students. *Computer Education, 58*(2), 732–739. doi:10.1016/j.compedu.2011.09.025

W3C. (2014). *The web standards model – HTML CSS and JavaScript.* Accessed: http://www.w3.org/wiki/The_web_standards_model_-_HTML_CSS_and_JavaScript

Zuckerberg, M. (2017). *Building Global Community.* Retrieved on Nov 30, 2017 from https://www.facebook.com/notes/mark-zuckerberg/building-global-community/10154544292806634/

This research was previously published in Innovative Methods, User-Friendly Tools, Coding, and Design Approaches in People-Oriented Programming; pages 407-440, copyright year 2018 by Engineering Science Reference (an imprint of IGI Global).

Chapter 21
Use of Novel Ensemble Machine Learning Approach for Social Media Sentiment Analysis

Ishrat Nazeer

School of Computer Science and Engineering, Lovely Professional University, Jalandhar, India

Mamoon Rashid

ⓘ https://orcid.org/0000-0002-8302-4571

School of Computer Science and Engineering, Lovely Professional University, Jalandhar, India

Sachin Kumar Gupta

School of Electronics and Communication Engineering, Shri Mata Vaishno Devi University, Jammu, India

Abhishek Kumar

School of Computer Science and IT, Jain University, Bangalore, India

ABSTRACT

Twitter is a platform where people express their opinions and come with regular updates. At present, it has become a source for many organizations where data will be extracted and then later analyzed for sentiments. Many machine learning algorithms are available for twitter sentiment analysis which are used for automatically predicting the sentiment of tweets. However, there are challenges that hinder machine learning classifiers to achieve better results in terms of classification. In this chapter, the authors are proposing a novel feature generation technique to provide desired features for training model. Next, the novel ensemble classification system is proposed for identifying sentiment in tweets through weighted majority rule ensemble classifier, which utilizes several commonly used statistical models like naive Bayes, random forest, logistic regression, which are weighted according to their performance on historical data, where weights are chosen separately for each model.

DOI: 10.4018/978-1-6684-7123-4.ch021

INTRODUCTION TO SENTIMENT ANALYSIS

In the current world of technology everyone is expressive in one or other way. People want to express their opinions about various issues be it social, political, economic or business. In this process social media is helping people in a great way. Social networking sites like Facebook, twitter, WhatsApp and many others thus become a common tool for people to express themselves. Analyzing the opinions expressed by the people on different social networking sites to get useful insights from them is called social media analytics. The insights gained can then be used to make important decisions. Among all the networking sites twitter is becoming most powerful wherein people express their opinions in short textual messages called tweets. Analyzing the tweets to retrieve insight information is called twitter sentiment analysis (SA) or opinion mining. Sentiment analysis classifies the sentiment of a tweet into three classes of positive negative and neutral (Ahuja, Ret al. 2019). Twitter sentiment analysis is helping the modern world in a great way as an example SA can help a company in knowing the customer reviews about a particular product and will help customers to select the best product based on opinion of people.

Figure 1. General steps in Twitter sentiment analysis process

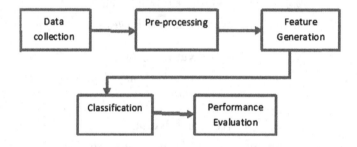

Figure 1 shows five main steps required in Sentiment Analysis.

1. **Data Collection**: Process of SA begins by collecting the tweets from twitter using Application Programming Interface (API). API will allow us to interact with the twitter and extract the tweets in a programmatic way. The extracted tweets are then used for further processing,
2. **Pre-Processing**: Data preprocessing is done to remove extra features from the tweets. It decreases the size of tweets and makes them suitable for classification (Rane, A et al. 2018). The feature that are removed include following:
   a. The user name which is preceded by @ symbol.
   b. The retweets which are preceded by RT.
   c. Hashtags denoted by #.
   d. Slang words are replaced with words of equivalent meanings.
3. **Feature Extraction**: Feature extraction steps are responsible for extracting the features from the tweets. Different types of features are there like twitter specific features (includes features like hashtags, retweets, user names, URL), textual features (includes feature like length of tweet and length of words, emoticons, number of question marks), Parts Of Speech (features like nouns,

verbs, adverbs, adjectives etc.), Lexicon Based features (comparison of positive and negative word percentages)(Permatasari, R. Iet al. 2018).

4. **Classification**: This step is responsible for determining whether the tweet expresses a positive, negative or neutral sentiment. There are three main approaches to classify the sentiment of a tweet they are, machine learning approach, lexicon based approach and deep learning approach. All these methods classify the polarity of the tweet with varying accuracy levels.

5. **Performance Evaluation**: This step is useful in determining the accuracy of the particular classifier used in the classification stage of the process. Performance is usually determined in terms of accuracy, precision, recall, and f-measure (Gamal, D et al. 2019).

Classification of Sentiment Analysis

Sentiment analysis is done at three different levels they are as follows:

1. **Document Level:** In document level sentiment analysis a document is analysed and the review got from it is classified as being positive negative or neutral. In document level sentiment analysis each document expresses opinion on a single entity (1 from proposal page).

2. **Sentence Level:** In sentence level sentiment analysis a sentence rather than a document is analyzed and classified as being positive negative or neutral. Sentences can be of two types subjective (sentence with opinion) or objective (sentence with factual knowledge). In sentence level classification the type of sentence is first identified and then if it contains an opinion it is classified (Behdenna, Set al. 2018).

3. **Aspect Level:** In aspect level sentiment analysis each aspect of a tweet or sentence is classified individually. The process first identifies the entity and its aspects then classifies the identified aspects.

Use of Twitter Micro-blogging for Sentiment Analysis

Twitter has become an important source of knowledge for people. It acts as a platform where people express themselves using short text messages called tweets. Sentiment analysis is mostly performed on twitter data because of the following reasons:

- It is the most popular micro-blogging site.
- It has 240+ million active users.
- About 500 million tweets are generated each day.
- Tweets are small in length and thus easy to analyze.
- It has variety of users.

Challenges in Twitter Sentiment Analysis

The task of sentiment analysis on twitter data is most challenging. The most common challenges associated with twitter sentiment analysis are as follows:

1. Use of highly unstructured and non-grammatical language in tweets.

2. Use of slang words.
3. Use of sarcasm in tweets.
4. Use of words which have subjective context in one sentence and objective in another.
5. Use of negative words to oppose the sentiment of tweet.
6. Use of acronyms and abbreviations.
7. Use of out of vocabulary words.

INTRODUCTION TO MACHINE LEARNING

Machine learning is a branch of artificial intelligence that gives machines the ability to learn from their own experience without being programmed. Machine learning is trying to impart human learning in computers. Humans learn by reasoning while computers learn by using algorithms. Based on the approach of learning used algorithms are classified into following general categories.

- **Supervised Learning**: Supervised learning algorithms are fed with a labelled dataset. Labelled dataset contains both input and output. The algorithm uses this dataset to train itself. After the training is over the algorithm is tested on a testing dataset, which is similar in dimensions to the training dataset, for predication or classification.
- **Unsupervised Learning**: Unsupervised learning algorithms are fed with an unlabeled dataset. Unlabeled dataset contains only input data and no information about the outputs. The algorithm has to learn by itself as no training is involved (Portugal, I et al. 2018). The algorithm classifies the data based on similarities or differences or patterns present in it.
- **Semi Supervised Learning**: Semi supervised learning algorithms are fed with a labelled dataset which is not complete and has missing information. The algorithm although goes through training but has to learn by itself as well because of the missing information (Portugal, I et al. 2018).
- **Reinforcement Learning**: Reinforcement learning is based on rewards. In this type of learning if algorithm makes a correct decision it is rewarded else it is punished. This type of learning is mostly used in game playing. In game playing if the algorithm makes a correct move the step will be repeated and learned however if an incorrect move is made then the step won't be repeated.

Overview of Machine Learning Classifiers

The different types of machine learning algorithms are given below:

- **Naive Bayes**: Naive Bayes algorithm is a statistical model of classification based on conditional probability. Conditional probability defines the probability of an event given that some other event has already occurred. The formula of Naive Bayes is given by:

$$P\left(H/X\right) = \frac{P\left(X/H\right)P\left(H\right)}{P\left(X\right)}$$

- **Support Vector Machine (SVM):** SVM classifier is mostly used for binary classification as shown in Figure 2. SVM is based on the construction of a hyperplane which acts as decision boundary between the two classes to be classified. The hyperplane is defined by w*x+b=0. Where w is the weight vector and b is the bias. Data point with w*x+b>=0 will be classified into a positive category and if w*x+b<0 then it is classified into a negative category (B, V et al. 2016).

Figure 2. Binary classification using SVM
(Mubaris NK, 2017)

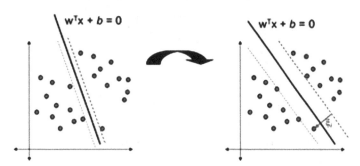

- **Random Forest:** Random forest algorithm builds a multitude of decision trees from the given dataset as shown in Figure 3. It then uses the result of each tree to find the class of data point using majority voting method (Rane, Aet al. 2018).

Figure 3. Illustration of Random forest
(Brendan Tierney, 2018)

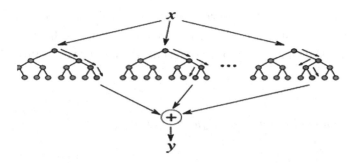

- **Decision Tree:** Decision tree algorithm works by constructing a decision tree from the given data. Each node of the tree represents the attribute of data and branch represents the test on attributes. Leaf nodes of the tree represent the final classes. Decision tree is constructed using the information gain of each node. Figure 4 shows the decision tree constructed for the shown dataset.
- **K Nearest Neighbour (KNN):** KNN classifier can be used for classification and regression and its illustration is shown in Figure 5. It is based on similarity index. The algorithm first identifies the K nearest neighbors of a data point using a distance measure like Euclidian distance. The data point is then assigned to the class that is most common among its K neighbours.

Figure 4. Classification of data set using Decision tree classifier
(Upasana Priyadarshiny, 2019)

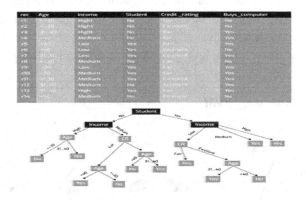

Figure 5. Classification of a data point using KNN classifier
(Avinash Navlani, 2018)

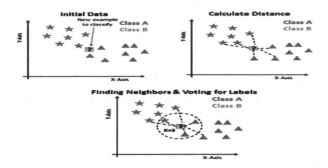

- **K Means Clustering**: K means clustering is an unsupervised learning technique. In this algorithm each data point is assigned to a cluster to which it resembles the most. The grouping of data points in clusters is shown in Figure 6. K represents the number of distinct clusters formed (Dey, A. 2016)

Figure 6. Grouping of data points into three different clusters
(Arun Manglic, 2017).

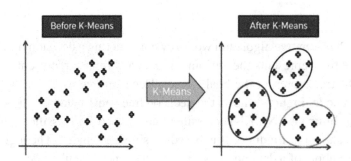

Applying Machine Learning Classifiers for Twitter Analysis

Machine learning involves a set of methods used to identify the features of text. Machine learning enables a computer to learn from the patterns of data and experiences. Thus the computer needs not be programmed explicitly. Machine learning has been successfully used in twitter sentiment classification. Machine learning classifiers have shown a good rate of accuracy in sentiment classification. Some of the recent works done on twitter sentiment analysis are mentioned below.

(Nanda, Cet al. 2018) used machine learning algorithms on movie review tweets to classify the tweets into positive and negative. The algorithms used were Support Vector Machine (SVM) and Random Forest (RF). An accuracy of 91.07 and 89.73 was achieved by RF and SVM respectively. (Rathi, M et al. 2018) used an ensemble machine learning algorithm. Ensemble was created by using merging SVM and Decision Tree (DT) algorithms. The algorithm achieved an accuracy of 84% which was greater than the accuracy provided by the individual SVM and DT. (El-Jawad, M. H. A et al. 2018) compared different machine learning and deep learning algorithms. They developed a hybrid model using Naive Bayes, Decision Tree, Convolution Neural Network (CNN) and Recurrent Neural Network (RNN). The model gives an accuracy of 83.6%. (Arti et al. 2019) used Random Forest algorithm on tweets related to Indian Premier League 2016. The classifier achieved an accuracy of 81.69%. (Alrehili, A et al. 2019) combined Naive Bayes, SVM, Random Forest, Bagging and Boosting to create ensemble algorithm for the customer reviews about a product. (Naz, S et al. 2018) used sentiment analysis on SemEval twitter dataset. The machine learning algorithm was SVM which uses multiple features of data to perform better accuracy. (Goel, A et al. 2016) used Naive Bayes algorithm to classify a movie review twitter dataset. (Jose, R et al. 2016) combined machine learning classification approach with lexicon based sentiment classification. The authors combined SentiWordNet classifier, Naive bayes classifier and hidden Markov model classifier to achieve better accuracy.An attempt to fetch twitter data has been done by (Rashid, M et al. 2019). This research used Hadoop distributed file system for storage of data which were fetched with the help of flume. Decision Tree and Naïve Bayes classifiers were used for sentiment analysis. The clustering approach has been used for managing web news data in (Kaur, S et al. 2016). This research has used Back Propagation Neural Network and K-Means Clustering for classifying the news data.

DATA EXTRACTION AND FEATURE SELECTION

When twitter sentiment analysis is done using machine learning approach, feature extraction plays an important role. Features represent the information that can be extracted from the data. Features define the unique property of a data sample. In Machine Learning the feature of data are projected on a higher dimensional feature space. To achieve better accuracy in classification higher dimensional data needs to be mapped onto low dimensional feature space. Feature extraction acts as a dimensional reduction technique. Each machine learning classifier uses most appropriate feature set to classify the sentiment of tweet as positive, negative or neutral (Avinash, M et al. 2018).

El-Jawad, M. H. A *et al.*, (2018) in their study divides features into following categories.

1. **Bag of Words (BOW):** BOW is basically a feature representation technique wherein tweets are commonly converted into an array of numbers. It first learns all the words present in a tweet and

then describes the presence of words in a tweet. BOW uses ngram_range as a parameter. ngram range represents number of words taken together. Range can be 1 (unigram), 2 (bigram) or multiple.

2. **Lexicon Based Feature:** In this feature representation technique a comparison is made between percentage of positive and negative words present in a tweet. Positive words include words like good, great, excellent etc. Negative words include words like bad, poor, dangerous etc.

3. **Parts of Speech Feature Representation:** In this feature representation technique the count of nouns, verbs, adverbs, adjectives present in the tweet is determined. By identifying each word of tweet as a different POS it becomes easy to get the context in which each word is used thus helping in analyzing the sentiment of tweet.

4. **Emoticon Based Feature Representation:** Emoticons are used in tweets to represent the feeling an individual has related to a particular event. The number of emoticons present in each tweet represents its feature set. Emoticon based features have been used by many researchers to effectively classify the tweets.

Feature Selection

Feature selection technique is used to select the relevant features and eliminate the irrelevant ones from a tweet. It thus helps in reducing the feature dimensionality of a data set. Lower dimensional feature space provides better accuracy in classification. There are different feature selection methods some of them are discussed below.

1. **Information Gain (IG):** Information gain is used to measure dependencies between the class and the feature. If dependencies are present we select the feature else not. If x is a feature and c1 and c2 are the two classes then the information gain is given by:

$$IG(x) = -\sum_{j=1}^{2} P(C_j) \log(P(C_j)) + P(x) \sum_{j=1}^{2} P(C_j \mid x) \log(P(C_j \mid x))$$
$$+ P(\bar{x}) \sum_{j=1}^{2} P(C_j \mid \bar{x}) \log(P(C_j \mid \bar{x}))$$

2. **Chi- Square:** Chi square is used when tweets contain categorical features. Chi square is used calculated between feature and the class. The features with best chi-square scores are selected. Chi–square is calculated as follows

$$c^2 = \sum_{i=1}^{k} \left| \frac{(O_i - E_i)^2}{E_i} \right|$$

Here O denotes the observed frequency, E denotes expected frequency and "i" denotes "ith" position in the contingency table. Expected frequency is the number of expected observations of class when there is no relationship between the feature and the target class and observed frequency is the number of observations of class.

3. **Minimum Redundancy method:** in this method of feature selection the features which are highly dependent on class and minimally dependent on other features are selected. It is also called as Minimum Redundancy Maximum Relevance feature selection. If two features possess redundant information then if only one is selected it does not affect the classification accuracy much.

Training and Testing Machine Learning Classifier for Twitter Sentiment Analysis

Once the data is pre-processed and ready, the next step is train this data to classifier for model preparation. However to evaluate the performance of model, it is very important to split the given data into training and test parts where the performance will be evaluated later by comparing the predictions from machine learning model with that of the target values in outcome variable of testing data. In some cases, separate datasets are to be used for training and tests purposes which is critical in correctly assessing the performance of classifier. The training and testing datasets. Keeping this challenge under consideration, we can use same dataset for training and testing iterations. The concept of k-fold cross validation is to be used where the data is divided into k units or blocks and then classifier is trained for all units except one unit which is to be used for testing purposes and later this process is repeated for all other units. If the value of K is equal to the number of observations, then this process is called as leave one out cross validation. Leave out one validation is turning biased for large value of K. However 10 fold cross validation is always a good choice (Hastie, T et al. 2009).

PROPOSAL OF NOVEL ENSEMBLE MACHINE LEARNING FOR TWITTER SENTIMENT ANALYSIS

In classical machine learning approach a single classifier is applied on the training data at once for classification. This produces different results of accuracy for different classifiers on same training dataset. Moreover if we have a set of classifiers all of which are providing a good accuracy result on same training dataset. Choosing a single classifier will not give us best and generalized results on unseen data. Thus using a single classifier will not help in selecting a best classifier among the competing ones. Also it is difficult to say which realization of a particular classifier will be best set to training data. All of these problems were solved by ensemble learning. Ensemble learning is a Machine Learning methodology in which different base models are combined to produce an optimal classification model. The optimal classification model formed is known as Ensemble classifier. Ensemble classifier combines output of different models to give best and generalized results in classification. The general ensemble classification approach is shown in Figure 7.

The outputs of different base classifiers are combined in multiple ways to get the final prediction. The different approaches by which the outputs of base classifiers can be combined are;

1. **Majority Voting:** In majority voting method the prediction is made by each base classifier. These predictions are deemed as votes. The final output of the ensemble classifier will be the prediction that is most common among the individual classifier predictions. For example if we are using three classifiers in the ensemble if two classifiers are predicting the tweet as positive and one as negative the final output of ensemble will be positive. Majority voting method is shown in Figure 8.

Figure 7. General ensemble classification approach

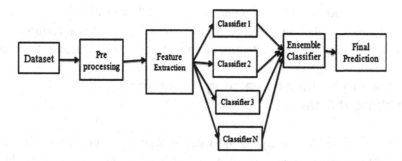

Figure 8. Majority voting method to classification using Ensemble classifier

2. **Maximum Probability:** In maximum probability rule the individual predictions of base classifiers are averaged. The final output of the ensemble classifier is the class with maximum average value. In case of Twitter Sentiment Analysis for each tweet probability of positive as well negative class is calculated. The ensemble classifier then finds the average of probabilities of all classes of each classifier and the class with maximum probability is assigned to the tweet. Maximum probability rule of ensemble classification is shown in Figure 9.

Figure 9. Maximum Probability method to classification using Ensemble classifier

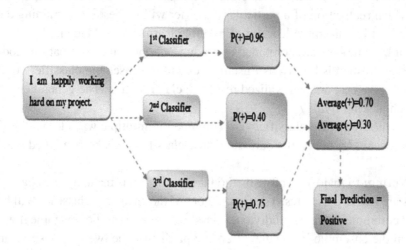

3.   **Weighted Average:** Weighted average method is similar to the maximum probability rule however in weighted average rule the base models are assigned with some weights. The weights are given according to the importance of each predictive model. The models which are more effective for a particular dataset will be assigned with larger weights and the models which are less effective are assigned comparatively smaller weights.

The algorithm for ensemble classification is as follows.

ALGORITHM

Step 1: Extraction of data from twitter using twitters API.

Step 2: Pre-processing the data to remove unwanted symbols and words which are of no use in predicting the sentiment of the tweet.

Step 3: Extracting the features from preprocessed tweets using Bag of Words technique.

Step 4: Applying each individual classifier on the extracted features to get individual predictions.

Step 5: Using majority voting technique on the individual predictions to get the final prediction by ensemble classifier.

Step 6: Output the sentiment of the tweet.

CONCLUSION AND FUTURE DIRECTIONS

In this chapter, the authors proposed novel machine learning approach for the sentiment analysis classification. This proposed algorithm is based on ensemble approach which will identify sentiment in tweets through - Weighted Majority Rule Ensemble Classifier where several commonly used statistical models like Naive Bayes, Random forest, Logistic regression will be utilized and weighted according to their performance on historical data and weights will be chosen separately for each model. In future, this proposed ensemble model will be used for training datasets for the classification of sentiments. This model will also be extended by the application of optimization algorithms for further refining the feature set for better results of classification in sentiment analysis.

REFERENCES

Ahuja, R., Chug, A., Kohli, S., Gupta, S., & Ahuja, P. (2019). The Impact of Features Extraction on the Sentiment Analysis. *Procedia Computer Science*, *152*, 341–348. doi:10.1016/j.procs.2019.05.008

Alrehili, A., & Albalawi, K. (2019). Sentiment Analysis of Customer Reviews Using Ensemble Method. *2019 International Conference on Computer and Information Sciences (ICCIS)*. 10.1109/ICCISci.2019.8716454

Arti, D. K. P., & Agrawal, S. (2019). An Opinion Mining for Indian Premier League Using Machine Learning Techniques. *2019 4th International Conference on Internet of Things: Smart Innovation and Usages (IoT-SIU)*. doi: 10.1109/iot-siu.2019.8777472

Avinash, M., & Sivasankar, E. (2018). A Study of Feature Extraction Techniques for Sentiment Analysis. *Advances in Intelligent Systems and Computing Emerging Technologies in Data Mining and Information Security*, 475–486. doi:10.1007/978-981-13-1501-5_41

B., V., & M., B. (2016). Analysis of Various Sentiment Classification Techniques. *International Journal of Computer Applications, 140*(3), 22–27. doi:10.5120/ijca2016909259

Behdenna, S., Barigou, F., & Belalem, G. (2018). Document Level Sentiment Analysis: A survey. *EAI Endorsed Transactions on Context-Aware Systems and Applications*, *4*(13), 154339. doi:10.4108/eai.14-3-2018.154339

Dey, A. (2016). Machine learning algorithms: A review. *International Journal of Computer Science and Information Technologies*, *7*(3), 1174–1179.

El-Jawad, M. H. A., Hodhod, R., & Omar, Y. M. K. (2018). Sentiment Analysis of Social Media Networks Using Machine Learning. *2018 14th International Computer Engineering Conference (ICENCO)*. doi: 10.1109/icenco.2018.8636124

Gamal, D., Alfonse, M., El-Horbaty, E.-S. M., & Salem, A.-B. M. (2019). Implementation of Machine Learning Algorithms in Arabic Sentiment Analysis Using N-Gram Features. *Procedia Computer Science*, *154*, 332–340. doi:10.1016/j.procs.2019.06.048

Goel, A., Gautam, J., & Kumar, S. (2016). Real time sentiment analysis of tweets using Naive Bayes. *2016 2nd International Conference on Next Generation Computing Technologies (NGCT)*. doi: 10.1109/ngct.2016.7877424

Hastie, T., Tibshirani, R., Friedman, J., & Franklin, J. (2005). The elements of statistical learning: Data mining, inference and prediction. *The Mathematical Intelligencer*, *27*(2), 83–85. doi:10.1007/BF02985802

Jose, R., & Chooralil, V. S. (2016). Prediction of election result by enhanced sentiment analysis on twitter data using classifier ensemble Approach. *2016 International Conference on Data Mining and Advanced Computing (SAPIENCE)*. 10.1109/SAPIENCE.2016.7684133

Kaur, S., & Rashid, E. M. (2016). Web news mining using Back Propagation Neural Network and clustering using K-Means algorithm in big data. *Indian Journal of Science and Technology*, *9*(41). Advance online publication. doi:10.17485/ijst/2016/v9i41/95598

Manglic, A. (2017). *Artificial Intelligence and Machine/ Deep Learning*. Retrieved from http://arun-aiml.blogspot.com/2017/07/k-means-clustering.html

Mubaris, N. K. (2017). *Support Vector Machines for Classification*. Retrieved from https://mubaris.com/posts/svm

Nanda, C., Dua, M., & Nanda, G. (2018). Sentiment Analysis of Movie Reviews in Hindi Language Using Machine Learning. *2018 International Conference on Communication and Signal Processing (ICCSP)*. 10.1109/ICCSP.2018.8524223

Navlani, A. (2018). *KNN Classification using Scikit-learn*. Retrieved from https://www.datacamp.com/community/tutorials/k-nearest-neighbor-classification-scikit-learn

Naz, S., Sharan, A., & Malik, N. (2018). Sentiment Classification on Twitter Data Using Support Vector Machine. *2018 IEEE/WIC/ACM International Conference on Web Intelligence (WI)*. 10.1109/ WI.2018.00-13

Permatasari, R. I., Fauzi, M. A., Adikara, P. P., & Sari, E. D. L. (2018). Twitter Sentiment Analysis of Movie Reviews using Ensemble Features Based Naïve Bayes. *2018 International Conference on Sustainable Information Engineering and Technology (SIET)*. 10.1109/SIET.2018.8693195

Portugal, I., Alencar, P., & Cowan, D. (2018). The use of machine learning algorithms in recommender systems: A systematic review. *Expert Systems with Applications*, *97*, 205–227. doi:10.1016/j. eswa.2017.12.020

Priyadarshiny, U. (2019). *How to create a Perfect Decision Tree*. Retrieved from https://dzone.com/ articles/how-to-create-a-perfect-decision-tree

Rane, A., & Kumar, A. (2018). Sentiment Classification System of Twitter Data for US Airline Service Analysis. *2018 IEEE 42nd Annual Computer Software and Applications Conference (COMPSAC)*. doi: 10.1109/compsac.2018.00114

Rashid, M., Hamid, A., & Parah, S. A. (2019). Analysis of Streaming Data Using Big Data and Hybrid Machine Learning Approach. In *Handbook of Multimedia Information Security: Techniques and Applications* (pp. 629–643). Springer. doi:10.1007/978-3-030-15887-3_30

Rathi, M., Malik, A., Varshney, D., Sharma, R., & Mendiratta, S. (2018). Sentiment Analysis of Tweets Using Machine Learning Approach. *2018 Eleventh International Conference on Contemporary Computing (IC3)*. 10.1109/IC3.2018.8530517

Silva, N. F. D., Hruschka, E. R., & Hruschka, E. R. (2014). Tweet sentiment analysis with classifier ensembles. *Decision Support Systems*, *66*, 170–179. doi:10.1016/j.dss.2014.07.003

Tierney, B. (2018). *Random Forest Machine Learning in R, Python and SQL - Part 1*. Retrieved from https:// blog.toadworld.com/2018/08/31/random-forest-machine-learning-in-r-python-and-sql-part-1

This research was previously published in Analyzing Global Social Media Consumption; pages 16-28, copyright year 2021 by Information Science Reference (an imprint of IGI Global).

Chapter 22
Extending the Apprenticeship Model of Music Instruction in Higher Education with Facebook Groups

Tamara R Meredith
University of North Texas, USA

Scott J Warren
University of North Texas, USA

ABSTRACT

Although faculty may not believe that they are legitimately "teaching" while engaging with students via Facebook, results of interviews and publicly available Facebook data clearly document intentional music faculty activities that fit the description of teaching through enculturation. This situates the phenomenon of Facebook groups firmly within the larger apprenticeship model in use in music departments; the process of enculturation through Facebook is used to teach new apprentices how to become functional members of their musical communities. Recommendations generated from the research and discussed in this chapter include addressing faculty concerns about personal and professional risk, departmental development of guidelines for Facebook group use and management that is based in enculturation theory, and training for music faculty in the use of social media channels as opportunities for teaching and learning.

INTRODUCTION

The master-apprentice dyadic roles assumed by applied music faculty and their students are well documented in educational literature addressing pedagogic styles in conservatories and university music departments (Burwell, 2012; Daniel & Parkes, 2015; Gaunt, Creech, Long, & Hallam, 2012). The applied teacher is the focal point for most educational direction during a student's tenure at an institution since weekly study usually occurs with the same teacher every semester until graduation. As with all master-apprentice

DOI: 10.4018/978-1-6684-7123-4.ch022

relationships, it is the eventual goal of the student (apprentice) to become a master him/herself. In the context of applied studio music study in higher education, this results in the eventual "mastery" of an instrument or voice by an apprentice through training. Training may include: performance, pedagogy, music business concepts, self-promotion, social skills, or other practices and behaviors that are deemed important by the master for successful enculturation into the profession.

Music students often select their schools based upon prior interaction with, or the reputation of, a single music faculty member who is, or has been, a professional performer of the highest caliber (Nerland & Hanken, 2011). The perceived authority and professional reputation of the master is key to recruiting apprentices. Once enrolled, music students attempt to develop their professional identities through anticipatory socialization (Bouij, 2004) with respected faculty, peers, and others in the music profession. It is through the apprenticeship model, paired with anticipatory socialization efforts, that music students acquire the skills, knowledge, and professional connections that they will use in their future lives as musicians within the professional musical community. In short—music students (apprentices) work to become professionals by seeking out faculty (masters) who will teach them the requisite skills and behaviors and provide anticipatory socialization opportunities. Once necessary musical and social skills and behaviors are acquired, the apprentice assumes the role of master within a greater professional music culture, and often the cycle repeats with the new master in a position to take on new apprentices.

Studying the master-apprentice relationship in studio-based music education has previously been difficult as it exists in isolated, one-on-one lessons that occur behind closed doors. Additionally, asking musicians to reflect upon their experiences as students carries with it the challenge that these former apprentices are now masters and view themselves as such in their current practices. However, the recent availability and adoption of social media platforms as informal, non-academic communication and learning environments has provided a new level of visibility into these practices and discourses. Faculty now communicate with current and future students as well as colleagues from other institutions in social media's public environment. This environment provides researchers opportunities to document views, beliefs, and practices through social media exchanges. Advice and/or instruction that may have been previously imparted in an applied lesson—one-on-one, verbally, behind a closed door—is now shared widely via social media and archived, ostensibly for the foreseeable future. This new opportunity to share information carries with it potential benefits and pitfalls for both master and apprentice. It is further complicated by the fact that the current generation of music faculty masters often have little or no previous experience with, nor likely received guidance on, using social media as an informal learning environment. They are, in this case, first-generation masters with no previous experience as an apprentice to guide or inform their decision-making processes.

The social media tool often selected by music faculty for communication within their studios is called Facebook. Facebook is a social media platform started in 2006. It allows users to share information (text, media, links to other web content, etc.) with "friends" - a pre-approved group of other Facebook members with whom a user can interact. However, a challenge exists when attempting to research Facebook groups in that groups can be private (i.e., hidden from public view) and groups (visible or hidden) that have fallen into disuse are not automatically removed or disabled. This leads to an inability to quantify currently active Facebook groups or generate an approximate percentage of use by higher education music faculty.

Educators have used Facebook directly and indirectly for communication and educational purposes since its inception over a decade ago (Sumuer, Esfer, & Yildirim, 2014). The literature reviewed in this study showed substantial inquiry into using Facebook and other social media platforms to extend the formal learning environment of the classroom into an informal space where students are already participating in social discourse. There is a noticeable lack of literature that addresses potential impacts of extending the traditional, one-to-one, private master-apprentice relationship into an environment that is one-to-many or many-to-many in nature, with indefinitely retained documentation of all discourses. Furthermore, music faculty and students may still assume the roles of master-apprentice even when interacting in online environments, but this may not be explicitly understood by the participants. In addition, faculty "lived experiences" with social media may be imparted to students as examples of professional social interactions (i.e., positive or negative) in the music world—and, therefore, embedded into the apprenticeship/enculturation experience.

The purpose of this chapter is to document current practice, address current challenges and barriers to the effective use of Facebook groups as opportunities to extend teaching outside the physical studio, and share recommendations generated from recent research. Topics such as master/apprentice roles, enculturation, and anticipatory socialization are presented to reinforce the need to address music faculty and student social media use independently from typical higher education social media guidelines and institutional policy.

BACKGROUND

The field of classical music education (i.e., Western European musical practices) typically uses an apprenticeship educational model for instrumental and vocal instruction in university and conservatory settings (Burwell, 2012; Burwell, 2015; Haddon & Potter, 2014; Nerland & Hanken, 2011; Nielsen, 2006; Seaton, 1998). Therefore, this chapter's analysis of music faculty Facebook use is rooted in theories of apprenticeship (Pratt, 1998; Rogoff, 1990), enculturation, anticipatory socialization, and Lave and Wenger's (1991) concept of legitimate peripheral participation.

Apprenticeship

Apprenticeship is often considered the oldest educational practice in human history. Egan and Gajdamaschko (2003) refer to it as, "the first, and most ancient, conception" of education and point out that "this kind of learning has been perhaps the commonest in human cultures across the world" (p. 2). However, the definition of apprenticeship is less agreed upon. Apprenticeship (i.e., "traditional" apprenticeship), cognitive apprenticeship, and mentoring, are terms often used interchangeably by educators discussing one-to-one learning contexts (Burwell, 2012. However, all have distinct characteristics and applications.

Traditional apprenticeship is associated with occupation-based training, usually involving physical skills and practice. It is governed by an agreement stipulating the length of time and completion requirements, or competencies (Burwell, 2012; Nielsen, 2006; Pratt, 1998/2016;). Pratt (1998) notes that traditional apprenticeship is used to convey procedures rather than tacit knowledge. He also addresses the use of increasingly complex cognitive schemas to learn from, interpret, and predict outcomes of new experiences as part of an apprenticeship. Rogoff (1995) views apprenticeship through a sociocultural lens and includes the expectation that, "In apprenticeship, newcomers to a community of practice advance their skill and understanding through participation with others in culturally organized activities" (p. 143). Together, these observations suggest the practice as distinctly participatory, social, and situated in real-world contexts. However, traditional apprenticeship retains the characteristics of being governed by an agreement between master and apprentice (i.e., a degree plan) and focused on achieving master status of skill and knowledge within a profession of practice.

Cognitive apprenticeship is an educational approach that strives to "make thinking visible" (Collins, Brown, & Holum, 1991, p. 1) in disciplines that focus on intellectual tasks (i.e., in contrast to the physical, visible/tangible task of traditional apprenticeship). The master-apprentice dyad is still used. However, the master is responsible for explaining content knowledge rather than showing skills to be acquired. The master is also required to evaluate the apprentice's skill acquisition through tasks that allow the apprentice to demonstrate his/her cognitive processes rather than a physical product or performance. Cognitive apprenticeship theory has been applied to higher education music settings (Hennessy, 2000; Varvarigou & Durrant, 2011). However, it is more commonly applied to cognitive subjects like music theory and music education theory than studio-based instruction.

The term mentoring is also frequently used in literature addressing higher education music environments (Gaunt, Creech, Long, & Hallam, 2012; Haddon & Potter, 2014; Hays, Minichiello, & Wright, 2000; Liertz & Macedon, 2007; Renshaw, 2009). Many of the elements of mentoring discussed in the literature align with traditional apprenticeship practices in university music departments and conservatories. However, the mentors in these studies were often not the students' studio teachers and did not assume a "master" role toward the student's musical performance training. Renshaw's (2009) framework for mentoring students in music conservatories in the United Kingdom described a multi-year project to "foster personal growth and to help an individual place their artistic, personal and professional development in a wider cultural, social and educational context" (p. 63). Key elements of the framework included: incorporating professional musicians from outside the educational institution as mentors, mentor training for those participants, and extensive reflective and reflexive practices for students. Haddon and Potter (2014) suggested that students' creativity might be improved through the guidance of a mentor who was not an instrument or voice instructor. They were also concerned traditional apprenticeship practices could become goal-oriented, rather than process-oriented, leaving students without contextualized knowledge. Liertz and Macedon (2007) called for a more holistic approach to mentoring music students, including access to "a broad range of masters" (p. 8). They contrasted the single master-apprentice educational model of higher education music to athletics. That is, where numerous trainers/mentors (coach, nutritionist, psychologist, etc.) were available for each athlete, "music performance education needs to address performance confidence and learn from sport performance's success in this area, using sport psychology principles" (p. 3).

The literature's treatment of the terms traditional apprenticeship, cognitive apprenticeship, and mentoring make it clear that traditional apprenticeship is the model currently used in music department applied instrument and voice studios. Traditional apprenticeship, hereafter simply "apprenticeship," has been the primary training and knowledge delivery method for music education since the origin of guilds in Europe in the twelfth century. Pratt (1998) defines modern apprenticeship as "the process of enculturating learners into a specific community" (p. 11) and describes the master as both instructor and content in a single unit. Rogoff (1990) expands the understanding of traditional apprenticeship to "go beyond expert-novice dyads...focus[ing] on a system of interpersonal involvements and arrangements in which...apprentices become more responsible participants" (p. 143). Both theoretical descriptions of apprenticeship align with the basics of present-day music training in higher education.

Enculturation

Enculturation (Pratt, 1998; Kottak, 2004) is also key to understanding apprenticeship and the ramifications of social media participation by music faculty and students. Pratt (1998) defines apprenticeship as "a process of enculturation..." (p.11). Interestingly, Pratt's (2016) updated version of the same publication uses the word "socialization" in place of "enculturation." The reason for the change is unclear. However, recently published literature suggests that social science prefers the term "socialization" to anthropology's use of "enculturation." Additionally, Veblen (2012) points out that Schugurensky's (2000) description of socialization "...could also be termed tacit learning or enculturation" (p. 250). In this chapter, enculturation and socialization are understood to be interchangeable terms based upon current definitions of both to identify an individual learning the belief systems, values, and behaviors of a group/culture through engagement with it.

Enculturation is "...the process where the culture that is currently established teaches an individual the accepted norms and values of the culture or society... It teaches the individual their role within society as well as what is accepted behavior within that society and lifestyle" (Kottak, 2004, p. 209). Enculturation happens through direct and indirect instruction, consciously and unconsciously, through social events and interactions that include modeling, copying, and observation (Kottak, 2004). Music education – specifically studio-based music training in higher education that is intended to lead to a career in music – fits the definition of enculturation.

Published studies of enculturation and music have frequently focused on children's music education (Corrigall & Trainor, 2010; Hannon & Trainor, 2007; Morrison, Demorest, Campbell, Bartolome, & Roberts, 2013) and ethnomusicological research (Otchere, 2015). Additional studies of enculturation focus on world cultures which remain primarily in the ethnomusicological field. For example, Cawley's (2013) dissertation on enculturation describes how Irish traditional musicians learn in formal and informal environments. She suggested, "While learning repertoire and instrumental skills are significant parts of musical enculturation, they are only part of the process of 'becoming' a musician" (p. 14). Nettl's (1992) work in ethnomusicology posited "one can hardly comprehend a musical system without knowing how it is taught, learned and transmitted in its own society" (p. 389).

Lucy Green's (2002) book, *How Popular Musicians Learn,* provides in-depth coverage of enculturation in studio-based music education. For Green, enculturation is defined as "the acquisition of musical skills and knowledge by immersion in the everyday music and musical practices" (p. 22). She advocates for more modeling, observation, and listening in the classical music studio. She argued,

...an apprenticeship involving exposure to a number of different ways of playing...is just as likely...to equip learners with the wider understanding necessary for the development of their own, 'individual' expression' (Green, 2003, p. 188)

These descriptions and definitions of enculturation suggest that studio-based music training in higher education is, in fact, an example of enculturation. Both formal and informal learning is necessary for students to become successful participants in professional musical culture.

Legitimate Peripheral Participation

Both Rogoff (1995) and Pratt (1998) invoked Lave and Wenger's (1991) concepts legitimate peripheral participation as a critical element of apprenticeship. This concept of legitimate peripheral participation is illustrative of higher education music environments in that it describes the movement of a new group member (apprentice) from a position of observation-only and non-participation, through active participation, and into the role of expert (master) within a community. This transition is an accurate description of a music student entering a new program of study at a university or conservatory. That is, the student initially learns through observation (of both master and peers), begins to execute by imitating what is heard/seen, and eventually moves into a position of expert within the studio. This is generally completed after three to four years of study as part of an undergraduate degree program.

Anticipatory Socialization

Anticipatory socialization (Kramer, 2010; Bouij, 2004) is another key component of understanding music student and faculty motivation for Facebook use. The concept of anticipatory socialization was first defined and presented by Robert Merton (1968) as a way of describing "the acquisition of values and orientations found in statuses and groups in which one not yet engages but which one is likely to enter" (pp. 438-439). It is also sometimes referred to as vocational anticipatory socialization (Putnam & Jablin, 2001) when addressing career development. Students participate in anticipatory socialization when they select a major degree stream (or profession), and seek to understand and acquire the normative behaviors necessary for success in that role or career. Students who have decided to major in music, and pursue a career as a professional musician, look for social opportunities to enhance their knowledge of, and professional standing, in the field. Bouij (2004) found that music educators used anticipatory socialization to establish their role-identities through routine social interaction with music teachers and peers. Facebook studio groups allow for increased social contact between faculty, students, and other professionals in the field, which improves opportunities for anticipatory socialization activities before, during, and after an apprenticeship.

DOCUMENTING CURRENT PRACTICE: FACEBOOK STUDIO GROUPS

Currently, there is a lack of research that addresses the specific potential impact of expanding master-apprentice relationships into informal learning environments via social media. With the long-term, familiar nature of master-apprentice relationships in academic music fields, it may suggest that previous studies of social media communication practices between or among teachers and students in higher education may not be generalizable to music schools. However, music faculty members' personal and professional social media interactions with students and colleagues, made visible through Facebook applied studio groups, might affect how music students perceive the value of and expectations for use of social media in the context of professional practice. Remarkably, these potential effects on student perception have yet to be documented in academic literature.

Recently, there have been published concerns related to the use of social media and other web resources by music students who are no longer restricted to hearing and communicating with a single master (Nerland & Hanken, 2011). This has the potential to upset the traditional vertical authority structure of the master-apprentice mode. Students are now able to "shop around" for multiple interpretations and pedagogical approaches with a simple web search. This decentered apprenticeship model (Nielsen & Kvale, 1997) is a recent phenomenon in the realm of higher education music study. The examination of belief systems of music faculty using Facebook studio groups is a step toward understanding potential impacts on the traditional educational model.

The information in this chapter is based on Meredith's (2017) 2016 study on experiences of music faculty. The purpose of the study was to investigate the social media-related belief systems, intended uses, and lived experiences of applied music faculty in higher education. It provided a comprehensive view of current beliefs and practices, generated a process for phenomenological study and analysis in this type of informal learning environment, and identified future topics of inquiry for social media dialogues between or among music faculty members and students. Analyses were interpreted through the lens of apprenticeship and enculturation so that they could be more easily communicated with academic music faculty, for whom apprenticeship is the most common teaching model.

Method

This study used Interpretative Phenomenological Analysis (IPA) within the constructivist paradigm. Inherent in IPA is the understanding that it is the researcher's job to document a participant's interpretation of a phenomenon as well as the researcher's own perception of the participant's interpretation. IPA uses a double hermeneutic—that is, "...the researcher is trying to make sense of the participant trying to make sense of what is happening to them" (Smith, Flowers, & Larkin, 2009, p. 3). It requires the application of three theoretical constructs throughout the study: phenomenology (the study of a phenomenon through lived experiences), hermeneutics (interpretation of text and authors' meanings), and idiography (concern for individual, contextualized accounts of lived experiences). Because IPA focuses on individual experiences as interpreted through participant and researcher lenses, IPA research is understood to be non-generalizable. Instead, it results in incredibly rich, detailed descriptions of experiences with phenomena that assist with understanding a participant's lived experiences and sense-making of a phenomenon. Readers are then able to use their own experiences and professional knowledge to interpret the results and apply the information as they deem relevant.

Participants

Participants in this study included four full-time music faculty members in universities across the United States. Each was assigned a pseudonym (Berlioz, Gordeli, Mozart, and Stamitz) to protect participant anonymity. Requirements for inclusion were tenured, tenure-track, or full-time academic status, typical studio teaching responsibilities (one-to-one weekly lessons), and regular use of a Facebook group to communicate with students for purposes other than academic coursework. Participants' years of experience in their current positions and years spent using Facebook as a communication tool were varied (Table 1), but all four shared similar perceptions of themselves as "administrators" for their Facebook groups. Additonally, all stated that they had not received any type of formal social media training by their institutions.

Table 1. Participant descriptions

Pseudonym	Position	Years in Position	Years w/Facebook studio group
Berlioz	Professor	37	6
Gordeli	Associate Professor	9	2
Mozart	Assistant Professor	2	2
Stamitz	Senior Lecturer	6	4

Types of Data

Data for this study were collected through demographic surveys, semi-structured interviews, and public Facebook studio group transcripts. The initial demographic survey collected information that included participant position title, years in position, Facebook group creation and management responsibilities, and prior social media training. Each participant was then interviewed, synchronously, over the internet via http://www.Zoom.us due to geographical distance and time constraints. For each participant's public Facebook studio group, all content from January 1 to May 30, 2016, was collected and transcribed/described. Detailed demographic and interview questions can be found in Meredith (2017, pp. 140-146).

Findings

The findings of the study were reported through narrative retellings of each participant's lived experiences with Facebook studio groups as well as tables of emergent themes (Table 2) and the super-ordinate themes identified through grouping (Table 3).

When all emergent themes from the four cases were analyzed and grouped for similarities, three super-ordinate themes emerged. They were: Impact of Social Media on Studio Teaching and Learning; Learning through Enculturation, and; Faculty Lived Experiences with Facebook Studio Groups.

The *Impact of Social Media on Studio Teaching and Learning* theme encompassed participant observations of, opinions about, and reaction to social media's impact on teaching and learning in music studio environments. *Student Skill Acquisition through Enculturation* addressed participant intent when using a Facebook studio group with students. The emergent themes clustered here reflected participant use of Facebook to facilitate student acquisition of skills required for successful membership in the studio as well as enculturation into the broader field/culture of professional musicianship. *Faculty Lived Experiences with Facebook Studio Groups* contained emerging themes that document participants' practices, lived experiences, and reflective opinions of Facebook as a tool, based upon personal knowledge and experience.

Impact of Social Media on Studio Teaching and Learning

Evident with all four faculty were awareness of and response to recent changes in technology, higher education policy, and student behavior/actions. The role of social media as a primary instigator or contributing factor was noted multiple times and by multiple participants. The impact of social media, especially Facebook, on teaching and learning in the music studio was interpreted as positive by some and negative by others. The cluster of emergent themes within this super-ordinate theme suggests that social media's impact on studio teaching and learning affects more than just the members of the Facebook page. Social media, as a phenomenon, has significantly altered how faculty interact with their students and how they teach.

Table 2. All emergent themes developed from data analysis

Theme	Participant(s)
Role Definition	All participants
Student Agency/Influence	Gordeli, Mozart, Stamitz
Institutional Oversight	Berlioz, Gordeli
Learning with Facebook	Berlioz, Stamitz
Celebrating Studio Success	Berlioz
Networking and Promotion	Berlioz
Studio Tradition	Berlioz
Value of Facebook	Gordeli
Intentional Group Use/Management	Gordeli
Social Media's Influence on Instructor Relationships with Students	Gordeli
Negative Impacts of Facebook/Social Media	Mozart
Skeptical of Facebook as Educational Tool	Mozart
Uncertain, but Curious	Mozart
Developing and Maintaining Relationships	Stamitz
Concerns about Social Media Use in Higher Ed	Stamitz
Facebook vs. Face-to-Face Environments	Stamitz

Table 3. Super-ordinate themes with associated emergent themes

Super-Ordinate Themes	Emergent Themes
Impact of Social Media on Studio Teaching and Learning	• Facebook vs. Face-to-Face • Student Agency/Influence • Institutional Oversight • Social Media's Influence on Relationships • Skepticism and Concern
Learning through Enculturation	• Role Definition • Student Agency/Influence • Learning with Facebook • Celebrating Studio Success • Studio Tradition • Networking and Promotion
Faculty Lived Experiences with Facebook Studio Groups	• Affordances of Facebook • Negative Impacts • Developing and Maintaining Relationships • Networking and Promotion • Group Management

The most significant effect of social media—and specifically Facebook—on studio teaching and learning is that the master-apprentice relationship is no longer built solely upon the professional reputation of the master and weekly face-to-face interactions in the studio. Gordeli pointed out that students she connected with on Facebook can "see my life." Faculty who make themselves available to students through social media are no longer simply training students in a traditional apprenticeship model where they are responsible for teaching/modeling skills and practices. Instead, they have adopted the position of teaching/modeling through their *lives*, including personal interests, family activities, beliefs, etc. This contrasts with previous generations of music masters and apprentices who communicated primarily through face-to-face conversations and written documents. Masters could easily select what type of personal information to give out, if any, and to which apprentices. The use of a tool such as Facebook might be seen as democratizing the process, allowing equal access to faculty information and teaching for all students. However, Stamitz noted that she found herself self-censoring to avoid potential conflict or other issues when sharing information on Facebook. This suggests the possibility that when masters make themselves more visible through social media, they may actually reduce the amount of personal insight and opinion shared, and that the lives they teach and model for students could be less than authentic.

Tied closely to faculty authenticity and identity is social media's impact on faculty exposure to risk. As institutions develop and implement policies to cover any social media interaction between faculty and students—whether as part of formal classroom tasks or informal learning and social environments—faculty are forced to take on an additional level of responsibility, and therefore risk, if they want to engage in using social media for learning. Unlike a classroom or studio setting, however, a faculty member has little to no control of the space or what happens within it. As the participants in this study related, there are currently several ways this is being handled by faculty. Gordeli basically ignored or performed minimal diligence to meet the institutional policies based on her perception that she knew more than the policy makers and a belief that her Facebook studio groups offered little to no risk to herself or the university. Berlioz heeded the institutional policies that minimized risk to himself and the university, even though they frustrated him and restricted his ability to share timely information. He believed that his Facebook studio group provided a valuable service to his students, even if content is delayed. Mozart was unwilling to accept any significant risk and so restricted his Facebook studio page interaction and content sharing to minimal levels. Even with this small sample size, it is clear that a faculty member's comfort with risk can significantly influence willingness to use social media for learning, regardless of its educational potential or ability to meet student needs.

Social media's impact on interpersonal formality in studio teaching and learning was also present in the emergent themes. Gordeli noted that her students expected more casual, informal relationships with her than she had with her teachers, suggesting this is related to her students seeing her informally through social media. This further suggests that master-apprentice roles would be impacted if apprentices viewed their masters more as colleagues or friends instead of the traditional authority figures. The fact that most students come to Facebook already fluent in the platform—and sometimes more so than the faculty member—adds another potential element of equalization between master and apprentice. Gordeli observed that, while she was comfortable with her less formal teaching role, her students still feared her. She wanted her students to continue to view her as an authority figure, even as relationships with her students became less rigid and formal. This is an excellent example social media's contribution to shifting levels of formality in a master-apprentice environment where traditional dynamics of authority remain desirable.

Skepticism and concern surrounding the impacts of social media on teaching and learning are plentiful in the literature and are borne out in the participants' comments and observations. Only Gordeli had nothing but positive reflections on social media's impact on teaching and learning. Mozart's observation that "social networking causes latent laziness" was based upon his perception that students who use social media require more reminders and do not record scheduled events in calendars. Berlioz and Stamitz, on the other hand, viewed their Facebook studio groups as tools for providing reminders and event information to meet student needs. This contrast in views of the same phenomenon could be related to professional experience in that Mozart had fewer years in his position. It may also result from a pedagogical belief system, as Berlioz and Stamitz approach their roles on Facebook similarly—as motivators/cheerleaders—with instructor/master roles saved for the studio.

Other concerns about social media impacts on studio teaching and learning were also espoused. Stamitz expressed concern that it wass too easy to quickly change lesson times or rearrange schedules with social media tools, suggesting that it encourages a lack of organization or preparation. She also worried that the "always connected" nature of technology and social media prevented students from disconnecting and taking time away during academic breaks, with the implication that disconnecting is necessary and beneficial for learning. Mozart was annoyed by colleagues who "show off" their large studios, without regard for the actual academic skills of the studio members. He voiced resentment of those who used Facebook to promote their studios based upon size rather than skillset. Mozart noted that prospective students were likely impressed by the pictures, without regard for the academic underpinnings. This was interpreted as concern for students who may select a university/studio based upon size rather than quality, and receive an inferior education as a result. However, Gordeli countered this negative view of studio pictures by clarifying that the picture of her studio posted to Facebook was not bragging—instead, it is a way to celebrate and look forward to the coming school year.

Social media's impacts on studio teaching and learning detailed here show that they can significantly affect not only a student's quality of education, but the basic fabric of traditional master-apprentice teaching present in most university music departments and conservatories today. The ubiquitous nature of social media has resulted in institutional oversight and personal role definition and re-definition by faculty who use it. Inherent in its adoption is faculty awareness of risk, both personal and professional, which could impact the quality and authenticity of communication and content delivery. However, there is no agreement among faculty participants in this study as to what level of risk is acceptable or at what point student learning is positively or negatively impacted. Concerns about a lack of ability to disconnect from social media and school were voiced, as well as mixed reactions to posting images of studios to Facebook. From the data and themes presented in this chapter, the perceived impacts of social media on studio teaching and learning can be interpreted as either positive and negative, depending upon faculty members' prior experiences and comfort with risk.

Learning Through Enculturation

Two of the four participants, Berlioz and Stamitz, explicitly stated that they did not assume the role of pedagogue when using their Facebook studio groups. Mozart was skeptical that Facebook has any educational purpose. However, all faculty members discussed taking specific, intentional actions that provided students the opportunity to learn critical skills, generally through enculturation in this informal learning environment. Faculty members may not perceive their actions as teaching—but when viewed through the lens of apprenticeship, the recommendation of field-specific resources and modeling of professional practice on Facebook meet traditional expectations for master-apprentice education.

Educational content was intentionally shared on Facebook by all faculty in some way. All four shared links to videos or other media that they had determined was professionally relevant for their students. Stamitz and Mozart referred to posting articles or information about practicing techniques. Fourteen of Mozart's sixteen posts were instructional or provided guidance for performance issues. Participants discussed these materials as resources they had selected and wanted their students to view; this suggests an unspoken expectation that students would learn something from those materials. Mozart noted that when he posted videos to his Facebook studio page, he could not verify that students had actually viewed it. Therefore, he shared the same content during a face-to-face lesson, which validates the educational intent of sharing the content on Facebook. This example may partially explain why music faculty are reluctant to state that they are teaching with their Facebook pages—although there is clear intent to share educational content and help students build skills, they are not aware of a way to measure student learning if or when students engage with it.

A significant opportunity for student skill acquisition through Facebook studio groups or pages is faculty members' modeling of professional practices and behaviors. Gordeli attempted to show "the career of a musician as a whole" by allowing her students to see both her personal and professional activities, thereby modeling her own expectations and discipline norms. Berlioz focused significant effort on connecting his students to other professionals in the field, including alumni this provided documented examples of professional interactions as models for his students' future interactions with colleagues. Stamitz' commented about self-censorship which reflected her desire to avoid conflict and present a positive model for discourse on her Facebook studio group. As modeling is a standard practice for traditional apprenticeship teaching and learning, the modeling performed via Facebook studio groups can be viewed as a simple extension of teaching practices used in the studio with face-to-face instruction.

The establishment and reinforcement of studio traditions is also part of the enculturation that leads to learner skill acquisition. Visible documentation and celebration of student and studio successes assists with student recruitment and students' desire for studio membership. As students participate in anticipatory socialization activities through Facebook studio groups, they acquire the skills necessary for full participation in the studio, its traditions, and the greater musical community. Berlioz requested alumni to post their professional activities and whereabouts was done to let "current students know about former students so that they feel like they're part of tradition." Gordeli commented that she wanted to inspire her students "to get them more interested in what we do," which suggested an internalized sense of heritage and/or community with its own norms and traditions. Three of the faculty mentioned hosting annual studio parties, gatherings held at faculty members' houses for all the current members of the studio. Berlioz posted pictures from a studio party hosted at his home, further reinforcing studio tradition and making it visible.

Although teaching with Facebook studio groups is not an explicit goal for the faculty interviewed, their interview responses and Facebook posts suggested that they participate in activities that provide learning materials and opportunities for their students. Modeling professional practices and behaviors occurs frequently on Facebook studio groups by faculty and mirrors similar modeling practices in face-to-face apprenticeship environments. Facebook also provides a space for students to practice their online behaviors and communication through anticipatory socialization activities. Finally, Facebook studio groups contribute to the visibility of studio traditions, which provides motivation for student membership and enculturation. As part of that enculturation process, students are able to acquire professional skills and behaviors that will aid in their future successful careers.

Faculty Lived Experience With Facebook Studio Groups

The third super-ordinate theme identified from participants' responses emerged from their commentary on their lived experiences with Facebook. Although the homogenous sample solicited and enlisted for the study shared similar academic and career backgrounds, each faculty member voiced a distinctive view on Facebook studio group management, purpose for its use, and perspective on its value in higher education. These unique experiences and opinions are documented here to convey the diverse practices and values currently in place for music faculty using Facebook studio groups.

Management and administration practices were discussed by each faculty member, and several similar topics were addressed by multiple participants. Advertising by group members was commented on by both Berlioz and Gordeli. Each noted that when they had first created Facebook studio groups there were individuals who joined for the sole purpose of advertising instruments or other things for sale. This surprised both of them and resulted in decisions to restrict or remove those types of posts. Stamitz' Facebook studio group, on the other hand, showed commercial activity but only within its core membership—members actively seeking instruments for purchase for themselves or their students and getting retailer recommendations from each other.

Another page management/use topic that arose was the use of Facebook studio group/page posts for communication with students versus traditional email methods. All participants stated that they used both mediums for communication with current students, and all noted that personal conversations were kept in face-to-face or institutional email environments. Gordeli mentioned that she does not use the Messenger (instant messaging) application in Facebook with her students because she did not use Messenger frequently enough to consistently answer individual student questions; instead, she used email for that purpose. Mozart stated that he duplicated all of his Facebook studio page posts in email form to his students because they get an alert of some type through the LMS when a new email message arrives. This suggests that faculty decisions to use Facebook versus email may influenced by the mechanics of the tools themselves as well as the content and/or personal nature of the communications.

Each faculty member voiced strong convictions for the reasoning used when managing his/her Facebook group/page, including who can view the page, become a member, and post materials. The variety of management practices led to very different types of membership, purposes, and intended audiences for each Facebook studio group/page. Each of the four used a different combination of administrative settings. Table 4 shows a comparison of the participants' management practices.

Berlioz created and managed one Facebook studio group with membership that included current and former students, parents, colleagues, and other professionals in the field. He actively promoted the interaction of current and former students toward building a sense of tradition and noted that parents enjoyed seeing their children's contributions in that forum. Berlioz posted information that is directed to the Facebook studio group members as well as about them when he introduces current students. He also occasionally responded to others' posts.

Gordeli maintained two separate Facebook studio groups; one was for current students and was private, the other public and for alumni (although anyone may view content and request membership). Her concerns about student privacy and creating a safe space to let them develop their own community influenced her decision to split her audiences. Gordeli stated that she posted information daily to her private

Table 4. Facebook studio page management comparison

	Berlioz	**Gordeli (Public)**	**Gordeli (Private)**	**Mozart**	**Stamitz**
Who can view:	Public/ anyone	Public/ anyone	Current students & professor	Public/ anyone	Public/ anyone
Membership/ Followers:	Current students, professor, alumni, parents, other professional musicians	Alumni, professor	Current students, professor	Current students, professor, other professional musicians	Current students, alumni, professor
Who can post:	All members	All members	All members	Professor only; any other posts require moderation/ permission	All members

Facebook studio group and communicated regularly with her students. She posted less frequently—and in a uni-directional manner—to the public Facebook studio group.

Mozart's page audience was primarily current students, although a few other colleagues/professionals had interacted and viewed his page. His posts were entirely uni-directional, and in fact, no one was allowed to post information to the Facebook studio page without his moderation/approval. Followers of the page could respond to his posts, however. Mozart's page was aimed entirely at providing educational information (videos, websites, etc.) to his studio. His students maintained their own separate Facebook group, to which he did not have access and did not wish to access.

Stamitz managed a group that was originally co-created with students and had a membership that included current and former students. Her group displayed a focus on satisfying current students' needs in real time as well as providing a link to resources and information for those that had graduated and no longer had university resources available to them. Stamitz used her Facebook studio group regularly as someone who posts new information and responded to others' posts.

Other lived experiences related by the participants included frequent reference to using Facebook to build and maintain relationships. Stamitz and Berlioz noted the importance of their studio groups for keeping in touch with alumni; Gordeli also used Facebook in this manner, but created a separate group to continue her connection to former students. Gordeli and Stamitz discussed using their groups to connect to colleagues at their own institutions, and Stamitz also used her personal Facebook page to connect with colleagues across the country. This communicative affordance (Hutchby, 2001; Schrock, 2015) of the Facebook platform is valued highly by all of the faculty interviewed, even Mozart, who expressed interest in using Facebook to "see what other studios around the country are doing." This is understandable since most applied music faculty are singular in their departments—most music departments only have one instructor per instrument or voice, so feelings of isolation are plausible.

Beyond student/faculty interactions and relationship-building activities, individual participants mentioned lived experiences that are wide-ranging in scope. Berlioz noted that he discovered Facebook was a tool shared by students, parents, and other professionals, so using it allowed him to quickly get information to the widest demographic audience possible. Gordeli saw her students creating their own peer-oriented community within her private Facebook studio group, something she viewed as positive. Stamitz found that Facebook provided access to a supportive network of colleagues across the country with whom she could share frustrations. Mozart saw potential negative implications of using Facebook

Live and feared that sharing a poor performance might impact student respect and recruiting efforts. Each of these experiences influenced the faculty member's perception of Facebook. This study's documentation of first-generation music faculty use of Facebook studio pages illuminates the varied lived experiences and practices currently employed.

DISCUSSION

The super-ordinate themes discerned from the study provided a frame for discussing faculty members' current beliefs, intent, and lived experiences with Facebook studio pages. The first super-ordinate theme, *Impact of Social Media on Studio Teaching and Learning*, can be understood to represent the beliefs of the music faculty. It described their reasons for using Facebook studio groups, concerns about risk, and addresses the challenge of moving from an educational model of apprenticeship involving limited master-apprentice contact to one that involves faculty sharing their entire musician lives/lifestyles with students. The second super-ordinate theme, *Learning through Enculturation*, was interpreted as faculty intent when actively using a Facebook studio group/page. Although teaching and learning were not stated goals by participants, faculty intentions voiced in interviews and visible activity on their Facebook studio groups fit the description of teaching through enculturation as described by Kottak (2004). The final super-ordinate theme, *Lived Experiences with Facebook Studio Groups,* shared the diverse and unique lived experiences of each participant. These themes are discussed in detail below.

Impact of Social Media on Studio Teaching and Learning

The faculty members who participated in this study acknowledged the impact of social media on their studio teaching resulting from creating and using Facebook studio groups in response to student wants and behaviors. The concerns voiced by previous researchers (Oliver & Clayes, 2014; Cain et al, 2013; Mathieson & Leafman, 2014) about potential student resentment emanating from instructor decisions to use social media tools that students were already using—and thereby invading their (students') space— were not apparent in this study. In fact, participants' respect for student agency was demonstrated through their reflections about why they began using Facebook or creating a studio group. Gordeli was challenged by her students to create a Facebook profile not long after the platform emerged, and so she did.

We have a Christmas party like most flute studios do now. And my students said, "Why don't you go on Facebook?" and I was like "Because that's for people your age." And they gave me an assignment... they told me that I had Christmas break to get on my own Facebook page.

Her subsequent experience with Facebook encouraged her to use it for studio communication. Similarly, Stamitz heeded student requests to have an informal space for sharing information and connecting with others and is now an administrator for that Facebook studio group. Berlioz mentioned his surprise at how much his students enjoyed sharing their own work on the Facebook group as well as the fact that parents and other group members loved it—acknowledging that student and parent positive response was impactful on his perception and continued use of the tool. Mozart went so far with student agency he sought not to intrude on a pre-existing Facebook studio group created and managed by students when he arrived at the institution. Instead, he created a new group to avoid entering their personal virtual space.

They have their own [group]...I have yet to really infiltrate that page, because I'm debating whether or not I really need to...I'm not here to babysit them...I'm not really here to debate whether or not they should have their own...conversations.

In each of these cases, faculty reaction to student wants and behaviors—recognizing student agency/influence—was the key to establishing the current set of Facebook studio groups included in this study. The "creepy treehouse" analogy used by Cain and Policastri (2011) was avoided by participants' willingness to respect students' personal space and build their own Facebook studio groups, then invite students and others to join or follow. This suggests a shift toward greater acknowledgement and respect for student agency in social media environments by the participants in this study as compared to those in earlier studies.

A shift from modeling skills and practices in a face-to-face studio environment to modeling all elements of musician life/lifestyle is another sizable impact of social media on studio teaching and learning. Previous generations of masters modeled skills, practices, and behaviors for apprentices in the studio and in other school (i.e., classrooms or school ensemble rehearsals) or professional events (i.e., rehearsals and concerts) where both master and apprentice were acting in a professional capacity. Faculty who choose to have and use a social media profile visible to current students, alumni, and others must be willing to accept a new role of modeling all aspects of life as a musician – extra-musical activities, family events, and other elements of a musician's life that would not have been previously available to students except through face-to-face conversations or during instructional time. The purposeful crafting of social media identities discussed by Karl and Peluchette (2011) and Kimmons and Veletsianos (2014) is less possible here. Students interact with their applied faculty teacher face-to-face, weekly and for several years; an inauthentic social media presence would be noticeable if it were different from the faculty member's real-life persona. Chen and Breyer's (2012) observation that crafting an identity for social media only including positive or selected parts of self would be detrimental to teaching would seem to apply directly to this situation.

When reflecting on their own pre-social media academic communication with students, Gordeli and Berlioz commented that their only communications with their teachers were in face-to-face settings or through notes left on studio doors. Berlioz remembered:

My teacher at [institution] was old school, and messages were always by phone call or face to face – no written communication or even group messages via memo... A sign on the door might be as close as it got and that was rare!

Stamitz recalled that a former teacher might leave a telephone message regarding a lesson or rehearsal time, but otherwise all communication was only during an academic class/meeting time or occasionally sending email.

My studio teacher communicated with primarily by making announcements in weekly studio classes... maybe sometimes sending emails... If [someone needed] to cancel a lesson or reschedule a lesson, you just made a phone call.

Making oneself visible and available, and sharing personal information about family, travel, and the entire life of a musician is a striking contrast to only seeing and talking to students during a single weekly lesson or in a classroom setting. Veletsianos (2013) and Metzger et al. (2010) pointed out potential positive effects of instructor self-disclosure and authenticity with social media profiles. Metzger et al. (2010) suggested that this approach "may lead to higher anticipated motivation among students, affective learning, and a more comfortable classroom climate" (p. 2).

However, one of the challenges of adapting to a new communication medium and frank social presence is the lack of training for faculty who choose to do so. It is unsurprising that some faculty find themselves being criticized by colleagues or the institution for their social media activities. Intentionally sharing one's entire life/lifestyle as a master within a traditional apprenticeship seems relevant and expected, and historical accounts of apprenticeship validate this observation. However, for many generations music faculty in higher education have used traditional apprenticeship practices in one-on-one settings behind closed doors. This meant little interaction with apprentices outside limited fixed hours in the studio. The cognitive shift in role-identity is significant, and it is evident even within this small study that faculty reactions to this shift are variable and inconsistent.

Another significant impact of social media on studio teaching and learning is the element of perceived risk to the faculty member personally or professionally. A Kansas faculty member's suspension based upon his "improper use of social media" (Jaschik, 2013), an aborted hiring in Illinois related to a perceived "lack of civility" on the candidate's Twitter feed (Jaschik, 2015), and other impacts to faculty employment based on social media use have been reported by the Chronicle of Higher Education. Lupton (2014) commented on the risk of an instructor becoming a target for abuse or unprofessional conduct by students or colleagues, but no existing academic literature addressed faculty perception of risk due to violation of institutional rules and regulations that govern social media use with students.

Faculty assume some level of responsibility for students and the accompanying data in their classrooms and studios. This is contained within a controlled, physical environment. However, faculty have been told by institutions that similar levels of responsibility will be assigned for virtual settings where they have little to no control over student behavior and data. This elevates the level of risk that faculty assume if they choose to create and use Facebook studio groups with their students.

Participants in this study reacted to institutional oversight and rules governing responsibility when using social media with students in different ways. Mozart expressed his concerns about posting content to his Facebook studio group that might be considered inappropriate by the institution – his fear of legal action and/or job loss affected him strongly enough that his engagement and activities in his Facebook studio group are minimal and restricted.

There's a fine line, and I'm just going to play it safe. I don't want to see a university lawyer.

Berlioz was also aware of the risk of violating a recently instituted a policy that allows the institution to fire employees for violating its social media regulations:

I can actually be fired for posting something that's embarrassing to the university... I would not want to be a test case of that.

This perception of risk encourages him to follow the rules requiring social media releases from every student before posting a picture to Facebook, even though the delay frustrates him. Gordeli, however, acknowledged institutional oversight rules governing social media, but ignored them.

[The university] want us to clear our Facebook pages with them which I don't do... The university just wants to make sure that they can control it and they haven't yet realized that maybe there are some things that they want to fuss with and...they should just let go... I think my public page is cleared but my private [page] is not.

Her personal assessment of the low risk to herself and her students is grounded in her perception that she knows more than the institution's rule-makers and maintains appropriate conduct on her Facebook studio groups in the same way that she would in a classroom. These examples suggest that reactions to institutional oversight are grounded in risk appraisal, not ethical assessment of potential harm to self or students. None of the participants expressed antipathy for the ethical justification of the rules, guidelines, or restrictions. They were cognizant of the personal risks they were taking by assuming responsibility for their students in an online environment and did not challenge the reasoning behind the rules and restrictions. The faculty in this study each chose to maintain active Facebook studio groups regardless of the level/type of institutional oversight, and appear to have evaluated the educational value of the tool's use in a holistic sense, including factors such as perceived risk and ease of use. It is unknown how strongly that perceived risk may impact faculty willingness to use Facebook studio groups or the type of activities and content they decide to post.

Learning Through Enculturation

Several participants stated that they were not intentionally teaching through their Facebook studio groups, but those comments reflect a narrow definition of teaching and learning. Faculty who viewed teaching as direct instruction, delivered in a studio or classroom, and formally assessed in an academic environment do not feel that their activities on Facebook constitute teaching. However, Berlioz clearly considered the possibility mid-interview with his think-aloud "that's a thought...how we can teach using this page...." Expanding the concept of teaching and learning to include enculturation as a legitimate learning process, however, situates the Facebook studio groups securely within the definition of an informal learning environment.

Pratt (1998) defined the apprenticeship model of education as "the process of enculturating learners into a specific community" (p. 11). Kottak (2004) described enculturation as a conscious and unconscious process, employing three different stages: direct instruction, indirect instruction (modeling/copying) that is a conscious act, and observation or awareness of events through unconscious acts. The latter two stages – conscious and unconscious indirect instruction and observation – nicely encapsulate the documented faculty content and activities found on each of the Facebook studio groups. Viewed through this lens, the Facebook studio groups are extensions of the apprenticeship, and support the enculturation process by providing a virtual space for both direct, through resources posted by faculty for student learning/ consumption, and indirect instruction. The indirect instruction manifests through faculty modeling of behavior and administrative decisions on the groups, and students may consciously or unconsciously learn from their engagement with or observation of those modeled activities.

Participants' desire to show students what they do and share the non-academically-focused activities in their musical lives is a significant contribution to the enculturation process. Consciously or unconsciously, students come to understand the culture of their musical community through the representative behaviors and beliefs they encounter in face-to-face and virtual settings with their faculty member/ master. Facebook studio groups provide a free virtual space for music faculty to expand the enculturation process and provide visible models of behavior that represent the largely unseen extra-academic life of professional musicians. The study participants may not consciously teach with their Facebook studio groups, but theories of apprenticeship and enculturation suggest that their students both consciously and unconsciously learn from them. This confirms the researcher's definition of Facebook studio groups as informal learning environments.

Lived Experiences With Facebook Studio Groups

Each of the participants related unique lived experiences with a Facebook studio group. Group management and administrative practices were diverse, leading faculty members to interact with different audiences and tailor posted content to their group membership or followers. This, in turn, led to different philosophies regarding the use of Facebook studio groups, which is evident in the varied data sets collected from Spring 2016. Each group contained significantly different numbers of posts, types of content posted, and frequency of faculty/student interaction. For that reason, the researcher chose to illustrate the individual participant cases and the emergent themes in the study before developing super-ordinate themes. The homogenous population solicited and selected for this study was discovered to be highly heterogeneous in practice.

Some similarities were discerned from participants' discussion of lived experiences. All four stated that they had not participated in any training for the use of social media with students in higher education. Two—Berlioz and Mozart—expressed an interest in receiving training and seemed to see value in learning about other uses for Facebook as an informal learning environment, while Gordeli and Stamitz felt that training would not provide them with anything they did not already know. A call for faculty and student training for social media use in the areas of ethics, security, and equitable access evident in previous literature (Veletsianos, 2013; Oliver & Clayes, 2014; Chen & Bryer, 2012; Lee, 2013; Mathieson & Leafman, 2014) has not yet been heeded by many institutional leaders.

All four participants also acknowledged the power of Facebook to provide free and easy access to developing and maintaining relationships with colleagues, students, and/or alumni who are geographically distant from the physical studio. The Facebook platform was also recognized as a tool for event promotion and marketing, providing a no-cost way to potentially reach a larger audience than the members of the institution and local community. However, there is disagreement about the appropriateness of marketing one's studio. Mozart believes that colleagues who post pictures and promotional information about their studios are showing off, focusing on studio size and activities rather than academic prowess. He complains:

I see my colleagues constantly posting pictures of what their studio's doing and...their giant [instrument] choirs... You're honestly showing off. I don't like that.

Gordeli's commentary on posting information about her studio at the beginning of the year is counter to Mozart's view. She explicitly states that she is not bragging, but wants to convey a sense of excitement about her studio's potential in the upcoming year.

I do it for, you know, reasons of promotion...it's not about, look at how many students I have. It's "aren't they great? You know this is gonna be a great year"

This disagreement about marketing and/or promoting one's studio exemplifies the lack of conformity in the lived experiences of the participants in this study.

Overall, participants' lived experiences with their Facebook studio groups were discussed positively. None related stories of negative impacts or actions/posts that were problematic. Three of the four participants – Berlioz, Gordeli, and Stamitz – held positive opinions of the affordances of Facebook based upon their perceptions of it as an easy-to-use, valuable tool for communication. Mozart is skeptical of the platform as an educational or communication tool, but recognized its popularity with students. He also freely admitted that he may not know how to use it well and gave it the benefit of the doubt as a potentially useful tool for teaching and learning. For the four music faculty members in this study, perceived risk or skepticism about using Facebook to interact with their students in an informal learning environment was outweighed by their beliefs in its potential for positive impacts within their studios.

Challenges of a New Communication Medium

Five topics were discerned from the results that are believed to require further discussion. They are: faculty members' perception of risk, sharing one's musical and extra-musical life with students, enculturation, informal vs. formal learning through observation, and the lack of uniformity of Facebook page management/administration. These elements are expanded upon below.

Risk was a key concern voiced by participants. Institutional oversight of social media interactions between faculty and students has resulted in the creation and adoption of rules that require faculty to assume responsibility—and therefore a level of risk—if they choose to interact with their students through social media. Consequences of violating those rules and responsibilities carry heavy penalties, often involving legal action and/or job loss. Literature exists that addresses faculty awareness (or lack thereof) of institutional rules and ethical concerns with regard to using social media in higher education, but there is a gap in the published literature that might address how perception of risk/risk aversion may impact teaching and learning once faculty understand the institution's rules and regulations. In this study, two faculty members followed the rules, and one of those severely restricted his Facebook studio group activity to avoid any possible perception of impropriety. The other two faculty members were unconcerned, and one went so far as to actively ignore the institution's request for oversight/approval of her group. Further study is warranted to determine whether a faculty member's aversion to risk may impact willingness to enhance their instructional methods through social media use, or if there is a tipping point at which taking on added responsibility/risk becomes justifiable if particular outcomes are guaranteed.

The issue of sharing one's entire musical life/lifestyle with students is also significant. The expansion of studio-based music education from limited weekly contact with a master to nearly continuous visibility and contact outside the physical studio has far-reaching implications. Providing students with a glimpse of all aspects of a musical career may assist with the transition from college to the professional workforce. It can also allow students to determine that a particular career is desirable or undesirable before making academic and financial commitments, and humanize the faculty member to his/her students in a way that is not possible with limited contact and visibility. However, such humanization carries with it the likelihood of increasing informality between faculty and students, if only through more frequent communication. This was noted by one participant in her interview, and evident in the Facebook data of another—increased visibility of personal lives and frequency of communication can lead to less formal interactions and speech. The participants in this study did not have a problem with a move toward more informal discourse, although Mozart maintained his desire to keep professional and friend-oriented interactions separate. However, this is a significant change from previous generations of studio-based music teaching in higher education and it is worth documenting this first generation of faculty who have acknowledged and embraced the shift toward sharing all of themselves with students and participating in less formal interactions.

Though unnoticed by the participants, it was evident that enculturation was a central teaching and learning concept during this study. Although it is not routinely discussed in studio teaching literature, the concept is situated within the core principles of apprenticeship that are the foundation of studio-based music education. Facebook studio groups provide a virtual space for teaching through enculturation, and provide a platform for the stages involved: direct instruction, indirect instruction (through conscious perception) and subconscious observation/involvement. Even when activities were not identified as "teaching" by the participants in this study, students were provided the opportunity to learn through faculty members' modeling of behavior and activities. All four study participants used Facebook in this manner. Direct instruction was provided through recommended articles and videos. Indirect instruction was enacted by modeling behaviors and communication with colleagues in a visible forum.

Subconscious learning through observation was facilitated by faculty sharing their own personal experiences and musical lives as exemplars of professional musical culture. Viewing Facebook studio groups from the perspective of enculturation dynamically expands justification for their use as an educational tool, and could provide guidance toward assessing educational value of content and activities. However, if fully integrated as part of the apprenticeship model that originated in studio-based music teaching, the label "informal learning environment" might have to be re-evaluated. Approaching Facebook studio groups as an extension of the studio for learning purposes could re-situate them as part of the "formal" learning environment.

A final discussion point that emerged from the study is the lack of uniformity displayed in Facebook studio group management and administration. One of the features of Facebook is administrator ability to control membership, audience/visibility, and who can post content. Every participant used a group where all content was visible to the public. However, this was the only consistent element across the four groups that were analyzed. Each Facebook studio group had a different membership composition or target audience – some included other professionals and colleagues, others targeted alumni and current students only, etc. In Mozart's Facebook studio group, only he—the administrator—could post new content; however, students were allowed to comment and react to the posts. Management diversity makes it difficult to compare groups or evaluate engagement levels, a critical task if guidance or training is to be implemented by institutions.

Limitations

This study's findings are a new addition to the literature in the area of first-generation social media use by music faculty. The Interpretative Phenomenological Analysis (IPA) methodology employed in the study resulted in thick, rich descriptions of lived experiences and practices for four participants on a topic that had yet to be addressed in published literature. However, several study limitations were identified and are addressed below.

First, although the sample size was adequate for the use of IPA as a qualitative methodology and a homogenous sample was used, the diversity of Facebook group management practices displayed by the four participants suggest that a larger sample might assist with discerning super-ordinate themes. Second, limiting Facebook data collection to publicly available content may have contributed to more conservative data sets since participants were all aware that their groups could be viewed by anyone. Third, it was not possible to tell who was responding to participants' posts. Based upon the types of responses and inferences from profile images, it seems that most activity was generated by students. However, it is possible that alumni and other professionals were also commenting and there was no way to differentiate.

The greatest limitation of this study was that several of the participants did not view themselves as "teaching" when using their Facebook studio groups and so did not discuss their activities using pedagogical vocabulary. In several instances, it was necessary for the researcher to interpret responses using personal knowledge and experience from the music field to translate what was being said into a description of the activity using teaching/learning terminology. The use of IPA assisted greatly with this task as it expects this type of interpretive act by the researcher and provides a theoretical foundation for execution and later explanation. However, embedding this layer of interpretation into the findings challenges the reader to accept this second hermeneutic, and without a background in studio-based music instruction readers may be less receptive to the conclusions reached.

A final limitation of this study was the dearth of existing literature about studio-based music instruction and social media use. Previous studies of social media communication practices between or among teachers and students in higher education did not address the unique nature of master-apprentice relationships. The findings of this study demonstrated marked differences in music faculty beliefs, intent, and lived experiences from those higher education faculty interviewed in previous studies. In this study, no evidence of a true virtual community of practice was uncovered, participants were adamant about maintaining a single profile that spanned personal and professional presence. Also, there was no sense of faculty intrusion into student personal space by using Facebook; indeed, several Facebook studio groups were created at the request of the students. Readers wishing to investigate this study's topic further will find the lack of similar literature to be challenging. However, it is hoped that this study will provide an impetus for other researchers to pursue this topic and remedy that issue.

The variety of management approaches used by faculty in this study resulted in each Facebook studio group having a different composition of member types (students, alumni, faculty colleagues, etc.). However, the manner in which faculty use the groups fits well into the theory of enculturation, in which case a Facebook studio group can be viewed as an additional feature of the traditional apprenticeship model and not an independent community.

SOLUTIONS AND RECOMMENDATIONS

The study was exploratory and not intended to generate practical solutions to an identified problem. However, the findings indicate that there are several specific challenges endured by music faculty that impact their beliefs, intent, and lived experiences when using Facebook to communicate with their students. Several recommendations for practice were generated, and are intended to assist the broader population of music faculty engaged in studio-based instruction who currently use, or may use in the future, Facebook studio groups.

The first recommendation is that music faculty receive training on social media skills and appropriate norms for use that acknowledges the master-apprentice relationship, helping to situate Facebook studio groups within the enculturation process of students pursuing a career in music. This study suggests that music faculty may not recognize that Facebook can be used in this manner, but could be receptive to the idea if prompted to consider it. Social media training by institutions is likely to focus on issues of ethics, security, and equitable access—not on educational theories for use that are field-specific. Therefore, training should be provided to music faculty that addresses not only institutional requirements and guidelines but the capacity of platforms such as Facebook to act as an extension of the studio environment and enculturation process.

The second recommendation is that music departments develop their own set of guidelines for Facebook studio group creation and management based upon their institution's rules and oversight procedures. The concern about personal and professional risk that was evident in participants in this study might be at least partially alleviated with the knowledge that they had followed a set of practices adopted at the departmental level. Also, this would create more consistency in membership management, group visibility, and posting rights. If a level of uniformity in group management is reached, then instruction and training can more easily be developed and implemented that would aid with marketing events, student recruitment and retention, and other studio-oriented promotion topics.

The final recommendation is that exemplar Facebook studio groups be shared by professional music education organizations to encourage a discussion of best-practices for teaching and learning. At this time, first-generation faculty using Facebook studio groups are creating policy and practice independently from one another, without consultation or collaboration. If these types of informal learning environments are to be better understood, managed, and use for educational purposes, it is critical that current practices are shared to promote discussion and debate. National and international organizations could support this goal by initiating conversations within the field and soliciting examples from practitioners to share.

FUTURE RESEARCH DIRECTIONS

This study investigated a phenomenon that had not yet been documented and analyzed in academic literature. While studies have been undertaken with a few faculty members that used it for direct, intentional instruction, the use of Facebook studio groups by music faculty is a relatively recent activity since the platform has only been available to the public for ten years. Therefore, there are several additional research opportunities regarding the use of social media tools by music faculty who teach in studio-based music education environments.

First, it is recommended that a similar, if not identical, study be performed using the same methodology with students as participants instead of faculty. This study was limited to faculty lived experiences to establish "why" the Facebook studio groups were being used in certain ways. The next step is to determine if the enculturating activities that faculty engage in are having the desired effect on students and student learning. IPA has proved to be an effective methodology for investigating beliefs, intent, and lived experiences. A parallel study of music students who participate in Facebook studio groups would significantly enhance the results and findings of this study.

Second, a recommendation is made for a study of music faculty that discerns instructor perception of personal and professional risk when using Facebook studio groups. The effects of risk aversion on faculty willingness to use social media with their students or types of activities and interaction is unknown, but perceived risk was mentioned multiple times by participants in this study. Understanding how risk aversion impacts use would help with training and guideline development for music faculty using or considering starting a Facebook studio group.

Third, now that emergent themes and super-ordinate themes have been developed from this study, a discourse analysis of Facebook group data could be implemented that addresses the types of posts and the engagement/learning they appear to effect in students. It has been possible to execute a Computer-Mediated Discourse Analysis (CMDA) of Facebook group data using previously established methods and techniques. However, the faculty beliefs, intent, and lived experiences documented here could improve how such a CMDA is tailored to the culture and practices of music faculty and students in studio-based music education environments.

Finally, future studies should address faculty response to training efforts once they have been implemented. Pre- and post-instruction perception of Facebook affordances and values could be assessed through traditional quantitative studies. Faculty, student, and general public response to targeted marketing and recruitment efforts could be evaluated through qualitative, quantitative, and/or mixed paradigm approaches. Once training has been developed and implemented, the possibilities for iterative research designs that address teaching, learning, marketing/promotion, and student recruitment are extensive.

CONCLUSION

This chapter contributes to a gap in literature by documenting the first generation of music faculty social media masters and their beliefs/intentions as they engage with their apprentices through Facebook groups. Findings included faculty concerns about personal and professional risk and the observation that teaching and learning are occurring through these Facebook studio groups by way of the process of enculturation, even when faculty are not consciously and intentionally doing so. This reinforces the need to study the use of Facebook groups as an extension of the higher education music studio and potential impacts on traditional master-apprentice roles. However, diverse and unregulated Facebook group management practices make it difficult to measure and evaluate those impacts.

The information gleaned from the 2016 study provides a solid foundation from which to generate recommendations for current and future music faculty to improve the informal learning capacity of social media with their students. Those recommendations include training in social media use that acknowledges the master-apprentice roles adopted by music faculty, independent social media guidelines developed by and for music departments, and the sharing of exemplar Facebook groups as part of academic discourse. Future studies addressing students' perceptions of Facebook groups and faculty perception of risk/risk aversion will be useful for gaining a fuller understanding of Facebook studio groups' impact on the higher education music studio and traditional master-apprentice roles.

ACKNOWLEDGMENT

This research received no specific grant from any funding agency in the public, commercial, or not-for-profit sectors.

REFERENCES

Bouij, C. (2004). Two theoretical perspectives on the socialization of music teachers. *Action, Criticism, and Theory for Music Education*, *3*(3), 1–14.

Burwell, K. (2012). *Studio-based instrumental learning*. Burlington, VT: Ashgate Publishing, Ltd.

Burwell, K. (2015). Dissonance in the studio: An exploration of tensions within the apprenticeship setting in higher education music. *International Journal of Music Education*, *34*(4), 499–512. doi:10.1177/0255761415574124

Cain, J., & Policastri, A. (2011). Using Facebook as an informal learning environment. *American Journal of Pharmaceutical Education*, *75*(10), 207. doi:10.5688/ajpe7510207 PMID:22345726

Cain, J., Scott, D. R., Tiemeier, A. M., Akers, P., & Metzger, A. H. (2013). Social media use by pharmacy faculty: Student friending, e-professionalism, and professional use. *Currents in Pharmacy Teaching and Learning*, *5*(1), 2–8. doi:10.1016/j.cptl.2012.09.002

Cawley, J. (2013). *The musical enculturation of Irish traditional musicians: An ethnographic study of learning processes* (Ph.D. Dissertation). University College Cork.

Chen, B., & Bryer, T. (2012). Investigating instructional strategies for using social media in formal and informal learning. *The International Review of Research in Open and Distributed Learning*, *13*(1), 87–104. doi:10.19173/irrodl.v13i1.1027

Collins, A., Brown, J. S., & Holum, A. (1991). Cognitive apprenticeship: Making thinking visible. *American Educator*, *15*(3), 6–11.

Corrigall, K. A., & Trainor, L. J. (2010). Musical enculturation in preschool children: Acquisition of key and harmonic knowledge. *Music Perception*, *28*(2), 195–200. doi:10.1525/mp.2010.28.2.195

Daniel, R. J., & Parkes, K. A. (2015). Assessment and critical feedback in the master-apprentice relationship: rethinking approaches to the learning of a music instrument. In Assessment in Music Education: from Policy to Practice (pp. 107-124). Springer International Publishing. doi:10.1007/978-3-319-10274-0_8

Egan, K., & Gajdamaschko, N. (2003). Some cognitive tools of literacy. In A. Kozulin (Ed.), *Vygotsky's Educational Theory in Cultural Context* (pp. 83–98). New York, NY: Cambridge University Press. doi:10.1017/CBO9780511840975.006

Gaunt, H., Creech, A., Long, M., & Hallam, S. (2012). Supporting conservatoire students towards professional integration: One-to-one tuition and the potential of mentoring. *Music Education Research*, *14*(1), 25–43. doi:10.1080/14613808.2012.657166

Green, L. (2002). *How popular musicians learn: A way ahead for music education*. Burlington, VT: Ashgate Publishing, Ltd.

Haddon, E., & Potter, J. (2014). Creativity and the Institutional Mindset. In Advanced Musical Performance: Investigations in Higher Education Learning (pp. 129-41). Abingdon, UK: Routledge.

Hannon, E. E., & Trainor, L. J. (2007). Music acquisition: Effects of enculturation and formal training on development. *Trends in Cognitive Sciences*, *11*(11), 466–472. doi:10.1016/j.tics.2007.08.008 PMID:17981074

Hays, T., Minichiello, V., & Wright, P. (2000). Mentorship: The meaning of the relationship for musicians. *Research Studies in Music Education*, *15*(1), 3–14. doi:10.1177/1321103X0001500102

Hennessy, S. (2000). Overcoming the red-feeling: The development of confidence to teach music in primary school amongst student teachers. *British Journal of Music Education, 17*(02), 183–196. doi:10.1017/S0265051700000243

Herring, S. C. (2007). A faceted classification scheme for computer-mediated discourse. *Language@ internet, 4*(1), 1-37.

Hutchby, I. (2001). *Conversation and Technology: From the Telephone to the Internet.* Cambridge, UK: Polity.

Jaschik, S. (2013, December 19). Kansas regents adopt policy on when social media use get faculty fired [Blog post]. Retrieved from: https://www.insidehighered.com/news/2013/12/19/kansas-regents-adopt-policy-when-social-media-use-can-get-faculty-fired

Jaschik, S. (2015, January 2). U. of Illinois faculty panel issues mixed report on aborted hiring of Steven Salaita [Blog post]. Retrieved from: https://www.insidehighered.com/news/2015/01/02/u-illinois-faculty-panel-issues-mixed-report-aborted-hiring-steven-salaita

Karl, K. A., & Peluchette, J. V. (2011). "Friending" professors, parents and bosses: A Facebook connection conundrum. *Journal of Education for Business, 86*(4), 214–222. doi:10.1080/08832323.2010.507638

Kimmons, R., & Veletsianos, G. (2014). The fragmented educator 2.0: Social networking sites, acceptable identity fragments, and the identity constellation. *Computers & Education, 72*, 292–301. doi:10.1016/j.compedu.2013.12.001

Kottak, C. P. (2004). Window on humanity. *Urban Anthropology, 11*, 11.

Kramer, M. W. (2010). *Organizational socialization: Joining and leaving organizations* (Vol. 6). Polity.

Lave, J., & Wenger, E. (1991). *Situated learning: Legitimate peripheral participation.* New York, NY: Cambridge University Press. doi:10.1017/CBO9780511815355

Lee, B. (2013). Social media as a non-formal learning platform. *Procedia: Social and Behavioral Sciences, 103*, 837–843. doi:10.1016/j.sbspro.2013.10.405

Liertz, C., & Macedon, M. (2007). New Frameworks for Tertiary Music Education–A Holistic Approach for Many Pyramids of Excellence. In *Australasian Piano Pedagogy Conference.* Retrieved from http://www.appca.com.au

Lupton, D. (2014). *'Feeling Better Connected': Academics' use of social media.* Canberra, Australia: News & Media Research Centre, University of Canberra.

Mathieson, K., & Leafman, J. S. (2014). Comparison of student and instructor perceptions of social presence. *Journal of Educators Online, 11*(2). doi:10.9743/JEO.2014.2.3

Meredith, T. (2017). *Extending the Apprenticeship through Informal Learning on Facebook: An interpretative phenomenological analysis of the lived experiences of music faculty* (Unpublished Ph.D. Dissertation). University of North Texas.

Merton, R. K. (1968). *Social theory and social structure.* New York, NY: Simon and Schuster.

Metzger, A. H., Finley, K. N., Ulbrich, T. R., & McAuley, J. W. (2010). Pharmacy faculty members' perspectives on the student/faculty relationship in online social networks. *American Journal of Pharmaceutical Education*, *74*(10), 188. doi:10.5688/aj7410188 PMID:21436929

Morrison, S. J., Demorest, S. M., Campbell, P. S., Bartolome, S. J., & Roberts, J. C. (2013). Effect of intensive instruction on elementary students' memory for culturally unfamiliar music. *Journal of Research in Music Education*, *60*(4), 363–374. doi:10.1177/0022429412462581

Nerland, M., & Hanken, I. M. (2011). Apprenticeship in transition? New configurations of teacher-student relationships in higher music education. Musik och kunnskapsbildning. En festskrift till Bengt Olsson, 129-136.

Nettl, B. (1992). *Recent directions in ethnomusicology. In Helen Myers: Ethnomusicology: An Introduction* (pp. 375–399). New York, NY: Norton.

Nielsen, K. (2006). Apprenticeship at the academy of music. *International Journal of Education & the Arts*, *7*(4), 1–15.

Nielsen, K., & Kvale, S. (1997). Current issues of apprenticeship. *Nordisk Pedagogik*, *17*(3), 160–169.

Oliver, P. G., & Clayes, E. (2014). Issues of Using Information Communication Technologies in Higher Education. In Proceedings *of the European Conference on Social Media*. University of Brighton.

Otchere, E. D. (2015). Music teaching and the process of enculturation: A cultural dilemma. *British Journal of Music Education*, *32*(3), 291–297. doi:10.1017/S0265051715000352

Pratt, D. D. (1998). *Five perspectives on teaching in adult and higher education*. Melbourne, FL: Krieger Publishing Co.

Pratt, D. D. (2016). *Five perspectives on teaching: Mapping a plurality of the good*. Melbourne, FL: Krieger Publishing Co.

Putnam, L. L., & Jablin, F. M. (Eds.). (2001). *The new handbook of organizational communication: Advances in theory, research and methods*. Thousand Oaks, CA: Sage Publications.

Renshaw, P. (2009). *Lifelong learning for musicians: The place of mentoring*. Groningen, The Netherlands: Lectorate Lifelong Learning in Music & the Arts.

Rogoff, B. (1990). *Apprenticeship in thinking: Cognitive development in social context*. New York, NY: Oxford University Press.

Rogoff, B. (1995). Observing sociocultural activity on three planes: Participatory appropriation, guided participation, and apprenticeship. In J.V. Wertsch, P. del Rio, & A. Alvarez (Eds.), Sociocultural studies of mind (pp. 139-164). Cambridge, UK: Cambridge University Press.

Schrock, A. R. (2015). Communicative affordances of mobile media: Portability, availability, locatability, and multimediality. *International Journal of Communication*, *9*(0), 1229–1246.

Schugurensky, D. (2000). *The Forms of Informal Learning: Towards a conceptualization of the field*. NALL Working Paper No. 19, Centre for the Study of Education and Work, Department of Sociology and Equity Studies in Education, Ontario Institute for Studies in Education of the University of Toronto, Toronto.

Seaton, D. (1998). *Music and American Higher Education.* Reston, VA: National Association of Schools of Music.

Smith, J. A., & Eatough, V. (2007). Interpretative phenomenological analysis. In E. Lyons & A. Coyle (Eds.), *Analysing qualitative data in psychology* (pp. 35–50). Thousand Oaks, CA: SAGE Publications, Ltd. doi:10.4135/9781446207536.d10

Smith, J. A., Flowers, P., & Larkin, M. (2009). *Interpretative Phenomenological Analysis: Theory, Method and Research.* London: Sage Publications.

Sumuer, E., Esfer, S., & Yildirim, S. (2014). Teachers' Facebook use: Their use habits, intensity, self-disclosure, privacy settings, and activities on Facebook. *Educational Studies*, *40*(5), 537–553. doi:10.1 080/03055698.2014.952713

Varvarigou, M., & Durrant, C. (2011). Theoretical perspectives on the education of choral conductors: A suggested framework. *British Journal of Music Education*, *28*(03), 325–338. doi:10.1017/ S0265051711000325

Veblen, K. K. (2012). Adult music learning in formal, nonformal, and informal contexts. The Oxford Handbook of Music Education, 2, 243-256.

Veletsianos, G. (2013). Open practices and identity: Evidence from researchers and educators' social media participation. *British Journal of Educational Technology*, *44*(4), 639–651. doi:10.1111/bjet.12052

KEY TERMS AND DEFINITIONS

Anticipatory Socialization: An individual's adoption of group behaviors and norms through social activities before group membership is granted.

Apprenticeship: Associated with occupation-based training, usually involving physical skills and practice, and is governed by an agreement stipulating the length of time and requirements/competencies that must be fulfilled before the apprenticeship is complete.

Enculturation: The manner in which an individual learns his/her role, cultural norms, and a society's acceptable behavior and values.

Facebook: A social media platform begun in 2006 that allows users to share information (text, media, links to other web content, etc.) with "friends," a pre-approved group of other Facebook members with whom a user can interact.

Facebook Studio Group: Virtual spaces within Facebook that are created and maintained by music faculty; within a group, membership includes students in the faculty member's studio and anyone else the faculty member allows to participate.

Lived Experiences: Participants' experiences which contribute to their understanding and interpretation of phenomena.

Phenomenology: The study of a phenomenon through participants' experience with that phenomenon.

This research was previously published in Pedagogy Development for Teaching Online Music; pages 136-163, copyright year 2018 by Information Science Reference (an imprint of IGI Global).

Chapter 23
Engaging Millennial Students Through Social Media Usage and Its Impact on HBCU Persistence

Antwon D. Woods
Belhaven University, USA

Kenisha Shelton
Hinds Community College, USA

ABSTRACT

This chapter will explore the perception millennial college students hold regarding the engagement of social media use and its impact on their college persistence at Historically Black Colleges and Universities (HBCUs). The topic of student persistence in postsecondary education continues to be a matter of significant importance. A third or more students leave four-year public colleges and universities at the end of their first year, and about 40% of students who begin college will never earn a degree. Despite all the attention to improving student retention, most institutional persistence rates have remained stagnant.

INTRODUCTION

In today's society, millennials build and partake in extensive digital social networks. Recent studies in both the U.S. and the U.K. have also found a widespread youthful interest in social media (Ofcom, 2012). In 2007, 30 percent of social network members accessed sites at least once a day (Lenhart, Purcell, Smith, & Zickuhr, 2010); by 2010 this grew to 67 percent. Studies reported that on average, young people stayed in touch with 300 Facebook friends and followed 79 Twitter accounts (Lenhart, et al., 2010). The 2014 Canadian-based Media Smarts survey of 5,000 students found a proliferation of mobile devices devoted almost entirely to social networking (Steeves, 2014). Acknowledging this increase in time spent "socializing," Sherry Turkle (2012) wondered whether as Facebook friends grow, real friends diminish. New

DOI: 10.4018/978-1-6684-7123-4.ch023

media, Turkle argued, constructs a space in which the young are alone together (Turkle, 2012). Turkle's interviewees reported that when social situations are really problematic or troubling, they turn to family members, not friends (Turkle, 2012).

According to Pew Internet and American Life Project(2010), 79% of adults say that they use the Internet and nearly half (47%), or 59% of Internet users, say that use a least one social networking site. This is nearly double the number of users found in a Pew study conducted in 2008 (Pew Internet and American Life Project, 2010). In addition to the number of users increasing dramatically, Pew's research also found that the population of users of social media has gotten older. More than half of all adult social networking site users are over the age of 35 (Pew Internet and American Life Project, 2010).

Pew Internet and American Life Project (2010) study provided insight into the popularity among the sites. The dominant platform was Facebook, with more than 90% of people surveyed. Next, 29% of individuals surveyed stated LinkedIn was second dominant platform, followed 18% for Twitter. Pew Internet and American Life Project (2010) also found that there is variance in the way that people use various social media: 52% of Facebook users and 33% of Twitter users engage with the platform daily; while only 7% and 6% of LinkedIn users do the same (Pew Internet and American Life Project, 2010).

In a separate study, the Pew report found that Millennials, will lead society into "a new world of personal disclosure and information sharing using new media" (Pew Internet and American Life Project, 2010). In this study, researchers interviewed 895 technology stakeholders and critics. Nearly 70% of the respondents agreed that by 2020, Generation Y, also known as Millennials, will continue to be "ambient broadcasters who disclose a great deal of personal information in order to stay connected and take advantage of social, economic and political opportunities. However, 29% of those surveyed posited that as the population group ages, they will grow out of their desire to use social networks, multiplayer online games and other time consuming, transparency engendering online tools (Pew Internet and American Life Project, 2010).

According to the ComScore report, Facebook is the leader in time spent on social media. A study in October 2011 found that Facebook reached more than half of the world''s global audience (55%) and accounted for approximately 3 in every 4 minutes spent on social media and 1 in every 7 minutes spent online around the world (ComScore, 2012). As the report states, "The importance of Facebook cannot be overstated." However, the ComScore report says that Facebook is not the only major player in the world of social media, and there is evidence to suggest that disruptive innovation may be taking place within the industry. Microblogging, a style of communicating through short-form content, has taken hold as a wildly popular social networking platform in recent years, due in large part to the emergence of Twitter – which saw its audience begin to erupt in the spring of 2009. To date, Twitter reaches 1 in 10 Internet users worldwide to rank among the top social networks, and posted an impressive growth rate of 59% over the past year. Interestingly, the use of Twitter around the world has not been limited to interpersonal communication among friends (ComScore, 2012).

In 2011, Twitter was used as a central means of communication during events of worldwide and national significance, ranging from political uprisings in the Middle East to disasters, such as the earthquake and tsunami in Japan. Among the most tweeted moments in 2011 according to Twitter were political events such as the death of Osama bin Laden, celebratory moments such as New Year, and news about Steve Jobs'' resignation from Apple and consequent passing. The announcement of the singer Beyoncé's pregnancy at the Video Music Awards broke Twitter records as users generated 8,868 tweets per second around the event (ComScore, 2012). The rise of the use of social networks to communicate is prevalent among the age group that this study focused on: 15-24 year olds. The ComScore study found from July

2010 to October 2011, 15-24 year olds had the largest decrease in the use of emails and instant messaging to communicate with their peers (ComScore, 2012). At the same time, the ComScore study show this age group had the largest increase in time spent on social media using these sites as the basis of their communication. The ComScore study posits that this adoption signifies a shift in how people communicate, a shift that will have repercussions going forward as this age group, which contains the typical college age, will only continue to rely on social media as the basis of their communication.

Social media's role in higher education is a topic of emerging debate and research. To date, there are only a few studies available that have measured the role of social media, such as Facebook and Twitter, in the ability of students to engage in the campus environment and persist toward graduation. The most frequently referenced scholars, on this topic, are Reynol Junco and Sheila Cotton. Though these scholars have contributed significantly to the discussion, their research has offered little in understanding how social media may specifically impact millennial college students.

There are five main areas that emerge within research articles that will direct this chapter. In spite of a rigorous search, there was a lack of research that seeks to understand exactly how social media impacts the persistence of millennial college students at Historically Black Colleges and Universities (HBCUs). The following sections will be explored throughout this chapter: 1) Students, Academics, and Social Media, 2) The Encouragement of Student Engagement and Social Capital at HBCUs, and 3). Social and Academic Sense of Belonging.

STUDENTS, ACADEMICS, AND SOCIAL MEDIA

Social media is more than just technology. It is a set of collaborations and the active participation of detailed principles that exemplify our current social movement (The Paradox of Social Media, 2011). Systems of education are dealing with the pressure to retain students, to improve the first year experience for students, and to improve the overall educational environment (Hung & Yuen, 2010). Technology has played a huge role in retaining students by utilizing creative and collaborative innovations, promoting a means of classroom community, and ensuring better communication within this specific population (Hung & Yuen, 2010).

Putnam (2000), discussed the role the social networking website had on the development of three kinds of social capital: Bridging Social Capital, Bonding Social Capital and Maintained Social Capital was examined. Bridging Social Capital and Bonding Social Capital have been defined by Putnam (2000). Putnam claims that Bridging Social Capital are loose connections between individuals who provide useful information or new perspectives but little, if any, emotional support. Given the level of social media usage among Millennials, there is a growing body of research into the use of social media to enhance student engagement. Though there is little research about the impact of social media in higher education, there is related research on the impact of the intensity of Facebook usage on such things as civic participation, life satisfaction and social trust.

When social capital declines, a community experiences increased social disorder, reduced participation in civic activities and distrust among community members (Ellison et al., 2007). Enhanced social capital increases commitment to community, improves the ability to mobilize collective actions, and brings other benefits. For an individual, social capital has a positive association with psychological well-being, and satisfaction with life (Ellison et al., 2007).

There is a lack of consensus about social media's ability in higher education. Although there could be benefits to using social media to engage students, there are some barriers to the adoption of such initiatives. Some pitfalls to using social media include misuse or poor displays of social media etiquette; that it can eliminate face to face interaction; not everyone is familiar with it; and it can be distracting from work and academics (Hardin, McClure, Alspach, & Cooper, 2012).

A study by Mazer, Murphy and Simonds (2007) found negative associations between faculty use of Facebook and their credibility with students. The study revealed that students were concerned about their teacher's professionalism, although they did like learning more about their personality. However, the students were concerned that faculty members would judge them or use Facebook as a means of judging them, to get gossip or spy on them (Mazer, Murphy, & Simonds, 2007). Reiner (2012) says that social media prevent students from developing the level of intimacy with the world that is necessary to be successful in personal interactions and in academia. Reiner (2012) writes that students have become too concerned with keeping up with the flow on social media. Students should be encouraged to take a social media Sabbath to enable them to disconnect from technology and the continuous flow of information with the hope of spending time on necessary inner reflection (Reiner, 2012).

Marquis (2012) acknowledges Reiner's points as valid, but offers that in a controlled environment, social media can be beneficial in higher education He offered several suggestions for how professors might utilize social media to promote student engagement, which include encouraging students to use social media to connect with experts outside the classroom and to conduct research they can share with class; promoting the continuous sharing of ideas and opinions on theories and discussions and posting class lectures and other resources to be shared with the global community and enable learning and remediation to occur at a student's pace (Marquis, 2012). Due to its potential pitfalls, social media should be used in collaboration with traditional student affairs practices, according to Hardin, McClure, Alspach, and Cooper (2012).

The Encouragement of Student Engagement and Social Capital at HBCUs

Researchers have emphasized that student engagement and a strong support system are influential factors in the decision-making process of students remain enrolled. According to Love (2008), African American students may encounter unwelcoming campus climates, racial stereotypes and poor faculty relationships. This problem is greatest at Predominantly White Institutions (PWIs), where 70% of African American students drop out prior to obtaining their baccalaureate degree, compared to 20% at HBCUs (HBCUs) (Love, 2008).

According to Tinto (2011), persistence occurs when a student successfully integrates into the institution academically and socially. Integration, in turn, is influenced by pre-college characteristics and goals, interactions with peers and faculty, and out-of- classroom factors (Jensen, 2011). Gray, Vitak, Easton, and Ellison (2013) asserted that HBCUs offer more supportive and positive learning environments, which can lead to higher grades, higher occupational aspirations, support, connection and feelings of acceptance, than other institutions.

The support system that is provided at HBCUs and being in a positive learning environment presentes the likelihood that African American students will remain engaged in college and complete their degree (Gray et al, 2013). Until the mid-1960s, the majority of people of African descent received their post-secondary education at HBCUs (Kim & Conrad, 2006). Kim and Conrad (2006) alluded that these institutions were founded starting in the 1830s to serve African Americans. Over time, HBCUs have become a diverse group. They are public and private, four-year and two-year institutions, co-educational and single-sex institutions, research universities and professional schools. Their size varies from several hundred students to more than 10,000 (Media, 2007). There are 105 institutions classified as HBCUs, representing 3% of all institutions of higher education (Kim & Conrad, 2006). These institutions enroll 15% of all black college students and produce nearly 30% of all black graduates. Roughly 75% of all African Americans who have received doctoral degrees earned them at an HBCU (Wilson, 2007).

Wilson (2007) mentioned that there has recently been renewed research interest in the role, accomplishments and future of HBCUs. This interest has been motivated by the financial failures of some institutions, litigation to re-enforce the obligation of state governments to provide equal access to education to all people and Supreme Court decisions on the use of race in admissions decisions (Wilson, 2007). The competition that HBCUs face to attract and educate African American and other students presents both challenges and opportunities. Though numerous studies have shown that HBCUs are more effective than predominantly white colleges at retaining and graduating African American students, the HBCUs still have detractors (Media, 2007). The detractors say that the financial pressures and waning public support will make it difficult for some public HBCUs to survive. The private HBCUs may be better poised to adapt to the changing landscape due to their relative autonomy (Wilson, 2007).

To support this literature, research has been establish to support the belief that African American students feel a greater level of support at HBCUs than at PWIs. Chen, Ingram, and Davis (2006) compared the levels of educational engagement and satisfaction for African American students in their research study. Their study, entitled *Engaging African American Students: Comparing Student Engagement and Student Satisfaction at HBCUs and their Self-Identified Predominantly White Peer Institutions,* included a data sample of 1,631 seniors from 17 HBCUs and 2,939 seniors from 246 PWIs. The results of the study show that African American seniors at HBCUs are generally equally or more engaged in educationally purposeful activities than their peers at PredominantlyWhite Institutions. But the study also found that this level of engagement does not translate into higher student satisfaction. One factor in the level of satisfaction was the student relationship with administrative personnel and their respective offices (Chen, Ingram, & Davis, 2006).

Chen, Ingram, and Davis (2006) study also referenced a 1992 study, which found that students who have a good relationship with faculty and had good grades in high school usually accomplish a higher level of academic achievement in college. In study conducted by St. John (2010) examined the strategies for success at HBCUs. The results of the study were presented at a symposium in June 2010, entitled Setting an Agenda for HBCUs (St. Johns, 2010). It was a summary of the findings from Pathways to Academic Success: Expanding Opportunity for Underrepresented Students (St. John, 2010). The study found that from 2002 to 2007, the six-year graduation rates for African American college students in the state of North Carolina remained at 48% while other groups increased. This, as the study points out, merits attention because research data found that the number of African American students graduating from high school in North Carolina was increasing (St. John, 2010). This helps to build a case for investigating the experiences that African American students have in college and which procedures might help increase engagement and degree completion. Racial minorities are disproportionately more likely to be from families with fewer resources to invest in education and are forced to live in neighborhoods with failing schools. The result is that minorities are less likely to perform well in secondary schooling and thus face greater obstacles to achieving success in college (Servertis & Christie-Mizell, 2007). Researchers have begun to examine other routes to educational success, including the use of social networks or social capital, to help improve college persistence and completion (Servertis & Christie-Mizell, 2007).

Social and Academic Sense of Belonging

Many student retention theories have emerged as a result of Tinto's theoretical model of persistence. A student's decision to continue the pursuit of postsecondary education is directly impacted by the student's ability to assimilate into an institution, socially and academically (Tinto, 1975). The "sense of belonging" is applicable to many facets of life so the correlation to an academic environment is practical. In accordance with Hurtado and Ruiz (2012), students' sense of belonging is delineated as their psychological connection to an academic community. The sense of belonging for students correlates to their ability to better adjust socially and academically, though not directly to their academic performance (Hurtado, Han, Saenz, Espinosa, Cabrera, & Cerna, 2007). Interaction with peers and faculty, involvement in extracurricular activities, and classroom engagement, all contribute to students' sense of belonging. Students' social and academic involvement is critical to their persistence (Astin, 1984).

Students who perceived their social interactions to be positive during their first semester of enrollment were more likely to enroll in a second semester (Heaney & Fisher, 2011). The more involvement in an academic community, the greater sense of belonging for students, thus these students are more likely to continue pursuing their postsecondary education. Students who reported increased social involvement on campus also indicated more social integration equating to commitment to the institution and the intent to return to the institution (Hausmann, Ye, Schofield, & Woods, 2009). Astin's (1984) model highlights that student involvement promotes learning and development resulting in increased persistence. Though the sense of belonging socially in an academic setting is important (Pascarella & Terenzini, 2005), the sense of belonging academically is of equal importance (Gray et al, 2013).

The faculty-student relationship impacts students' persistence and, ultimately, academic success (Wood & Turner, 2011). Positive interactions between faculty members and students contribute to the overall learning experience. Student classroom involvement may be reduced in the absence of positive interactions with faculty members, thereby inhibiting a beneficial learning experience (Wood & Turner, 2011). Classroom interaction with peers is also essential to gaining the full benefits of the learning environment (Tinto, 1997). Collaborative peer support was of noted importance to motivating students (Enstrom & Tinto, 2008). Those who perform poorly academically may feel uncomfortable in a classroom setting with those students who perform well. On the other hand, students who excel academically can be hesitant to exhibit their knowledge in the classroom in trepidation of embarrassment from being viewed as an outsider (Swenson, Nordstrom, & Hiester, 2008). While theorists have provided substantial insight into academic and social integration, theory does not provide administrators with a blueprint for what is necessary to achieve academic and social integration within their particular institutional setting (Tinto, 2006).

CONCLUSION

It is important that higher education professionals at HBCUs have an appreciation of the students' knowledge base of social media and how they employ it in their construction of knowledge and reality. It is also valuable for professionals in the industry, who are hiring recent college graduates, to gain insight into how students perceive social media in their own lives and as strategic tools. Thus, educators must expose students using social media as tools to solve an authentic problem, which in turn creates participatory learning experiences. Educators can facilitate learning by creating inventive ways of engaging students in meaningful practices, providing access to resources that enhance their participation, opening their horizons so they can put themselves in learning trajectories they can identify with, and involving them in actions, discussions, and reflections that make a difference to the communities that they value. By including social media as a tool that students can use and see actual results in real time, they will become more engaged and better educated in the tools and knowledge of communicating strategically. According to Heaney and Fisher (2011), employers are expecting interns and recent college graduate to be "experts" in social media due to their high consumption. By teaching students how to effectively use social media strategically, HBCU instructors are developing students become more marketable in the job market and more effective in the work force by helping them provide what employers are expecting through enriching their educational experiences (Heaney & Fisher, 2011).

Millennial students prefer moderate use of technology in the classroom. In fact, the actual use of technology is not as important as the activity the technology allows students to do (Oblinger & Oblinger, 2005). When technology is used in class, it should vary; use different tools such as PowerPoint presentations, social networks, podcasts, streaming videos, blogs, virtual games, and also video clips. Kvavik and Caruso (2005) referred to this as "Edutainment." HBCUs educators should balance the use of technology in classes with other activities such as lectures, guest speakers, group assignments, interactive and hands-on activities, and class discussions. These efforts will support millennial student's desire for team collaboration, as well as satisfy the millennial' preference for moderate use of technology in the classroom. Similarly, institutions should consider revising policies, which require students to read hard copy material. Instead, HBCUs should consider integrating electronic books, as well as other electronic versions of informational material, to increase the academic development of millennial students.

According to Gray et al (2013), faculty members should consider assignments that include active involvement such as volunteering, environmental causes, fund raising, and other civic duties will help satisfy millennial' need to be socially responsible and allow them to feel they can contribute value and meaning through their education. Smith (2008) suggests assigning peer reviewed projects to get the students involved with more team collaboration. Educators also need to provide detailed assignments, grading rubrics (to show fairness), syllabi, examples, and deadlines to the millennial students (Smith, 2008; Shih & Allen, 2007). Lippincott and Pergoal (2009) asserted that HBCUs should also utilize simulations when appropriate. The researchers stated that a simulation allows students to be more actively engaged and in greater control of their own learning should enhance student learning since research indicates this type of environment is beneficial for the Millennials. Faculty members can aid in persistence as it relates to millennial college students by assessing student goals, and attempting to meet student needs (Myers, 2008). The millennial generation presents to college with a history of success and are confident about their ability to succeed; however, their continued success can be significantly impacted by their communication of expectations with their faculty members.

REFERENCES

Astin, A. W. (1984). Student involvement: A developmental theory for higher education. *Journal of College Student Personnel, 25,* 297–308.

Chen, P.S. D., Ingram, T. N., & Davis, L. (2006). *Engaging African American students: comparing student engagement and student satisfaction at historical Black colleges and universities and their self-identified predominately White peer institutions*. Academic Press.

ComScore. (2012). *The state of social media*. Retrieved January 3, 2013 from: http://www.slideshare.net/karanbhujbal/the-state-of-social-media2012-comscorereport

Ellison, N. B., Steinfield, C., & Lampe, C. (2007). The benefits of Facebook friends: Social capital and college students use of online social network sites. *Journal of Computer-Mediated Communication*, *12*(4), 1143–1168. doi:10.1111/j.1083-6101.2007.00367.x

Gray, R., Vitak, J., Easton, E. W., & Ellison, N. B. (2013). Examining social adjustment to college in the age of social media: Factors influencing successful transitions and persistence. *Computers & Education*, *67*, 193–207. doi:10.1016/j.compedu.2013.02.021

Hausmann, L. R., Schofield, J. W., & Woods, R. L. (2007). Sense of belonging as a predictor of intentions to persist among African American and White first-year college students. *Research in Higher Education*, *48*(7), 803–839. doi:10.100711162-007-9052-9

Heaney, A., & Fisher, R. (2011). Supporting conditionally-admitted students: A case study of assessing persistence in a learning community. *The Journal of Scholarship of Teaching and Learning*, *11*, 62–78.

Hung, H., & Yuen, S. (2010). Educational use of social networking technology in Higher Education. *Teaching in Higher Education*, *15*(6), 703–714. doi:10.1080/13562517.2010.507307

Hurtado, S., Han, J. C., Sáenz, V. B., Espinosa, L. L., Cabrera, N. L., & Cerna, O. S. (2007). Predicting transition and adjustment to college: Biomedical and behavioral science aspirants' and minority students' first year of college. *Research in Higher Education*, *48*(7), 841–887. doi:10.100711162-007-9051-x

Hurtado, S., & Ruiz, A. (2012). *The climate for underrepresented groups and diversity on campus*. Los Angeles, CA: Higher Education Research Institute.

Junco, R., & Cotten, S. R. (2012). No A 4 U: The relationship between multitasking and academic performance. *Computers & Education*, *59*(2), 505–514. doi:10.1016/j.compedu.2011.12.023

Kim, M. M., & Conrad, C. F. (2006). The impact of historically Black colleges and universities on the academic success of African-American students. *Research in Higher Education*, *47*(4), 399–427. doi:10.100711162-005-9001-4

Kvavik, R. B., & Caruso, J. (2005). *ECAR study of students and information technology, 2005: Convenience*. Connection, Control, and Learning.

Lenhart, A., Purcell, K., Smith, A., & Zickuhr, K. (2010). *Social Media and Mobile Internet Use Among Teens and Young Adults*. Retrieved by http://www.pewinternet.org

Lippincott, B., & Pergola, T. (2009). Use of a job-cost simulation to engage Gen Y students. *Journal of the International Academy for Case Studies*, 107-112.

Love, D. (2008). Revitalizing retention efforts for African-American college students at Predominantly White Institutions. *Proceedings of the Allied Academies*.

Marquis, J. (2012). *The advantages and disadvantages of student social media use.* Retrieved from Online Universities: http://www.onlineuniversities.com/blog/2012/10/balancing-advantagesdisadvantages-student-social-media-use/

Mazer, J., Murphy, R. E., & Simonds, C. J. (2007). "I'll see you on Facebook": The effects of computer-mediated teacher self disclosure on student motivation, affective learning and classroom climate. *Communication Education, 56*(1), 1–17. doi:10.1080/03634520601009710

Myers, C. B. (2008). Divergence in learning goal priorities between college students and their faculty: Implications for teaching and learning. *College Teaching, 56*(1), 53-58.

Oblinger, D.G., & Oblinger, J.L. (2005). *Educating the Net Generation.* Academic Press.

Ofcom. (2012). *Adults media use and attitudes report.* Retrieved from http://stakeholders.ofcom.0rg.uk/bmaries/research/media-literacy/media-use attitudes/adults-media-use-2012.pdf

Pascarella, E., & Terenzini, P. T. (2005). *How college affects students: A third decade of research.* San Francisco, CA: John Wiley & Sons.

Pew Internet and American Life Project. (2010). *Technology trends among people of color.* Retrieved December 27, 2012, from pewinternet.org: http://www.pewinternet.org/Commentary/2010/September/Technology

Putnam, R. N. (2000). *Bowling Alone: The collapse and revival of American community.* Simon and Schuster.

Reiner, A. (2012). Only disconnect. *The Chronicle of Higher Education.*

Servertis, R., & Christie-Mizell, C. A. (2007). *Greek letter membership and college graduation: Does race matter?* Academic Press.

Shih, W., & Allen, M. (2007). Working with Generation-D: Adopting and adapting to cultural learning and change. *Library Management, 28*(1/2), 89–100. doi:10.1108/014351207107235 72

Smith, L. (2008). Grading written projects: What approaches do students find helpful? *Journal of Education for Business, 83*(6), 322–330. doi:10.3200/JOEB.83.6.325-330

St. John, E. (2010). Student access and success: Strategies for historically Black colleges and universities. Setting an Agenda for Historically Black Colleges and Universities. Academic Press.

Steeves, V. (2014). *Young Canadians in a wired world, phase III: Life online.* Ottawa: MediaSmarts.

Swenson, L. M., Nordstrom, A., & Hiester, M. (2008). The role of peer relationships in adjustment to college. *Journal of College Student Development, 49*(6), 551–567. doi:10.1353/csd.0.0038

Tinto, V. (1975). Dropout from higher education: A theoretical synthesis of recent research. *Review of Educational Research, 45*(1), 89–125. doi:10.3102/00346543045001089

Tinto, V. (1993). Leaving college: Rethinking the causes and cures of students and attrition (2nd ed.). Chicago, IL: University of Chicago Press.

Tinto, V. (1997). Classrooms as communities: Exploring the educational character of student persistence. *The Journal of Higher Education*, *68*(6), 599–623. doi:10.2307/2959965

Tinto, V. (2006). Research and practice of student retention: What next? *Journal of College Student Retention*, *8*(1), 1–19. doi:10.2190/4YNU-4TMB-22DJ-AN4W

Tinto, V. (2011). *Completing College: Rethinking Institutional Action*. Chicago, IL: University of Chicago Press.

Turkle, S. (2012). *Alone together: Why we expect more from technology and less from each other*. New York, NY: Basic Books.

Wilson, V. R. (2007). The effect of attending an HBCU on persistence and graduation outcomes of African American college students. *The Review of Black Political Economy*, *34*(1-2), 11–52. doi:10.100712114-007-9006-7

KEY TERMS AND DEFINITIONS

Academic Excellence: Students who achieve grade point averages ranging from 3.0-4.0 and graduate.

Historically Black Colleges and Universities (HBCUs): Institutions of higher education in the United States that were established before 1964 with the intention of serving the Black community.

Involvement: The amount of time and energy that a student dedicates to the collegiate experience.

Millennial Students: Are students that grew up with the internet and was born between 1985-2003.

Persistence: The desire and action of a student to stay within the system of higher education from beginning year through degree completion.

Predominantly White Institutions (PWIs): A term used to describe institutions of higher learning in which Caucasians account for 50% or greater of the student enrollment.

Retention: Institutional measure of student persistence at a college or university until the completion of the degree.

Social Media: Is a web-based service that allows individuals to (1) construct a public or semipublic profile within a bounded system, (2) articulate a list of other users with whom they share a connection, and (3) view and traverse their list of connections and those made by others within the system.

Student Engagement: The amount of time and effort a student devotes toward his or her studies and other educationally purposeful activities is called student engagement.

This research was previously published in Examining Student Retention and Engagement Strategies at Historically Black Colleges and Universities; pages 83-97, copyright year 2019 by Information Science Reference (an imprint of IGI Global).

Chapter 24
Mobile Technology and Social Media Literacy:
Exploring Architecture and Interior Architecture Students' Practices

A.Tolga Ilter
🆔 https://orcid.org/0000-0002-7868-900X
Istanbul Technical University, Turkey

Pelin Karacar
Istanbul Medipol University, Turkey

ABSTRACT

Advancing information and communication technologies (ICT) are reshaping our daily lives. Mobile communication devices, especially the introduction of smartphones, changed the way we communicate both professionally and socially. Mobile technologies are spreading our daily lives with the help of social media applications. Implementation of social networks to the education programs may encourage students to reach information, share their work, get feedback more easily, and produce content that will build up their portfolios and professional identities for their future career. However, in order to achieve such a goal, it is quite important to understand their behavioural patterns on social networks and mobile technology use. In this context, this research tries to explore architecture and interior architecture students' social network patterns under the social media literacy framework.

INTRODUCTION

Information and Communication Technologies (ICT) are restructuring our everyday daily life with an increasing pace. An important part of this accelerating change is driven by advancing mobile communication devices. Enhanced by the introduction of smart phones, mobile technologies are spreading our daily lives along with the social media applications. This technological advancement changed the way we communicate both professionally and socially. Mobile devices, especially smart phones are literally

DOI: 10.4018/978-1-6684-7123-4.ch024

becoming our extensions and people who use them are being drawn in to these social media applications as if they are neural networks of our natural bodies just as Marshall McLuhan predicted more than half a century ago in his book 'Understanding Media: The Extensions of Man' (McLuhan, 1964)

The generation born roughly after 1980 is called "generation Y", "Millennials" or "Net Generation". The Net Generation is considered to have grown up in an environment they were regularly exposed to computer based technology. Not surprisingly, technology marketing seems to aim more at the Net Generation as a substantial consumer group. Consequently, current higher education is being shaped by these tech-savvy millennials and the advent of web 2.0. Technology is a critical part of learning environments (Gikas & Grant, 2013), that is valid for traditional brick-and-mortar classrooms as well as e-learning settings.

Alter (2017) indicates that, the average time spent on telephone has increased from 18 minutes to an average of 3 hours a day and underlines the attribution of the social media applications on that change. Under the light of this substantial transformation, it is quite liable to acknowledge smartphones as the dominant driver of social media. However, there are some serious side effects of these technological advancement that should also be mentioned. Social media applications seem to be creating digitized medium for a virtual social life instead of boosting our personal social interactions that we used to have face-to-face. Similarly, Greenfield (2012) quotes the Internet as "… a socially connecting device that's socially isolating at the same time". Social and technological existence that are all online increases the flow of information day by day and by the time you finish checking your e-mails and social networks, it is time to check your e-mail and social media accounts again. Alter (2017) call this a ludic loop that is a process that puts you into a state of serenity such as the soothed state people are in while playing slot machines at casinos. This state of comfort relieves the anxiety we live in and has a strong potential to drag us into an addiction if it begins to fulfil a missing psychological motive. The addictive use of Internet is not a new phenomenon. This condition is commonly cited as Internet addiction disorder (IAD) whereas there are other terms used such as pathological Internet use, Internet abuse, digital media compulsion and virtual addiction (Greenfield, 2012). It is considered quite similar to other addictions like drug, alcohol and gambling which results in social, academic, and occupational impairment (Young, 1998).

Although the debate about the definition and extent of IAD is still going on, studies reveal that young users are more at risk (Ferraro, Caci, D'Amico, & Blasi, 2007).Teenagers and young adults are among the highest percentage of smartphone and social media application users (Perrin, 2015). As an apparent result, colleges and higher education institutions are in a challenge to limit and control students' smartphone and social network use as these practices are considered as distracting for the conventional education practices. On the other hand, academicians are tending to spend more time with their mobile devices and use social networks similarly. Moreover, we are on the verge of a connected world with the 'internet of things' that will be a breakthrough innovation in technological advancements and our digital environment. Under the light of all these forthcoming developments, it seems things will get tougher to leave these devices out of classrooms.

The idea of using mobile devices and social media applications for the benefit of education is being discussed by various researchers like Gikas & Grant (2013), Liu (2010), but research on using such tools and technologies for undergraduate architecture and interior architecture students is far from being extensive. Besides, existing data and insights are in line for becoming irrelevant with an unusual pace. It is essential to understand the nature of the social media context and to what extent students can reach, understand, practice and benefit social media applications in order to propose educational solutions using mobile technologies.

The motivation behind using social media can be classified under three main topics. First type of the social media use is for building networks. These networks can be professional or interest based. Second reason for using social media is to find and evaluate information which means using it as a type of information source. Third type of social media use is for producing information or knowledge generation. This last type enables users to be an active participant in the content production process instead of being just a consumer. The technology enabling user participation forms the internet medium called web 2.0. In this context, institutions of education may use this potential of interest into an opportunity to enhance both the content and the process of learning. We may well argue that using social media as an information source and as a tool for education would be much easier for design oriented programs such as architecture or interior architecture since the social network interfaces are more graphic oriented. A properly programmed implementation of social networks to the education program may encourage students to reach information, share their work, get feedback more easily as well as producing content that will build up their portfolios and professional identities for their future career. However, in order to achieve such a goal it is quite important to understand their behaviour patterns on social networks and mobile technology usage. In this context this research tries to explore architecture and interior architecture students' social network patterns under the social media literacy framework.

By the help of a series of survey data this study tries to explore undergraduate architecture and interior architecture students' smartphone and social network practice under the social media and technology literacy frameworks. These data include but not limited to their operating medium, active social network memberships, time spent online, time spent with social networks, weather they go online during classes and check their social networks, frequency of sharing new posts, their intentions about following accounts about their soon to be profession and their social interaction with academicians on these social networks. Considering the fast-track changes in social media environments and mobile technologies, a comparison between years 2017 and 2019 is also added to this research following a previous study by the authors.

MOBILE TECHNOLOGY AND SOCIAL MEDIA LITERACY

Technology is defined as a system that uses knowledge and organization to develop objects and techniques for achieving defined roles. In addition, the term "technology literacy" can be adopted in a variety of contexts adhering to the term technology. Technology literacy is defined as 'an individual's skills to adopt, adapt, invent, and evaluate technology to positively affect people's life, environment and community (Hansen,2003). It is technology literacy that contributes both to building trust in learning processes and to creating new environments for advanced learning opportunities. Personal, portable, wireless network technologies are becoming widespread in the lives of learners today.

Technology, which is identified as "uninterrupted learning spaces and marked by the continuity of the learning experience in different scenarios or contexts, appears to create potential for a new stage in the evolution of advanced learning. It enables students to learn through mobile technology whenever they are curious, between formal and informal contexts, between individual and social learning, as well as between different contexts and by expanding the social spaces in which students interact with each other.

It is technology and society that implies a special approach of mutual forming that adds the idea that technological development interacts with social contradictions. What is based on dialectical reasoning is the important theory of media and technology.

In this way, a particular media / technology has at least two potential effects on society and on social systems that can co-exit or may conflict with one another so we can see the causal relationship of media / technology and society in a multidimensional and complex way. Social networking sites, which combine different media, information and communication technologies, at least provide information that displays information describing users, links are displayed and links between displayed users provide link lists and communication between users. It is also true that social media literacy is defined as being capable of communicating appropriately, responsibly and critically evaluating conversations in the field of social-based technologies. (Tillman, 2010).

Users who gain a personal reputation for their actions on the platforms they use should be aware of this. Anyone can post something online, so the user needs to know that critical thinking is key to determining what is critical and what is not. In terms of personal or corporate branding, it is therefore important to determine which networks to use, to find people and to participate in the interaction from a brand management perspective. There is an available Oxford glossary (n.d.), which defines social media as websites and applications that let users to create and share the content of news or articles or join social networks. Some examples of social media are; Facebook, Twitter, Instagram, Pinterest and LinkedIn.

What is accessible on the Internet and can be used to share information and ideas can be regarded as social media. Social media improves itself with computer and internet technologies and in some environments it is also called new media. Social media (new media) is also used especially by young people, adults and children. However, it is not known exactly what it will bring to humanity. It makes communication relatively easy, but it raises many problems. The main reason for these problems is to use social media in an unconscious manner.

UNESCO's definition of Media and Information Literacy (MIL) is as follows and Social Media Literacy can be defined from this definition: *a set of competencies that empowers citizens to access, retrieve, understand, evaluate and use, create as well as share information and media content in all formats, using various tools, in a critical, ethical and effective way in order to participate and engage in personal professional and societal activities. This means that a 'media and information literate person must not only be a consumer of information and media content, but also a responsible information seeker, knowledge creator and innovator, who is able to take advantage of a diverse range of information and communication tools and Media.*Social media literacy (SML) can therefore be understood as the *...specific set of technical, cognitive and emotional competencies that are required when using social media to search for information, for communication, content creation and for problem-avoiding and problem-solving, both in both professional and social context* ("What is Social Media Literacy?," n.d.).

What the media literacy research reveals is a rich and productive, yet controversial work structure. Media literacy is a widely accepted definition, although it is difficult to define, as it has the capacity to communicate, understand, evaluate and communicate in all forms. (Aufderheide, 1993). While the concept of media literacy has recently been expanded, sometimes digital literacy or digital media literacy has been re-labelled (Hobbs, 2008).

Today's social media community, discussions on the experience and information, ability, competencies and attitudes or orientations needed to successfully access and succeed were distorted and framed in connection to the concept of literacy (Banaji, 2015). When this approach is adopted, a technologically deterministic perspective is clearly avoided. It also opens up skill discussions for a number of key supporting but important skills and competences, such as experimentation, problem-solving skills, or the ability to gather information and move towards a common goal with others.

The adoption of new media literacy can be defined as cultural competences and social skills developed through collaboration and networking. Jenkins & Foundation (2006) identifies eleven different skills that underlie traditional literacy, research skills and critical thinking skills considered in the traditional education system.

Jenkins & Foundation (2006) suggested the following new skills indispensable for new media literacy:

- **Play:** It is the capacity to experience problems as a way of solving.
- **Performance:** It is the ability to obtain alternative identities for improvisation and discovery purposes.
- **Simulation:** It is the ability to interpret and establish dynamic models of real-world processes.
- **Appropriation:** It is the ability to sample and remix media content in a meaningful way.
- **Multitasking:** It is the ability to scan a person's environment and change the focus as needed for outstanding details.
- **Distributed Cognition:** It is the ability to make meaningful interaction with the tools that increase their mental capacity.
- **Collective Intelligence:** It is the ability to gather information together and compare notes with others for a common goal.
- **Judgment:** It is the ability to evaluate the reliability and validity of information sources from different locations.
- **Transmedia Navigation:** It is the ability to follow story and information flow in multiple modalities.
- **Networking:** It is the ability to search, synthesize and disseminate information.
- **Negotiation:** It is the ability to travel in different places, to distinguish different perspectives and to respect them and to understand and follow alternative norms.

For people who can distribute messages from economic information to political, economic, social and cultural and defence and security, mass media means a source of information. There is an increase in information dissemination channels and easy access to all kinds of information in today's digital age. In the 21st century, when the network society was widely discussed, it became a social network community. Political and personal agendas are including social media. Official and nonofficial education, information search, introduction of oneself, entertainment, games, socialization, CV creation, job search, archiving, networking, cyber activism and civil and political campaigns are among these agendas. There are people with relatively unobstructed attainment of internet, and they are getting increase residing in a hyperlinked arena. Private and corporate profiles are profiles that can be created (individually or jointly), divided, maintained, linked to, and updated on a range of platforms, both static and mobile.

The discussions of mass media, such as Facebook, Twitter or Wikipedia, which always pursue the next innovation, emerge with discussions of social media. These online spaces are geographically dispersed and bridged, apparently not hierarchical, and it is said that their architecture is to provide more recent and o from time to time more egalitarian learning, sociality and policy forms (Bennett & Segerberg, 2012).

In this framework, multiple profiles, groups and pages are created and maintained in different platforms and ways in which social media is used and accessed. Therefore, some questions arise for teaching and research. For example, what does literacy history mean in a social media age? Can a particular literacy be distinguished from what is related to social media that does not require an additional legion of literacy? Can they be social, political or technological? Is social media really 'social'? Or does it mean that individuals remain alone by making them dependent on them? In this perspective, the outlines of the study have started to be formed. (Sabancı, 2018).

In addition to contextual information, tendencies and orientations are observed more prominently in teens's social media literacy in the age of social media. The use of Facebook is researched, and at the end of this research reveals that the distinction among a skill-based approach to media/social media literacy and a critical/political approach is typical of this research context (Selwyn & Grant, 2009).

A social media literate can find, participate or found and protect relevant communities of interest in relation, for example, entertainment or politics; present ideas for different contexts and audiences using codes and rules of individual and co-written texts and platforms. It is possible for these people to find and track information on resources on tweets, hyperlinks and social networks. Relevant skills and competences may include, but are not limited to, decoding and interpreting data hyperlinked or embedded in social networks; separation of large amounts of data; finding, merging, and using networks or applications; effective use of privacy settings; customize profiles within the boundaries of certain social media platforms; effectively implement online rules, agreements, and codes of conduct online; recognize, report and avoid bullying, exacerbation and trolling, including unpleasant or controversial content on the accounts, pages and networks of friends, groups or unknown persons; and distinguishing ad from non-commercial content (Selwyn & Grant, 2009). Therefore, social media literacy studies will include research on how property, social media website profitability, governance and social control, as well as pleasure, identity, expression and participation are facilitated by social media.

RESEARCH METHODOLOGY

To assess the social media literacy of architecture and interior architecture students, a cross sectional descriptive study is used. Semi structured questionnaire forms are applied both in the researchers' institutions and also sent to academicians known by the researchers, with a request to disseminate their students of different universities.

Data collection is done by conducting two separate questionnaires in April 2017 and April 2019 respectively. In both cases, the structure of the questionnaire is developed using recent research studies (Vural & Bat, 2010), (Tektas, 2014), (Liu, 2010) in order to obtain data about the mobile technology practices and social media literacy of architecture and interior architecture students. Survey questions are not grouped structurally on the form but planned in groups as follow: (1) Students' general perception and habitual approaches towards Internet usage, (2) Social media literacy, social networks they actively use, (3) Internet and social network practices during the time they spend in their university, (4) Their interest in architects, architectural offices and architecture schools on social networks and which of them they follow, (5) Demographic questions pertaining students' institution, department, grade and gender.

The link for reaching the questionnaire was sent to the students by e-mail. Students of architecture and interior architecture/design departments of three universities in 2017 and five universities in 2019 were included in the research as the request was accepted by relevant department academics. While the majority of the Universities in both surveys are located in Istanbul, students of a university in the western province of Edirne also joined both surveys. Duration for both surveys were limited by 15 days. During this time period two separate e-mails with the questionnaire link are sent as a reminder to draw attention and increase the participation.

The collected data are analysed by using Microsoft Excel and SPSS software. Microsoft Excel is used for the descriptive analysis of the results, where SPSS is used for variance analysis between different groups of students. As the initial findings of the first questionnaire was summarized in a previous paper (Ilter & Karacar, 2017) this article reports the difference between the two time periods using the gathered descriptive data. Number of universities conducted and the limited time assigned for the answers were significant limitations of this research.

FINDINGS

The first questionnaire, that forms the first stage of this research was applied in 2017. It was sent to 1126 students of department of architecture and interior architecture in three different Universities in Turkey. At the end of the given time period, 240 valid questionnaire forms were received. The amount of valid answers were corresponding to 21,3% of the total population and at a confidence level of 95% margin of error was 5,6%. The second set of questions used in 2019 are meticulously revised for minor changes in social network brand names and mobile technologies. All revisions are made staying authentic to the purpose and construct of the questions. As the second stage of the research, a similar questionnaire is sent to 844 students and the number of responses to this second questionnaire is 136. The amount of valid answers are corresponding to 16.70% of the total population and at a confidence level of 95% margin of error is 7,7%. As the number of responses are well behind the first questionnaire, the change in the margin of error should be considered while interpreting the two sets of data.

In this section, descriptive analysis and comparison of the survey data gathered from 2017 and 2019 surveys are reported according to the planned groups in this order: (1) Demographic questions pertaining students' institution, department, grade and gender, (2) Students' general perception and habitual approaches towards Internet and smartphone usage, social networks they actively use, (3) Internet and Social network practices at the university and for their education, (4) Their interest in architects, architectural offices and architecture schools on social networks and which of them they follow, (5) General insights for using social media for architectural education.

Demographic Data

Representing over two thirds of the total population, 68% of the respondents were female in 2017 survey where this percentage is 71% in 2019. In 2017 survey, about 65% of them were architecture students compared to 35% interior architecture students. Similarly, 63% of them are architecture students and 37% are interior architecture students in 2019. In both surveys, most of the students are at their first year at their University with 41% and 46% for 2017 and 2019 respectively. However, compared to 35% second year students in 2017, this rate is 13% in 2019. Third year students are represented with 14% and fourth year students 6% in 2017. These ratios are slightly different in 2019 survey with 20% and 15% respectively. In 2017 survey, 3% of the students were studying in their department for more than four years. In the recent survey this ratio is 6%.

General Perceptions: Internet, Smartphones, and Social Networks

All the students answered the questionnaire are regular Internet users. Meanwhile students using mobile phones to go online have increased from 76% to 89% in last two years. As a result, notebook computer users to go online decreased from 21% to 9% and common desktop computer users and tablet computer users to connect Internet, which were smaller than 1% in 2017 seem to prefer other tools as no one did select this option in 2019. However, students using private desktop computers to go online are stable with 2%. Most of the students are spending between 2-6 hours going online with 51%. For about 30% of them this time extends to 6-12 hours. Going online more than 12 hours represent %10 and less than 2 hours %9. Percentage of students using mobile phones to go online is 97,5%, where the smartphone owners are a noble 99,2%. Around 57% of these phones are using iOS, 42% Android and less than 1% of the students claim using "other" operating systems for both time periods.

99,3% of the students state that they have active accounts in social networking sites raising from 96,7% in 2017. Instagram is still the most popular social network with 94,1% followed by 74,8% Pinterest. However, as Pinterest has a slide of around 2%, Facebook accounts lessened from 74,7% to 50,4%, twitter from 65,7% to 55,6% and Google+ from 57,1% to 43,7%. With these percentage changes, YouTube became the third most popular social network by 68,9% followed by Twitter and Facebook. LinkedIn accounts have an increase around 2%. On the other side, students stating 'other' social network accounts have a significant drop around 5% and became 6,7%. Distribution of the social networking sites that students have accounts and the change between 2017 and 2019 are shown on Figure 1". Students have 4-6 social network accounts on average with 64,81%.

Figure 1. Percentage distribution and change of the students' social network accounts 2017-2019 (%)

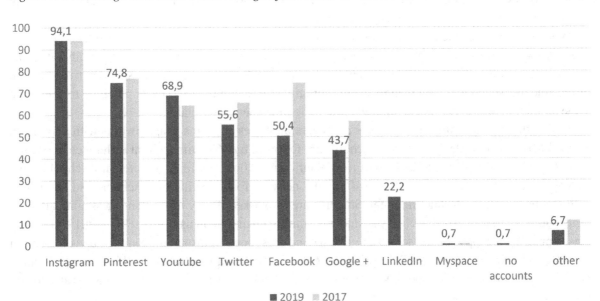

Students are also asked about their preference to use the social network accounts they have with a grade of 1-5, where 1 is the most preferred and the others follow up to the fifth preference. Instagram is again the most preferred social network by 56,7% raised from 55,2% in 2017. Second one is YouTube by 28,4% up from 20,5% and the third is now Pinterest defeating Facebook by 21,6%. These preference percentages also strengthen the change in the account holders. 25% of the students have their personal weblog and about 30% of the students visit weblog sites regularly. These percentages were 10,4% and 20,25% in 2017 survey respectively. Regular visitors of the blog sites are asked about the weblog sites they visit and the blog owners about the weblog sites they own a blog. Answers show that Tumblr is both the most visited and most blog owned social network site between the ones that have interest. That one is followed by Blogger, Weebly and WordPress in popularity.

A significant amount of students with 87% are checking their social media accounts many times daily which raised from 71% in 2017. However, students stating that they check their social network accounts less than once in a week have also raised from 1% to 3%.

Using Social Networks at the University

Students' answers show that about 70% of them can reach Internet using their University's wi-fi infrastructure and 67% of the students use that connection for reaching their social networks. These ratios display a change over 10% as these numbers were both 78% in 2017.

In the 2017 survey, 3,8% of the students admitted that they never go online during the classes. In 2019 this ratio is 7,9%. In 2017, 10% of students were admitting that they never check their social network accounts during the classes. In 2019 this ratio raised to 13,5%. Similarly, students that rarely check their accounts have raised from 26,5% to 34,9% and answers for "occasionally I do" dropped from 41,2% to 31%. Answers for "I do most of the time" and "I regularly do" seems alike. 4% is regularly checking social network accounts during the class activities.

When students are asked about the daily average time they spend online, 39,7% of students state they spend between 4 to 8 hours, 35,7% between 2 to 4 hours and 15,1% less than 2 hours daily. Students who admit spending more than 8 hours daily online are 9,5%. When it comes to social networks, none of the students stated that they plan to spend more time for social media. 51% is planning to spend the same amount of while 49% is planning to reduce the time spent on social media.

85% of the students follow architects or architectural offices on their social networks with a rise from 70% in 2017. Meanwhile Architectural schools are followed by 46% with a slight difference compared to 48,6% in 2017. Notable in 2019, apart from their own schools, a foreign architectural school is also stated by a significant ratio of 4,4%. Most popular network for following both schools and architects/ architectural offices is Instagram by far. Students are also asked if they use instant messaging applications. Quiet similar to 2017, 99% of the students admitted using them as it was 97% in 2017. Between these apps, WhatsApp is on top with 97%. The second most popular instant messaging app is Instagram by 80%, which was Snapchat in 2017 with about 61%. In 2019, Snapchat becomes third with 25% which is in close proximity with Facebook Messenger with 23,4%. However Facebook Messenger is also losing ground as it's ratio was about 35% in 2017.

Friending, Following, and Posting for Architecture

When students are asked if they use their real name on social networking activities, 84,1% admitted doing so. In 2017, the same ratio was 89,7%. When asked about further personal content they would share in their posts, 59% admitted sharing their school, 53% personal photos, 48% birth date, 47% the city they live. Mobile phone numbers are the least shared personal detail of students with a sharing ratio of 10%. Another question was about students' friending patterns. Students are asked if they accept friending requests of strangers on their social network accounts in three different categories. While 22% admitted that they will accept all requests in professional networks, this ratio became 8,7 in personal networks and 4,7% in instant messaging apps. Answers for students' behaviour against friending requests is shown in Figure 2.

Figure 2. 'Do you accept strangers' friending requests in social networks?' 2019 (%)

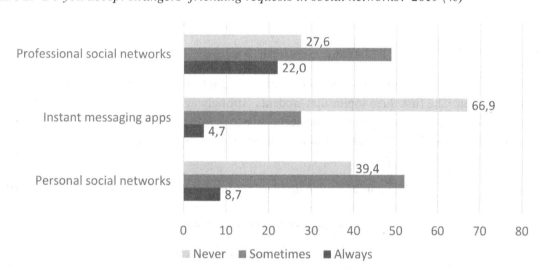

2019 results show that 29% of the students also follow their academician's social networks, joined by another 43,5% who do the same occasionally. These numbers were 41% and 36% in 2017 respectively, showing a fall of around 5%. In the latest survey, Students state that 63% of their design course lecturers share course documents and information on social networks at least occasionally. However in 2017 this ratio was 78%, showing a sharp fall for lecturers sharing course information and material on social networks. When students are asked about posting course related online documents to the social networks, 17% of the students admit posting documents regularly and 45% admit occasionally. In 2017, the same question was answered as 31% and 39% respectively. Meanwhile, in 2019 the ratio of the students who "strongly agree" or "agree" that their lecturers are efficient users of the social networks is 35%. The same ratio in 2017 was 45%. Percentage ratio of the answers for the question 'Do you think your lecturers use social networks effectively?' in the 2019 survey are shown in Figure 3.

Figure 3. 'Do you think your lecturers use social networks effectively?'2017-2019 (%)

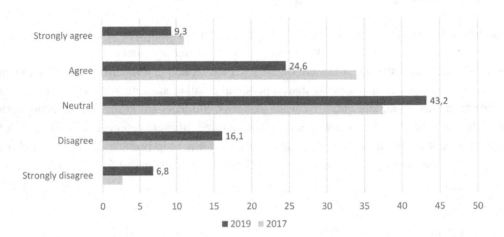

Social Networks for Education

Students are asked if they agree that social media networks can be helpful for proposed topics concerning their education. The first three topics that students 'strongly agreed' are 'Reaching sample project and details' with 59,3%, 'Finding similar projects' images' with 56,8 and contacting architects and architectural offices by 52,5. All the result of this question are shown in Figure 4.

Figure 4. 'Do you think social networks can help your education by reaching these features?'2019 (%)

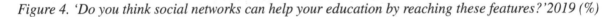

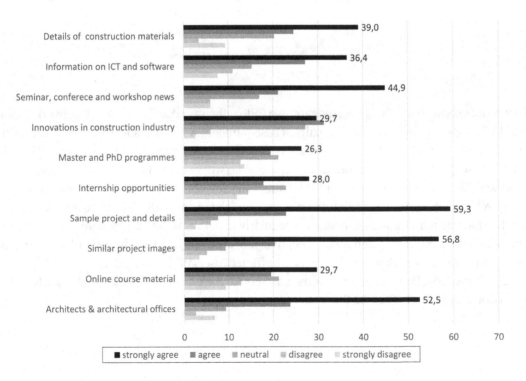

As the last question of the questionnaire, students were asked to indicate their thoughts about using social networks as a tool for their design education. In 2019, about 55 students out of 136 have expressed their thoughts and ideas with 40,4% in this open ended question. In 2017, it was 52 students out of 240 with 21,6%. With nearly the same number of students in two subsequent surveys, initially, all the students who answered this question are affirmative and demanding from using social networks as an educational intermedium.

Most of them are asking for a dynamic portal that will contain an archive of photos, videos, detail drawings, sample projects, presentations, book recommendations, articles, architectural terminology in both Turkish and English, interviews with famous architects and their work, enabling sharing and brain storming between students and lecturers. They request video tutorials and an archive about current lectures and/or technical drawing, like CAD, BIM lectures, announcements about architectural competition and apprenticeship opportunities. They want to freely express their design work and also want to see other project groups' and university students' work and evaluation. There is also a demand for the social networks to be introduced by lecturers and professionally managed faculty and department social media accounts behaving like social platforms between students and lecturers globally. Students are also asking for establishing mobile ready social networks and offer social responsibility projects for the community. These demands are more or less the same in both 2017 and 2019.

There are also complaints about divergent practices of different architecture schools, starting from unclear jury and grading criteria to social media abuse by students. Although some students criticise their peers for using social network sites such as Pinterest as cheat sheets, they are still positive about the idea of using social media for educational purposes. Nevertheless, in the 2019 survey, two students stated that social networks are being effective enough for their education and the rest should be more personal.

SOLUTIONS AND RECOMMENDATIONS

Results and comparison of the two surveys highlight some changes and affinities about both mobile device and social media use for interior architecture and architecture students. Students using mobile phones to go online have increased from 76% to 89% in last two years while notebook computer users to go online decreased from 21% to 9%. These ratios show us the change towards the mobile devices. However notebook or the so called laptop computer genre is no more considered as mobile for the 'Net Generation'.

Besides the change towards mobile, smart phone or up to 'Phablet' devices which are hybrid devices of mobile phones and tablets, we are so close to the point where every student has a social media account. And again the ratios show us that the social networks are moving towards being a monopolistic corporations as the number of students who admitted using other than the most known brand name social networks lessened down under ten percent as they have a share about 6,7% in 2019 survey. The number of monopolistic corporations are decreasing too. One network buying the other or supplementing new features like adding instant messaging function to an image sharing network enables them to secure more shares of the social media market for the acquiring company.

In this context, nearly nine in ten students are checking their social network accounts daily with an addition of two in ten in the past two years time. On the other hand, number of students who pay less attention to social media are quiet few in ratio but the number of this students have tripled since 2017 and raised to 3%. In the 2019 survey, none of the students stated that they plan to spend more time for social media. 51% is planning to spend the same amount of while 49% is planning to reduce the time spent on social media. Findings of the two consequent surveys discussed here both have similarities with other researchers work like Vural & Bat (2010), Tektas (2014) and Liu, (2010). However, global survey results about smart phone and social media use put forward a consistent amount of difference between different cultures (Poushter, Bishop, & Chwe, 2018). Besides, during the literature analysis, similar research work dealing with architecture and interior architecture students could not be identified which restraints subject specific comparisons.

Although the sample size of this research is not sufficient to test and validate more wide-ranging implications, interior architecture and architecture students are drawing a picture where we have an almost full-time online generation who are feeling a bit distracted by the social media and trying to limit or at least stop the amount of time they spend on. Results show an up to date mobile technology infrastructure afforded by the students themselves and an increasing interest towards social networks on the student side. However, academic institutions and the system of education seems to lag behind. Such an output shows that this highly opportunistic environment brings us challenges. We are paying attention to using social media and investing on mobile technologies but on the other hand struggling to put these technologies on the right track to improve the system of higher education.

Mobile devices and social media applications can help students learn new skills such as Jenkins & Foundation (2006) suggests. Architecture and interior architecture students can be motivated to blog their design work, share their studio work on mediums like Instagram, Facebook or similar sharing platforms. Follow and comment on their classmates designs as well as famous architects and designers. During the practice, academicians' active involvement is needed to motivate the students and manage the process to reach aimed results. These activities are considered to be promising for some of the needed skills in the new media culture such as play, simulation, networking and collective intelligence.

FUTURE RESEARCH DIRECTIONS

In a digitized world, reaching any kind of information is getting easier everyday by undeniable contribution of social media. However while the amount of information on any kind of subject extends beyond our imagination by using social media tools, it is getting more and more complex to reach precise and unmanipulated information in a highly complex and 'polluted' nature of this clutter. As the students also mention in both surveys, social media slightly moderated by academic institutions or lecturers have the potential of eliminating the negative connotation attached to it. As well as a major number of citizens in our global village Turkish interior architecture and architecture students are spending a remarkable amount of time within the social media. This opportunity to use the potential for developing new educational mediums is worth making further research. As an initial stage, using social networks such as blogs, dedicated networking groups or pages where studio work can be posted, commented, archived and shared with a wider community seems worth looking for as a future direction.

CONCLUSION

Mobile technologies have spread into our lives initially as tools enabling verbal communication and short message services. They got adopted by businesses as they enabled reaching people anytime and anywhere who are considered lucky enough to be under the coverage of phone operators. In a couple of decades, while the limited coverage area enlarged and the data transmission speed increased multiple times, the simplistic need to speak to other people for doing business turned into streams of data flow forming networks of a virtual world that is for business as much as any other need or desire of mankind.

Social media evolved as a dynamic virtual network that has broad effects on social life and business environment globally. While the access speed increased with an unbelievable pace, number of social media accounts have soared globally. However the limited control over the internet and social media caused security concerns as well as a serious issue of identifying the pure form of the information and it's manipulated state. Although it still seems quiet far to identify social media slightly moderated by academic institutions or lecturers have the potential of eliminating the negative connotation attached to it.

It is obvious that more detailed enquiries should be made to go further in understanding and improving social media literacy and use these findings to adopt and develop the tools and technologies for educational purposes. We need more research on social media literacy, how they identify, understand, use and adapt to these technologies. Understanding perceptions towards social networks and their 'designed' online existence in wider communities seems to be the key to enable researchers to identify new ways for education and to develop next generations' knowledge and potential.

REFERENCES

Alter, A. L. (2017). *Irresistible : the rise of addictive technology and the business of keeping us hooked.* New York: Penguin Press.

Aufderheide, P. (1993). Media Literacy: A Report of the National Leadership Conference on Media Literacy. *Media Literacy in the Information Age Current Perspectives.*

Banaji, S. (2015). Social Media and Literacy. In *Major Reference Works* (pp. 1–6). The International Encyclopedia of Digital Communication and Society. doi:10.1002/9781118767771.wbiedcs078

Bennett, W. L., & Segerberg, A. (2012). The Logic Of Connective Action. *Information Communication and Society, 15*(5), 739–768. doi:10.1080/1369118X.2012.670661

Ferraro, G., Caci, B., D'Amico, A., & Di Blasi, M. (2007). Internet Addiction Disorder: An Italian Study. *Cyberpsychology & Behavior, 10*(2), 170–175. doi:10.1089/cpb.2006.9972 PMID:17474832

Gikas, J., & Grant, M. M. (2013). Mobile computing devices in higher education: Student perspectives on learning with cellphones, smartphones & social media. *The Internet and Higher Education, 19,* 18–26. doi:10.1016/j.iheduc.2013.06.002

<edb> Greenfield, D. (2012). The Addictive Properties of Internet Usage. In Internet Addiction (pp. 133–153). Academic Press. doi:10.1002/9781118013991.ch8</edb>

Hobbs, R. (2008). Debates and challenges facing new literacies in the 21st century. In *The International Handbook of Children.* Media and Culture. doi:10.4135/9781848608436.n26

<conf>Ilter, A. T., & Karacar, P. (2017). Mobile Technology And Social Networks: Mapping Architecture Students' Practice And Awareness For Educational Possibilities. 9th International Conference on Education and New Learning Technologies, 6820–6827. doi:10.21125/edulearn.2017.2573</conf>

Jenkins, H., & Foundation, J. D. (2006). *Confronting the Challenges of Participatory Culture: Media Education for the 21st Century.* An Occasional Paper on Digital Media and Learning. John D. and Catherine T. MacArthur Foundation.

Liu, Y. (2010). Social Media Tools as a Learning Resource. *Journal of Educational Technology Development and Exchange, 3*(1), 101–114. doi:10.18785/jetde.0301.08

McLuhan, M. (1964). *Understanding media : the extensions of man.* New York: McGraw-Hill.

Oxford Dictionary. (n.d.). *social media | Definition of social media in English by Lexico Dictionaries.* Retrieved August 9, 2019, from https://www.lexico.com/en/definition/social_media

Perrin, A. (2015). *Social Media Usage: 2005-2015 | Pew Research Center.* Retrieved from https://www.pewinternet.org/2015/10/08/social-networking-usage-2005-2015/

Poushter, J., Bishop, C., & Chwe, H. (2018). *Social Media Use Continues to Rise in Developing Countries but Plateaus Across Developed Ones Digital divides remain, both within and across countries for media or other inquiries* (Vol. 19). Retrieved from www.pewresearch.org

Sabancı, Y. S. (2018). *Sosyal Medya Okuryazarlığı: Facebook Ve Instagram Örneği.* Marmara Üniversitesi.

Selwyn, N., & Grant, L. (2009). Researching the realities of social software use – an introduction. *Learning, Media and Technology, 34*(2), 79–86. doi:10.1080/17439880902921907

Tektas, N. (2014). A Research On University Students' Social Networking Habits. *Journal of History School, 7*(17), 851–870. doi:10.14225/Joh474

Tillman, K. (2010). *Do Media Literacy, Digital Literacy, and SM Literacy Intersect?* Retrieved August 10, 2015, from http://www.edelmandigital.com/2010/04/01/do-media-literacy-digital-literacy-and-social-media-literacy-intersect/

Vural, Z. B. A., & Bat, M. (2010). Yeni Bir İletişim Ortamı Olarak Sosyal Medya: Ege Üniversitesi İletişim Fakültesine Yönelik Bir Araştırma. *Social Media as a New Communication Environment: A Research on Ege University Faculty of Communication, 5*(20), 3348–3382.

What is Social Media Literacy? (n.d.). Retrieved from http://fcl.eun.org/sml4change/what-is-social-media-literacy

Young, K. S. (1998). Internet Addiction: The Emergence of a New Clinical Disorder. *Cyberpsychology & Behavior, 1*(3), 237–244. doi:10.1089/cpb.1998.1.237

ADDITIONAL READING

Alvermann, D. E., & Sanders, R. K. (2019). Adolescent Literacy in a Digital World. In R. Hobbs & P. Mihailidis (Eds.), *The International Encyclopedia of Media Literacy.*, doi:10.1002/9781118978238. ieml0005

Fonseca, D., Villagrasa, S., Martí, N., Redondo, E., & Sánchez, A. (2013). Visualization Methods in Architecture Education Using 3D Virtual Models and Augmented Reality in Mobile and Social Networks. *Procedia: Social and Behavioral Sciences*, *93*, 1337–1343. doi:10.1016/j.sbspro.2013.10.040

Livingstone, S. (2014). Developing social media literacy: How children learn to interpret risky opportunities on social network sites. *Communications*, *39*(3), 283–303. Retrieved11Sep.2019. doi:10.1515/commun-2014-0113

Moran, M., Seaman, J., & Tinti-Kane, H. (2011). Teaching, learning, and sharing: How today's higher education faculty use social media. Babson Survey Research Group, and New Marketing Labs, Retrieved August 1, 2018 from http://www.pearsonlearningsolutions.com/educators/pearson-social-media-survey-2011-bw.pdf

Rogers, D. L. (2000). A paradigm shift: Technology integration for higer education in the new milleninum. *Educational Technology Review*, *13*, 19–33.

Soliman, A. M. (2017). Appropriate teaching and learning strategies for the architectural design process in pedagogic design studios. *Frontiers of Architectural Research*, *6*(2), 204–217. doi:10.1016/j.foar.2017.03.002

Tess, P. A. (2013). The role of social media in higher education classes (real and virtual)–A literature review. *Computers in Human Behavior*, *29*(5), A60–A68. doi:10.1016/j.chb.2012.12.032

KEY TERMS AND DEFINITIONS

Following: Social media users that choose to see all the posts of other users in a social network platform.

Friending: Act of adding or granting someone to a list of 'friends' on a social network that allows that person special privileges of viewing and posting to that person's 'timeline'.

Instant Messaging App: Usually a mobile device or online computer service that provides text as well as voice communication.

Mobile Technology: Generally referring to hand-held computer devices such as smart phone and tablet computers.

Posting: Act of sending or 'sharing' content in a social network that can be both private or public.

Social Media: Web-based platforms that people broadcast text, images, graphical expressions, images, video etc.

Social Network: Web-based platforms that people that people interact with one another in which the communication has a two-way nature.

Chapter 25
Educators' Participatory Practices and Development of Professional Identities in a Twitter Online Professional Learning Network (PLN)

Krista Welz
New Jersey City University, USA

ABSTRACT

Twitter, a popular social networking application, is being recognized as a tool for changing how people share their knowledge and experience, as well as collaborate with one another. Twitter is being recognized for not only how people network with one another, but as a multipurpose learning tool. Originally designed as an application where users could update and share their statuses with friends, Twitter has become an essential tool for learning and developing online communities. Various studies feature Twitter's potentialities to promote the work of K-12 teachers. Within these studies, Twitter (1) enables educators to interact with other educators besides those in their own school districts, (2) decreases different kinds of isolation in workplaces, and (3) provides personalized and collaborative communities as well as PLNs.

INTRODUCTION

Social networking applications are now being recognized in transforming how educators distribute their knowledge and network with others. With the advancement of online social networking applications, educators are engaging in networked communities that provide them with the assistance they need to obtain particular necessities, respond to problems, and develop professional knowledge (Nelson, 2012). Educational technology is developing options such as professional learning communities (PLCs) and PLNs that are not limited to social networks. Networking can take place within school meetings, online, and at state and national conferences through formal and informal discussions. Reading, reflecting, and

DOI: 10.4018/978-1-6684-7123-4.ch025

sharing through media also avail professional opportunities (Nelson, 2012). Educators can share sources, exchange stories, and assist each other.

Twitter, a popular social networking application, is being recognized as a tool for changing how people share their knowledge and experience, as well as collaborate with one another. Twitter is being recognized for not only how people network with one another, but as a multipurpose learning tool (Komorowski, Do Huu, & Deligiannis, 2018). Originally designed as an application where users could update and share their statuses with friends (Bilton, 2013), Twitter has become an essential tool for learning and developing online communities. Various studies feature Twitter's potentialities to promote the work of K-12 teachers. Within these studies, Twitter (a) enables educators to interact with other educators besides those in their own school districts, (b) decreases different kinds of isolation in workplaces, and (c) provides personalized and collaborative communities as well as PLNs.

Being able to connect with others for the intent of learning, such as discovering new resources, creating and sharing their own content, participating in discussions, exploring best practices, and seeking examples of innovation in schools, helps educators strengthen their practice. Web 2.0 technology, such as Twitter, can help them gain knowledge and experience from other educators who are either beginners or experts (Nelson, 2012). By engaging in an online Twitter PLN, educators have a place to discover the practices of other educators around the world, explore innovative ideas and trends, expand their overall thinking, and become familiar with educational leaders who are transforming the field and education.

Twitter can present a powerful digital environment for the analysis of social and informational practices within an online CoP. Because the quality and amount of school district professional learning can be unpredictable for many educators, many of them are in search of other ways to acquire support and access to beneficial resources, such as online communities. Harlan (2009) exclaims that an online community can help develop learning beyond direct school environments, such as remaining current with the dynamic realm of technology. Educators need to remain relevant with current and fluctuating educational and technological trends, which does not come easily if they are isolated in their workplace.

With the options of joining and exploring online communities, such as Twitter, remaining current has become simpler for educators. Changes in educational theory, technology, current and award-winning literature, advocacy issues, and other helpful trends or resources that may affect student learning can be explored in an online community (Harlan, 2009). Online communities play an essential part in encouraging and supporting modern practices, as educators are subject to a variety of innovative concepts and viewpoints from outside their school practice.

Educators may develop continuous learning opportunities using Twitter. Harlan (2009) asserts that to be highly effective in their practice, educators need to explore beyond their school's walls and persist in discovering innovative and inspiring ideas. Twitter, like many online communities, can help its users explore their individual interests, desires, and necessities, which may help lessen the feelings of isolation. Hathcock (2017) states that some of the most constructive and inspiring conversations for educators are occurring on Twitter. Twitter has become a popular online community for connecting with other educators, taking part in discussions, learning, and growing professionally. Twitter's ability to build communities through the use of micro-dialogues, made up of 280 characters, has become of specific significance to educators who are exploring ways to develop practical social significance from like-minded individuals with shared interests and visions (Hathcock, 2017). From Twitter chats, sharing resources and ideas, and searching subject-specific hashtags, to establishing professional and personal connections, educators are discovering many ways to connect through Twitter.

Twitter can be extremely valuable for educators who participate in its online community. Along with its many ways of establishing connections and providing a space to share valuable information and resources, Hathcock (2017) asserts that Twitter can also provide educators with a space to self-reflect and can help them establish their professional identities. Whether or not an educator self-identifies with a PLN on Twitter, Twitter's public, communicative space allows them to share their viewpoints on what their online communities are or what they could possibly be. In addition, Willemese (2014) supports Twitter's effective implementation of peer mentoring, where users participate in discussions that often provide rich, varied interactive perceptions – supporting the essential concept of PLNs. Hurt (2013) commends these highly applicable mentoring moments as Twitter users take the time and sincere interest in assisting other users that seek their help and support. Because of its positive environment of sharing information and resources, Twitter can be an ideal tool to augment and encourage the formation of a Twitter online community of educators.

The utilization of social media networking tools, such as Twitter, can offer its users many opportunities to gather and share information and resources, as well as help enable and encourage interaction. Of specific interest is whether Twitter can be used to form a CoP where its participants share a communal interest and desire to discuss ideas, experiences, and share knowledge (Lewis & Rush, 2013). The term *community of practice* (CoP) was originally coined by Lave and Wenger (1991) to assert that people learn by not only obtaining and grasping individual information, but by learning from one another. In Wenger's (1998) revolutionary publication of *Communities of Practice: Learning, Meaning, and Identity*, he concentrated on learning in workplaces, essentially developing upon the concept of communities of practice. Wenger (1998) expressed how social learning formed people's paths of learning and their professional identity. The developments of CoPs can be applied to various contexts, including administrative design and educational leadership.

It is imperative to consider that the concept of a CoP has continued to develop in intricacy and focus. CoP is one of the most extensively cited and significant perceptions of social learning used in research (Smith, Hayes, & Shea, 2017). In 2011, Wenger, Trayner, and de Laat (2011) further defined CoP as a learning cooperative among participants who found it beneficial to learn from one another about a specific domain. Participants could ask each other questions, discuss concepts, develop products, share resources, decipher problems, seek emotional encouragement, and utilize each other's experience of practice as a knowledge source (Trust & Horrocks, 2018). Each CoP is distinctive and contains resources, experiences, methods for tackling habitual tribulations, and advice for participants – differentiating it from other communities and networks (Trust & Horrocks, 2018). There is a similarity, however, in the participants of a CoP. This similarity is determined by both the participants' shared interests and identities that ultimately result in communal goals and practices (Warden & Ogbamichael, 2018). Participation is different for every individual member – some choose to ask questions and actively contribute to the CoP, while others may benefit from simply observing and learning from the sidelines (Trust & Horrocks, 2018). If a CoP's participants do not dynamically participate in sharing, communicating, and collaborating with each other, participation may begin to wither, and participants may visit less often. The CoP may also decrease in its overall size, ultimately giving the small gathering of participants control over what type of information is shared (Seo, 2014). Moreover, learning is defined by the participants amongst a CoP (Trust & Horrocks, 2018). Because CoPs are based on the values of social learning, a successful CoP is generally dependent on the participants (Trust & Horrocks, 2018). Participants can choose to communicate in-person within a CoP, but are now more likely to engage virtually with each other.

Twitter strengthens the development of connectivity amongst users through the use of text, called tweets. Tweets can also include hashtags, which consist of the # symbol followed by a word or phrase. Twitter's easy-to-use interface enables users to quickly search for tweets that include specific hashtags. The ability to search for hashtags enables users to discover new content and, most importantly, connect with new users. Weller, Bruns, Burgess, Mahrt, and Puschmann (2014) describe Twitter as a networked world where conversations are dispersed. Tweets serve as micro-content or "nanostories" (p. 6) that move in a continuous flow of knowledge within a user's personal timeline. These personal timelines offer a wealth of information and access to meaningful conversations. As Stephen Colbert, actor and comedian, states – "Don't these little tweets, these little sips of online connection, add up to one big gulp of conversation?" (Turkle, 2016, p. 19). Indeed they do.

Being connected in an online community can make participants feel like they belong. The online community's digital place is a space that allows us to explore a multitude of knowledge, network with other users, and most importantly, explore the self. When participants engage in online communities, they may not alter their true selves. Turkle (2016) states that members' online identities are features of their own true selves that some may find difficult to express in real-life. For this reason, the online environment is a fascinating space that cannot only help a person develop professionally, but personally as well. People can work on their aspired qualities in the online world and steadily carry them into their real worlds. Profiles, tweets that include shared content and reflections, and connections made with other users allow people to represent themselves and grasp at chances to reconsider and develop their identities.

IDENTITY AND EDUCATION

Creating a practice involves developing a community where participants can connect with each other. Connecting with each other allows participants to acknowledge each other. In a CoP, there is an association between practice and identity. Identity is defined on how a person views and recognizes himself or herself. It is also the self-conception on how a person is perceived by others (Wenger, 1998). The concept of identity is an equal, main component of CoP theory. A person's identity includes his or her own capability and incapability to construct the values that characterize their communities and their practices of fitting in. By fitting into his or her own community, a person establishes a distinctive identity (Brown & Heck, 2018). In a CoP, people learn and develop particular ways of how to interact with each other, how to behave toward each other, and how to work well together.

A person fundamentally becomes who they are by performing a part in the associations of engagement that establish his or her community. Wenger (2010) describes the three different modes of belonging in identity development in communities of practice: engagement, imagination, and alignment. Engagement is the most active, direct participation of shared practices in forming a CoP. Through active engagement, participants are negotiating their meanings by engaging in activities, such as conversing, contributing, and utilizing resources with each other. People start to become aware of their own competencies (or inabilities) and whether they develop identities that will be participative or non-participative. By participating, they are assisting in the formation of the practice and gaining competence and respect by other members of the community. Through imagination, participants start to form new perceptions and awareness of the world, along with forming models and ideas while co-reflecting on practice. For example, if participants work as educators they begin to use their own imagination in forming a representation of the educator model, imagining themselves as one of them. They are positioning themselves as educators, perceiving themselves from several perspectives, reflecting on their own positions, and exploring new potentials as an educator. Wenger (1998) states that the world offers people with a variety of imagination tools, such as role models, stories, and languages. When participants use their imagination, they can form associations of identification that are as meaningful as those obtained from engagement. Through alignment, participants organize activities and resources to fit within wider formations and accomplish outcomes. Through alignment, participants are developing communications, best practices, mutual meanings, and leadership skills. Alignment includes defining roles, norms, mutual values, and negotiated obligations and expectancies that embrace the community together.

Taking part in new practices allows people to venture into uncharted areas. People experience and manifest themselves by what they know and do not know, what they understand and cannot comprehend, what makes them feel accepted and isolated, and what they can and cannot implement into their professional services (Wenger, 1998). By focusing on our identity, we construct an apprehension amongst our experience and competence. This focus adds an aspect of determination and changeability to the formation of practice as we strive to discover our place in a community (Wenger, 2010). In practice, people know who they are by what they find familiar, reasonable, practical, and open for discussion to them.

Studies have claimed that communities of practice can improve professional identities through social networking applications and online communities. Goodyear, Casey, and Kirk (2014) studied how teachers utilized social media in order to enable instructional change within a developing online Twitter CoP. The researchers discovered that Twitter helped teachers develop a professional identity as a direct result of contributing their knowledge via tweets, ultimately demonstrating social proficiency amongst other participants in their CoP. The Twitter conversations that occurred amongst participants added to the development of a shared collection, inclusive of best practices, resources, and so on, and it helped them to develop each other's practice and achieve common objectives. The study's findings suggested that each participant becomes genuinely situated in a social space where they individually develop a professional identity. The teachers felt that they acquired statuses as innovative practitioners as a result of working within an effective online Twitter CoP. The development of an online Twitter CoP helped develop participants' professional identities, reinforced focused communications amongst other teachers, and encouraged professional learning that resulted in instructional transformation.

One must remember that establishing an identity is a continuous practice. It is not a predetermined set part of our personality. Our identities are in a continuous mode of renegotiation. In a CoP, participants must realize the past experiences of their practice, the importance of what guides their community, the associations between other participants that form the practice, and the identities of the participants that contribute knowledge and content for learning – for both novices and experts (Wenger, 2010).

In a CoP, education is the leading factor that must be attempted, as it unlocks aspects for self-negotiation. Wenger (1998) states, "If learning is a matter of identity, then identity is itself an educational resource" (p. 277). Education situates participants on an ongoing path towards an extensive domain of potential identities. Educational imagination enables participants to explore themselves and their situations with new perceptions through the act of reflection. They learn to become aware of the various ways they can interpret their lives. Their identities are perceived as self-recognition. Educational imagination is the process of participants learning that they do not necessarily have to accept the way things are, but experiment and discover various prospects by recreating themselves and the world (Wenger, 1998). The development of identities involves participants choosing what to become aware of and what to experience. By experimenting with new things, new experiences are formed and different prospective futures are considered. In this awareness, identity is considered as a creation. Information on its own account is insignificant unless it catches and develops participants' identities.

TWITTER AS A LEARNING TOOL

There have been a variety of research studies that have explored the utilization of Twitter by educators in different sectors. The variety of research studies include Twitter use amongst teachers in K-12 school districts, those in higher education, pre-service teachers, and those who use it exclusively for backchanneling at conferences. Carpenter and Krutka (2015), Davis (2015), Visser, Evering, and Barrett (2014), and focused their studies primarily on K-12 teacher use of Twitter. Davis (2015) explored how teachers in the United States were using Twitter as a method for self-directed professional development. Davis not only wanted to explore their use of Twitter as a tool, but to learn more about their engagement in an online CoP. Davis focused on the #Edchat Twitter chat that many educators participate in. Tweets with the #edchat hashtags were collected, along with interviews with educators who participated in the chat. After coding the tweets and interview data, Davis discovered several themes and subthemes. These themes included teachers' perceptions of sharing information and resources, attaining an awareness of belonging by being a part of a community, and Twitter being an effective tool for professional development. Twitter was expressed as a useful method for teachers to reflect on their own practices, receive advice from those with experience, and engage with other compassionate educators.

The awareness of being part of a community and the encouragement that it provides helps educators discover the benefits of Twitter as a constructive, learner- focused tool. Similar to Davis's (2015) study, Visser, Evering, and Barrett (2014) also conducted a study on how K-12 teachers use Twitter. Instead of applying a qualitative, online ethnographic method for collecting data like Davis's study, Visser, Evering, and Barrett conducted their study using a mixed-methods approach. Data was collected through a survey that consisted of both closed and open-ended questions. The researchers wanted to explore how teachers were using and accessing Twitter, along with their opinions of the tool. Similar to Davis's (2015) results, the study revealed that teachers who used it several times a day were more likely to utilize it as a form of self-directed professional development. Acquiring both content knowledge and forming connections with other educators seem to be the most popular benefits for educator use of Twitter. In addition, Carpenter and Krutka (2015) published a study on the use of Twitter amongst teachers (K-12), administrators, and instructors in higher education. They both proclaim that conventional, mandated professional development established in school districts decide what educators need to learn about to become more efficient at their jobs. By implementing the participatory, informal environment of Twitter, educators can take control of their own learning. By surveying educators' use of Twitter for professional purposes, Carpenter and Krutka's study revealed that Twitter was being used for many different educational purposes. Twitter was perceived as resourceful, available at any time of the day, and highly collaborative in the sense of connecting with others. It was also favorable among other social media applications because of its open, public access in connecting educators with others outside of their school districts. Twitter also provided educators with opportunities to gain access to innovative concepts shared by other educators and remain up-to-date with educational and technological trends. Furthermore, the educators noted how the use of Twitter assisted them in preventing many kinds of isolation – a recurring problem both observed in the professional lives of school librarians and pre-service teachers.

Twitter has benefitted in its ability to globally connect individuals and provide resources so that its users gain a deeper sense of knowledge. While various studies include Twitter and its use of professional development in educators, there are few studies on the use of Twitter by pre-service educators and their journey in acquiring relevant knowledge that might support them. Lemon (2014) studied how the formation of knowledge through tweets can support constructive, logical, and thoughtful thinking for pre-service teachers in undergraduate pre-service teachers in Australia. Lemon focused her study on how the teachers accessed Twitter in order to reflect upon their experiences of studying and practicing on becoming a fully licensed teacher. The focus was mainly concerned on how theory and connections to other educators were created. The pre- service teachers' instructor demonstrated how to use Twitter and then integrated it into the curriculum. The pre-service teachers' reflections were shared through their tweets in order to facilitate online conversation. Lemon stressed that educators should build a professional identity on Twitter to actively engage with each other while in or away from educational environments.

Throughout the years, Twitter has not only provided its users with valuable content and enabled them to connect with others around the world, it has also become a popular choice for virtual backchannel communication and participation at events, especially in educational environments (Justice, 2015). Because of its use of formal and informal learning, many educators often use Twitter as a backchannel for conferences. In conferences, a backchannel is indicated as an "informal secondary or background communication channel that exists while a formal front channel speaker, lecturer, or panel is presenting" (Justice, 2015, p. 234). Li and Greenhow (2015) developed a study on the use of Twitter as a conference backchannel at the 2013 American Educational Research Association (AERA) annual conference. Within the AERA Twitter backchannel, faculty and student groups actively developed their PLNs, casually contributed content, collaborated with other users for resolutions to problems, composed tweets in the same style as they would if they took notes during conferences, and discussed sessions in their tweets. They would also often quote conference presenters in their tweets. Many of the faculty groups felt that possessing an online identity associated with their occupation was of great value in a Twitter backchannel, while the graduate students felt that using it was a chance to learn about upcoming conferences and conference-related resources. Li and Greenhow discussed how using a Twitter backchannel could potentially help graduate students effectively manage a continuous flow of information during a conference (i.e. Twitter feed) and consider how to create and manage their self-presentation in public communities.

In most online communities, asynchronous textual communication is used in place of synchronous live gatherings. The on-demand, asynchronous digital environment of Twitter provides participants with an accessible and flexible space to effortlessly explore content-specific information and encourage users to contribute their own content with like-minded individuals who share similar interests. For newcomers who are starting to form their Twitter PLN, the easiest method to start contributing content is to simply retweet others' tweets (Stranack, 2012). Retweeting others' tweets is the same as reposting their content so that the participant's own followers can view it. A simple retweet can quickly spread valuable information. Retweeting enables information to be seen by many more participants on Twitter and suggests new participants to follow – ultimately helping participants grow their PLN.

In order for tweets to reach a larger audience, participants can add designated hashtags to their tweets. Hashtags are specific word tags preceded by a hashtag (#) symbol, i.e. #edutwitter in tweets (Huang, Thornton & Efthimiadis, 2010). Through the use of implementing hashtags in tweets, participants can easily collect content, discover upcoming learning opportunities such as professional development events, engage and collaborate in threaded discussions through Twitter chats, and bookmark tweets that they find relevant to their professions.

An extensive variation of educational and library-specific resources is accessible on Twitter. As participants start sharing content through tweets and interact with others in their PLN, they begin to discover (or rediscover) their own viewpoints and maintain their sense of involvement in a CoP. They begin to establish a trusting bond with others and can comfortably post questions in their tweets and within hours can receive a fair amount of advice and other helpful tips. Participants can choose to either interact with those who they are following or with other experts in their field. The variations of participants' professional backgrounds enable Twitter to be a community where distinctive knowledge, experiences, and reflections are contributed (Gilbert, 2016). By actively contributing and engaging in discussions with others, participants can further build their online PLN and attain a wealth of knowledge that pertains to their specific professional field.

EMERGENT THEMES OF AN EDUCATIONAL TWITTER PROFESSIONAL LEARNING NETWORK (PLN)

Being an active participant in Twitter, a thorough observation of educator tweets during a six-week period during 2018 provided me with a number of emergent themes:

Twitter Chats for Professional Development

Many educators who I follow on Twitter engaged in a variety of Twitter chats. Many used Twitter chats to focus on their professionalism, contribute ideas, share work-related experiences with others in the chat, connect with other like-minded individuals, tweet about programs and events they implemented in their schools, share professional resources, and advocate issues pertaining to education. From observing their tweets, one can surely sense the appreciation for the sense of community and learned-centered professional development that took place in their CoP. The emerging themes of this study coincide with some of the themes in Davis's (2015) qualitative study of teachers participating in the weekly #EdChat Twitter chat that discusses educational issues. Some of main themes that emerged from the study were teachers sharing their knowledge and resources through the #EdChat Twitter chat, the sense of belonging that Twitter provided, and the use of Twitter for on-demand professional development.

The CoP model includes various forms of exchanges, which are classified into three sections: domain, community, and practice. As I observed the educators participate in their Twitter chats, they acknowledged what area of interest they wanted to learn more about by choosing which chat to participate. These areas of interests represented the domain section of the CoP model. As they socially interacted with one another, they were participants of the Twitter chat community. Furthermore, as they shared their experiences, knowledge, and resources, they represented the practice of the CoP model. Participating in an online CoP can help offer its participants support, especially in professions that can be isolating (Mawhinney, 2008). Twitter chats can help provide educators a helpful learning community and the professional development they desire for those who do not have this type of support throughout their regular workdays (Davis, 2013). Twitter can provide educators a chance to interact with other like-minded individuals. By forming a Twitter online CoP, educators can have a place where they find support from each other, share resources, and converse with other professionals outside of their school district.

Although some educators do participate in Twitter chats, many like to be passive participants and simply observe and learn from others within the chat. Lave and Wenger's (1991) discussed the act of lurking in their theory of legitimate peripheral participation. Participation in a CoP involves both active contribution and observation. Definitive of Wenger's CoP (1998), the observed Twitter chats were perceived to be groups of educators who shared a common interest who wanted to learn more about a certain topic in order to improve it. During the Twitter chats, the participants were creating their own questions and applying their knowledge in order to answer them. Learning was situated in a social environment and was collaborative as the participants were "coproducing knowledge at a self-directed level" (Megele, 2014, p. 48). The findings of my observation period in regards to participating in Twitter chats indicated that Twitter is an exceptional example on how online environments can be used to develop CoPs. Because the chats are focused on a shared domain of interest and enables live collaboration amongst its participants, it meets the standards of an effective online CoP.

Incorporating and Practicing Educational Technology

The second largest observed theme of the educators' Twitter participatory practices included tweeting and retweeting about the technological utilization of Flipgrid, coding, Bloxels, augmented and virtual reality, and Skype. Many of the educators actively utilized Flipgrid in their schools and composed tweets in order to share how they were using the tool. Flipgrid can be very beneficial in enabling social learning amongst students and help improve digital media skills. From observing the tweets, many used Flipgrid to promote self-reflection and global collaboration amongst students. In Stoszkowski's (2018) study of using Flipgrid to develop social learning, Flipgrid was projected to inspire reflective and honest peer communication and cooperative discussions on the conventional matters students are facing in their everyday lives. According to Torrie (2017), Flipgrid can be categorized into the social constructivist model because its users are forming their own understanding in a shared social environment. Users can provide their own video responses, reply to others' video posts, and interact with subject matter to formulate their own viewpoints. For those users who are more reserved, they can observe others' responses and eventually participate in order to express their own viewpoints. From viewing the observed tweets of the educators, Flipgrid seemed to fit the CoP theory because of the users' interests in Flipgrid, the gathering of users who interacted with each other on Flipgrid, and the practice of utilizing it in classrooms.

Several of the observed educators on Twitter engaged in the annual Hour of Code, utilization of Bloxels, and augmented and virtual reality apps and devices. They tweeted about their students' coding creations and shared coding lessons and resources. Many of them shared their coding creations, lessons, and resources on Twitter because they wanted to inspire others to do the same. As they tweeted about using Bloxels in their classrooms, the participants were demonstrating how their students engaged in critical thinking, expressed their creativity and innovative reasoning, and how inclusive technology can be applied with all students. By taking part in an active CoP, the educators were sharing coding ideas, approaches, resources, and essentially inspiring each other to grow and adapt in their profession. In addition, many of the participants tweeted and retweeted about the utilization of augmented and virtual reality in their classrooms. From using apps (3DBear and Quivervision) and devices (Merge goggles), their tweets demonstrated a group of people who enjoyed sharing and learning from each other. This common interest in augmented and virtual reality was guided by their desire and need to share their best practices, visions, difficulties, and self-created lessons using a variety of AR and VR products. The participation observed from the Twitter activity demonstrated shared learning and interest amongst the educators.

Promoting the School and Professional Branding

From discussing literacy events, activities that included a variety of educational technologies, candid moments, interacting with research projects, and promoting the school was evident in many of the educators' tweets. Just from observing their tweets, the promotion of their schools and classrooms encouraged lively discussions, including compliments and questions from others in their PLN. Tweets consisted of activities and events that included photos, tagging educational sources, such as ReadWriteThink.org and BrainPop, collaborating with other educators, engaging with technology (i.e. Quizlet Live), promoting books, and more. The activities and events being promoted in the classrooms on Twitter enhanced the knowledge amongst the educators, essentially helping them improve their practice.

As many of the educators took advantage of Twitter in order to promote their practice, others took the time to professionally promote themselves. A number of educators promoted their individual blogs and projects they were collaborating on. Two classifications of the observed tweets included institution promoted (i.e. new services initiated) and self-promotional (i.e. tweets about themselves and how they contributed to their work) tweets. When educators tweet about their success, they are inspiring and providing ideas to those in their PLN. It was observed that the educators in the PLN were creating and exchanging knowledge with each other about personal knowledge about the best practices in terms of school promotion and how these practices can be incorporated into their profession. Through the information provided in tweets, many of the educators were considering their current knowledge in various domains and combining it into innovative means of new competency (Sánchez-Cardona, Sánchez-Lugo, & VŽlez-González, 2012). This type of interaction validates the importance of collaboration and knowledge sharing among CoP participants. In addition to improving their current learning, the interaction in the Twitter CoP also promotes contemporary practices among educators.

In regards to building their school's brand and professional image, several of the educators tweeted about distinctive features that made their schools and themselves prominently noticeable on Twitter. Some promoted their classroom's makerspace and fundraising events. Various tweets included photos of the students interacting in activities in order to help others in the PLN come up with similar ideas on their own. Educators often tagged educational associations in their tweets that contained photos of schools and educational products. Through Twitter, the educators were notably visible. Their virtual presence offered exclusive insights that highlighted their work practices, ethics, outlooks, personal and professional activities. According to Brems, Temmerman, Graham, and Broersma (2017), "with the development of social media the individual is placed on a pedestal" (p. 445). They state that anyone can design a profile for many reasons such as sharing and networking with others. Professional branding can be an important part of any practice. Branding does not only showcase their work in schools, but encourages them to be "accepted by their audience – independent of the organization they are working for" (Brems, Temmerman, Graham, & Broersma, 2017, p. 445). For many of the educators, building an image and identity on Twitter was distinctively made apparent.

Participating in Twitter Backchannel

Several educators engaged in Twitter backchannels, such as educational conferences. Backchanneling through Twitter enabled them to post about the different sessions they presented or attended, their interactions with each other, and the ability to engage with others at the conferences. When tweeting before, throughout, and after the conferences, the educators developed their own CoP and situated learning through the use of a Twitter backchannel. As observed through their tweets, situated learning occurred from the active discussions, collaborations, and shared content (i.e. hyperlinks to presentations) through the use of the backchannel. Justice (2015) suggested that participating in a CoP via a backchannel delivers both educational and social support. Backchanneling via Twitter offers educators many viewpoints and learning approaches. Justice (2015) also suggests that educators make sense of knowledge when they actively participate through conversing and deliberating with each other, forming inquires, and rationalizing rather than passively listening to conference presenters.

From perceiving the tweets and conversations that took place during my observation, I observed that the educators used Twitter as a backchannel in order to discuss presentations and keynote speeches with each other, promote themselves and their sessions, record memorable moments during the conferences, shared useful resources, and shared what they were learning. Some of the conferences' hashtags were used during the conferences' timeframes (event-based), while others lasted even though the conferences had ended. The educators' use of Twitter as a backchannel coincided with both Li and Greenhow's (2015) and Kimmons and Veletsianos's (2016) studies. In both studies, the participants use of utilizing Twitter as a backchannel helped share content, enabled discussion in the newly formed CoP during conferences, and augment their PLNs. Many of the participants composed tweets instead of writing notes during keynotes and sessions in order to share the information with others and posted reflections in their tweets about sessions. Bates and Wilson (2012) state that by participating in backchannels, users can find like-minded individuals, create trust and an awareness of community, discover a variety of pedagogical methods, reflect on educational products and technology, and share content. In brief, using Twitter as a backchannel can provide participants the chance to connect and learn in a single, collaborative place.

Twitter as a Positive Learning Experience

The educators shared information and resources they discovered on Twitter with other educators in their Twitter PLN. Many of the educators modified the ideas they discovered on Twitter so that they would be more suitable for their own schools. Some of the participants would share their own blog posts via Twitter. Because of their active involvement on Twitter, they effectively knew their CoP audience and wanted to share their blog posts with them. From analyzing the blog posts, the educators provided information that was relevant and specific to their practice. Blog topics were relevant to the participants' Twitter CoP, such as literacy (i.e. diversity in literature), technology, and notable activities performed in schools. Including the links to blog posts in tweets was seen as a beneficial practice in order for a CoP to acquire more valuable information through textual content and media.

Some actively tweeted about educational technology resources that could benefit students. From creating YouTube tutorials and links to supplemental Google Docs and Slides lessons, these participants were adamant in actively sharing educational technology information with their Twitter CoP. Many discovered educational technology products and apps, such as Merge Cube and Periscope, and ideas on how to collaborate with global audiences, such as Mystery Skype and Skype with a Scientist. From analyzing these types of tweets, technology was observed to be a determined activity practiced by many of the educators. Combined with their many different levels of knowledge and experience, they were perceived as practitioners in implementing technology into real-world problems and enhancing lessons in their schools. Technological practice takes place within, and is influenced by, "social contexts" (Ministry of Education, 1995, p.6). Educational technological practice was observed as a social activity on

Twitter. They were proud of their work in implementing technology in their schools and actively shared it with others in their Twitter CoP.

According to Courduff and Szapkiw (2015), effective integration of technology requires both the knowledge of that specific technology and an understanding of how to implement it in everyday situations. In Lave's (1998) work on situated learning theory, she heavily emphasized that the application of knowledge within social settings is crucial to learning. As a result, if on-demand professional development for educational technology is going to be successful for educators in a Twitter CoP, it must include the opportunity for its participants to actively apply what they are learning in their current workplace. Lave and Wenger (1991) also stressed the importance of social collaboration as being vital to effective learning, as observed in the observed educators' Twitter CoP. The formation of a Twitter CoP definitely improved both learning and implementation. Through lurking and active participation in the Twitter CoP, the participants increased their levels of knowledge, abilities, and implementation of educational technology into their schools.

Many of the participants were interested in trying or incorporating different things into their lesson planning and curricula, as well as providing bite-sized professional development for their school. For example, a few were adamant in integrating student digital portfolios into their school's curriculum, while some actively searched for lesson plan ideas to use with their class's special needs classes. Some liked to monitor websites for updates or new information so that they could share them with their school's teachers. In addition, A few of the educators also liked to browse Twitter for educational technology ideas so that they could successfully design bite-sized professional development flyers for their school's teachers.

From observing and analyzing the tweets, the educators were developing an improved intelligibility on how to enhance or implement different things into their lesson plans or curricula by gathering evidence of learning on Twitter. Twitter was a place they navigated to in order to develop, implement, converse and improve their ideas. They were also able to encourage each other through their learning experiences.

Through the Twitter CoP, the educators were able to reflect upon their new ideas and gather evidence of how others were implementing them in their own schools and districts. From actively interacting with others, they were able to modify existing practices in favor of other techniques that were better suited for their students. These types of additions or modifications require reflection and time. A Twitter CoP can provide this time and opportunity for educators.

Many of the educators shared their admiration of using Twitter for professional learning. Twitter was regarded as a positive and worthy learning experience for those who took advantage of its benefits for professional learning.

Establishing Trust, Building Professional Relationships, and Defeating Isolation

The educators being observed on Twitter were active in composing tweets, retweeting, and conversing with each other, and most importantly, establishing mutual trust and forming professional relationships with each other. This type of active participation helped the educators connect with other educators, as well as assist in defeating some of their workplace isolation. It was a pleasure to observe the conversations they had with each other, especially during Twitter chats and when they made personal connections, such as with authors. Willemese (2017) states that Twitter is indeed a valuable tool for establishing professional relationships. From reading some of their replies to others via tweets, some of them stated that they had finally met some of the Twitter members in their PLN in real life. Because of their shared interests over time, they finally got to meet those who shared particular passions - collaborating with them on projects and receiving the support they needed.

The observation period demonstrated that some online relationships could help establish the foundation for success in real life collaborations. Two of the educators successfully co-authored a book together. The emphasis of both a CoP and PLN is people coming together to practice a shared interest or passion. They learn while they help each other, as many of them have something to offer and voices to be heard. Willemese (2017) also suggested that Twitter facilitates discussions and supports the sharing of knowledge and content, ultimately making it a great tool to strengthen and encourage ideas amongst participants. A variety of features such as communal support, implied trust, and the act of sharing, were apparent and benefited most of the observed educators on Twitter. Hart (2019) states that Twitter is a great learning tool because it is centered on learning, in comparison to the modern workplace. Through social collaboration, people share their knowledge and experiences as they work together, most often seen in communities of practice.

It was apparent how beneficial Twitter was to the observed educators because it helped them feel less isolated in an online community of unlimited educational opportunities. Compared to many of the studies on the work of K-12 educators, such as Carpenter and Krutka (2014), Rosell-Aguilar (2018), Greenhalgh and Koehler (2017), Davis (2015), Trust, Carpenter and Krutka (2018), Wesley (2013), and Cho (2016), participating in a Twitter PLN helped the observed educators decrease their feelings of isolation in their workplaces. For example, one of the educators compared her Twitter PLN to a "support group of like-minded educators". Another educator enjoyed using Twitter in order to "see" what others in her profession were doing. These educators rook the initiative and sought out their own professional development through Twitter in order to learn about innovative educational trends, technologies, and other pertinent information that is significant to their daily practice. Through the years, educators must understand that learning is not an isolated activity and need to remain up-to-date with the new demands of information and literacy, along with new technologies and pedagogical practices. As noted from Mulatiningsih, Partridge and Davis (2013), Twitter can help lessen the costs of professional development for educators and alleviate the isolation that may occur. The on-demand learning that Twitter provides is useful for those who are geographically isolated from each other. Similar to Rosell-Aguilar's study of language teachers on Twitter, the observed educators regarded the important connections they made with their Twitter PLN and how the support they received from each other lessened their feelings of isolation. From observing the tweets, I discovered that besides sharing resources and other helpful content amongst the participants in their Twitter PLN, the educators were also sharing their feelings and worries about their profession. However, they also shared how much their profession makes a difference in educating students. It was observed that by sharing their feelings, experiences, exploring, and discussing ideas, the educators were connecting with other like-minded individuals, which helped them reduce their feelings of isolation. An important component of a CoP is not only the significant knowledge sharing opportunities, but the recognition of belonging that participation makes.

Developing Professional Identities

In order to make sense of the development of identities in the educators' online Twitter communities of practice, I will reflect on the Wenger's (1998) three modes of belonging: (a) engagement, (b) imagination, and (c) alignment in regards to the educators' participation in a Twitter CoP from my six-week observational period in 2019. Combining these three modes of belonging can change an online CoP into an effective online learning community for educators. Engagement is the effort of participation. An example of engagement within the observational period is the educators realizing that they need to seek out and participate in learning opportunities. This includes turning to Twitter as a learning tool. Although some participants might have initially lurked through tweets when they first joined Twitter, through time active engagement enables them to be visible amongst other like-minded educators. Wenger (1998) discussed the act of engagement as identity work or "gaining a lived sense of who we are" (p. 192). The educators developed this sense through their participation and the communications with others in their Twitter PLN. Imagination involves the method of shifting past the present and envisioning future opportunities. Imagination was often seen through the educators' tweets when they collaborated on projects with others in their PLN or when they asked if anyone would want to collaborate on certain events (e.g. using Skype and Flipgrid with other classrooms). They anticipated what their students would be doing and imagined the effects of their collaborations. Imagination amongst the educators was observed as innovative and entailed both engagement and alignment in order to establish its practice. Alignment connected the educators to a wider purpose and enabled them to direct their strengths. They were aligning themselves with expectations or standards, such as enhancing STEM activities through the use of making in their classrooms, or organizing programs towards a shared purpose (i.e. bringing diverse literature into the curriculum). According to Wenger, these three modes of belonging essentially support each other. Educators' obligations in a Twitter CoP involve interacting with those who are engaged, imaginative, and aligned with a mutual intention – to support and learn from one another. A CoP enables its participants to organize their shared passions and interests as they participate with one another. Participating in a CoP helps educators develop their professional identity, recognition amongst others, and an authentic self.

Recognized and Remembered

Several of the educators associated being recognized with being remembered. Others recognized many of them during conferences. Being recognized not only helped establish their professional identities, it helped recognize the work they contributed to the innovation and development of educational practices. Centerwall (2016) stated that educators require a need to be seen and recognized for the work that they do. If they were recognized, they were remembered. In Goodyear, Casey, and Kirk's (2014) study of using social media in order to facilitate pedagogical change in an emerging CoP, recognition was an essential theme amongst teachers. The researchers discovered that Twitter helped teachers develop a professional identity as a direct result from contributing their own knowledge. The teachers were recognizing that their own practices would benefit others. They were also strengthening their statuses as being innovative practitioners. In addition, Wenger (1998) states that there is a similarity among identity and practice. Developing a practice requires forming a community of those who share a mutual concern or passion for something. As participants interact with each other, they acknowledge each other. This practice of recognition generates a negotiation of its participants' identities. Wenger (1998) states "identity and practices are mirror images of each other" (p. 149). As a result, educators can utilize Twitter to practice professional identities. As they gather and share information, they become recognized as a member of the education community and their authenticity is acknowledged by others.

Authenticity and Acknowledgement

Building an authentic professional identity is essential when sharing knowledge and conversing with others in a Twitter online CoP. According to Cho (2016) participants should tweet on a regular basis and also respond to those who seek advice. The more engaged a participant, the more active the Twitter CoP will be. Specifically, an essential feature of a professional online identity includes providing others the sense that you are an active participant of a Twitter CoP. This is crucial in ascertaining authenticity.

From observing the tweets in the 2018 six-week period, all educators had something valuable to contribute. Whether it was showcasing their students' work, promoting literacy, conversing in Twitter backchannels, collaborating with each other in educational technologies, the educators established their voices within their Twitter CoP. By increasing their public presence through active participation, they further developed their professional identities. Through recognition and authenticity, their Twitter CoP acknowledged their valuable contributions to the practice of educational leadership.

IMPLICATIONS FOR PRACTICE

Based on the acquired knowledge and emergent themes during the 2018 six-week observational period on Twitter, I believe that teachers, educational specialists, and school administrators can take advantage of its results. Because of the isolation and lack of professional development many educators face in their school districts, they often need to self-direct their own professional learning and locate like-minded individuals to communicate with (Frye, 2018). As educators find alternative forms of professional development and form their own PLNs, school administrators should encourage this type of self-directed professional learning. Voluntary professional development should be encouraged amongst all staff.

As educators take the time to engage in their professional Twitter CoPs, Twitter professional development should count towards their school district's requirement of PD hours. Twitter PD should also be an option that educators can use when devising their annual professional development plans (PDPs) and can be included in self-evaluations (i.e. Danielson Framework for Teaching – Domain 4 – 4d and 4e). If school administrators grasp the benefits of Twitter for professional learning, they might also learn to incorporate it into their school cultures that support the constructive and proficient use of social media. If educators learn the benefits of using Twitter for professional learning, they can then provide their own PD to other educators in their schools (for example, Carpenter & Krutka, 2015). As educators and school administrators grasp the advantages of Twitter for PD, they might also want to consider other informal learning approaches, such as edcamps and CoffeeEDUs (Burns, 2017). Twitter, edcamps, and CoffeeEDUs can help educators build their own PLNs and help bring passionate, like-minded individuals together to discuss the work they are doing in their schools.

Administrators in higher education may also benefit from the results of this study. Many educators often face isolation as a result of their subject-specific position in their school(s). Many work with little to no supervision from an immediate supervisor (Hornung, 2013). College professors and adjuncts need to remind their prospective students that they might not have another subject-specific teacher in their building (or school district) that they can turn to for advice. Educators might converse with others at educational conferences or other online communications (i.e. educational listservs). Although these conventional techniques of meetups have their benefits, they also have limitations. Educators often leave conferences with excellent ideas, but have little assistance in implementing or improving those ideas. They need to engage in continuous conversations even after the conferences have ended. As a result, implications for practice in teacher and educational specialist certification programs should incorporate the advantages of forming online communities of practice through social media into their curricula. Courses that incorporate the benefits of joining online communities of practice, including social media platforms such as Twitter, can actively engage new educators in sharing information and conversing with others in different geographical locations. The observed educators during this six-week observational period in 2018 used Twitter as a tool to develop their own online communities of practice in order to engage in conversations with others and practice their shared interests and passions. The Twitter CoPs provided a sense of solidarity, belonging, and helped develop professional identities. Twitter CoPs can hopefully inspire new educators and educational specialists who are in need of professional development and those who need to establish their voice in the education community.

REFERENCES

Bates, M., & Wilson, M. (2012). Vendor Support of PLNS. *Knowledge Quest, 4*(2), 22–25.

Bilton, N. (2013, October 9). All is fair in love and Twitter. *New York Times*. Retrieved from https://www.nytimes.com/2013/10/13/magazine/all-is-fair-in-love-and-twitter.html

Brems, C., Temmerman, M., Graham, T., & Broersma, M. (2017). Personal Branding on Twitter: How employed and freelance journalists stage themselves on social media. *Digital Journalism, 5*(4), 443-459.

Brown, R., & Heck, D. (2018). The construction of teacher identity in an alternative education context. *Teaching and Teacher Education, 76*, 50–57. doi:10.1016/j.tate.2018.08.007

Burns, M. (2017). *Tasks before apps: Designing rigorous learning in a tech-rich classroom*. ASCD.

Carpenter, J., & Krutka, D. (2014). How and why educators use twitter: A survey of the field. *Journal of Research on Technology in Education, 46*(4), 414–434. doi:10.1080/15391523.2014.925701

Carpenter, J. P., & Krutka, D. G. (2015). Engagement through microblogging: Educator professional development via twitter. *Professional Development in Education, 41*(4), 707–728. doi:10.1080/19415257.2014.939294

Centerwall, U. (2016). Performing the school librarian: Using the butlerian concept of performativity in the analysis of school librarian identities. *Journal of Librarianship and Information Science*, (1), 1–13.

Cho, V. (2016). Administrators' professional learning via twitter. *Journal of Educational Administration, 54*(3), 340–356. doi:10.1108/JEA-03-2015-0024

Courduff, J., & Szapkiw, A. (2015). Using a Community of Practice to Support Technology Integration in Speech-Language Pathologist Instruction. *Journal of Special Education Technology, 30*(2), 89–100. doi:10.1177/0162643415617373

Davis, K. (2015). *Teachers' perceptions of Twitter for professional development*. Academic Press.

Davis, K. (2015, August 14). Teachers' perceptions of Twitter for professional development. *Disability and Rehabilitation, 37*(17), 1551–1558. doi:10.3109/09638288.2015.1052576

Davis, K. J. (2013). Exploring Virtual PLCs: Professional development for the busy practitioner. *Perspectives on School-Based Issues, 14*(2), 28–32. doi:10.1044bi14.2.28

Frye, J. M., & Ph, D. (2018). Assimilation or Humiliation? An Analysis of Professional Identities after Critical Events in the Workplace. *School Library Research, 21,* 1-27. Retrieved from http://www.ala.org/aasl/sites/ala.org.aasl/files/content/ aaslpubsandjournals/slr/vol21/SLR_AssimilationorHumiliation_V21.pdf

Goodyear, V. A., Casey, A., & Kirk, D. (2014). Tweet me, message me, like me: Using social media to facilitate pedagogical change within an emerging community of practice. *Sport Education and Society, 19*(7), 927–943. doi:10.1080/13573322.2013.858624

Greenhalgh, S., & Koehler, M. (2017). 28 days later: Twitter hashtags as "just in time" teacher professional development. *Techtrends: Linking Research and Practice to Improve Learning - a Publication of the Association for Educational Communications & Technology, 61*(3), 273-281.

Harlan, M. A. (2009). *Personal learning networks: Professional development for the isolated school librarian.* Libraries Unlimited.

Hart, J. (2019). *Modern workplace learning 2019.* Lulu Press.

Hathcock, A. (2017). Cultivating Critical Dialogue on Twitter. *Using Social Media to Build Library Communities: A LITA Guide,* 137.

Hornung, E. (2013). On your own but not alone: One-person librarians in Ireland and their perceptions of continuing professional development. *Library Trends, 61*(3), 675–702. doi:10.1353/lib.2013.0007

Huang, J., Thornton, K. M., & Efthimiadis, E. N. (2010, June). Conversational tagging in Twitter. In *Proceedings of the 21st ACM conference on Hypertext and hypermedia* (pp. 173-178). ACM. 10.1145/1810617.1810647

Hurt, K. (2013, April 30). *Mentoring moments: Just in time support* [Blog post]. Retrieved from http://letsgrowleaders.com/2013/04/30/mentoring_moments/

Justice, L. J. (2015). *Using a Backchannel to Build a Community of Practice in a Professional Development.* Association for Educational Communications and Technology. Retrieved from https://members.aect.org/pdf /Proceedings/proceedings15/2015i/15_06.pdf

Kimmons, R., & Veletsianos, G. (2016). Education scholars' evolving uses of twitter as a conference backchannel and social commentary platform: Twitter backchannel use. *British Journal of Educational Technology, 47*(3), 445–464. doi:10.1111/bjet.12428

Komorowski, M., Do Huu, T., & Deligiannis, N. (2018). Twitter data analysis for studying communities of practice in the media industry. *Telematics and Informatics, 35*(1), 195–212. doi:10.1016/j.tele.2017.11.001

Lave, J. (1988). *Cognition in practice: Mind, mathematics and culture in everyday life (Learning in doing).* Cambridge University Press. doi:10.1017/CBO9780511609268

Lave, J., & Wenger, E. (1991). *Situated learning - Legitimate peripheral participation.* Cambridge University Press. doi:10.1017/CBO9780511815355

Lemon, N. (2014). Twitter and teacher education: Exploring teacher, social, and cognitive presence in professional use of social media. *Teacher Education and Practice, 27*(4), 532.

Lewis, B., & Rush, D. (2013). Experience of developing twitter-based communities of practice in higher education. *Research in Learning Technology, 21*(3). Advance online publication. doi:10.3402/rlt.v21i0.18598

Li, J., & Greenhow, C. (2015). Scholars and social media: Tweeting in the conference backchannel for professional learning. *Educational Media International, 52*(1), 1–14. doi:10.1080/09523987.2015.1005426

Mawhinney, L. (2008). Laugh so you don't cry: Teachers combating isolation in schools through humour and social support. *Ethnography and Education, 3*(2), 195–209. doi:10.1080/17457820802062466

Megele, C. (2014). Theorizing twitter chat. *Journal of Perspectives in Applied Academic Practice, 2*(2). Advance online publication. doi:10.14297/jpaap.v2i2.106

Ministry of Education. (1995). *Technology in the New Zealand Curriculum.* Learning Media.

Mulatiningsih, B., Partridge, H., & Davis, K. (2013). Exploring the role of twitter in the professional practice of LIS professionals: A pilot study. *The Australian Library Journal, 62*(3), 204–217. doi:10.1080/00049670.2013.806998

Nelson, C. J. (2012). RIF or VIP? *Knowledge Quest, 41*(2), 70.

Rosell-Aguilar, F. (2018). Twitter: A Professional Development and Community of Practice Tool for Teachers. *Journal of Interactive Media in Education, 2018*(1), 6. doi:10.5334/jime.452

Sánchez-Cardona, I., Sánchez-Lugo, J., & Vžlez-González, J. (2012). Exploring the potential of communities of practice for learning and collaboration in a higher education context. *Procedia: Social and Behavioral Sciences, 46*, 1820–1825. doi:10.1016/j.sbspro.2012.05.385

Seo, K. (2014). Professional learning of observers, collaborators and contributors in a teacher-created online community in Korea. *Asia Pacific Journal of Education, 34*(3), 337–350. doi:10.1080/02188791.2013.860004

Smith, S., Hayes, S., & Shea, P. (2017). A critical review of the use of Wenger's community of practice (CoP) theoretical framework in online and blended learning research, 2000-2014. *Online Learning, 21*(1), 209–237. doi:10.24059/olj.v21i1.963

Stoszkowski, J. R. (2018). Using Flipgrid to develop social learning. *Compass (Eltham), 11*(2). Advance online publication. doi:10.21100/compass.v11i2.786

Stranack, K. (2012). The connected librarian: Using social media for "do it yourself" professional development. Partnership. *The Canadian Journal of Library and Information Practice and Research, 7*(1), 1. doi:10.21083/partnership.v7i1.1924

Torrie, R. (2017, September 13). *Flipgrid: Video Discussion Tool for Fostering a Community of Learners.* Retrieved February 3, 2019, from Learning Theories website: https://www.learning-theories.com/flipgrid-video-discussion-tool-fostering-community-learners.html

Trust, T., Carpenter, J., & Krutka, D. (2018). Leading by learning: Exploring the professional learning networks of instructional leaders. *Educational Media International*, *55*(2), 137–152. doi:10.1080/09523987.2018.1484041

Trust, T., & Horrocks, B. (2016). 'I never feel alone in my classroom': The value of participating in a blended community of practice. *Professional Development in Education*, *43*(4), 1–21.

Turkle, S. (2016). *Reclaiming Conversation: The Power of Talk in a Digital Age.* Penguin Books.

Visser, R. D., Evering, L. C., & Barrett, D. E. (2014). TwitterforTeachers: The implications of twitter as a self-directed professional development tool for K-12 teachers. *Journal of Research on Technology in Education*, *46*(4), 396–413. doi:10.1080/15391523.2014.925694

Warden, S., & Ogbamichael, H. (2018). Information and knowledge sharing within virtual communities of practice. *South African Journal of Information Management*, *20*(1), 1–11.

Weller, K., Bruns, A., Burgess, J., Mahrt, M., & Puschmann, C. (2014). Digital Formations: Vol. 89. *Twitter and Society.* Peter Lang Inc., International Academic Publishers. doi:10.3726/978-1-4539-1170-9

Wenger, E. (1998). *Communities of Practice: Learning, Meaning, and Identity.* Cambridge University Press. doi:10.1017/CBO9780511803932

Wenger, E. (2010). Communities of Practice and Social Learning Systems: The Career of a Concept. In C. Blackmore (Ed.), *Social Learning Systems and Communities of Practice* (pp. 179–198). Springer. doi:10.1007/978-1-84996-133-2_11

Wenger, E., Trayner, B., & de Laat, M. (2011). *Promoting and assessing value creation in communities and networks: A conceptual framework.* Ruud de Moor Centrum, Open University of the Netherlands.

Wesely, P. M. (2013). Investigating the community of practice of world language educators on Twitter. *Journal of Teacher Education*, *64*(4), 305–318. doi:10.1177/0022487113489032

Willemse, A. (2014, February 13). *Librarians using social media: The role of Twitter in forming and cultivating mentoring relationships.* Retrieved September 21, 2018, from Library and Information Association of New Zealand Aotearoa website: https://lianza.org.nz/librarians-using-social-media-role-twitter-forming-and-cultivating-mentoring-relationships

Willemse, A. (2017). TwitMentoring: Librarians Using Twitter in Forming and Cultivating Mentoring Relationships. In *Beyond Mentoring* (pp. 75–92). Chandos Publishing. doi:10.1016/B978-0-08-101294-9.00007-6

This research was previously published in Emerging Realities and the Future of Technology in the Classroom; pages 242-260, copyright year 2021 by Information Science Reference (an imprint of IGI Global).

Chapter 26
The Social Media Imperative:
Adopting Social Media Usage Practices That Support Faculty Career Advancement

Elsa Camargo

https://orcid.org/0000-0002-1965-2901

University of Arkansas, USA

ABSTRACT

As the usage of social media among faculty increases, it has become pressing for institutions to find ways to monitor and support this activity. In some cases, academic administrators have responded by reprimanding faculty members through suspension and forced leaves of absence. This chapter focuses on the role social media play in the careers of faculty, the function a mature workforce (senior faculty and administrators) has in adequately supporting junior faculty's use of social media, and on how institutions equip mature senior faculty and administrators (MSFAs) with the necessary skills to manage junior faculty's use of social media for the purpose of balancing a mature workforce in academia.

INTRODUCTION

The internet has accelerated the dissemination of knowledge among higher education professionals. This is especially true for faculty members who, in addition to publishing in referred journals, can now disseminate their expertise using media platforms with a quicker and wider impact. Many faculty members develop blogs and have social media accounts. Through these platforms they share information about their research and views about existing social issues that may be tied to their areas of investigation. But what happens when these views enter the public domain and are perceived as unpopular or controversial? What role does academic freedom play as faculty publicize their research expertise on social media platforms where they are subject to more scrutiny by a more varied audience?

Faculty members' comments in social media have subjected some institutions to negative publicity. In many cases, academic administrators have responded by reprimanding faculty members through suspension and forced leaves of absence, which has resulted in outrage from other academics. Yet, the

DOI: 10.4018/978-1-6684-7123-4.ch026

use of social media platforms especially among junior faculty members remains a necessary tool of the craft; emerging scholars rely heavily on social media to build their reputation as emerging experts in their fields and rely on platforms like Mendeley and Academia.edu to publicize their research (Mohammadi, 2014; Sugimoto, Work, Lariviere, & Haustein, 2017). The manner in which faculty members are being treated has called into question the validity of academic freedom and freedom of expression. Academic freedom's volatility can make professors feel unprotected and censored. In some cases, academic freedom has been guarded in conjunction with the university's reputation, limiting faculty's ability to freely exchange ideas.

There are a variety of categories of social media and platforms within these categories, making it difficult to comprehensively discuss faculty's use of social media. However, "most [academic context, definitions, and classifications] identify the following major social media categories as "social networking, social bookmarking, blogging, wikis, and media and data sharing" (Sugimoto, Work, Lariviere, & Haustein, 2017, p. 2038). Although many social media platforms cannot be easily classified, this chapter defines "social media" as online platforms that include and are not limited to Facebook, Twitter, Instagram, Google+, Mendeley, ResearchGate, LinkedIn, blogs (e.g., Academia.org), where social networking, social bookmarking, blogging, wikis, and media and data sharing occur. Furthermore, in this chapter, mature workers are defined in alignment with the Discrimination in Employment Act (ADEA) as anyone age 40 or older. "Mature faculty" are those 40 or older and with the rank of associate professor or professor. "Mature senior faculty and administrators (MSFAs)" are those 40 or older, with rank of associate or professor and who may also have administrative or leadership roles in the institution. In this chapter the term "mature workers" is used interchangeably with "MSFAs."

Purpose of Chapter

With the rise of social media usage among faculty, especially among those in early stages of their careers, it becomes important for MSFAs to be equipped with skills needed to lead institutions on these issues and mentor early career faculty on their use of social media. Such mentorship can contribute to early career faculty more successfully becoming mature workers, ultimately contributing to balancing a mature workforce in academia. This chapter focuses on the role social media play in the careers of faculty, the important function a mature workforce has in adequately supporting such use of social media, and how workforce development can equip MSFAs with the necessary skills to manage faculty's use of social media. The first section of the chapter includes a description of the mature workforce in academia. The second section focuses on the relationship between academic freedom, First Amendment rights and social media. This section also reviews previous case law on faculty's academic freedom. The third section examines the importance that social media play in balancing a mature workforce. The fourth section articulates some of the social media usage polices that exist at various higher education institutions. The fifth section discusses recent cases in which faculty have made controversial statements on social media that have resulted in faculty being reprimanded or dismissed. The last section provides recommendations for human resources and faculty leadership development on how to equip MSFAs with skills to navigate faculty's social media usage in a way that is supportive of junior faculty's career advancement and productive for balancing a mature workforce.

ACADEMIA AND ITS MATURE WORKFORCE

Recent studies demonstrate that while in the past 10 years, some disciplines in higher education have experienced an increase in the percentage of faculty 44 and younger (ASHA Wire, 2018), there has also been an increase in the average age of retirement among faculty, increasing the amount of time mature workers remain at their jobs before retiring (Nakada & Xu, 2018). In 1993, Congress allowed for an exemption that existed as part of the Higher Education Act of 1965 relieving faculty from being subject to the mandated retirement age (Weinberg & Scott, 2013). Weinberg and Scott (2013) examined faculty retirement patterns at one higher education institution and found that the uncapping in 1993 changed faculty's retirement behavior. Prior to the uncapping period, 25% of mature faculty who were 69 years old had not retired, however between 1993 to 2009 (post uncapping), it was estimated that 25% of mature faculty at 78 years of age had yet not retired, and 15% would likely retire at the age of 80 or older (Weinberg & Scott, 2013). Findings from this study are in alignment with data from the Bureau of Labor Statistics, demonstrating that between 2000 and 2011, the number of mature faculty over the age of 65 doubled (June, 2012). Similar trends also exist in some administrative professions. According to the American College President Study from the American Council on Education (2017), 58% of college presidents are older than 60, compared to 20 years ago when it was only 14%. Additionally, university presidents are serving on average 6.5 years.

As faculty continue to have longer careers in higher education, their levels of experience inevitably lead to them influencing universities' policymaking processes and governance structures. Organizational theorists such as Schein (2010), note that it is those who have stable membership within an organization who possess shared assumptions that maintain the core of culture. These assumptions drive other elements of an institution's culture, including its values and artifacts (e.g., policies). Therefore, considering the level of influence and presence those with a stable membership have at an institution, it is imperative that MSFAs be equipped with technology skills to lead colleges and universities in a manner that is protective of academic freedom and supportive of junior faculty's use of social media for the purposes of career advancement and balancing a mature workforce. After all, junior faculty's successes, like those of all faculty cumulatively, are critical to institutional success and the ability to cultivate a mature workforce in academia.

ACADEMIC FREEDOM AND SOCIAL MEDIA

Before discussing in greater detail faculty's use of social media, it is important to understand the relationship between social media, academic freedom, and the First Amendment. By understanding this relationship, the ways in which faculty's speech on social media are protected will become clearer. This section will discuss the existing relationship between academic freedom and social media established by the American Association of University Professors (AAUP) and examine previous case law on academic freedom and freedom of expression. Overall, this section will highlight the complexities that exist when applying this principle to the use of social media.

In 1915, the AAUP developed the *Declaration of Principles on Academic Freedom and Academic Tenure*, which was the first defense for academic freedom in higher education in the U.S. In 1940, the AAUP updated this statement, today known as the *1940 Statement of Principles on Academic Freedom and Tenure*. It provides that with academic freedom:

Teachers are entitled to full freedom in research and in the publication of the results, subject to the adequate performance of their other academic duties; but research for pecuniary return should be based upon an understanding with the authorities of the institution.

Teachers are entitled to freedom in the classroom in discussing their subject, but they should be careful not to introduce into their teaching controversial matter which has no relation to their subject. Limitations of academic freedom because of religious or other aims of the institution should be clearly stated in writing at the time of the appointment.

College and university teachers are citizens, members of a learned profession, and officers of an educational institution. When they speak or write as citizens, they should be free from institutional censorship or discipline, but their special position in the community imposes special obligations. As scholars and educational officers, they should remember that the public may judge their profession and their institution by their utterances. Hence, they should at all times be accurate, should exercise appropriate restraint, should show respect for the opinions of others, and should make every effort to indicate that they are not speaking for the institution. (p.14)

In 2013, The American Association of University Professors (AAUP) updated their 2004 report, "Academic Freedom and Electronic Communications." The updated reported sought to apply the principle of academic freedom from 2004 to the social media environment, by including social media activity as a form of "electronic communications." The 2004 report assumed that electronic communications were either personal such as with email or public such as websites, blogs, etc. (American Association of University Professors, 2014). However, in this report AAUP acknowledges that social media blurs the designations between personal and public communications. The 2013 report includes a section for social media that details recent cases in which faculty have misused social media platforms and have been reprimanded by their employers. The report recommends that institutions develop social media polices by working with faculty and following a shared governance process. Institutional policies should also recognize that faculty may engage with social media extramurally and that any extramural utterances are subject to the Association-supported principles of academic freedom, which encompass such utterances. Furthermore, the report also established that "faculty members cannot be held responsible for always indicating that they are speaking as individuals and not in the name of their institution, especially if doing so will place an undue burden on the faculty member's ability to express views in electronic media" (American Association of University Professors, 2014, p. 50).

As such, the social media environment is a space in which borders of geography, disciplines, industries, professional careers, and personal identities become blurred. Faculty's frequent use of social media allows them to share their expertise beyond their professional jobs and impact society at large. Unfortunately, readers and creators of these profiles do not always acknowledge the distinction between the types of profiles, causing readers to see ideas shared as representative of the faculty member's employer—the institution. The real debate on whether faculty members have the right to voice their unpopular opinions stems from being one individual with multiple roles, each carrying different rights and responsibilities. As citizens, faculty members have First Amendment rights and as employees they receive academic freedom. These roles are highly convoluted in social media, making it hard to distinguish which hat a faculty member is wearing and which rights apply when a thought, observation, or critique is posted.

Faculty members have at least two roles in society: citizen and employee. Within an instructional environment, faculty are greatly protected by academic freedom in their duties as researchers, teachers, scholars, and advocates, especially within the classroom. Out-of-class academic freedom can still protect faculty members if it is in the interest of teaching and learning. Simultaneously faculty members' roles as citizens also provide them freedom of speech in some of their daily activities (e.g., advocate). While these roles are easier to define when bounded to a place and time, the use of Internet profiles blurs these boundaries causing for freedom of speech and academic freedom to be reanalyzed in relation to a faculty member's usage of social media. In a qualitative study that examined the experiences with social networking sites of three faculty members at a research-intensive institution, Veletsianos and Kimmons (2013) found that the participants saw their social networking sites activity as part of their personal and professional identities; yet, they felt that they had little control over how others would perceive their use of social platforms. For example, when using platforms like Facebook, to whom they are connected as "friends" can have an impact on how they are perceived (Veletsianos & Kimmons, 2013). In this manner, faculty did not feel that they were in full control of their image on social media.

Some of the first disputes on freedom of speech and education trace back to the *Pickering v. Board of Education* (1968) case. In this case, the Supreme Court established that there needed to be a balance between the rights of the individual to voice issues of public concern and the state, as an employer to operate efficiently when providing services through its employers. Furthermore, the court in *Connick v. Myers* (1983) declared that public employees' speech was only protected when it was about a public concern. In addition to the First Amendment, public institutions of higher education have also historically given faculty members academic freedom to pursue research and teaching. Academic freedom is defined as "[the freedom of] faculty and students to pursue research, teaching and learning without interference from their institutions or the government" and it is protected by "law or by custom and usage" (Kaplin & Lee, 2014, p.671). First Amendment and employment contracts can also protect academic freedom.

Urofsky v. Gilmore (2000) addressed the level of academic freedom that faculty members have while using the institution's computer equipment. The increased level of technology has created more opportunities to practice speech in less formal ways. Although technology may present unique issues, these can be addressed by applying some of the traditional legal principles connected to academic freedom such as those found in *Levin v. Harleston* (1992). In this case Michael Levin, professor from the City College of the City University of New York published negative remarks about the intelligence of blacks in three publications: a letter to the *New York Times*, a book review for *Quadrant*, and a letter for the American Philosophical Association Proceedings. Students complained about his remarks for which university officials created shadow sections of his course to give students the option to have a different professor. University administrators also created a committee to investigate Levin's views. The United States Second Circuit Court ruled that Levin's speech was "protected expression" because his remarks and writings were "issues of public importance" and that the institution had infringed upon his rights by creating an environment that had a "chilling effect" that threatened his job security (*Levin v. Harleston*, 1992). The *Levin v. Harleston's* court ruling demonstrates that the issue continues to be about whether a faculty member is expressing a matter of public concern regardless of the platform being used. *Urofsky v. Gilmore* reinforces this and at the same time acknowledges that university equipment is an important factor, therefore allowing university administrators to develop protocols that will keep them abreast of how university equipment is being used. These protocols' objective is about informing administrators on campus of the usage of equipment and not about attempting to control faculty members' voices.

In recent years the concern defining "issues of public importance" and determining when a public employee is speaking as a "citizen" has continued to resurface as faculty members voice their opinions. More recent cases have cited *Garcetti v. Ceballos* (2006), which was not a higher education case, yet the court's ruling has influenced lower court post-secondary cases. The *Gracetti v. Ceballos* (2006) United States Supreme Court case involved Gil Garcetti, a deputy district attorney in Los Angeles who challenged actions taken against him by his office when he questioned an affidavit. The Supreme Court ruled that "when public employees make statements pursuant to their official duties, the employees are not speaking out as citizens for First Amendment purposes, and the Constitution does not insulate their communication from employer discipline" (*Gracetti v. Ceballos*, 2006, p. 3). This case ruling was later cited in *Renken v. Gregory* (2008) and *Gorum v. Sessoms* (2009). After the court decisions of *Hong v. Grant* (2007), *Renken v. Gregory*, and *Gorum v. Sessoms*, the AAUP (2009) published a report declaring that the *Garcetti v. Ceballos* court ruling presented a threat to academic freedom. The AAUP's 2013 report explains that although *Garcetti v. Ceballos* focuses on public employees, it does not account for faculty members' academic freedom and their ability to serve on university committees. The report provides the academic community with ways to protect academic freedom and urges faculty senates to develop policy statements that protect faculty academic freedom even when performing governance affairs (American Association of University Professors, 2009).

Renken v. Gregory (2008) involved Kevin J. Renken, a professor at the University of Wisconsin at Milwaukee who after receiving a grant from the National Science Foundation (NSF) expressed his opinion and filed complaints with university committees about the way the institution had planned to use grant funds he had secured. He not only disagreed with how the grant's funds would be used, but also argued that it violated federal law. Following his complaint, officials at the university reduced his pay and terminated his role in the NSF grant. Although Renken argued that he was exercising his First Amendment rights when he made his critique, the United States Court of Appeals for the Seventh Circuit ruled that the complaints made about the institution's management of the grant were part of his official duties and therefore he was speaking as a "faculty employee" and not as a "private citizen" (*Renken v. Gregory*, 2008, p. 4). Therefore, Renken's speech was not protected by the First Amendment and the court ruled in favor of the institution.

In this manner it becomes a complicated balance for institutions to support faculty's professional use of social media without attempting to also regulate their personal use of platforms. Consequently, it is difficult for institutions to be fully supportive of faculty's professional use of social media without being concerned of how faculty's overall social media presence reflects on their university. Yet, it is important for MSFAs to receive the necessary training on social media usage to in turn provide mentoring to junior faculty on how to manage their professional and personal social media profiles. As previous case law has demonstrated, academic freedom does not protect faculty's speech when speaking as citizens. Yet social media profiles are not always distinguished as either professional or personal. The following section describes the faculty's usage of social media, both professional and personal. Ultimately this section highlights the important role that social media play in balancing a mature workforce.

THE IMPORTANCE OF SOCIAL MEDIA IN BALANCING A MATURE WORKFORCE

Today, social media are challenging the boundaries of academic freedom and the First Amendment. Traditionally, academia has been a place where knowledge is created through research and disseminated through highly specialized publications, and other formal outlets of communication. With the introduction of social media, academics no longer have to wait long to voice some of their ideas. Ideas flourish and limitless teaching and learning occur via social media. It has become a means to more fully accomplish the goal of teaching, research, and learning without being bounded to time, place, or audience. Social media provide a place for disciplines and industries to converge and for ideas to be shared. For this reason and others, today faculty members find themselves becoming more active in social media and they may even create separate personal and professional profiles.

According to Chmura (2011), faculty are *twice* as likely as workers in other industries to use social media as part of their job. Through the use of social media, faculty are able to communicate with peers worldwide. In 2011, Pearson Learning Solutions conducted a nationwide study to investigate social media usage among faculty members ($n = 1,920$). "Social media" included personal and professional use of Facebook, Twitter, Myspace, LinkedIn, SlideShare, Flickr, blogs, wikis, YouTube, and podcasts (Moran, Seaman, & Tinti-Kane, 2011, p. 4). Findings revealed that faculty use social media to support their professional careers. The most frequently used platforms were YouTube, Facebook, and blogs. In fact, at the time 57% of faculty reported having visited Facebook within the previous month and 43% of those who visited posted one or more comments. Most faculty reported using at least one social media platform for personal use, and more than 30% visited a total of three or more platforms (Chmura, 2011). As for blogs, 22% of respondents visited them and only 11% posted in the previous month. These findings demonstrate the level of involvement that faculty members have with social media.

Additional studies (Bowman, 2015; Haustein et al., 2014) have examined the social networking of scholars and found that it is used for professional and personal purposes. The percentage of academics who use social networking for personal purposes is much higher than those who use it for professional reasons (Netwick & Konig, 2014). Facebook was the most highly used platform, followed by LinkedIn, and ResearchGate (Bowman, 2015). Meanwhile, Academia.edu had lower rates of use (Bowman, 2015).

The primary reasons for academics' scholarly use of social networking sites is to connect with researchers, dissemination of research, and tracking the research output of colleagues (Nández & Borrego, 2013). More specifically, the reasons for academics' social networking varied by rank. Gruzd, Staves, and Wilk (2012) found in a qualitative study focused on faculty in the field of Information Science and Technology that assistant professors were likelier than associate and full professors to use digital social networking platforms to create and maintain connections with other researchers. Additionally, in a mixed-methods study, Grande and colleagues (2014) found that junior faculty in Public Health were likelier than associate and full professors to believe that using social media was an efficient way to disseminate research. Differences by rank may be an indication that a shift in values related to social networking is occurring in academia. Mature workers may have fewer social media options since they are already recognized scholars. More importantly this data demonstrate that junior scholars find social media to be useful as they seek to make their research more widely known and establish networks with other researchers. Junior faculty place a high value on social media for advancing their careers, making it imperative for MSFAs to take on an active role in mentoring and supporting early career faculty in using social media positively and efficiently.

While some scholars argue that certain social media networks require a level of scholarliness, others believe that blogs supplement the conventional form of publication and serve as an alternative and more transparent form of peer review (Solum, 2006). For example, authors of blogs often reference peer-reviewed research, creating a community of scholarship that pushes for public engagement (Sugimoto, Work, Lariviere, & Haustein, 2017). Additionally, blogs serve as sources that are critical of underlying academic systems.

Yet, recent studies have documented that junior faculty hesitate to use social media for professional purposes due to this being a nonconventional way of disseminating research and therefore the perceptions of using them for academic promotion purposes are unknown (Grande et al., 2014). In part, some of the perceptions of faculty's use of social media is due to the lack of clarity that can exist between a personal and a professional profile. While academics use social networking for multiple purposes there are tensions between the professional and personal identity. This phenomenon is documented in recent cases questioning the "civility" of academics on these platforms (Sugimoto, Work, Lariviere, & Haustein, 2017). The following section discusses cases in which faculty members have been reprimanded or terminated by their institutions for improper use of social media, which can potentially hurt efforts seeking to balance a mature workforce in academia.

RECENT CONTROVERSIAL SOCIAL MEDIA CASES

Institutions get negative publicity for comments and blogs made by their faculty members in social media and academic administrators' reactions have only escalated the issues. In November 2013, Chicago State University (CSU) had a group of eight faculty members that wrote a blog entry on their blog site called "Crony $tate University" to criticize administrators for creating fake job applications and resumes. The blog was created in 2009 with the purpose of critiquing school leaders, exemplified by their slogan, "where competent people are fired and our friends are hired. The blog's URL includes "csu," the initials of the institution, causing for it to be a search result when looking for information about CSU. Therefore, CSU officials demanded the blog be removed because it damaged the university's reputation. The bloggers refused to delete the blog because it allows them to express their perspectives (Watson, 2014). The Illinois Conference of the American Association of University Professors (IL-AAUP) encouraged the bloggers remain firm against the university's request because such demand indicates that academic administrators want to silence faculty voices (Reichman, 2013).

In 2013, university officials demanded professors, Robert Bionaz and Phillip Beverly shut down the blog because it was an improper use of the university's trade names and marks, and also violated the university's policy on faculty's civility and professionalism (Rhodes, 2019). Then again in 2014, university officials demanded the blog change its cover photo and domain name. In 2015, as a means to silence Phillip Beverly, the university president, Wayne Watson asked a high-level administrator, LaShondra Peebles to accuse Beverly of sexual harassment, even though this was false (Bowean, 2015). Yet, both professors argued that CSU's demands to shut down or change the blog site constituted a violation of their free-speech rights and submitted court claims to which, in 2017, a federal judge ruled that the professors could sue Chicago State University (Bergner, 2017). In January 2019, the lawsuit was settled when Chicago State agreed to pay $650,000 in damages and attorney fees to professors, Bionaz and Beverly (Rhodes, 2019). To date, the blog continues to exist. The bloggers were mature faculty and their purpose for using social media was different from creating a professional presence to advance their careers. Yet, this case demonstrates how mature workers may find social media usage important in relation to their careers and the structural differences they seek to make in academia. Furthermore, their use of social media serves as guidance for junior faculty. However, it is important to highlight that while the CSU case ended in favor of the faculty who own the controversial blog, junior faculty could have a different outcome due to academic freedom functioning differently for mature faculty than for early career faculty.

In 2013, David Guth, an associate professor at Kansas University used his Twitter account to tweet controversial comments about the Navy Yard shootings, which he connected to the National Rifle Association (Jones, 2013). A few days after his tweet, Guth wrote a blog on his personal site, "Snapping Turtle," further explaining his comment and claimed that even if he was criticized, he had the right to express himself (Guth, 2013). Soon after, Guth was placed on administrative leave and Chancellor Bernadette Gray-Little at the time expressed that such action was taken to "prevent disruptions in the learning environment...." She also announced that Professor Guth's classes would be taught by other faculty members (University of Kansas, 2013). Additionally, the Kansas Board of Regents developed an elaborate social media policy for which it has received a lot of criticism nationwide because of the threat it represents to faculty members' academic freedom. The American Association of University Professors (AAUP) condemned "[the Kansas Board of Regents social media] policy as a gross violation of the fundamental principles of academic freedom that have been a cornerstone of American higher education for nearly a century" (American Association of University Professors, 2013, p. 2). The AAUP continues to affirm that the benefits of academic freedom extend beyond higher education and to the general public. While university policies are important for regulating social media usage, if mature faculty were equipped with knowledge on how social media could positively support junior faculty's career development, mentorship would serve as proactive guidance for junior faculty's social media usage, decreasing the number of faculty who are reprimanded by universities.

Furthermore, that same year, one of the most controversial cases of academic freedom and social media cases occurred when Steven Salaita, a professor from Virginia Tech published an opinion piece on *Salon,* a news and opinion website in the U.S., in which he was critiquing the phrase "support our troops" (Salaita, 2013). His critique of this phrase outraged many readers since he is employed at an American state institution and many were asking administrators at Virginia Tech to take action and dismiss him. Upon not seeing any action from the institution many critiqued the university for being anti-military (Ruth, 2013). The institution's spokesman at the time, Larry Hinckler, explained in a letter that academic freedom allowed professors to voice their opinions, but that these did not reflect the beliefs of the institution (Moxley, 2013). Furthermore, Hinckler explained that not taking any action against Salaita did not mean that the institution is anti-military and reminded all of the 1,000 Corps of Cadets at Virginia Tech and other forms of support the university offers student veterans (Ruth, 2013). Nonetheless, the professor received many threats from people who felt that he should have been fired from Virginia Tech (Ruth, 2013).

Salaita then applied to work at the American Indian Studies Program at the University of Illinois at Urbana-Champaign (UIUC) and in 2014 received an offer of employment pending approval from the Board of Trustees for a tenured position (Cohen, 2015). The conditional offer was withdrawn after the university's chancellor at the time, Phyllis M. Wise, reviewed Salaita's Twitter account which included anti- Israel tweets that were deemed ant-Semitic. The Chancellor decided to withdraw the offer and the Board of Trustees supported the Chancellor's decision (Cohen, 2015). The withdrawal of the offer resulted in Salaita suing the institution for breach of contract and violation of his rights to free speech. Salaita and his lawyers called for him to be hired as faculty at UIUC. Additionally, the American Association of University Professors added UIUC to the list of censured institutions. In 2015, after a year of litigation, the university trustees did not hire him, but did approve a settlement of $875,000 to end the dispute (Cohen, 2015). This controversy ultimately resulted in Salaita not being hired by any other institution of higher education, bringing his faculty career to an end. Salaita's case highlights the degree to which controversial comments on social media can negatively impact faculty careers. In Salaita's case, his career ended even though he was tenured. Perhaps if academia recognized the active role that social media play in faculty's lives, trainings, and other forms of social media could be provided to mature workers. In turn these mature faculty could provide more formal mentorship to faculty who actively engage with social media. By actively equipping mature workers with knowledge about social media usage in the academy, better measures could be taken in ensuring talented faculty are retained to complete full careers in this profession.

More recently, there have also been cases in which faculty members have been denied tenure, in which some suspect such denial is due to comments faculty have made using Twitter. In February 2019, BethAnn McLaughlin a faculty member at Vanderbilt University founded the website MeTooSTEM.com, a non-profit organization dedicated to raise awareness of the harassment women in academic science fields face (Jashchick, 2019). She has been outspoken in calling out scientists by name and questioning their treatment of women. Upon her tenure review, a faculty committee endorsed her tenure bid, but it was later reversed. The reversal came in 2015 when she testified in a sexual harassment case of another professor who asked for McLaughlin to be investigated for posting anonymous derogatory comments about colleagues (Goldstone & Partan, 2019). She was denied tenure at Vanderbilt as of April 2019, in spite of a petition being signed requesting for McLaughlin to be granted tenure (Goldstone & Partan, 2019) and in July 2019 she left the institution (Taylor, 2019). Similar to Salaita's case, McLaughlin was not allotted an opportunity to continue her career in academia. While the reasons as to why she did not earn tenure are unclear, her social media usage has been often cited on media coverage, making it clear that faculty are using social media to voice their concerns and opinions about controversial topics. The ways in which faculty are using social media require for academia to address faculty's use of social media in a manner that is proactive in preserving their faculty for them to become mature workers. A key way in ensuring this is by making sure current mature workers are actively engaging in conversations with junior faculty about ways to properly use social media for the purposes of career advancement.

EXISTING UNIVERSITY SOCIAL MEDIA USE POLICIES

In response to faculty's use of social media, university administrators have followed nonuniform protocols to protect their institutions' reputations. Some administrators have been detailed and provided written concrete policies about how faculty members need to manage their personal social media interactions (e.g., posts) and even outline the various forms of consequences, including employment termination if any of the polices are violated. Meanwhile, administrators at other institutions merely provide loose recommendations about things to consider when faculty members post in personal accounts. In cases like the latter, academic freedom has been guarded in conjunction with the university's reputation and in cases like the former it has been reduced and is highly limiting faculty's ability to exchange ideas freely. As social media continues to permeate academia, university administrators must create sustainable social media protocols to not only protect institutions' reputation and legal liability but higher education's duty to continue evolving in areas like social media. Institutional social media usage policies have to be written in a way that ensures that junior faculty are able to have a presence on social media for the purpose of advancing in their careers. If junior faculty are able to advance in their careers, institutions are likelier to have balanced mature workforces.

With faculty members' increased usage of social media, chancellors and public relations representatives have found themselves having to make remarks about how faculty members' opinions do not represent the institutions' points of view. Other institutions have taken this a step further and have placed faculty members on leave. To further regulate faculty members' involvement in social media and prevent additional issues, some administrators have developed social media use policies, the goals of these policies being to prevent future dilemmas and to aid in distinguishing faculty members' "employee role" from their "citizen role."

Many institutions have social media policies that address how employees must manage university entity social media profiles, but not all address how to handle personal accounts. Universities that have policies advising employees on ways to manage their personal accounts often list things to consider when creating their profiles online and when posting on these. For example, Oregon State University (OSU) employs a much broader approach on how employees should use their personal social media accounts. The policy begins by explaining that everything said reflects on the university including what is articulated on personal social media accounts. The policy explains that "if you work in the field of communications, what you say on your personal accounts and networks will reflect directly on the university and on your career. The blending of public and private communications is a new reality" (Oregon State University, 2019). It is further explained that personal accounts are not as private as one thinks and that personal and professional opinions are hard to distinguish, especially when accounts make reference to their employer, the university.

Furthermore, OSU's document explains that "what we do and say reflects directly back to the institution, including our activity on social media...realize that whatever you post can eventually be seen by coworkers, bosses, friends, family and even future employers" (Oregon State University, 2019). Additionally, Oregon State University (2019) asks that employees follow these five steps before posting:

1. *Avoid anonymity, and represent yourself. Anonymous profiles can lead to more negative content.*
2. *Post within reason, no different than you would offline.*
3. *Accuracy. Be sure that what you put on the web is factually correct and doesn't reveal sensitive information.*
4. *Once it's out there, it's out there forever. Think of yourself as always being on record. Avoid saying anything you wouldn't be comfortable saying to your co-workers.*
5. *Proof and reproof. Before you hit the 'post' button, reread what you've written. What you are about to post will be associated with your name forever.* (Oregon State University, 2019*)*

Meanwhile other universities go into even more detail on their employees' social media personal use policies. The University of Wisconsin-Madison (UW-Madison) adapted their use of social media guidelines document from a document created by the University of Michigan (Office of University Relations, 2019). UW-Madison's document includes a section of social media guidelines for when employees post as individuals. In this section, UW-Madison encourages its employees to share news and events that are "a matter of public record" with family and friends, as this is a way to help promote the university's mission and build community (Office of University Relations, 2019). Furthermore, employees are asked that in personal posts employees can identify themselves as faculty of the university, but when expressing personal views, they should include a disclaimer that informs the public that the opinions shared are their personal views and not the university's (Office of University Relations, 2019). When discussing higher education on personal social media sites, employees, especially those in leadership roles are asked to include a statement that reads "The views expressed on this [blog, Web site] are mine alone and do not necessarily reflect the views of the University of Wisconsin–Madison" (Office of University Relations, 2019).

Furthermore, if employees publish on any website other than the university's and the content is related to work they do or "subjects associated with UW-Madison" then they should use a disclaimer that states that the postings on that site are personal and do not reflect the university's position, strategies, or opinions (Office of University Relations, 2019). The university also advises employees to not use "ethnic slurs, personal slurs, profanity or engage in a manner that is not acceptable by the UW- Madison community. Moreover, it recommends that employees filter social media sites' comments, by changing settings to require that comments be approved before they appear. Finally, the university also asks that employees remember that even if they include a disclaimer people may still associate them with UW-Madison. Therefore, ideas should be discussed civilly, and employees should not "pick fights online" (Office of University Relations, 2019).

While policies at OSU and UW-Madison are positive steps towards the direction of providing faculty with guidance when engaging with social media, there are other ways beyond policies in which mature workers can further mentor junior faculty. As seen in past controversial cases, sometimes social media posts are deemed controversial. In these instances, it is the stance that faculty take on certain issues what can end in a controversial social media case. In these types of situations, faculty require complex mentorship from mature workers that focuses on how to best publish unpopular ideas as scholars on non- academic journals.

Institutions like Kansas University were among the first institutions to enact more stringent policies to regulate faculty members' social media communications. During December 2013, the Kansas Board of Regents proposed and approved a policy that cited precedent U.S. Supreme Court free-speech cases including *Garcetti v. Ceballos* (2006). At the time the policy gave administrators the authority to suspend, dismiss or terminate any university employee who misuses social media regardless of tenure status (Kansas Board of Regents, 2013, p. 85). Today, the university's social media policy has been situated in the context of academic freedom and freedom of speech rights. Prior to introducing the policy, the document highlights that the Kansas Board of Regents strongly supports principles of academic freedom and values the work that faculty members do at the university. In addition, the document cites the statement from the 1940 Statement of Principles of the American Association of University Professors:

College and university teachers are citizens, members of a learned profession, and officers of an educational institution. When they speak or write as citizens, they should be free from institutional censorship or discipline, but their special position in the community imposes special obligations. As scholars and educational officers, they should remember that the public may judge their profession and their institution by their utterances. Hence they should at all times be accurate, should exercise appropriate restraint, should show respect for the opinions of others, and should make every effort to indicate that they are not speaking for the institution. (AAUP, 1940)

The institution also expresses their recognition of the First Amendment rights that their employees have as private citizens when speaking on issues of public concern. Therefore, the document states that "for both faculty and staff, any communication via social media that is protected by the First Amendment and that is otherwise permissible under the law is not precluded by this policy" (Kansas Board of Regents, 2018, p.98).

Therefore, the institution asks that the policy be applied in a manner that is consistent with the First Amendment and academic principles. Similar to UW-Madison, KU also acknowledges that social media play a role in advancing the institution's mission, but at the same time can put at risk the reputations of individuals and the "efficient operation of the higher education system" (Kansas Board of Regents, 2018, p.98). Proper use of social media (individual and on KU's social media sites) includes any expressions made in accordance with university policies. However, improper use of social media gives the institution authority to discipline their employees. Employees can therefore be disciplined for speech that:

i. *is directed to inciting or producing imminent violence or other breach of the peace and is likely to incite or produce such action;*

ii. *when made pursuant to (i.e. in furtherance of) the employee's official duties, is contrary to the best interests of the employer;*

iii. *discloses without lawful authority any confidential student information, protected health care information, personnel records, personal financial information, or confidential research data; or*

iv. *subject to the balancing analysis required by the following paragraph, impairs discipline by superiors or harmony among co-workers, has a detrimental impact on close working relationships for which personal loyalty and confidence are necessary, impedes the performance of the speaker's official duties, interferes with the regular operation of the employer, or otherwise adversely affects the employer's ability to efficiently provide services.*

In determining whether an employee's communication is actionable under subparagraph iv., the interest of the employer in promoting the efficiency of the public services it performs through its employees must be balanced against the employee's right as a citizen to speak on matters of public concern. (Kansas Board of Regents, 2018, p.98)

Additionally, when reviewing a case of improper use of social media the institution has the right to also consider if the communication was made during work hours and if it was transmitted using university systems or equipment (Kansas Board of Regents, 2018, p.98). Finally, the university has authority to discipline an employee for improper use of social media. Disciplinary measures that may be taken include suspension, dismissal, or termination. KU's social media policy is therefore much better defined than those of other institutions. The policy does not only guide employees on what to do in their personal and professional social media profiles, but also includes actions the university can take against employees who use social media improperly. KU's social media policy has been criticized for requiring employees, specifically faculty, to balance academic freedom against four factors: "the employee's position within the university," "whether the communication was made during the employee's working hours," "whether the communication was transmitted utilizing university systems or equipment," and "whether the employee used or publicized the university name, brands, website, official title or school/department/college or otherwise created the appearance of the communication being endorsed, approved or connected to the university in a manner that discredits the university" (Kansas Board of Regents,

2018, p.98). Such balance is likely to result in academic freedom being outweighed by one of the other four factors. Therefore, while the policy claims to not violate academic freedom and Freedom of Speech principles, it does foment fear among faculty (Wilson, 2016).

Such fear can lead to faculty feeling surveillance and can result in faculty restraining themselves from engaging on social media and losing out on connecting with colleagues and potential research collaborators through these means. While social media is not necessary to advance in faculty careers, research shows (Mohammadi, 2014; Sugimoto, Work, Lariviere, & Haustein, 2017) that the various platforms can facilitate the process of establishing a reputation online. Therefore, it is important for institutions to find ways to be more supportive of faculty's use of social media as these can serve as tools to more easily share their research and establish networks online. In other words, in an interest to have junior faculty become mature workers, institutions should seek to find ways to support all the avenues that promote career advancement for early-career faculty rather than dissuade them by invoking fear.

University social media personal use policies are much more common today than they were five years ago. In large part this is due to the increase in usage of social networking of employees and universities' desire to protect their reputation. According to Wilson (2016), social media platforms can serve as tools for academics to reach a wider public and challenge the "narrow norm of scholarly restraint." Therefore, university trustees and regents seek to regulate faculty's social media use. While the AAUP rejects that there be a clear distinction between intramural and extramural utterances, Wilson (2016) argues that trying to also create a distinction between expert and non-expert is a mistake because it makes it difficult for faculty to speak on any topic unless they lack expertise, as this would mean they are speaking as a "citizen" rather than an "employee."

In many instances institutional polices for employees' use of social media on university websites is quite similar to the policies for personal use of social media. Such similarities in these policies highlight how social media have limited freedom of speech for employees. It is crucial for higher education institutions to create policies supportive of faculty's need to engage in social media use so that they can be as productive and as competitive as possible in order to achieve academic promotion. Their ability to succeed as faculty depends on higher education's mature workforce being equipped with the necessary tools and knowledge to create a supportive culture of junior faculty who rely on social media to advance their careers.

RECOMMENDATIONS

As it becomes harder to decipher between professional and personal social media profiles and as junior faculty's presence on these platforms continues to increase, it becomes more important to understand how institutions can support such activity in their careers. Through such support junior faculty can advance throughout their careers and become mature workers: balancing a mature workforce in academia. Therefore, it becomes imperative that universities and colleges provide adequate training for MSFAs who shape organizational culture through policymaking and daily interactions. In this section, I provide recommendations for ways in which human resources and faculty development units can equip MSFAs.

Provide Mature Workers With Training on Social Media and Faculty Careers

Given that social media are constantly evolving, it is important that MSFAs be aware of the positive impact these can have on faculty's careers. Some scholars argue that institutional social media usage policies are more about protecting the institution than they are about supporting faculty's use of social media (Wilson, 2016). In many ways, because of the governance responsibilities that MSFAs have, it is not unusual that they are more concerned with managing the enterprise than with any other aspect. Therefore, to increase their awareness of the role of social media in faculty career advancement and how in this manner social media also benefit the institution, it is essential that faculty development training on this topic is provided for MSFAs. Such training must be ongoing as social media platforms evolve and may serve faculty in different ways.

Provide Mature Workers With Informative Sessions on Social Media and Altmetrics

Furthermore, in a more concrete way, training programming that links social media to faculty career advancement must also expose MSFAs to recent research on social media and altmetrics. Recent research evaluation (Brown, Cowan, & Green, 2016) on faculty's usage of social media, has sparked a conversation within academia on how to include the use of social media as a measurement of faculty productivity. That is, can the use of social media's impact be measured as part of faculty productivity? As faculty are increasingly using social media, it has become increasingly important to find ways in which mature administrators can value and measure the contributions that faculty make to their fields (Brown, Cowan, & Green, 2016). While historically faculty have reported the measurement of their scholarly impact as part of their overall productivity, this measurement is highly dependent on the number of times their work has been cited by other scholars. However, with faculty using social media platforms (e.g., blogs) to disseminate their research and expertise, these forms of scholarship are often cited in non-traditional forms of scholarship and linked to various platforms of social media (Brown, Cowan, & Green, 2016). In this manner, social media use serves as a form of scholarly activity with the potential to reach beyond traditional audiences.

This new line of scholarship can be used in shaping promotion and tenure policies. In which case faculty can be given credit for the amount of impact their scholarship has on a broader audience, beyond the traditional journals. For example, some count "social media metrics" under "scholarly metrics" as indicators of overall citations. This is one way to reimagine the role of social media in faculty's careers. It allows for the institution to take credit for the level of a faculty member's social media presence in a way that is more tightly linked to their profession and expertise. Simultaneously, it allows for a clearer distinction between a faculty's personal versus professional social media activity. By only counting the professional activity, the institution reinforces that only that piece of a faculty member's communication is being endorsed by the institution. Furthermore, such approach further enhances First Amendment rights of faculty by no longer asking them to constantly distinguish if they are speaking as a private citizen or as an employee. Under such new structure, faculty would have greater agency in labeling whether communications should be counted as professional or as personal.

Provide Mature Workers With Training on Academic Freedom and First Amendment Rights for Faculty

Not all MSFAs have received formal training on how issues of academic freedom and First Amendment rights can be handled by the institution. As faculty's use of social media increases and conversations about "proper use of social media" are occurring on campuses, it is imperative that MSFAs will receive legal training on these topics. Through this training MSFAs will be able to more easily develop policies and practices that provide a healthy balance between academic freedom and First Amendment rights. More importantly, MSFAs will be better able to creatively support junior faculty's use of social media in a way that highly benefits both the institution and its employees. To be sure, university legal units will play a central role in this type of training, as they can speak to the role of the institution in monitoring such balance as well as to faculty members' rights. Additionally, such training programs can also include experts from the AAUP, who can speak directly to MSFAs about ways to further interpret academic freedom in social media. Such trainings can be organized by faculty leadership development and human resources. These trainings will encourage MSFAs to have ongoing informed conversations about ways to manage and support faculty's use of social media. Such ongoing conversations will allow for them to be more effective leaders as they stay abreast of changes need for policymaking.

Provide Mature Workers With Informative Sessions on Social Media University Policies at Other Institutions

As MSFAs continue to craft how to support faculty's use of social media, it is important that they are having conversations with faculty and administrators from other institutions with similar missions on strategies that they are using. Again, social media are constantly changing, and some institutions are better at developing innovative policies that can be adopted by other institutions. Therefore, conversations about policies that impact faculty and social media must also be occurring across institutions. For example, some institutions today are already finding ways to give faculty credit for their social media professional activity on annual reports. These are conversations from which MSFAs who may be developing ways to integrate social media activity in reward systems can benefit. These informative sessions should be headed by universities' faculty leadership development units and must also be ongoing.

Provide Mature Workers With Informative Sessions on Social Media Platforms and Faculty Usage Behavior

As existing social media platforms change and new ones are created, MSFAs should be aware of the differences between them and develop their understanding of how these operate. As research shows, mature faculty are less likely to use social media compared to junior faculty for developing collaborations (Gruzd, Staves, & Wilk, 2012). This is one way in which their behavior is different. Such difference highlights the need for mature faculty who are creating policies related to social media and faculty to learn why and how faculty use these platforms. Therefore, informative sessions should showcase social media platforms, the capabilities that these have for academics, and how faculty's use varies by platforms and demographics. These types of sessions should also be provided by the faculty leadership development units on campus in collaboration with representatives from the various social media platforms.

FUTURE RESEARCH DIRECTIONS

Research related to altmetrics and social media is a fairly new area for research. Further research needs to be done to better determine how to best measure the impact of social media and how to design a mechanism to measure impact across the various platforms. Research in this area will provide institutions of higher education with more concrete ways on how to reward faculty for their social media use during academic promotion and annual reviews.

Further research on faculty's use of social media by rank is also needed as we continue to find ways for a mature workforce in academia to best mentor and support junior faculty. Additional research in this area would help MSFAs better detect how junior faculty are using the various social media platforms to provide tailored mentorship and support. Additionally, such research would also aid institutions in understanding how mature faculty are using social media. With a better understanding of mature faculty use of social media, institutions can enhance their understanding of these platforms and equip them with the necessary tools to effectively lead in their governing practices.

CONCLUSION

Social media are critical to the democratization of knowledge developed by researchers in colleges and universities. As academia becomes more accessible to the larger society through the use of social media, we will see the interpretation of faculty's academic freedom change and the First Amendment protection of speech become more intricate. While institutions often rely on past case law to craft existing employees' social media usage policies, social media is constantly changing, requiring for administrators to constantly undergo review of policies related to faculty and social media. More importantly, faculty's use of social media for the purposes of advancing their careers and balancing a mature workforce will require that institutions provide substantial support. Due to the amount of influence MSFAs have in shaping institutional cultures, it is essential that human resources and faculty leadership development equip them with skills that prioritize innovation when promoting and monitoring junior faculty's use of social media in a manner that supports their career advancement.

This chapter has presented information on academia's mature workforce, described the relationship between academic freedom, the First Amendment and social media for faculty, discussed the importance of social media in faculty careers and in balancing a mature workforce, presented recent headlines of faculty members' controversial comments made on social media, discussed existing university social media use policies for employees, and provided recommendations for human resources and faculty leadership development to equip MSFAs with the necessary tools to govern social media use in a manner that is supportive or junior faculty's career advancement while protecting institutional standing.

REFERENCES

American Association of University Professors. (1940). *1940 statement of principles on academic freedom and tenure.* Retrieved from the American Association of University Professors website: https://www.aaup.org/report/1940-statement-principles-academic-freedom-and-tenure

American Association of University Professors. (2009). *Protecting an independent faculty voice: Academic freedom after Garcetti v. Ceballos*. Retrieved from the American Association of University Professors website: http://www.aaup.org/file/Protecting-Independent-Voice.pdf

American Association of University Professors. (2013). *AAUP statement on the Kansas board of regents social media policy*. Retrieved from the American Association of University Professors website: http://www.aaup.org/news/social-media-policy-violates-academic-freedom

American Association of University Professors. (2014). *Academic freedom and electronic communications*. Retrieved from the American Association of University Professors website:https://www.aaup.org/file/Academic%20Freedom%20%26%20Electronic%20Communications.pdf

American Council on Education. (2017). *American college president study 2017*. Retrieved from the American Council on Education website: http://www.aceacps.org/

ASHA Wire. (2018). Younger phd faculty on the rise. *The ASHA Leader*. Retrieved from the ASHA Wire website: https://leader.pubs.asha.org/doi/10.1044/leader.AAG.23022018.30

Bergner, G. F. (2017). Blogging professor can sue school officials on free-speech claims. *Courthouse News Service*. Retrieved from https://www.courthousenews.com/blogging-professors-can-sue-school-officials-free-speech-claims/

Bowean, L. (2015). Chicago State president is accused of pushing fake claims of sex harassment. *Chicago Tribune*. Retrieved from https://www.chicagotribune.com/news/ct-chicago-state-sexual-harassment-lawsuit-met-0320-20150319-story.html

Bowman, T. D. (2015, July). *Investigating the use of affordances and framing techniques by scholars to manage personal and professional impressions on Twitter* (Dissertation). Indiana University, Bloomington, IN. Retrieved from http://www.tdbowman.com/pdf/2015_07_TDBowman_Dissertation.pdf

Brown, A., Cowan, J., & Green, T. (2016). Faculty productivity: Using social media and measuring its impact. *Educausereview*. Retrieved from https://er.educause.edu/articles/2016/5/faculty-productivity-using-social-media-and-measuring-its-impact

Chmura, M. (2011). New survey finds more than ninety percent of college faculty use social media in the workplace: A new survey from Babson Survey Research Group and Pearson. *Babson Centenial, 1919-2019*. Retrieved from: https://www.babson.edu/about/news-events/babson-announcements/survey-finds-more-than-ninety-percent-of-college-faculty-use-social-media/

Cohen, J. S. (2015). University of Illinois oks $875,000 settlement to end Steven Salaita dispute. *Chicago Tribune*. Retrieved from https://www.chicagotribune.com/news/breaking/ct-steven-salaita-settlement-met-20151112-story.html

Connick v. Myers, 461 U.S. 103 (1983).

Garcetti v. Ceballos, 547 U.S. 410; 126 (2006).

Glodstone, H., & Partan, E. (2019). The cost of speaking out? #MetooSTEM activist may lose her job. *WCAI: Local NPR for the Cape, Coast, & Islands*. Retrieved from https://www.capeandislands.org/post/cost-speaking-out-metoostem-activist-may-lose-her-job#stream/0

Gorum v. Sessoms, 561 F. 3d 179 (2009).

Grande, D., Gollust, S. E., Pany, M., Seymour, J., Goss, A., Kilaru, A., & Meisel, Z. (2014). Translating research for health policy: Researchers' perceptions and use of social media. *Health Affairs*, *33*(7), 278–1285. doi:10.1377/hlthaff.2014.0300 PMID:24907363

Gruzd, A., Staves, K., & Wilk, A. (2012). Connected scholars: Examining the role of social media in research practices of faculty using the UTAUT model. *Computers in Human Behavior*, *28*(6), 2340–2350. doi:10.1016/j.chb.2012.07.004

Guth, D. (2013, September 16). Where do you stand? [Web log post]. Retrieved from http://snapping-turtle.us/blog2013.html

Haustein, S., Peters, I., Bar-Ilan, J., Priem, J., Shema, H., & Terliesner, J. (2014). Coverage and adoption of altmetrics sources in the bibliometric community. *Scientometrics*, *101*(2), 1145–1163. doi:10.100711192-013-1221-3

Jaschik, S. (2019). Will me too activism cost professor her job? *Inside HigherEd*. Retrieved from https://www.insidehighered.com/news/2019/02/22/scientists-rally-around-vanderbilt-professor-whose-tenure-bid-appeared-hit

Jones, C. (2013). KU decries journalism professors Navy Yard shooting comments. *Topeka capital-Journal (Kansas)*. Retrieved from http://cjonline.com/news/2013-09-19/ku-

June, A. W. (2012). Professors are graying and staying creating a faculty bottleneck. *The Chronicle for Higher Education*. Retrieved from https://www.chronicle.com/article/Professors-Are-Graying-and/131226

Kansas Board of Regents. (2013). *Discussion agenda: Governance*. Retrieved from Kansas Board of Regents website: http://www.kansasregents.org/regents_agendas_meetings

Kansas Board of Regents. (2018). *Kansas board of regents policy manual*. Retrieved from http://www.kansasregents.org/resources/062018_Policy_Manual_revised.pdf

Kaplin, W. A., & Lee, B. A. (2014). *The law of higher education, Student version* (5th ed.). San Francisco, CA: Jossey-Bass.

Levin v. Harleston, 966 F. 2d 85 (1992).

Moran, M., Seaman, J., & Tinti-Kane, H. (2011). *Teaching, learning, and sharing: How today's higher education faculty use social media*. Boston, MA: Pearson Learning Solutions. Retrieved from http://eric.ed.gov/?id5ED535130

Moxley, T. (2013, August 30). Virginia Tech professor's 'troops' remark stirs up anger. *The Roanoke Times*. Retrieved from http://www.roanoke.com/

Nakada, M. R., & Xu, L. W. (2018). No room for new blood: Harvard's aging faculty. *The Harvard Crimson*. Retrieved from https://www.thecrimson.com/article/2018/5/23/yir-aging-faculty/

Nández, G., & Borrego, A. (2013). Use of social networks for academic purposes: A case study. *The Electronic Library*, *31*(6), 781–791. doi:10.1108/EL-03-2012-0031

Nentwich, M., & Konig, R. (2014). Academia goes facebook? The potential of social network sites in the scholarly realm. In S. Bartling & S. Friesike (Eds.), *Opening science* (pp. 107–124). Cham: Springer International Publishing. doi:10.1007/978-3-319-00026-8_7

Office of University of Relations. (2019). *Policies and guidelines: social media.* University of Wisconsin-Madison. Retrieved from the University of Wisconsin-Madison webpage: https://universityrelations.wisc.edu/policies-and-guidelines/social-media/

Oregon State University. (2019). *Social media policy.* Oregon State University. Retrieved from Oregon State University webpage: https://osucascades.edu/social-media-policy

Pickering v. Board of Education, 391 U.S. 563 (1968).

Reichman, H. (2013). Chicago state targets faculty critics. *American Association of University Professors.* Retrieved from Illinois AAUP webpage: http://www.ilaaup.org/Fall201312.asp

Rhodes, D. (2019). State to pay $650K to end lawsuit over faculty blog criticizing school leaders. *Chicago Tribune.* Retrieved from https://www.chicagotribune.com/news/breaking/ct-met-chicago-state-university-faculty-blog-lawsuit-20190107-story.html

Ruth, S. L. (2013). Stop saying "support our troops" rants VA tech professor. *The Washington Times Communities.* Retrieved from The Washington Times Communities webpage: http://communities.washingtontimes.com/neighborhood/metro-news/2013/sep/4/stop-saying-support-our-troops-rants-va-tech-profe/

Salaita, S. (2013, August 25). No, thanks: Stop saying "support the troops" [Web log post]. Retrieved from http://www.salon.com/2013/08/25/no_thanks_i_wont_ support _the _troops/

Schein, E. H. (2010). *Organizational culture and leadership* (4th ed.). San Francisco, CA: Jossey-Bass.

Solum, L. B. (2006). Blogging and the transformation of legal scholarship. *Washington University Law Review, 84,* 1071.

Sugimoto, C. R., Work, S., Lariviere, V., & Haustein, S. (2017). Scholarly use of social media and altmetrics: A review of the literature. *Journal of the Association for Information Science and Technology, 69*(9), 2037–2062. doi:10.1002/asi.23833

Taylor, A. P. (2019). #MeTooSTEM founder BethAnn McLaughlin has left Vanderbilt. *The Scientist.* Retrieved from https://www.the-scientist.com/news-opinion/-metoostem-founder-bethann-mclaughlin-has-left-vanderbilt-66135

Urofsky v. Gilmore, 216 F. 3d 401 (2000).

Veletsianos, G., & Kimmons, R. (2013). Scholars and faculty members' lived experiences in online social networks. *Internet and Higher Education, 16,* 43–50. doi:10.1016/j.iheduc.2012.01.004

Watson, A. (2014). Fight over faculty blog escalates. *Inside HigherEd.* Retrieved from http://www.insidehighered.com/news/2014/01/13/chicago-state-again-seeks-changes-highly-critical-faculty-blog

Weinberg, S. L., & Scott, M. A. (2013). The impact of uncapping of mandatory retirement on postsecondary institutions. *Educational Researcher, 6*(42), 338–348. doi:10.3102/0013189X13497993

Wilson, J. K. (2016). The changing media and academic freedom. *Academe*. Retrieved from https://www.aaup.org/article/changing-media-and-academic-freedom#.XQjn_tNKgWo

ADDITIONAL READING

Adie, E., & Roe, W. (2013). Altmetric: Enriching scholarly content with article-level discussion and metrics. *Learned Publishing, 26*(1), 11–17. doi:10.1087/20130103

Bornmann, L. (2014a). Do altmetrics point to the broader impact of research? An overview of benefits and disadvantages of altmetrics. *Journal of Informetrics, 8*(4), 895–903. doi:10.1016/j.joi.2014.09.005

Ehrenberg, R. (2000). *The survey of changes in faculty retirement policies*. Washington, DC: American Association of University Professors. Retrieved from http://www.aaup.org/issues/retirement/survey

Herman, B. (2014, September 5). Steven Salaita twitter scandal: University offers settlement, but free speech questions Linger. *International Business Times*. Retrieved from http://www.ibtimes.com/steven-salaita-twitter-scandal-university-offers-settlement-free-speech-questionslinger-1678854

Kaskie, B., Leicht, K., & Hitlin, S. (2012). Promoting workplace longevity and desirable retirement pathways within academic institutions. *TIAA-CREF Institute: Trends and Issues*. Retrieved from: https://www.tiaainstitute.org/sites/default/files/presentations/2017-02/ti_promotinglongevity0312.pdf

McMurtrie, B. (2015, July 6). Nearly a year later, fallout from Salaita case lingers on campuses. *The Chronicle of Higher Education, 231365*, ●●●. Retrieved from http://chronicle.com/article/Nearly-a-Year-Later-Fallout/

Nakada, M. R., & Luke, X. W. (2018). No room for new blood: Harvard's aging faculty. *The Harvard Crimson*. Retrieved from: https://www.thecrimson.com/article/2018/5/23/yir-aging-faculty/

Nicholas, D., Watkinson, A., Volentine, R., Allard, S., Levine, K., Tenopir, C., & Herman, E. (2014). Trust and authority in scholarly communications in the light of the digital transition: Setting the scene for a major study. *Learned Publishing, 27*(2), 121–134. doi:10.1087/20140206

O'Neil, R. M. (2004, January 16). Controversial weblogs and academic freedom. *The Chronicle of Higher Education*. Retrieved from http://chronicle.com/

O'Neil, R. M. (2016). Academic freedom: Past, present, future. In N. M. Bastedo, P. G. Altbach, & P. J. Gumport (Eds.), *American higher education in the twenty-first century: Social, political and economic challenges* (4th ed., pp. 25–47). Baltimore, NJ: Johns Hopkins University Press.

Rothschild, S., & Unglesbee, B. (2013, September). Kansas University professor receiving death threats over NRA tweet. *The Dispatch*. Retrieved from http://www.shawneedispatch.com/news/2013/sep/24/kansas-university-professor-receiving-death-threat/

KEY TERMS AND DEFINITIONS

Academia: A community often composed of universities and colleges that is concerned with the pursuit of knowledge through research, scholarship, and education.

Academic Freedom: The protection of expression that faculty members receive while performing in their duties as researchers, scholars, and teachers.

Junior Faculty: Faculty members that are early in their careers in academia. This often includes someone with assistant professor rank.

Mature Faculty: Are those 40 or older and with the rank of associate professor or professor.

Mature Senior Faculty and Administrators (MSFAs): Faculty members who are age 40 and above and are associate or full professors and may also serve in an administrative position. In this chapter this term is used interchangeably with "mature workforce."

Mature Workforce: Are those 40 or older, with rank of associate or professor and who may also have administrative or leadership roles in the institution. In this chapter the term "mature workers" is used interchangeably with "MSFAs."

Social Media: Online platforms that include and are not limited to Facebook, Twitter, Instagram, Google+, Mendeley, ResearchGate, LinkedIn, blogs (e.g., Academia.org) where social networking, social bookmarking, blogging, wikis, and media and data sharing occur.

Social Media Use Policies: University and colleges policies used to guide or regulate employees use of social media. This use can sometimes include both personal and professional.

This research was previously published in Strategies for Attracting, Maintaining, and Balancing a Mature Workforce; pages 208-236, copyright year 2020 by Business Science Reference (an imprint of IGI Global).

Index

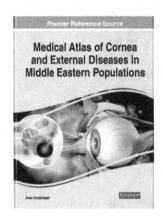
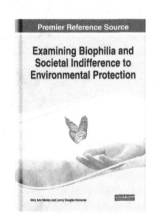
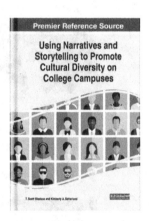

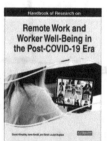

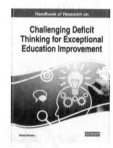

Printed in the United States
by Baker & Taylor Publisher Services